Lasers and Light

Lasers and Light

Readings from
SCIENTIFIC AMERICAN

With Introductions by
Arthur L. Schawlow
Stanford University

W. H. FREEMAN AND COMPANY
San Francisco

Each of the SCIENTIFIC AMERICAN articles
in *Lasers and Light* is available as a
separate Offprint. For a complete listing
of approximately 700 articles now
available as Offprints, write to
W. H. Freeman and Company,
660 Market Street, San Francisco,
California 94104.

Preface

There is surely no branch of science more ancient than the study of light. For thousands of years it has attracted the attention of some of the greatest minds: the early Greeks, Isaac Newton, and many others. In the past century, the interaction of light with matter, as revealed by the spectroscope, has been at the heart of the scientific revolution which introduced quantum mechanics. Thus we know a good deal about the physical nature of light. But we are only beginning to unlock the rich storehouse of devices that have been made possible by the understanding of quantum mechanics and by the subsequent discoveries of solid-state, atomic, molecular and plasma physics. The process began with the transistor in the 1940's, followed by atomic clocks, low noise maser amplifiers, optically pumped magnetometers, and frequency standards in the 1950's. Near the end of that decade, it was realized that the new quantum electronics could be extended all the way from radio waves to the visible part of the spectrum. The result was the creation of the optical maser or, as it is now called, a laser. The impact of lasers on many branches of science and technology has been great.

Yet light has many aspects, and scientists and engineers from very different disciplines have been attracted to it. These men have employed the techniques and concepts of their own fields, and more than one have made significant advances that have lent freshness and vigor to the subject of light as well as providing new tools for the other branches of science. The richness and diversity of modern optics are exemplified by the eleven articles that made up the September, 1968, issue of *Scientific American*. All of those articles are reprinted in this collection. Also included are a number of other previously published *Scientific American* articles—10 on various aspects of lasers and 12 pertaining to other aspects of modern optics that are of special interest.

To the physicist, light is an electromagnetic wave, and thus akin both to the infrared and the long, low-frequency radio waves at one extreme and to the x-rays and gamma rays beyond ultraviolet light at the other. Much of what is learned about one of these electromagnetic waves applies directly to the others, but the differences are instructive too. The wave nature of light links it to other kinds of waves, such as sound waves, water waves, and even the wave aspects of matter. But light, like matter, can appear to behave as particles rather than waves under some conditions. The two aspects—particle and wave—are linked by the theory of quantum mechanics, whose implications are still being realized. Thus, although we have understood for some time the emission, absorption, and refraction of light as it interacts with matter, it is only recently that we have learned that light can also be amplified by suitably prepared matter and can interact with it in other subtle and complex ways.

The wave properties of light are extremely important in the formation of images. Our understanding of the ways in which light waves are shaped by optical elements such as lenses has continued to increase, and we now have totally new ways to convey and direct light waves by bundles of transparent fibers. Ultimately, the image is detected by a photoelectric or photochemical device—be it a photographic film, an electronic detector, or an eye.

The photochemical processes that occur in living matter are essential to most forms of life, especially for vision. Other photochemical effects are utilized for processes as diverse as bleaching, photography, and the hardening of liquid plastics. With the advent of lasers to provide very intense beams of pure light, the number of such applications is likely to increase.

The most common use of light is for seeing. There must be enough light of the proper quality, and there are new ways to provide this. Eyes and brain combine in complex ways to respond to the message of the light. The study of vision draws on many disciplines—optics, chemistry, biology and psychology—and many techniques, one important one being the study of the eye movements that take place as an observer views a scene.

But not all electromagnetic waves are visible to the eye. X-rays have long been used to photograph the interior of opaque objects, such as the human body, and their wave nature enables us to use them to discern the arrangement of atoms in crystals, even those composed of molecules as complex as DNA. Infrared waves can be detected and converted to visible representations of the sky or landscapes, and this different way of observation reveals new information. The long low-frequency radio waves, too, interact with matter, and it was through the study of these that the first quantum electronic amplifier, the maser, was developed.

In the years since the late 1950's we have learned that masers can be made at many wavelengths extending from the radio region through the infrared and visible into the ultraviolet. These devices, the lasers, can produce intense beams of highly monochromatic, coherent light. Already many kinds of lasers have been developed that make use of insulating solids, semiconductors, liquids, and gases. Their energy can come from light, electrical discharges, or chemical processes.

These lasers are opening up many new scientific and other applications, which are closely linked to the particular properties of the light produced by the various devices. Under the enormous intensity of the beam from a high power laser, matter behaves in strange new ways, generating beams of different wavelengths or even producing delayed echoes. Light waves have long been used for communication, but now one laser beam can carry as much information as all radio channels. But if we are to make use of even a fraction of the enormous transmission capacity of a laser beam, new and sophisticated methods must be developed for handling the information and impressing it on the light beam. Lasers are also making practical the lensless, truly three-dimensional method of photography known as holography.

The study of light encompasses fundamental discoveries of the deepest and most far-reaching kind as well as immediate and practical applications. On these foundations surprising advances have been built, and others will surely follow. It is hoped that this collection, as a supplementary volume in undergraduate optics courses, will convey some sense of the excitement that pervades this living branch of science.

March 1969   ARTHUR L. SCHAWLOW

Contents

I
Light

Light

In this section we consider the physical nature of light, revealed by its interaction with matter. In the first three articles the topic is surveyed from different viewpoints. Gerald Feinberg, in the first article, discusses the dual nature of light, summarizes the historical evidence for both the wave and the particle properties, and shows how these aspects are reconciled in the quantum-mechanical picture, which encompasses both. Actually, light behaves in a more complex way than either waves or particles, but these are useful approximations. It might be likened to the elephant, as perceived by the blind men in the fable: to the one who touched the tail, the elephant was like a rope; to another, who touched a leg, it was like a tree; to others it was like a wall or a hose. The quantum-mechanical theory of light is not only comprehensive but precise: it describes the interaction of light and electrons as accurately as the best experiments can demonstrate. Yet even the simplest nucleus, the proton, has an internal structure so complex that even quantum mechanics has not yet fully elucidated its interaction with light.

If we examine light and matter in bulk, as Victor Weisskopf does in his article, an enormous variety of phenomena are revealed: light can be absorbed, refracted, reflected, or scattered. It is these processes that determine how much of the illuminating light comes to the eye from each point on an object, and thus determine how the object looks to us. Each of these phenomena can be explained in terms of what is known about the structure of matter and the ways in which the electrons and atoms in materials can respond to light.

In Ali Javan's article, a more recently discovered kind of interaction—stimulated emission—is described. Because it can occur only when some of the electrons, atoms, or molecules are excited, it is not ordinarily noticeable. Nevertheless it can be produced, and it is essential for the operation of masers and lasers.

Some light sources, such as incandescent lamps, emit light spread across a broad range of wavelengths or colors. Others, such as neon signs, emit only a few narrow bands of wavelengths. The sorting and measuring of these wavelengths is done by spectroscopy, and most of our knowledge of atoms and molecules has been deduced from the results of spectroscopic studies. For faint sources like astronomical objects, the traditional spectrographs with their prisms and gratings are being replaced by techniques of interferometry. These methods measure a wavelength by dividing the light into two parts, which are made to travel different distances and are then recombined. If the difference between the path lengths is a whole number of wavelengths the waves arrive in the same phase and reinforce each other, thus giving a maximum intensity. For other path lengths they will partially or completely cancel each other on recombining. As the difference between the path lengths is varied, the corresponding intensities are measured. If there is light of only one wavelength entering the inferometer, the distance between successive intensity maxima is just that wavelength. When many different wavelengths are present at the same time, the intensity changes in a complicated way, but the intensity variation is equivalent to each individual wavelength having a series of successive maxima and minima as the path length changes. The individual wavelengths and intensities could be derived by filtering each periodicity separately by tuned filters. The common procedure is to record all the resultant intensities digitally and extract the individual wavelengths by a computer calculation. Pierre Connes, in his article, describes some of the techniques of modern spectroscopy.

Some of the most refined and delicate methods of studying certain spectra in detail are those of optical pumping, described by Arnold L. Bloom in the concluding article in this section. Whenever atoms absorb light, they are raised to higher energy levels. Usually an infinitesimal fraction of the atoms are excited at any one time, and they quickly return to their original state. The experiments in optical pumping are concerned with just those atoms which are excited. The atoms may emit light of some characteristic polarization, or they may return to a different state, showing a changed absorption spectrum. In a broad sense, as the term "optical pumping" is now used in connection with devices such as lasers, it is an old phenomenon. Atoms were excited by light long ago, or we would not have observed such effects as bleaching, fluorescence, and phosphorescence. On the other hand, the techniques of optical pumping —beginning with the work of Kastler to selectively populate atomic levels split by a magnetic field—are new, delicate, and powerful. They have provided us with further knowledge of atoms and led to the development of such devices as sensitive magnetometers and precise atomic clocks.

3

1
Light

Gerald Feinberg   *September 1968*

The prevailing view of the nature of light has changed several times in the past three centuries. Each time the answer to the question "What is light?" has assumed more fundamental importance in the physicist's picture of the universe.

Isaac Newton (in his *Opticks,* printed in 1704) described light as a stream of particles, partly because it "travels in a straight line." Out of his experiments with color phenomena in glass plates ("Newton's rings") he also recognized the necessity for associating certain wavelike properties with light beams. These properties he called "fits of easy reflection and easy transmission." Careful not to make hypotheses, he let the matter rest. His authority was so compelling, however, that the corpuscular theory of light held sway for a century, his successors being more persuaded to this view than Newton himself.

Early in the 19th century the notion that light consists of waves, a view already expressed by Christiaan Huygens in the 17th century, came into ascendance. A decisive experiment performed in 1803 by Thomas Young, a London physician, demonstrated that a monochromatic beam of light passed through two pinholes would set up an interference pattern resembling those observed "in the case of the waves of water, and the pulses of sound." At about this time Augustin Jean Fresnel and Dominique François Arago came forward with the correct interpretation of an experiment

performed by Huygens. They showed that the light transmitted by Huygens' blocks of calcite crystal is polarized and that light waves therefore cannot be longitudinal compression waves as Huygens had thought but must be transverse waves oscillating at right angles to their direction of propagation [*see bottom illustration on page* 7].

This elucidation of the wave nature of light fit nicely into the electromagnetic theory of light propounded later in the century by James Clerk Maxwell. In Maxwell's equations light is described as a rapid variation in the electromagnetic field surrounding a charged particle, the variations in the field being generated by the oscillation of the particle.

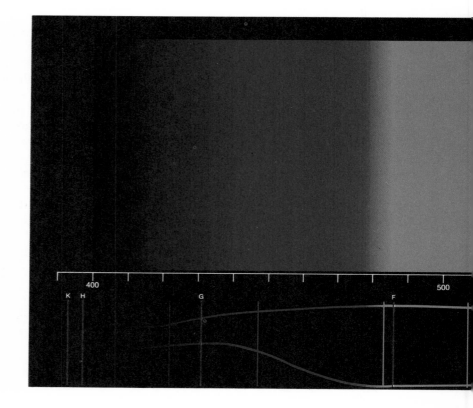

As such a varying field, light takes its place beside a number of other forms of radiant energy that were discovered in the 19th century. The different kinds of electromagnetic radiation—radio waves on one side of the spectrum of visible light and X rays on the other—correspond to different rates of variation of the field. Thus in Maxwell's theory light appears not as an independent element in nature but rather as an aspect of the fundamental phenomenon: electromagnetism.

The momentous developments in physics in this century have reopened and then resolved the old wave-particle controversy. Whereas the association of light with electromagnetism remains valid, the interpretation of this connection has changed. It has been shown that such wave properties as interference and polarization, so well demonstrated by light, are also exhibited under suitable circumstances by the subatomic constituents of matter, such as electrons. Conversely, it has been shown that light, in its interaction with matter, behaves as though it is composed of many individual bodies called photons, which carry such particle-like properties as energy and momentum.

As a result of these developments most physicists today would answer the question "What is light?" as Newton would have: "Light is a particular kind of matter." The differences between

light and bulk matter are now thought to flow from relatively inessential differences between their constituent particles. Particles of both kinds—of all kinds—exhibit wave properties.

Much of this understanding has been acquired, of course, by means of light. In a subsequent article in this volume, Pierre Connes observes that the analysis of light "provides the best evidence for our belief in the homogeneity of the universe." In a wider context Victor F. Weisskopf shows that sight is our most important link to the world around us.

Indeed, life itself is a manifestation of radiant energy in the visible spectrum; Sterling B. Hendricks describes how light starts up life, governs growth and stimulates behavior by the excitation of specialized light-absorbing molecules. The occasion for these observations and for the dedication of this issue to the topic of light is provided by an unexpected departure in the classic discipline of optics. That is the discovery of ways to synchronize the oscillation of electrons and thus produce coherent light, waves of the same length propagating in step.

SPECTRUM OF LIGHT encompasses the narrow band of radiant energy to which the human eye is sensitive, a portion of the electromagnetic spectrum from about 400 to about 700 nanometers in wavelength that is reproduced on these two pages. (A nanometer is 10^{-9} meter, or a billionth of a meter.) The upper of the two curves, with its peak at 483 nanometers, gives the energy distribution in sunlight at the earth's surface. The lower curve is the double-peaked absorption spectrum of chlorophyll, the green pigment of plants. The Fraunhofer lines (*gray*) mark the chief wavelengths at which solar radiation is absorbed by elements in the cooler atmosphere of the sun: oxygen (*B*), hydrogen (*C, F*), sodium (*D1, D2*), iron (*E, G*) and calcium (*G, H, K*). At 530 is the green emission line of heavily ionized iron in the sun's corona that was once attributed to the hypothetical element "coronium." A helium emission line is at 422, the principal emission line of a mercury arc at 546. The three cone-cell pigments of human color vision absorb most strongly at 447, 540 and 577, setting the peak of daylight vision at 555; the rod cells of night vision have their absorption peak at 507. The "red shift" of the astronomer is represented here by the line at 564, to which the Fraunhofer *F* line is shifted in the emission spectrum of the quasar 3C 273. The world's standard of length, the emission line of krypton 86, is at 606; the standard was formerly a cadmium line at 644. The helium-neon and ruby laser emit their monochromatic, coherent light at 633 and 694 respectively. This printed spectrum is not a reproduction, as is usually the case, of an actual spectrum captured photographically. Instead the color separations were prepared at the Eastman Kodak Research Laboratories by calibrating color patches prepared with cyan (blue), magenta (red), yellow and black inks and then making four negatives, each with a calculated density for each wavelength of the spectrum.

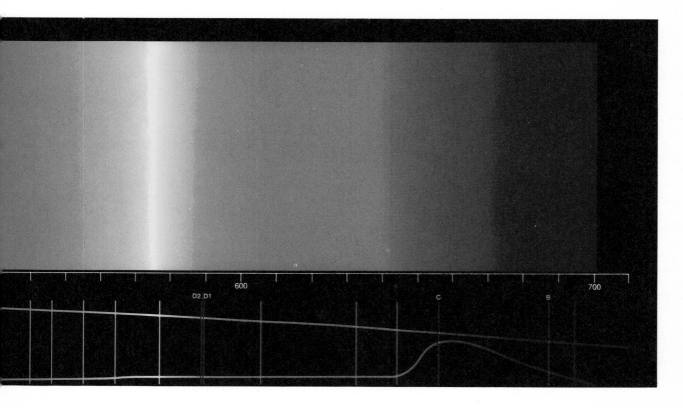

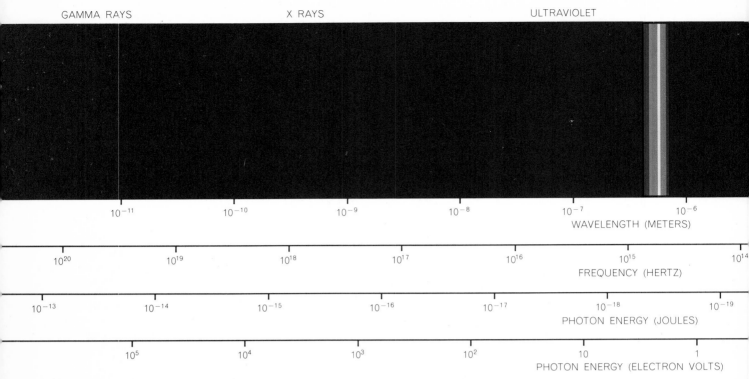

GAMMA RAYS   X RAYS   ULTRAVIOLET

10^{-11} 10^{-10} 10^{-9} 10^{-8} 10^{-7} 10^{-6}

WAVELENGTH (METERS)

10^{20} 10^{19} 10^{18} 10^{17} 10^{16} 10^{15} 10^{14}

FREQUENCY (HERTZ)

10^{-13} 10^{-14} 10^{-15} 10^{-16} 10^{-17} 10^{-18} 10^{-19}

PHOTON ENERGY (JOULES)

10^5 10^4 10^3 10^2 10 1

PHOTON ENERGY (ELECTRON VOLTS)

ELECTROMAGNETIC SPECTRUM, of which the visible spectrum on the preceding two pages is only a small part, is a continuum of electromagnetic radiation, the energy of which is carried in the quanta called photons. This diagram extends from gamma rays to high-frequency radio waves. The upper scales give the radiation's frequency (in hertz, or cycles per second) and wavelength;

The laser has given physics a powerful instrument for study of the interaction of light and matter [see "Laser Light," by Arthur L. Schawlow, page 282]. In technology laser light is finding uses in surveying and metrology, in cutting and welding, in communication and information storage [see "Applications of Laser Light," by Donald R. Herriott, page 313].

The operation of the laser exploits one of those inessential differences between photons and other particles. Let us now examine more closely the similarities and differences between the particles of light and ordinary matter and see how what is known about light can be understood in such terms.

One phenomenon that serves this purpose well is diffraction. It plainly demonstrates the wave properties of light and matter. If a beam of monochromatic light from a small source, or a stream of particles such as electrons, is directed at a screen with a small hole in it, the light or the particles that get through the hole will produce a characteristic pattern on a second screen placed beyond the first. The pattern is easy to understand in the case of light regarded as a wave, and it was cited in the 19th century as evidence in favor of the wave theory of light. Diffraction shows that light waves do not exactly travel in straight lines but diffract, or spread, as other waves do, and so find different pathways to the collecting screen. The interference of wavelets that in consequence arrive out of phase with one another at the collecting screen sets up the diffraction pattern.

In order to demonstrate the simple form of interference described above, a source of monochromatic light is required. Ordinary light sources are not monochromatic. Light from a luminous gas, for example, is emitted independently by many atoms in the gas. Furthermore, because collisions between the atoms excite and de-excite them, the light is emitted in pulses that have a finite length in time rather than an infinite length as is suggested by the textbook sine wave. Such a pulse can be resolved into a sum of pure sine waves of different wavelengths. The range of wavelengths in the pulse is inversely proportional to its duration; therefore the shorter the pulse in time, the greater the spread in wavelengths. Interference patterns are not usually detected in light from such a source. The reason is that the different wavelengths will interfere constructively in different places and the overall pattern will approximate constant illumination. Light of this kind is said to be incoherent. Conversely, light that yields interference patterns is said to be coherent. To obtain coherent light from natural sources one must narrow the range of wavelengths by means of a monochromatic filter and reduce the size of the source to a small area, as with a pinhole. With the advent of the laser we can now obtain highly coherent light without the loss of intensity involved in these procedures.

The exact shape of the diffraction pattern obtained from a given light source depends on the color of the light, objectively measured as wavelength. In the case of electrons the wavelength, and therefore the pattern, depends on the electrons' energy. In either case if diffraction is to be observed, the hole must be small with respect to the wavelength. For visible light, with wavelengths from 400 to 700 nanometers (4×10^{-7} to 7×10^{-7} meter), deviations from straight-line propagation are small unless the hole is very small. A barely visible pinhole will just produce a perceptible diffraction pattern. Electron and other subatomic particles usually have wavelengths of 10^{-9} meter or less, so that diffraction of these particles can be demonstrated only with crystals in which the "holes" are spaces between atoms about 10^{-10} meter apart.

It is this difference in the characteristic wavelength that explains why wave

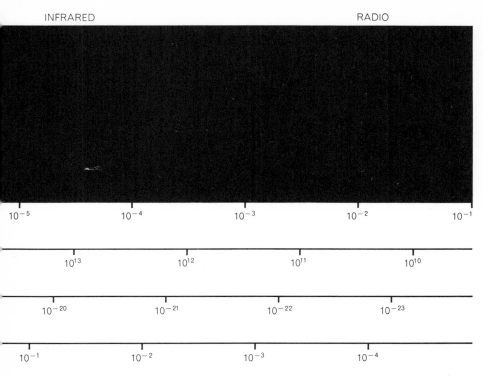

INFRARED   RADIO

10^{-5}	10^{-4}	10^{-3}	10^{-2}	10^{-1}

10^{13}	10^{12}	10^{11}	10^{10}

10^{-20}	10^{-21}	10^{-22}	10^{-23}

10^{-1}	10^{-2}	10^{-3}	10^{-4}

their product at any wavelength is the speed of light. The lower scales give the energy of the corresponding photons first in joules, or watt-seconds, and then in terms of the electron volt, the energy imparted to an electron falling through a potential difference of one volt.

properties were so easy to demonstrate for light beams and so much harder to discover for matter beams. Diffraction was first shown in electrons in 1927. All the wave properties characteristic of light, however, have now been demonstrated in electron and neutron beams, and there is little doubt that they hold also for other particle beams.

An important step in establishing the underlying resemblance of the particles of matter to the particles of light was the recognition that for both kinds of particle wavelength is related to the momentum, and hence to the energy, of the particles constituting the beam. The same equations show for all cases that wavelength is inversely proportional to momentum [see top illustration on page 10]. The equations also bring out the

difference between photons and the particles of ordinary matter. In the case of the electron, for example, the energy must include the rest mass of the particle. Photons, on the other hand, have zero rest mass, and so the term for rest mass drops out of the equations.

It is the rest-mass energy ($E = mc^2$) of the electron and other matter particles that gives them wavelengths so much shorter than light beams. A photon of blue light has an energy of about 3×10^{-19} joule, which corresponds to a wavelength of 4×10^{-7} meter. If this photon energy is transferred as kinetic energy to an electron, which starts with a rest-mass energy of 8×10^{-14} joule, the total energy is changed very little (by less than 10 parts in a million) and the wavelength is about 10^{-9} meter. The

wavelength is still shorter, of course, for particles that have larger rest-mass energies.

The inverse proportionality of wavelength to momentum is governed in these equations by the constant h, known as Planck's constant. It may be helpful to recall how this constant entered physics; the story is a significant chapter in the recognition of the particle nature of light. In 1900 Max Planck was concerned to explain the relation between wavelength and intensity in the radiant energy from a hot body. According to classical electromagnetic theory, the intensity was supposed to increase as the square of the frequency; by this reckoning an infinite amount of energy should be radiated at the higher frequencies or shorter wavelengths. Actual measurement had shown a quite different distribution of intensity with respect to wavelength for any given temperature [see bottom illustration on page 10]. Planck found an empirical formula that described this distribution. It contained a constant, the value of which Planck chose in order to produce the best agreement with the observations. To explain why this formula should work he had to assert that light must exchange its energy with the matter of the hot body in quanta, or packets. His equation showed that the amount of energy in each quantum would be equal to the frequency multiplied by the constant $h = 6.63 \times 10^{-34}$ joule-second. (The frequency is equal to the speed of light divided by the wavelength.) The constant h has since proved to be a fundamental constant of nature.

In 1905 Albert Einstein was prompted by another failure of classical electromagnetic theory to extend Planck's quantum concept further. Einstein asserted that not only is the energy of the light exchanged in quanta; the energy of the light beam is itself always divided into discrete quanta. His argument was based on his analysis of the photoelectric effect. It had been observed that negatively charged plates of certain metals

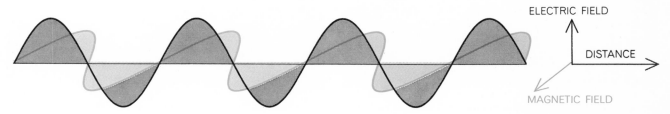

ELECTRIC FIELD

DISTANCE

MAGNETIC FIELD

ELECTROMAGNETIC WAVES, including light waves, are transverse: the electric and the magnetic fields are each at right angles to the direction of propagation. This illustration is a perspective view of a graph of the two fields at a given instant (electric field is vertical, magnetic field horizontal). The intensity of the radiation (light, for example) varies with the square of the peak amplitude of the electric field and is proportional to the number of photons in the field. The color of the light is governed by the wavelength.

lose their charge when they are exposed to ultraviolet radiation; in other metals the reaction could be triggered by visible light. It is now known that every metal has a critical wavelength for the effect. The emission of electrons will occur only on exposure of the metal to light of this wavelength or a shorter one. The effect depends entirely on wavelength and is independent of the intensity of the light. Furthermore, even for very weak light sources, the ejected electrons may come out simultaneously with the incidence of the light, without any time being required for the accumulation of energy.

It was impossible to understand these aspects of the photoelectric effect on the basis of a model in which the energy of light is uniformly distributed over the whole of an incident wave. In light of low intensity there would be insufficient energy at any one place in the beam to eject an electron. On the other hand, the observed results follow directly from Einstein's description of the photoelectric effect, according to which each quantum of light, or photon, carries an energy inversely proportional to the wavelength of the light, the proportionality being governed by Planck's constant. In this model a light beam contains a large number of photons (about 10^{18} per second in the beam of a flashlight), and the photoelectric effect occurs

when a given photon is absorbed by a particular electron, with the total energy of the photon being transferred to the electron. The relation between the energy transferred to the electron and the wavelength of the light has been precisely measured and found to be in accord with the prediction from Einstein's hypothesis.

The Compton effect provides further evidence that electrons interact with light through encounters with discrete bodies in the light beam that carry momentum and energy. Here it had been observed that X rays passing through matter often increase in wavelength. This was interpreted by Arthur Holly Compton as a loss of energy due to collisions between the highly energetic X-ray photons and the electrons. From the equation showing the relation of wavelength to energy Compton argued that the wavelength shift in the X rays would have a simple dependence on scattering angle, and this was in fact observed. It was shown soon afterward by the use of coincidence counting techniques that an electron recoils from each scattered photon and carries off the energy and momentum given up by the photon. These billiard-ball collisions plainly show that an X-ray beam behaves like a stream of particles. Similar behavior has been demonstrated for electromagnetic radiation of other wavelengths.

Although photons obey the same equations governing the relation of momentum and energy as other particles do, the relation is a special one in the case of the photon, owing to its vanishing rest mass [see top illustration on page 10]. The relative prominence of the wave properties of photons is therefore a consequence of the vanishing of the rest mass, rather than a qualitative difference between photons and other particles. The same characteristic accounts for the fact that the speed of light is independent of its energy. The velocity of particles with nonzero rest mass increases as their energy increases. For the photon velocity does not change with energy at all.

The discovery that both light and matter have wave and particle properties has made it easier to understand how these properties can exist together in either light or matter. This understanding is set out in the new description of nature, perfected in the 1920's, known as quantum mechanics. The basic objects described by the quantum mechanics of either light or matter are particles that are at least somewhat localized in space. The wave aspects of light and matter express the fact that these particles do not obey deterministic laws of motion, as they would in classical mechanics. Instead the laws they obey govern only

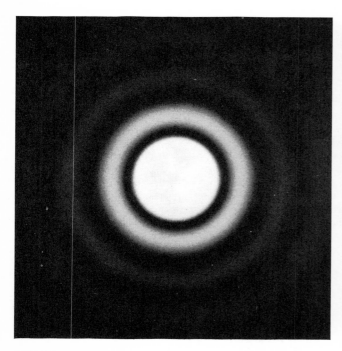

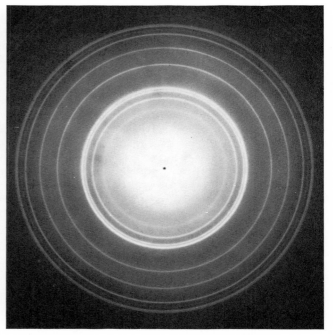

WAVE NATURE of light and of electrons is demonstrated by diffraction effects. The diffraction image (left) of light from a point source was caused by interference among waves from different parts of a .2-millimeter aperture. The photograph was made with coherent light by Brian J. Thompson of Technical Operations, Inc. An electron diffraction pattern (right) is created when a beam of electrons passed through a crystal lattice, in this case beryllium, forms an image. The photograph is from the RCA Laboratories.

the relative probabilities of motion at different speeds in different directions, even for a single particle in a known field of force. The waves associated with light and matter are a way of describing these probabilities. Hence when a light beam passes through a hole, there is some probability, related to the wavelength of the light, that the photons in the beam will not go straight through, giving a geometrical image of the hole, but instead will be deflected, ending up in the geometrical shadow region. The intensity of the waves in the diffraction pattern is a measure of this probability.

Let us see how the probabilities that quantum mechanics associates with particles (of light or other matter) explain the Young experiment that historically "proved" the wave nature of light. The experiment is usually performed with parallel narrow slits, to yield an interference pattern of alternating bright and shadowed lines. If the photons followed classical trajectories, the total probability of a photon's hitting a given point on the collecting screen would be the sum of the probabilities of this happening for each path; in other words, the light pattern would be a simple sum of the independent intensities of the two parts of the divided beam. Instead the collecting screen displays an interference pattern. The pattern is perfectly intelligible according to laws governing wave motion, in which the intensity at any given point is the sum of the amplitudes of the waves (whose squares are the intensities) reaching that point along paths of different length and thus in different phase. In quantum theory this experiment is interpreted as indicating that the motion of the photons depends on the complete physical system. If we allow the photon to go through either slit without determining which, the experiment will yield the interference pattern that reflects the probabilities—or rather the interference of probabilities—that a photon will find this or that path to the collecting screen. If we could instead monitor the photons to find out which slit they passed through on their way to the screen, the interference pattern would disappear and we would see the sum of the independent intensities [see illustrations on page 13].

The development of the pattern does not depend at all on the intensity of the beam, that is, on the number of photons going through the slits. As long as 50 years ago G. I. Taylor of the University of Cambridge performed an experiment with a light source so attenuated that most of the time there was no more than

NEWTON described light as corpuscular but noted wavelike properties in color phenomena such as the rings formed when glass plates are placed in contact. Lines AB and CD are glass surfaces in this diagram from the *Opticks*. The light, he suggested, undergoes "fits" of reflection and transmission as it passes through varying distances of air between the two plates.

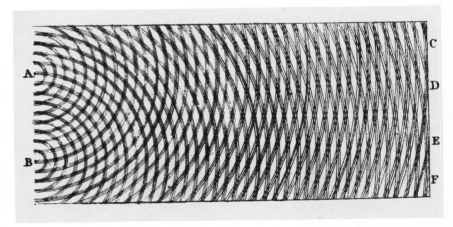

YOUNG explained interference among light waves by analogy with water waves, as in this illustration from a book of his lectures published in 1807. Where the two sets of waves from two apertures are in phase (where the curves intersect), they reinforce each other.

one photon on its way to the collecting screen. Yet after an exposure time of several months the photographic plate showed the interference pattern!

A similar experiment, employing laser light, has recently been performed by Robert L. Pfleegor and Leonard Mandel of the University of Rochester. Monitoring the arrival of each photon as they came through one by one, the counters showed that each photon found a random location at the detector. Yet when a sufficient number of photons had come through, they formed the expected interference pattern. Thus the number of photons arriving at a given position on the screen is proportional to the intensity of the interference pattern at that point, calculated according to the wave theory for the wavelength of the light in question. This shows that the wave

properties must be associated with each photon rather than with the entire beam.

The wave properties of light are examples of a universal behavior of objects, contained in the quantum-mechanical description of nature. From this standpoint contemporary physicists interpret experiments such as Young's interference experiment as showing not that light is a moving wave but rather that the probabilities of various photon motions are described by a wave equation. We might say that photons are the components of a light beam whereas the wave is a description of it. The waves are not vibrations of a new substance distinct from matter, as in the old ether theories. Rather they are a means of mathematically describing the probabilities that particles will do various things. No

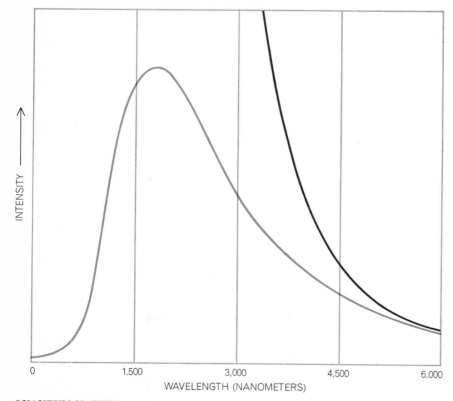

GENERAL CASE   PHOTONS (m = 0)

$$p = \frac{\sqrt{E^2 - m^2c^4}}{c} = \frac{E}{c}$$

$$\lambda = \frac{h}{p} = \frac{hc}{\sqrt{E^2 - m^2c^4}} = \frac{hc}{E}$$

$$v = \frac{pc^2}{E} = c\sqrt{1 - \frac{m^2c^4}{E^2}} = c$$

LIGHT differs from other forms of matter primarily in that photons have zero rest mass. The relation between momentum (p) and energy (E) takes on a special form for photons (*top row*). Wavelength (λ) depends on momentum and Planck's constant (h); when this universal relation is reexpressed as a dependence on energy, two forms result (*middle*). Similarly, particle velocity (v) depends on energy except in the case of photons (*bottom*).

ether-like carrier is needed for them. Nor is there any paradox involved in the occurrence of both wave and particle phenomena in light. The particles composing light and matter do not follow classical laws. If anything is surprising, it is that the behavior of the particles can be described by a concept that is as familiar as a wave satisfying a simple equation.

It is natural to ask how this picture of light as a stream of photons can be made to conform with the relation between light and electromagnetism, the discovery of which was a high point of 19th-century physics. Perhaps the most instructive way to view the relation is to say that, rather than considering light as an aspect of electromagnetism, we now think of electromagnetic phenomena as one manifestation of photons. It is easy enough, in accordance with this policy, to think of the transmission of radiant energy from place to place as being due to photons traveling across the gap. With a little more difficulty we can visualize the static electric and magnetic forces that occur between charges and currents as being due to an exchange of photons between them. In this latter case the photons are called virtual photons because the relation between their energy and their momentum is different. Quantum physics invokes this notion of virtual-particle exchange to account for forces between particles in cases other than electromagnetic forces. Nuclear forces, for example, are described as being due to the exchange of virtual mesons. Here again we are dealing with a special case of a general phenomenon.

Carrying the generalization further, we can say that all electromagnetic fields are to be thought of as being composed of photons. One result is that electromagnetic fields cannot always be taken as having determined values in space and time. Instead their values generally have associated indeterminacies; it is impossible to measure exactly the value of both the electric and the magnetic fields at the same point in space and time. The exact knowledge of one generates a necessary uncertainty in the value of the other.

Although this reduction of electromagnetism to optics can be carried through generally, it must be recognized that in many circumstances there is justification for thinking of the electromagnetic field as a special entity, as Faraday and Maxwell did. Again this is a result of specific properties of photons. Because the photon has zero rest mass it is possible for a physical system to contain many low-energy photons without its total energy becoming very great. That is the situation, for example, with the electric field between macroscopic charges. If we analyze such a field into photons, there will be a high probability of finding many photons of low energy, and also varying probabilities that different large numbers of photons of other energies are present. In these cases it is more useful to use the older field description, since the addition or subtraction of a single photon makes little difference in a state containing many photons. To put the statement another way, the fluctua-

QUANTUM NATURE of light was recognized as a result of Max Planck's explanation of the spectral distribution of electromagnetic radiation from a hot, black (fully absorbing) body. The classical theory predicted infinite radiation at short wavelengths (*black curve*). The observed distribution (*color*) was explained by introduction of quantum constant h.

tions in the field strength arising from the quantum properties of the photons that compose it are small compared with the average value at the field. In short, the particle aspects of electromagnetism and light are unimportant in many cases.

There is another property of photons that is important in situations involving many similar photons. It is termed Bose statistics. Most other stable subatomic particles, such as electrons, follow Fermi statistics. As a consequence electrons must satisfy the Pauli exclusion principle, which forbids the existence of more than one electron with any given value of momentum and angular momentum at any given time. For photons, on the other hand, not only is it allowed but also there is a tendency for photons to be produced in this way—in large numbers of the same momentum. Of all the stable elementary particles (except for the hypothetical graviton, or quantum of gravity), photons alone can occur in the combinations necessary to produce classical fields that have well-defined values over large regions. It is therefore not surprising that electromagnetism is the only case where the field aspects were recognized first.

This is the property, incidentally, that is exploited in the laser. What the laser does is to produce vast numbers of particles of exactly the same energy and wavelength. With no other stable particle but the photon is such a feat possible. The laser beam's remarkable macroscopic properties arise from the fact that its constituent photons are precisely identical. Whether the laser could have been invented without quantum mechanics is an interesting question!

In order to fully understand the properties of light it is important to know about the fundamental interaction process through which light and matter particles influence each other. Although photons do interact with most other subatomic particles, whether charged or neutral, it is believed (it is not completely proved) that the basic interaction is between photons and charges. According to this model, sometimes called Ampère's assumption, the fact that photons can be emitted and absorbed by electrically neutral objects such as neutrons is a consequence of the fact that these objects, although neutral as a whole, have a structure of opposite charges distributed throughout their volume. Supposedly it is these internal charges that do the emitting and absorbing of photons.

The simplest charged particle to consider is the electron, which does not have any known structure. An electron

at rest can be taken as a point charge, and its fundamental interaction with light is the emission and absorption of photons, one at a time, from this point. If there is a photon at the point where the electron sits, there is some probability that the photon will be absorbed by the electron and so will disappear. Similarly, an electron can spontaneously emit a photon even if no photon was present. The probability of these events is proportional to the square of the charge of the electron.

It should be noted that in the fundamental interaction process the number of photons changes while the number of electrons remains the same. There is no conservation law for photons as there is

for charged particles. As a consequence of this fact, and of the fact that photons can have arbitrarily low energy because of their vanishing rest mass, it is easy to produce them in very large numbers, as in a flashlight beam. All of the many photons in such a beam, however, are produced one at a time by individual electrons in the atoms of the flashlight's incandescent-lamp filament.

Starting with Ampère's assumption that photons interact only with charges, and applying the principles of special relativity and quantum mechanics, a mathematical theory known as quantum electrodynamics has been developed that provides detailed and accurate pre-

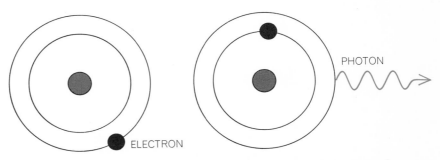

LIGHT IS EMITTED when an electron drops from a higher energy state to a lower state in an atom or a molecule. This process is reversed in most cases in which light is absorbed.

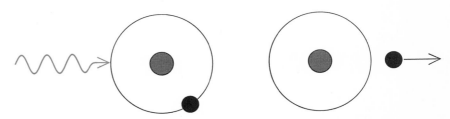

PHOTOELECTRIC EFFECT is an alternate means of light absorption, in which an electron is knocked out of an atom or a molecule by a photon. It was Einstein's explanation of the photoelectric effect as the absorption of a quantum of energy and the emission of an electron carrying the same amount of energy that established the quantum nature of light.

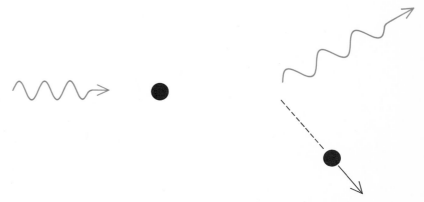

COMPTON EFFECT explained how X rays passing through matter may increase in wavelength. An X-ray photon that strikes an electron is deflected and loses energy; the wavelength shift and scattering angle are related by the dependence of wavelength on energy.

INTERFERENCE FRINGES from an experiment like Young's were photographed by Brian Thompson. Two apertures 1.4 milli- meters in diameter, 22 millimeters apart, were set in front of a lens (focal length 1.52 meters) and illuminated with mercury-arc light.

FORMATION OF FRINGES is evident in this diagram, in which slits are used instead of holes. Light from a source is passed through a single slit to attain some coherence and then diffracted into fans by two slits. The fans interfere to form fringes (right).

0 INTENSITY →

WAVE EXPLANATION OF FRINGES is evident in a plan view of the two sets of wave fronts that emerge from the slits. As the wave fronts move outward, "beams" of high intensity (solid color) de- velop where wave crests from both slits travel together and are therefore in phase (as are the troughs also along the same direc- tions). At right is a plot of the resulting wave intensity: the fringes.

dictions for the entire range of phenomena involving light and electrons. Some of these predictions (for example the response of hydrogen atoms to microwaves) have been verified to one part in a billion. Indeed, of all the theories physicists have constructed, the quantum electrodynamics of electrons is rivaled only by the gravitational theory of planetary motion in its agreement with observation. Since a large fraction of the phenomena involving ordinary matter occur through the interaction of light with matter, or through the play of the electromagnetic forces between charges that this interaction produces, we can agree with P. A. M. Dirac in his statement that this theory "explains all of chemistry and most of physics." As the present discussion has emphasized, the theory uses the same criteria to describe and distinguish photons as it does to specify the other particles. The success of the quantum electrodynamics of electrons can therefore be taken as testimony to the idea that all matter is similar, insofar as it is described by the same general principles.

The interaction of light with other charged particles, such as protons, is less well understood theoretically. These particles have a spatial structure arising from their rapid conversion into one another through the strong interaction that generates the force holding the atomic nucleus together. The details of the scattering of light by protons have not been adequately derived from any theory. Most physicists, however, consider this a result of our inability to deal with strong interactions rather than of a failure in our understanding of the properties of light. It is believed the interaction of light with charges is basically simple and universal, even when these charges have strong interactions as well. Techniques have been devised in the past few years to circumvent in part our inability to deal with the strong interactions, and some progress has been made in calculating the interaction of light with all the other charged particles. Whether or not our understanding of this interaction will approach our understanding of the interaction of light with electrons remains to be seen.

At several times in the past physicists have thought they understood the fundamental nature of light, and they were mistaken. Is it possible that our present view is also mistaken, that it will be radically modified in the future? Predicting the future of physics is a hazardous task; the most likely outcome of such predictions is that they will provide a source of amusement for future physicists. The

question nevertheless must be faced. Since our present description holds light to be similar to other forms of matter, it seems likely that any fundamental modification in the description would include all kinds of matter, not just light. The need for such a new description is perhaps indicated by the bewildering number of types of matter and of laws governing their behavior that the study of "elementary" particles has revealed. It could be that particles are not the ulti-

mate constituents of light and matter after all but rather manifestations of something deeper.

At present the photon theory gives an accurate description of all we know about light. The notion that light is fundamentally just another kind of matter is likely to persist in any future theory. That idea is the distinctive contribution of 20th-century physicists to the understanding of light, and it is one of which we can well be proud.

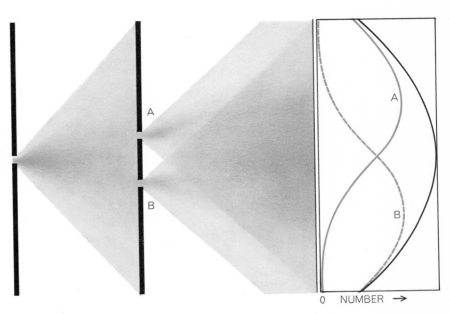

CLASSICAL PARTICLE DESCRIPTION of the two-slit experiment would say that the distribution of all particles that arrive at the screen is the sum (*black curve*) of the distribution curves for particles from the upper slit (*solid color*) and lower slit (*broken color*).

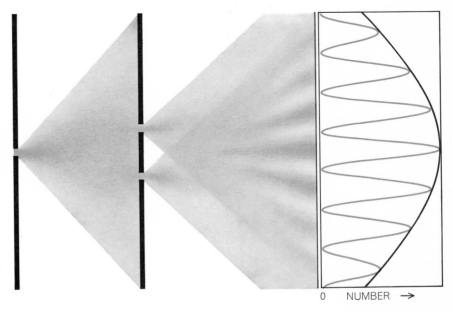

QUANTUM PARTICLE DESCRIPTION says the distribution of particles will show a distribution pattern typical of wave phenomena, but only if *each* particle can go through *both* slits. Observation shows clearly that this description, and not the classical one, is correct.

2

How Light
Interacts with Matter

Victor F. Weisskopf   *September 1968*

The overwhelming majority of things we see when we look around our environment do not emit light of their own. They are visible only because they reemit part of the light that falls on them from some primary source, such as the sun or an electric lamp. What is the nature of the light that reaches our eyes from objects that are inherently nonluminous?

In everyday language we say that such light is reflected or, in some cases, transmitted. As we shall see, however, the terms reflection and transmission give little hint of the subtle atomic and molecular mechanisms that come into play when materials are irradiated by a light source. These mechanisms determine whether an object looks white, colored or black, opaque or transparent. Most objects also have a texture of some kind, but texture arises largely from the interplay of light and shadow and need not concern us here. I shall restrict my discussion mainly to the effect of white light on materials of all kinds: solids, liquids and gases.

White light, as it comes from the sun or from an artificial source, is a mixture of electromagnetic radiation, with wavelengths roughly between 400 and 700 nanometers (billionths of a meter) and an intensity distribution characteristic of the radiation from a body that has a temperature of about 6,000 degrees Celsius. When such light impinges on the surface of some material, it is either reemitted without change of frequency or it is absorbed and its energy is transformed into heat motion. In rare instances the incident light is reemitted in the form of visible light of lower frequency; this phenomenon is termed fluorescence. In what follows I shall take up the commonest forms of secondary light emission. I shall undertake to answer such familiar questions as: Why is the sky blue?

Why is paper white? Why is water transparent? What causes objects to appear colored? Why are metals shiny?

The answers are all based on the fact that the electrons of atoms are made to perform tiny vibrations when they are exposed to light. The amplitudes of these vibrations are extremely small: even in bright sunlight they are not more than 10^{-17} meter, or less than 1 percent of the radius of an atomic nucleus. Nevertheless, all we see around us, all light and color we collect with our eyes when we look at objects in our environment, is produced by these small vibrations of electrons under the influence of sunlight or of artificial light.

What happens when matter is exposed to light? Let us go back to the simplest unit of matter and ask what happens when an isolated atom or molecule is exposed to light. Quantum theory tells us that light comes in packets called photons; the higher the frequency of the light (and the shorter the wavelength), the more energy per packet. Quantum theory also tells us that the energy of an atom (or a system of atoms such as a molecule) can assume only certain definite values that are characteristic for each species of atom. These values represent the energy spectrum of the atom. Ordinarily the atom finds itself in the ground state, the state of lowest energy. When the atom is exposed to light of a frequency such that the photon energy is equal to one of the energy differences

between an excited state and the ground state, the atom absorbs a photon and changes into the corresponding excited state. It falls back to a lower state after a short time and emits the energy difference in the form of a photon [*see illustration on page 17*].

According to this simple picture the atom reacts to light only when the frequency is such that the photon energy is equal to the difference between two energy levels of the atom. The light is then "in resonance" with the atom. Actually the atom also reacts to light of any frequency, but this nonresonant reaction is more subtle and cannot be described in terms of quantum jumps from one energy level to the other. It is nonetheless important, because most of the processes responsible for the visual appearance of objects are based on responses to nonresonant light.

Fortunately the interaction of light with atoms can be described rather simply. One obtains the essential features of that interaction—in particular the reemission without change of frequency—by replacing the atom with electron oscillators. An electron oscillator is a system in which an electron vibrates with a certain frequency designated ω_0. One can imagine the electron bound to a center with a spring adjusted so that there is a resonance at the frequency ω_0. The electron oscillators we are using to represent an atom are designed so that their frequencies ω_0 correspond to transitions from the ground state to higher states.

LIGHT AND COLOR were brilliantly manipulated by the medieval artisans who created the stained-glass windows of the Gothic cathedrals. The photograph on the opposite page shows a detail of the Passion Window, in the west façade of the Cathedral of Notre Dame at Chartres. The window was made in the 12th century. Stained glass is given its color by adding metal oxides directly to molten glass or by burning pigments into the surface of clear glass. Both coloring methods are evident in the example on the opposite page. The details in the faces and in the folds of the garments were produced by painting the glass with an opaque brown pigment, which was then permanently fused to the glass.

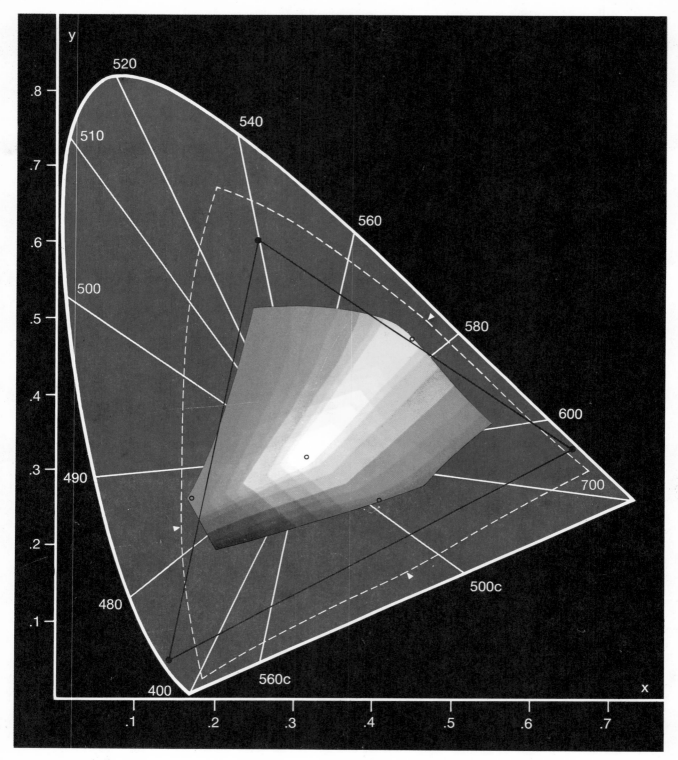

COLOR-QUALITY MAP, technically known as a chromaticity diagram, indicates how closely the colors of printing inks, color film and color television can approach the fully saturated colors of the visible spectrum, represented by the boundaries of the white horseshoe-shaped curve. The numbers around the curve indicate wavelength in nanometers. The straight line at the bottom of the horseshoe marks the boundary of the nonspectral colors from bluish purple to purplish red. When mixed with the spectral color at the opposite end of the axis, these "c" (for "complementary") colors form white. Inward from the horseshoe colors decrease in saturation, meaning that they contain more than one wavelength. The area printed in color shows the range of hues and saturations attainable with inks of three colors: magenta ("red"), yellow and cyan ("blue"). The open circles at the perimeter indicate the pure inks at full density. The open circle in the center is the white of average daylight. The colored area is actually a continuum; the steplike structure simplified the specification of ink combinations. An optimum set of dyes for color film (*white triangles*) can reproduce all the printing-ink colors plus all the more saturated tones that lie between the colored area and the broken white outline. The red, green and blue phosphors (*black dots*) used in color television picture tubes can re-create all the colors inside the black triangle. The x axis specifies the proportion of red in a particular color, the y axis the proportion of green. The rest is blue and need not be specified.

They represent the resonance frequencies of the atom in the ground state. Each of these oscillators has a certain "strength," a measure of the probability of the transition it represents. Usually the first transition from the ground state has the largest strength; that being so, we can replace the atom with a single oscillator.

Another quantity that characterizes these oscillators is their resistance coefficient, or friction. Friction causes a loss of energy in the oscillating motion. It describes a flow of energy away from the vibration into some other form of energy. It indicates that energy is being transferred from the excited state by some route other than the direct transition back to the ground state. Thus whenever the excited state can get rid of its energy by means other than reemission of the absorbed quantum, the corresponding oscillator must be assumed to suffer some friction. This is an important point in our discussion, because excited atoms in solids or liquids transmit their excitation energy mostly into heat motion of the material. Unlike the isolated atoms found in rarefied gases, they have only a small chance of returning directly to the ground state by emission of a light quantum.

Henceforward I shall discuss the effect of light on atoms in terms of this oscillator model. We can now forget about photons and excited quantum states because one obtains correct results by considering the incoming light as a classical electromagnetic wave acting on classical electron oscillators. The effects of quantum theory are taken care of by the appropriate choice of oscillators to replace the atom. One can interpret the results of the oscillator model in such a way that under the influence of light the motion of the oscillators is superposed on the ordinary state of motion of the electron in the ground state. Whenever a light wave passes over the atom, a general vibration is set up in the ground state of the atom, a vibration of a kind and strength equal to the vibrations the oscillators of our model would perform if they were exposed to the light wave. The electron cloud of each atom vibrates under the influence of light. The cloud vibrates with the same frequency as the incoming light and with an amplitude corresponding to that of one of the model oscillators. It is this vibration, amounting to less than 10^{-17} meter in amplitude, that reemits the light by which we see the objects around us.

The light from the sun or from artificial sources is a mixture of light of many frequencies. The motion of an oscilla-

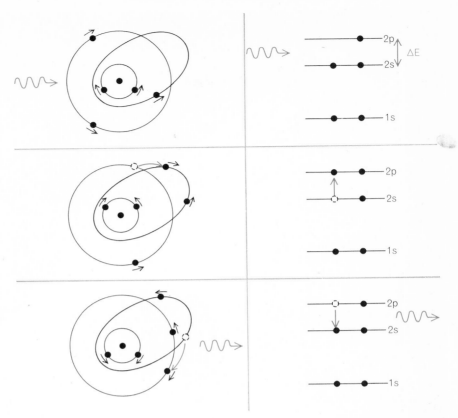

INTERACTION OF LIGHT WITH MATTER involves the absorption of a photon, or quantum of light, by an atom or a molecule. If the photon has the required energy, the atom or molecule will be raised from a low energy state to one of higher energy. After a short time the atom or molecule falls back to a lower state and the energy difference is emitted as a photon. Two simple pictures of the interaction are presented here. At the left a photon (*wavy arrow*) interacts with a Bohr model of an atom with five electrons (*top*). The photon raises an electron from the second, or 2s, orbit to the third, or 2p, orbit (*middle*). When the excited electron drops back to its former orbit, a photon is emitted (*bottom*). At the right the sequence is depicted in terms of energy-level diagrams. The photon supplies exactly the energy (ΔE) required to raise an electron from the 2s to the 2p level. These simple pictures are inadequate, however, for describing the typical interaction of visible light with matter, dealt with in this article. First, photon energy usually does not correspond to the energy difference between orbits. Second, when atoms in bulk matter are excited, they normally get rid of their energy by means other than the emission of a photon.

tor exposed to such a mixture is simply a superposition of all the motions it would perform if exposed separately to light of each frequency contained in the mixture. Hence all one needs to know for the study of atoms under the influence of light is the motion of oscillators driven by an electric wave of a specific frequency.

If an electromagnetic wave of frequency ω passes over an electron oscillator, the electric field exerts a periodic force and leads to certain characteristic responses [*see illustration on next page*]. First of all the periodic electric field induces a vibration of the oscillator so that it oscillates with the frequency ω of the field, not with its own resonance frequency ω_0. The amplitude and the phase of this motion depend on the relative values of ω and ω_0. If ω is much

smaller than ω_0, the oscillation is weak and in phase with the driving electric force of the light. If ω is much larger than ω_0, it is also weak but opposite in phase to the driving force. If ω is in resonance (in which case ω equals ω_0), the oscillation is strong and out of phase. That is, when the driving force is at its crest, the oscillation goes through the zero point. The amplitude of the oscillation follows a fairly simple mathematical formula that need not concern us here. The formula shows that if ω is much smaller than ω_0, the amplitude is small but is almost independent of the driving frequency ω. If ω is much larger than ω_0, the amplitude decreases with increasing ω at a rate proportional to $1/\omega^2$. Only the resonance case ($\omega = \omega_0$) corresponds to the simple picture of a transition to another quantum state.

What are the resonance frequencies in different atoms and molecules? Most of the simple atoms such as hydrogen, carbon, oxygen and nitrogen have resonances with frequencies higher than visible light; they lie in the ultraviolet. Molecules, however, can perform vibrations in which the atoms move with respect to one another within the molecule. Because of the large mass of the nuclei, such vibrations have very low frequencies; the frequencies are lower than those of visible light, in the infrared region. Hence most simple molecules such as O_2, N_2, H_2O and CO_2 have resonances in the infrared and ultraviolet and no resonances in the visible region. They are transparent to visible light. Nevertheless, visible light has an influence on them, which can be described by our oscillator picture. We replace the molecules by two kinds of oscillator, one representing the ultraviolet resonances, the other the infrared resonances. The latter are not really electron oscillators; they are "heavy" oscillators in which the mass of the oscillating charge is as large as the mass of the vibrating atoms, since they are supposed to represent the motions of atoms within the molecule.

We are now ready to understand one of the most beautiful colors in nature: the blue of the sky. The action of sunlight on the molecules of oxygen and nitrogen in air is the same as the action on the two kinds of oscillator. Both oscillators will vibrate under the influence of visible sunlight. The amplitude of the infrared oscillators, however, will be much smaller than the amplitude of the ultraviolet oscillators because of their higher vibrating mass. Accordingly we need to consider only the oscillators with ultraviolet resonance. When the oscillators are under the influence of visible sunlight, the force that drives them is below the resonance frequency. Therefore they vibrate with an amplitude that is roughly equal for all visible frequencies [see *illustration on opposite page*].

We must now take into account the fact that a vibrating charge is an emitter of light. According to a principle of electrodynamics an electron oscillating with an amplitude A emits light in all directions with an intensity given by a formula in which the intensity of the radiation is proportional to the fourth power of the frequency. (The formula is $1/3(e^2/c^3)\omega^4 A^2$, where e is the charge of the electron, c the velocity of light and ω the frequency of oscillation.) Hence the molecules of air emit radiation when they are exposed to sunlight. This phenomenon is known as Rayleigh scattering. It is called scattering because part of the incident light appears to be diverted into another direction. Whenever we look at the sky but not directly at the sun, we see the light radiated by the air molecules that are exposed to sunlight. The scattered light is predominantly blue because the reradiation varies with the fourth power of the frequency; therefore higher frequencies are reemitted much more strongly than the lower ones.

The complementary phenomenon is the color of the setting sun. Here we see solar rays that have traveled through the air a great distance. The higher-frequency light is attenuated more than light of lower frequency; therefore the reds and yellows come through more strongly than the blues and violets. The yellowish tint of snowy mountains seen at a distance is a similar phenomenon. The stronger attenuation of higher frequencies is a consequence of the conservation of energy: the energy for the reradiation must come from the incident sunlight, and because there is stronger reradiation at the higher frequencies more energy is taken from the sunlight at higher frequencies.

In actuality Rayleigh scattering is a very weak phenomenon. Each molecule scatters extremely little light. A beam of green light, for example, goes about 150 kilometers through the atmosphere before it is reduced to half its intensity. That is why we can see mountains at distances of hundreds of miles. Lord Rayleigh exploited the phenomenon of light scattering to determine the number of molecules in a unit of volume in air. In 1899 he was admiring the sight of Mount Everest from the terrace of his hotel in Darjeeling, about 100 miles away, and he concluded from the dimness of the mountain's outline that a good part of its light was scattered away. He determined the scattering power of each molecule from the index of refraction of air, and he found the number of air molecules per cubic centimeter at sea level to be 3×10^{19}, which is very close to the correct value.

Now we know why the sky is blue. Why, then, are clouds so white? Clouds are small droplets of water suspended in air. Why do they react differently to sunlight? The water molecule

RESPONSE OF OSCILLATOR TO PERIODIC DRIVING FORCE serves as a model of how the electrons of an atom respond to the driving force of light. The response of each oscillator (b, c, d, e) depends on its particular resonance frequency, ω_0. The driving force (a) has a frequency of ω. When ω_0 is much greater than ω, the oscillator responds in phase but only weakly (b). When ω_0 equals ω, the response reaches a maximum and is 90 degrees out of phase (c). When ω_0 is much less than ω, the response is again weak and 180 degrees out of phase (d). This weak response closely resembles the response of a free electron (e).

also has resonances in the infrared and in the ultraviolet, resonances not much different from those of oxygen and nitrogen molecules. Water molecules should react to sunlight in a similar way. There is, however, an essential difference. We determined the scattering of sunlight in air by assuming that each molecule reradiates independently of the others, so that the total scattered intensity is the sum of the individual molecular intensities. That is correct for a gas such as air because gas molecules are located at random in space, and thus there is no particular interference among the individual radiations of the molecules in any direction other than the direction of the incident sunlight.

That is no longer the case when the molecules or atoms take on a more orderly arrangement, as they do in solids and liquids and even in the droplets of a cloud. In order to understand the effect of light on matter in bulk, we must study how electromagnetic waves react to a large number of more or less regularly arranged oscillators, when the average distance between the oscillators is small compared with the wavelength of visible light. As we have seen, under the influence of incident light every oscillator emits a light wave. Because the oscillators are no longer randomly spaced, however, these waves tend to interfere with one another in a definite way: there is constructive interference in the forward direction (the direction of the light path) and destructive interference in all other directions. The individual waves build up to a strong wave called the refracted wave; in any other direction the waves tend to cancel one another. If the oscillators are in a regular array, the cancellation is complete [see illustration on next page].

The refracted wave travels with a velocity v that differs from the ordinary light velocity c. The ratio c/v is called the refractive index n of the medium. There is a simple relation connecting the value of n with the amplitude A of the oscillator vibrations. The greater this amplitude is under the influence of a given and fixed driving force, the more n departs from unity. Knowing the refractive index of air, Lord Rayleigh used this relation to find the amplitude in sunlight of the oscillators representing the air molecules.

In a regular and uniform arrangement of atoms the reemitted waves build up to a single refracted wave. There is no individual, or incoherent, scattering by each oscillator, as occurs in a gas such as air. As long as a crystal or a liquid contains heat it cannot be

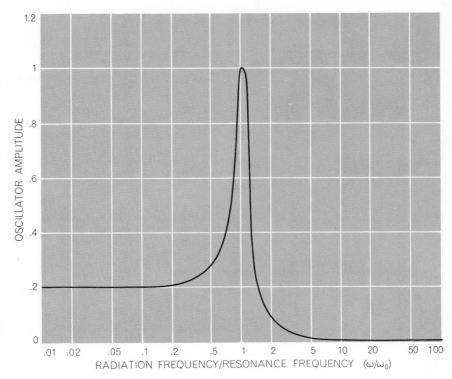

OSCILLATOR AMPLITUDE is a function of the ratio between the frequency of the driving force, ω, and the oscillator's resonance frequency, ω_0. This ratio, ω/ω_0, is expressed in the horizontal scale, which is logarithmic. The amplitude approaches a constant value (*left*) when the driving frequency is much below resonance. This is the situation when molecules of nitrogen and oxygen in the atmosphere are exposed to visible light. When the driving frequency is much above resonance, the amplitude decreases as the square of ω/ω_0.

completely regular. The atoms or molecules are constantly vibrating, and in addition there are always some irregularities and imperfections in the crystal structure. These irregularities scatter some of the light away from the direction of the refracted wave. This scattering, however, is much weaker than the scattering in air, assuming equivalent numbers of atoms. For example, water is 1,000 times denser than air, but its incoherent molecular scattering is only five times greater per unit volume than the scattering in air that makes the sky blue.

Now let us see what happens when light impinges on the surface of a liquid or a solid or a cloud droplet. Again we replace each atom by an oscillator. These oscillators vibrate under the influence of the incident light and emit light waves. In the bulk of the material all these light waves, apart from the weak incoherent scattering, add up to one strong refracted wave. This is not so, however, near the surface of the material. There is a thin layer of oscillators at the surface (about as deep as half a wavelength) for which the back radiation is not completely canceled by interference. The radiations backward of

these oscillators add up to a "reflected" wave [see illustration on page 21].

What is the color of this reflected light if the incident light is white? One might perhaps conclude that it should be as blue as the sky, since it too comes from the reradiation of oscillators and we have learned that the intensity of this reradiation is proportional to the fourth power of the frequency. Actually it is as white as the incident light. The intensity of the reflected light with respect to the incident light in water, glass or crystals is practically independent of the frequency.

The explanation is that the reflected wave is a coherent composite of many individual reradiations. The oscillators, since they are not randomly distributed, reradiate in unison. That by itself would not yet explain the difference; it would only tell us that the reradiated intensity is high. In a coherent radiation it is the amplitudes that add up and not the intensities. Hence N coherent oscillators give N^2 times the intensity of one individual radiation. It still would seem that the reradiation should be blue, inasmuch as the radiation intensity of each oscillator increases strongly with frequency. What happens, however, is that the

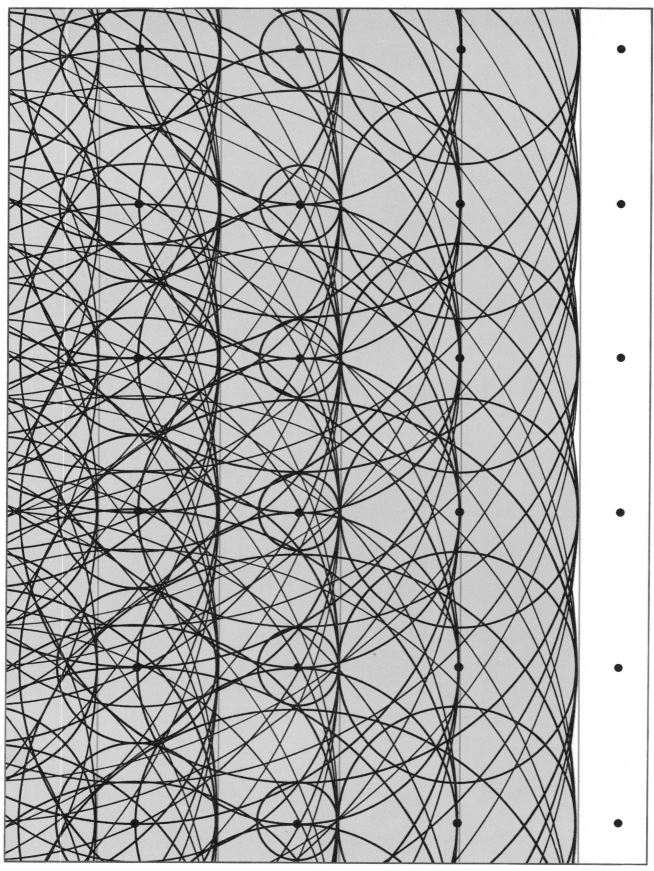

REFRACTED WAVE IN CRYSTAL consists of a parallel series of plane waves (*dark color*) formed by the crests of many spherical waves (*black circles*). The spherical waves depicted here represent light reemitted by the atoms (*black dots*) in a crystal that is exposed to a light beam entering from the left. The refracted wave is traveling to the right. The situation in glass and water is similar.

number of oscillators acting in unison also depends on the frequency: the layer that gives rise to reflection is half a wavelength deep, and the area of the layer whose reflected light arrives in step, or with the same phase, at a given point in space is also proportional to the wavelength. (This area is known as the first Fresnel zone. The radiations from all other parts of the surface interfere with one another, so that they give no light at that point.) Hence the number N of oscillators producing light in unison is proportional to the square of the wavelength. The intensity of this light is proportional to N^2. The net effect is to cancel the fourth power of the frequency, because higher frequency means smaller wavelength and a smaller value of N. As a consequence the reflected-light intensity is independent of frequency. Therefore clouds are white: the incident sunlight is reflected at the surface of the water droplets without change in spectral composition.

On the same basis we can understand the transparency of water, of glass and of crystals such as salt, sugar and quartz. If light impinges on these substances, it is partially reflected at the surface but without preference for any color. The rest of the light enters the substance and propagates as a refracted wave within it. Therefore these objects look colorless. Their outlines are nonetheless visible because of the reflection of the light at the surfaces.

Sometimes such objects may exhibit color under special circumstances. Reflection and refraction are only approximately independent of frequency. Both increase slightly at higher frequencies because such frequencies are a little closer to the natural resonance of the atom. Although these differences amount to only a few percent, they can become important if the details of refraction and reflection are critically involved in the way the light returns to the observer. Then, as in the case of a rainbow, these small differences may spread white light into its constituent colors.

Transparent substances with a large smooth surface reflect part of the incident light in a fixed direction according to the familiar laws of reflection. Therefore extended plane surfaces of colorless substances (windowpanes, water surfaces) can produce mirror images. If such colorless substances are in the form of small grains, each grain being larger than the wavelength of light, the substances appear white, like clouds. The incident white light is partially reflected in many directions, depending on the orientation of the grain surfaces. The light that penetrates the grains is again partially reflected at the inside surfaces, and after several reflections and refractions it comes back to the eye of the observer from various directions. Since none of these processes discriminates against any color, the returning light will be white and diffuse. This explains the color of snow, of salt and sugar in small grains and of white pills and powders: all consist of small crystals of molecules with resonances only in the infrared and in the ultraviolet. The whiteness of paper has the same origin. Paper consists of an irregular weave of transparent fibers [*see illustrations on next page*]. The molecules of the fibers also have no resonances in the visible region. The fibers reflect and refract light in the same way as fine grains of salt or snow.

If the grains are smaller than the wavelength of light, there are not enough oscillators in the grain to establish ordinary reflection and refraction. The situation is then more as it is in a gas of independent molecules, and the substance looks bluish. One can see this on a dry day when a cloud disappears. What often happens is simply that the droplets become smaller and smaller by evaporation until the cloud appears blue. The blue color of cigarette smoke is also evidence that the particles are smaller than the wavelength of visible light. The color of the sky above our cities is largely determined by the way sunlight is scattered by particles of smoke or dust, some larger than the wavelength of light, some smaller. That is why the city sky is a pale mixture of white and blue—far from the deep, rich blue that prevails where the air is clear.

Although water is transparent because

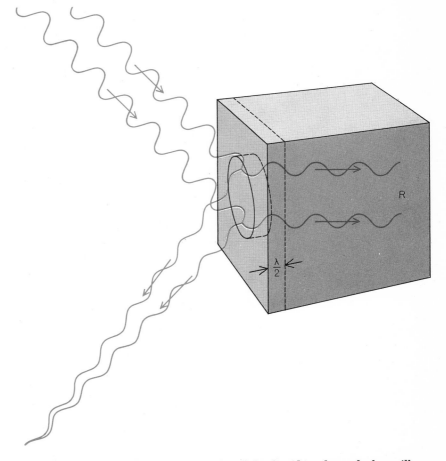

REFLECTION OF LIGHT from the surface of a solid or liquid involves only the oscillators (electrons) located in a small, pillbox-shaped volume at the surface of the material. When light (I) impinges on a smooth surface, part of the light proceeds into the material as a refracted wave (R) and part is reflected toward the observer (P). The radiation that makes up the reflected wave originates in a thin layer whose thickness is about half the wavelength of the incident light. The oscillators whose radiation adds up coherently at P are contained in a flat cylinder whose top surface is about λd in area, where λ is the wavelength of the light and d is the distance from the surface to the observer. This area is called the first Fresnel zone. For a spherical surface of radius R the area of the first Fresnel zone is equal to $\pi \lambda R$, provided that the distance to the observer is large compared with R.

it has strong resonances only in the infrared and the ultraviolet, it does have a slight color of its own. This is not the wonderful deep blue one often sees on the surface of a lake or an ocean. That blue is the reflected color of the sky. The intrinsic color of water is a pale greenish blue that results from a weak absorption of red light. Because of its strong electric polarity the water molecule vibrates readily when it is exposed to infrared radiation. Indeed, its infrared resonances are so strong that they reach even into the visible red [*see top illustration on page 24*].

These resonances represent true absorptions of light because the energy of the light quantum absorbed is transformed into heat motion. The weak resonances in the visible red therefore cause a slight absorption of red light in water. Fifteen meters of water reduces red light to a quarter of its original intensity. Practically no red sunlight reaches a depth below 30 meters in the sea. At such depths everything looks green. Many deep-sea crustaceans are found to be red when they are raised to the surface. In their normal environment they appear black. The selection mechanisms of evolution could not distinguish between black and red under such conditions.

The greenish-blue color of water is different in kind from the blue color of the sky. It is a color produced by the preferential absorption of the red and not by the preferential reemission of the blue, as it is in the sky. One way to be convinced of this difference between air and water is to look at a white object under the surface of water: it looks bluish green. On the other hand, a snowy slope seen through many miles of air looks yellowish. In the first instance the red light was absorbed; in the second the blue light was scattered away.

Most of the colors we see around us are due to preferential absorption: the colors of leaves, flowers, birds, butterflies, rubies, emeralds and the whole gamut of paints and dyes. What accounts for the preferential absorption in such a diverse range of things and substances? Most atoms and molecules have resonances only in the infrared and the ultraviolet. In order to produce a resonance in the visible region the excitation energy must be between 1.5 and three electron volts. These are rather small values for electron excitations and large values for molecular vibrations. There are, however, atoms and molecules that do have excited states in that region. They are atoms with several electrons in incomplete shells and certain organic compounds: the dyestuffs. Such atoms can be excited by rearranging the electrons in the incomplete shell, which requires less energy than excitation to a higher shell. The dyestuffs are chain or ring molecules in which the electrons move freely along the chain or the ring. They are spread out, so to speak, over larger distances than electrons in ordinary atoms and molecules. The excited states in such a system are of lower energy than they are in atoms, because larger size gives rise to longer electron wavelengths, and this in turn is associated with lower frequency and thus lower excitation energy. Thousands of chemists have devoted their professional lives to the synthesis of organic molecules that have resonances in one part or another of the visible spectrum [*see illustration on opposite page*].

Although low-lying excited states give rise to resonance frequencies in the visible region, other conditions must be fulfilled before a molecule will serve as a dye. First, one must be sure that the light quantum is not simply reemitted after its absorption has lifted the molecule into the excited state. One wants the energy of the excited state to be transformed preferentially into heat motion. This will be the case if we deal with matter in

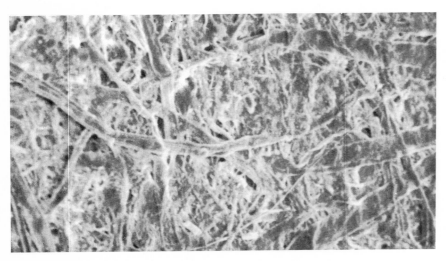

ORDINARY PAPER consists of a random mesh of translucent cellulose fibers. This 125-diameter magnification was made with a scanning electron microscope by Consolidated Papers, Inc. In such a micrograph the object appears to be tilted at an angle of 45 degrees.

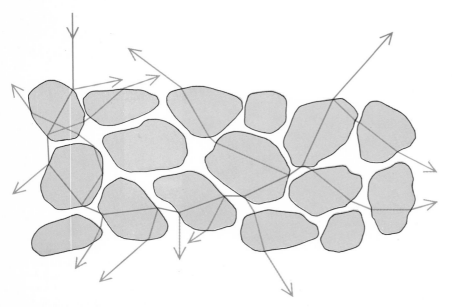

REFLECTION OF LIGHT FROM PAPER SURFACE involves many refractions and reflections as the rays of incident light perform a random walk through a mesh of translucent fibers, represented here in cross section. The multiple refractions of a single entering beam are traced in dark color; beams reflected from various surfaces are shown in light color.

bulk, liquid or solid. Under such circumstances reemission of light is very improbable. Second, the resonance frequencies must be spread over a broad interval. A dye with a narrow absorption band would reflect most wavelengths and thus look practically white. Here again matter in bulk contributes to the desired effect. In liquids and solids the energy levels of atoms or molecules are expanded into broad energy bands, with the result that resonances are spread over broad ranges of frequency. For example, a red dye absorbs light of all visible frequencies except the red. A green paint absorbs red and yellow as well as blue and violet. The absorption of a dye covers the visible spectrum with the exception of the actual color of the material. Some people may have wondered why a mixture of paint of all colors gives rise to a dirty black, although we are told that white is the sum of all colors. Colored paints function not by adding parts of the spectrum but by subtracting them. Hence a mixture of red, green and blue paints will absorb all wavelengths and look virtually black.

A simple and striking color effect is the one produced by a stained-glass window. The dyestuff is contained in the glass. When light falls on stained glass, it is partially reflected at the surface, just as it is by ordinary glass. Indeed, the reflection is a little stronger for those frequencies that are absorbed, because, as we saw earlier, the amplitude of vibration is larger when the frequency is in resonance with the system. This effect, however, is usually not very pronounced, since the main reflection comes from the oscillators with resonances in the ultraviolet, as it does in ordinary glass. The part of the light that penetrates the body of the glass—the refracted wave—is subjected to the absorbing effect of the dye. Accordingly only light of the frequency that is not absorbed will pass through the glass. That is why one obtains such impressive color effects when white light penetrates stained glass. The color of the glass is less strong when one looks at the side that is illuminated. The reflection from the surface is practically colorless; the principal color one sees is from light that has penetrated the glass and is reflected again by the second surface [see bottom illustration on next page].

A painted sheet of paper will serve as an example of ordinary painted objects. The paint causes the fibers of the paper to become impregnated with dye. When white light falls on paper, it is reflected and refracted many times before it comes back to our eyes. Whenever the

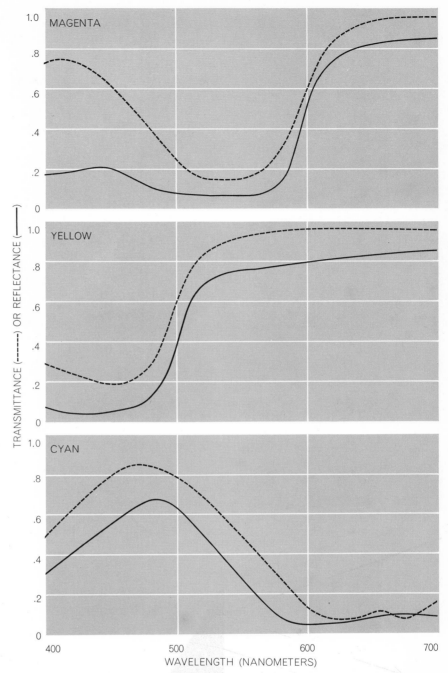

SPECTRAL CHARACTERISTICS of colored inks (*solid curves*) and of an optimum set of dyes for color film (*broken curves*) are plotted in these three panels. The inks and dyes are those represented in the illustration on page 16. There it can be seen that the dyes of color film can produce colors that are more highly saturated than those attainable with printing inks. The reason becomes clear in these curves: each of the color film dyes transmits more of the desired wavelengths than the corresponding printing ink is able to reflect.

light penetrates a fiber, the dye absorbs part of it: the fibers act as small pieces of stained glass. The best color effect is achieved when the reflecting power of the fiber is not too strong, so that most of the light enters the fiber. One remembers childhood experience with watercolors, which are most intense while the paper is still wet. The water reduces the difference in refraction between the fibers

and the interstices, thereby reducing the reflection of the fiber surfaces.

Glossy colored paper has a smooth surface. Its irregularities are small compared with the wavelength of light. The incident light is partially reflected without much preference for one color over another, but it is reflected by the smooth surface at a fixed angle according to the familiar laws of reflection. At any other

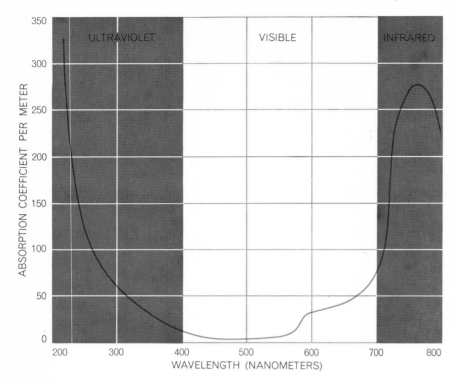

LIGHT ABSORPTION BY WATER is negligible between 400 and 580 nanometers in the visible part of the spectrum. The absorption increases in the orange and red region and rises steeply in the near infrared. Absorption is also strong in the ultraviolet. The absorption is caused by resonances of the water molecule in response to various wavelengths.

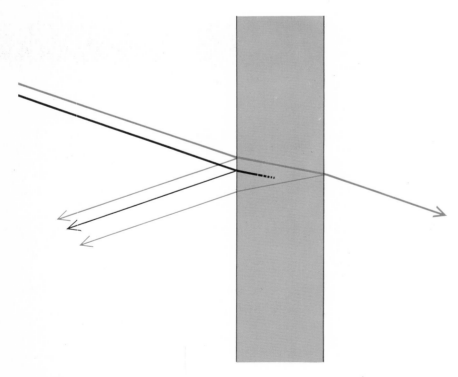

COLOR OF STAINED GLASS depends on which wavelengths the glass absorbs. Here it is assumed that the glass absorbs the shorter wavelengths so that primarily red light is transmitted. Thus blue light, represented here by black, enters the glass and is absorbed; it is also partially reflected. Red light is reflected from the rear surface as well as from the front, so that the total reflected light is predominantly red. Thus red stained glass looks red by reflected as well as by transmitted light; the transmitted color is purer, however.

angle most of the light that reaches the eye will have made several passages through the fibers before leaving the paper. That is why the color of the light is clear and deep: it is free of any uncolored direct reflection. Sometimes glossy paper demonstrates the fact that being in resonance implies larger amplitudes and therefore stronger reflection. One often notices an increased reflection of the deeply colored parts of a glossy picture, but only when the dye is deposited in the uppermost layer. Examine the colored illustrations in this article.

Objects are black when there is absorption for all visible frequencies. Well-known examples are graphite and tar. Black objects do not absorb all light that falls on them. There is always some reflection at the surface. Think of the reflection of the polished surface of a black shoe. A dull black surface reflects as strongly as a polished one but the reflected rays are distributed in all directions. A black surface with very low reflectivity can be produced by placing a few hundred razor blades in a stack. When the edges of the blades are viewed end on, they appear to be nearly dead black even though they are highly polished [see illustrations on opposite page]. The explanation is that light is trapped between the closely spaced edges and is absorbed after being reflected many times.

The most beautiful colors of all—the colors of plants, trees and flowers—are based on the same principle of preferential absorption. The cells of plants are filled with dyes: chlorophyll in green leaves and blades of grass, other dyestuffs in the petals of flowers. White light that falls on plants is reflected and refracted by the cells; a large part of the light enters the cells, in the same way it does the fibers of paper. When it returns to the eye, all the colors but one or two are strongly reduced by absorption. Only green light escapes from chlorophyll-containing cells, only red light from the petals of red flowers.

We now turn to the visual appearance of metals. A metal is characterized by the fact that within the confines of the material there are many electrons —the conduction electrons—extending over many atomic diameters. These electrons are most important for the optical properties of metals. There is one, two or sometimes three electrons per atom among the conduction electrons. The rest of the atomic electrons remain bound to the atoms. The conduction electrons can be regarded as an electron gas that penetrates the crystal lattice

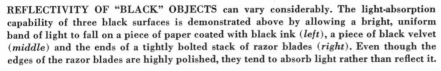

REFLECTIVITY OF "BLACK" OBJECTS can vary considerably. The light-absorption capability of three black surfaces is demonstrated above by allowing a bright, uniform band of light to fall on a piece of paper coated with black ink (*left*), a piece of black velvet (*middle*) and the ends of a tightly bolted stack of razor blades (*right*). Even though the edges of the razor blades are highly polished, they tend to absorb light rather than reflect it.

RAZOR-BLADE LIGHT TRAP consists of some two hundred blades bolted together. Light that enters the wedges between adjacent blades is reflected so many times that most of it is absorbed before it can escape.

without much hindrance. The reason for this quasi-free motion lies in the wave nature of the electron. Although it is true that an electron wave is scattered by each of the metal atoms, the regular arrangement of atoms in the lattice makes the scattered waves interfere in a definite way: the waves all add up to one undisturbed wave in the forward direction. The corresponding electron motion is therefore the motion of a free particle. This is a phenomenon closely related to the formation of a refracted wave when light penetrates a crystal.

The motion of the conduction electrons is not completely free, however. Thermal agitation of the crystal lattice and other lattice imperfections produce some scattering away from the main electron wave. This is closely analogous to the weak scattering of the refracted light wave in a crystal. The effect can be expressed as a kind of friction of the conduction electrons. It is the cause of the electrical resistance in metals. In the reaction of electrons to visible light, however, friction does not play an important role; we are allowed to consider the electrons as freely moving.

What is the behavior of a free electron under the influence of light? It performs vibrations of the same frequency as the frequency of the driving force but of opposite phase. When the force is moving in one direction, the electron moves in the other one. It is the same kind of movement an oscillator performs when the driving frequency is much higher than its resonance frequency. A free electron in plain sunlight performs vibrations with an amplitude about 10

times larger than the amplitude of electrons in water and in crystals, or several times 10^{-17} meter.

What happens when light impinges on a metallic surface? The answer is, very much the same as happens when light strikes the surface of a liquid or a crystal, but there is one important difference. Since the resonance frequencies of a liquid or a crystal are higher than the frequency of light, they vibrate in phase with the light. In a metal, however, the electrons vibrate in *opposite* phase. Under these conditions a refracted light wave cannot be propagated if the density of electrons and the amplitude of their vibration is above a certain limit. The limit can be expressed in terms of the "plasma frequency" ω_p, which is given by the equation $\omega_p = (Ne^2/m)^{\frac{1}{2}}$, where N is the number of electrons per cubic centimeter and m is the electron mass. This frequency usually is in the ultraviolet. Whenever the light frequency is less than ω_p, as it always is for visible light, no refracted wave can develop in the medium; there are too many electrons inside moving in phase opposite to the light.

Since no light energy can propagate into the material, all energy of the incoming light must go into the reflected wave. Just as with water or glass, the reflected light wave is produced in a thin layer at the surface of the metal, a layer no thicker than the wavelength of the light. A more exact calculation shows that in a metal this thickness is equal to the wavelength corresponding to the plasma frequency divided by 2π. This value is less than 10^{-7} meter. Unlike the

wave reflected from water and glass, however, the wave reflected from a metal surface has almost the full intensity of the incoming wave, apart from small energy losses due to the friction of the vibrating electrons in the surface. This is why "white" metals such as silver and aluminum are so shiny: they reflect almost all visible light regardless of its frequency. Smooth surfaces of these metals therefore are ideal mirrors.

In colored metals such as copper or gold there are additional losses apart from the electron friction. These losses come from absorption by electrons other than the conduction electrons. Each atom in a metal is surrounded by shells of those electrons that remain with the atoms after the conduction electrons have detached themselves and formed the gas of free electrons. The resonance frequencies of the remaining electrons are usually in the ultraviolet and thus do not contribute to any color. In copper and gold, however, the bound electrons are part of an incomplete shell and do have resonances in the blue-violet that lead to absorption. As a result copper and gold have a reddish-yellow appearance.

Many color phenomena have not been treated here: the color of thin films, of fluorescent materials, of light emitted by flames, of electric discharges as produced in neon tubes and many others. We have taken up only the most common features of colored objects in order to provide some insight into the optical processes that occur on the surface of things when they are illuminated by light and seen by our eyes.

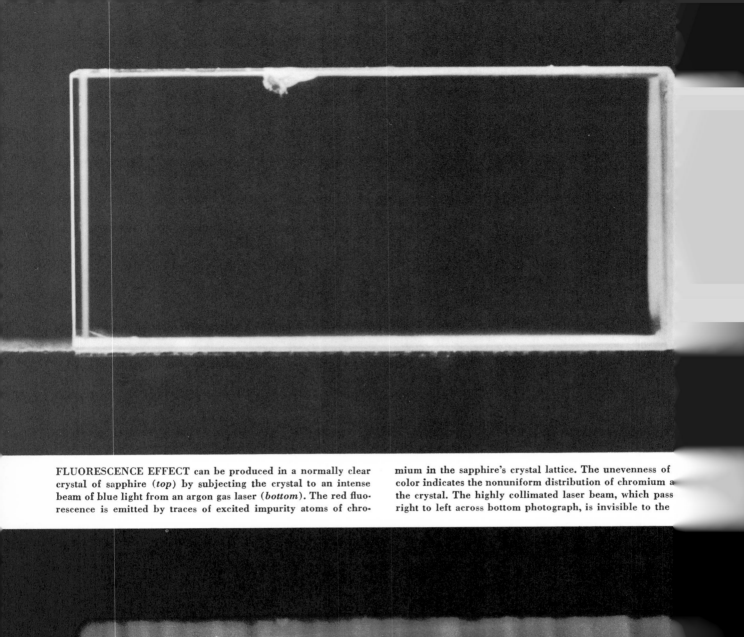

FLUORESCENCE EFFECT can be produced in a normally clear crystal of sapphire (*top*) by subjecting the crystal to an intense beam of blue light from an argon gas laser (*bottom*). The red fluorescence is emitted by traces of excited impurity atoms of chro- mium in the sapphire's crystal lattice. The unevenness of color indicates the nonuniform distribution of chromium a the crystal. The highly collimated laser beam, which pass right to left across bottom photograph, is invisible to the

3

The Optical Properties of Materials

Ali Javan   September 1967

Before the advent of quantum physics one could give only very crude answers to such elementary questions as: Why do materials have characteristic colors? Why do all materials glow when they are heated? What makes one material transparent and another opaque?

We now know that all these optical properties are intimately related to the way electrons are deployed in a material. This article explains how the modern theory of quantum mechanics accounts for the optical properties of materials in terms of their electronic structure, and shows how this knowledge is being used in the development of new materials for optical applications. For historical as well as expository reasons I shall begin by describing the optical behavior of isolated atoms, such as one finds in a gas, and then proceed to show how this comparatively simple picture is related to the complex many-body problem presented by a typical solid material.

The insights of quantum mechanics have come in large part from spectroscopy, which began more than 300 years ago with the experiments of Isaac Newton. In his *Opticks* Newton wrote: "In a very dark Chamber, at a round Hole, about one third Part of an Inch broad, made in the Shut of a Window, I placed a Glass Prism, whereby the Beam of the Sun's Light, which came in at that Hole, might be refracted upwards toward the opposite Wall of the Chamber, and there form a colour'd Image of the Sun." It was this experiment that led Newton to discover that his observed solar spectrum did not originate in the glass prism but was a property of the sunlight itself. The prism merely refracted the different colors at different angles. This simple arrangement was the first spectroscope, and Newton's experi-ment marked the first application of spectroscopy to the study of the interaction of light and matter.

It is now common knowledge that the colors observed by Newton correspond to electromagnetic waves of various frequencies, each with a specified wavelength: the higher the frequency, the shorter the wavelength, and vice versa. For example, the frequency of visible light extends from about 4,300 to 10,000 trillion cycles per second, corresponding to wavelengths of about 7,700 to 3,900 angstrom units (ten-billionths of a meter). The angle of refraction of a particular colored ray through a piece of glass is a unique function of its wavelength: the shorter the wavelength, the larger the angle of refraction. Although Newton did not advocate a wave theory of light, he described the various colors by their "degree of refrangibility" as they passed the prism of his spectroscope.

A great deal of useful information is contained in the characteristic spectra associated with the various species and states of matter. Indeed, one might say that matter communicates with us by means of the spectrum of light that it emits and with which it interacts. Consider the visible spectrum of the sun as seen through Newton's prism. The dominant feature of the solar spectrum is a color continuum extending over the entire visible range from red to violet. The distribution of intensity among these colors is governed by the temperature of the emitting surface of the sun. The particular color combination that appears to us as white sunlight indicates a surface temperature of about 6,000 degrees centigrade.

In fact, at a given temperature all hot bodies, regardless of their composition, emit a continuous spectrum of rays with an identical distribution of intensity. As the temperature of the body is increased, this distribution changes: the color being emitted at maximum intensity shifts toward the violet end of the spectrum. Thus stars that have higher surface temperatures than the sun appear blue against the night sky. Similarly, as the filament of an incandescent electric light bulb is gradually heated, its dominant color changes from an initial dull red to a bright yellowish white.

If Newton had made a very narrow slit instead of a hole in the "shut" of his window, he would probably have discovered that his solar spectrum also contained a sprinkling of narrow, dark lines. A century passed, however, before these delicate features came to the attention of Joseph von Fraunhofer, a German master of optical devices. Fraunhofer

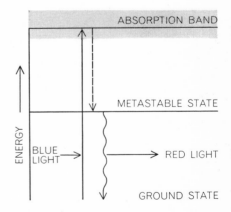

ENERGY-LEVEL DIAGRAM of an isolated chromium atom shows how the red fluorescence effect originates in a clear sapphire. The chromium atom absorbs a photon of blue light, causing an electron in the atom to be excited from its ground state to a broad upper absorption level. A nonradiative process involving an exchange of energy with the crystal lattice then causes the electron to decay to a lower metastable energy state, from which it decays spontaneously to the ground state, emitting a photon of red light.

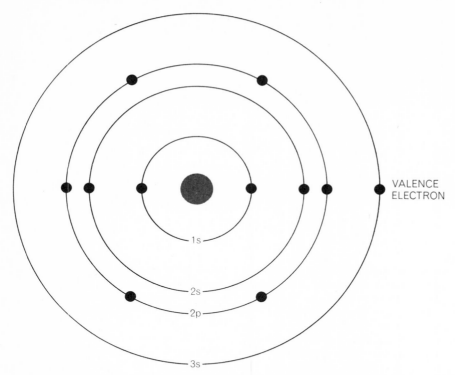

VALENCE
ELECTRON

SODIUM ATOM has 11 electrons, one of which—the valence electron—occupies the atom's outer boundary and is responsible for the chemical behavior of sodium as an alkali metal. The distinct quantum states of this single valence electron are also responsible for the optical properties of an isolated sodium atom. The rest of the electrons form closed inner shells and are tightly bound to the nucleus. In spectrographic terminology the electron shells of the elements are designated 1, 2, 3, 4, 5 and so on. The subshells are designated *s*, *p*, *d* and *f*.

mapped hundreds of these dark lines, lettering eight of the most prominent *A* through *H*. Another 50 years passed before Fraunhofer's work led to the exciting discovery that many elements found on the earth also exist on the sun. It then became clear that the Fraunhofer lines were caused by the passage of solar rays through the sun's outer atmosphere. Layers of gas in this atmosphere contain isolated atoms of certain elements, which characteristically absorb the sun's rays only at sharp and well-defined wavelengths. For example, a pair of closely spaced dark lines in the yellow region of the solar spectrum—Fraunhofer's *D* lines—are due to the absorption of sunlight by sodium atoms.

The absorption lines of sodium and other elements can be reproduced in the laboratory by means of a simple absorption spectroscope. When one views an ordinary incandescent lamp through a prism spectroscope with a narrow slit, one sees a continuous spectrum of color extending from red to blue. Now, if one places a flame containing sodium atoms between the lamp and the slit, the continuous spectrum is altered in the yellow region, where the Fraunhofer *D* lines are located. In fact, the intensity of the light is diminished by an appreciable

amount precisely at the wavelengths of the two *D* lines. This reduction in intensity is caused by the absorption of light by the sodium atoms in the flame. An element that strongly absorbs an incident light ray at a definite wavelength may become entirely transparent at a slightly different wavelength. The width of such an absorption line is defined by the range of wavelengths within which strong absorption takes place.

The existence of characteristic absorption lines is an important aspect of the optical properties of matter in all three of its states: gas, liquid and solid. Isolated atoms or molecules in a gas at moderate pressure yield sharp, narrow absorption lines, which become somewhat broader as the pressure is raised. In liquids and solids these absorption lines become very broad, in some cases encompassing sizable regions of the visible spectrum. Thus red glass examined through an absorption spectroscope shows a strong absorption band covering the green and blue regions and leaving the red region transparent, whereas blue glass shows a strong absorption band in the red and yellow regions and is transparent in the blue region. A completely transparent glass of course shows no ab-

sorption bands in the visible region of the spectrum.

The absorption characteristics of materials are not restricted to the visible region of the spectrum. A crystal transparent to visible light may be completely opaque in the infrared and ultraviolet regions. Metals, on the other hand, reflect visible light and hence are opaque in this region, but they are often transparent at short ultraviolet wavelengths.

Simultaneous with the discovery that elements have characteristic absorption lines, it was found that elements are also capable of emitting characteristic radiation at well-defined wavelengths. These emission lines were first observed in flames and later in electrically excited gases. In recent years they have also been produced by electrically or optically excited impurity atoms in certain solids, a situation that is quite similar to that in a gas. When the spectra of such light sources are analyzed in a prism spectroscope, a series of sharp bright lines is obtained. The wavelengths of the emission lines for a particular element coincide exactly with that element's characteristic absorption lines. Sodium, for example, which strongly absorbs at the Fraunhofer *D* lines, also emits radiation at these wavelengths.

During the 1850's it was further recognized that some of an element's emission lines could be strongly "reabsorbed" by the same element. A related optical property has been added to this list in our own century. Under appropriate conditions matter is capable of amplifying instead of absorbing an incident light ray. This property—the basis of the modern laser—will be discussed later in this article.

Toward the end of the 19th century there was collected a vast body of data on the precise wavelengths of the absorption and emission lines in the spectra of a great many elements. Moreover, curious regularities were recognized in some of these spectra. The interpretation of these regularities became a major challenge of the time. The precision with which the spectral lines were charted provided one of the keys to quantum mechanics—the ultimate interpretation of the optical properties of matter.

In the initial formulation of quantum mechanics hydrogen played a decisive role. Its simple atomic structure of one electron bound to one proton produced a line spectrum that revealed the quantum nature of an atom's electronic structure in its barest essentials. These laws were then generalized and applied to the optical properties of more complex atoms containing many electrons and finally to atoms in the liquid and the solid states.

In their present form the laws of quantum mechanics in principle embrace all the optical properties of gases, liquids and solids. The mathematical manipulation of these laws becomes exceedingly intricate, however, when one is dealing with many-body interactions, particularly in solids. For the purposes of this article, therefore, the hydrogen atom will serve as a starting point for further generalization about more complex systems.

The hydrogen atom can be described in quantum-mechanical terms as an electron "cloud" surrounding a single proton nucleus, the volume of the cloud being much larger than that of the nucleus. Although the electron behaves in some respects as a pointlike particle with a definite charge and mass, in other respects its position can be regarded as being spread over an extended volume whose size and shape depend on the electron's motion. The density of this cloud at each point around the nucleus represents the probability of finding the electron at that point. The total internal energy of the atom is uniquely determined by the configuration of the electron cloud, and the configuration is in turn is governed by the wavelike behavior of the electron.

An atom can exist in only one of a number of quantized energy states, each state corresponding to an electron cloud of a different size or shape. Accordingly an atom can change its energy only in distinct quantized steps, each step a transition from one energy state to another. The various states, arranged in order of increasing energy, constitute the energy-level diagram of the atom.

Atoms that have more than one electron can be similarly described. In that case, however, the different electrons occupy different quantum states, and the internal energy arises from electron-electron interactions as well as from electron-nucleus interactions. Most of the chemical and optical properties of an atom are determined by the quantum states of its valence electrons, which occupy the atom's outer boundary. The rest of the electrons form closed inner shells and are tightly bound to the nucleus. An atom of sodium, for example, has 11 electrons, one of which is the valence electron responsible for the chemical behavior of sodium as an alkali metal [*see illustration on opposite page*]. The distinct energies associated with the various quantum states of this single valence electron are responsible for the optical

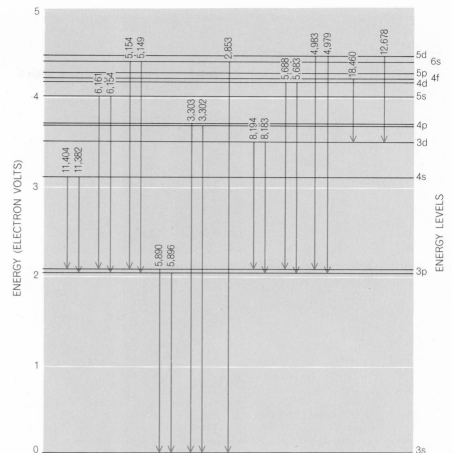

ENERGY-LEVEL DIAGRAM OF SODIUM ATOM shows some of the upper energy levels to which the valence electron (normally at the 3s level) can be excited by the input of energy to the atom. An excited electron can return to the 3s level by a variety of routes (*colored arrows*); for each transition from an upper level to a lower one the atom emits a photon of light with a characteristic wavelength, which is indicated in angstrom units on the arrow representing that transition. The two transitions from the split 3p level to the 3s level are responsible for the characteristic yellow *D* lines in the spectrum of sodium.

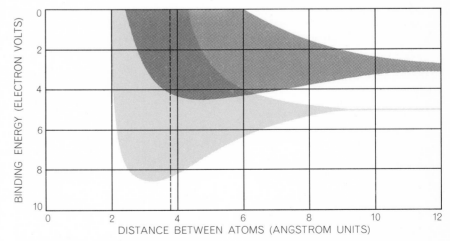

QUANTUM STATES OF SOLID SODIUM can be traced back to their origin as energy levels in the isolated sodium atom. This is done by assuming that the atoms of the solid are arranged on a fictitious crystal lattice with interatomic separations many times larger (*right*) than those found in the actual solid. As the interatomic separation is gradually reduced toward the value corresponding to that for the actual crystal lattice of sodium (*broken vertical line*), the energy levels of the atoms split into broad bands (*left*). The overlapping of the various bands in metals is responsible for their distinctive optical properties, such as color and opacity. Only the 3s (*color*) and 3p (*gray*) bands of sodium are shown here.

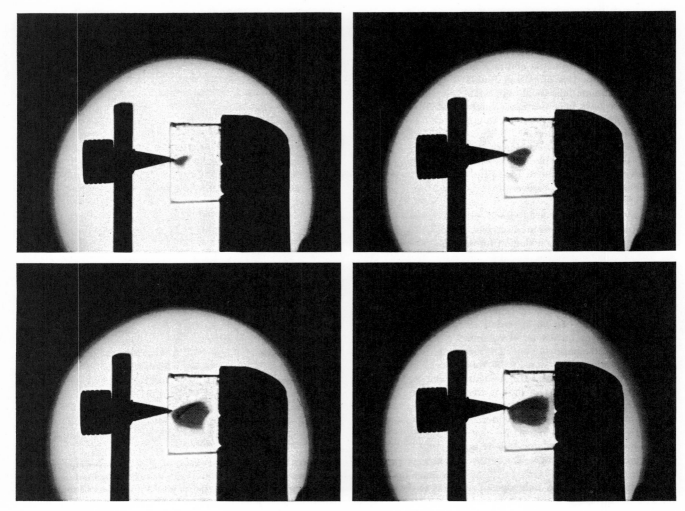

DIFFUSION OF COLOR CENTERS in a normally clear crystal of potassium chloride is demonstrated in this apparatus devised by R. L. Wild of the University of California at Riverside. The transparent crystal contains an equal number of positive and negative vacant lattice sites. A color center is an electron in one of the negative vacant lattice sites that is capable of absorbing light in the visible region of the spectrum. The extra electrons are injected into the crystal by means of a pointed stainless-steel electrode. A voltage of about 300 volts is applied to this electrode. The crystal and the electrodes are located in an oven maintained at about 550 degrees centigrade. At this temperature the color centers appear deep blue; at room temperature they would be purple. The interval between pictures in this sequence is about one second. The crystal is about 10 millimeters square and three millimeters thick.

properties of isolated sodium atoms in the gaseous phase.

There are several ways of looking at the system of quantum states in a solid. One of these views—the energy-band model—traces the quantum states of the solid back to their origin in the isolated atom. This is done by assuming that the atoms of a given solid are perfectly arranged on a fictitious crystal lattice with interatomic separations many times larger than those found in an actual solid. The quantized states of this fictitious solid are simply duplicates of the states of an isolated atom that undergoes negligible interactions with its neighbors. As the interatomic separation is gradually reduced toward the value corresponding to that for an actual crystal lattice, however, the energy levels of the atoms split into broad bands [see *bottom illustration on preceding page*]. This splitting occurs when the valence electron clouds of adjacent atoms begin to overlap appreciably, giving rise to strong interactions among the atoms. The overlapping of the various bands in metals is at the root of both their electrical conductivity and their distinctive optical properties, including such absorption characteristics as color and opacity. On the other hand, in an insulator such as sodium chloride or calcium fluoride the valence electrons occupy nonoverlapping bands and the crystals are generally transparent.

In addition there exist a variety of colored materials that derive their optical properties from the quantum states of impurity atoms embedded in the crystal lattice of an otherwise transparent solid. The width of the energy level of the impurity atom depends on the extent of its interaction with the host lattice. For a strongly interacting state the level is broad and forms a band similar to that of a pure solid; otherwise the level is narrow and resembles that of an isolated atom. For example, sapphire is a transparent ionic crystal consisting of aluminum oxide with traces of titanium and chromium, whereas ruby has the identical composition but with a few percent of the chromium. The absorption spectrum of a ruby shows wide absorption bands in the blue region, resulting in the ruby's characteristic pink color. The chromium ions, which substitute for aluminum ions in the crystal lattice of the ruby, are solely responsible for this absorption spectrum. The width of the bands shows that the chromium atom interacts quite strongly with the lattice.

A closely associated substitution can

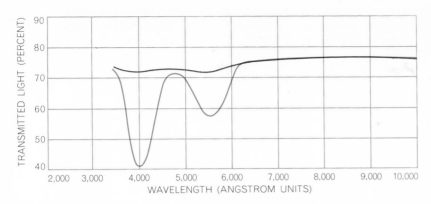

ABSORPTION SPECTRA of a clear sapphire (*gray curve*) and a pink ruby (*colored curve*) are compared. Both are ionic crystals of aluminum oxide with traces of certain impurities. The only difference between the crystals is that ruby has considerably more chromium, amounting to a few percent. As a result the absorption spectrum of the ruby shows strong absorption bands in the blue region, and this gives the ruby its characteristic pink color.

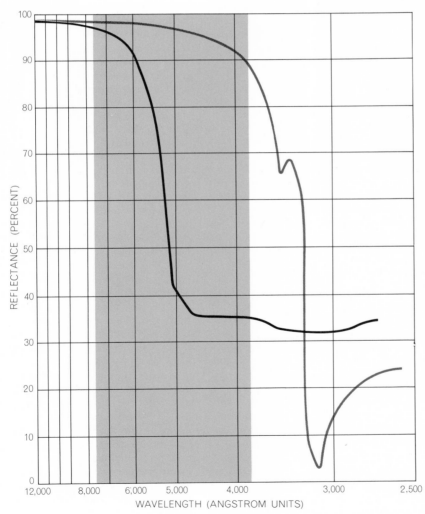

REFLECTANCE SPECTRA of gold (*black curve*) and silver (*gray curve*) are compared. Gold reflects red and yellow light strongly at the surface but allows some penetration by green rays, which are then completely absorbed within a small thickness of the bulk of the metal. Silver, on the other hand, strongly reflects incident light over most of the visible region of the spectrum (*color*) but allows considerable transmission in the ultraviolet.

take place in certain ionic crystals such as potassium chloride. In this case missing chlorine atoms in the crystal lattice are replaced by free electrons, creating "color centers" with a characteristic absorption spectrum that gives the normally transparent crystal a purple or blue color depending on the temperature.

When an atom is in its lowest energy state, it prefers to stay there for an indefinite time unless it is disturbed by some external means. Such a disturbance can take the form of a collision with an external electron, causing the atom to be excited suddenly to a higher energy state. Once the atom is in an excited state, it tends to decay spontaneously to a lower energy level. The decay is accompanied by the emission of a light wave at a frequency that is uniquely and universally proportional to the change in the energy of the atom. This universal relation of energy change to frequency defines a resonance frequency for each pair of levels. In fact, whenever a spontaneous transition from a higher to a lower level occurs, an electron in the atom exhibits a decaying oscillatory motion at the resonance frequency of the corresponding pair of levels. The oscillation, in turn, is responsible for the light wave radiated at that frequency. When the emission ends, the emitted energy in the light wave precisely equals the change in energy of the atom. Thus the energy in the emitted light wave is also universally related to the frequency of that wave. Here the quantized nature of the atom goes hand in hand with the quantized state of the radiation field; one photon, or quantum of light, is emitted when one atomic transition occurs. The laws of quantum mechanics make it possible to calculate exactly the probability of spontaneous emission from one level to a lower one. The probability is high for some pairs of levels and exceedingly low for others.

In brief, the quantum states of an atom are defined by a set of energy levels, with a resonance frequency associated with each pair. An atom can decay with a predictable probability from a higher to a lower level by spontaneously emitting a photon at the corresponding resonance frequency. It must be emphasized that the exact energies of an atom's quantized states are predictable theoretically; one merely needs to know the number of electrons in the atom and the nature of its nucleus. The rest follows from the universal laws of the interactions of the electrons with the nucleus and with other electrons.

The emission line spectra of isolated

atoms can now be interpreted in terms of this quantum-mechanical picture. For instance, the energy-level diagram of a sodium atom contains two closely spaced levels immediately above its lowest energy state. The spontaneous transitions from these two levels to the lowest energy state are responsible for the emissions at the two closely spaced Fraunhofer *D* lines. Precise measurements of the difference in wavelength between these two lines reflect the difference in energy between the two excited levels. This "level-splitting" is a manifestation of an important property of the electron known as spin. In a crude sense an electron can be visualized as a spinning entity with a fixed angular momentum. In the more sophisticated theory the electron spin and its resulting interaction are shown to be necessary consequences of the laws of quantum mechanics when they are formulated in a manner consistent with the theory of relativity. These fundamental insights have all emerged from delicate experimental observations of the optical line spectra of the elements.

The structural detail of an atomic nucleus introduces additional minute features in the energy-level structure of an atom; these generally appear as further level-splittings or small energy shifts. The study of these effects in optical emission-line spectra has yielded a wealth of information about atomic nuclei, including their size, charge distribution and spinning behavior.

Let us turn now to the interaction of an isolated atom with an incident light wave. This interaction is particularly strong if the wavelength of the incident light is close to that of one of the atom's emission lines. In other words, strong interaction occurs when the incident light frequency is near or at the resonance frequency of a given pair of energy levels. When the atom is found in the lower level, it undergoes a transition to the upper level by absorbing energy from the incident light ray. The amount of absorbed energy is exactly the amount gained by the atom. The opposite happens when the atom is found in the upper level: the atom decays to the lower level by giving its energy change to the incident light wave. The latter process is an emission act induced by the applied field and drastically different from the spontaneous emission described above. In the induced emission the emitted light wave cannot be distinguished from the incident light. Spontaneous emission, however, is independent of an incident light ray and generally occurs isotropic-

ally—the emission probability is the same in any direction in space.

The induced emission probability, which is proportional to the intensity of the incident light, is exactly identical with the probability of the absorption process of an atom initially found in the lower level. An induced emission, however, must compete with the act of spontaneous emission, and at a low intensity spontaneous emission may predominate. Finally, the induced emission (or absorption) probability diminishes considerably if the frequency of the incident radiation is appreciably different from the resonance frequency of the atomic transition.

Induced emission by atoms in the upper level enhances the incident light, whereas absorption by atoms in the lower level attenuates it. Accordingly when the average number of atoms in the lower level exceeds that in the upper one, the absorbing transitions would prevail and a total attenuation of the light wave would result. The reverse process, called population inversion, occurs if the average number of atoms in the upper level is larger than the number in the lower—the incident light is then amplified as it passes through the medium. This kind of amplification, "light amplification by stimulated emission of radiation," is the underlying principle of the laser.

There exist a host of nonradiative processes that also cause transitions among atomic energy levels. These play an important role in determining the average number of atoms in each level and therefore establish the main absorption and emission characteristics of an ensemble of atoms. For instance, the impact of a free electron with an atom or the collision of two or more atoms can induce transitions among various atomic energy states without requiring either the emission or the absorption of a light wave. In such cases the quantized change in the internal energies of the atoms is determined by the kinetic energies of the collision partners.

For matter in thermal equilibrium the exact number of atoms in each level is uniquely determined by the temperature of the system. It is a general property of this thermal distribution that the average number of atoms in a lower level is always larger than that in an upper one. Because of this, matter in thermal equilibrium always attenuates an incident radiation at a frequency on or very near any atomic resonance frequency.

A broad class of systems exist that, though in a steady state, are not in thermal equilibrium and therefore cannot be

described in terms of temperature. Most of the universe is composed of such nonthermal systems. In these cases the average number of atoms may be larger in a lower or an upper level, depending on their excitations and decays. These systems allow amplification of an incident radiation when an upper level is more populated than the lower one.

Consider an ordinary neon lamp, essentially a glass tube filled with neon gas at low pressure. An electric voltage applied across a pair of electrodes at opposite ends of the tube causes the ionization of a small fraction of the neon atoms. This results in a stream of free electrons—an electric current—passing through the tube. The electrons collide with neon atoms and excite them into higher energy levels. The spontaneous emission from the various excited levels is responsible for the color of the lamp.

In such an electrically excited gaseous discharge the atomic population distribution is completely nonthermal. Under the proper conditions it could allow population inversion among some level pairs and amplification of light waves at the corresponding resonance frequencies. It was an oversight in scientific history that this possibility passed unrecognized in the late 1920's, since by that time quantum mechanics had successfully formulated the principles of induced emission and absorption of light, and the excitation processes in electrically excited gas discharges were also fairly well explored. All the necessary theoretical and technical information for the achievement of light amplification in an electrically excited gas was close at hand. However, physicists of the time were so preoccupied with the emission and absorption line spectra and the characteristics of matter in thermal equilibrium that they missed this exciting possibility. Thus laser amplification, based on the principle of population inversion in a gas discharge, was achieved some 30 years late.

A medium capable of a sufficient light amplification becomes unstable if it is placed between a pair of parallel mirrors. The light wave, propagating at right angles to the mirrors, will be reflected back and forth and enormously amplified by the medium. This process can be initially triggered by the spontaneous emission of a light ray in the amplifying medium itself. Output coupling can be provided by allowing a small beam of light to be transmitted through the surface of a mirror. This system, commonly called the laser, generates an intense directional light with a minute frequency spread. Several general types of laser exist, each of them using a different method to prepare level pairs with inverted populations. Among the major types are gas-discharge lasers, chemical lasers, semiconducting-diode lasers and homogeneous optically pumped liquid and solid-state lasers. These devices, useful in many practical applications, have also provided a new tool for research into the nature of matter.

Consider now an atom in its lowest energy level interacting weakly with a light ray whose energy does not correspond to the separation of any upper level from the ground state. It is no longer appropriate to describe this interaction in terms of absorption and emission accompanying a real atomic transition, since the frequency of the light is appreciably different from the resonances of atomic transitions. Actually the atom serves to weakly scatter the incident light in all directions while essentially remaining in its unperturbed energy state. The incident radiation will force an atomic electron to oscillate at the frequency of the light wave itself; the electron, in turn, radiates the scattered light wave in all directions at its oscillating frequency. The intensity of the reemitted light is generally a function of the incident light frequency and the proximity of this frequency to various atomic resonances.

When a collection of atoms is subjected to such an incident light wave, the atoms' reemitted waves interfere with one another. The propagation pattern of the resultant sum of the reradiated light waves depends on the density and spatial distribution of the scattering atoms. This effect is responsible for the index of refraction of a transparent material,

giving rise to the reflection and refraction of light. The reflection of an incident light by a transparent solid with a uniform density comes from the superposition of reemitted light waves by atoms at the surface boundary of the medium. The refracted light ray results from this superposition of reemitted light by atoms in the bulk of the solid.

In metals the reradiation at the boundary interface is so strong that most of the incident radiation is reflected over a wide range of the spectrum. This phenomenon differs, however, from the partial reflection of light at the boundary of a transparent dielectric crystal. The conduction electrons in metal behave collectively as a highly dense plasma, and cause total reflection of long-wavelength incident light; at shorter wavelengths there is partial transmission. Gold, for example, reflects red and yellow light strongly but allows some penetration by green rays, which are then completely absorbed within a small thickness of the bulk of the metal. Silver, on the other hand, reflects strongly over most of the visible spectrum but allows considerable transmission in the ultraviolet [see bottom illustration on page 31].

There are in addition a number of light-scattering processes in which an incident ray at one frequency is absorbed by an atom and then reemitted at an entirely different frequency. When the absorption and reemission occur simultaneously as part of a single transition, the phenomenon is called the Raman effect. Here the difference in frequency between the two light waves must exactly equal a resonance frequency between a pair of atomic levels; the individual light frequencies, however, are not required to be near any of the atomic

resonances. Raman scattering, which can take place in gases, liquids or solids, is usually weak unless the intensity of the incident light is very high.

Light absorption at one frequency and light emission at another frequency can also take place in two separate steps. An incident ray at the resonance frequency of a pair of levels is first absorbed in the usual way, causing an atomic transition from a lower level to an upper one. After a certain delay the atom spontaneously undergoes a transition involving a third level, emitting a light ray at the appropriate frequency. In some cases the delay may be as short as a microsecond or less, in which case the phenomenon is called fluorescence. In other cases the delay can be for seconds or even days, allowing the emitted light to be observed after the incident light is turned off; this phenomenon is called phosphorescence.

The absorption and emission characteristics of matter outlined in this article of course extend far beyond the visible region of the electromagnetic spectrum. On the long-wavelength side there are the infrared, far-infrared, microwave and radio-wave regions, and on the short-wavelength side the ultraviolet, X-ray and gamma-ray regions. The optical properties of materials in all these regions are similar to those in the visible region in their basic relation to the quantum-mechanical interactions of electrons, but they are vastly different in detail. In these ranges spectroscopy requires a diversity of experimental techniques, ranging from Newton's prism to radio-wave and gamma-ray spectrometers.

4

How Light is Analyzed

Pierre Connes   *September 1968*

The efforts of ancient philosophers to analyze matter began with an intuitive but basically sound concept: Matter can be separated into its elementary constituents. The concept that light might be analyzed was much less obvious. Men looked at rainbows for millenniums without devising any kind of rational explanation for them. Even when René Descartes noted that the colors of a rainbow were like those produced by a prism, he was giving an analogy and not an explanation.

It was Isaac Newton who formulated the basic concept: Light from ordinary sources is complex. By "complex" he meant that such light can be analyzed into colors and that conversely the colors can be used to synthesize light. An optician should be allowed to rank this concept with Newton's discovery of gravitation.

Here I shall describe the rise of instrumental spectroscopy, which is the technique of analyzing light. From other articles in this issue it will be evident to the reader that much of the information we get about the physical world is carried by light and that analyzing light is highly rewarding. Spectroscopy is the first tool of astrophysics; the analysis of the light from planets, stars and galaxies is the means of determining what they are made of. Spectroscopy thus provides the best evidence for our belief in the homogeneity of the universe. At the same time spectroscopic analysis is used in every chemical plant to follow the progress of reactions.

In short, the complexity of light is today an exceptionally valuable source of information. To Newton and his contemporaries, however, the complexity of light was only a nuisance. Newton had been led to study the subject of light by the need to improve optical instruments. The images produced by lenses were then extremely poor. The worst defect was the persistence of strange colored edges that nobody was able to explain. It was clear that the colored edges arose within the instruments; indeed, the colors were to some extent responsible for the skepticism that greeted many of the early discoveries made with telescopes and microscopes. Newton provided the explanation and, believing (wrongly) the defect could not be cured, he invented the reflecting telescope, which was achromatic, or free of color.

By the 18th century the technique of building optical instruments had been greatly improved. Achromatic lenses were developed for telescopes. The technique of photometry, by which the intensity of light is measured, had grown out of the work of the French physicist and mathematician Pierre Bouguer, who measured and compared the intensity of the light from the sun and the moon. As a result of these developments all the tools needed for the evolution of spectroscopy were in hand. Strangely enough, however, no progress was made beyond Newton's crude division of visible light into seven colors. Apparently nobody conceived of a need to improve the analysis of light.

The change in outlook came in the first year of the 19th century, when the English astronomer Sir William Herschel became interested in the distribution of radiant heat according to color in light from the sun. In 1800 he investigated the matter by placing several thermometers across a solar spectrum that had been dispersed by a prism in the same way that Newton had dispersed sunlight. In modern terms Herschel built the first spectrometer equipped with a thermal receiver. (It is noteworthy that thermometers, which were crude but adequate for the experiment, had been available for more than a century.)

With this experiment Herschel made the unexpected discovery of invisible but heat-carrying radiation beyond the red end of the visible spectrum—in the region that has since been named the infrared. Obviously it was worth looking at the region beyond the other end of the visible spectrum, but the amount of heat carried by solar ultraviolet radiation happened to be too weak for Herschel's thermometer. He had nonetheless shown the way, and only a year later Johann Wilhelm Ritter of Germany and William Hyde Wollaston of England did detect ultraviolet rays by virtue of the fact that they blackened crystals of silver chloride just as well as visible light did. Eventually experiments showed that both infrared and ultraviolet rays could also be refracted, reflected and polarized.

What was then clearly needed was a finer analysis; today it would be called an increase in resolving power. From the early 19th century to the present the improvement of resolving power has been the first aim of spectroscopists. As we shall see, each large advance has invariably paid off in new discoveries.

The first step was taken by Joseph Fraunhofer, a highly skilled Bavarian optician, between 1815 and 1825. By a simple but adept use of lenses and slits he was able to produce a "pure" solar spectrum in which light from a given color did not fade gradually into other colors. The spectrum showed many sharp dark lines that ever since have been called Fraunhofer lines.

Fraunhofer also took the second step toward finer resolving power. He built a new tool, the diffraction grating, which far exceeded prisms in its ability to disperse light [*see top illustration on page 41*]. The invention of the grating was made possible only by the upheaval that had taken place in optics. Mostly as a

INTERFERENCE FRINGES were photographed as they appeared in an interferometer of the Michelson, type illuminated by light from a helium-neon laser at a wavelength of 6,328 angstroms, equivalent to the color in which the photograph is printed. The small ring patterns are attributable to the laser. Fringes yield information about wavelength of the light and thus about the source.

consequence of the work of Augustin Jean Fresnel of France, the Newton emission theory of light was being replaced by the wave theory originally put forward by Newton's contemporary Christiaan Huygens.

This is not the place to discuss light theories; indeed, so far we have seen the analysis of light progressing quite independently of theory. The working of a diffraction grating, however, can only be understood in the context of wave theory. Moreover, Fresnel, in bringing about the acceptance of wave theory, had substituted for the subjective concept of color a precisely measurable quantity: wavelength. (His own measurements of wavelength were not accurate because he worked only with ordinary white light that had been more or less crudely filtered.)

Fraunhofer accomplished two important things with his diffraction grating. First, he was able to isolate within the light emitted by a sodium flame a pair of lines that appeared to be monochromatic, meaning that they represented light that could not be decomposed further by increasing the dispersion. (This result was only apparent; the resolving power was still insufficient to break the sodium line down further.) Second, Fraunhofer made the first accurate measurements of wavelength, obtaining figures that do not differ from modern ones by more than a tenth of 1 percent.

It took until the middle of the 19th century to achieve a complete explanation of the dark lines in the spectra obtained by Fraunhofer. The significance of the achievement was that it demonstrated that the lines corresponded to def-

GIRARD GRID on the opposite page was devised recently by André Girard of the French Office of Aeronautical Research to analyze light by a technique that is explained in the bottom illustration on page 44. A pair of grids replace the input and output slits of a grating spectrometer and create a high-luminosity means of directly scanning a spectrum of light.

inite elements in the source of light. Each element gave rise to a characteristic pattern of lines—a fingerprint, as it were.

When this relation became clear, the missing incentive to develop spectroscopy was at last found. Now in the laboratory the spectroscope could be used instead of tedious chemical analysis to detect elements in trace amounts and to provide a quantitative estimate of abundance. In astronomy the spectroscope could be applied to solve the problem that had been declared unsolvable only a few years earlier by the philosopher Auguste Comte: the identification of the matter in stars.

It is possible to mention only a few of the workers who contributed thereafter to instrumental spectroscopy. In Germany, Robert Bunsen and Gustav Kirchhoff brought the prism spectroscope to a high degree of perfection. As methods of casting and polishing glass improved, however, it became clear that resolving power could not be increased indefinitely by merely improving existing techniques. Lord Rayleigh showed that the limitation was a fundamental one: Because of diffraction—the spreading of a beam that takes place when light goes through a finite aperture—even a perfect prism cannot resolve two lines whose difference in wavelength is less than a certain amount. (This difference is now known as the Rayleigh limit.)

The resolving power—defined as the ratio of the mean wavelength of two lines to the minimum resolvable difference—is proportional to the total thickness of the glass. One cannot increase resolving power indefinitely by using thicker glass, however, because any substance that disperses light also absorbs it. Beyond a certain thickness nothing is to be gained.

The resolving power of gratings is also related to their size, which in principle can be increased without limit. Ruling a large grating is the most difficult mechanical operation known, however, and progress has been very slow. One of the most notable contributors was Anders Ångström, a Swedish physicist who made such remarkably accurate

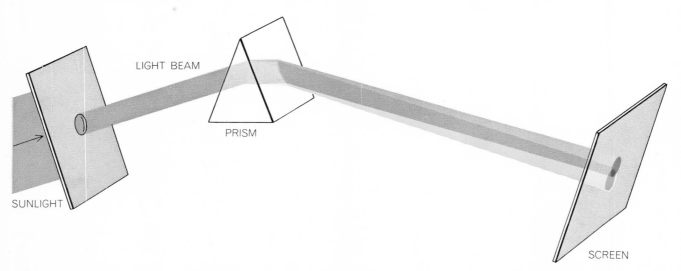

FIRST STEP in analyzing light was made by Isaac Newton in 1666. Through a small hole in a window shutter he admitted a beam of sunlight to a darkened room and directed the beam through a prism. Because light of different colors is refracted, or bent, at different angles in passing through a prism, the constituent colors of the sunlight appeared like a rainbow on the wall opposite the window. Newton then used another prism to reunite the colors. With these experiments he demonstrated the composition of white light.

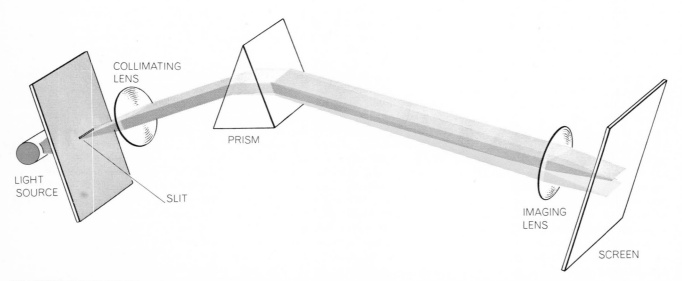

SHARPER SEPARATION of the components of white light was achieved early in the 19th century by the Bavarian optician Joseph Fraunhofer. He passed light through a slit. A collimating lens made the light parallel and directed it into a prism. Each color emerged from the prism in a different direction. A second lens converted the pattern into distinctly separated lines on the screen.

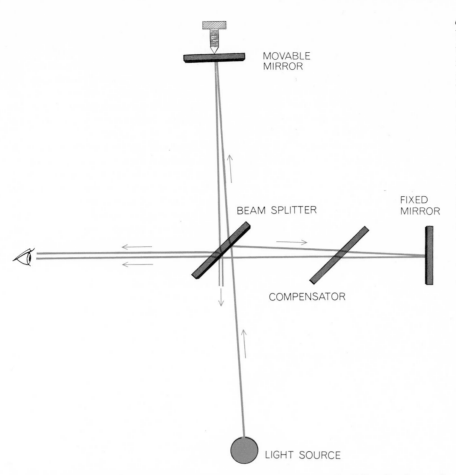

MOVABLE
MIRROR

BEAM SPLITTER

FIXED
MIRROR

COMPENSATOR

LIGHT SOURCE

MICHELSON INTERFEROMETER, devised by A. A. Michelson of the U.S., split a beam of light into two beams with a half-reflecting glass plate (*center*). One beam went on to a movable mirror and the other one was deflected 90 degrees to a fixed mirror. The two beams were reconverged on the glass plate, producing constructive or destructive interference, visible as bright or dark fringes, as the movable mirror was adjusted. When white light is used, a compensator plate equalizes the lengths of the paths in glass of the two light beams.

at left]. The light waves of the two beams interfere with each other. If the two component beams are in phase, or in step, the recombined beam is bright; if they are out of phase, the recombined beam is dark. The two situations are respectively termed constructive and destructive interference. If the difference in the length of the two paths varies from one part of the beam to another, there will be constructive interference in some places and destructive interference in others. To the observer the result appears as the series of bright and dark lines called interference fringes. The spacing between fringes is proportional to the wavelength of light.

A recording of the intensity output of the interferometer while the path difference is varied in a uniform manner is called an interferogram. It is utterly unlike a direct recording of the source spectrum. The spectrum can be reconstructed from the interferogram, however, by applying the mathematical operation known as the Fourier transform. (Baron Jean Baptiste Joseph Fourier, a French mathematician of the early 19th century, applied his findings to several physical problems but never dreamed about their possible bearing on spectroscopy.) The interferogram can be said to contain all the needed information about the spectrum in a coded form.

The extreme elegance of Michelson's method arises from the fact that resolving power is no longer related to the path length within an absorbing medium or to the width of the ruled surface of a grating. It is purely a function of the path difference between the two beams. The path difference can be increased almost without limit, not only in theory but also in practice.

Today we can record interference fringes. Michelson, however, had to rely on his eyes. Moreover, performing a Fourier transform is easier said than done: the interferogram is an experimentally determined curve and does not fit any simple analytical formula. The decoding can be done by numerical computation. The basic rules are simple and the whole process can be broken down into elementary arithmetic operations, but their number can be enormous if the resolving power is high and the spectral range is an extended one.

Because of these difficulties Michelson did not attempt to use his method in the general case, that is, for extended, complex and unknown spectra. He restricted himself to the study of just one apparently monochromatic line. The curve he plotted was not the interfero-

measurements of wavelength that his name was given to a unit of length used for evaluating wavelengths. (One angstrom is a ten-millionth of a millimeter.) Toward the end of the century Henry Rowland of Johns Hopkins University produced gratings, and with them spectra, that nobody was able to duplicate during his lifetime—an achievement that is rare in the experimental sciences.

The beginning of the modern period is clearly marked by the work of A. A. Michelson of the U.S. Michelson was dissatisfied with the limitations of gratings and devised a radically different method of spectroscopy. His vehicle was an optical instrument that he invented in 1880 and named the interferometer. For this instrument he received the seventh Nobel prize in physics and the first Nobel prize to be awarded to an American. (Among the many uses Michelson found for his versatile tool was the ether-drift experi-

ment that established his reputation with the general public. The experiment was designed to determine the velocity of the earth through the "ether" that many scholars, believing electromagnetic radiation could not be transmitted through a vacuum, thought filled the voids in the universe. The experiment, which involved measuring the speed of light, ultimately showed that there is no ether.) A Michelson interferometer works quite differently from a prism or a grating. The role of a prism or a grating is to disperse light, that is, to separate the different spectral elements into different directions so that they can be individually measured. Michelson reasoned that such spatial separation is not basic to spectroscopy and can be dispensed with. The interferometer makes no use of dispersion. In Michelson's interferometer light is split into two beams by a half-reflecting glass plate, follows two paths of unequal length and is recombined on the beam-splitting plate [see illustration

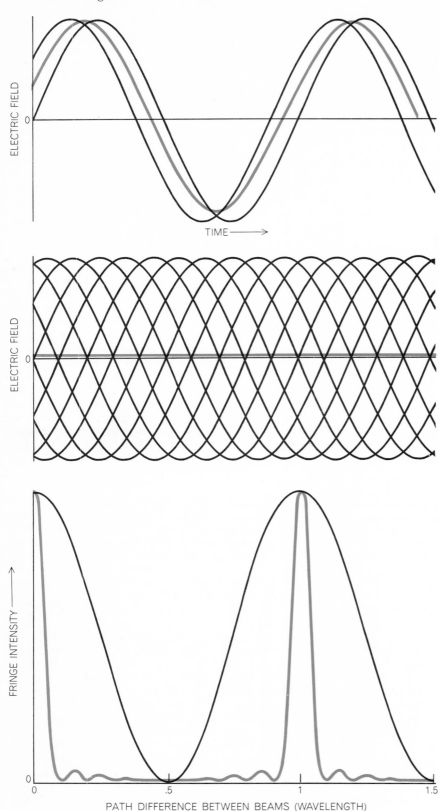

ELECTRIC FIELD

0

TIME ⟶

ELECTRIC FIELD

0

FRINGE INTENSITY ⟶

0

0   .5   1   1.5

PATH DIFFERENCE BETWEEN BEAMS (WAVELENGTH)

APPEARANCE OF FRINGES is compared for three devices. If in a two-beam interferometer two beams of equal amplitude are combined after paths differing in length by a tenth of the wavelength (*top*), the resulting amplitude (*color*) is nearly the same as if the two paths had been the same length. If in a multiple-beam device 10 equal-amplitude waves are each delayed a tenth of a wavelength from the preceding one (*middle*), the resulting wave (*color*) has zero amplitude. At bottom is the intensity resulting when two beams (*black*) or 10 beams (*color*) are interfered as a function of the path difference between successive beams. Multiple-beam devices, such as a Fabry-Perot interferometer, produce the sharpest fringes.

gram itself but the fringe-visibility curve, which is a smoothed-out version of the interferogram. The curve enabled him to discriminate among certain assumed spectra, but he could not unambiguously define the true spectral distributions. As a result his computed spectra show errors when they are checked with modern results.

Michelson's errors, however, are trivial compared with the importance of the discoveries he made. One was that lines believed to be monochromatic in actuality had several different components. This splitting is called the hyperfine structure of optical lines, and it yields information about the structure of atomic nuclei. Second, Michelson showed that a line that has been split as much as possible exhibits a continuous distribution of frequency, or energy. A "monochromatic" line thus has to be regarded as a theoretical concept with no physical existence, although today lasers come closer than any other source of light to generating such lines.

The interferometer could also be used to measure the wavelength of sharp spectral lines. This part of Michelson's work ultimately led to the adoption (in 1960) of an optical line as the primary standard of length. The reason is simply that wavelengths can now be measured more accurately than the length of any material body.

Another form of interferometer was invented in 1897 and applied to spectroscopy by the French optician Charles Fabry and his collaborator Alfred Perot. It is extremely simple—just two plane-parallel plates with highly reflecting surfaces [*see the bottom illustration on page 41*]. The Michelson type of interferometer has two equal beams; the Fabry-Perot interferometer has an infinite number with decreasing intensity. The fringe pattern of a Fabry-Perot interferometer is quite different from one generated by a Michelson interferometer, and it makes possible a direct recording of the spectrum. A Fourier transform of the experimental data is not needed, and there is no ambiguity of interpretation.

For these reasons the Fabry-Perot interferometer was widely taken up for high-resolution spectroscopy. The Michelson fringe-visibility method, although it still holds a place of honor in all textbooks, is used in only a few cases. Nonetheless, the Fabry-Perot arrangement does have limitations. Its very simplicity makes it impossible for it to approximate theoretical performance. The two surfaces have to be polished

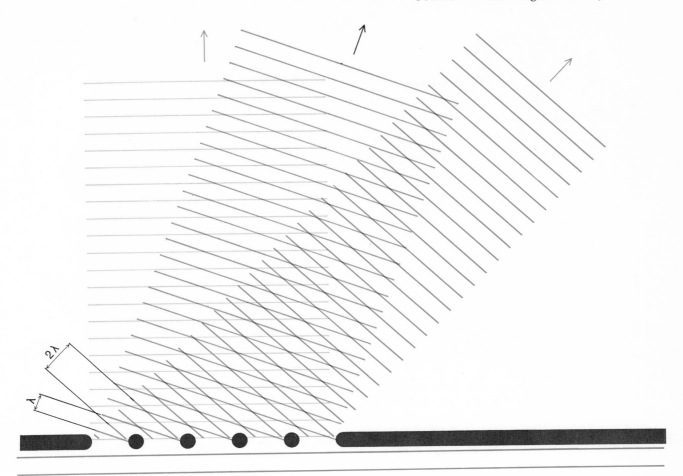

DIFFRACTION GRATING devised by Fraunhofer consisted of many fine, parallel wires. Four wires are shown here in cross section. Part of the light travels straight through (*light color*). For each wavelength, some light will be deflected in each of several other directions. The angle through which it is deflected is deter- mined by the requirement that the light through each opening should travel an integral number of wavelengths farther than light through an adjacent opening. Here a first-order beam (*gray*) and a second-order beam (*dark color*) are shown. Since the angle de- pends on the wavelength, the colors of the light are separated.

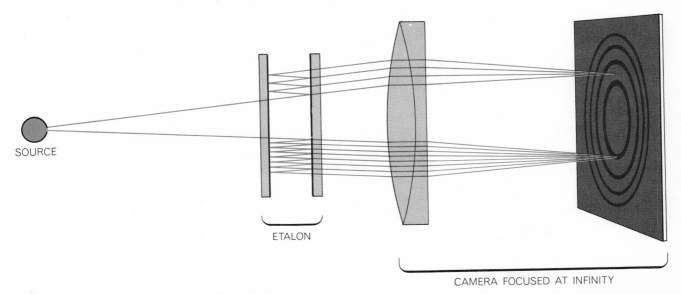

FABRY-PEROT INTERFEROMETER was invented in 1897 by the French opticians Charles Fabry and Alfred Perot. It consists of two highly reflecting parallel plates called an etalon. When light waves reflected between the plates interfere destructively (*top*), canceling each other out, darkness appears on the screen. When the waves interfere constructively (*bottom*), reinforcing each other, the point of focus is bright. The result is a ring pattern such as the one on the cover of this issue. Unlike the Michelson interferometer, in which two beams interfere, the Fabry-Perot interferometer com- bines a large number of parallel beams of decreasing intensity.

LAMELLAR GRATING devised by John D. Strong of the University of Massachusetts consists of two sets of strip mirrors that can be moved with respect to each other. Here the two sets are shown separately. When they are assembled, they create an interferometer that is like Michelson's in producing only two beams but differs from a Michelson interferometer in requiring no beam splitter.

glass or quartz, and even when they are made with all possible care, they show small residual ripples. The reflecting surfaces are coated with evaporated layers of metals or dielectrics that cannot be made perfectly uniform. Finally, the plates and the spacers that are supposed to keep them parallel are subject to flexion and thermal expansion.

The best the present state of the art can provide is an accuracy of the order of a hundredth of a visible-light wavelength. This means in turn that at best the peaks cannot be made sharper than a hundredth of their spacing. The spectrum to be studied cannot then contain more than about 50 separate lines, and even this is a highly optimistic figure. No order-of-magnitude improvements are in sight.

We now have to introduce a few modern concepts that dominate the recent evolution of spectroscopy. Direct recording of spectra with photomultipliers and photoconductive or thermal receivers has come into play. Spectra on photographic plates are scanned by densitometers. Electronic amplifiers can expand traces from weak lines without limit—one just has to turn a knob! It soon becomes obvious, however, that mere amplification is useless. When the spectral curve is sufficiently blown up, it always shows the meaningless fluctuations

called noise. The important consideration thus becomes signal-to-noise ratio; it is the one basic limitation to the accuracy of photometric measurements.

Signal-to-noise ratio depends on several factors. The first is the monochromatic brightness of the source. Even when the source is a terrestrial one, this factor is not completely under the spectroscopist's control. For instance, putting more electric power into the gaseous-discharge sources used for studying atomic emission spectra broadens their emission lines, which cannot be tolerated.

The second factor is the "receiver noise equivalent power": the light power that, if it impinged on the receiver, would give rise to the same output as the output of the receiver operating in the dark. From the far ultraviolet to the far infrared detectors are now available that operate close to the fundamental limitations imposed by thermodynamic and quantum-mechanical laws. Hence large improvements in detectors can no longer be expected.

The third factor is the recording time. Unfortunately signal-to-noise ratio increases only as the square root of the total time during which energy is collected. The price for obtaining improved signal-to-noise ratios by this means is therefore very high. In all practical cases the recording time is limited, and one can only try not to waste any of it.

The fourth factor is the resolving power. When a spectrum is divided into more and more separate portions, the energy per portion unavoidably goes down. For a continuous spectrum—all other factors being held constant—the energy and the signal-to-noise ratio are inversely proportional to the resolving power.

The spectroscopist has a measure of control only over the recording time and the resolving power. A requirement for high resolving power forces him to longer recording time. The theoretical maximum resolving power of a slit instrument, which is limited by diffraction, may become irrelevant; with a weak light flux the practical resolving power, which is limited by the available energy, is much lower than the theoretical limit. This practical resolving power can be improved only by increasing the light-gathering capacity of the instrument, that is, the size of the beam that can be fed through the spectrometer. Such a move means increasing the size of the disperser, and practical limits are again soon in view.

The Fabry-Perot interferometer represents a marked improvement over slit devices in light-gathering power. The reason is that it needs no sharp slits to record a spectrum. The interference filters now commonly used to isolate a narrow band of optical wavelengths are simply thin, low-resolution Fabry-Perot interferometers.

An altogether different way of producing spectra was proposed in 1950 by Peter B. Fellgett, who was then working at the University of Cambridge. He reasoned as follows. All spectrometers, which scan a spectrum bit by bit, waste most of the available light, whereas spectrographs, which record a spectrum photographically, do not. The reason is that the receiver behind the output slit in a spectrometer is a single-channel device: it can gather information about only one spectral element at a time, unlike the photographic plate, which contains a large number of individual detectors (the silver grains in the emulsion).

Fellgett concluded that the waste of light in a spectrometer could be eliminated if information about all spectral elements were fed through the receiver at the same time. (In the language of communications technology the receiver would be said to be multiplexed.) He looked around for ways to achieve the necessary encoding of the spectrum.

Although several approaches seemed to be feasible, the most promising one was Fourier spectroscopy, which had to be discovered anew because everyone had forgotten that Michelson had (in a rather obscure paper, to be sure) given all the essentials. The method had never been made to work; as I said earlier, Michelson in his experiments had used only the smoothed-out fringe-visibility curve and not the complete interferogram curve. As a matter of fact he could hardly have done more than he did, given the state of instrumentation at the time and the lack of high-speed automatic computers to work out the necessary Fourier transforms.

Multiplexing can be achieved with the two-beam interferometer because there is no dispersion and all the light is being utilized all the time. The gain to be expected, compared with the scanning of a spectrum, is greatest for extended spectral ranges and is manifest even at low resolving power. (These are circumstances Michelson never dreamed of; he applied the Fourier technique only to high-resolution spectrograms covering a narrow range.) Multiplexing has proved most useful in the infrared,

for reasons that have to do with the different types of detector. Fellgett's idea received little notice at the time, and many technical difficulties had to be solved before skeptics could be convinced by actual results.

In France, at the Bellevue Laboratories of the National Center for Scientific Research, Pierre Jacquinot also rediscovered Fourier spectroscopy, but from a different viewpoint. He had greatly contributed to the improvement of Fabry-Perot interferometer spectroscopy, which means that he was well aware of its limitations and was looking for ways of overcoming them. He found that the spectral range could be increased by using only two beams and unscrambling the data later by Fourier analysis. Jacquinot set his disciples, of whom I am one, to work in that direction.

The first spectra recorded by Fellgett, which were spectra of cool stars in the near infrared, had very low resolving power, but the results were encouraging because the objects are so faint. Other early workers in the Fourier field (around 1955) were Lawrence Mertz of Harvard University, John D. Strong and George Vanasse of Johns Hopkins and H. A. Gebbie of the British National Physical Laboratory. Strong, Vanasse and Gebbie initiated the use of the technique in the far infrared.

During the past 10 years the contributors to Fourier spectroscopy have become numerous. At an international conference on instrumental spectroscopy at Bellevue two years ago more than half of the papers dealt with Fourier spectroscopy. We shall indicate only the general trends. Most of the work has been done in the far infrared (wavelengths greater than about 50 microns), where the use of the method is now so common that commercial Fourier spectrometers are available. This is no accident; the accuracy required in the construction of the interferometer is less when the wavelength is greater. Moreover, the energy available in that range is very low, so that the results given by scanning spectrometers are comparatively poor and easy to improve on.

Fourier spectroscopy is also sometimes employed because of advantages we have said nothing about since they are not fundamental—which does not mean they are negligible. Two-beam interferometers, in particular those developed by Mertz, can be made very small and light. They lend themselves well to spectroscopic observations from aircraft, balloons, artificial satellites and deep-space probes.

Much effort is being devoted to the

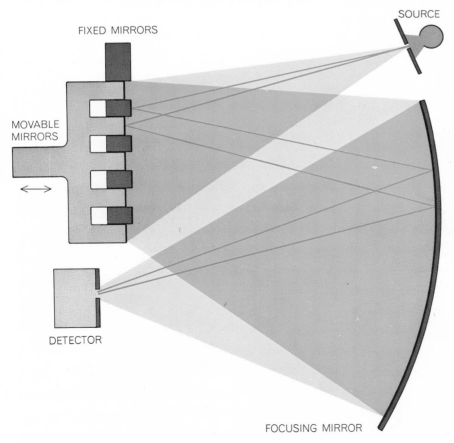

FIXED MIRRORS

SOURCE

MOVABLE MIRRORS

DETECTOR

FOCUSING MIRROR

OPERATION of lamellar grating is indicated. The detector records the zero-order diffraction beam. If path lengths (*colored lines*) of light reflected from movable mirrors and from fixed mirrors differ by half a wavelength, the beam will be dark at the detector. As one set of mirrors is moved at a constant rate with respect to the other one, the light of each color will fluctuate at detector with frequency inversely proportional to wavelength.

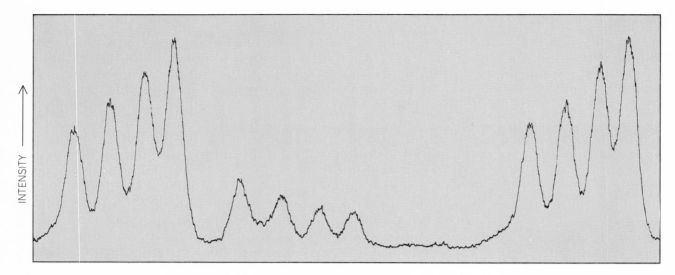

FABRY-PEROT RECORDING was made by a photometer that scanned across a Fabry-Perot ring pattern. The four peaks at left show four clearly resolved components of one blue line of terbium, which is a rare earth. The four lower peaks show four components of another line, and then the first pattern is repeated. Separation of the first two peaks at left is .01 angstrom. The small ripples are caused by noise in the detector. Such noise sets an ultimate limit on the accuracy of measurements that can be made of light intensity.

still difficult problems of computing the Fourier transform. Several types of special-purpose computers have been built. Some operate in real time: they actually plot the spectrum while the interferogram is being recorded. The main tool, however, is still the general-purpose computer. Striking advances have recently been made in the art of programming Fourier transforms, and optical spectroscopy will be the main beneficiary of these advances.

The reader may have guessed that the author, being a confirmed Fourier spectroscopist, is about to discuss his own contribution. (To choose to devote more space to one's own work than to Newton's is disturbing, to say the least, but one should understand that this huge distortion is a perspective effect and make the proper correction.) At Bellevue we have been from the start aiming at very high resolving power in the visible or the near infrared, because this is

what the theoreticians in the group were asking for. (They deal mostly with the hyperfine structure of atomic energy levels.)

Briefly summarized, the difficulties were connected with the high accuracy required for both intensity and path-difference measurements in the interferogram. Errors in path difference distort the computed spectrum in the same way that imperfections in the construction of a slit spectrometer do. For in-

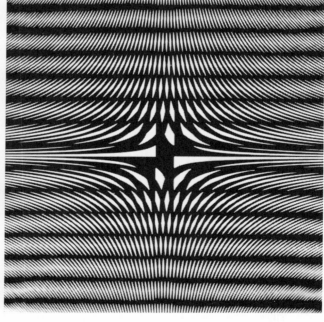

MOIRÉ PATTERNS are produced with Girard grids such as the one shown on page 36. For each frequency of light the spectrometer will form an image of the input grid on the output grid. If one grid is oscillated slightly, the output of light will be modulated by the varying overlap of the image and the output grid. The modulation is greatest when the output grid exactly lines up with the input grid. The overlapping images located a short distance apart, which correspond to different colors, can be separately discriminated.

stance, a grating ruled with periodic errors produces ghosts, or spurious lines. Similarly, if the device that measures the displacement of the interferometer carriage is afflicted with a periodic error, the Fourier-computed spectrum will also exhibit ghosts, and of much greater intensity. That is why the requirements for mechanical accuracy are even more stringent in a Fourier interferometer than in the ruling engine used to make gratings.

Errors in intensity produce additional noise in the spectrum. The difficulty is greatest in the very circumstances where the largest gain from multiplexing is sought. The problem is particularly severe when the intensity of the source fluctuates rapidly, which is what happens with all astronomical sources because of air turbulence.

These problems have now been solved, but the steps are too technical to warrant description here. They involve sophisticated electronics and servo-control devices and also the development of new computer programs to extend the number of interferogram samples that can be transformed. This latter part of the work is the responsibility of Janine Connes, the author's wife, at the Numerical Computation Center of the Meudon Observatory.

Applications are progressing in two directions. Spectra of laboratory sources have been recorded (in collaboration with Jacques Pinard) that clearly exceed those given by the best gratings in resolving power and those given by Fabry-Perot interferometers in spectral range. Greater accuracy in determining wavelengths is being achieved, together with more freedom from ghosts and stray light.

The improvement is perhaps even more striking for infrared astronomical spectra because the energy from the sources is low and the observing time is sharply limited. In a program executed jointly with the Jet Propulsion Laboratory of the California Institute of Technology, where the author spent a year, spectra of Venus, Mars, Jupiter and a dozen red stars have been recorded. They show an improvement in resolving power by a factor of 100 or more compared with the best spectra previously obtained [see illustration at left]. The near-infrared spectrum of Mars and Venus is now known more accurately than the spectrum of the sun was a few years ago. Three new trace gases (hydrochloric acid, hydrofluoric acid and carbon monoxide) have been found in the atmosphere of Venus. Very large infrared telescopes will soon be specially built for multiplex spectroscopy.

Making predictions about the future of this both old and young method is obviously risky. One cannot be far wrong, however, in stressing the importance of having nonoptical techniques intrude on what has so far been the purely optical approach to light analysis. Opticians have to acknowledge that the tools of their trade progress very slowly. The methods by which lenses are polished today do not differ markedly from those of Galileo or Newton. Mirrors and glass plates used by Michelson or Fabry could be incorporated quite satisfactorily in the latest interferometers.

On the other hand, the elaborate, fully transistorized servo system I built three years ago for my astronomical measurements has today only one possible future—providing parts for my son to play with. The immediate question is whether the new all-integrated-circuited servo now being completed will produce anything before it becomes obsolete. The time is long past when experimenters could afford to let technical improvements lie idle for 100 years.

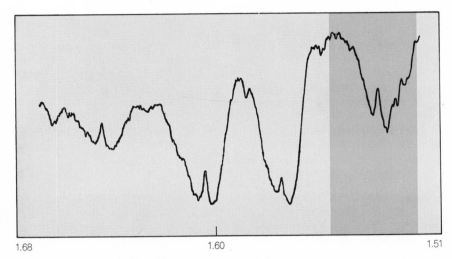
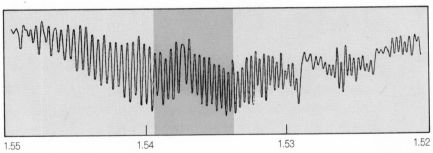
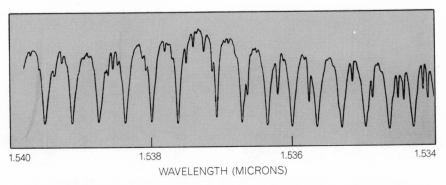

WAVELENGTH (MICRONS)

SPECTRA OF VENUS have improved greatly with improved techniques. At top is a curve covering part of the near-infrared spectrum of the planet's atmosphere; it was obtained in 1962 with a grating spectrometer. The area in darker color is covered in the middle spectrogram, obtained by the author in 1964 with multiplex spectroscopy. It gives more detail of one of the four carbon dioxide bands of the top spectrogram. Author's later results (bottom) show with even higher resolution the part of the middle spectrogram that is in darker color. Little dips between major ones are partly due to less abundant isotopes of carbon and oxygen.

5

Optical Pumping

Arnold L. Bloom   *October 1960*

The rather odd term optical pumping means just what it says. In general "pumping" is a process of raising matter from lower to higher energy; for example, raising the potential energy of water by moving it from an underground well to an elevated tank. In this article we shall be concerned with the pumping of individual atoms from lower to higher states of internal energy. The word optical refers to the light energy that is the source of power for the pump.

Why pump atoms? The purpose is to prepare them for a special kind of spectroscopic analysis. When we think of a spectrum, we usually visualize bands of color. Actually atomic spectra extend far beyond the wavelengths of visible light (a few hundred thousandths of a centimeter) in both directions. Atoms can emit and absorb electromagnetic radiation ranging from radio waves (whose length is measured in hundreds of meters) to X-rays (a thousandth as long as light waves). The visible spectrum has been intensively studied for a century, and the X-ray spectrum for about 50 years. Among the results of these investigations is the quantum theory of atomic structure. But spectroscopy in the radio-frequency region is a very recent development, in part made possible by the technique of optical pumping, and only now beginning to be exploited. Paradoxically, long-wave studies are now revealing fine detail in the structure of atoms that is invisible at shorter wavelengths. And optical pumping has already led to a number of practical applications.

The reason for both the effectiveness and the difficulty of using radio waves for spectroscopy lies in their low energy. Like all other electromagnetic radiations, radio waves are divided into discrete packets, or photons, the energy of which varies directly with their frequency, or inversely with wavelength. Having frequencies millions or even billions of times lower than the frequencies of visible light, their energy is less in the same proportion.

When photons are absorbed or emitted by an atom, the atom gains or loses the energy they contain, changing its physical state in some way. The photons of light, with their comparatively high energy, involve the transition of an electron from one orbit to another. The photons of radio waves merely shift the axes of spinning electrons within an orbit. Since the electrons are tiny magnets with fields aligned along their axes, such a

RUBIDIUM IS PUMPED by beaming light from a rubidium-vapor lamp (*far left*) through a circular polarizer (*square at left center*) and a plastic condensing lens into an

shift produces a small change in the magnetic energy of an atom.

The transition between energy states, or levels, is a two-way street: atoms at a higher level tend to fall spontaneously into the lower one; those at the lower level will jump to the higher one if the requisite quanta of energy are available. If a transition is to be detected spectroscopically in a sample of matter, there must be a net excess either of upward or of downward jumps among its atoms. In jumping up, the atoms subtract photons from a transmitted beam of radiation, producing an absorption spectrum; in jumping down, they send out photons, producing an emission, or "bright line," spectrum. Generally speaking, matter must be in the form of a gas or a vapor to exhibit sharp emission or absorption lines. In solids and liquids interactions of neighboring atoms broaden the energy levels, so that the spectra consist not of lines but of wide bands of frequencies.

Now the energy associated with a quantum jump can be exchanged through the direct collision of atoms as well as by radiation. At room temperature atoms are not moving fast enough to raise one another up to the levels required for the emission of visible light. Therefore they are in a position to absorb energy from an external light source. On the other hand, by raising the temperature of a substance, collisions between its atoms can be made sufficiently energetic to excite them so that they emit light.

The situation is otherwise for the radio-wave spectrum. The minute quantity of energy necessary to shift atoms between the closely spaced levels is available many times over in thermal motion at room temperature. As a result the atoms continually shift back and forth, and those in the emitting state are almost exactly counterbalanced by those in the absorbing state. In order to do spectroscopy some way must be found to put a majority of atoms into one state or the other.

There are a few ways to accomplish this. The most direct is to cool a material to a point where it no longer has enough thermal energy to produce transitions even between closely spaced levels. Normally this means bathing the material in liquid helium. Another rather difficult technique is to pass a beam of atoms through a magnetic field, which separates them according to their energy states. More recently experimenters have been reluctant to use these relatively cumbersome approaches and have developed extremely sensitive radio receivers to detect emissions or absorptions arising out of the tiny differences in energy population (measured in parts per million) that exist naturally.

About 10 years ago A. Kastler and J. Brossel of the Ecole Normale Supérieure in Paris and Francis Bitter of the Massachusetts Institute of Technology hit upon a better idea, which Kastler named optical pumping. To understand the principle, consider a simplified atom with only three energy levels, which we shall call A, B and C [see illustration on next page]. Levels A and B are low-lying and very close together; the energy difference between them corresponds to a radio-frequency spectrum line, and ini-

absorption cell (*center*). Coil around cell sets up a fluctuating magnetic field. Some of the energy of the light beam is absorbed to pump atoms in cell to higher energy-levels; the rest passes through the absorption cell and is measured by the photocell at far right.

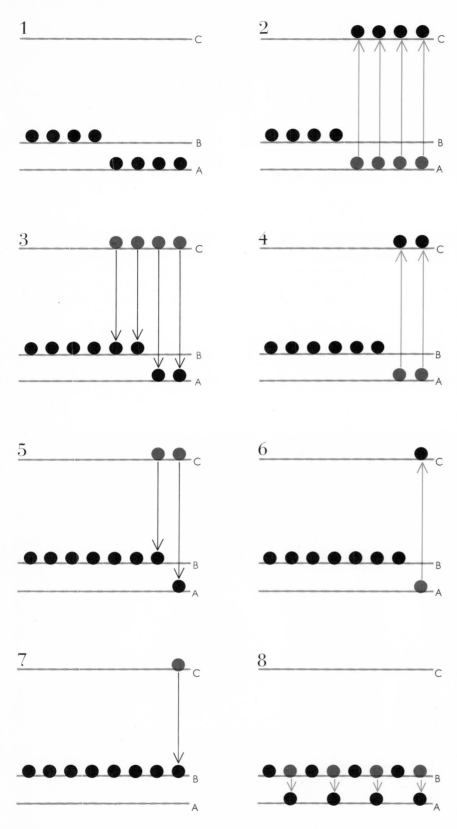

tially all the atoms are distributed equally between them. Level C is much higher; the transitions A-C and B-C correspond to lines in the optical part of the spectrum. Suppose we irradiate a sample of these atoms with a light beam from which the spectral line BC has been filtered. The beam contains photons that can excite atoms in level A but not in level B. Atoms excited out of A absorb energy and rise to C. They will remain there for a short time (as little as a ten millionth of a second) and then emit energy, dropping back either to the A or B state.

The proportion going to each state depends on the structure of the atoms, but the important thing is that occasionally an atom drops into B. When it does, it can no longer be excited by the incident light. If it returns to A, the light will raise it to the C state again, and again it will have some probability of dropping to B. Given enough time, every atom must end up in the B state, and the material is then completely pumped.

Once this condition has been attained, there are a number of ways to detect it. The simplest and most effective is the method developed by H. G. Dehmelt of the University of Washington. It depends on the fact that the transparency of the sample to the light beam varies with the degree of pumping. As atoms are removed from the A state, the material can absorb less and less of the pumping light, and more of it passes through, reaching a maximum when pumping is complete. Now if some atoms are suddenly returned to the A state, light will again be absorbed, and the brightness of the transmitted beam will drop sharply.

This can be accomplished by irradiating the atoms with radio waves at the frequency corresponding to the energy of transition between levels A and B. The effect is rather complicated in its details, but roughly speaking the radio-frequency photons cause the atoms to shuttle back and forth between the two states, thus effectively transferring some of them from B to A.

The technique is extraordinarily sensitive. A sample of vapor at a pressure of a ten millionth of a millimeter of mercury can reduce the transmitted light intensity by as much as 20 per cent when the correct radio frequency is applied. In effect every photon of radio-frequency energy undoes the pumping of at least one optical photon. Since the latter's energy is perhaps a billion times greater than that of the radio-frequency

PUMPING PROCESS is depicted schematically in this diagram of the energy states of atoms. Before pumping, the atoms are divided evenly between energy levels A and B, as in 1. After absorbing photons from a beam of light (2) and being raised to energy level C, atoms drop back in equal numbers to energy levels A and B (3). As the process continues, only one atom is left in level A (5); finally it, too, ends up in level B (7). The atoms are then completely pumped. Pumping can be removed by a radio-frequency signal (8).

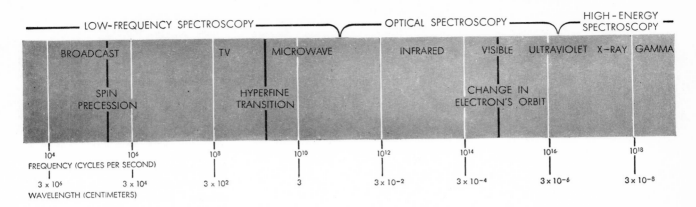

ELECTROMAGNETIC SPECTRUM ranges from low-frequency radio waves (*left*) to high-frequency gamma rays (*right*). Vertical black lines show three spectral lines of sodium; labels on lines indicate corresponding transitions in energy levels of an electron.

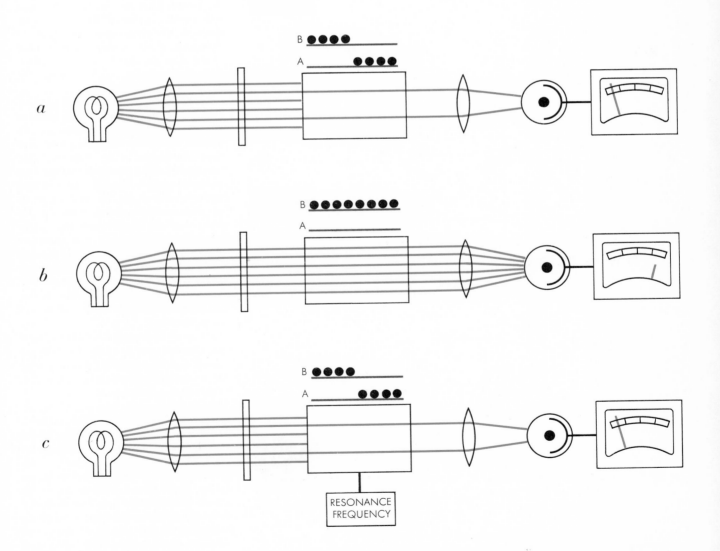

EFFECT OF PUMPING on the transmission of a beam of pumping light is depicted schematically. Rectangles at center represent absorption cells; circles above them show energy levels of atoms within them. Little light gets through unpumped cell in row *a*, as is shown by the reading on meter connected to photocell at right. Completely pumped cell in row *b* is optically transparent; when pumping is removed by applying magnetic field that fluctuates at radio frequency, cell again becomes almost opaque (*c*).

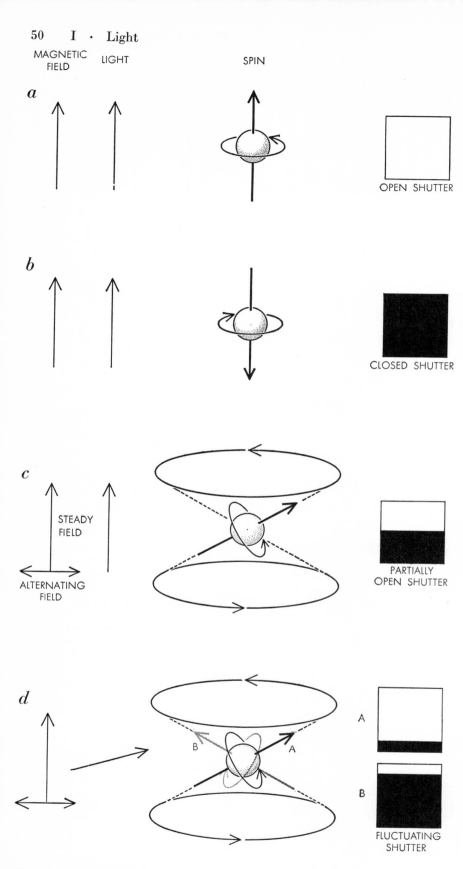

MAGNETIC FIELD　LIGHT　SPIN

a

OPEN SHUTTER

b

CLOSED SHUTTER

c

STEADY FIELD

ALTERNATING FIELD

PARTIALLY OPEN SHUTTER

d

A

B

FLUCTUATING SHUTTER

ELECTRON SPIN determines whether absorption cell will act as an "open shutter" that transmits pumping light or as a "closed shutter" that blocks it. When spin axis of electron is parallel to that of magnetic field across cell, and to the polarization of the light, as in diagram *a*, electron acts as a miniature open shutter. When spin is reversed, electron acts as closed shutter (*b*). When an alternating magnetic field is applied (*c*), electron precesses and acts as partially open shutter. When polarization of light is changed, the presence of the alternating field causes electron to act as a fluctuating shutter (*d*).

photon, we have in effect an amplifier whose gain is a billion!

Our description thus far has glossed over a complication that accounts for the fact that this basically simple effect was not discovered long ago. When atoms arrive in the B state, they are not firmly caught there, but "leak" back into the A state through collisions with one another or with the walls of the container. To be effective, pumping must be faster than the leaks. Even in extremely dilute gases, where collisions between atoms are infrequent, each atom will bump into the walls of the container perhaps 10,000 times a second. Since an atom can absorb no more than about 1,000 photons per second from existing spectral lamps, the leak is clearly much too fast. Successful optical pumping had to await the discovery of methods for slowing down the leak.

The discovery came through one of those happy accidents that every scientist hopes for. Kastler and his associates did their early experiments on sodium vapor contained in highly evacuated glass bulbs. They were barely able to keep ahead of the leaking, but they did observe a very small pumping effect. Then one day in 1955 a defective vacuum system filled one of the bulbs with hydrogen instead of evacuating it. When this bulb was tested, it was found, to everyone's amazement, to show a much larger pumping effect. The investigators had known that a foreign gas could act as a buffer and slow the drift of sodium atoms to the walls. What they had failed to realize was that collisions between the sodium atoms and the buffer atoms would not undo the pumping. The reason is that the shapes of the electron orbits of the sodium atoms and the buffer atoms prevent the magnetic interaction of their electrons. And it is by this interaction that pumped atoms leak back to the unpumped state.

Capitalizing on the lucky error, Kastler began to try hydrogen and helium as buffers, and was able to use them at pressures as high as one millimeter of mercury. Further he could not go, because the buffer interfered with the process by which he detected the pumping effect. At about that time Dehmelt was developing his method of monitoring transmitted light, which is much less sensitive to the presence of buffer gas. Thus he was able to work at much higher pressures. In a sodium experiment with an argon buffer at 40 millimeters of mercury, he found that the time required for the pumping to leak away could be made as long as a 10th of a second. Thus he had achieved a "relaxation time" 100 times longer than the time between photon absorptions.

This was a remarkable result, but Dehmelt then proceeded to do even better without the buffer gas! He reasoned that, since the gas does not completely stop atoms from hitting the walls, a better solution would be to coat the walls themselves with a buffer. The coating should resemble argon in its electronic structure, but should remain solid near 130 degrees centigrade, the temperature at which sodium is pumped. Dehmelt concluded that the requirements could best be met by hydrocarbons with long, straight-chain molecules. Using substances with as many as 40 carbon atoms per molecule, Dehmelt and others have obtained relaxation times as long as two seconds. These experiments are performed with rubidium and cesium, which behave like sodium but which can be pumped at lower temperatures. Apparently the only reason relaxation occurs at all is that once in every 20,000 collisions or so an atom hits the tiny spot of rubidium or cesium metal placed in the vessel to maintain the vapor.

The actual pattern of energy states in sodium, cesium and rubidium that makes them suitable for optical pumping is a bit more complicated than that of our example. Their atoms contain a single, unpaired electron in their outermost electron shells. According to the rules of quantum mechanics the magnetic field of the electron (and therefore its spin axis) can take only two directions with respect to an external field: parallel or antiparallel. The two conditions correspond to our levels A and B. They are distinguished not only magnetically, but also in terms of the "angular momentum" associated with the spin. When the electron's axis points one way (the B state, say) the atom as a whole has one more quantum unit of angular momentum than when the direction is reversed (the A state). In many of their excited states the atoms can have still greater angular momentum than in the B state. The important point, as we shall see in a moment, is that at least one level (our level C) can have no more angular momentum than the B state.

It is important because light photons also have one unit of spin or angular momentum. In an ordinary light beam the spins take on all directions. However, it is possible to restrict them to a single direction, in which case the light is said to be circularly polarized. When atoms absorb photons from a polarized

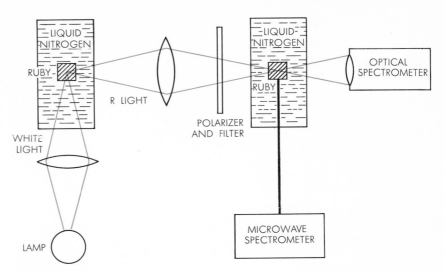

RUBY IS PUMPED by red light from another ruby. First ruby (*left*) fluoresces in the red (R) region of the spectrum when illuminated by intense white light. Pumping effect was detected by the optical spectrometer at right, but not by the microwave spectrometer at bottom.

beam, their angular momentum necessarily changes by one unit, increasing or decreasing depending on the direction of polarization.

Suppose we have a mixture of atoms in the A and B states and illuminate them with light of the proper wavelength to raise them to C. If the light is polarized so as to increase angular momentum, then the atoms in A can absorb it. They move up to C, gaining one unit of angular momentum in the process. But the atoms in B already have as much angular momentum as the maximum allowable in state C. Hence they cannot absorb the light. This is precisely the condition for optical pumping.

In Dehmelt's classic sodium experiment [*see top illustration on next two pages*] pumping light is obtained from a sodium-vapor lamp. Its beam is directed parallel to the earth's magnetic field, which serves as the external field to distinguish the A and B states. After passing through a circular polarizer, the light enters the sample cell: a glass bulb containing sodium metal and a trace of vapor plus argon as a buffer gas. Around the bulb are two sets of coils, one to feed in radio waves and the other to vary the strength of the earth's field slightly. Light transmitted by the bulb falls on a photocell, the output of which is amplified and displayed on an oscilloscope.

When the experiment begins, comparatively little light reaches the photocell because half the sodium atoms are in the light-absorbing state. As pumping proceeds, the vapor rapidly increases in transparency, giving rise to a sharp upward curve on the oscilloscope. The

trace soon levels off, showing that pumping is complete. Now the pumping can be undone by applying radio-frequency energy to flip the electrons over. The exact energy, and hence frequency, required to do this depends on the strength of the magnetic field; in a field of one half gauss, typical of the earth's magnetism at middle latitudes, the frequency at which sodium resonates between the A and B states is about 350 kilocycles per second. The most convenient way to observe the resonance is by varying the earth's field a little in recurrent cycles, or "sweeps." Each time the field passes through the correct value for the radio frequency the brightness of the transmitted light drops sharply, and the drop registers as a dip in the oscilloscope trace. If the field strength is known, the resonance serves as a measure of the radio frequency. Conversely, if the frequency is known, the experiment can be used to determine the earth's magnetic field with high accuracy.

A still more sensitive method of measuring the geomagnetic field takes advantage of an auxiliary resonance-effect. Dehmelt had predicted that, under certain conditions, resonance would not only decrease the over-all intensity of the transmitted light, but would also make it flicker at the radio frequency. The effect was soon observed experimentally by W. E. Bell and the author at Varian Associates in Palo Alto, Calif. It can best be understood in terms of the classical picture of electrons in a magnetic field. On this view the radio waves do not flip the electrons back and forth, but cause them to wobble, or precess, around the field direction at the radio frequency, much as a top precesses around the gravitational field. With respect to the pumping light, the wobbling electrons act as a shutter that is open widest when the axes tip one way and almost closed when they tip the other way [*see illustration on page 50*]. Since the shutter opens and closes about 350,-000 times a second, it produces a flicker at the same rate in the transmitted light. This flicker allows us to "watch" the electrons precess in more than a figurative sense.

When the flickering light strikes the photocell, the electrical output pulsates at the same frequency. Suppose this oscillation is suitably amplified and fed back into the radio-frequency coils around the bulb. Now the circuit can produce its own radio waves. In other words, it is an atomic oscillator. As we have said, the resonant frequency of the electrons depends on the strength of the external field. Hence the frequency of our oscillator, which can be determined very accurately, is a direct measure of the earth's magnetic field.

Magnetometers using pumped rubidium as an atomic oscillator have been built in the author's laboratory. They are more sensitive than any previous instrument, and yet the entire electronic circuit, aside from the lamp, consists of one amplifier. Installed in satellites and rockets, they should be able to measure fields in outer space as weak as a hundred thousandth of a gauss.

The second important application of optical pumping to appear thus far is in atomic clocks and frequency standards. Here the magnetic field that distinguishes the energy levels is supplied not from the outside, but by the nucleus of the atom itself. Until this point in the discussion we have been able to ignore the fact that the nucleus has a spin and a magnetic field. In an alkali atom, such as that of sodium or rubidium, the magnetism of the nucleus and of the outer electron are strongly coupled, and the two precess about an external magnetic field as though they were a single particle. By exciting the atom with microwaves, however, it is possible to uncouple them and make the electron precess about the nucleus. Since the strength of the nuclear magnet is a constant of nature, the frequency at which the electron resonates is precisely determined.

Atomic clocks employing cesium atoms in a beam had been in existence for several years when it occurred to

Robert H. Dicke of Princeton University that pumped rubidium vapor in a glass bulb might provide a more convenient and stable standard. However, if the container held only rubidium atoms, their irregular thermal motion would cause Doppler effects, shifting the resonant frequency by a different amount for each atom, and thus smearing out the resonance line. Dicke proposed that the effect might be reduced by adding a buffer gas. (At the time the effectiveness of a buffer in enhancing optical pumping had not been discovered.)

Trying out various gases and using the monitoring technique that Dehmelt had recently developed, a number of workers soon discovered that a buffer did sharpen the resonance line, and that it also shifted the resonant frequency by a small amount. The shift turned out to be directly proportional to the pressure of the buffer gas, and to be upward in light gases such as hydrogen or helium, and downward in heavy gases such as krypton. Because of the pressure shift, an optically pumped atomic clock is not an absolute standard, as is an atomic beam. Instead it is a highly accurate secondary standard that can be precisely tuned, within a narrow range, by adjusting the gas pressure.

In the past few years a number of workers, notably Peter L. Bender of the National Bureau of Standards, have built optically pumped atomic clocks. Bender's rubidium cell, pumped with light from a rubidium lamp, resonates to a microwave-resonance signal at about 6,834 megacycles per second that is stable to within one part in 100 billion. The device is sufficiently compact to be carried in a satellite, where it could be used to check the gravitational red-shift predicted by the general theory of relativity.

In addition to its practical usefulness, optical pumping offers considerable promise as a research tool. Studies of the pressure shift itself, which is not too well understood, should tell a good deal about the forces between atoms when they collide. A variety of substances other than the alkali metals can be pumped. Experiments on mercury vapor, applying the combined techniques of optical and radio-frequency resonance, have yielded information about details in the optical spectrum that are too fine to be resolved by the best optical spectrograph. Helium atoms, although they do not have the proper structure for optical pumping in their normal state, can be raised to a long-lived, or

metastable, excited state that is amenable to pumping. As shown by Peter Franken of the University of Michigan, low-frequency spectroscopy can then be used to measure the lifetime of the metastable state. Here again, as with sodium, the frequency of the resonance is directly

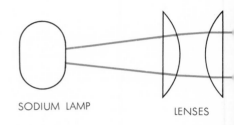

SODIUM IS PUMPED by light from a sodium-vapor lamp (*left*). Absorption cell

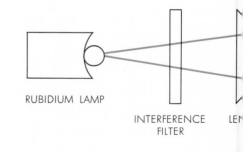

RUBIDIUM MAGNETOMETER is actually an atomic oscillator. Feedback circuit that

proportional to the strength of the applied magnetic field, and very sensitive measurements of the earth's field can be made in this way.

It is also possible to do low-frequency spectroscopy on vapors that cannot themselves be optically pumped. This is accomplished by mixing them with atoms of a pumpable substance and taking advantage of a process known as "spin exchange," in which angular momentum is transferred between the materials. Nitrogen and hydrogen have already been investigated, and there is no reason why the method cannot be extended to many other vapors:

A particularly interesting development is the recent discovery that optical pumping can be applied to certain solids. It has been known for some time that a ruby, stimulated by a strong white

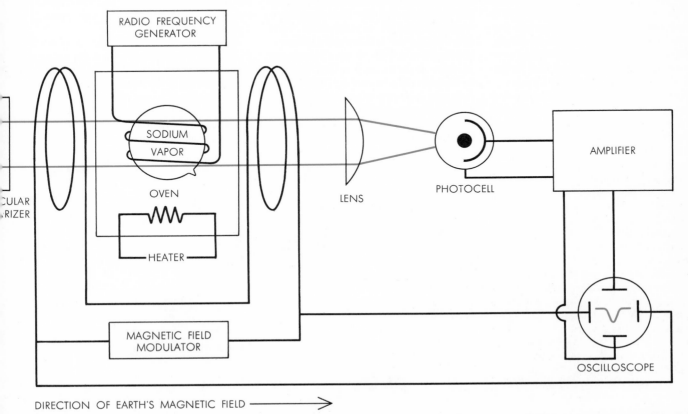

at center contains sodium that is vaporized by a heater. Light (*colored lines*) transmitted by cell reaches photocell at right. Amplified signal from photocell is fed to oscilloscope. Coils at center are used to vary the magnetic field across absorption cell.

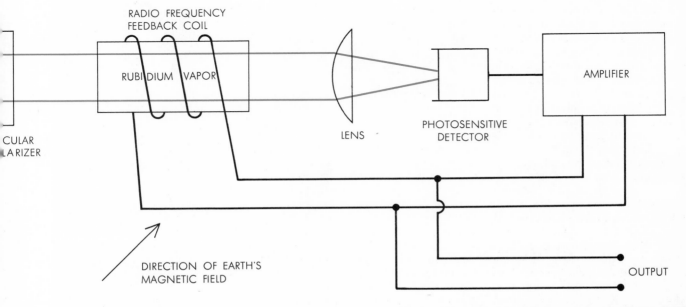

connects the photosensitive detector to the amplifier and the coils causes the light transmitted by the absorption cell to flicker at a radio frequency. The frequency of output signal at terminals at bottom depends on the strength of the earth's magnetic field.

light, will emit a red glow, known as R light, in a very narrow band of wavelengths. Irwin Wieder of the Westinghouse Research Laboratories has successfully used the R light to pump a second ruby in a conventional radio-frequency resonance experiment.

Of much greater potential importance is the first step, in which white light is converted to R light. Again we can picture the process in terms of three energy-levels, but now the large gap is between A and B rather than B and C. Furthermore, C is not a single energy but a rather broad band. Thus the atoms in A can absorb photons of various energies in the white light, and move up to the C band. Thermal motions then cause them

to leak, or rather spill, into the B level almost immediately. From here they fall to the A level far below, emitting light photons of sharply defined energy and frequency.

In this way the energy spread over a wide range of frequencies has been channeled into a narrow band. In effect the energy in this band has been enormously amplified. Moreover if the white light is applied in extremely powerful pulses, then *all* the atoms are pumped at once to level B and fall back to A almost simultaneously. When this happens, a co-operative effect can take place between the atoms that causes them to emit their R photons in unison, or coherently. It is as if the atoms, emit-

ting light waves, are so engulfed by the waves produced by their neighbors that they are forced to radiate synchronously with them. Such coherent radiation in the visible range, now available for the first time, makes possible light devices of unprecedented efficiency. For example, coherent light can be focused into a pencil beam that will not spread more than five feet in 12 miles.

T. H. Maiman at the Hughes Aircraft Company has already observed some degree of coherent emission from a ruby, and he as well as workers at several other laboratories are trying to put R light to practical use. Although a working light amplifier may still be some time away, its prospects now seem excellent.

FREQUENCY STANDARD is tuned by regulating the pressure of buffer gas in a rubidium vapor cell (*inside aluminum cylinder at center*) while it is still connected to the vacuum system. Rubidium lamp is in tube at right. Large coils control magnetic field.

II

Forming and
Detecting Images

Forming and Detecting Images

Light is used primarily for making and viewing images. Whenever an object is illuminated by white light, the intensity and wavelengths of the light that comes from each point on the object depend on the material at that point. The light from each point is conveyed by some means to a corresponding point on an image, which in turn is somehow converted by the brain into meaningful information. The articles in this section describe some of the significant advances in our understanding of the principles and new methods of conveying and detecting the optical image.

The usual way to form an image is, of course, by a lens. Usually one begins to learn about lenses by considering rays of light which diverge from each object point, and are bent by the lens to converge at an image point. The lens may have to be composed of several elements, as in a good camera, if it is to focus sharply on all parts of the image without undesirable separation of colors. However, there are ultimate theoretical limitations for even the best lenses because light consists of waves, whose lengths are quite short but not negligible. The nearest equivalent to a ray is a narrow pencil of waves. Image formation, then, can be described as the refraction and interference of light waves as they travel through different parts of the lens. With wave methods, modern computers, and a wide variety of possible optical materials, it is possible to design and construct a lens as close to the theoretical limits as necessary for the purpose. The quality of a given lens can be described by various indices, one of which is the spatial frequency response of the lens. For example, when a camera lens is carefully focused on a point object, instead of specifying the size of the image the lens produces, we may say that it can resolve so many lines per millimeter on the film. More quantitatively, instead of giving the intensity distribution in the image from a point object, we can specify the contrast ratio for images of lattices of regular rulings of different spatial repetition rate. These methods of producing and evaluating images are described in the article by F. Dow Smith.

A very different way to transmit light from object points to corresponding image points is discussed in the article by Narinder S. Kapany. In fiber optics, bundles of glass or plastic rod pipes are used to guide light from one small area on the object to a corresponding area on the image. The fibers can be either quite short or several meters long, they can either contract or increase in diameter from one end to the other, and they can be rigidly fused or assembled in flexible bundles. These useful optical elements are now finding many uses.

However the image is formed, ultimately the light at each point must be detected. The human eye is a remarkably sensitive instrument but its response is confined to the small visible part of the spectrum. Various kinds of electronic sensors, some of which have larger apertures than the eye and thus gather more light, can respond to wavelengths in the ultraviolet and infrared regions. There are also photographic films and electron devices that can accumulate signals from weak light until there is enough for a satisfactory image. Other devices can intensify the light image, making it easier to see or photograph. These various methods for detecting light are discussed and compared in the article by R. Clark Jones.

Another way to form an image is by the method of holography. The basic idea of holography was proposed by Dennis Gabor in 1948 and demonstrated with conventional light sources. Since then, lasers have greatly facilitated holography and expanded its scope and uses. For this reason, the holographic method of forming images will be discussed in Section VII, which treats some applications of lasers.

57

6

How Images are Formed

F. Dow Smith   September 1968

Because light wavelengths are short light can convey a remarkable quantity of information. The fidelity with which this information is ultimately presented in an image depends on the physical characteristics of the optical system that forms the image. In recent years optical technology has made dramatic advances; aerospace photography from very high altitudes and photomicrographic techniques for producing integrated circuits are just two applications of the remarkable optical systems that are now being developed. The new technology is based on a comprehensive new discipline of image formation that combines traditional geometric optics with the wave and diffraction theory of modern physical optics, and brings to bear new mathematical routines executed by high-speed computers.

The behavior of light was one of the first aspects of the physical world to be observed and investigated by the ancient philosophers. They learned by experiment that rays of light striking a surface at an angle are reflected at precisely

HIGH INFORMATION CONTENT in an image is demonstrated by the photographs on the opposite page. The contact print is a strip from a portion of a negative exposed at a high altitude east of Los Angeles by an advanced Itek Corporation aerial camera. The scale is 1 : 36,000 (one inch equals 3,000 feet). The print covers about 7.5 square miles, ranging from Baldwin Park in the west (*top*) to Charter Oak in the east (*bottom*). A small segment of the contact print (*center, about four inches from the top*) was enlarged 25 diameters and the resulting print is reproduced here at a total enlargement of 31.5 diameters. The detail revealed in the enlargement includes the lane markers in the swimming pool, runners on the track and players on the football field.

the same angle. A general law of refraction—the change in angle of a ray passing from one transparent medium into another—was more elusive, although about A.D. 150 Ptolemy was able to measure the bending of a beam of light as it passed from air into water or glass (and in the opposite direction). Johannes Kepler found that when light struck a glass surface nearly perpendicularly the angles of incidence and refraction were in the ratio of 3 : 2. Finally in 1621 the Dutch mathematician Willebrord Snel (not Snell, as it is commonly given) found the correct relation for all angles of incidence, including large ones. At about the same time René Descartes derived the correct mathematical expression. Isaac Newton showed that the angle of refraction also depended on the color of the incident light. Thus the simple geometrical relation was established: the sines of the angles of incidence and refraction are inversely proportional to the indexes of refraction of the two mediums. For light of any color the index of refraction of a medium is inversely proportional to the speed of that light in that medium. Snell's law, as this relation is called in English-speaking countries, is a sufficient physical basis for all geometrical optics, the high development of which in the late 19th and early 20th century made possible great achievements in the design of complex lenses and optical instruments [*see illustrations on next page*].

From the optical designer's point of view, a practical lens for a camera or other instrument consists of a set of refracting or reflective surfaces, usually spherical in form, arranged along a common axis. A lens "formula" consists of a set of numbers giving the thicknesses and spacing of the various elements and the indexes of refraction of the glasses

of which they are made. The aim is to bring bundles of light rays from some "object point" to a single point, the image, and to do this simultaneously for many points and for light of many wavelengths.

It is not possible simply to solve a set of algebraic equations and come up with a complete lens formula. There are, however, formulas that express the general behavior of rays of light, particularly those close to the lens axis, the "paraxial" rays. These formulas show that all the rays typically do not come to the same focus and this results in image errors known as aberrations. It is not possible or indeed desirable to reduce all these errors to zero in a practical system. Instead the usual practice is to allow a specified amount of a certain aberration to occur and to cancel its effect by introducing an opposite error from a different kind of aberration. Formulas derived from aberration theory can be a general guide to lens design, but the formulas are approximate at best.

The classic and continuing method of lens design is therefore "ray-tracing," a trigonometric process by which an individual ray is traced through the lens. Its change in direction at each surface is computed by Snell's law. In this way the position at which each ray intersects the desired image plane can be determined. In the very early days these computations were done with logarithms to six or more decimal places; the process was laborious and only a few rays could be traced. Later the process was speeded up by the introduction of mechanical desk calculators. The designer would select a number of rays from one object point and determine where each intersected a plane near the image, and then do the same for other points in the field of view and for light of various wavelengths. After making a set of calcula-

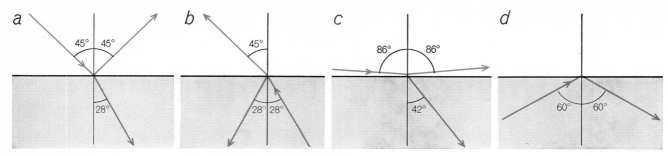

REFLECTION AND REFRACTION are shown for light passing from air (index of refraction 1) to glass (index 1.5). The angle of reflection equals the angle of incidence and the sines of the angles of incidence and refraction vary inversely with the indexes of re-

fraction (*a*). Reversing the direction of light propagation does not change the angles (*b*). A grazing incident ray is refracted at a limiting angle (*c*). When the direction is reversed, at any larger angle a ray is totally reflected within the denser medium (*d*).

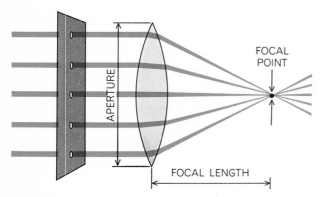

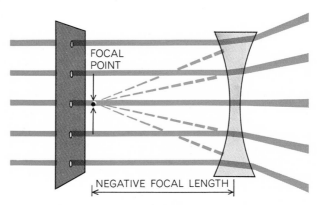

LENSES refract light rays. Parallel rays (pencils of light formed by holes in a screen) are converged to the focal point by a convex

(positive) lens (*left*). Rays are diverged by a concave (negative) lens so as to seem to originate at the negative focal point (*right*).

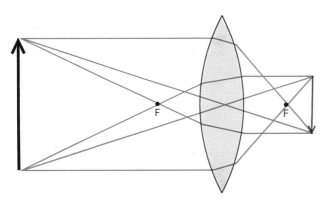

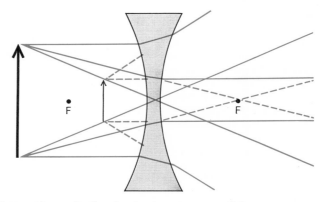

RAYS from points on an object (*black arrows*), refracted by a lens, converge to establish corresponding points on an image (*gray arrows*). Parallel rays are refracted through the focal point; rays

intersecting at the first focal point emerge parallel; rays through the center of a thin lens are not deviated. A convex lens forms a real image, as on film; a concave lens forms only a "virtual" one.

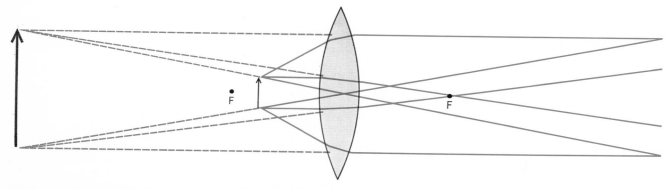

MAGNIFICATION can occur when an object is located inside the focal point of a converging lens, which forms a virtual, enlarged

and upright image. In microscopes and telescopes the object to be magnified is an image that has been formed by an objective lens.

tions he would evaluate the resulting image, adjust his lens elements accordingly and do the calculations again.

The design process was greatly accelerated with the advent of high-speed digital computers, which also made possible the development of a new pictorial tool, the spot diagram. With the computer a very large number of rays can be traced for a single object point. The interactions of these rays on the image surface provide a dot pattern that represents the image of that point [*see illustration at right*]. Such diagrams, determined geometrically, are good representations of the image when the aberration is large, but the better the lens, the less adequate they become. The reason is that diffraction effects (discussed in the opening article of this issue) become relatively more important as aberration effects are reduced. It is possible with a computer actually to calculate the diffraction image, but the procedure is cumbersome and not generally appropriate for engineering applications. The real importance of the computer in optics has been in the development of remarkable new processes of "automatic lens design," processes that are able to cope with the complexity of modern high-quality lenses that must perform near the physical limit set by diffraction.

The problem of the lens designer is essentially to adjust the variables of the lens formula so as to bring the quality of the image to some predetermined level. A lens may have as many as 10 or more elements, and so the number of variables affecting it (curvature, thickness, spacing and glass type of the elements) can add up to 50 or more. The number of variables defining image quality is also large because a number of different things must be considered for several different object points and for several different colors of light.

The designer usually begins by assuming an approximate lens configuration and then adjusts the elements in an orderly way, testing his results as he goes along, until he achieves the desired image quality. His problem has been compared to the situation of the explorer dropped without maps into the Himalayas and asked to find Mount Everest: he can always find a local peak by climbing upward, but he can never know it is the highest peak in the range until he descends into a valley and tries a new direction—and even then he has limited data on the basis of which to avoid another false ascent. Similarly, the designer, in his multidimensional space, can arrange for a suitably programmed com-

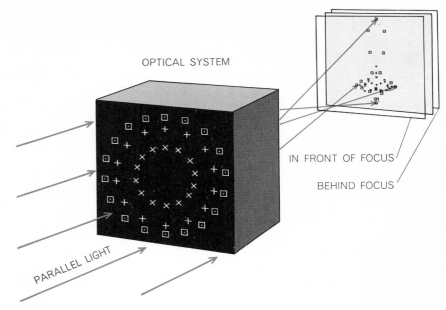

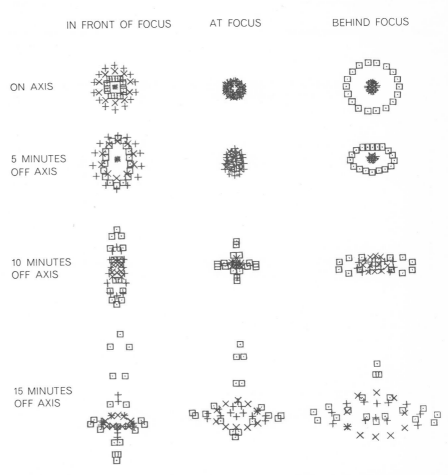

SPOT DIAGRAM was constructed by computer by D. H. Schulte to test his design for a 150-inch telescope. The diagram shows how the system would handle rays of parallel light entering its aperture (as from a distant point source) at many different points, each represented by a symbol in the schematic diagram (*top*). Ideally the image should be a point. In fact it varies from a good circle only about .25 second of arc (1/14,000 degree) in diameter (*spot at top center*) to more spread-out patterns as the image plane is moved (*columns*) and as the angle the rays make with the system's axis goes from zero to 1/4 degree (*rows*).

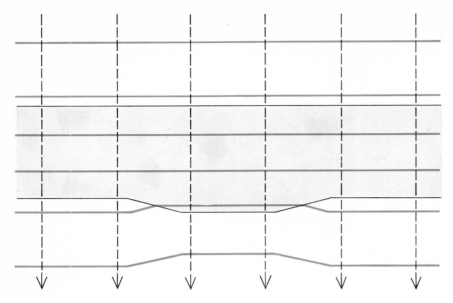

ERROR IN A LENS is manifested in the emerging wave front. In this diagram (with large vertical exaggeration) a straight-line wave front (*color*) formed by parallel light rays (*broken lines*) moves through a faulty piece of flat glass and is deformed from flatness by a bump.

ceptable solution but one composed of practical lens elements that can be manufactured. Every designer remembers his frustrations with computer programs that produced lenses of negative thickness or other physically impossible—let alone undesirable—configurations.)

Automated lens design or not, the main problem remains of choosing the image-quality variables: the terms in which the optimum solution is to be described. That depends in turn on an analysis of the objects of which images are to be formed. In discussing ray-tracing I referred to object points, and one can indeed treat the image of an extended object as a superposition of images of individual points on the object. This is possible because one can assume that each point is an independent radiator of light and that the light from the various points has no phase relation, or coherence. If the object is illuminated by laser light, the radiation will be coherent, and that is something else again [see "Applications of Laser Light," by Donald R. Herriott, page 313].

If an object can be regarded as an array of independent point sources of light, then it is important to consider how a lens system forms an image of such a point source. The fact is that, for fundamental reasons arising from the wave nature of light, a geometrical point

puter to begin with the trial lens configuration and quickly adjust the variables to find the local optimum. If a suitable optimum is not achieved, the computer programs can move across the "valley" to a nearby "peak"—a slightly different lens design. If an adequate solution is not found nearby, however, the designer himself must take some action to move

to a quite different region of the mountain range to find a new area of solution. The computer programs devised by a number of independent workers in different parts of the world to solve these problems are among the most complex ever developed. (Much of the complexity lies in the fact that these programs must produce not just a mathematically ac-

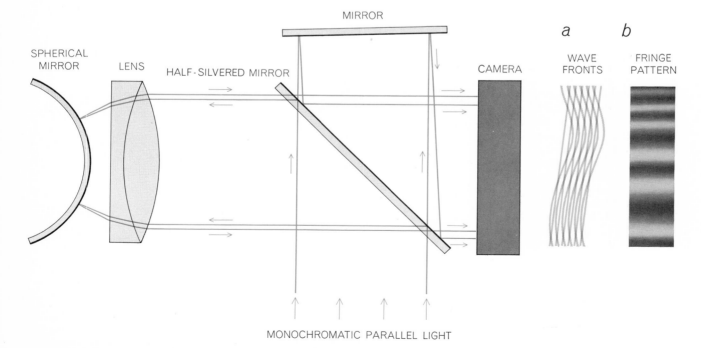

INTERFEROMETER is set up to measure the wave aberration, or error, in a lens or mirror by the Twyman method. Light deflected by the half-silvered mirror through the lens is reflected by the mirror. Any error in the lens or mirror will be manifested as a devia-

tion from flatness in wave fronts returned by the lens-mirror combination to the beam splitter. When the light is recombined, perfect wave fronts from the flat mirror (*top*) and deformed ones from the test element interfere (*a*), forming fringes on film (*b*).

object cannot be imaged as a perfect point; at best it can form a diffraction pattern of a finite size. In the case of a circular aperture and an aberration-free lens, the pattern is the familiar one analyzed by the English astronomer George Biddell Airy in 1834: a central bright disk containing some 85 percent of the energy, surrounded by equally spaced and successively fainter rings [*see photograph at left on page* 8]. The diameter of the bright disk is a function of the wavelength of the light and the *f* number (the focal length divided by the aperture) of the lens. A perfect *f*/8 lens, for example, produces an Airy disk about eight microns (thousandths of a millimeter) in diameter. When the aberrations have been made very small, the spreading of each point of light by diffraction may become the main factor reducing the quality of the image, and must therefore be considered in the design of very good lenses.

The best way to do this is to regard each point object as the origin of a wave that enters the aperture of the lens system and is there converted into a wave emerging from the rear of the lens. Any error in the lens will be manifested as an error in the emerging wave front, as is most clearly seen in the case of a straight-line wave front moving through a flat piece of glass [*see top illustration on opposite page*]. In a lens the ideal emerging wave front is spherical, with its center of curvature at the image point (the focal point, in the case of a plane incident wave from a distant source). In a practical lens there will usually be errors in the sphericity of this emerging wave front. The errors are described by the wave aberration (*W*) of the lens, a function that gives, for each point in the emerging wave front, the linear separation (generally expressed in wavelengths) between the actual wave and some reference surface. A convenient reference is a sphere centered on the paraxial image, the image formed by rays near the axis of the lens [*see illustration on page* 65]. The concept of wave aberration is of such a fundamental nature that, as we shall see, it provides the most general single description of the optical performance of the lens. The importance of the concept was first recognized by Lord Rayleigh, who pointed out that reducing the wave aberration below a quarter of a wavelength often brought no practical improvement in the quality of the image.

The process of geometrical ray-tracing I described earlier can provide an exact determination of the shape of the emerging wave front since the wave

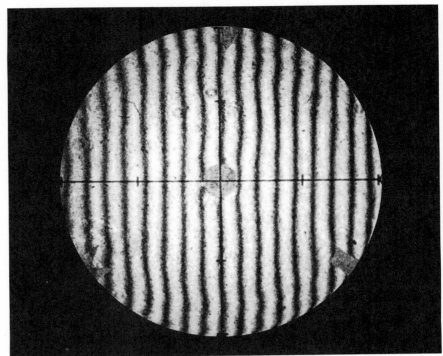
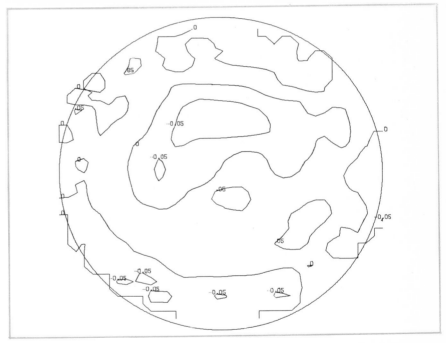
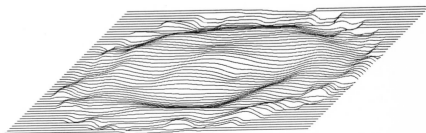

FRINGE PATTERN (*top*) is from a 50-inch mirror tested with a laser by a modified Twyman method. Several such patterns were automatically scanned and the resulting data were averaged by a computer to plot the contours (*middle*) and the perspective drawing (*bottom*) of the wave aberration. The "root mean square" aberration, or departure from a perfect wave front, is 1/34 wavelength, the maximum "peak to valley" distance 1/6 wavelength.

front is, at each point, perpendicular to the rays. Moreover, the wave-front shape is the traditional and correct starting point for calculating the diffraction pattern. Clearly, then, the wave front contains a full description of the image as it might be given by either geometrical or diffraction optics. What is even more important, the wave-front error of an actual lens or mirror can be measured, making it possible for the optician who is building the element to know the exact nature of the error in its surface and indeed giving him a map showing where the surface is too high and where it is too low. The wave front produced by a complete system can also be measured. The wave front thus connects the work of the designer of a system with the work of its builder.

For the designer the wave front provides the most convenient single criterion of lens performance and one that is preeminently suitable for computer programs. From the tentative design the values of the wave aberration W are determined with respect to a nearest-fitting reference sphere. The values are squared to eliminate negative numbers and averaged over the aperture, and the square root of this average is taken to yield the root-mean-square (RMS) wave aberration. This number turns out to be well correlated, in the case of high-quality images, with the overall quality of the image. Automatic design programs are often written to optimize the system specifically by adjusting for the minimum RMS wave aberration.

Although it is valid to consider an incoherently lighted object as an array of points to be examined one at a time, the designer often finds it better to evaluate the input to his system as an extended array of points in a particular pattern. Somewhat surprisingly, it is possible to analyze the complex, irregular pattern of light and dark that constitutes the surface of an object and predict how it will be formed into an image by a given optical system. The basis of the method is the "transfer function," which was developed as a theoretical concept over the past 20 years and has recently become available as a practical engineering tool now that certain difficult computational problems have been solved. The transfer function describes the ability of an optical system to form images of a particular class of extended objects: incoherently illuminated arrays of bars each of which has a sinusoidal variation in brightness. The point is that any physical scene can be regarded as a superposition of sinusoidal patterns (and

can be analyzed into such patterns by the process of Fourier analysis), just as a complex musical sound can be treated as a superposition of sinusoidal tones. This being so, one ought to be able to consider the behavior of an optical system in imaging individual spatial-frequency components much as one describes the fidelity of a sound system in reproducing tones over its required range. The transfer function is analogous to the frequency-response curve of a sound system.

Any optical system, no matter what its aberrations, forms a sinusoidal image of a sinusoidal object. The image has the same spatial frequency as the object (multiplied by the system's constant magnification). That is, the system is linear. However, the image is not identical with the object because in any practical optical system there will be some loss of contrast: the light-to-dark ratio is reduced as some light spills from the light bands into the dark ones. The spillage increases as the bands are more closely spaced, so that the contrast eventually drops to zero. The ratio of the contrast of the image to that of the object, arbitrarily set at one for the limit of infinitely coarse bars, is the value of the transfer function at a particular spatial frequency. The transfer function is therefore a curve that gives the image contrast as a function of spatial frequency, usually expressed in cycles of light and dark per millimeter at the image plane [*see illustration on page 68*].

The transfer function provides a basis for predicting the performance of a single element or the overall performance of an optical system. For example, in an aerial camera the velocity of the vehicle usually causes a predictable amount of blurring in the image. The image motion can be described by a transfer function that, when multiplied by the function for the lens, gives an exact function for the combination of the two. The result can be combined with a transfer function for the photographic emulsion to predict the performance of the total system. (This last step is less exact because the emulsion's response is nonlinear; a sine-wave exposure does not always produce

a sine-wave image in the emulsion.) Similarly, the transfer function can predict the image quality a lens will yield when it is combined with an electronic image detector such as a television camera tube.

The transfer function can be calculated from a description of the wave front, either from a computed wave front during the design stage or from an actual wave front measured in the laboratory. In the case of a perfect lens the computation is done rather easily. When the wave aberration is not zero, however, the calculation is complex and requires a large computer. Moreover, a number of similar calculations must be made for various orientations of the input sine-wave bars, since the optical system may respond to the different orientations quite differently.

A more powerful approach is to obtain the transfer function by first calculating the energy distribution in the image of a point source, that is, the extent to which light from a point source is spread out in the image. This procedure is possible because one can regard the point source as being composed equally of sinusoidal components with all possible wavelengths. Therefore if the image is decomposed into its sinusoidal components by a spatial Fourier analysis, the result is the transfer function. Recently Robert R. Shannon and his associates at the Itek Corporation, notably Steven H. Lerman and William A. Minnick, have worked out a practical system for making these computations through advanced programming methods. Their work used a new theoretical approach to the diffraction calculation of point images from wave-front data developed in England by Harold H. Hopkins, now at the University of Reading. The necessary Fourier decomposition had only recently been made practical for digital computers by a method of fast Fourier transformations that was introduced by James W. Cooley of the International Business Machines Corporation and John W. Tukey of Princeton University. Richard L. Mitchell, then at the Aerospace Corporation, developed a computer program with which

ABERRATIONS can be controlled by combining them. In a hypothetical example (*opposite page*) one lens has been fully corrected for simple chromatic aberration but its combined focus for red and blue light is still different from the focus for green (*a, b, c*). Another lens (*d, e, f*) has spherical aberration that varies with the color of the light. Combining the errors in the two lenses makes a lens with improved performance in blue light (*g, h, i*). In each diagram the marginal and paraxial rays are shown in color and their wave front (*color*) is compared with a perfectly spherical reference wave front (*black*); the broken line is the desired image plane and the arrows mark the best image attained by each lens. The curves below the diagrams give the wave aberration W of each lens in wavelengths.

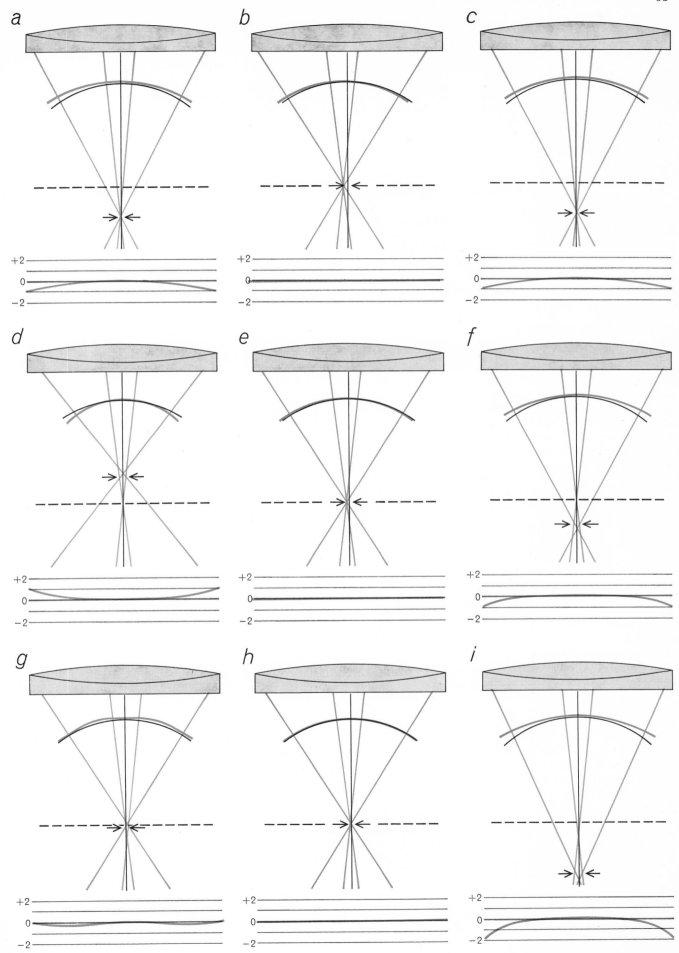

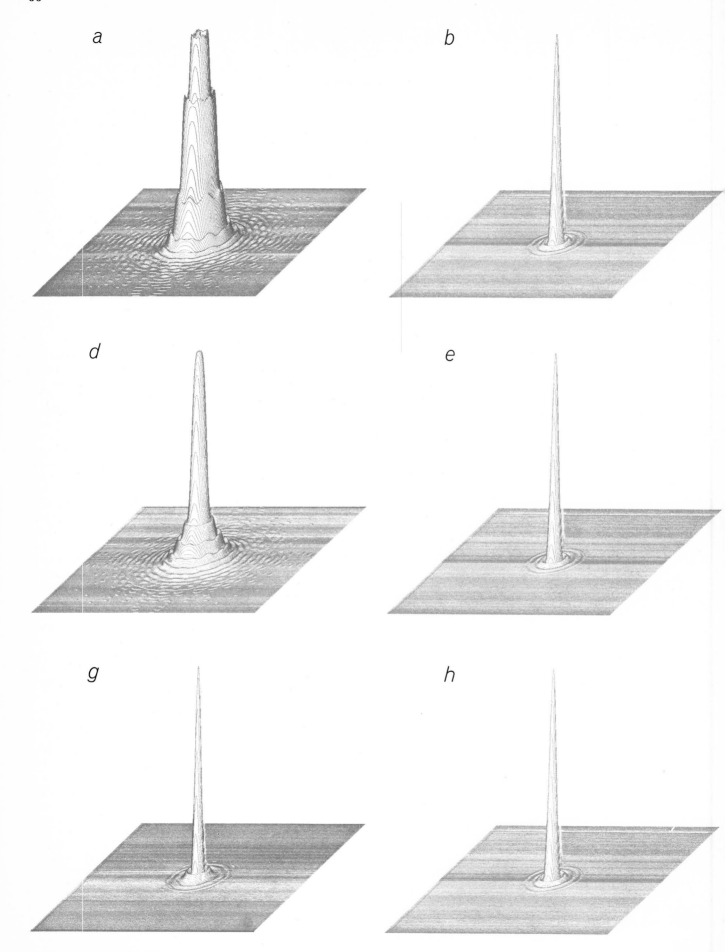

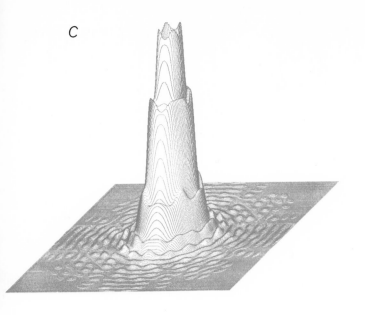

c

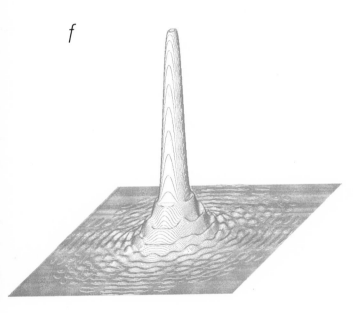

f

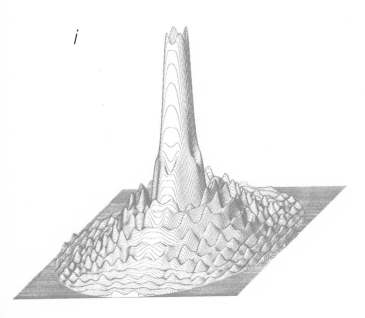

i

energy distribution and transfer function results can be automatically plotted in perspective [*see illustrations on these two pages and at top of page 69*].

As I pointed out earlier, one of the great advantages of the new methods of optical designing is that they enable the designer of a lens and the man who must evaluate its performance to speak the same language—wave-front language. It is the laser that has made practical the actual measurement of wave-front aberrations for a wide range of lenses, but the basic procedure was worked out in England more than 40 years ago by F. Twyman, who devised a modification of the Michelson interferometer [see "How Light Is Analyzed," by Pierre Connes, page 35]. In the Twyman procedure light from a monochromatic source is divided by a half-reflecting mirror, with one part going to the lens under test and the other to a precisely flat optical surface. When the light beams are recombined, the resulting interference between the two produces a fringe pattern directly related to the wave aberration W. The pattern is interpreted as the contour lines on a topographic map are, except that the contour interval is half a wavelength instead of many feet. (The factor of one-half arises because the light passes twice through the lens being tested.)

Prior to the introduction of the laser, this method suffered from several limitations. Since the two interferometer beams must be in phase to produce useful interference, the two light paths cannot differ by more than the length of a single train of waves emitted by the light source, a few centimeters in the case of a pure mercury arc. Moreover, the test setup must be kept vibration-free through the required exposure time, which was particularly difficult in the case of large lenses and mirrors. The laser solved both problems. Continuous gas lasers provide coherence lengths of many feet and sufficient power to allow fast recording of fringe patterns and thus minimize vibration effects.

A basic limitation of the interferom-

PERFORMANCE of each lens-light combination diagrammed on page 103 is represented visually in computer-plotted graphs of the distribution of energy in point images (*left*), each a three-dimensional graph of light intensity (*vertical*) against distance in the image plane. A slender peak means a good image (*b, e, g, h*). The large aberration of the third lens in red light is evident (*i*). (Small, asymmetrically distributed irregularities are artifacts of computer process.)

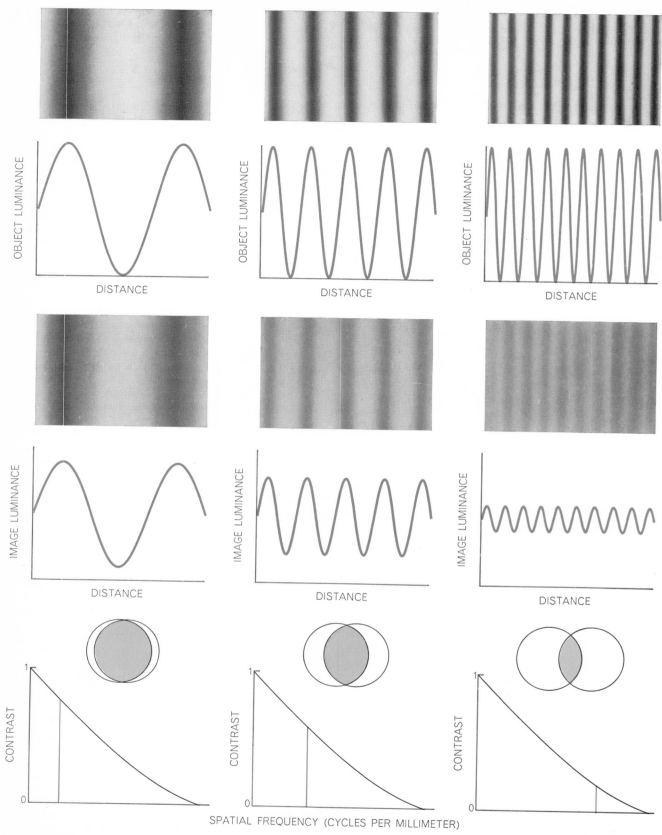

TRANSFER FUNCTION, a description of an optical system's ability to preserve contrast, is based on the change of contrast with decreasing spacing of an array of bars having a sinusoidal variation in contrast. Three such arrays and their intensity-v.-distance curves are shown (top) along with their images (middle). For a perfect system the falloff in contrast is given by the transfer-function curves (bottom). The value of the function at each spatial frequency (the ratio of the amplitudes of the sine waves above) is given by the colored vertical lines. The ratio is also given by the areas common to each pair of circles representing the aperture.

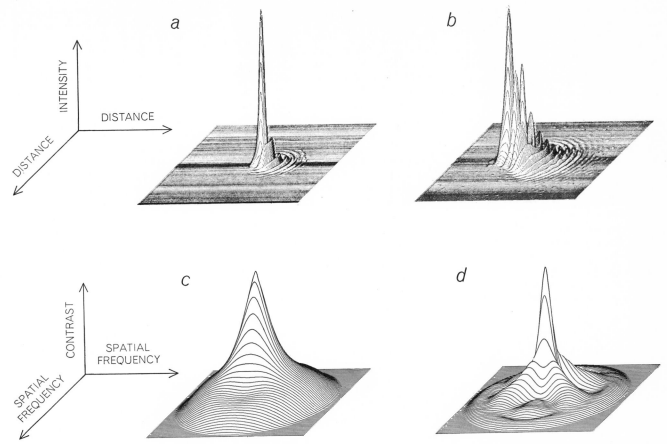

WAVE-FRONT DATA can be used to give the energy distribution, from which in turn the transfer function can be calculated. The transfer function can be plotted in three dimensions. Here energy-distribution (*top*) and associated transfer-function (*bottom*) graphs are shown for two instances of coma, an aberration in which light at an angle to the lens axis is focused asymmetrically.

eter method has to do with extracting data from the fringe pattern; specifically, it is not easy to determine the reference surface from which the aberration distance to the wave front should be measured. Large computers can solve this problem. At the Itek Corporation, for example, we now scan the fringe pattern automatically; from the resulting data, the computer determines the "best fit" reference surface with the smallest average separation from the measured wave front and then maps the error contours at height intervals much smaller than the one-wavelength intervals of the original fringe data [*see illustration on page 63*]. The wave front map can be used to guide a technician in further stages of manufacture, to compare his result with the original design or to compute the transfer function and other criteria of image quality, such as the image of a point source or of more complex objects. The contour map, in other words,

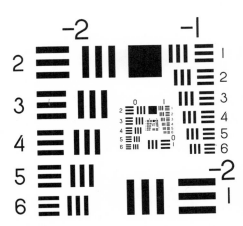
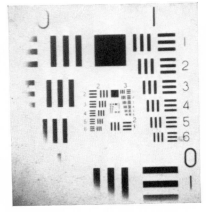
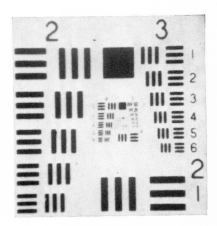

BAR TARGET can be used to test the resolving power of a lens-film combination. The Air Force target reproduced here actual size (*left*) has groups of six target pairs, each group half as large as the preceding one. The large numbers give the lines per millimeter in powers of 2; for example, 2^0 means one line per millimeter, 2^3 eight lines. The smaller numbers specify intermediate sizes. Images (*center and right*) of successively smaller parts of the target were formed, after five-diameter reduction, by a large $f/3.5$ lens on aerial film. Read with a microscope, the image at the right indicates that the system can resolve to about 300 lines per millimeter.

bridges gaps between divisions of optical technology more satisfactorily than earlier methods.

The importance of this bridge cannot be overestimated. The creation of an optical instrument such as an aerial camera or a telescope involves a number of steps. An overall design concept sets specifications for mechanical components as well as the lens itself, taking into account the relation with the image detector: photographic emulsion, television camera or photometer, for example. For the lens, there follow separate stages of design, fabrication and testing, each of which demands evaluation. Are the design aberrations small enough? Is a lens that is being polished smooth enough? Does the assembled lens produce a good enough image? Does the completed system produce test pictures on film that meet the original specifications? Over the years different criteria were developed for answering such questions at different stages, and the criteria could not be related accurately one to another. Now finally the optician can be sure when his optical surface is good enough and the assembler can be sure that the image he observes in the finished lens is what the designer predicted.

The developments I have described constitute important changes in optical technology. For decades much of optics has been an art, with craftsmanship and intuition playing dominant roles. Now there begins to be a connected scientific base for new technological developments. The advanced optical systems needed for space astronomy will be the first beneficiaries of this new technology, but the impact is already being felt in the development of commercial optics. Until recently commercial optical elements have had wave aberrations of from one to a few wavelengths. In that aberration range, ray optics provides an adequate description of performance, with light from each region of the aperture contributing incoherently to the image. When the wave aberration becomes a fraction of a wavelength, contributions from each part of the aperture combine coherently. As this begins to happen the energy within the image begins to concentrate rapidly and there is an improvement in quality quite out of proportion to the reduction in aberration. Even commercial lens systems are moving into this fractional-wavelength region. The new computer and measurement technologies will make practical increasingly complex optical systems of unprecedented performance.

7

Fiber Optics

Narinder S. Kapany   November 1960

As long ago as 1870 the British physicist John Tyndall demonstrated that light, which, as everyone knows, travels in straight lines, can be conducted along a curved path. His "light pipe" was simply a thin stream of water issuing from a hole in the side of a tank. Light shined into the tank emerged at the hole and followed the downward-curving stream. Most of us have seen the effect in illuminated fountains, and it has also been applied in advertising displays, with glass or plastic rods rather than liquid jets serving as conductors. Recently, however, light conductors of a special type have been transformed from trivial curiosities to important optical devices.

In this form they are made of bundles of very thin, and therefore flexible, glass fibers, usually coated with a layer of

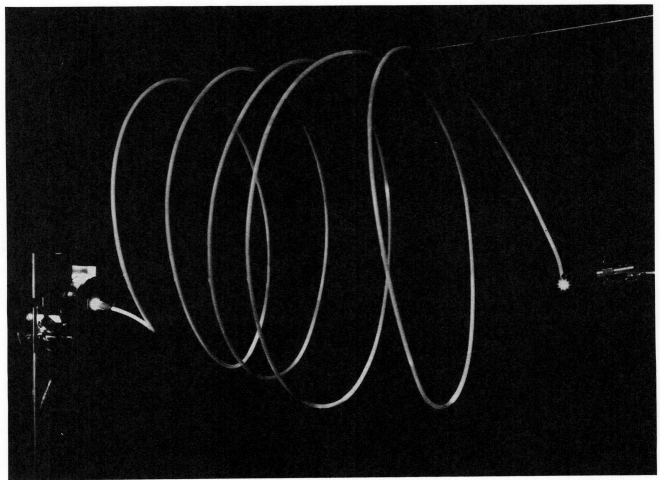

LIGHT IS TRANSMITTED from light source at left through a 23-foot-long "light pipe" made up of fibers. "Pipe" is looped over a rod. "Star" at right is light coming out of fiber bundle at far end, which is clamped to laboratory stand and points at camera.

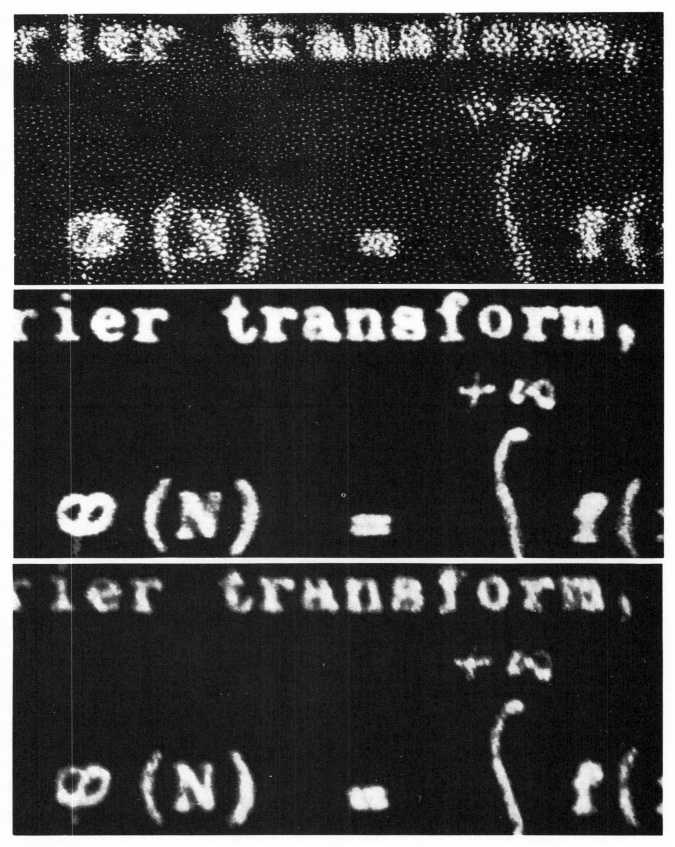

THREE DIFFERENT IMAGES through same bundle of 50-micron fibers are shown here. At top grainy "static" image is projected by immobile bundle. In center, bundle is vibrated in plane of image to produce "dynamic scanning." The image does not move, but motion of bundle wipes out edges of fibers, removing grain. At bottom, "space filtering" is produced with layers of different thicknesses of transparent material over the lens that receives image from bundle. Image is poorer than that in dynamic scanning.

glass of a different kind. Such bundles can not only transport an optical image over a tortuous path, but can also transform it in a number of useful ways.

Although a curved rod of glass or other transparent material appears to bend light rays passing through it, it does not actually do so. Instead the light follows a zigzag path down the rod, traveling always in straight lines and caroming repeatedly off the surface. Since the surface is transparent, the rays might be expected to cross it and escape from the conductor. The reason they do not is to be found in the phenomenon known as total internal reflection.

When light falls obliquely on the dividing surface, or interface, between two transparent media, part of it is invariably reflected back through the medium in which it was traveling. Another part may pass into the second medium, the rays being bent or refracted at the surface. (This is the effect that accounts for the familiar illusion that a stick thrust into the water is bent.) The amount of the refraction depends on the difference between the speeds of light in the two media; its direction depends on whether the speed is greater in the first or the second medium. When a ray travels from the medium of lower velocity to that of higher, it bends away from the perpendicular to the surface [see top illustration at right].

If the angle between the incident ray and the perpendicular is great enough, the refracted ray bends 90 degrees from the perpendicular, or along the interface. The angle of incidence at which this happens is called the critical angle. It depends, obviously, on the ratio of the speeds, or to put it another way, on the ratio of the indexes of refraction of the two media. (A higher refractive index means a lower speed, and vice versa.)

At angles of incidence greater than the critical angle no light passes into the second medium; it is entirely reflected back through the first. If the interface is very smooth and is protected from contaminating influences, virtually no light is lost in this total internal reflection. The process is thus much more efficient than reflection from an ordinary opaque mirror, where considerable energy is absorbed at the surface.

Transparent rods operate as light conductors by means of total internal reflection. They can contain a ray, bouncing it from one side to the other, as long as it always strikes their surface at an angle greater than the critical one. In a straight rod the angle of incidence is the same from one reflection to the next.

This angle is determined by the angle at which the light enters the end of the rod. Hence the smaller the critical angle, the wider the external cone of rays that can be trapped and transported by the conductor. Furthermore, as the diagram on the next page shows, bending a rod decreases the angles of incidence of the shuttling ray. Hence the degree of curvature allowable also depends on the smallness of the critical angle.

The narrow conductors used in fiber optics are usually made in two parts: a cylindrical fiber of glass with a high index of refraction surrounded by a thin coating of glass with a low index. Total reflection takes place between the two. The coating serves to protect the fire-polished reflecting surface and also separates the conducting cylinders in the bundle from one another. With glasses now available we can make fibers with a critical angle as small as 50 degrees. Such a conductor can trap a cone of light 180 degrees wide.

In a properly made fiber almost all the light loss is due to absorption in the glass and very little to reflection. The high-refraction glass used in fiber cores absorbs less than a quarter of 1 per cent of light energy per inch. A bundle seven feet long delivers 50 per cent of the entering light at the far end, and 25-foot bundles transmit enough for certain applications. Tests on individual fibers have shown a measurable amount of transmission over 150 feet. Considering that a ray inclined at 30 degrees to the axis undergoes 692,880 reflections per 100 feet, even in a comparatively thick fiber, one can see that there must be almost no loss at each reflection.

Two examples of the image-conveying property of an aligned assembly of fibers are to be found in nature. The human retina consists of an assembly of rods and cones, and the image formed by the eye lens is focused upon them. It has been established that the rods and cones have a higher refractive index than the surrounding material, and that the light falling on them is transported down their length by total internal reflection and then converted into the visual stimulus. The eye of an insect has a somewhat similar, though simpler, construction. Another example of natural fiber optics is a borax deposit commonly known as ulexite, which sometimes occurs as a fibrous crystal. It can transmit a fairly good image, but it admits too small a cone of light to serve as a practical light conductor.

While a bundle of thin fibers has the

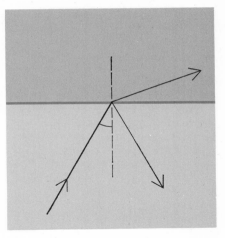

AT SHALLOW ANGLE to perpendicular most of light traveling through one transparent medium will cross interface (*heavy colored line*) into another such medium.

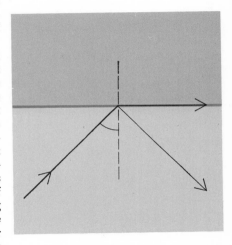

AT CRITICAL ANGLE most of the light will travel along the interface, and remainder is reflected within the first medium.

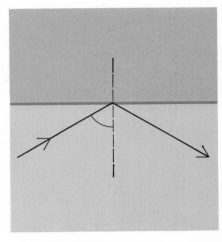

AT STEEP ANGLE all the light is reflected from the interface and continues its journey wholly within the original medium.

desired flexibility, it also necessarily dissects an image into separate spots of light. If the image is not to be distorted, the fiber ends must occupy the same position at both ends of the bundle. This is not in itself a disadvantage. It is not difficult to align the fibers. Moreover, as we shall see, we have the opportunity to change the positions, producing deliberate distortions that are advantageous in some cases. Another consequence is an inherent graininess in the image, which limits the resolution of fine detail. The finer the individual fibers, the greater the resolution that can be achieved.

Fibers are drawn from thick glass rods in a specially designed furnace. If they are to be coated, the inner rod of higher-refraction glass is inserted in a tubing of lower-refraction glass, and the two are drawn together. The emerging filament is wound in orderly layers on a revolving drum. When the successive layers are taken off the drum and stacked precisely one above the other, the fibers are properly aligned.

With this arrangement we can draw fibers down to about a thousandth of an inch in diameter, controlling their thickness within narrow limits. A bundle of such fibers can resolve lines a twentieth of a millimeter apart. To achieve still finer grain, a few hundred coated fibers

can be fused together and then drawn out a second time. Such a "multiple fiber," made up of units eight hundred-thousandths of an inch (two microns) in diameter, resolves 250 lines per millimeter. By means of a technique to be described later, the resolution can be increased to 500 lines per millimeter. It is possible to draw still thinner fibers, but they no longer act as simple light pipes. Their diameters are now comparable to the wavelength of the light, and they act as wave guides, transmitting energy in complex patterns that are no longer isolated from one another. A diameter of one micron, corresponding to about two wavelengths of visible light, is the approximate lower limit for simple image transmission.

By means of a flexible light pipe we can look around corners and see things that are hidden from direct view. Physicians may soon be examining interior parts of the body with "fiberscopes." The periscope type of instrument now used for stomach examination has several blind spots, and its rigidity causes the patient considerable discomfort. A fiber bundle will be able to reach every part of the stomach, and even the duodenum beyond it, and will be much easier on the patient. Illumination has always been a problem in this type of work. In

the fiberscope it is solved by enclosing the instrument proper in a sheath of unaligned fibers that conduct light from a bright lamp into the stomach. Other regions can also be reached. A thin fiberscope should even make it possible to scan the interior of the heart!

Bending is not the only advantage to be gained from transporting an image through fiber bundles. Because of their ability to accept a wide cone of entering light, they can increase the effective brightness of faint or fleeting objects. For example, the face of a cathode-ray or television tube gives off its light in all directions. If we place a camera in front of the tube to photograph it, the lens gathers only a small fraction of the total light emitted. By placing one end of a fused, air-tight fiber bundle against the tube face (or depositing a phosphorescent layer directly on the bundle, which then becomes the face of the tube), and putting a photographic plate at the other end of the bundle, much more light is delivered to the film.

For certain applications the effect can be further enhanced by drawing out a bundle so that it is narrower at one end than at the other. Now it serves as a funnel, gathering light over a large area and concentrating it on a small one.

Still another technique is available to make images sharper as well as brighter. Lens designers know that in certain optical systems resolution is improved by forming the image on a curved rather than a flat surface. In this form the image does not focus sharply on an ordinary photographic plate. But if one end of a fiber bundle is curved to fit the image surface, and the other is made flat, the image can be delivered undistorted to the focal plane of a camera or to the eyepiece of a high-powered microscope. The fibers can also be arranged to correct unwanted distortions introduced by the lens system. Both functions can be combined with the funneling effect of a conical bundle in a device called the "Focon."

As we have mentioned, the image emerging from a fiber bundle is inevitably grainy. However, a technique called dynamic scanning offers a means of eliminating the grain and improving resolution. The method involves moving both ends of the bundle in an identical random pattern, shifting the system a few fiber diameters at a time. In cases where this synchronous motion can be accomplished, the image is completely smoothed and the resolving power is increased by 100 per cent. For purposes of visual observation the bundle ends

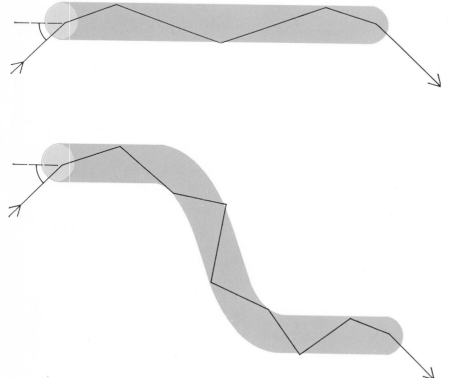

ANGLE OF EXIT of light emerging from a fiber (*top*) is same as angle of entry. Even if the fiber is bent many times (*bottom*) the light will travel all the way through it.

THREE GLASS FIBERS in this photomicrograph are of different diameters. Top fiber is uncoated and 37 microns wide. (A micron is a 10,000th of a centimeter.) Middle fiber is coated and 25 microns wide; bottom fiber is also coated and 62 microns wide.

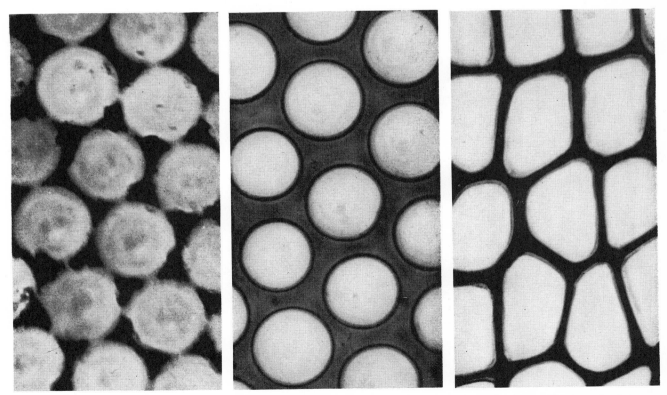

FIBERS ARE SEEN FROM THE END in these photomicrographs. Fibers at left are uncoated and are embedded in plastic. Coated fibers in middle are fused; coat has lower softening point than core. Fibers at right, with core of lower softening point, are distorted.

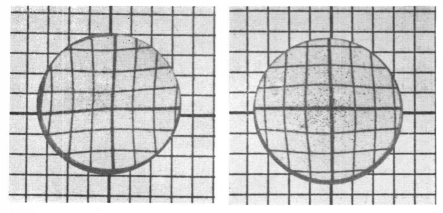

PLATES COMPOSED OF FIBERS, here lying on graph paper, can correct optical distortions. The plate at left can remove "barrel" distortion; that at right, "pincushion" distortion.

need only scan at a frequency considerably slower than the flicker frequency of the eye (about four to five times per second). On the other hand, in photography a minimum of about five oscillations are required during the period of exposure.

Of course not every application of fiber optics can accommodate dynamic scanning. Recently another way of improving image quality, known as "spatial filtering," has been developed. Passing the image through a pattern of thin films of varying thickness partially suppresses the graininess.

If the fibers in a bundle are not aligned, but rather are interwoven at random, the emerging image will be scrambled. Nevertheless the image will contain just as many units of information as the pattern at the other end. If it could be sent backward through the bundle, or transmitted through a second identical bundle, it would be reconverted to the original form. This suggests that fiber bundles would make convenient coder-decoder devices. With, say, a quarter of a million fibers whose positions can be manipulated, the scrambled image produced by a random fiber array would be virtually impossible to reconstitute without a decoder. The problem is finding a way to make several bundles incorporating the same complex pattern of interweaving. No satisfactory method is yet available, but one should not be too hard to find.

Other types of assembly take apart images and put them together in more convenient form. For example, in high-speed motion-picture photography, the film could be moved more slowly if the image were flattened to a horizontal line. This can be accomplished by a bundle that is square at one end but tapers and spreads to a line at the other. The camera lens forms its image on the square end, and the film, on a rotating drum, is placed opposite the slit end. To reconstitute the image, the finished print is projected backward through the bundle.

The tapered bundle may also act as a simple funnel, gathering light over a comparatively wide area and directing it into a narrow slit. It is a valuable tool in astronomical spectroscopy, where a substantial fraction of the light in the circular image formed by the telescope is lost at the slit of the spectroscope.

As a final example of the many and varied applications of these new devices, let us see how a single uncoated rod can serve as a refractometer, that is, an instrument for measuring the index of refraction of liquids. When a light-con-

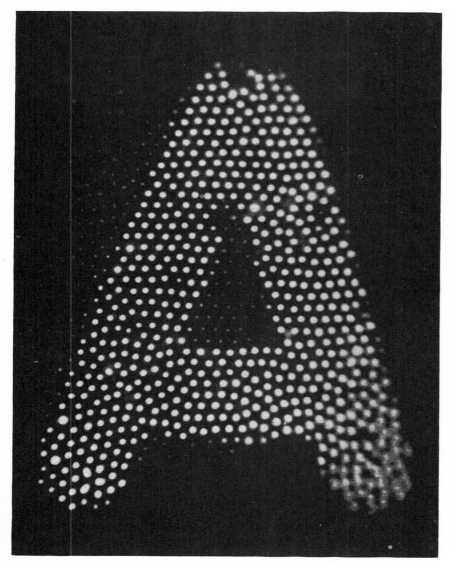

FIBERS ONE MICRON IN DIAMETER, the thinnest ever incorporated into a bundle, project letter "A" in photomicrograph of end of bundle. They are enlarged 3,500 times.

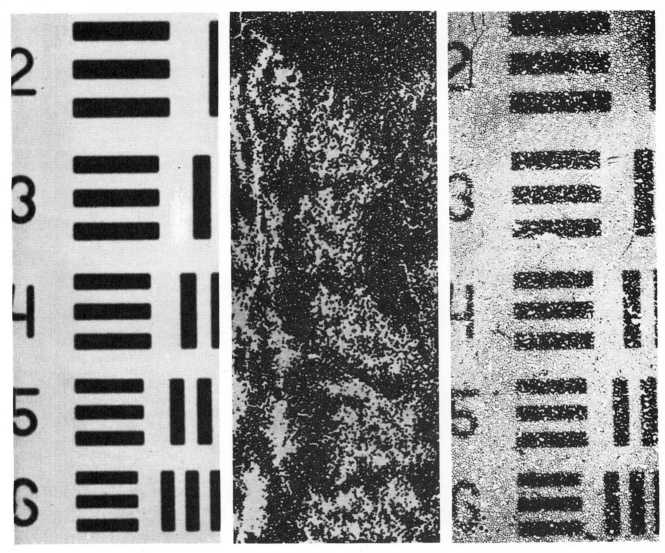

CODER-DECODER DEVICE employs scrambled fibers. Test pattern at left was placed at one end of bundle; photographic film at other end recorded pattern in center. Pattern at right was seen when center pattern was projected "backward" through the bundle.

OPERATION OF CODER-DECODER is depicted schematically. At left is the image of a cross projected on a rectangular array of fibers. Scrambled fibers in bundle produce image at right. Viewed through the same bundle, the latter image would be a cross.

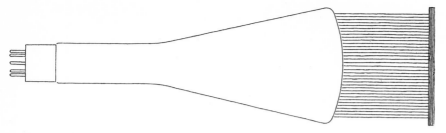

INTENSIFICATION OF IMAGE from cathode-ray tube is achieved when fibers gather light rays that would normally scatter, and channel them to surface of fiber "lens" (*right*).

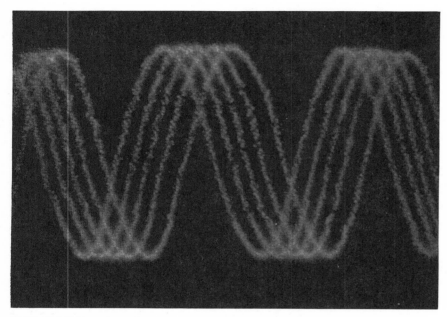

SINE CURVES on face of cathode-ray tube have been transmitted here through a fiber bundle, as diagrammed at top of page. Each dot represents end of one fiber in the bundle.

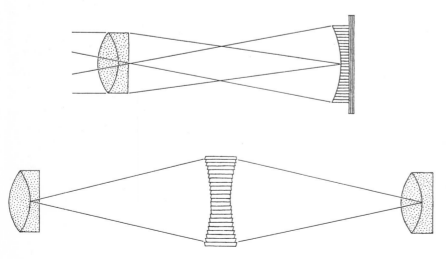

CURVED IMAGES from lenses are flattened by bundles of fibers. At top fibers (*right*) project image onto photographic plate. At bottom fibers (*center*) flatten image between lenses.

ducting rod is immersed in a liquid, the critical angle depends on the difference between the indexes of refraction of the two materials. The closer the refractive index of the liquid approaches that of the rod, the greater the critical angle. And the greater the critical angle, the more nearly a light ray must graze the surface of the rod to be totally reflected. Thus, if a constant wide cone of light is directed at one end of the rod, the amount that reaches the other end will vary as the index of refraction of the liquid changes.

Light emerging from the rod falls on a photocell whose output indicates the index of refraction of the liquid. This simple instrument detects a change in refractive index with an accuracy of one part in 100,000 to a million over a limited range. To extend this range it is necessary to use several rods of different refractive indexes, mounted on a turret. By feeding the photocell output to an appropriate servo system, the instrument can be adapted for automatic chemical-process control. The instrument has the unique advantage of working on opaque liquids as well as on transparent ones.

At the Armour Research Foundation of the Illinois Institute of Technology we are working on extending fiber optics techniques in several directions. We are experimenting with fibers of scintillating materials for use in tracking nuclear particles. Transparent materials that also conduct electricity should make possible a number of interesting devices. Perhaps the most immediately promising area is the infrared region of the spectrum. We have found materials that make satisfactory fibers to handle wavelengths up to about six microns. We are now trying to extend the range to 25 microns. With further technological advance, fiber optics will become an important adjunct in infrared scanning and guidance systems and in infrared spectroscopy.

In almost all of the discussion thus far, the wave properties of light have been ignored. Actually, of course, there is no such thing as a "ray" of light, if we are not talking about quantum effects. A ray simply represents the direction along which part of a wave front is advancing. An analysis of the behavior of light as an electromagnetic wave shows that the fundamental process of fiber optics—total internal reflection—is not so simple as was indicated earlier. Instead of bouncing off the interface between two media, a wave train actually penetrates the second medium for a short distance before turning back into the original material. The strength of the electromagnetic field carried by the wave decreases rapidly in the second medium, dying away to a negligible amount at little more than a wavelength from the interface.

Suppose that two pieces of material of high refractive index are placed very close together—say within a quarter of a wavelength—and that they are separated by a layer with low refractive index. In this arrangement light will not be totally reflected in either piece of material, even if it strikes the low-refraction layer at an angle greater than critical. The neighboring high-refraction material picks up the energy that has penetrated the separating layer, frustrating its attempt to reflect back into the original medium.

Because of frustrated total reflection, as the phenomenon is called, the coating on the fibers in a bundle must be thick enough to keep them adequately separated. The required separation depends on the diameter of the core, the refractive index of core and coating, and on the angular spread of the incoming light. For fibers down to a few wavelengths in diameter a separation of one wavelength

CONICAL FIBER-BUNDLES can enlarge or diminish optical images. At bottom is a plate of glass with illuminated sample words (including the names of three pioneers in optics). The non-conical fiber bundle at lower left picks up but does not change size of letters in the word "Fabry." Above it the tall conical bundle over the letter "R" produces a tiny "R," visible upside down in mirror at top. The conical bundle at right has a similar but less pronounced effect upon the letter "S" in the word "optics."

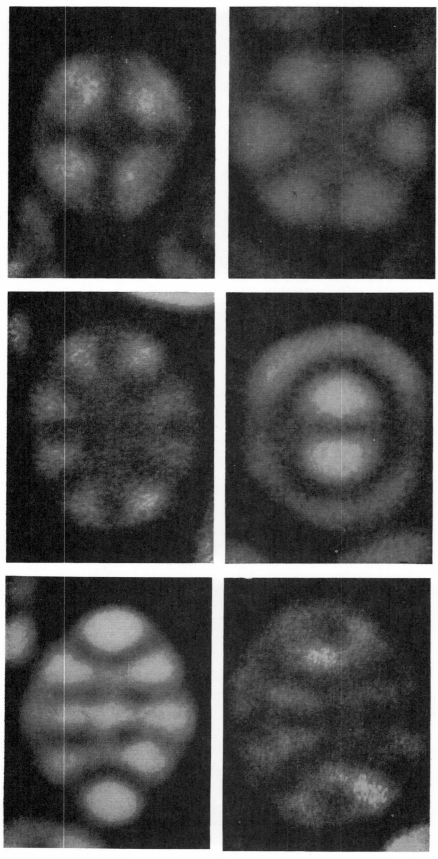

(about .5 micron for visible light) is sufficient under most conditions.

As we have already mentioned, when the fiber diameter becomes less than about two wavelengths, light conduction comes to resemble the transmission of microwaves by wave guides. My colleagues and I have extended conventional wave-guide theory to optical wavelengths. The calculations indicate that to be carried down a fiber, light waves must strike the sides not at any angle greater than critical, but only at certain "characteristic" angles. Each such angle corresponds to one mode of transmission in which the light energy is delivered in a distinctive pattern [see illustration at left]. In a fiber many wavelengths wide there is a great number of characteristic angles, and the various modes blur together. As the diameter decreases, however, the possible angles also decrease, until finally, when the conductor measures less than one wavelength across, only one angle and one mode are possible.

A second consequence of reducing fiber diameter is that more and more energy travels down the outside of the conductor rather than inside it. (A similar effect occurs in guides for microwaves.) This means that transmission through one fiber can excite reactions in neighboring ones.

As the technology advances, fiber optics will no doubt find wider applications in various areas of research and engineering. The field still offers a number of interesting and challenging problems to the investigator. The theoretical treatment of dielectric wave guides must be extended to explain fully how light behaves in transparent fibers with diameters comparable to the wavelength. A more detailed analysis is needed of the radiation patterns, with particular emphasis on the coupling of energy between one fiber and another. It has already been mentioned that, as fiber diameter decreases, more energy is transmitted outside the fiber than inside. Therefore absorption by the glass becomes less important. Eventually it should be possible to apply this effect to the conduction of light by fibers much finer than those discussed previously. This technique would be particularly valuable at infrared frequencies, where longer wavelengths place a higher limit on the diameter of fibers that can be used at present.

WAVE-GUIDE PATTERNS appear when diameter of fibers approaches wavelength of light. Then light that can travel in the fibers is limited to certain "characteristic angles" which produce interference and reinforcement patterns such as those seen in these six photomicrographs of ends of fibers. Wave guides for microwaves also behave in this way.

8

How Images are Detected

R. Clark Jones   *September 1968*

Today images are widely detected by such means as photographic emulsions and specialized electron tubes, but the most versatile detector of images remains the visual system of vertebrates. Even so, artificial image detectors can now outperform biological systems in certain highly important ways. In this regard it is instructive to compare the performance of the human visual system with artificial image detectors. The comparison can be made quantitatively by means of a measure called the detective quantum efficiency, or DQE. The DQE indicates the degree to which the signal-to-noise ratio in the output of the detector approaches the signal-to-noise ratio in the light image. In less exact language, the DQE is the ratio of the information in the detector's output to the information in the light image.

The train of thought that gave rise to the DQE, and the means of computing the DQE, are best dealt with later. The results of several computations, however, are shown in the illustration on page 86. It is evident from the illustration that over certain limited ranges of light intensity such electronic devices as the image orthicon tube (used in television) and the Carnegie image tube (used in astronomy) have a higher DQE than the eye does. Many photographic emulsions have a DQE nearly equal to the DQE of human vision but only over a very narrow range of light intensity.

The remarkable fact about the human visual system is that its DQE is substantially constant over an enormous range of light intensity. If the luminance of the scene is expressed in millilamberts, the visual system has a nearly constant DQE from 10^{-5} millilambert to 1,000 millilamberts—a range of 100 million to one. Considered on the same scale the typical image orthicon tube has a range of about 500 to one, and the range of the photo-graphic emulsions listed in the illustration is about 50 to one.

The vast working range of the human visual system is the despair of the designers of image detectors but it is also their goal. How does this system achieve its remarkable performance? Let us briefly consider the structure and function of the eye.

The retina consists of millions of individual detectors: the rod cells and cone cells. There are about 100 million rods and five million cones, each of which has a firing rate proportional to the amount of light it receives at low firing rates and roughly proportional to the logarithm of the light intensity at higher firing rates. The rods and cones of course function as an assemblage, and their output is correlated in various ways along the visual pathway from the retina to the cortex of the brain.

The rods are involved in the detection of light at low levels of intensity. The cones function at higher levels. At very low levels, close to the threshold at which the dark-adapted eye can detect light, many of the rods—those in a region about one degree in diameter on the spherical surface of the retina—are connected so that they all feed one giant ganglion cell. If just a few rods in this region are triggered by absorbing as small a number of photons as one per rod, a flash of light is perceived. Indeed, a group of investigators in the Netherlands (led by Maarten A. Bouman of the State University of Utrecht) believes that only two rods need to be fired by one photon each to yield the perception of a flash. It is important that at least two rods be fired; otherwise the inevitable random thermal firing of the rods would give rise to constant spurious sensations of light.

As the luminance increases, the inter-connection of the receptors is changed. When the luminance has reached the normal reading level of between 10 and 100 millilamberts, the best DQE is obtained for objects only a tenth of a degree in diameter. (The full moon is half a degree in diameter.) A comparison of the eye's DQE at various levels of illumination is shown in the illustration on page 87.

Over the eye's working range of 100 million to one in light intensity the speed of response changes by a factor of five. The area of best DQE changes by a factor of 100. The contrast that can be perceived runs from 100 percent to 2 percent. The area of the pupil changes by a factor of 10.

Not the least of the eye's remarkable capacities is that its gain control, which is roughly analogous to the automatic volume-control circuit of a radio receiver, is kept adjusted over the entire range so that the noise in the perceived image is held at just about the threshold of perception. The gain adjustment takes time, particularly when one is moving into a dark environment from a light one. Complete adaptation to darkness from sunlit conditions takes about 30 minutes. That period of time is entirely appropriate for the gradual darkening of the evening, but it can put serious limits on vision in other circumstances. An example is the demand placed on the vision of an airplane pilot facing the setting sun just before he descends through a heavy overcast for a landing.

The capability of the human visual system can be described in various other ways. Let us consider the system's ability to perceive stars. In a completely dark room an observer adapted to the darkness could detect with the unaided eye a star with a magnitude of +7. (The higher the positive magnitude number, the fainter the star. The brightest

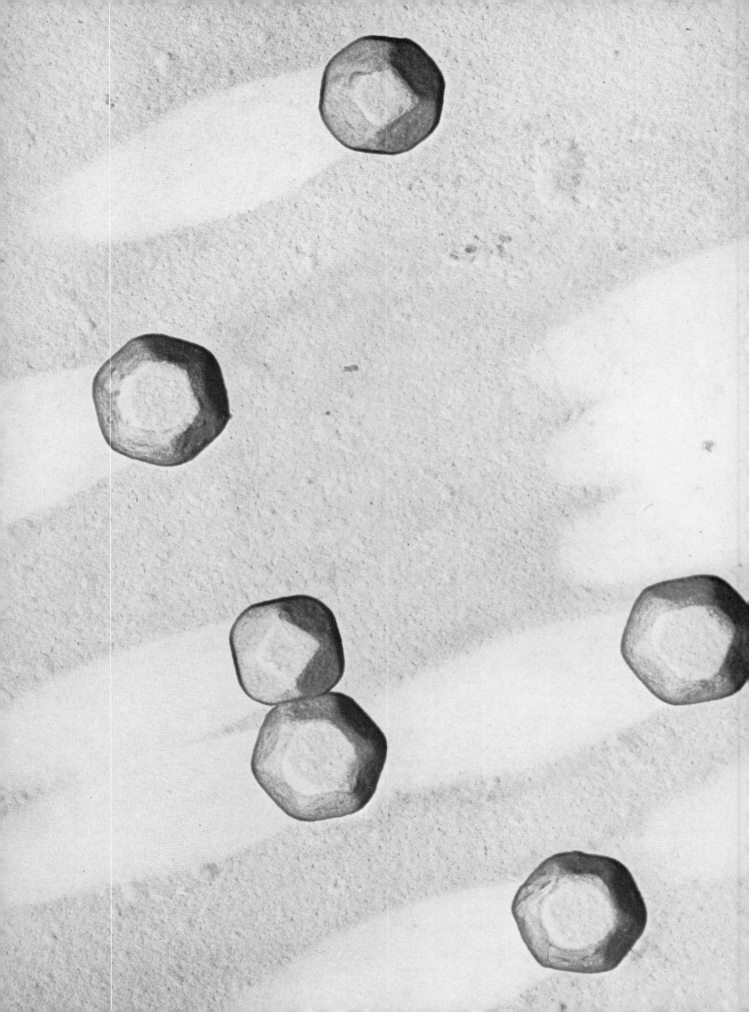

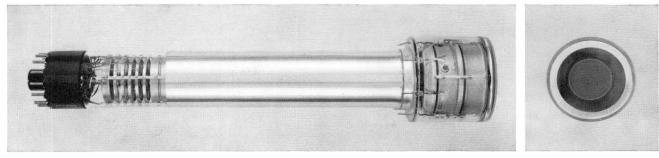

IMAGE ORTHICON TUBE used in television cameras is 15 inches long. Its three-inch light-detecting surface, which is at right in the side view, is shown end on in the adjacent view. Operating principle of an image orthicon tube is shown in the illustration below.

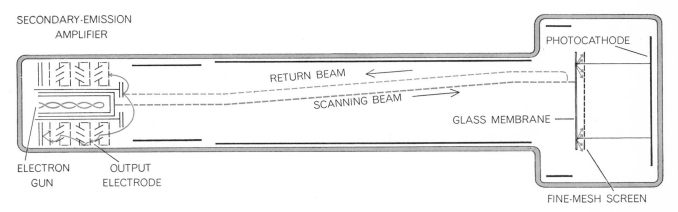

SECONDARY-EMISSION AMPLIFIER

PHOTOCATHODE

RETURN BEAM

SCANNING BEAM

GLASS MEMBRANE

ELECTRON GUN

OUTPUT ELECTRODE

FINE-MESH SCREEN

FUNCTIONING of an image orthicon tube is based on a photocathode on which light is focused by the lens of the television camera. The lens is not shown but in this instance would be to the right of the photocathode. The light causes the emission of electrons from the left side of the photocathode. They are accelerated by an electric charge and strike the glass membrane, where they are held briefly by a positive charge augmented by the fine-mesh screen that is 50 microns from the membrane. A beam of electrons from the gun at left scans the membrane and carries off the image. The return beam is amplified at left to yield output of tube.

star in the Little Dipper, the star at the end of the handle, has a magnitude of +2.) The background light of the night sky limits this performance; outdoors on a dark night the best an observer can do is to perceive a star of about magnitude +5 at sea level and about +6 at mountain altitudes, where the background light of the sky is fainter.

The assistance provided by a telescope is in magnification rather than brightness. The largest telescope that could usefully be employed for direct viewing of stars should magnify the faintest visible star so that the image on the retina is about one degree in diameter. When stars are viewed through large telescopes at mountain observatories, the images under the best conditions are about one second in diameter; if conditions are poorer, the images are larger. To increase the size of the image from one second to one degree requires a magnification of 3,600 diameters. The magnification will be excessive and pointless, however, unless the light falls on the eye across the entire pupil. Since the pupil is about .8 centimeter in diameter under starlit conditions, the collecting lens must be 3,600 × .8, or nearly 30 meters in diameter. Inasmuch as the largest telescope—the one on Palomar Mountain—has a collecting mirror only five meters (200 inches) in diameter, it follows that no telescope in existence can do an optimal job of enabling the human eye to detect stars. On this basis the maximum useful magnification of a five-meter telescope for single stars is about 600. For larger and much brighter objects or systems such as the moon and close double stars, however, higher magnifications are useful.

Quite another kind of instrument used to aid vision is the image-intensifier tube, which has evolved in several forms. The key feature in each case is that the instrument has a collecting lens or mirror that, like the lens or mirror of a telescope, is much larger in diameter than the pupil of the eye. Within its range of light intensity the tube also has a better DQE than human vision does. For these reasons the tube greatly increases the signal-to-noise ratio in the output image that is viewed by a human observer. He is thus able to see things he could not see with unaided vision.

An intensifier tube, unlike a telescope, increases the luminance of the image. Moreover, there is no optical limit to the size of the collecting lens that can be used. Suppose one is looking at a starlit landscape or a very dim fluorescent X-ray screen at a luminance of 10⁻⁵ millilambert. The unaided visual system can perceive the scene, but the perception is slow. One reason is that the visual system is intrinsically slower at low levels of light. Moreover, one must slightly avert one's eyes, because the fovea—the small rodless area of the retina that provides the most acute vision—does not function at low levels of light, and one's perception of relations in the field of vision is slow with averted vision.

Suppose the luminance of the scene is

SILVER HALIDE GRAINS that are the light detectors in photographic emulsions appear greatly enlarged in the electron micrograph on the opposite page. The actual size of the grains is between 600 and 800 nanometers. Detection of an image begins when a photon of light from the image strikes a grain and changes the arrangement of electrons in the grain.

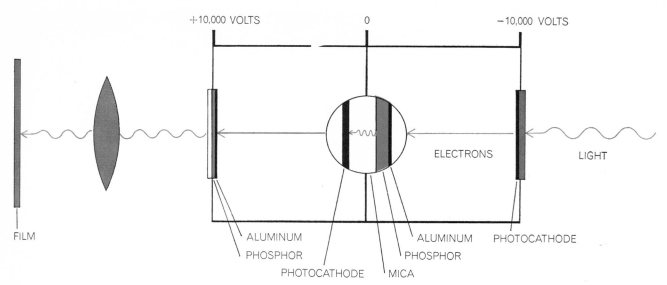

+10,000 VOLTS 0 −10,000 VOLTS

ELECTRONS LIGHT

FILM

ALUMINUM

PHOSPHOR

PHOTOCATHODE

MICA

ALUMINUM

PHOSPHOR

PHOTOCATHODE

CARNEGIE IMAGE TUBE was devised as an image intensifier for use with astronomical telescopes. Light from the telescope enters the glass window at right and strikes the photocathode, causing the emission of electrons. They are accelerated to a mica sandwich in the middle of the tube. There, with an aluminum film preventing feedback, they are absorbed by a phosphor. Resulting light strikes the second photocathode, producing an increased number of electrons that strike phosphor at left. Its light is recorded on film.

ELECTRODE ARRANGEMENT of a Carnegie image tube is evident when the tube (center) is separated from the telescope with which it is usually associated. The electrodes carry the charges that accelerate the electrons in the tube. Cylindrical objects to the left and right of the tube are plastic insulators that hold it in its operating position and prevent the 20,000-volt tube from sparking.

increased to 10 millilamberts—that is, by a factor of a million—by an image tube. If one has been using magnification to bring the diameter of the object of interest to one degree, the magnification can be reduced by a factor of 10, since at 10 millilamberts the critical object can be best perceived at a diameter of .1 degree. In addition the increase in luminance means that the visual system can use foveal vision, can scan the scene quickly and can use its normal ability to rapidly perceive the relations between the parts of the scene.

The principal use for image tubes to assist vision has so far been military. A recently developed device used by the U.S. Army employs six fiber-optic faceplates, together with electrostatic focusing to avoid the weight of the magnets used in the astronomical image tubes. It amplifies by a factor of 40,000 the light the unaided eye could receive from a scene. The tube has three stages of amplification, each consisting of a photocathode at the forward end and a phosphor at the rear. When light strikes the photocathode, electrons are ejected toward the phosphor. The beam of electrons is accelerated by an electrostatic field and focused on the phosphor, which converts the energy of the beam into visible light. The third stage of the device is coupled to a magnifying eyepiece. Power is supplied by a battery.

An important class of image detectors is made up of instruments that involve scanning with an electron beam, so that the light image is converted into a video signal. A convenient but not too specific term for the class is electronic image detectors. Their major role is in technology: they are the image detectors in television cameras. Such detectors are also becoming increasingly useful in astronomy.

Most of the electronic image detectors are photoemissive. When a photoemissive surface absorbs light, it emits electrons. One kind of device, the modern vidicon used in television cameras, is photoconductive: when the light-sensitive surface absorbs light, its electrical conductivity changes.

All the photoemissive devices receive the light image on a semitransparent photocathode that is on the inside of an evacuated chamber. Light striking one side of the photocathode causes photoelectrons to be ejected from the other side into the vacuum. The spatial distribution of the electrons as they leave the photocathode is an excellent replica of the light that falls on the photocathode.

The emissive devices differ only in the

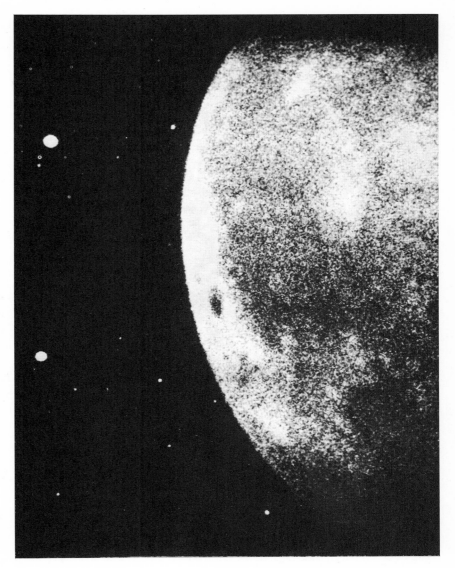

MOON IN ECLIPSE by the earth was photographed during totality through a telescope equipped with an image orthicon. Because the image orthicon has a higher level of efficiency in detecting light than photographic emulsion does, the half-second exposure was only about a fiftieth as long as would have been needed otherwise. The photograph was made by J. R. Dunlap of Northwestern University's Corralitos Observatory in New Mexico.

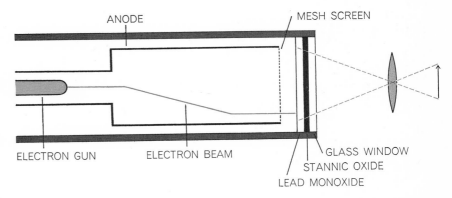

VIDICON TYPE of image detector for television cameras operates by photoconductivity. In the Philips Plumbicon, for example, a glass window (right) has on its inside a transparent layer of stannic oxide and a photoconducting layer of lead monoxide. Light striking the stannic oxide is conducted as a current by the lead monoxide. The photoconducting layer is scanned by an electron beam that is accelerated by the anode. The fine-mesh screen makes the electric field between the anode and the photoconducting layer more uniform.

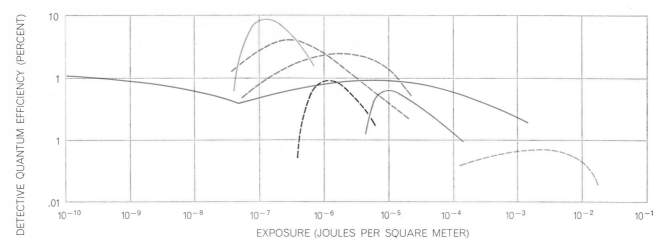

CAPABILITY OF DETECTORS over a range of light intensity is compared by means of the detective quantum efficiency, a measure of performance. The three top curves represent respectively the Carnegie image tube used in astronomy and two of the orthicons used in television cameras. The long colored curve represents human vision; the notch in the curve indicates where the system switches from rod to cone vision. Black curves represent two kinds of photographic film. Colored curve at right reflects the performance of an early-model vidicon used in television cameras; vidicons have been considerably improved since evaluation was made.

way they convert the image formed by the photoelectrons into an image that is visible to a human observer. One such device, the image orthicon, is used both in television cameras and in astronomy. Two others, the Lallemand electronic camera and the Carnegie image intensifier, are used only in astronomy.

The development of the image orthicon tube by the Radio Corporation of America in the late 1930's made commercial television practical. In an image orthicon tube the photoelectrons from the photocathode are accelerated by a charge of about 300 volts and are magnetically focused on a glass membrane that is only two microns thick [see lower illustration on page 83]. Each electron that hits the glass membrane ejects several secondary electrons. Since the electrons have a negative charge, the result is that the membrane acquires a positive charge whose magnitude is several times the charge of an electron. A metal screen with a very fine mesh is located about 50 microns from the membrane and held at a potential one or two volts positive with respect to the resting potential of the membrane. The effect of the screen is to increase the length of time the glass membrane can hold its charge and to make the potential of the membrane more nearly proportional to the charge; the result is that the membrane holds a replica of the original image.

Each point on the membrane is scanned every thirtieth of a second by a beam of electrons from an electron gun; the beam is focused and deflected by magnetic fields. The negative electrons discharge the positive membrane and carry away its image. The beam is carefully adjusted in two ways. First, its electrons are given just enough energy to return the glass membrane to zero potential. Second, the current of the beam—the number of electrons per second—is adjusted so that the beam can supply just enough charge to return the membrane to zero potential at the places where the membrane charge is greatest. At other places, where the membrane has less charge, some of the electrons will be reflected. They return toward the electron gun and there are deflected into a secondary-emission amplifier. The output of the amplifier is the television signal, which can be used to produce a visible image on the cathode ray tube of a television set.

When the image orthicon is used in astronomy, the glass membrane is usually replaced by a thin sheet of magnesium oxide. The magnesium oxide has a higher secondary-emission gain than the glass membrane and allows the charge to be stored for a much longer time. A telescope equipped with an image orthicon is particularly useful for astronomical problems where short exposures are essential. It is conceivable that a telescope thus equipped could be programmed to survey galaxies automatically so that they could be checked for supernovas by the comparison of two photographs made at different times.

In the Lallemand electronic camera, invented by André Lallemand of the Paris Observatory, the electrons from the photocathode are accelerated by a potential of between 20 and 40 kilovolts. They fall directly on an electron-sensitive photographic plate [see illustration on page 88]. This camera has been used successfully in France at a number of observatories and in the U.S. at the Lick Observatory and the Flagstaff Branch of the U.S. Naval Observatory. It is not likely to come into wide use, however, because great skill and application are required to operate it.

The basic difficulty is that the photocathode requires a very high vacuum for good performance. In such a vacuum it is extraordinarily difficult to handle the gases that leave the photographic plate. They can easily contaminate the photocathode, which is specially designed to release electrons easily but for that reason is highly reactive and readily oxidized. As a result the apparatus requires rigorous cleaning of internal parts, refrigeration of the photographic plate to hold down the escape of gas and various other steps to protect the cathode. For these reasons it requires about eight hours of painstaking work to prepare the Lallemand camera for a night's use.

A variant of the Lallemand tube has been developed by J. D. McGee of the Imperial College of Science and Technology. In it the electrons go through a mica window about 4.5 microns thick. The mica protects the cathode because it is impermeable to oxygen, but with 40-kilovolt acceleration most of the electrons go through. When the window is made in the form of a long, narrow strip (seven by 30 millimeters), it will withstand atmospheric pressure, but it requires very careful handling.

Under the best conditions the Lallemand camera has a DQE of 10 percent. This enables it to reduce exposure times by a factor of 10. These cameras also yield an image density that is directly proportional to the light exposure, which is not the case with photographic emulsions exposed to light. This feature simplifies the photometric analysis of spectrograms.

The Carnegie image tube arose from the desire of a number of astronomers for an image detector that would provide the gain of 10 to 20 in DQE that photocathodes have over photographic film. The Carnegie Institution of Washington initiated a project to develop such a detector. Under the leadership of Merle A. Tuve the group considered a wide variety of approaches and finally settled on a type of image intensifier.

In the Carnegie image intensifier, which is manufactured by RCA, the electrons from the photocathode are accelerated by about 10 kilovolts and are magnetically focused on a membrane formed like a sandwich [*see top illustration on page 84*]. The sandwich is a sheet of mica four microns thick with a phosphor on one side and a photocathode on the other. As the electrons from the first photocathode reach the sandwich they pass through an opaque film of aluminum, which prevents the feedback of light to the first photocathode, and then are absorbed by the phosphor. The light produced by the phosphor goes through the sheet of mica and produces photoelectrons at the second photocathode. The electrons from this photocathode are accelerated by 10 kilovolts and focused on a second phosphor screen, the image on which is focused on a photographic film by a lens system.

The sandwich has a gain of about 50, that is, about 50 electrons leave the second photocathode for every electron that strikes the adjacent phosphor. The total light gain of the tube is about 3,000. The lens system, however, can deliver only a small fraction of the phosphor's light output to the photographic film, so that the overall gain is only about 15. Some 35 of these tubes have been delivered to observatories, mostly in the U.S. They are used chiefly for spectroscopy of dim objects.

The vidicons, which operate on the principle of photoconductivity, surpass orthicons in simplicity and ease of operation. The early vidicons, however, were of limited usefulness because the picture they supplied was uneven at low levels of light and also because the vidicons had too slow a response at low levels. The vidicons were therefore restricted to applications where very high illumination could be provided; a typical

use was in scanning motion-picture film for television broadcasting.

Vidicons have been considerably improved in recent years. As a result they have partly supplanted orthicons as the image detectors in television cameras. They are particularly valuable in the cameras used for color television.

A widely used modern device of the vidicon type is the Plumbicon, which was developed at the Philips Research Laboratories in the Netherlands. The heart of the device is a glass plate coated with a thin, transparent conducting layer of stannic (tin) oxide. A thin layer of lead monoxide, which is a photoconducting material, is deposited on the stannic oxide.

The scene to be transmitted is projected through the glass plate and the layer of stannic oxide onto the lead monoxide. A beam of slow electrons scans the other side of the lead monoxide layer; the current that flows to the stannic oxide varies with the conductivity of the lead monoxide and hence with the light level at different points in the scene. Thereafter the image is amplified by conventional means and delivered to the transmitter.

The Philips Plumbicon differs from earlier arsenic trisulfide vidicons in that the photoconductive layer is a sandwich of three layers. The vacuum side of the lead monoxide layer is made positive (*p*-type) by chemical processing. The side of the lead monoxide layer adjacent to the stannic oxide is strongly negative (*n*-type). The major part of the layer is "intrinsic," or not active, so that the layer is a *p-i-n* junction. This structure is responsible for the low dark current of the vidicon—the fact that it conducts only a small amount of current in darkness—and for several other advantages.

Photographic emulsions clearly con-

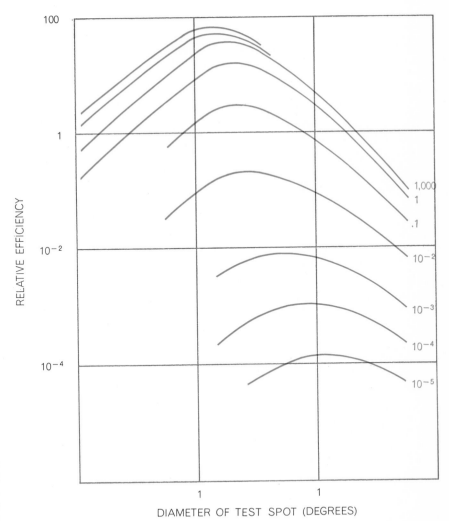

HUMAN VISION'S capabilities are indicated in curves that show by their height on the vertical scale how the detective quantum efficiency of the visual system varies with changing diameter of test spot. Colored numbers give background luminance in foot-lamberts. The curves cannot be compared with one another. The vertical scale is actually the reciprocal of the square of the product of the test-spot diameter and the threshold contrast.

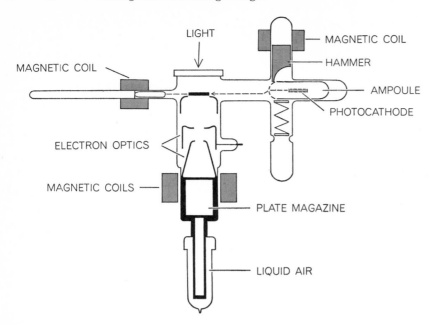

LALLEMAND ELECTRONIC CAMERA employs a photocathode that is stored in an ampoule to prevent its contamination by gases. After the camera has been prepared and a high vacuum has been established the ampoule is broken by the hammer, and the photocathode is magnetically pulled into position over the photographic plate. Light striking the photocathode causes the emission of electrons that strike the electron-sensitive photographic plate.

stitute another major class of image detectors. Every photographic film or plate has a layer about 100 microns thick that is a suspension in solidified gelatin of a myriad of grains of silver halide. Each grain is about one micron in size.

The grains are laid down rather rapidly so that they will be irregular, with numerous points of imperfection on the surface. After deposition the grains are subjected to processing designed to increase their sensitivity to photons. Finally the surface is partly covered with a single layer of dye molecules.

When light strikes one of the grains, the blue part of the light is absorbed by the grain; the green and red parts are absorbed by the molecules of dye. In either case what happens is that an electron is put into the conduction band of the silver halide crystal. As a result the electron is free to move around. Many things can happen to the electron, but the important thing for photography is that the electron may be trapped at an imperfection. If it is, it may convert a silver ion into a silver atom.

This atom cannot exist long by itself, but if a second photoelectron neutralizes a second silver ion at the same imperfection within about a second, the two-atom combination is more stable and will last for several weeks. If two more silver atoms are produced by two photoelectrons at the same site, the four-atom combination is quite stable and is large

enough to catalyze the development of the grain. (For astronomical purposes the single-atom decay time of roughly a second can be increased to as much as an hour by making the environment of the grains more reducing. This increase in decay time is achieved at the cost of rapid fogging at room temperature, so that the plates must be shipped and stored under refrigeration.)

After the film has been exposed to light, it must of course be developed to make the image visible. Developing involves immersing the film in a water solution that contains a reducing agent. The agent is carefully chosen so that it does not have the ability to develop an unexposed grain during the normal duration of developing, but when the agent is aided by the group of silver atoms at the imperfection, it is able to start the reduction. Once the reduction begins, more silver is formed and the entire grain is converted to silver.

The amplification involved in the developing process is enormous. As few as four photons effectively absorbed in a grain of silver halide with a volume of one cubic micron will produce more than 10^{10} silver atoms. This is an amplification of more than a billion.

It is important for the success of the photographic emulsion that more than one photon must be received within a short time. If only one photon were needed, thermal excitation would soon

make all the grains developable. As we have noted, the human visual system uses a similar method of avoiding thermal excitation. Both systems employ what electrical engineers call a coincidence gate.

Judging the efficiency of an image detector is more difficult than one might expect. The judgment is straightforward enough if one merely wants to establish the ratio of photoelectrons to incident photons—the output to the input—in the operation of a photocathode. That is a ratio of countable events. The ratio establishes what can be called the responsive quantum efficiency of the photocathode.

The trouble with the concept is that one cannot extend it to other detectors without ambiguity. In a photoconductor, for example, is the output event an electron in the conduction band, or is it the flow of an electron in the external circuit? These two phenomena can have greatly different counts, so that the distinction is an important one.

What is the output event in photographic film? Is it an electron in the conduction band of the silver halide grain, a silver atom added to the latent image or a grain made developable? Again, the different events have greatly different counts.

What is the output event in human vision? Is it the firing of the nerve cell connected to a rod? Or is it the perception of a flash or the perception of the color of a flash?

Uncertainties of this nature led Albert Rose of RCA to develop an important new concept that he called performance. This is the concept I have termed detective quantum efficiency. The DQE is defined not by comparing input and output counts but by comparing input and output signal-to-noise ratios. The formula for calculating a DQE is to divide the output signal-to-noise ratio by the input signal-to-noise ratio and then to square the result.

With human vision the output noise cannot be measured directly. Instead one tests the performance of the visual system on certain well-defined tasks and compares the result with the performance of an ideal device that uses all the incident photons. The task is then varied until the level at which the eye performs best is found. The result is the DQE of vision.

The significant point about the DQE of any detector is that it allows unambiguous evaluation of the detector's efficiency. The DQE is thus a key to the understanding of all detectors.

III

Chemical and Biological Effects of Light

Light, upon being absorbed by a substance, can sometimes change the substance. Common examples of such photochemical changes are sunburn and the bleaching of dyed materials, both of which can be produced by ultraviolet light. The radiation excites the atoms or molecules of the material, and for that instant they are capable of reacting more readily and so can combine chemically with their neighbors. Gerald Oster, in his article, reviews some of the processes of photochemistry and the methods for investigating them. These include the techniques of flash photolysis, in which an intense flash of light excites the materials that have been mixed together. The progress of the subsequent reaction is followed by photographing the absorption spectrum. Photochemical processes occur in simple compounds, in large organic molecules, and in the very large, complex molecules of biological materials. Indeed, photosynthesis is indispensable for life as we know it. George Wald explains why the particular wavelengths in and near the visible region, which are so strongly produced by the sun, are those most suitable for life processes: Wavelengths that are longer are not suitable because they have smaller quanta which are not photochemically potent; the more energetic quanta of shorter wavelengths are too disruptive.

The eye is our ultimate receptor for light images, no matter how much the light has been processed by lenses, cameras, image intensifiers, or other devices. We know that its structure is like a camera's in that the lens forms an image on the retina, as the camera lens does on a film, but have yet much to learn about the complex optical, photochemical and electrical processes that occur in the rods and cones. Sterling B. Hendricks describes the structure of the eye and the way in which it converts light patterns to nerve impulses.

More specifically, he discusses some of the particular biological pigments and the way in which they are activated by light. The activation of these pigments, which are sensitive to particular wavelengths or colors, is responsible for three important processes of life: photosynthesis, vision, and the periodic response of plants and animals to the light and dark cycles of the day. Some photobiological processes can be reversed by a change in the color of the light; others are altered by a relative duration of light and darkness. These features can be related to the several stages of chemical activation by light and to the transfer and storage of the excitation energy within and between molecules.

Chemical and Biological Effects of Light

91

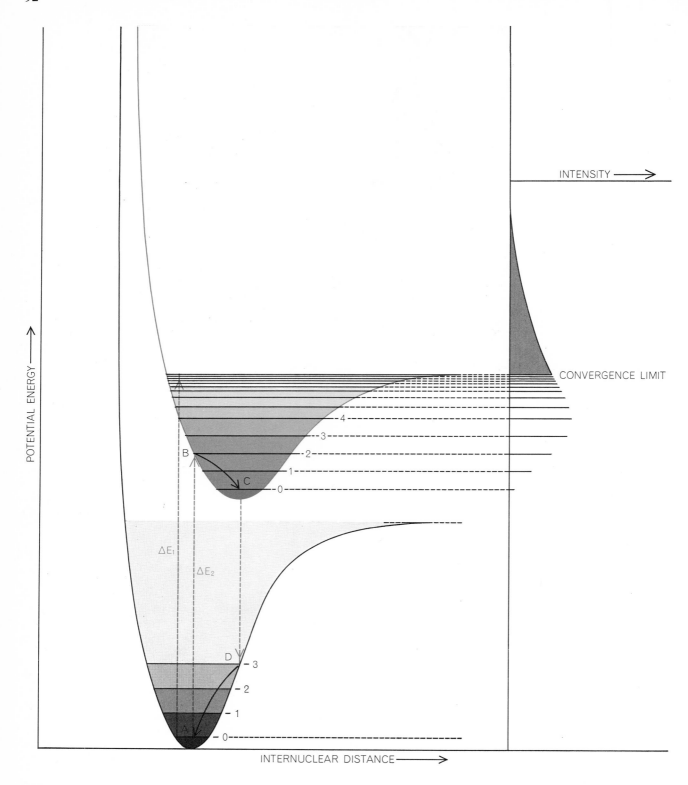

INTENSITY ⟶

POTENTIAL ENERGY ⟶

CONVERGENCE LIMIT

4
3
2
1
0

ΔE₁

ΔE₂

B

C

A

D
3
2
1
0

INTERNUCLEAR DISTANCE ⟶

RESPONSE OF SIMPLE MOLECULES TO PHOTONS can be followed with the help of potential-energy curves. The lower curve represents the potential energy of a typical diatomic molecule in the ground state; the upper curve represents its potential energy in the first excited electronic state. Because the two atoms of the molecule are constantly vibrating, thus changing the distance between atomic nuclei, the molecule can occupy different but discrete energy levels (*horizontal lines*) within each electronic state. The molecule in the lowest ground state can be dissociated, or photolysed, if it absorbs a photon with an energy equal to or great-

er than ΔE_1. This is the energy required to carry the molecule to or beyond the "convergence limit." The length of the horizontal lines at the right below that limit represents the probability of transition from the ground electronic state to a particular vibrational level in the excited electronic state. Thus a photon with an energy of ΔE_2 will raise the molecule to the second level (*B*) of that state. There it will vibrate, ultimately lose energy to surrounding molecules and fall to *C*. It can now emit a photon with somewhat less energy than ΔE_2 and fall to *D*. This is called fluorescence. After losing vibrational energy molecule will return to *A*.

9

The Chemical Effects of Light

Gerald Oster   September 1968

Our everyday world endures because most substances, organic as well as inorganic, are stable in the presence of visible light. Only a few complex molecules produced by living organisms have the specific property of responding to light in such a way as to initiate or participate in chemical reactions [see "How Light Interacts with Living Matter," by Sterling B. Hendricks, page 115]. Outside of living systems only a few kinds of molecules are sufficiently activated by visible light to be of interest to the photochemist.

The number of reactive molecules increases sharply, however, if the wavelength of the radiant energy is shifted slightly into the ultraviolet part of the spectrum. To the photochemist that is where the action is. Thus he is primarily concerned with chemical events that are triggered by ultraviolet radiation in the range between 180 and 400 nanometers. These events usually happen so swiftly that ingenious techniques have had to be devised to follow the molecular transformations that take place. It is now routine, for example, to identify molecular species that exist for less than a millisecond. Species with lifetimes measured in microseconds are being studied, and new techniques using laser pulses are pushing into the realm where lifetimes can be measured in nanoseconds and perhaps even picoseconds.

The photochemist is interested in such short-lived species not simply for their own sake but because he suspects that many, if not most, chemical reactions proceed by way of short-lived intermediaries. Only by following chemical reactions step by step in fine detail can he develop plausible models of how chemical reactions proceed in general. From such studies it is often only a short step to the development of chemical processes and products of practical value.

When a quantum of light is absorbed by a molecule, one of the electrons of the molecule is raised to some higher excited state. The excited molecule is then in an unstable condition and will try to rid itself of this excess energy by one means or another. Usually the electronic excitation is converted into vibrational energy (vibration of the atoms of the molecule), which is then passed on to the surroundings as heat. Such is the case, for example, with a tar roof on a sunny day. An alternative pathway is for the excited molecule to fluoresce, that is, to emit radiation whose wavelength is slightly longer than that of the exciting radiation. The bluish appearance of quinine water in the sunlight is an example of fluorescence; the excitation is produced by the invisible ultraviolet radiation of the sun.

The third way an electronically excited molecule can rid itself of energy is the one of principal interest to the photochemist: the excited molecule can undergo a chemical transformation. It is the task of the photochemist to determine the nature of the products made, the amount of product made per quantum absorbed (the quantum yield) and how these results depend on the concentrations of the starting materials. His next step is to combine these data with the known spectroscopic and thermodynamic properties of the molecules involved to make a coherent picture. It must be admitted, however, that only the simplest photochemical reactions are understood in detail.

There is also a fourth way an excited molecule can dissipate its energy: the molecule may be torn apart. This is called photolysis. As might be expected, photolysis occurs only if the energy of the absorbed quantum exceeds the energy of the chemical bonds that hold the molecule together. The energy required to photolyse most simple molecules corresponds to light that lies in the ultraviolet region [see illustration on page 94]. For example, the chlorine molecule is colored and thus absorbs light in the visible range (at 425 nanometers), but it has a low quantum yield of photolysis when exposed to visible light. When it is exposed to ultraviolet radiation at 330 nanometers, on the other hand, the quantum yield is close to unity: each quantum of radiation absorbed ruptures one molecule.

Albert Einstein proposed in 1905 that one quantum of absorbed light leads to the photolysis of one molecule, but it required the development of quantum mechanics in the late 1920's to explain why the quantum yield should depend on the wavelength of the exciting light. James Franck and Edward U. Condon, who carefully analyzed molecular excitation, pointed out that when a molecule makes a transition from a ground state to an electronically excited state, the transition takes place so rapidly that the interatomic distances in the molecule do not have time to change. The reason is that the time required for transition is much shorter than the period of vibration of the atoms in the molecule.

To understand what happens when a molecule is excited by light it will be helpful to refer to the illustration on the opposite page. The lower curve represents the potential energy of a vibrating diatomic molecule in the ground state. The upper curve represents the potential energy of the excited molecule, which is also vibrating. The horizontal lines in the lower portion of each curve indicate the energy of discrete vibrational levels. If the interatomic distance

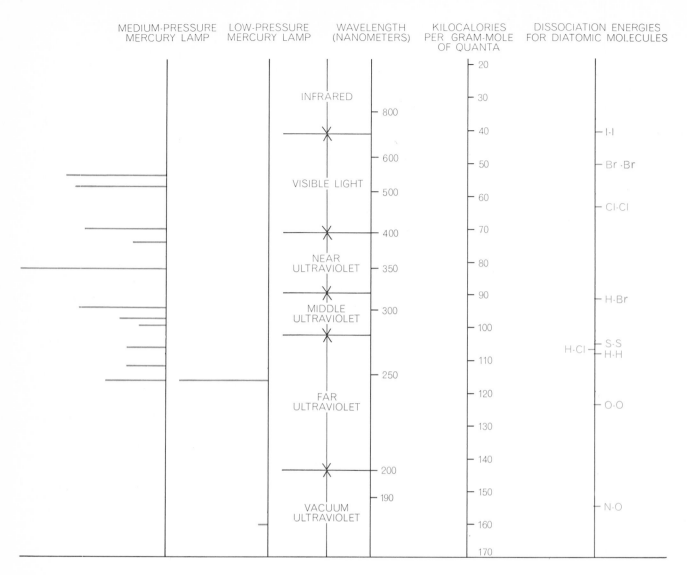

MEDIUM-PRESSURE   LOW-PRESSURE   WAVELENGTH   KILOCALORIES   DISSOCIATION ENERGIES
MERCURY LAMP   MERCURY LAMP   (NANOMETERS)   PER GRAM-MOLE   FOR DIATOMIC MOLECULES
                                                      OF QUANTA

INFRARED

800

VISIBLE LIGHT
                                    600   40   I-I
                                    500   50   Br-Br
                                                       60   Cl-Cl
                                    400   70
NEAR
ULTRAVIOLET   350   80
                                                       90   H-Br
MIDDLE
ULTRAVIOLET   300   100   S-S
                                                       110   H-Cl   H-H
                                    250   120
FAR
ULTRAVIOLET   130   O-O
                                                       140
                                    200   150
                                    190   160   N-O
VACUUM
ULTRAVIOLET   170

DISSOCIATION ENERGIES of most common diatomic molecules are so high that the energy can be supplied only by radiation of ultraviolet wavelengths. The principal exceptions are molecules of chlorine, bromine and iodine, all of which are strongly colored, indicating that they absorb light. The energy carried by a quantum of radiation, or photon, is directly proportional to its frequency, or inversely proportional to its wavelength. There are 6.06×10^{23} photons in a gram-mole of quanta. This is the number required to dissociate a gram-mole of diatomic molecules (6.06×10^{23} molecules) if the quantum yield is unity. A gram-mole is the weight in grams equal to the molecular weight of a molecule, thus a gram-mole of oxygen (O_2) is 32 grams. The principal emission wavelengths of two commonly used types of mercury lamp are identified at the left. Lengths of the bars are proportional to intensity.

becomes large enough in the ground state, the molecule can come apart without ever entering the excited state. The curve for the excited state is displaced to the right of the curve for the ground state, indicating that the average interatomic distance (the minimum in each curve) is somewhat greater in the excited state than it is in the ground state. That is, the excited molecule is somewhat "looser."

The molecule can pass from the ground state to one of the levels of the excited state by absorbing radiation whose photon energy is equal to the energy difference between the ground state and one of the levels of the excited state. Provided that the quantum of radiation is not too energetic the molecule will remain intact and continue to vibrate. After a brief interval it will emit a quantum of fluorescent radiation and drop back to the ground state. Because the emission occurs when the excited molecule is at the lowest vibrational level, the emitted energy is less than the absorbed energy, hence the wavelength of the fluorescent radiation is greater than that of the absorbed radiation.

When the absorbed radiation exceeds a certain threshold value, the molecule comes apart; it is photolysed. At this point the absorption spectrum, shown at the right side of the illustration, becomes continuous, because the molecule is no longer vibrating at discrete energy levels. As long as the molecule is intact only discrete wavelengths of light can be absorbed.

It is possible for the excited state to pass to the ground state without releasing a quantum of radiation, in which case the electronic energy is dissipated as heat. Franck and Condon explained that this was accomplished by an overlapping, or crossing, of the two potential-energy curves, so that the excited molecule slides over, so to speak, to the ground state, leaving the molecule in an abnormally high state of vibration. This vibrational energy is then readily transferred to surrounding molecules.

As far as life on the earth is concerned, the most important photolytic reaction in nature is the one that creates a canopy of ozone in the upper atmosphere. Ozone is a faintly bluish gas whose molecules consist of three atoms of oxygen; ordinary oxygen molecules contain two atoms. Ozone absorbs broadly in the middle- and far-ultraviolet regions with a maximum at 255 nanometers. Fortunately ozone filters out just those wavelengths that are fatal to living organisms.

Ozone production begins with the photolysis of oxygen molecules (O_2), which occurs when oxygen strongly absorbs ultraviolet radiation with a wavelength of 190 nanometers. The oxygen atoms released by photolysis may simply recombine or they may react with other oxygen molecules to produce ozone (O_3). When ozone, in turn, absorbs ultraviolet radiation from the sun, it is either photolysed (yielding O_2 and O) or it contributes to the heating of the atmosphere. A dynamic equilibrium is reached in which ozone photolysis balances ozone synthesis.

Early in this century physical chemists were presented with a photolytic puzzle. It was observed that when pure chlorine and hydrogen are exposed to ultraviolet radiation, the quantum yield approaches one million, that is, nearly a million molecules of hydrogen chloride (HCl) are produced for each quantum of radiation absorbed. This seemed to contradict Einstein's postulate that the quantum yield should be unity. In 1912 Max Bodenstein explained the puzzle by proposing that a chain reaction is involved [see upper illustration at right].

The chain reaction proceeds by means of two reactions, following the initial photolysis of chlorine (Cl_2). The first reaction, which involves the breaking of the fairly strong H-H bond, creates a small energy deficit. The second reaction, which involves the breaking of the weaker Cl-Cl bond, makes up the deficit with energy to spare. Breaking the H-H bond requires 104 kilocalories per gram-mole (the equivalent in grams of the molecular weight of the reactants, in this case H_2). Breaking the Cl-Cl bond requires only 58 kilocalories per gram-mole. In both of the reactions that break these bonds HCl is produced, yielding 103 kilocalories per gram-mole. Consequently the first reaction has a deficit of one kilocalorie per gram-mole and the

second a surplus of 45 (103 − 58) kilocalories per gram-mole. The two reactions together provide a net of 44 kilocalories per gram-mole. Thus the chain reaction is fueled, once ultraviolet radiation provides the initial breaking of Cl-Cl bonds.

The chain continues until two chlorine atoms happen to encounter each other to form chlorine molecules. This takes place mainly at the walls of the reaction vessel, which can dissipate some of the excess electronic excitation energy of the chlorine atoms and allow chlorine mole-

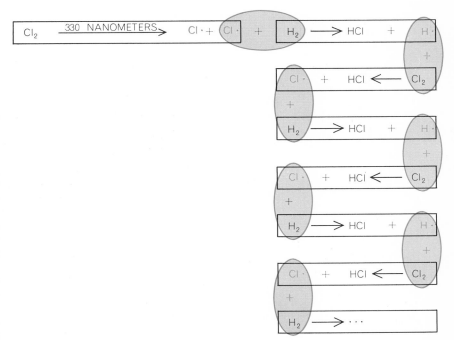

CHAIN REACTION is produced when pure chlorine and hydrogen are exposed to ultraviolet radiation. A wavelength of 330 nanometers is particularly effective. Such radiation is energetic enough to dissociate chlorine molecules, which requires only 58 kilocalories per gram-mole, but it is too weak to dissociate hydrogen molecules, which requires 104 kilocalories per gram-mole. The formation of HCl in the subsequent reactions provides 103 kilocalories per gram-mole. Since 104 kilocalories are needed for breaking the H-H bond, the reaction of atomic chlorine (Cl·) and H_2 involves a net deficit of one kilocalorie per gram-mole. However, the next reaction in the chain, involving H· and Cl_2, provides a surplus of 45 kilocalories (103 − 58). This energy surplus keeps the chain reaction going.

PHOTOLYSIS OF ACETONE, which yields primarily ethane and carbon monoxide, is a much studied photochemical reaction. It was finally understood by postulating the existence of short-lived free radicals, fragments that contain unsatisfied valence electrons.

cules to form. The free atoms may also be removed by impurities in the system.

Bromine molecules will likewise undergo a photochemical reaction with hydrogen to yield hydrogen bromide. The quantum yield is lower than in the chlorine-hydrogen reaction because atomic bromine reacts less vigorously with hydrogen than atomic chlorine does. Bromine atoms react readily, however, with olefins (linear or branched hydrocarbon molecules that contain one double bond). Each double bond is replaced by two bromine atoms. This is the basis of the industrial photobromination of hydrocarbons. Bromination can also be carried out by heating the reactants in the presence of a catalyst, but the product itself may be decomposed by such treatment. The advantage of the photochemical process is that the products formed are not affected by ultraviolet radiation.

An important industrial photochlorin-ation process has been developed by the B. F. Goodrich Company. There it was discovered that when polyvinyl chloride is exposed to chlorine in the presence of ultraviolet radiation, the resulting plastic withstands a heat-distortion temperature 50 degrees Celsius higher than the untreated plastic does. As a result this inexpensive plastic can now be used as piping for hot-water plumbing systems.

A much studied photolytic reaction is one involving acetone (C_2H_6CO). When it is exposed to ultraviolet radiation, acetone gives rise to ethane (C_2H_6) with a quantum yield near unity, together with carbon monoxide and a variety of minor products, depending on the wavelength of excitation. The results can be explained by schemes that involve free radicals—fragments of molecules that have unsatisfied valence elec-trons. Photolysis of acetone produces the methyl radical (CH_3) and the acetyl radical (CH_3CO). Two methyl radicals combine to form ethane [see lower illustration on page 95].

W. A. Noyes, Jr., of the University of Rochester and others assumed the existence of these free radicals in order to explain the end products of the photolysis. Because the lifetime of free radicals may be only a ten-thousandth of a second, they cannot be isolated for study. Since the end of World War II, however, the technique of flash spectroscopy has been developed for recording their existence during their brief lifetime.

Flash spectroscopy was devised at the University of Cambridge by R. G. W. Norrish and his student George Porter, who is now director of the Royal Institution. They designed an apparatus [see figure on page 98] in which a sample is illuminated with an intense burst of ultraviolet to create the photolytic products. A small fraction of a second later weaker light is beamed into the reaction chamber; at the far end of the chamber the light enters a spectrograph, which records whatever wavelengths have not been absorbed. The absorbed wavelengths provide clues to the nature of the short-lived species produced by photolysis. In 1967 Norrish and Porter shared the Nobel prize in chemistry with Manfred Eigen of the University of Göttingen, who had also developed techniques for studying fast reactions.

Flash spectroscopy has greatly increased chemists' knowledge about the "triplet state," an excited state that involves the pairs of electrons that form chemical bonds in organic molecules. Normally the spins of the paired electrons are antiparallel, or opposite to each other. When exposed to ultraviolet radiation, the molecules are raised to the first excited state and then undergo a nonradiative transition to an intermediate state in which the spins of two electrons in the same state are parallel to each other. This is the triplet state. If it is again exposed to ultraviolet or visible radiation, the triplet state exhibits its own absorption spectrum, which lies at a longer wavelength than the absorption spectrum of the normal ground state, or state of lowest energy [see illustration at left].

The concept of the triplet state in organic molecules is due mainly to the work of G. N. Lewis and his collaborators at the University of California at Berkeley in the late 1930's and early 1940's. These workers found that when

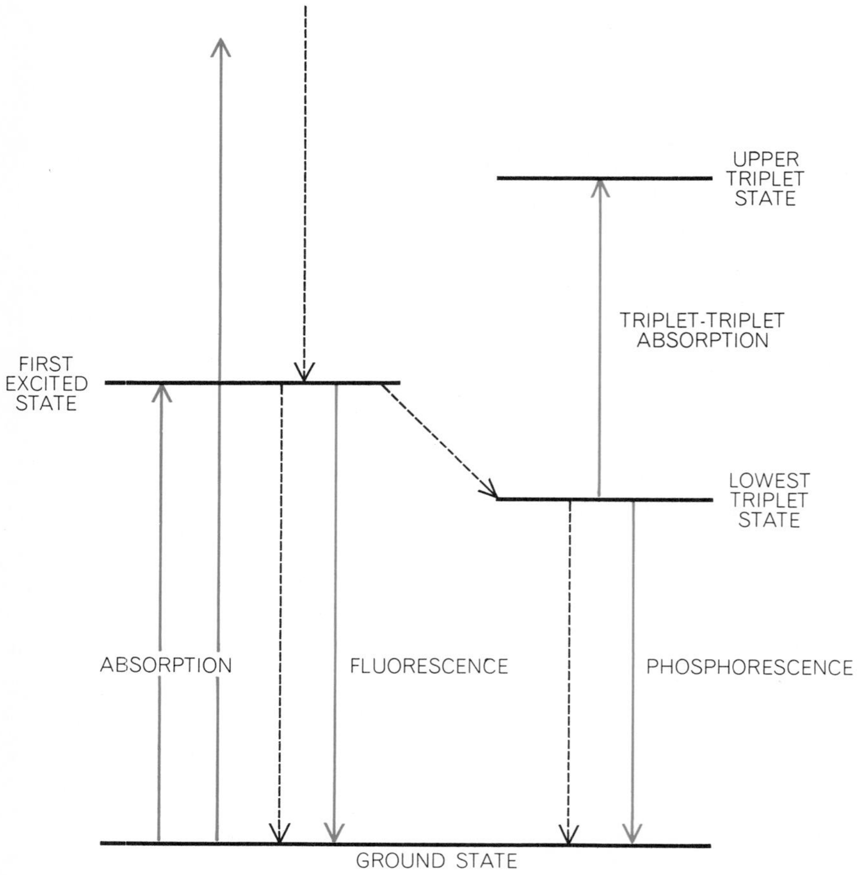

TRIPLET STATE has become an important concept in understanding the photochemical reactions of many organic molecules. Like all molecules, they can be raised to an excited state by absorption of radiation. They can also return to the ground state by normal fluorescence: reemission of a photon. Alternatively, they can drop to the triplet state without emission of radiation. (Broken lines indicate nonradiative transitions.) The existence of this state can be inferred from the wavelength of the radiation it is then able to absorb in passing to a higher triplet state. The triplet state arises when the spins of paired electrons point in the same direction rather than in the opposite direction, as they ordinarily do.

dyes (notably fluorescein) are dissolved in a rigid medium such as glass and are exposed to a strong light, the dyes change color. When the light is removed, the dyes revert to their normal color after a second or so. This general phenomenon is called photochromism. Lewis deduced the existence of the triplet state and ascribed its fairly long duration to the time required for the parallel-spin electrons to become uncoupled and to revert to their normal antiparallel arrangement.

In 1952 Porter and M. W. Windsor used flash spectroscopy to search for the triplet state in the spectra of organic molecules in ordinary fluid solvents. They were almost immediately successful. They found that under such conditions the triplet state has a lifetime of about a millisecond.

In his Nobel prize lecture Porter said: "Any discussion of mechanism in organic photochemistry immediately involves the triplet state, and questions about this state are most directly answered by means of flash photolysis. It is now known that many of the most important photochemical reactions in solution, such as those of ketones and quinones, proceed almost exclusively via the triplet state, and the properties of this state therefore become of prime importance."

While studying the photochemistry of dyes in solution, my student Albert H. Adelman and I, working at the Polytechnic Institute of Brooklyn, demonstrated that the chemically reactive species is the triplet state of the dye. Specifically, when certain dyes are excited by light in the presence of electron-donating substances, the dyes are rapidly changed into the colorless ("reduced") form. Our studies showed that the reactive state of the dye—the triplet state—has a lifetime of about a tenth of a millisecond. The dye is now a powerful reducing agent and will donate electrons to other substances, with the dye being returned to its oxidized state [*see illustration on page* 99]. In other words, the dye is a photosensitizer for chemical reductions; visible light provides the energy for getting the reaction started.

In the course of these studies I discovered that free radicals are created when dyes are photoreduced. The free radicals make their presence known by causing vinyl monomers to link up into polymers. The use of free radicals for bringing about polymerization of monomers is well known in industry. It occurred to me that adding suitable dyes to monomer solutions would provide the basis for a new kind of photography. In such a solution the concentration of free radicals would be proportional to the intensity of the visible light and thus the degree of polymerization would be controlled by light. It has turned out that very accurate three-dimensional topographical maps can be produced in plastic by this method.

The use of dyes as photosensitizing agents is, of course, fundamental to photography. In 1873 Hermann Wilhelm Vogel found that by adding dyes to silver halide emulsions he could make photographic plates that were sensitive to visible light. At first such plates responded only to light at the blue end of the spectrum. Later new dyes were found that extended the sensitivity farther and farther toward the red end of the spectrum, making possible panchromatic

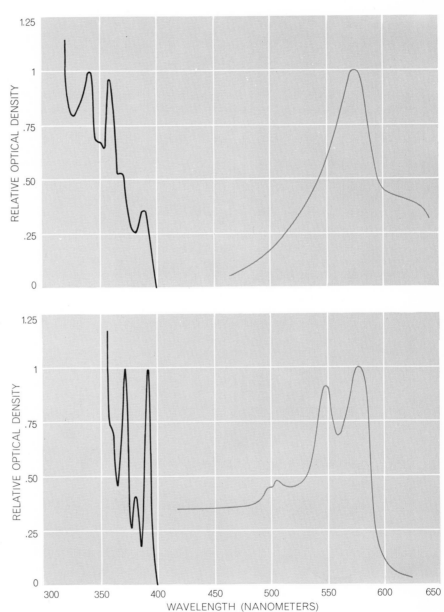

TRIPLET-TRIPLET ABSORPTION OF VISIBLE LIGHT has been observed in the author's laboratory at the Polytechnic Institute of Brooklyn. His equipment sends a beam of ultraviolet radiation into samples embedded in a plastic matrix in one direction and visible light at right angles to the ultraviolet radiation. The visible absorption spectra are then recorded in the presence of ultraviolet radiation. The black curves at the left in these two examples show the absorption of the electronic ground state. The colored curves at the right show the absorption of visible wavelengths that raises the excited molecule from the lowest triplet state to upper triplet states. The top spectra were produced by chrysene, the lower spectra by 1,2,5,6-dibenzanthracene. Both are aromatic coal-tar hydrocarbons.

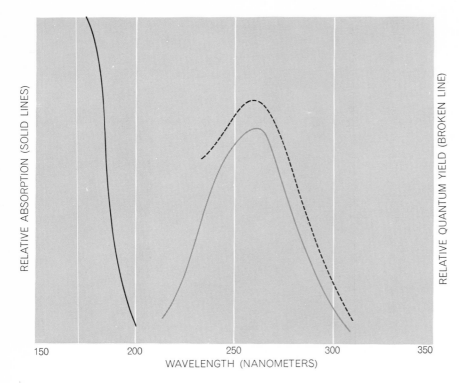

ABSORPTION SPECTRUM OF OZONE (*solid curve in color*) peaks at about 250 nanometers in the ultraviolet. As a happy consequence, the canopy of ozone in the upper atmosphere removes the portion of the sun's radiation that would be most harmful to life. The biocidal effectiveness of ultraviolet radiation is shown by the broken black line. The solid black curve is the absorption spectrum of molecular oxygen. For reasons not well understood, ultraviolet radiation of 200 nanometers does not penetrate the atmosphere.

emulsions. Photographic firms continue to synthesize new dyes in a search for sensitizers that will act efficiently in the infrared part of the spectrum. The nature of the action ot sensitizers in silver halide photography is still obscure, nearly 100 years after the effect was first demonstrated. The effect seems to depend on the state of aggregation of the dye absorbed to the silver halide crystals.

The reverse of photoreduction—photooxidation—can also be mediated by dyes, as we have found in our laboratory. Here again the reactive species of the dye is the dye in the triplet state. We have found that the only dyes that will serve as sensitizers for photooxidation are those that can be reduced in the presence of light.

The oxidized dye—the dye peroxide—is a powerful oxidizing agent. In the process of oxidizing other substances the dye is regenerated [*see figure on right*]. My student Judith S. Bellin and I have demonstrated this phenomenon, and we have employed dye-sensitized photooxidation to inactivate some biological systems. These systems include viruses, DNA and ascites tumor cells. That dyes are visible-light sensitizers for biological inactivation was first demonstrated in 1900 by O. Raab, who observed that a dye that did not kill a

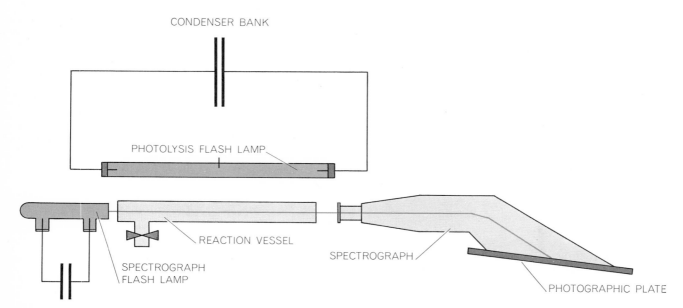

APPARATUS FOR FLASH PHOTOLYSIS was devised by R. G. W. Norrish and George Porter at the University of Cambridge. With it they discovered the short-lived triplet state that follows the photolysis of various kinds of molecules, organic as well as inorganic. The initial dissociation is triggered by the photolysis flash lamp, which produces an intense burst of ultraviolet radiation. A millisecond or less later another flash lamp sends a beam of ultraviolet radiation through the reaction vessel. Free radicals in the triplet state absorb various wavelengths ("triplet-triplet" absorption) and the resulting spectrum is recorded by the spectrograph.

culture of protozoa did so when the culture was placed near a window.

The inactivation that results from dye sensitization is different from the inactivation that results when biological systems are exposed to ultraviolet radiation.

ABSORPTION OF VISIBLE LIGHT ⎯ D DYE IN GROUND STATE

D* FIRST EXCITED STATE

D′ TRIPLET STATE

OXYGEN   ELECTRON DONOR

D PEROXIDE   D REDUCED

+   +

SUBSTRATE S   S SUBSTRATE

OXIDIZED S   D   S REDUCED

(DYE REGENERATED)

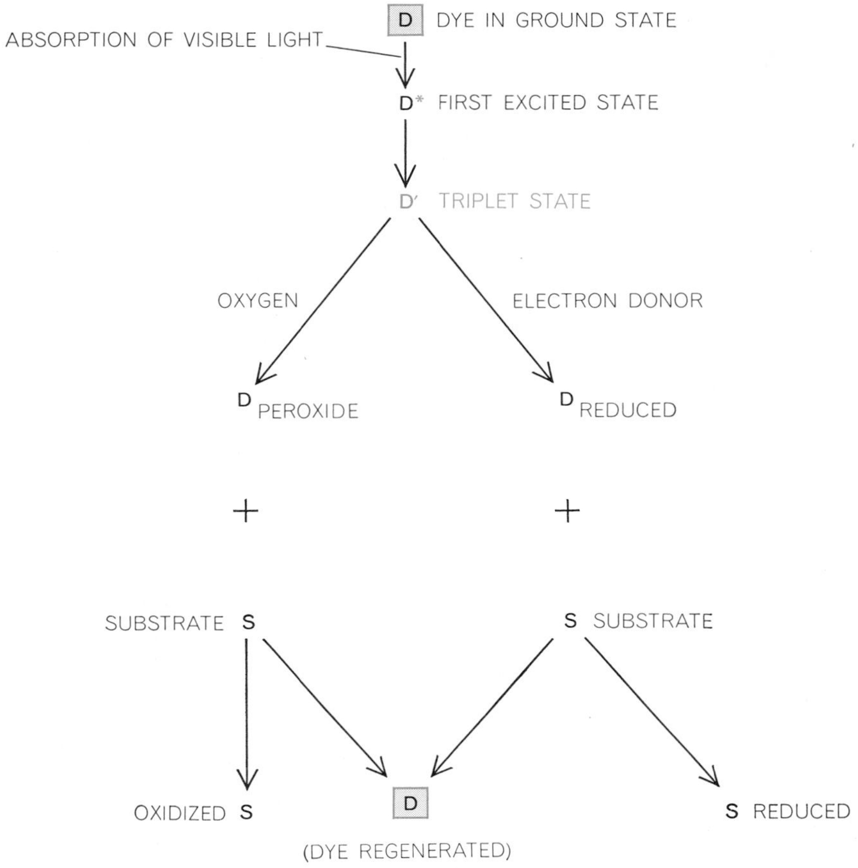

UNUSUAL PROPERTIES OF TRIPLET STATE have been explored by the author. Certain dyes in the triplet state can act either as strong oxidizing or as strong reducing agents, depending on the conditions to which the triplet state itself is exposed. In the presence of a substance that donates electrons (i.e., a reducing agent), the dye is reduced and can then donate electrons to some other substance (*substrate S*). In the presence of an oxidizing agent, the dye becomes highly oxidized and can then oxidize, or remove electrons from, a substrate. In both cases the dye is regenerated and returns to its normal state. The author's studies show that the reactive state of the dye lives only about .1 millisecond.

Here the inactivation often seems to result from the production of dimers: the cross-linking of two identical or similar chemical subunits. Photodimerization is implicated, for example, in the bactericidal action of ultraviolet radiation. It has long been known that the bactericidal action spectrum (the extent of killing as a function of wavelength) closely parallels the absorption spectrum of DNA, the genetic material. If dried-down films of DNA are irradiated with ultraviolet, they become cross-linked. According to one view the cross-linking occurs by means of the dimerization of thymine, one of the constituent groups of DNA.

Although this may well be the mode of action of ultraviolet radiation, my own feeling is that insufficient consideration has been given to the photolysis of the disulfide bonds of the proteins in bacteria. This bond is readily cleaved by ultraviolet radiation and has an absorption spectrum resembling that of DNA. Disulfide bonds are vital in maintaining the structure and activity of proteins; their destruction by ultraviolet radiation could also account for the death of bacteria.

In using dyes as sensitizers for initiating chemical reactions we are taking our first tentative steps into a realm where nature has learned to work with consummate finesse. Carbon dioxide and water are completely stable in the presence of visible light. Inside the leaves of plants, however, the green dye chlorophyll, when acted on by light, mediates a sequence of chemical reactions that dissociates carbon dioxide and water and reassembles their constituents into sugars and starches. A dream of photochemists is to find a dye, or sensitizer, that will bring about the same reactions in a nonliving system. There is reason to hope that such a system could be a good deal simpler than a living cell.

10

Life and Light

George Wald   October 1959

All life on this planet runs on sunlight, that is, on photosynthesis performed by plants. In this process light supplies the energy to make the organic molecules of which all living things are principally composed. Those plants and animals which are incapable of photosynthesis live as parasites on photosynthetic plants. But light—that form of radiant energy which is visible to the human eye—comprises only a narrow band in the spectrum of the radiant energy that pervades the universe. From gamma rays, which may be only one ten-billionth of a centimeter long, the wavelengths of electromagnetic radiation stretch through the enormous range of 10^{16}—10,000 million million times—up to radio waves, which may be miles in length. The portion of this spectrum that is visible to man is mainly contained between the wavelengths 380 to 760 millimicrons (a millimicron is ten millionths of a centimeter). By using very intense artificial sources one can stretch the limits of human vision somewhat more widely: from about 310 to 1,050 millimicrons. The remarkable fact is that, lying altogether within this slightly wider range of wavelengths, and mainly enclosed between 380 and 760 millimicrons, we also find the vision of all other animals, the bending of plants toward light, the oriented movements of animals toward or away from light and, most important, all types of photosynthesis. This is the domain of photobiology.

Why these wavelengths rather than others? I believe that this choice is dictated by intrinsic factors which involve the general role of energy in chemical reactions, the special role that light energy plays in photochemical reactions, and the nature of the molecules that mediate the utilization of light by living organisms. It is not merely a tautology

to say that photobiology requires the particular range of wavelengths we call light. This statement must be as applicable everywhere in the universe as here. Now that many of us are convinced that life exists in many places in the universe (it is hard to see how to avoid this conclusion), we have good reason to believe that everywhere we should find photobiology restricted to about the same range of wavelengths. What sets this range ultimately is not its availability, but its suitability to perform the tasks demanded of it. There cannot be a planet on which photosynthesis or vision occurs in the far infrared or far ultraviolet, because these radiations are not appropriate to perform these functions. It is not the range of available radiation that sets the photobiological domain, but rather the availability of the proper range of wavelengths that decides whether living organisms can develop and light can act upon them in useful ways.

We characterize light by its wave motion, identifying the regions of the spectrum by wavelength or frequency [*see illustration, top of pages 102 and 103*]. But in its interactions with matter—its absorption or emission by atoms and molecules—light also acts as though it were composed of small packets of energy called quanta or photons. These are in fact a class of ultimate particles, like protons and electrons, though they have no electric charge and very little mass. Each photon has the energy content: $E = hc/\lambda$, in which h is Planck's universal constant of action (1.58 $\times$ 10^{-34} calorie seconds), c is the velocity of light (3 $\times$ 10^{10} centimeters per second in empty space) and λ is the wavelength. Thus, while the intensity of light is the rate of delivery of photons, the work that a single photon can do (its energy content) is inversely proportional

to its wavelength. With the change in the energy of photons, from one end of the electromagnetic spectrum to the other, their effects upon matter vary widely. For this reason photons of different wavelengths require different instruments to detect them, and the spectrum is divided arbitrarily on this basis into regions called by different names.

In the realm of chemistry the most useful unit for measuring the work that light can do is the "einstein," the energy content of one mole of quanta (6.02 $\times$ 10^{23} quanta). One molecule is excited to enter into a chemical reaction by absorbing one quantum of light; so one mole of molecules can be activated by absorbing one mole of quanta. The energy content of one einstein is equal to 2.854 $\times$ 10^7 gram calories, divided by the wavelength of the photon expressed in millimicrons. With this formula one can easily interconvert wavelength and energy content, and so assess the chemical effectiveness of electromagnetic radiations.

Energy enters chemical reactions in two separate ways: as energy of activation, exciting molecules to react; and as heat of reaction, the change in energy of the system resulting from the reaction. In a reacting system, at any moment, only the small fraction of "hot" molecules react that possess energies equal to or greater than a threshold value called the energy of activation. In ordinary chemical reactions this energy is acquired in collisions with other molecules. In a photochemical reaction the energy of activation is supplied by light. Whether light also does work on the reaction is an entirely separate issue. Sometimes, as in photosynthesis, it does so; at other times, as probably in vision, it seems to do little or no work.

Almost all ordinary ("dark") chemical

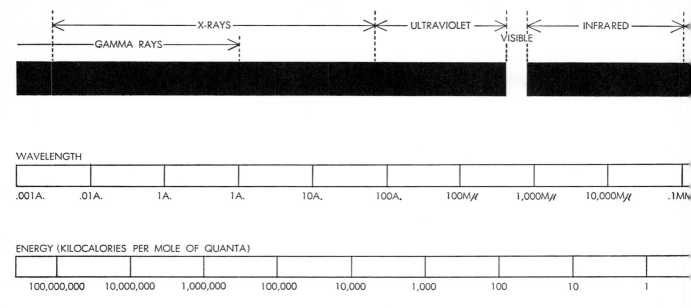

ELECTROMAGNETIC SPECTRUM is divided by man into qualitatively different regions (*top bar*), although the only difference between one kind of radiation and another is difference in wavelength (*middle bar*). From gamma rays, measured here in angstrom units, or hundred millionths of centimeter (A.), through light waves, measured here in millimicrons, or ten millionths of a centi-

reactions involve energies of activation between 15 and 65 kilogram calories (kilocalories) per mole. This is equivalent energetically to radiation of wavelengths between 1,900 and 440 millimicrons. The energies required to break single covalent bonds—a process that, through forming free radicals, can be a potent means of chemical activation—almost all fall between 40 and 90 kilocalories per mole, corresponding to radiation of wavelengths 710 to 320 millimicrons. Finally, there is the excitation of valence electrons to higher orbital levels that activates the reactions classified under the heading of photochemistry; this ordinarily involves energies of about 20 to 100 kilocalories per mole, corresponding to the absorption of light of wavelengths 1,430 to 280 millimicrons. Thus, however one approaches the activation of molecules for chemical reactions, one enters into a range of wavelengths that coincides approximately with the photobiological domain.

Actually photobiology is confined within slightly narrower limits than photochemistry. Radiations below 300 millimicrons (95 kilocalories per mole) are incompatible with the orderly existence of such large, highly organized molecules as proteins and nucleic acids. Both types of molecule consist of long chains of units bound to one another by primary valences. Both types of molecule, however, are held in the delicate and specific configurations upon which their functions in the cell depend by the relatively

weak forces of hydrogen-bonding and van der Waals attraction.

These forces, though individually weak, are cumulative. They hold a molecule together in a specific arrangement, like zippers. Radiation of wavelengths shorter than 300 millimicrons unzips them, opening up long sections of attachment, and permitting the orderly arrangement to become random and chaotic. Hence such radiations denature proteins and depolymerize nucleic acids, with disastrous consequences for the cell. For this reason about 300 millimicrons represents the lower limit of radiations capable of promoting photoreactions, yet compatible with life.

From this point of view we live upon a fortunate planet, because the radiation that is useful in promoting orderly chemical reactions comprises the great bulk of that of our sun. The commonly stated limit of human vision—400 to 700 millimicrons—already includes 41 per cent of the sun's radiant energy before it reaches our atmosphere, and 46 per cent of that arriving at the earth's surface. The entire photobiological range—300 to 1,100 millimicrons—includes about 75 per cent of the sun's radiant energy, and about 83 per cent of that reaching the earth.

From about 320 to 1,100 millimicrons —virtually the photobiological range— the sun's radiation reaches us with little modification. The atmosphere directly above us causes an attenuation, mainly by scattering rather than absorption of

light, which is negligible at 700 millimicrons and increases exponentially toward shorter wavelengths, so that at 400 millimicrons the radiation is reduced by about half. In the upper atmosphere, however, a layer of ozone, at a height of 22 to 25 kilometers, begins to absorb the sun's radiation strongly at 320 millimicrons, and at 290 millimicrons forms a virtually opaque screen. It is only the presence of this layer of ozone, removing short-wave antibiotic radiation, that makes terrestrial life possible.

At long wavelengths the absorption bands of water vapor cut strongly into the region of solar radiation from 720 to 2,300 millimicrons. Beyond 2,300 millimicrons the infrared radiation is absorbed almost completely by the water vapor, carbon dioxide and ozone of the atmosphere. The sun's radiation, therefore, which starts toward the earth in a band reaching from about 225 to 3,200 millimicrons, with its maximum at about 475 millimicrons, is narrowed by passing through the atmosphere to a range of about 310 to 2,300 millimicrons at the earth's surface.

The differential absorption of light by water confines more sharply the range of illumination that reaches living organisms in the oceans and in fresh water. The infrared is removed almost immediately in the surface layers. Cutting into the visible spectrum, water attenuates very rapidly in succession the red, orange, yellow and green. The short-wavelength limit is also gradually drawn

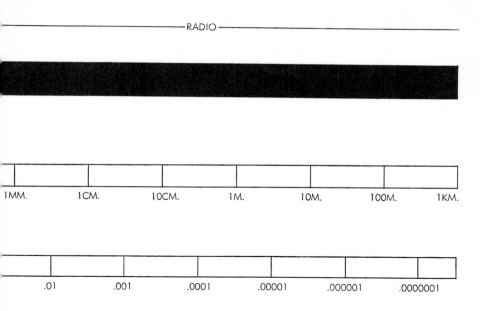

RADIO

1MM. 1CM. 10CM. 1M. 10M. 100M. 1KM.

.01 .001 .0001 .00001 .000001 .0000001

meter (Mμ), the waves range upward in length to the longest radio waves. The difference in wavelength is associated with a decisive difference in the energy conveyed by radiation at each wavelength. This energy content (*bottom bar*) is inversely proportional to wavelength.

matter once every 300 years. All the oxygen in our atmosphere, having been bound by various oxidation processes, is renewed by photosynthesis once in about 2,000 years.

In the original accumulation of this capital of carbon dioxide and oxygen, early in the history of the earth, it is thought that the process of photosynthesis itself profoundly modified the character of the earth's atmosphere and furnished the essential conditions for the efflorescence and evolution of life. Some of the oldest rock formations have lately been discovered to contain recognizable vestiges of living organisms, including what appear to have been photosynthetic forms. So for example iron gunflint cherts found in southern Ontario contain microscopic fossils, among which appear to be colonial forms of blue-green algae. These deposits are estimated to be at least 1.5 billion years old, so that if this identification can be accepted, photosynthesis has existed at least that long on this planet.

in, so that the entire transmitted radiation is narrowed to a band centered at about 475 millimicrons, in the blue.

Photosynthesis

Each year the energy of sunlight, via the process of photosynthesis, fixes nearly 200 billion tons of carbon, taken up in the form of carbon dioxide, in more complex and useful organic molecules: about 20 billion tons on land and almost 10 times this quantity in the upper layers of the ocean. All the carbon dioxide in our atmosphere and all that is dissolved in the waters of the earth passes into this process, and is completely renewed by respiration and the decay of organic

It now seems possible that the original development of the use of light by organisms, through the agency of chlorophyll pigments, may have involved not primarily the synthesis of new organic matter, but rather the provision of stores of chemical energy for the cell. A few years ago the process called photosynthetic phosphorylation was discovered, and has since been intensively explored,

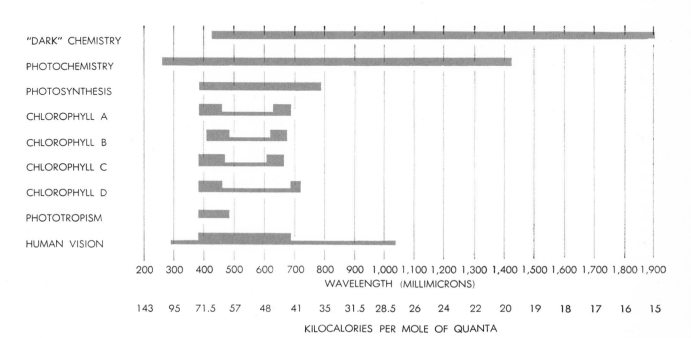

ENERGY CONTENT OF LIGHT is matched to the energy requirements of chemistry and photobiological processes and to the absorption spectra of photoreactive substances. The thicker segments of the bars opposite the chlorophylls indicate the regions of maximum absorption of light in each case, and the thicker segment in the bar opposite human vision indicates the normal boundaries.

mainly by Daniel I. Arnon of the University of California. By a still-unknown mechanism light forms the terminal high-energy phosphate bonds of adenosine triphosphate (ATP), which acts as a principal energy-carrier in the chemistry of the cell. One of the most interesting features of this process is that it is anaerobic; it neither requires nor produces oxygen. At a time when our atmosphere still lacked oxygen, this process could have become an efficient source of ATP. Among the many things ATP does in cells one of the most important is to supply the energy for organic syntheses. This direct trading of

the energy of sunlight for usable chemical energy in the form of ATP would therefore already have had as by-product the synthesis of organic structures. Mechanisms for performing such synthesis directly may have been a later development, leading to photosynthesis proper.

The essence of the photosynthetic process is the use of the energy of light to split water. The hydrogen from the water is used to reduce carbon dioxide or other organic molecules; and, in photosynthesis as performed by algae and higher plants, the oxygen is released into the atmosphere.

We owe our general view of photosynthesis in great part to the work of C. B. van Niel of the Hopkins Marine Station of Stanford University. Van Niel had examined the over-all reactions of photosynthesis in a variety of bacteria. Some of these organisms—green sulfur bacteria—require hydrogen sulfide to perform photosynthesis; van Niel discovered that in this case the net effect of photosynthesis is to split hydrogen sulfide, rendering the hydrogen available to reduce carbon dioxide to sugar, and liberating sulfur rather than oxygen. Still other bacteria—certain nonsulfur purple bacteria, for example—require organic

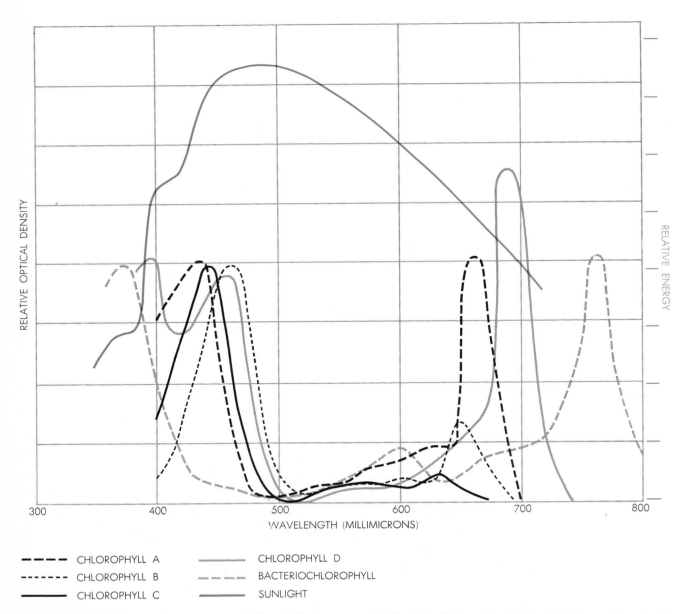

– – – – CHLOROPHYLL A	——— CHLOROPHYLL D
- - - - CHLOROPHYLL B	– – – BACTERIOCHLOROPHYLL
——— CHLOROPHYLL C	——— SUNLIGHT

ABSORPTION SPECTRA of various types of chlorophyll show the regions of the spectrum in which these substances absorb sunlight most effectively, measured on scale of relative optical density at left. Paradoxically the chlorophylls absorb best at the ends of the spectrum of sunlight, where energy, shown on scale at right, falls off steeply from the maximum around middle of the spectrum.

substances in photosynthesis. Here van Niel found that the effect of photosynthesis is to split hydrogen from these organic molecules to reduce carbon dioxide, liberating in this case neither oxygen nor sulfur but more highly oxidized states of the organic molecules themselves. Finally there are forms of purple bacteria that use molecular hydrogen directly in photosynthesis to reduce carbon dioxide, and liberate no by-product.

The efficiency of photosynthesis in algae and higher green plants is extraordinarily high—just how high is a matter of continuing controversy. The work of reducing one mole of carbon dioxide to the level of carbohydrate is in the neighborhood of 120 kilocalories. This energy requirement, though the exact figure is approximate, cannot be evaded through any choice of mechanism. Thanks to the selective absorption of the green chlorophyll pigment, light is made available for this process in quanta whose energy content is 41 or 42 kilocalories per mole, corresponding to quanta of red light of wavelength about 680 millimicrons. It is apparent, therefore, that several such quanta are required to reduce one molecule of carbon dioxide. If the energy of light were used with perfect efficiency, three quanta might perhaps suffice.

About 35 years ago the great German biochemist Otto Warburg performed experiments which appeared to show that in fact about four quanta of light of any wavelength in the visible spectrum are enough to reduce a molecule of carbon dioxide to carbohydrate. This might have meant an efficiency of about 75 per cent. Later a variety of workers in this country and elsewhere insisted that when such experiments are performed more critically, from eight to 12 quanta are required per molecule of carbon dioxide reduced. This discrepancy led to one of the bitterest controversies in modern science.

Many of us have grown tired of this controversy, which long ago bogged down in technical details and fruitless recriminations. I think it significant, however, that a number of recent, non-Warburgian, investigations have reported quantum demands of about six, and in at least one case the reported demand was as low as five. These numbers represent very high efficiencies (50 to 60 per cent), though not quite as high as Warburg prefers to set them.

Investigators have now turned from the question of efficiency to a more fruitful study of the specific uses to which quanta are put in photosynthesis. This is yielding estimates of quantum demand related to specific mechanisms rather than to controversial details of experimentation.

To reduce one molecule of carbon dioxide requires four hydrogen atoms and apparently three high-energy phosphate bonds of ATP. If we allow one quantum for each hydrogen atom (a point not universally conceded), that yields directly a quantum demand of four. If the ATP can be supplied in other ways, for example by respiration, four may be enough. If, however, light is needed also to supply ATP, by photosynthetic phosphorylation, then more quanta are needed; how many is not yet clear. Yet if one quantum were to generate one phosphate bond, the theoretical quantum-demand of photosynthesis, with all the energy supplied by light, would be four plus three, or seven. That would represent a high order of efficiency in the conversion of the energy of light to the energy of chemical bonds.

It is curious to put this almost obsessive concentration on the efficiency of photosynthesis together with what I think to be one of the most remarkable facts in all biology. Chlorophylls, the pigments universally used in photosynthesis, have absorption properties that seem just the opposite of what is wanted in a photosynthetic pigment. The energy of sunlight as it reaches the surface of the earth forms a broad maximum in the blue-green to green region of the spectrum, falling off at both shorter and longer wavelengths. Yet it is precisely in the blue-green and green, where the energy of sunlight is maximal, that the chlorophylls absorb light most poorly; this, indeed, is the reason for their green color. Where the absorption by chlorophyll is maximal—in widely separated bands in the violet and red—the energy of sunlight has fallen off considerably [see illustration on opposite page].

After perhaps two billion years of selection, involving a process whose efficiency is more important than that of any other process on earth, this seems an extraordinarily poor performance. It is a curious fact to put together with Warburg's comment (at one point in the quantum-demand controversy) that in a perfect nature, photosynthesis also is perfect. I think that the question it raises may be put more usefully as follows: What properties do the chlorophylls have that are so profoundly advantageous for photosynthesis as to override their disadvantageous absorption spectra?

We have the bare beginnings of an answer; it is emerging from a deeper understanding of the mechanism of photosynthesis, in particular as it is expressed in the structure and function of chlorophyll itself. Chlorophyll a, the type of chlorophyll principally involved in the photosynthesis of algae and higher plants, owes its color, that is, its capacity for absorbing light, to the possession of a long, regular alternation of single and double bonds, the type of arrangement called a conjugated system [see illustration on next two pages]. All pigments, natural and synthetic, possess such conjugated systems of alternate single and double bonds. The property of such systems that lends them color is the possession of particularly mobile electrons, called pi electrons, which are associated not with single atoms or bonds but with the conjugated system as a whole. It requires relatively little energy to raise a pi electron to a higher level. This small energy-requirement corresponds with the absorption of radiation of relatively long wavelengths, that is, radiation in the visible spectrum; and also with a high probability, and hence a strong intensity, of absorption.

In chlorophyll this conjugated system is turned around upon itself to form a ring of rings, a so-called porphyrin nucleus, and this I think is of extraordinary significance. On the one hand, as the illustration on these two pages shows, it makes possible a large number of rearrangements of the pattern of conjugated single and double bonds in the ring structure. Each such arrangement corresponds to a different way of arranging the external electrons, without moving any of the atoms. The molecule may thus be conceived to resonate among and be a hybrid of all these possible arrangements. In such a structure the pi electrons can not only oscillate, as in a straight-chain conjugated system; they can also circulate.

The many possibilities of resonance, together with the high degree of condensation of the molecule in rings, give the chlorophylls a peculiar rigidity and stability which I think are among the most important features of this type of structure. Indeed, porphyrins are among the most inert and stable molecules in the whole of organic chemistry. Porphyrins, apparently derived from chlorophyll, have been found in petroleum, oil shales and soft coals some 400 million years old.

This directs our attention to special features of chlorophyll, which are directly related to its functions in photosynthesis. One such property is not to utilize the energy it absorbs immediately in

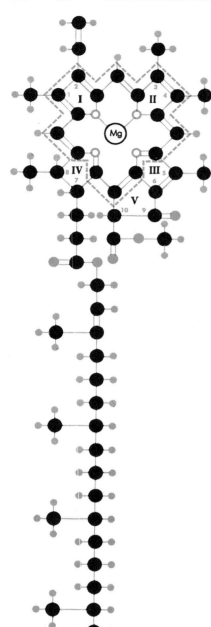

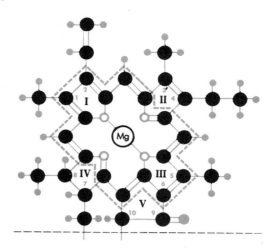

● CARBON   (Mg) MAGNESIUM

● OXYGEN   ○ NITROGEN

● HYDROGEN

CHLOROPHYLL MOLECULE, diagrammed in its entirety at left, owes its photobiological activity to the rigid and intricate porphyrin structure at top. The arrangement of the bonds in this structure may resonate among the configurations

reaction, but to trap it for a time, and pass it on intact to other, neighboring chlorophyll molecules. It has been shown that chlorophyll forms a long-lived metastable state, which, upon absorption of a quantum of light, retains a large part of the energy for a half-life of the order of five ten-thousandths of a second, perhaps 1,000 times longer than might otherwise be the case. In the structure of the chloroplasts, the functional assemblages of chlorophyll molecules in the cell, the chlorophyll molecules are in position to transfer energy from one to another, by a radiationless transfer akin to the way electrical energy is trans-

ferred in an induction motor. This capacity for transferring the energy about, so that it virtually belongs to a region of the chloroplast rather than to the specific molecule of chlorophyll that first absorbed it, makes possible the high efficiency of photosynthesis. While photosynthesis is proceeding rapidly, many chlorophyll molecules, having just reacted, are still in position to absorb light, but not to utilize it. In this way large amounts of absorbed energy that would otherwise be degraded into heat are retained and passed about intact until used photosynthetically.

One sign of the capacity to retain the energy absorbed as light and pass it on relatively intact is the strong fluorescence exhibited by chlorophyll. This green or blue-green pigment fluoresces red light; and however short the wavelengths that are absorbed—that is, however large the quanta—the same red light is fluoresced, corresponding to quanta of energy content about 40 kilocalories per mole. This is the quantity of energy that is passed from molecule to molecule in the chloroplast and eventually made available for photosynthesis.

The generally inert structure of chlorophyll must somewhere contain a chemically reactive site. Such a site seems to exist in the five-membered carbon ring, usually designated ring V in the structural diagrams. James Franck of the University of Chicago some years ago called attention to the possibility that it is here that the reactivity of chlorophyll is localized. Recent experiments by Wolf

Vishniac and I. A. Rose of Yale University, employing the radioactive isotope of hydrogen (tritium), have shown that chlorophyll, both in the cell and in solution, can take up hydrogen in the light though not in the dark, and can transfer it to the coenzyme triphosphopyridine nucleotide, which appears to be principally responsible for transferring hydrogen in photosynthesis. There is some evidence to support Franck's suggestion that the portion of chlorophyll involved in these processes is the five-membered ring.

Chlorophyll thus possesses a triple combination of capacities: a high receptivity to light, an inertness of structure permitting it to store the energy and relay it to other molecules, and a reactive site equipping it to transfer hydrogen in the critical reaction that ultimately binds hydrogen to carbon in the reduction of carbon dioxide. I would suppose that these properties singled out the chlorophylls for use by organisms in photosynthesis in spite of their disadvantageous absorption spectrum.

Photosynthetic organisms cope with the deficiencies of chlorophyll in a variety of ways. In 1883 the German physiologist T. W. Engelmann pointed out that in the various types of algae other pigments must also function in photosynthesis. Among these are the carotenoid pigments in the green and brown algae, and the phycobilins, phycocyanin and phycoerythrin (related to the animal bile-pigments) in the red and blue-green algae. Engelmann showed that each type

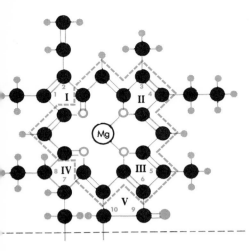

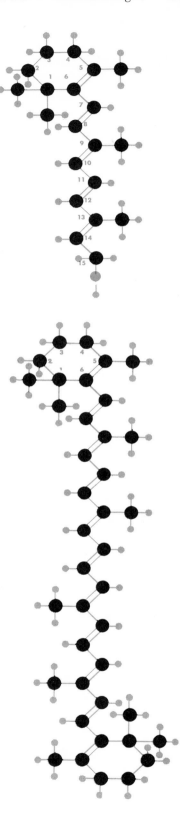

diagrammed in the middle and at the right. These and other possible configurations of the bonds help to make it possible for the chlorophyll molecule to trap and store energy which is conveyed to it by light quanta.

of alga photosynthesizes best in light of the complementary color: green algae in red light, brown algae in green light, red algae in blue light. He pointed out that this is probably the basis of the layering of these types of algae at various depths in the ocean.

All these pigments act, however, by transferring the energy they absorb to one another and eventually to chlorophyll *a;* whatever pigments have absorbed the light, the same red fluorescence of chlorophyll *a* results, with its maximum at about 670 to 690 millimicrons. The end result is therefore always the same: a quantum with an energy content of about 40 kilocalories per mole is made available to chlorophyll *a* for photosynthesis. The accessory pigments, including other varieties of chlorophyll, perform the important function of filling in the hole in the absorption spectrum of chlorophyll.

Still another device helps to compensate for the failure of chlorophyll to absorb green and blue-green light efficiently: On land and in the sea the concentration of chlorophyll and the depth of the absorbing layer are maximized by plant life. As a result chlorophyll absorbs considerable energy even in the wavelengths at which its absorption is weakest. Leaves absorb green light poorly, yet they do absorb a fraction of it. One need only look up from under a tree to see that the cover of superimposed leaves permits virtually no light to get through, green or otherwise. The lower leaves on a tree, though plentifully supplied with chloro-

plasts, may receive too little light to contribute significantly to photosynthesis. By being so profligate with the chlorophylls, plants compensate in large part for the intrinsic absorption deficiencies of this pigment.

Phototropism

The phototropism of plants—their tendency to bend toward the light—is excited by a different region of the spectrum from that involved in photosynthesis. The red wavelengths, which are most effective in photosynthesis, are wholly ineffective in phototropism, which depends upon the violet, blue and green regions of the spectrum. This relationship was first demonstrated early in the 19th century by a worker who reported that when he placed a flask of port wine between a growing plant and the light from a window, the plant grew about as well as before, but no longer bent toward the light. Recently, more precise measurements with monochromatic lights have shown that the phototropism of both molds and higher plants is stimulated only by light of wavelengths shorter than approximately 550 millimicrons, lying almost completely within the blue-green, blue and violet regions of the spectrum.

Phototropism must therefore depend on yellow pigments, because only such pigments absorb exclusively the short wavelengths of the visible spectrum. All types of plant that exhibit phototropism appear to contain such yellow pigments, in the carotenoids. In certain instances the carotenoids are localized specifically in the region of the plant that is phototropically sensitive. The most careful measurements of the effectiveness of various wavelengths of light in stimulating phototropism in molds and higher plants have yielded action spectra which resemble closely the absorption spectra of the carotenoids that are present.

A number of lower invertebrates—for example, hydroids, marine organisms that are attached to the bottom by stalks —bend toward the light by differential growth, just as do plants. The range of wavelengths which stimulate this response is also about the same as that in plants. It appears that here also carotenoids, which are usually present in considerable amount, may be the excitatory agents. Phototactic responses, involving motion of the whole animal toward or away from the light, also abound throughout all groups of invertebrates. Unfortunately no one has yet correlated accurately the action spectra for such re-

CAROTENE MOLECULE (*bottom*) is probable light-receptor in phototropism and is synthesized by plants. In structure it is a double vitamin A molecule (*top*). Vitamin A, in turn, is precursor of retinine molecule (*illustration, page 108*), which mediates vision.

sponses with the absorption spectra of the pigments that are present, so that no rigorous identification of the excitatory pigments can be made at present. This is a field awaiting investigation.

Vision

Only three of the 11 major phyla of animals have developed well-formed, image-resolving eyes: the arthropods (insects, crabs, spiders), mollusks (octopus, squid) and vertebrates. These three types of eye are entirely independent developments. There is no connection among them, anatomical, embryological or evolutionary. This is an important realization, for it means that three times, in complete independence of one another, animals on this planet have developed image-forming eyes.

It is all the more remarkable for this reason that in all three types of eye the chemistry of the visual process is very nearly the same. In all cases the pigments which absorb the light that stimulates vision are made of vitamin A, in the form of its aldehyde, retinene, joined with specific retinal proteins called opsins. Vitamin A ($C_{20}H_{29}OH$) has the structure of half a beta-carotene ($C_{40}H_{56}$), with a hydrogen and a hydroxyl radical (OH) added at the broken double bond.

Thus animal vision not only employs substances of the same nature as the carotenoids involved in phototropism of plants; there is also a genetic connection. Animals cannot make vitamin A *de novo*, but derive it from the plant carotenoids

consumed in their diet. All photoreception, from phototropism in lower and higher plants to human vision, thus appears to depend for its light-sensitive pigments upon the carotenoids.

The role of light in vision is fundamentally different from its role in photosynthesis. The point of photosynthesis is to use light to perform chemical work, and the more efficiently this conversion is accomplished, the better the process serves its purpose. The point of vision is excitation; there is no evidence that the light also does work. The nervous structures upon which the light acts, so far as we know, are ready to discharge, having been charged through energy supplied by internal chemical reactions. Light is required only to trigger their responses.

Because this distinction is not always understood, attempts are frequently made to force parallels between vision and photosynthesis. In fact, these processes differ so greatly in their essential natures that no deep parallelism can be expected. The problem of quantum demand, for example, raises entirely different issues in vision as compared with photosynthesis. In photosynthesis one is interested in the minimum number of quanta needed to perform a given chemical task. In vision the problem hinges not on energetic efficiency but on differential sensitivity. The light intensities within which animals must see range from starlight to noonday sunlight; the latter is about a billion times brighter than the former. It is this enormous range of intensities that presents organ-

isms with their fundamental visual problem: how to see at the lowest intensities without having vision obliterated by glare at the highest.

In the wholly dark-adapted state a vertebrate rod, the receptor principally involved in night vision, can respond to the absorption of a single quantum of visible light. To be sure, in the human eye, in which this relationship has been studied most completely, this minimal response of a single rod does not produce a visual sensation. In the dark-adapted state, seeing requires that at least five such events occur almost simultaneously within a small area of retina. This arrangement is probably designed to place the visual response above the "noise level" of the retina. From careful electrophysiological measurements it seems that a retina, even in total darkness, transmits a constant barrage of randomly scattered spontaneous responses to the brain. If the response of a single rod entered consciousness, we should be seeing random points of light flickering over the retina at all times.

The eye's extraordinary sensitivity to light is lost as the brightness of the illumination is increased. The threshold of human vision, which begins at the level of a few quanta in the dark-adapted state, rises as the brightness of the light increases until in bright daylight one million times more light may be needed just to stimulate the eye. But the very low quantum-efficiency in the light-adapted condition nonetheless represents a high visual efficiency.

The statement that the limits of human vision are 380 and 760 millimicrons is actually quite arbitrary. These limits are the wavelengths at which the visual sensitivity has fallen to about a thousandth of its maximum value. Specific investigations have pursued human vision to about 312 millimicrons in the near ultraviolet, and to about 1,050 in the near infrared.

In order to see at 1,050 millimicrons, however, 10,000 million times more light energy is required if cones are being stimulated, and over a million million times more energy if rods are being stimulated. This result came out of measurements made in our laboratory at Harvard University during World War II in association with Donald R. Griffin and Ruth Hubbard. As we exposed our eyes to flashes of light in the neighborhood of 1,000 millimicrons, we could not only see the flash but feel a momentary flush of heat on the cornea of the eye. At about 1,150 millimicrons, just a little farther into the infrared than our ex-

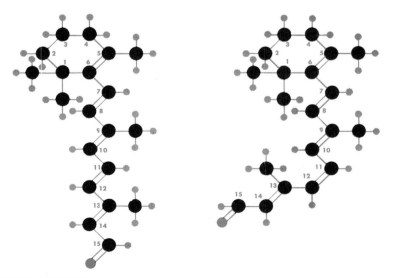

RETINENE MOLECULE is the active agent in the pigments of vision. Upon absorbing energy of light the geometry of the molecule changes from the so-called *cis* arrangement at left to the *trans* arrangement at right. This change in structure triggers process of vision.

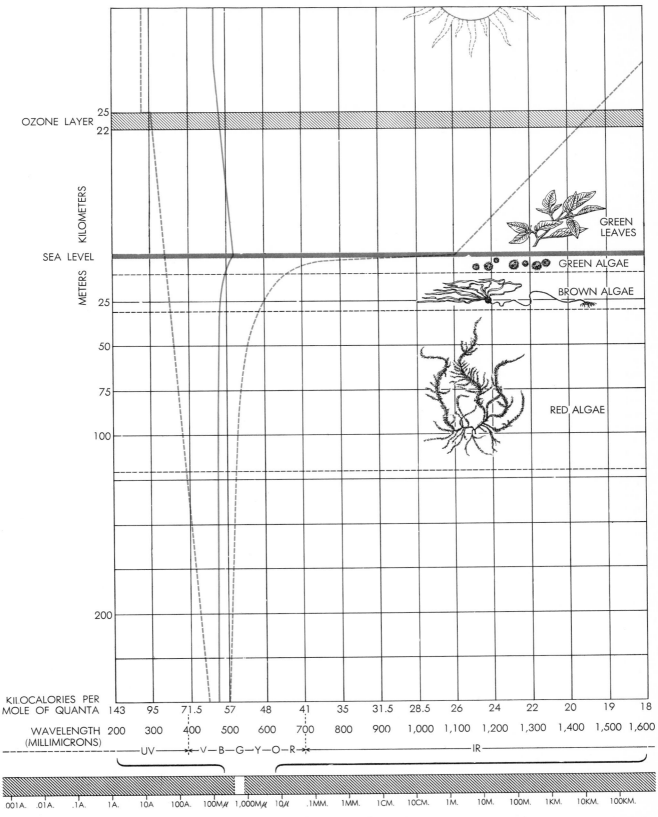

KILOCALORIES PER MOLE OF QUANTA	143	95	71.5	57	48	41	35	31.5	28.5	26	24	22	20	19	18
WAVELENGTH (MILLIMICRONS)	200	300	400	500	600	700	800	900	1,000	1,100	1,200	1,300	1,400	1,500	1,600

---------------------------- UV ---- V—B—G—Y—O—R --- IR ------------------------

| .001A. | .01A. | .1A. | 1A. | 10A | 100A. | 100Mμ | 1,000Mμ | 10μ | .1MM. | 1MM. | 1CM. | 10CM. | 1M. | 10M. | 100M. | 1KM. | 10KM. | 100KM. |

SPECTRUM OF SUNLIGHT at the earth's surface is narrowed by atmospheric absorption to the range of wavelengths (from 320 to 1,100 millimicrons) that are effective in photobiological processes. The sunlight reaching the domain of life in the sea is further narrowed by absorption in the sea water. The solid colored line locates the wavelengths of maximum intensity; the broken colored lines, the wavelength-boundaries within which 90 per cent of the solar energy is concentrated at each level in the atmosphere and ocean. The letters above the spectrum of wavelengths at bottom represent ultraviolet (UV), violet (V), blue (B), green (G), yellow (Y), orange (O), red (R) and infrared (IR). Other usages in the chart are explained in the illustration on pages 102 and 103.

periments had taken us, the radiation should have become a better stimulus as heat than as light.

The ultraviolet boundary of human vision, as that of many other vertebrates, raises a special problem. Ordinarily our vision is excluded from the ultraviolet, not primarily because the retina or its visual pigments are insensitive to that portion of the spectrum, but because ultraviolet light is absorbed by the lens of the eye. The human lens is yellow in color and grows more deeply yellow with age. One curious consequence of this arrangement is that persons who have had their lenses removed in the operation for cataract have excellent ultraviolet vision.

One may wonder how it comes about that man and many other vertebrates have been excluded from ultraviolet vision by the yellowness of their lenses. Actually this effect is probably of real advantage. All lens systems made of one material refract shorter wavelengths more strongly than longer wavelengths, and so bring blue light to a shorter focus than red. This phenomenon is known as chromatic aberration, or color error, and even the cheapest cameras are corrected for it. In default of color correction the lens seems to do the next best thing; it eliminates the short wavelengths of the spectrum for which the color error is greatest.

One group of animals, however, makes important use of the ultraviolet in vision. These are the insects. The insect eye is composed of a large number of independent units, the ommatidia, each of which records a point in the object, so that the image as a whole is composed as a mosaic of such points. Projection by a lens plays no part in this system, and chromatic aberration is of no account.

How does it happen that whenever vision has developed on our planet, it has come to the same group of molecules, the A vitamins, to make its light-sensitive pigments? I think that one can include plant phototropism in the same question, and ask how it comes about that all photoreception, animal and plant, employs carotenoids to mediate excitation by light. We have already asked a similar question concerning the chlorophylls and photosynthesis; and what chlorophylls are to photosynthesis, carotenoids are to photoreception.

Both the carotenoids and chlorophylls owe their color to the possession of conjugated systems. In the chlorophylls these are condensed in rings; in the carotenoids they are mainly in straight

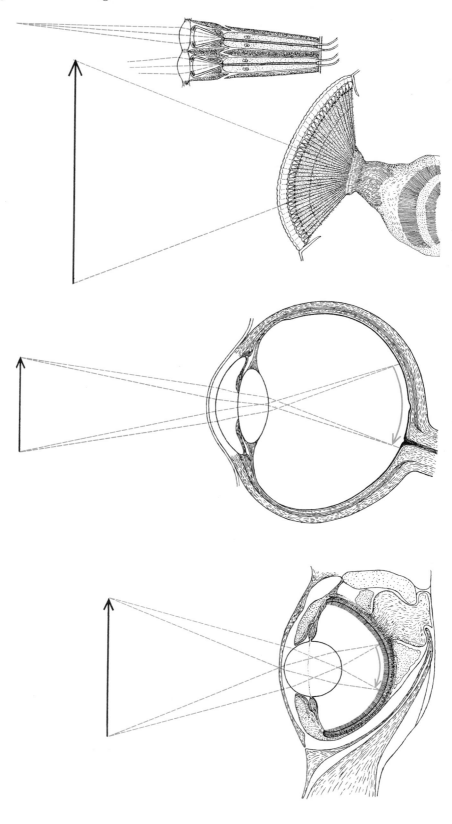

EYES of three kinds have evolved quite independently in three phyla: insects (*top*), vertebrates (*center*) and mollusks (*bottom*). In all three types of eye, however, the chemistry of vision is mediated by retinene derived from the carotenoids synthesized by plants.

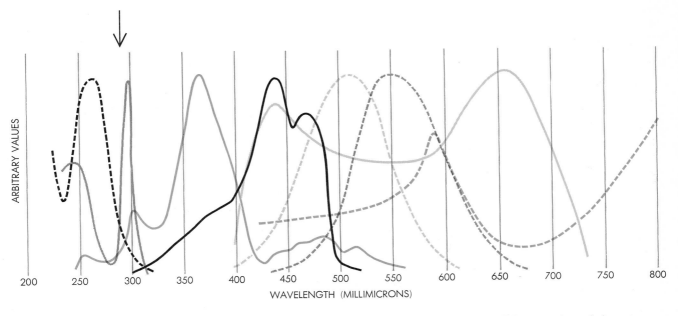

A - - - - -   E ————
B ░░░░░░   F - - - -
C ————   G ░░░░░░
D ————   H - - - -

PHOTOBIOLOGICAL PROCESSES are activated by different regions of the spectrum: killing of a bacillus (A), sunburn in human skin (B), insect vision (C), phototropism in an oat plant (D), photosynthesis in wheat (E), human "night" vision (F), human "day" vision (G), photosynthesis in a bacterium (H). Arrow at left marks limit of solar short waves.

chains. The chlorophylls fluoresce strongly; the carotenoids, weakly or not at all. Much of the effectiveness of the chlorophylls in photosynthesis is associated with a high capacity for energy transfer; there is as yet no evidence that such energy transfer has a place in vision.

I think that the key to the special position of the carotenoids in photoreception lies in their capacity to change their shapes profoundly on exposure to light. They do this by the process known as *cis-trans* isomerization. Whenever two carbon atoms in a molecule are joined by a single bond, they can rotate more or less freely about this bond, and take all positions with respect to each other. When, however, two carbon atoms are joined by a double bond, this fixes their position with respect to each other. If now another carbon atom is joined to each of this pair, both the new atoms may attach on the same side of the double bond (the *cis* position) or on opposite sides, diagonally (the *trans* position). These are two different structures, each of them stable until activated to undergo transformation—isomerization—into the other.

Carotenoids, possessing as they do long straight chains of conjugated double bonds, can exist in a great variety of such *cis-trans* or geometrical isomers. No other natural pigments approach them in this regard. Porphyrins and other natural pigments may have as

many or more double bonds, but are held in a rigid geometry by being bound in rings.

Cis-trans isomerization involves changes in shape. The all-*trans* molecule is relatively straight, whereas a *cis* linkage at any point in the chain represents a bend. In the composition of living organisms, which depends in large part on the capacity of molecules to fit one another, shape is all-important.

We have learned recently that all the visual pigments known, in both vertebrate and invertebrate eyes, are made with a specifically bent and twisted isomer of retinene. Only this isomer will do because it alone fits the point of attachment on the protein opsin. The intimate union thus made possible between the normally yellow retinene and opsin greatly enhances the color of the retinene, yielding the deep-orange to violet colors of the visual pigments. The only action of light upon a visual pigment is to isomerize—to straighten out—retinene to the all-*trans* configuration. Now it no longer fits opsin, and hence comes away. The deep color of the visual pigment is replaced by the light yellow color of free retinene. This is what is meant by the bleaching of visual pigments by light.

In this succession of processes, however, it is some process associated with the *cis-trans* isomerization that excites vision. The subsequent cleavage of reti-

nene from opsin is much too slow to be responsible for the sensory response. Indeed, in many animals the visual pigments appear hardly to bleach at all. This seems to be the case in all the invertebrate eyes yet examined, in which the entire transformation in light and darkness appears to be restricted to the isomerization of retinene. It seems possible that similar *cis-trans* isomerizations of carotenoid pigments underlie phototropic excitation in plants. Experiments are now in progress in our laboratory to explore this possibility.

Bioluminescence

In addition to responding to light in their various ways, many bacteria, invertebrates and fishes also produce light. All bioluminescent reactions require molecular oxygen; combustions of one kind or another supply the energy that is emitted as light. In photosynthesis light performs organic reductions, releasing oxygen in the process. In bioluminescence the oxidation of organic molecules with molecular oxygen emits light. I used to think that bioluminescence is like vision in reverse; but in fact it is more nearly like photosynthesis in reverse.

What function bioluminescence fulfills in the lives of some of the animals that display it is not yet clear. The flashing of fireflies may act as a signal for integrating their activities, and perhaps as a sexual excitant. What role may be fulfilled by the extraordinary display of red, green and yellow illumination in a railroad worm is altogether conjectural. There is one major situation, however, in which bioluminescence must play an exceedingly important role. This is in the sea, at depths lower than those reached by surface light, and at night at all depths. It would be difficult otherwise to understand how fishes taken from great depths, far below those to which light from the surface can penetrate, frequently have very large eyes. For vision at night or at great depths, it is not necessary that the organisms and objects that are visible themselves be bioluminescent. Bioluminescent bacteria abound in the ocean, and many submerged objects are coated sufficiently with luminous bacteria to be visible to the sensitive eye.

It has lately been discovered that the rod vision of deep-sea fishes is adapted to the wavelengths of surface light that penetrate most deeply into the water: the blue light centered around 475 millimicrons. Furthermore, sensitive new devices for measuring underwater illumination have begun to reveal the remarkable fact that deep-sea bioluminescence may also be most intense at about 475 millimicrons. The same selection of visual pigments that best equips deep-sea fishes to see by light penetrating from the surface seems best adapted to the bioluminescent radiation.

Just as light quanta must be of a certain size to activate or provide the energy for useful chemical reactions, so chemical reactions emit light in the same range of wavelengths. It is for this reason, and no accident, that the range of bioluminescent radiations coincides well with the range of vision and other photobiological processes.

Light and Evolution

The relationship between light and life is in one important sense reciprocal. Over the ages in which sunlight has activated the processes of life, living organisms have modified the terrestrial environment to select those wavelengths of sunlight that are most compatible with those processes. Before life arose, much more of the radiation of the sun reached the surface of the earth than now. We believe this to have been because the atmosphere at that time contained very little oxygen (hence negligible amounts of ozone) and probably very little carbon dioxide. Very much more of the sun's infrared and hard ultraviolet radiation must have reached the surface of

the earth then than now.

Some of the short-wave radiation, operating in lower reaches of the atmosphere and also probably in the surface layers of the seas, must have been important in activating the synthesis and interactions of organic molecules which formed the prelude to the eventual emergence of the first living organisms. These organisms, coming into an anaerobic world, surrounded by the organic matter that had accumulated over the previous ages, must have lived by fermentation, and in this process must have produced as a by-product very large quantities of carbon dioxide. Part of this remained dissolved in the oceans; part entered the atmosphere.

Eventually the availability of large amounts of carbon dioxide, much larger than are in the atmosphere today, made possible the development of the process of photosynthesis. This began to remove carbon dioxide from the atmosphere, fix-

ing it in organic form. Simultaneously, through the most prevalent and familiar form of photosynthesis, it began to produce oxygen, and in this way oxygen first became established in our atmosphere. As oxygen accumulated, the layer of ozone that formed high in the atmosphere—itself a photochemical process—prevented the short-wavelength radiation from the sun from reaching the surface of the earth. This relief from antibiotic radiation permitted living organisms to emerge from the water onto the land.

The presence of oxygen also led to the development of the process of cellular respiration, which involves gas exchanges just the reverse of those of photosynthesis. Eventually respiration and photosynthesis came into approximate balance, as they must have been for some ages past.

One may wonder how much of this history could have occurred in darkness,

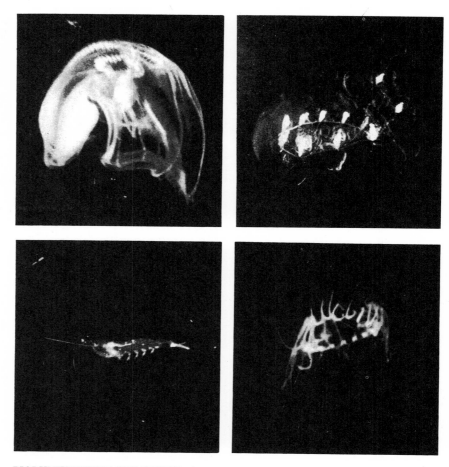

BIOLUMINESCENT CREATURES of the ocean were made to take these photographs of themselves by means of a camera designed by Harold E. Edgerton of Massachusetts Institute of Technology and L. R. Breslau of the Woods Hole Oceanographic Institution. The feeble luminescence of the animals was harnessed to trigger a high-speed electronic flash.

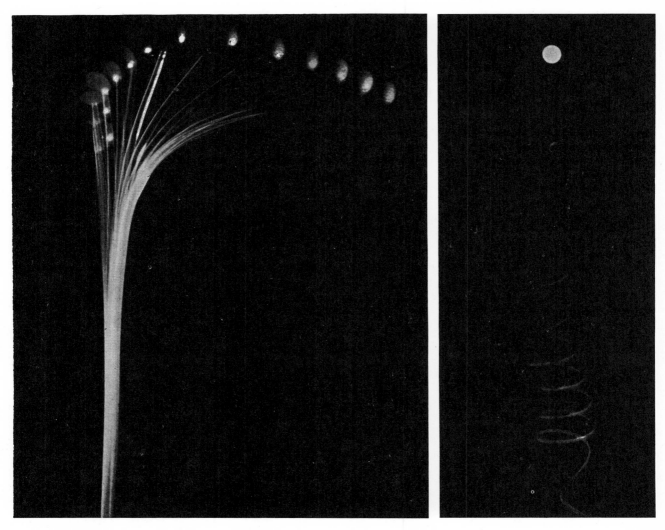

PHOTOTROPISM in the fruiting body of the mold *Phycomyces* is demonstrated in these photographs from the laboratory of Max Delbrück at the California Institute of Technology. The multiple photograph at left, with exposures made at intervals of five minutes, shows the fruiting body growing toward the light source. In the photograph at right, the stalk of the fruiting body has been made to grow in an ascending spiral by placing it on a turntable which revolved once every two hours in the presence of a fixed light-source.

by which I mean not merely the absence of external radiation but a much more specific thing: tne absence of radiation in the range between 300 and 1,100 millimicrons. A planet without this range of radiation would virtually lack photochemistry. It would have a relatively inert surface, upon which organic molecules could accumulate only exceedingly slowly. Granted even enough time for such accumulation, and granted that eventually primitive living organisms might form, what then? They could live for a time on the accumulated organic matter. But without the possibility of photosynthesis how could they ever become independent of this geological heritage and fend for themselves? Inevitably they must eventually consume the organic molecules about them, and with that life must come to an end.

It may form an interesting intellectual exercise to imagine ways in which life might arise, and having arisen might maintain itself, on a dark planet; but I doubt very much that this has ever happened, or that it can happen.

11

How Light Interacts with Living Matter

Sterling B. Hendricks   *September 1968*

Life is believed to have arisen in a primordial broth formed by sunlight acting on simple molecules at the surface of the cooling earth. It could have been sustained by the broth for aeons, but eventually, with the arrival of photosynthesis, some living things came to use sunlight more directly. So it remains today, with photosynthesis by plants serving to capture sunlight for the energy needs of all forms of life.

As various kinds of animals evolved, the ones that were best able to sense their surroundings were favored to survive. Because light acts over considerable distances it is well suited to sensing. To exploit light the animals needed some kind of detector: a tissue, an eyespot or an eye. The detector had to be coupled to a responding system: a ganglion or a brain. Signals from the system controlled locomotion toward food or away from danger.

Photosynthesis and vision do not exhaust the potential of the luminous environment. Both plants and animals have evolved mechanisms to respond to the changing daily cycle of light and dark. It is this photoperiodism that provides the seasonal schedule for, among other things, the flowering of plants, the pupation of insects and the nesting of birds.

To understand these phenomena one must ask how light acts in life. Part of the answer is very simple: it acts by ex-

citing certain absorbing molecules. What happens to the molecules in the course of absorption is more difficult to describe, but many details of the processes are now reasonably well known. On the other hand, our ideas about how the molecular events are coupled to the responses of plants and animals are still quite tentative.

In discussing the present state of knowledge about light and life I shall treat vision first because this phenomenon has some features in common with both photosynthesis and photoperiodism. In all three processes light acts through absorption by a small, colored molecule—a chromophore—that is associated with a large molecule of protein. In the case of vision the light-sensitive molecules are responsible for the pink and purplish color of the retina. In the retina of the human eye there are some 100 million thin rod-shaped cells and five million slightly cone-shaped ones. Each is connected through a synapse, or junction, to a nerve fiber leading to the brain. Electron micrographs show that the outer end of both rods and cones is packed with thin membranous sacs, and with these sacs are associated the light-absorbing chromophores. (Vision and photosynthesis share this association of a chromophore with a membrane.) Excitation of the chromophore by light caus-

es some kind of change in the membrane, and this change gives rise to a signal in the nerve fiber.

In vision the nature of the receiving chromophore and the manner of its excitation by light are well understood. Both have much in common with light reception in photoperiodism. As George Wald of Harvard University established, the receiving chromophore is vitamin-A aldehyde (in structural terms 11-*cis* retinal). The chromophore is found in association with a protein, opsin. The opsins are fatty proteins; thus they have an affinity for the sac membranes, which consist largely of lipid—that is, fatty—material. There are four types of opsin, one in the rods and three in the cones. Combined with 11-*cis* retinal, they respectively form rhodopsin and three kinds of iodopsin. On excitation by light all four opsins change in the same way.

In vision, photosynthesis and photoperiodism alike the chromophore molecule is notable for its alternating single and double chemical bonds. Known to chemists as conjugated systems, molecules of this kind are structurally quite stable because the groups of atoms attached by double bonds cannot rotate around the bonds. Each conjugated system, if it is adequately extended, has a rather low energy state that can be excited by visible light. When the system is excited, its double-bond character is somewhat relaxed, so that a *cis* configuration can change to a *trans* one [*see top illustration on next page*]. This ability to change form is a key element in vision and photoperiodism. In photosynthesis, however, no change of form takes place because the change is constrained by the ring structures of the chlorophyll chromophores.

The effects of light in vision and photoperiodism are determined by measur-

LIGHT-SENSITIVE PIGMENT that triggers photoperiodic responses in plants is shown in its two states in the photograph on the opposite page. Called phytochrome, the pigment, which is seen here in a .2 percent solution, is instrumental in a number of seasonal occurrences such as plants flowering and seeds germinating. In one state (*left*) phytochrome is excitable by far-red light, in the other (*right*) by red light. Alternating exposures to these colors change the pigment from one state to the other and back again. The phytochrome shown here was extracted from oat seedlings in the laboratory of F. E. Mumford and E. L. Jenner in the Central Research Department of E. I. du Pont de Nemours & Co. It is contained in square quartz cells designed for studies of light absorption. The faint numerals near the top indicates the length of the light path through the cell: 1.000 centimeter.

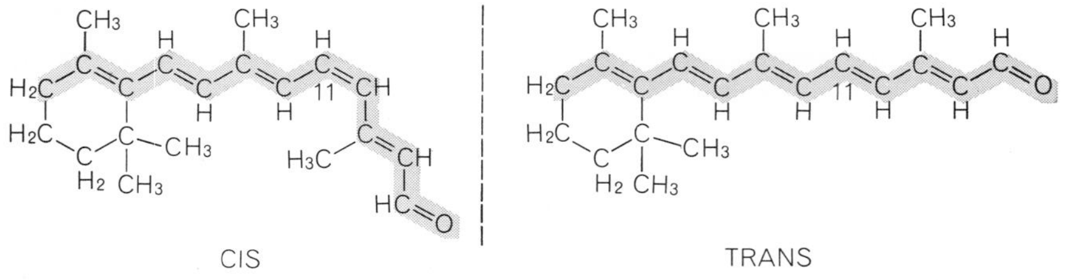

VISION depends on a light-sensitive chromophore molecule, 11-*cis* retinal (*left*), which has alternating single and double bonds (*color*). When light excites the molecule, its configuration changes from *cis* to the *trans* form (*right*), thereby setting in train a series of complex changes in the structure of the proteins with which the retinal chromophore is associated.

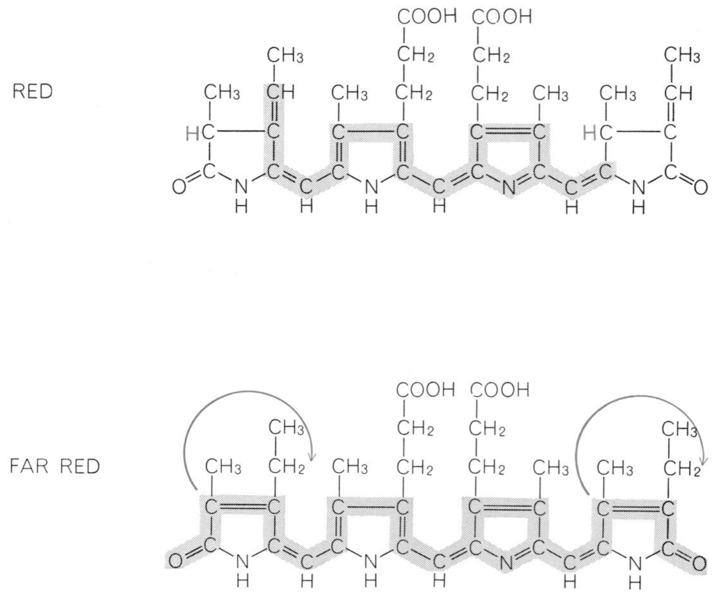

PHOTOPERIODISM in plants depends on phytochrome, another molecule that is sensitive to light. Like the retinal molecule, phytochrome has alternating single and double bonds (*color*). When excited by light, it changes from a configuration sensitive to red light (*top*) to one sensitive to far-red light, probably because two hydrogen atoms shift (*bottom*).

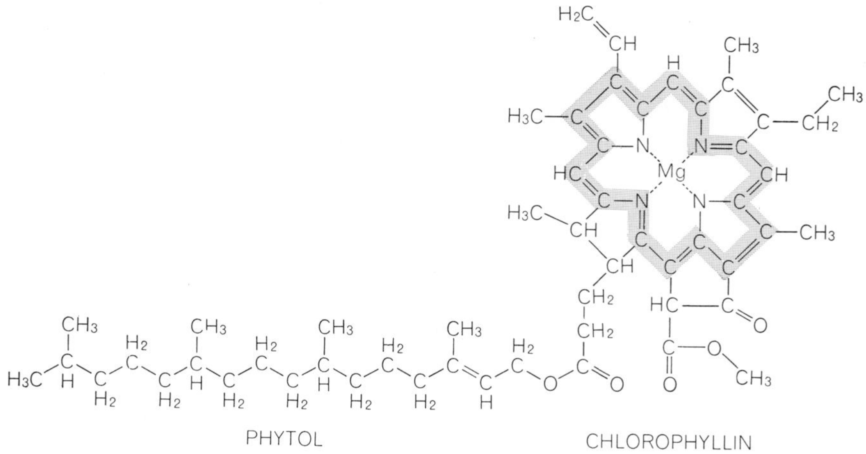

PHOTOSYNTHESIS depends on the light-sensitive chromophore molecules of several kinds of chlorophylls that have differing side groups. The molecule shown here is chlorophyll *a*. Like the vision and photoperiodism chromophores, chlorophyll molecules include singly and doubly bonded atoms, but these form a closed loop within the chlorophyllin portion of the molecule (*color*). When excited by light, chlorophylls forward the energy they receive to centers where it induces chemical changes (*see illustrations on page 123*).

ing the molecular changes produced by light excitation. Some of these changes are very rapid: they may occur in less than a millionth of a second. Changes as fast as this can be followed only if they are excited in an even shorter time, for instance by a very brief but intense flash of light. The measurement of the change also must be made quite rapidly. The method employed is flash excitation at room temperature or lower, followed by photoanalysis—the technique for which George Porter and R. G. W. Norrish shared (with Manfred Eigen) last year's Nobel prize in chemistry [see "The Chemical Effects of Light," by Gerald Oster, page 93]. Low temperatures slow down the molecular changes and make them more amenable to measurement.

When the vision chromophore is excited by light, it changes from the *cis* to the *trans* form. The result is the conversion of rhodopsin into prelumirhodopsin with an all-*trans* chromophore. The production of this single change is the one and only role that light plays in vision. The change is followed by several rapid shifts in the structure of the opsin and also changes in the relation of the chromophore to the opsin. To judge by the time it takes for a retinal-cell signal to arrive at a nerve ending, the signal is induced by the shifts that take place in the first thousandth of a second.

The course of the molecular changes can be traced by studying rhodopsin in solution. Prelumirhodopsin, identifiable by its maximum absorption of light at a wavelength of 543 nanometers, can be held at temperatures below −140 degrees Celsius and reversibly changed back into rhodopsin. When the prelumirhodopsin is warmed to −40 degrees C., it is converted into lumirhodopsin. The same conversion probably occurs at body temperature but much more rapidly. This change and subsequent ones, including the formation of metarhodopsins, involve shifts in the molecular configuration of opsin. Among vertebrates the changes finally lead to the dissociation of the chromophore from the protein. The released all-*trans* retinal then has to be reduced to the alcohol form and oxidized back to the aldehyde form to regenerate 11-*cis* retinal. Once the *cis* retinal is regenerated it spontaneously recombines with opsin to form rhodopsin again.

Analysis of the changes in electric potential that occur simultaneously with these molecular changes shows that a potential appears within 25 millionths of a second after a flash of light. The potential is positive with respect to the cornea in a circuit that includes neighboring tissues and the retina. The positive potential is followed in a thousandth of a second by a growing signal of the opposite sign. These events take place during the period when prelumirhodopsin and lumirhodopsin are present. The first potential probably accompanies the change of rhodopsin to prelumirhodopsin. The second depends markedly on the temperature at some distance from the place of light action, probably in the outer membrane of the rod or cone. Currently there is much interest in the possible identification of these changes in

potential as early steps in the eventual excitation of the nerve fiber. Another view is that nerve excitation is associated with the transitions involving metarhodopsin I and metarhodopsin II [see upper illustration below].

Color vision depends on the three opsins, each found in a different cone cell. Their absorption spectra have been measured, and curves were found with peaks at wavelengths of 450, 525 and 555 nanometers (respectively in the blue, green and yellow regions of the visible spectrum). Activation by light leads to the same sequence of molecular changes described for rhodopsin. The singularity of the nerve associations with the rod and

cone cells preserves the retinal detail, or register, in the transmission of the visual signal; the differences in absorption among the three kinds of cone retain the color pattern of the image.

The responses of plants to variations in the length of day and night involve light-induced molecular changes that closely parallel those involved in vision. Because photoperiodic responses are not as well known as visual ones I shall present some illustrative examples. Chrysanthemums and many other plants flower in response to the increasing length of the nights as fall approaches. If the long nights are experimentally inter-

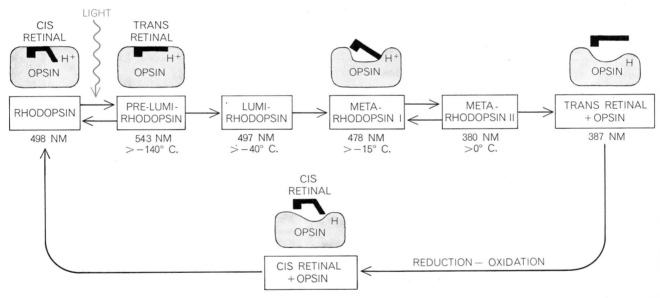

CHANGES IN RHODOPSIN, the visual pigment contained in the rod cells of the vertebrate eye, can be traced in the laboratory at low temperatures. Four successive forms of the pigment appear (*rectangles*) as the retinal molecule (*black*) first attains its *trans* configuration and then dissociates from the protein opsin. When it becomes *cis* retinal again, it recombines and completes the cycle.

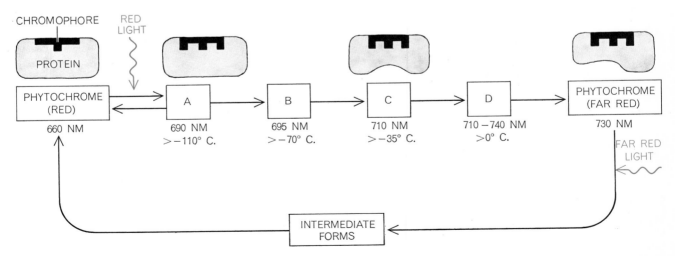

CHANGES IN PHYTOCHROME, the plant-photoperiodism chromophore, can also be traced at low temperature. As with rhodopsin, intermediate forms with characteristic light-absorption peaks appear before the initial red-absorbing form of the pigment is turned into the far-red-absorbing form. Unlike retinal, the chromophore (*black*) remains associated with its protein throughout the cycle.

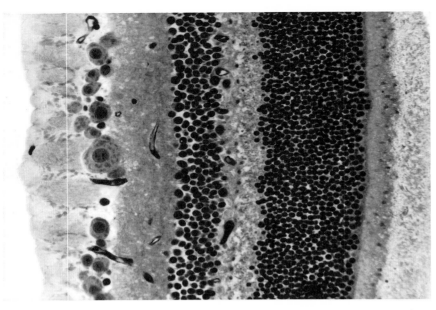

CAT RETINA is seen in cross section, enlarged 670 times. The nerve-fiber layer (*left*) is the part of the retina that lies in contact with the eye's vitreous body. The entering light must penetrate this and five additional layers of retinal tissue before reaching rods and cones (*right*). The micrograph was made by A. J. Ladman of the University of New Mexico.

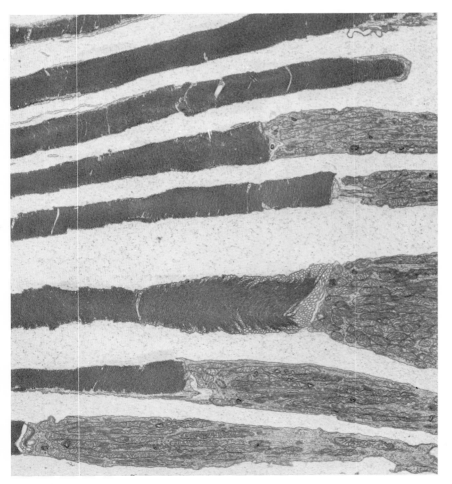

HUMAN RODS AND CONES, enlarged 7,200 times, are seen in an electron micrograph of retina. The visual pigments are concentrated in platelike layers of membrane called lamellae. The micrograph was made by Toichiro Kuwabara of the Harvard Medical School.

rupted by exposing the plants to short periods of light near midnight, the plants will not flower. Red light with an absorption maximum at a wavelength of 660 nanometers is most effective in preventing flower formation. Thus we anticipate that the light-receiving pigment in the plant is blue—the complementary color to the absorbed red. If shortly after exposure to red light the plants are exposed to light near the limit of vision in the far red (730 nanometers), they will flower.

The ornamental plant kalanchoe clearly illustrates the reversible response. The red light evidently converts the photoreversible pigment to a far-red-absorbing form. This changes the plant from the flowering state to the nonflowering one. The far-red light returns the pigment to its red-absorbing form, which enables flowering to proceed. Control of flowering by length of night is a very important factor in determining what varieties of soybean, wheat and other commercial crops are best suited for being grown in various latitudes with different periods of light and darkness.

Many kinds of seeds will germinate only if the photoreversible pigment has been activated. The seeds of some pine and lettuce species, for example, will not germinate in the laboratory unless they are briefly exposed to red light (or, to be sure, light containing red light). If the red-light activation of the seeds is followed by a short exposure to far-red light before the seeds are returned to darkness, the seeds remain dormant. The activation-reversal cycle can be repeated many times; germination or continued dormancy depends on the last exposure in the sequence.

The requirement of light for seed germination is a major cause of the persistence of weeds in cultivated crops. A seed that is dormant when it first falls to the ground is usually covered by soil in the course of the winter. As the seed lies buried the pigment that controls its germination changes into the red-absorbing form; now the seed will not germinate until it is again exposed to sunlight by cultivation or some other disturbance of the soil. When it is exposed, the sunlight converts some of the red-absorbing pigment back to the far-red-absorbing form, and germination begins. Seeds of one common weed, lamb's-quarters, are known to have lain buried for 1,700 years and then to have germinated on exposure to light.

The activation of the photoreversible pigment also controls the growth of trees and many common flowering plants. If

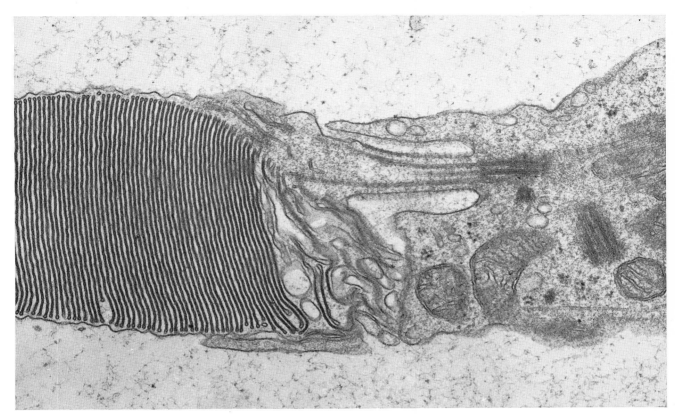

PART OF HUMAN ROD is magnified 44,000 times in electron micrograph. The outer segment of the rod (left) is filled with the membrane of the lamellae. The inner segment (right) is less complex in structure. This micrograph was also made by Kuwabara.

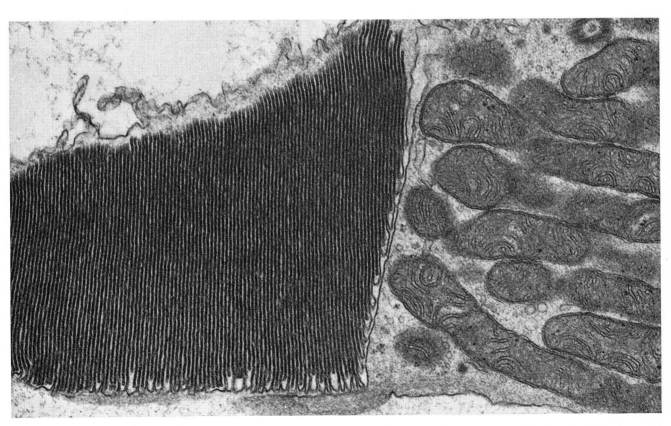

PART OF HUMAN CONE is magnified 44,000 times in another micrograph by Kuwabara that emphasizes the area connecting the structure's inner and outer segments. The lamellae differ from rod lamellae in being "packaged," some singly and some in groups.

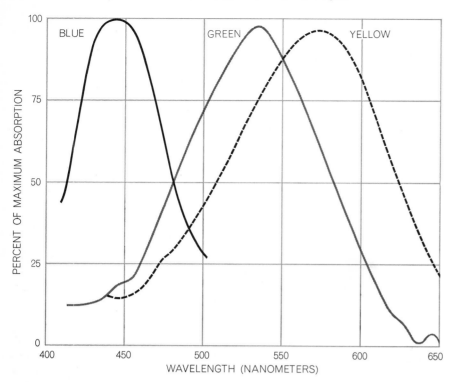

COLOR PERCEPTION in humans arises from the combination of retinal with three dissimilar opsins in the cones of the retina. The three different iodopsin pigments formed thereby absorb the greatest amount of visible light at three different wavelengths. The differences between the signals from each group of cones reflect the color pattern of the image.

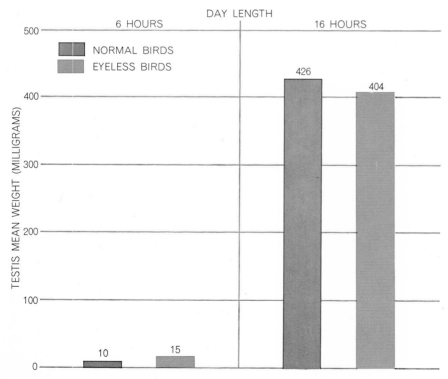

PHOTOPERIODISM IN SPARROWS has been shown to involve some light receptor other than the eye. The testis weight of both eyeless and normal sparrows remained low when their cages were lighted to simulate short days and long nights over a two-month period (left). When eyeless and normal birds instead underwent two months of long days and short nights, their testis weight showed a nearly identical increase (right). The experiment was conducted by Michael Menaker and Henry Keatts of the University of Texas.

such plants are to continue growing, they must have long periods of daylight. As the days become short growth stops and the plants' buds go into a dormant state that protects them against the low temperatures of winter.

The photoreversible pigment of plants has been named phytochrome. It is invisible in plant tissue because of its low concentration. It was isolated by methods widely used in the preparation of enzymes and other proteins. The pigment is indeed blue [see illustration on page 114]. Its photoreversibility is exactly what was expected on the basis of plant responses to light.

The chemical structure of the phytochrome molecule shows that it is related to the greenish-yellow pigments of human bile and the blue pigments of blue-green algae. The molecule comprises an open group of atoms that is closely related to the rings in the chlorophyll molecule. It has two side groups that can change from the cis form to the trans when they are excited by light. A more probable excitation change, however, is a shift in the position of the molecule's hydrogen atoms.

The changes in the phytochrome molecule following excitation by a flash of light are similar to those in rhodopsin. The first excitation response takes place in a few millionths of a second and gives rise to a form of the molecule that is analogous to prelumirhodopsin. The change stops at this point if the temperature is below −110 degrees C. At these low temperatures the molecule can be reconverted into its initial red-absorbing form by the action of light. At temperatures higher than −110 degrees several more intermediate phytochromes are formed before the final far-red-absorbing molecule appears. These intermediate stages also involve alterations in the molecular form of the protein associated with phytochrome, just as there are alterations in the form of opsin, the protein of rhodopsin. In its final form phytochrome differs from rhodopsin in that the molecule of phytochrome remains linked to the protein rather than being dissociated from it. Far-red light will reverse the process and convert the final form of phytochrome back to its initial red-absorbing form, although a different series of intermediate molecular forms is involved.

Flowering, seed germination and most other plant responses follow slowly on the excitation of phytochrome. Unlike vision, in which the response follows the rapid appearance of intermediate molecules, the photoperiodic response of plants depends on the presence of the final, far-red-absorbing form of phytochrome. Little is known about how the far-red-absorbing molecule does its work. One view is that it regulates enzyme production by controlling the genetic material in cell nuclei. Another view is that the molecule's lipid solubility results in its being attached to membranes in the cell, such as the cell wall and the membrane of the nucleus. Changes in the form of the phytochrome

molecule would then affect the permeability of the membranes and therefore the functioning of the cell.

The continuous exposure of plants to blue and far-red wavelengths in the visible spectrum opposes the action of the far-red-absorbing form of the phytochrome molecule. It may be that excitation by far-red light causes a continuous displacement of the far-red-absorbing molecules from cell membranes. Continuous excitation of this kind is what happens, for example, during the long

light periods that so markedly influence the growth of Douglas firs. If the trees are exposed to 12-hour days and 12-hour nights, they remain dormant. If the length of the day increases, however, they grow continuously.

Photoperiodism is not confined to the plant kingdom: animals also respond to changes in the length of the day. The migration and reproduction of many birds, the activity cycles of numerous mammals and the diapause (suspended animation) of insects are controlled in

LONG LIGHT PERIODS markedly influence the growth of Douglas fir. When exposed to short days, or days and nights of equal length, the tree will remain dormant (*left*). Excitation by additional light produces continuous growth. One tree (*center*) received an hour of dim illumination during its 12-hour night; the other (*right*) had its 12-hour day extended by eight hours of dim light.

this way. These examples of photoperiodism (and some less clear-cut responses in man) depend on the action of several hormones working in sequence. Such sequences of hormone action can have a regular rhythm. They provide a basis for the circadian (meaning about one day) rhythms of "biological clocks." The 24-hour cycle of such clocks is established by light.

The diapause of insects illustrates one form of the interplay of hormone action and light. Some silkworms and the larva of the codling moth, for example, go into a dormant form when the days are short. In this state, which helps the insects to survive the winter, the release of a hormone from a group of cells in the central part of the brain is suspended. The unreleased hormone is the first in a series that leads to a final hormone, ecdysone, that controls the metamorphosis of the pupa into an adult moth. When the brain cells of the dormant pupa are exposed to light for long days, the brain hormone is

released and triggers the metamorphosis. Ecdysone injected into a resting pupa brings on metamorphosis even when the days are short.

Here the sole action of the light is the release of a brain hormone. The pigment in the brain cells that absorbs the light has not yet been identified, but current work in the U.S. Department of Agriculture on the response to light by codling moths in diapause promises an answer. The blue-green part of the spectrum (between 500 and 560 nanometers), and probably shorter wavelengths as well, appears to be most effective for breaking diapause. The pigment is possibly of the porphyrin type, with a central structure resembling the ring system of chlorophyll.

Man's dependence on a biological clock is apparent in the unease he feels when the relation of his circadian rhythm to the actual cycle of day and night is quickly disrupted, as it is when he travels by air for distances measured

in many degrees of longitude. His hormonal controls are disturbed or out of phase. Deer mice and other small mammals also display cyclic periods of activity such as running that seem to be regulated by light.

Involved at an early stage in the release of the hormones that trigger activity cycles is the region of the brain known as the hypothalamus. Whether this region contains a pigment receptor for the small amount of light that might penetrate the skull or whether it is stimulated by a signal from the eye, or the region of the eye, is unknown. The hypothalamus also controls the pituitary, hormones from which affect the reproductive organs, the cortex of the adrenal gland and other target organs. At present, however, the existence of a pigment responsible for vertebrate photoperiodism, its physical location and the nature of its action on the molecular level remain to be established.

By exciting a chromophore light acts as a trigger both in vision and in photoperiodism, initiating processes that depend for their energy on the organism's own metabolism. In the third major area of light's interaction with living matter—photosynthesis—the opposite is true: the energy of light is utilized to manufacture the fuels that support life. For this to happen there must be (1) a system to receive the light, (2) an arrangement to transfer energy between molecules and (3) some means of coupling light energy to chemical change. Chlorophyll molecules (or rather the molecules of several chlorophylls that differ in their side groups) constitute the principal receiving system. An electron in the chlorophyll molecule is excited from its normal energy level to a higher level by the impact of visible light. The excited electron reverts to its normal state in less than a hundred-millionth of a second. This reversion might be accomplished by the reemission of visible light, but that, of course, would not advance the photosynthetic process. Instead the reversion proceeds in several steps during which the energy necessary for photosynthesis is transferred along a chain of molecules. A small part of the energy released by the reversion is reemitted as light of a longer wavelength, and hence of lower energy, than the light that was absorbed. (This is the dark red light characteristic emitted by chlorophyll when it is excited to fluorescence.) The remainder of the energy is transferred by way of other chlorophyll molecules to an ultimate recipient, a molecule that receives the energy and effects the chemi-

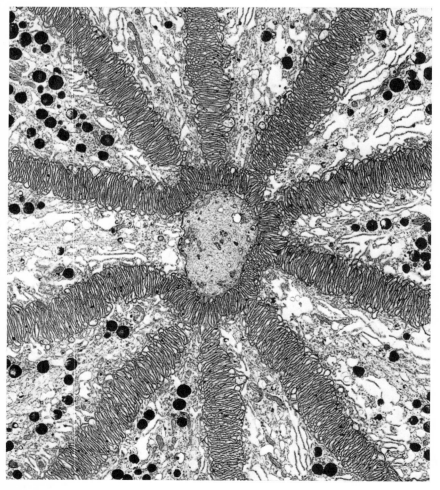

LIGHT-RECEPTOR ORGAN of an invertebrate is enlarged 8,000 times in an electron micrograph. Called an ommatidium, it is one of about 1,000 such units that comprise a horseshoe crab's compound eye. The spokelike arrays and the central ring are photosensitive. William H. Miller of the Yale University School of Medicine made the micrograph.

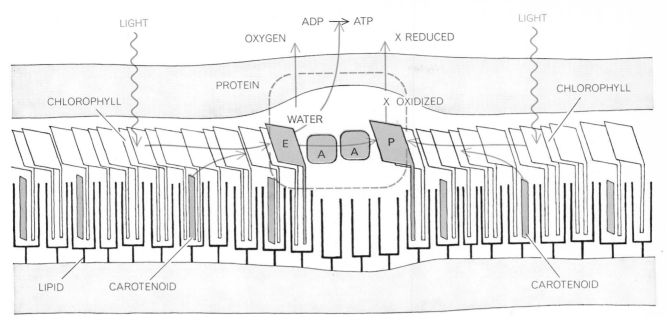

PLANT PHOTORECEPTORS contain molecular arrays, shown here in schematic form. Within the chloroplast, chlorophyll molecules are held together both by their mutual attraction and by the affinity of each molecule's phytol "tail" for lipids and its main body for proteins. Other molecules of pigment, such as carotenoids, are also embedded in the array. For each 500 or so chlorophyll molecules is found a specialized energy-transfer center, comprising two energy sinks, *E* and *P* (*color, center*), linked by a system for transferring electrons, represented here by units labeled *A*. The electron-cascade system by means of which this array of molecules turns energy from light (*colored inward arrows*) into chemical energy (*outward arrows*) is seen in detail in the illustration below.

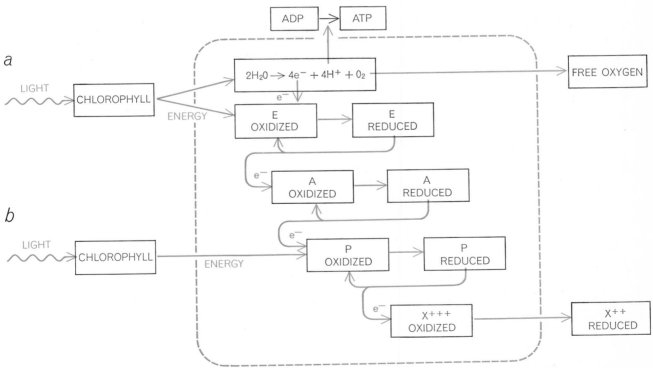

ELECTRON CASCADE that is responsible for the main action of photosynthesis, the use of energy from light to reduce carbon dioxide to sugar, is shown schematically here. Within a zone that contains two energy sinks, *E* and *P*, water and its components (*top rectangle*) are in a state of equilibrium until several chlorophyll molecules pass the energy received from light (*a*) to the first energy sink, *E*. This event starts the cascade; *E*, driven to a higher state of excitation by the energy it receives, seizes an electron (*colored arrow*) from a water component. Next *E* falls back to its lower state; the seized electron is released and cascades onward via the transfer system *A*. It arrives at the second energy sink, *P*, soon after that sink has received energy from other light-excited chlorophyll molecules (*b*). The cascade ends when *P* falls back to its lower state, passing both electron and energy to *X*, an electron-rich compound. The event energizes *X* sufficiently to let it power the carbon dioxide reduction process (*arrow, lower right*); this is the main photosynthetic action. Two other events, however, are also consequences of the cascade. Hydrogen ions (*top arrow*) provide the energy gradient needed to transform adenosine diphosphate (ADP) into adenosine triphosphate (ATP). Similarly, the ion neutralized by the electron loss that initiated the cascade joins with other components to form water, thereby freeing oxygen (*arrow, upper right*).

cal synthesis. For these energy transfers to be efficient the molecules in the chain must meet two criteria. First, they must be physically close together. Second, there must be a close match between the amount of energy available from the donor molecule and the amount acceptable by the recipient.

The plastids of plant cells, the microscopic bodies that contain the chlorophyll pigments, are made up of layered structures known as lamellae that have a high content of protein and lipid [see top illustration on preceding page]. The chlorophyll molecule has one end (the phytol end) that is soluble in lipid and a main body (the chlorophyllin end) that has an affinity for protein. These affinities give rise to a structural system in which the chlorophyll molecules are closely packed.

The lamellae also contain other molecules with conjugated bonds. These include carotenoids that are similar in structural arrangement to retinal, and phycocyanin, which has a chromophore closely related to the chromophore of phytochrome. These accessory molecules also absorb radiant energy and transfer it to the chlorophyll molecules.

The accumulated energy is finally transferred from the chlorophyll molecules to a relatively few molecules that act as energy-trapping "sinks." In each lamella there is about one sink for every 500 chlorophyll molecules. This small number, whereas it effects a desirable parsimony in the systems required for the chemical steps of photosynthesis, constitutes a bottleneck insofar as energy transfer is concerned. When light reach-

es a level of intensity about a fifth the intensity of full sunlight, energy arrives at the sinks faster than it can be utilized. Saturation at this level of intensity is nonetheless a good compromise because the average plant leaf is somewhat shaded and seldom receives energy much above the one-fifth level.

The energy accumulated by the sink molecules is ultimately applied to split water molecules into hydrogen and oxygen and to yield an electron-rich compound, which here I shall call "X," that acts as a final electron-acceptor. An oxidized material (that is, one that has given up electrons) is formed as a waste product. In green plants this material is oxygen. It is as a result of this aspect of photosynthesis that the earth's atmosphere contains the oxygen essential to all animal life.

Measured in terms of its products, the effectiveness of the photosynthetic chemical system decreases as the wavelength of the light being absorbed becomes longer. Absorption in the far-red region of the visible spectrum can be made effective, however, if supplementary light of shorter wavelength is also present. This suggests that two steps are involved in electron transfer rather than one; perhaps two energy sinks work together in some kind of booster action. The processes associated with each type of sink are a subject of current investigation, as is the manner in which electron flow might be coordinated between the two steps.

The electron-transport system, as it is now conceived, can be represented schematically [see illustrations on page 123]. Trapping centers are indicated as points E and P. An electron is thought to be transferred from P to X by one act of light absorption (b): the electron loss leaves P oxidized, whereupon X, the electron-acceptor, becomes an electron-rich, or reduced, compound. In close order a second act of light absorption (a) transfers an electron from water to point E, leaving E electron-rich and leading eventually to free oxygen as the oxidized substance in green plants. The scheme is completed by electron transfer from reduced E to oxidized P. Functioning of the electron transport steps from water to X again requires close association of the necessary parts in the lipid-rich lamellae of the plastids.

The bare skeleton of the scheme serves the purpose of exposition as far as the "photo" part of photosynthesis is concerned, but it leaves much to be told about the "synthesis" part. "Synthesis" implies an output that can be used in a

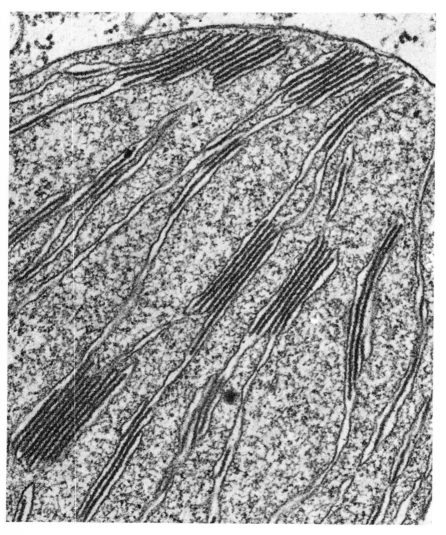

PART OF PHOTOSYNTHETIC ORGAN, a chloroplast of the alga *Nitella*, is seen enlarged 133,000 times in an electron micrograph made by Myron C. Ledbetter of the Brookhaven National Laboratory. Chlorophylls and other pigments involved in the process of photosynthesis are associated with the many lamellae scattered throughout the chloroplast.

life process. Oxygen, although it is an oxidized waste product of the scheme, eventually closes back on the electron-rich compound X through the process of respiration. X is an immediately useful product for reactions outside the lamellae. It serves as the chief energy-transferring agent in the reduction of carbon dioxide to sugar. A further reaction transforms X through intermediates, along with carbon dioxide and water, into electron-poor, or oxidized, X and phosphorus-containing sugars. The reaction needs more energy than can be supplied by X alone. This energy, as well as the needed phosphate, comes from adenosine triphosphate (ATP). ATP is formed by the removal of water from adenosine diphosphate (ADP) and the addition of a phosphate molecule. Energy for the transformation of X is available when the added phosphate of ATP is transferred to some other molecule or is split from ATP by water.

Returning to our illustration of the scheme, it appears that the energy difference in the electron transfer from E to P is adequate to make ATP. This until recently was thought to be the most likely way at least part of a plant's supply of ATP was produced. A view that is now being vigorously debated suggests that hydrogen ions appear inside the lamella in the electron transfer that follows light absorption. The enhanced acidity with respect to the outside of the retaining membrane that the ions inside the membrane provide would give an energy gradient adequate for the formation of ATP. With regard to the first action of light (b), electrons excited by that event can also be transferred through X back to the starting point P with coupling to ATP along the way—a process known as cyclic phosphorylation.

This broad outline of energy transfer in photosynthesis has been developed chiefly during the past 10 years. There is still much to be learned about the molecular details of oxygen liberation, the formation of ATP and the coordination of electron flow in various parts of the process. New discoveries may well alter some of today's concepts of photosynthesis at the most basic level. The situation is much the same with regard to our present understanding of vision and photoperiodism. Examination of the immediate changes after light absorption has proved to be a more fruitful realm of study than the search for the ensuing steps that lead to the responses of sight, growth and biological rhythm.

IV

Light and
Vision

If we are to see things, we must have light. Throughout most of history this has meant primarily sunlight. In the past century or so, many methods of artificial lighting have been discovered and developed for widespread use.

Human eyes are remarkably adaptable, and a person can see in light of many different colors and intensities. But because the eyes are best adapted to viewing objects illuminated by sunlight, vision is most comfortable if the illumination is fairly white, even, and of moderately high intensity. Thus, it is natural for us to use sunlight during the day and to try to approximate it at night. But sunlight itself is highly variable, its intensity, direction, and color depending on the time of day, the season, and the weather. James Marston Fitch describes in his article some of the ways in which architects are using and arranging new materials to provide the right kind of illumination for different visual tasks. For example, when sunlight is too bright, it can be reduced by absorbing or reflective glass, or it can be diverted by baffles of various kinds. For night illumination, indoor and outdoor, many kinds of lamps adapted to particular uses are available.

Upon being illuminated, objects scatter or reflect light, some of which enters the eye and is seen. The lens of the eye focuses the image on the retina, in which complex photochemical processes occur, such as those described by Hendricks in Section III. One is the bleaching of the pigment rhodopsin in the retinal rods by low-intensity light. In other such processes, important at higher intensities, light bleaches the appropriate opsin pigments in the cones, allowing the eye to discriminate colors. As a result of these processes, nerve impulses that somehow correspond to the pattern of light and darkness on the retina are sent to the brain.

The visual information is processed in ways that are still being explored. We do know that only the center of the visual field has good resolution, and also that we are hardly conscious of its lack elsewhere in the eye. What the eye does is to scan in complicated patterns, collecting details. With the aid of cues from the background and from successive views, the viewer interprets the image. In fact, he recognizes shapes even more easily when the eye is moving than when it is stationary. Also, the processes of recalling the image of something seen previously are remarkably similar to those of viewing the scene directly. In recall, too, the eye sometimes moves as details are sought from different parts of the recalled image. These processes of vision are discussed in the article by Ulric Neisser.

E. Llewellen Thomas describes methods used to record eye movements and some results of these observations. The article also gives some indication of the variety of ingenious techniques that are being used in experiments on vision. One remarkable device is a special camera that records the scene as viewed, marking the center of attention with a bright spot. The resultant findings have been noteworthy: for example, we have learned that the periphery of the eye, though less acute, detects interesting objects and forces the eye to look at them, and also that the eye, in searching for one particular object among many, may fixate on the object several times before it is consciously recognized.

Light and Vision

12

The Control of the Luminous Environment

James Marston Fitch   *September 1968*

We live in a luminous environment that is radically new for mankind. Until the 19th century life for most people was geared to the daily period of natural light between sunup and sundown. In George Washington's day 95 percent of Americans were farmers; daylight sufficed for their work, and they went to bed early not only because their hard labor made them sleepy but also because artificial lighting was primitive and expensive, illiteracy was general, books were few and the darkness of night still held much of its primordial menace. A symbolic illustration of the poverty of the luminous environment in the agricultural era is the picture of Abraham Lincoln heroically studying by the flickering light of an open fire.

The industrial revolution changed all of that. It created both the necessity and the means for a new order of artificial illumination. Machines could, and for efficient use should, be run around the clock. It became necessary not only to light up the nighttime but also to provide controlled illumination for the close and precise vision to which man now had to adapt himself—for operating machines and instruments, for reading and for the universal education that became an economic as well as a social and political necessity.

Today the majority of us work and spend most of our time in buildings, where the proper handling of daylight and the provision of artificial lighting are a *sine qua non*. In response to such needs artificial lighting, for both indoor and outdoor purposes, has been developed into a large and imaginative industry. Yet it cannot be said that many of the lighting systems are particularly well suited to the requirements of the job or to the health and comfort of the human eye. For one thing, they are often designed for appearance or for economy rather than for the utilitarian functions they are supposed to serve. For another thing, all too little study has been given to the psychology and physiology of vision in relation to illumination.

Within the visible portion of the spectrum the human eye is most sensitive to the yellow-green wavelengths at about 570 nanometers. The range of energies to which it responds is remarkable: the unaided eye can detect a lighted candle at a distance of 14 miles and at the other extreme is able to resolve the details of a landscape flooded by 8,000 foot-candles of sunshine. (The amount of light falling on a surface is measured in foot-candles; the reflected light, or brightness, of the surface is measured in foot-lamberts.) These figures refer to the responses of the normal eye under ordinary conditions; the actual performance of the visual system will vary, of course, according to external and internal circumstances, including stresses on the eye or fatigue. The causes and mechanism of visual fatigue are not entirely clear, but it is known that the fatigue rate rises in direct proportion to the dimming of the visual field; in other words, the brighter the illumination, the less the eye tires. The fatigue rate is also affected, however, by other factors, such as the distribution, direction and color of the light.

Generally speaking, the eye is most comfortable when the visual field has no great contrasts. This does not mean that it responds well to a field of uniform brightness; objects seen under diffuse light, for example, are difficult to make out. For optimal eye comfort the visual stimuli should vary somewhat in space and time but not strongly enough to produce stress. For tasks requiring fairly fine vision (such as proofreading, sewing or watch-repairing) the work should be illuminated by 100 to 150 foot-candles, and the surrounding surfaces should have a brightness of at least one-third of this value (35 to 45 foot-candles). Of course, many tasks require far higher levels of illumination: a surgeon at the operating table, for example, may need 1,000 foot-candles.

Apart from miscellaneous items of information such as these, the architect and the designer of illumination systems have little in the way of research findings on visual requirements to guide them in the creation of luminous environments for present-day needs. The questions that still need answers are numerous and important. It would be useful to know, for instance, if illumination should be increased as the day goes on and workers' eyes tire. What are the most effective forms of lighting for particular tasks? What is the optimal mix of natural and artificial illumination in the modern urban environment?

Illumination engineers tend to favor establishing complete control over the

FOUR PANES OF GLASS that modify daylight in different ways frame part of the midtown Manhattan skyline in the photograph on the opposite page. At top left is water-white glass; it absorbs no colors and transmits nearly 90 percent of the outdoor light. The other panes are examples of the wide range of "environmental" glasses available to architects today. The bronze-tinted glass (*top right*) transmits 51 percent of the light, the neutral gray glass (*bottom left*) 42 percent and the blue-green glass (*bottom right*) 75 percent. Environmental glasses also reject a large percentage of solar heat, thereby reducing the load on interior cooling systems. The glasses seen in the photograph are made by PPG Industries, Inc.

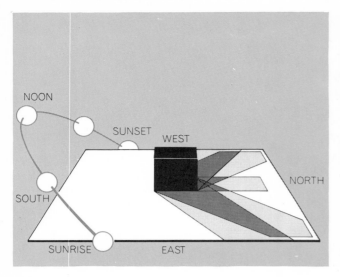

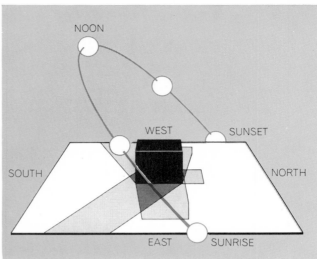

MOVEMENT OF THE SUN across the sky differs in azimuth and elevation with the seasons. The examples shown are summer (*left*) and winter (*right*) at 40 degrees north latitude. The seasonal variations alter the amount of solar energy that impinges on buildings.

luminous environment by employing fully artificial lighting in windowless buildings. For some functions this is obviously appropriate and essential. An outstanding example is the assembly tower at Cape Kennedy where the vehicle for the moon mission is to be constructed. In this structure (the world's largest building) the necessity for absolute control of all the environmental conditions is such that the enclosure must be hermetically sealed. For most purposes, however, the windowless building seems not only impracticable but also undesirable. Apart from the question of cost (involving the expense of the lighting system and the cooling needed to remove the waste heat

it produces), people do not relish being cooped up in a windowless building. Human vision and well-being apparently suffer when vision is restricted to the shallow frame of man-made perspectives and is denied the deep views of nature. The eye wants variety in the optical conditions and freedom for occasional idle scanning of a visual field broader than the work at hand. In the home and at work people hunger for view windows, if only to "see what the weather is like outside." And in many activities windows serve an essential function, for looking out or in or for both; one need only mention stores, banks, lobbies and airport control towers. Although artifi-

cial lighting will inevitably come into increasing use, the windowless building will certainly remain a special case.

Let us begin, then, with the first consideration in the illumination of a building interior: the appropriate use of sunlight. For this an architect now has a large variety of devices at his command. The first step, of course, is suitable orientation of the building toward the sun, so that sunlight will be admitted through transparent walls where it is wanted or excluded by opaque walls where it is not wanted, and a maximum of indirect daylight can be obtained throughout the day in parts of the building where direct

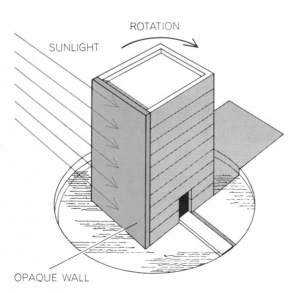

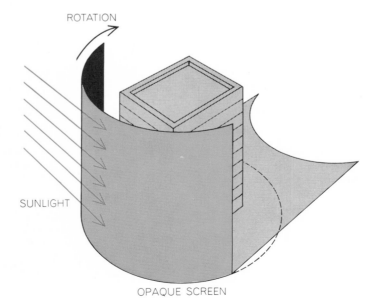

RADICAL SOLUTIONS to the problem of unwanted solar energy include construction of a revolving building (*left*) that would present the same windowless wall to the sun all day long, or a revolving sun screen (*right*) that would always intercept the sun's rays.

sunlight is undesirable. In regions of intense sunlight, such as the U.S. Southwest, or of feeble winter sunshine, such as the Canadian Arctic, effective use of the sunshine may be important not only for lighting but also for heating. Elsewhere, as in Lower California or the Persian Gulf region, cooling requirements demand that the building's interior be shielded from the sun. In any case, the orientation problem of course is complicated by the sun's movement across the sky and the seasonal variations in its angle. There are several possible means of coping with this movement. The building might be placed on a turntable that rotated it slowly in synchronization with the sun. Where the sunlight can be used for heating as well as lighting such a device might be economically feasible, particularly if an efficient and relatively frictionless turning apparatus were developed to minimize the power required to rotate the structure. Alternatively, the control of sunlight might be accomplished by a simpler mechanism: a solar screen that would run on a track and move around the building with the sun. It could be applied to large buildings as well as small and might serve as a windbreak in cold or stormy weather.

Both of these ideas, although still rather speculative, are actually extensions of a device that is already in fairly common use: namely, external sun shields consisting of large vanes that, like those of venetian blinds, can be changed in angle to keep out or let in sunlight as the sun shifts. With electronic controls these screens can rotate automatically in response to the sun's movement. They are particularly useful in warm, dry climates, where they are not subject to freezing or corrosion. Screens of this kind give far more satisfactory protection against the sun than the now common practice of building overhangs for windows, which often are more photogenic than useful because they do not allow sufficiently for variations in the angle of the sun.

Ralph Knowles of the University of Southern California has done some pioneering research on the surface responses of buildings to environmental forces—light, heat, gravity, air and sound. Using computerized techniques of analysis, he studied the surface response to light of structures in various shapes (cubic, tetrahedral, ellipsoidal and so on) and with various patterns of opaque walls. He concluded that rational parameters for the architectural control of sunlight effects and of other forces could be established. He is now studying the possibility

of extending the same criteria to the modification of environmental forces not only for buildings but also for urban districts and even entire cities.

Knowles's approach is to use the structure itself as a means of manipulation and control of daylight. Since structural materials are necessarily opaque, the effectiveness of the system depends on the way the geometry of the wall itself intercepts direct light or admits indirect light. There are now, however, a wide variety of nonstructural surfacing materials of every degree of transparency that can be employed as filters. Even with ordinary plate glass one can obtain certain desired effects simply by adjusting the orientation or shape of the glass window.

Curved glass that eliminates direct reflection of the bright outdoors can make a store window invisible for an observer looking in from the street; a glass wall angled from the vertical can likewise minimize disturbing reflections from indoor light sources and thus give a clear outward view, as in the famous Top of the Mark restaurant in San Francisco overlooking the city and the Golden Gate or the more mundane instance of airport control towers. Much more exciting, of course, are the effects now achievable with special glasses and other materials that filter, polarize, refract or focus light and thereby select the wavelengths of light to be admitted to the building or place the light where it is wanted.

GEOMETRY OF PROTECTION against unwanted solar radiation is studied by means of a model made at the Department of Architecture of Auburn University under the direction of Ralph Knowles. The design uses interlocking planes both to control the sunlight and to transfer building loads to the ground. J. H. R. Brady and D. L. Meador made the model.

CONTROL OF LIGHT AND HEAT is achieved at the Los Angeles Hall of Records by vertical louvers that resemble a venetian blind turned sideways. The angle at which the louvers are set is adjusted monthly to provide maximum shade throughout the year. Architects were Neutra and Alexander, Honnold and Rex, H. C. Light and James R. Friend.

The most familiar example—glass that is transparent to visible light but that blocks the infrared wavelengths—is now in wide use; in recent years it has been joined by new families of glasses and plastics that afford more subtle manipulations of sunlight.

One of the new glasses, coated with a thin film of metal on the inside face, acts as a one-way mirror, thus cloaking the interior of the building in privacy from outside observers in daytime while allowing the people inside to look out. (Actually on a bright day the exterior reflections on ordinary plate glass have much the same effect, making the interior almost as invisible to outsiders as if it were sheathed in polished granite.) The one-way mirror glass not only dispenses with the need for curtains or shades in daytime but also appears to be effective in blocking the entry of heat radiation.

A new type of glass now under development promises to introduce a novel mechanism for the management of sunlight. The glasses of this breed, called photochromic, are darkened by ultraviolet light, and oddly enough their reaction is reversible: as the ultraviolet intensity decreases, they recover their transparency proportionately. Hence the glass can maintain the intensity of the sunlight entering the building at a stable level. It should prove useful for classrooms, control towers, libraries and museums, where visual transparency is mandatory and a stable mix of natural and artificial light is desirable but difficult to maintain.

Another sophisticated innovation is embodied in a light-polarizing material formed by layers of plastics. It clarifies seeing and improves the efficiency of the use of light. Under ordinary illumination a surface is partly obscured by a "veil" of reflected light that tends to blur the colors and textures of the surface. Vertically plane-polarized light, which is absorbed by a surface and then reemitted, eliminates this veil and makes it possible to see the true qualities of the surface with greater ease and more accuracy. Polarized glass such as is used in sunglasses is not suitable, however, for purposes of illumination; it is effective only in certain directions, absorbs more than 50 percent of the light, is unpleasantly tinted and cannot be frosted to hide the light-bulb filament or soften the light. The new multilayer plastic polarizer avoids these shortcomings. The glare-reducing effect of this material on the illuminated surface varies, however, with the angle of vision from which it is viewed. Most desk work is done at angles between 0 and 40 degrees from the vertical, with the peak at 25 degrees, whereas the polarizer's most dramatic effects are from 40 degrees up, that is, in the field of middle vision. The plastic polarizer is not weatherproof and can only be used indoors, where it could serve well in ceiling fixtures and perhaps inside glass walls and skylights for daylight illumination of galleries and museums.

Another broadly applicable material for the manipulation of daylight is the so-called prismatic glass. Available in both sheet and block, it can deliver the incident daylight to any desired area of a room. It can be particularly useful for work that must be done under glareless light, such as matching colors, for illuminating paintings and for dramatic effects such as focusing a narrow beam of sunlight on an object—the "finger of God" effect that was cultivated by the baroque architects.

The sophisticated exploitation of sunlight is now more than matched by the ingenious exploitation of the possibilities of artificial illumination. Electricity, which in this century has supplanted all other sources of artificial lighting, has endowed us with an almost incredibly varied range of illumination devices.

Lamps, fixtures, accessories, controls and methods of disseminating light are available in great variety, and their permutations and combinations run into the thousands. The list of ways that have been found to generate light by electricity is itself a long one.

The first electric-lighting device was the arc lamp, which jumps a bridge of luminous current across the gap between two electrodes. Much too hot and inflexible to be used in interior lighting, it is employed principally for motion-picture and television photography, for illumination of parking lots and playing fields and in large searchlights. The second-oldest electric lamp is the incandescent filament (now made of tungsten) enclosed in a sealed glass bulb. It is inefficient: only 10 percent of its energy output is in the form of light (the rest being lost as heat) and an additional proportion of the light will be absorbed by any colored bulb or filter that is used to modify its yellow-white color. The incandescent lamp is so flexible and convenient, however, and is available in such a wide range of sizes, shapes and capacities that it is still by far the most popular type for general lighting, and its efficiency has been improved nearly tenfold in recent decades.

Artificial lighting is now largely dominated by the new and growing family of lamps based on the electrical excitation of luminous vapors, which already predominate in the fields of commercial, industrial and outdoor illumination. Sodium-vapor lamps, yielding an efficient output of 45 to 55 lumens of light per watt of power, have come into common use for the lighting of highways and bridges. Neon lamps in various colors, used mainly for signs, have become a ubiquitous—too ubiquitous—feature of the nighttime landscape. The most efficient of the vapor lamps are those employing mercury vapor; some produce more than 100 lumens per watt of power. Excited mercury atoms emit light at the blue-green end of the visible spectrum and into the near ultraviolet. Hence mercury-vapor lamps can be designed to serve as sunlamps, as light sources of high intensity or as fluorescent lamps, in which the ultraviolet emission from the mercury atoms is used to generate visible light from fluorescent material coated on the inside of a glass tube. The comparative coolness of a fluorescent lamp arises from the fact that mercury emits almost no energy at the red end of the spectrum and fluorescent emission itself possesses very little

SHADE WITHOUT SHADOW is obtained in the interior of the Van Leer Building in Amstelveen in the Netherlands by suspending horizontal panels of light- and heat-resistant glass at a distance from the southern wall of the building. Convection currents rise between the panels and the wall and help to dissipate the solar heat accumulation. The architects were Marcel Breuer and Associates.

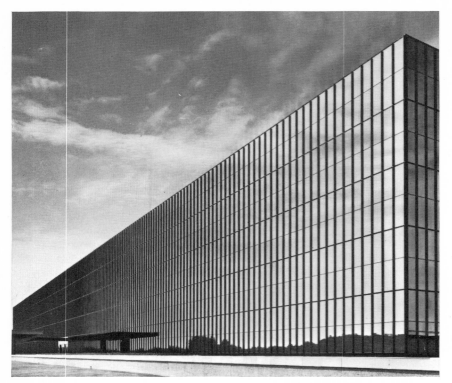

OPAQUE IN DAYLIGHT, the glass walls of the Bell Telephone Laboratories building at Holmdel, N.J., are mirrors to an observer standing outside the building. The building's occupants, however, have a clear, shaded view of the exterior. A thin metallic film deposited on one surface of the glass acts as a mirror on the side that is most strongly illuminated.

TRANSPARENT BY NIGHT, the Holmdel building emits a glow of light once the level of exterior illumination falls below that of the interior. The interior walls are now mirrors to the occupants. The glass rejects nearly 80 percent of the solar heat load. It is made by the Kinney Division of the New York Air Brake Co. Architects were Eero Saarinen and Associates.

heat. A fluorescent tube is only about a fourth or a fifth as hot as the ordinary filament lamp. Moreover, it produces from 25 to 75 lumens per watt, depending on the color, and it makes available a wide range of color in lighting, including a close approximation of the daylight spectrum. The linear shape of a fluorescent tube does not necessarily limit it to linear applications. The tube itself can be bent into circular, square or spiral forms; it can be installed in parallel rows, in conjunction with appropriate reflectors and diffusers, and it can be made into a planar light source ("luminous ceiling").

Given the present variety of sources and of accessory means of disseminating artificial light, one has indeed a great range of flexibility for adapting its application to particular needs and situations. The problem of specifying and evaluating the requirements in given cases is of course highly complicated; every lighting problem involves a number of factors, subjective as well as objective. There are, however, a few helpful principles that seem well established.

The first is that, as I have already mentioned, good seeing demands a high level of illumination. Within broad limits, the more light there is on the visual task, the easier vision becomes and the less stressful the task is on the organism as a whole. The second "law" of good lighting is that all areas of the room should be balanced in brightness, with no great contrasts between adjacent surfaces. The visual field surrounding the task should be at least a third as bright as the task itself and no part of it should be much brighter than the task. The third principle is that it is important to avoid glare, either from the light source or by reflection.

The optimal levels of illumination for specific visual tasks have not by any means been finally established; the recommended levels have steadily been raised over the past half-century and may well go higher still. Tasks that were once performed at only 10 to 15 footcandles are now believed to call for 100 to 200 foot-candles. For certain fine seeing tasks, such as microsurgery and autopsy, illumination as high as 2,500 footcandles is recommended. Incidentally, as illumination levels rise, the generated heat becomes more and more of a problem. In a space under 100 foot-candles of illumination the heat from the lamps may account for 37 percent of the load on the air-conditioning system in summer, and at the level of 400 foot-candles

SELF-DARKENING GLASS contains microscopic crystals of silver halide that react to near-ultraviolet wavelengths by absorbing as much as 75 percent of visible light. A masked pane of the glass is exposed to sunlight (top left). Its unmasked central rectangle darkens immediately (top right). Screened from further exposure to ultraviolet, the darkened area begins to fade; in five minutes it transmits about half as much light as the unexposed area (bottom left). In half an hour the darkened area has vanished (bottom right). Known as photochromic glass, the light-responsive material is made by the Corning Glass Works.

GLASS BRICK provides the architect with a translucent medium for bringing daylight indoors. At eye level or below, brick that acts as a general diffuser of daylight (left) is a practical wall material. Above eye level, prism-surfaced brick directs entering light up to ceilings to provide overall daylight (right). Bricks are made by the Pittsburgh Corning Corp.

the contribution to the cooling load may rise to 70 percent. When waste heat reaches such proportions, it becomes a major factor in summer cooling. By the same token, it can be employed in winter heating, sometimes to the extent of becoming the entire source of heat. In these installations current practice is to siphon off this heat before it enters the conditioned space, either exhausting it in summer or feeding it back to the heating system in winter. Since such installations usually involve fluorescent tubing used in luminous ceilings, there is less waste heat and less of it is radiant. As much as 76 percent can be siphoned off directly into the return air system.

For many lighting problems, particularly on the macroscale, there are no readily determinable criteria, nor have they been given much systematic study. The illumination of retail stores and showrooms, for example, involves subtleties in dramatizing the qualities of the merchandise. (Obviously jewelry and automobiles need point sources for shine and glitter; furs and velvets show up best under floodlighting at acute angles.) Restaurants, bars and cafés have their own special lighting needs; so do art galleries and museums, theaters and churches, exposition buildings and pleasure gardens. Whether or not the purely intuitive approach in creating "effects" in these situations produces truly effective results is a moot question. The vogue of "mood" lighting in restaurants and cafés, where current taste seems to dictate that the illumination level be low and the color pink, has the unfortunate effect of making one's companions only dimly visible and laying an unappetizing patina on food and complexions.

Just as a blind architect would be a contradiction in terms, so too would be a completely lightless room (tombs and photographic darkrooms would be among the few exceptions). All designed spaces are conceived in visual terms. Many of the architect's decisions as to interior proportions, colors and textures actually deal with matters of surface response to light. They are all made with an eye to "how it all will look." Such a conceptual approach assumes that a stable luminous state is desirable, that the room will "read" the same way day and night, winter and summer.

In any windowless enclosure this is a simple matter, but in any room where glass plays an important role the situation is entirely altered. Such transparent membranes are conceived as (1) being a source of light and (2) affording visual access to an illuminated outdoors. With

IMPROVEMENTS in new kinds of lamps include an increase in light emission per watt input and longer life. Two new lamps are compared here with the familiar incandescent household lamp (*left*). All three are drawing approximately 250 watts; distance of each lamp from the equally illuminated targets indicates its light output. This is 16.5 lumens per watt for the incandescent lamp, more than 80 for the sodium-vapor lamp (*center*) and 17.5 for the tungsten halide lamp (*right*). The tungsten halide lamp has a 2,000-hour life expectancy.

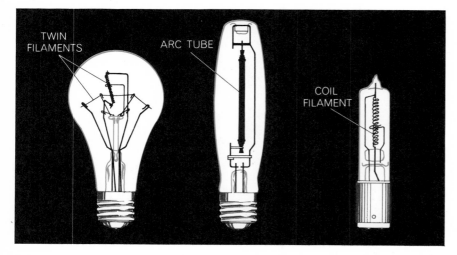

TWIN FILAMENTS

ARC TUBE

COIL FILAMENT

ANATOMY OF ADVANCED LAMPS is compared with that of a two-filament, three-way incandescent lamp (*left*). In the high-intensity sodium-vapor lamp (*center*) the vapor is contained in a translucent ceramic tube sturdy enough to allow operation at a temperature and pressure that spread the sodium-emission wavelengths over most of the visible spectrum. The filament of the tungsten halide lamp (*right*) is sealed in a quartz tube containing iodine gas; evaporating tungsten reacts with the gas and is redeposited on the filament, thereby increasing its life. The lamps are the ones shown in the photograph at top of page.

nightfall, however, both of these conditions change. Surfaces that were a source of light become open sluices for its escape, and the lighted outdoors is replaced by a dimly mirrored image of the room. Traditional architecture had no real difficulty with this paradox. Although natural lighting was very important, the high cost of glass and of heating tended to keep windows small or few. And since the windows were always covered at night with curtains or blinds whose reflectance value approached that of the walls, they did not seriously affect the luminous response of the walls.

In modern architecture, with its wide use of glass walls and wide misconceptions of their optical behavior, the problem of nocturnal disequilibrium reaches serious dimensions. In such cases the interior can only be restored to its daytime shape by one of two measures: (1) by covering the glass with a reflective membrane (shade, shutter or blind) and (2) by raising the illumination level outside the glass to that of the room itself. Both measures are technically quite feasible, although for obvious reasons the first is likely to be the simplest and least costly.

The uninhibited excursions in lighting at recent international expositions have demonstrated the great variety and brilliance of lighting effects that are now available through the use of color, both luminous and pigmental. There is a large and growing literature on the alleged subjective reactions to color. We are told that red is exciting, purple is stately or mournful, yellow is joyful, green is calming, and so forth. There are even reports on experiments in the therapeutic use of color for treatment of the mentally ill. The University of California at Los Angeles psychologist Robert M. Gerard, working with normal adults, has found that as a general rule people do indeed show differential responses to different colors. Red light apparently brings about a rise in blood pressure, respiration rate and frequency of blinking; blue light, on the other hand, depresses activity. He concludes that the entire organism is affected by color, that different colors evoke different emotions and degrees of activity and that activity rises with increases in the wavelength and the intensity of the light.

Nighttime illumination of the outdoors by artificial light is another factor with a profound potential for affecting human life and activity. It is hard for us to imagine how great a transformation of living was introduced by this development. In preindustrial times nightfall brought general movement and activity almost to a complete halt. For understandable reasons about the first application of gas and electrical illumination was for streetlights. The illumination of the urban environment at night doubled the daily period of mobility and activity for city dwellers. Moreover, it added a totally new aspect to the urban landscape.

Outdoor lighting has been carried further in the U.S. than anywhere else in the world; if not the best lighted, American cities are the *most* lighted on earth. Seen from the air on a clear night, with their structure vividly diagrammed by millions of lamps and illuminated signs, they are beautiful. Unfortunately at ground level the beauty and the clarity disappear. Grotesquely disparate in size and brightness, jostling one another in crowded profusion, garish and discordant in color, the lamps and signs are confusing to pedestrians, dangerously distracting to motorists and annoying to residents who must live in their nightly glare.

There are models showing how cities and their contents can be illuminated with highly aesthetic effects. The skillful lighting of the areas around Westminster Cathedral in London and the Louvre in Paris, of the Capitol in Washington and the Acropolis in Athens and of châteaus and gardens in France illustrates the possibilities in the urban use of illumination for spectacle. Most of these places are of course empty monuments. For inhabited areas of the city, designing systems of street and landscape lighting that will be functional but not disturbing to the residents is a more difficult and delicate matter. With skill and imagination, however, it should be possible to illuminate buildings, neighborhoods and the entire city in ways that will serve and satisfy everyone.

It is apparent that the nature of the luminous environment exerts profound physiological, psychological, social and economic effects on life in our urban culture. So far neither the effects nor the possible means of ameliorating them have been adequately analyzed. Obviously the establishment of a harmonious relation between man and his new environment of artificial illumination calls for cooperative studies by physical and biological scientists, engineers and architects.

NIGHT LIGHTING of New York's George Washington Bridge shows contrast between the illumination from mercury and sodium high-intensity lamps. When the photograph was made, lamp standards over outbound lanes (*left*) contained 400-watt mercury-vapor lamps and those over inbound lanes (*right*) 400-watt sodium-vapor lamps. The illumination of the inbound lanes is two to three times brighter than the illumination of the outbound lanes.

13

The Processes of Vision

Ulric Neisser *September 1968*

It was Johannes Kepler who first compared the eye to a "camera" (a darkened chamber) with an image in focus on its rear surface. "Vision is brought about by pictures of the thing seen being formed on the white concave surface of the retina," he wrote in 1604. A generation later René Descartes tried to clinch this argument by direct observation. In a hole in a window shutter he set the eye of an ox, just in the position it would have had if the ox had been peering out. Looking at the back of the eye (which he had scraped to make it transparent), he could see a small inverted image of the scene outside the window.

Since the 17th century the analogy between eye and camera has been elaborated in numerous textbooks. As an account of functional anatomy the analogy is not bad, but it carries some unfortunate implications for the study of vision. It suggests all too readily that the perceiver is in the position of Descartes and is in effect looking through the back of his own retina at the pictures that appear there. We use the same word—"image"—for both the optical pattern thrown on the retina by an object and the mental experience of seeing the object. It has been all too easy to treat this inner image as a copy of the outer one, to think of perceptual experiences as images formed by the nervous system acting as an optical instrument of extraordinarily ingenious design. Although this theory encounters insurmountable difficulties as soon as it is seriously considered, it has dominated philosophy and psychology for many years.

Not only perception but also memory has often been explained in terms of an image theory. Having looked at the retinal picture, the perceiver supposedly files it away somehow, as one might put a photograph in an album. Later, if he is lucky, he can take it out again in the form of a "memory image" and look at it a second time. The widespread notion that some people have a "photographic memory" reflects this analogy in a particularly literal way, but in a weaker form it is usually applied even to ordinary remembering. The analogy suggests that the mechanism of visual memory is a natural extension of the mechanisms of vision. Although there is some truth to this proposition, as we shall see below, it is not because both perception and memory are copying processes. Rather it is because *neither* perception *nor* memory is a copying process.

The fact is that one does not see the retinal image; one sees with the aid of the retinal image. The incoming pattern of light provides information that the nervous system is well adapted to pick up. This information is used by the perceiver to guide his movements, to anticipate events and to construct the internal representations of objects and of space called "conscious experience." These internal representations are not, however, at all like the corresponding optical images on the back of the eye. The retinal images of specific objects are at the mercy of every irrelevant change of position; their size, shape and location are hardly constant for a moment. Nevertheless, perception is usually accurate: real objects appear rigid and stable and appropriately located in three-dimensional space.

The first problem in the study of visual perception is therefore the discovery of the stimulus. What properties of the incoming optic array are informative for vision? In the entire distribution of light, over the retina and over a period of time, what determines the way things look? (Actually the light is distributed over two retinas, but the binocularity of vision has no relevance to the variables considered here. Although depth perception is more accurate with two eyes than with one, it is not fundamentally different. The world looks much the same with one eye closed as it does with both open; congenitally monocular people have more or less the same visual experiences as the rest of us.)

As a first step we can consider the patterns of reflected light that are formed when real objects and surfaces are illuminated in the ordinary way by

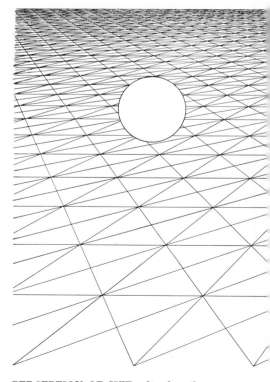

PERCEPTION OF SIZE relies heavily on cues provided by a textured surface. These five disks, if seen alone, would appear to lie

sunshine or lamplight. J. J. Gibson of Cornell University, who has contributed much to our understanding of perception, calls this inquiry "ecological optics." It is an optics in which point sources, homogeneous fields and the other basic elements of classical optics rarely appear. Instead the world we ordinarily look at consists mostly of *surfaces,* at various angles and in various relations to one another. This has significant consequences for the visual input.

One of these consequences (the only one we shall examine here) is to give the visual field a microstructure. Most surfaces have some kind of texture, such as the grain in wood, the individual stalks of grass in a field or the weave in a fabric. These textures structure the light reaching the eye in a way that carries vital information about the layout of environmental objects. In accordance with the principles of perspective the texture elements of more distant surfaces are represented closer to one another on the retina than the elements of surfaces nearby. Thus the microstructure of a surface that slants away from the observer is represented on the retina as a gradient of density—a gradient that carries information about the orientation of the surface.

Consider now an ordinary scene in which discrete figures are superposed on textured surfaces. The gradient of increasing texture density on the retina, corresponding to increasing distance from the observer, gives a kind of "scale" for object sizes. In the ideal case when the texture units are identical, two figures of the same real size will always occlude the same number of texture units, regardless of how far away either one may be. That is, the relation between the retinal texture-size and the dimensions of the object's retinal image is invariant, in spite of changes of distance. This relation is a potentially valuable source of information about the real size of the object—more valuable than the retinal image of the object considered alone. That image, of course, changes in dimension whenever the distance between the object and the observer is altered.

Psychologists have long been interested in what is called "size constancy": the fact that the sizes of real objects are almost always perceived accurately in spite of the linear dependence of retinal-image size on distance. It must not be supposed that this phenomenon is fully explained by the scaling of size with respect to texture elements. There are a great many other sources of relevant information: binocular parallax, shifts of retinal position as the observer moves,

relative position in the visual field, linear perspective and so on. It was once traditional to regard these sources of information as "cues" secondary to the size of the object's own retinal image. That is, they were thought to help the observer "correct" the size of the retinal image in the direction of accuracy. Perhaps this is not a bad description of Descartes's situation as he looked at the image on the back of the ox's eye: he may have tried to "correct" his perception of the size of the objects revealed to him on the ox's retina. Since one does not see one's own retina, however, nothing similar need be involved in normal perceiving. Instead the apparent size of an object is determined by information from the entire incoming light pattern, particularly by certain properties of the input that remain invariant with changes of the object's location.

The interrelation of textures, distances and relative retinal sizes is only one example of ecological optics. The example may be a misleadingly simple one, because it assumes a stationary eye, an eye fixed in space and stably oriented in a particular direction. This is by no means a characteristic of human vision. In normal use the eyes are rarely still for long. Apart from small tremors, their

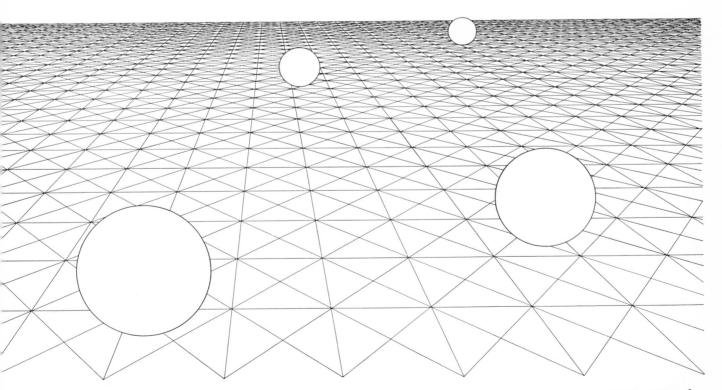

in one plane and be of different sizes. Against this apparently receding surface, however, they seem to lie in five different planes. Since each disk masks the same amount of surface texture, there is a tendency to see them as being equal in size. This illustration, the one at the bottom of the next two pages and the one on page 144 are based on the work of J. J. Gibson of Cornell University.

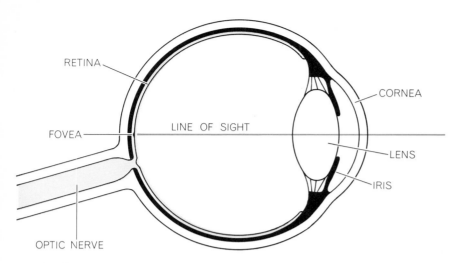

RETINA

FOVEA

LINE OF SIGHT

OPTIC NERVE

CORNEA

LENS

IRIS

SITE OF OPTICAL IMAGE is the retina, which contains the terminations of the optic nerve. In the tiny retinal depression known as the fovea the cone nerve endings are clustered. Their organization and dense packing make possible a high degree of visual acuity.

most common movement is the flick from one position to another called a "saccade." Saccades usually take less than a twentieth of a second, but they happen several times each second in reading and may be just as frequent when a picture or an actual scene is being inspected. This means that there is a new retinal image every few hundred milliseconds.

Such eye movements are necessary because the area of clear vision available to the stationary eye is severely limited. To see this for oneself it is only necessary to fixate on a point in some unfamiliar picture or on an unread printed page. Only a small region around the fixation point will be clear. Most of the page is seen peripherally, which means that it is hazily visible at best. Only in the fovea, the small central part of the retina, are the receptor cells packed close enough together (and appropriately organized) to make a high degree of visual acuity possible. This is the reason one must turn one's eyes (or head) to look directly at objects in which one is particularly interested. (Animals with non-foveated eyes, such as the horse, do not find this necessary.) It is also the reason why the eye must make several fixations on each line in reading, and why it roves widely over pictures.

Although it is easy to understand the function of saccadic movements, it is difficult or impossible to reconcile them with an image theory of perception. As long as we think of the perceiver as a homunculus looking at his retinal image, we must expect his experience to be one of almost constant interruption and change. Clearly this is not the case; one sees the page or the scene as a whole without any apparent discontinuity in

space or time. Most people are either unaware of their own eye movements or have erroneous notions about them. Far from being a copy of the retinal display, the visual world is somehow *constructed* on the basis of information taken in during many different fixations.

The same conclusion follows, perhaps even more compellingly, if we consider the motions of external objects rather than the motions of the eyes. If the analogy between eye and camera were valid, the thing one looked at would have to hold still like a photographer's model in order to be seen clearly. The opposite is true: far from obscuring the shapes and spatial relations of things, movement generally clarifies them. Consider the visual problem presented by a distant arrow-shaped weather vane. As long as the weather vane and the observer remain motionless, there is no way to tell whether it is a short arrow oriented at right angles to the line of sight or a longer arrow slanting toward (or away from) the observer. Let it begin to turn in the wind, however, and its true shape and orientation will become visible immediately. The reason lies in the systematic distortions of the retinal image produced by the object's rotation. Such distortions provide information that the nervous system can use. On the basis of a fluidly changing retinal pattern the perceiver comes to experience a rigid object. (An interesting aspect of this example is that the input information is ambiguous. The same retinal changes could be produced by either a clockwise or a counterclockwise rotation of the weather vane. As a result the perceiver may alternate between two perceptual experiences, one of which is illusory.)

Some years ago Hans Wallach and D. N. O'Connell of Swarthmore College showed that such motion-produced changes in the input are indeed used as a source of information in perceiving; in fact this kind of information seems to be a more potent determiner of what we see than the traditionally emphasized cues for depth are. In their experiment the subject watched the shadow of a wire form cast on a translucent screen. He could not see the object itself. So long as the object remained stationary the subject saw only a two-dimensional shadow on a two-dimensional screen, as might be expected. The form was mounted in such a way, however, that it could be swiveled back and forth by a small electric motor. When the motor was turned on, the true three-dimensional shape of the form appeared at once, even though the only stimulation reaching the subject's eyes came from a distorting shadow on a flat screen. Here the kinetic depth effect, as it has been called, overrode binocular stereoscopic information that continued to indicate that all the movement was taking place in a flat plane.

In the kinetic depth effect the constructive nature of perception is particularly apparent. What one sees is somehow a composite based on information accumulated over a period of time. The same is true in reading or in any instance where eye movements are involved: information from past fixations is used together with information from the present fixation to determine what is seen. But if perception is a temporally extended act, some storage of information, some kind of memory, must be involved in it. How shall we conceive of this storage? How is it organized? How

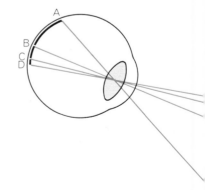

A

B

C

D

CONTRACTION OF IMAGE takes place as the distance between the viewer and the

long does it last? What other functions might it serve?

With questions like these, we have moved beyond the problem of specifying the visual stimulus. In addition to identifying the sources of information for vision, we want to know how that information is processed. In the long run, perhaps, questions about processes should be answered in neurological terms. However, no such answers can be given at present. The neurophysiology of vision has recently made great strides, but it is still not ready to deal with the constructive processes that are central to perception. We shall have to be content with a relatively abstract account, one that does not specify the neural locus of the implicated mechanisms.

Although seeing requires storage of information, this memory cannot be thought of as a sequence of superposed retinal images. Superposition would give rise only to a sort of smear in which all detail is lost. Nor can we assume that the perceiver keeps careful track of his eye movements and thus is able to set each new retinal image in just the right place in relation to the older stored ones. Such an alignment would require a much finer monitoring of eye motion than is actually available. Moreover, the similar synthesis of information that is involved in the kinetic depth effect could not possibly be explained that way. It seems, therefore, that perceiving involves a memory that is not representational but schematic. During a series of fixations the perceiver synthesizes a model or schema of the scene before him, using information from each successive fixation to add detail or to extend the construction. This constructed whole is what guides his

movements (including further eye movements in many cases) and it is what he describes when he is being introspective. In short, it is what he sees.

Interestingly enough, although the memory involved in visual synthesis cannot consist simply of stored retinal afterimages, recent experiments indicate that storage of this kind does exist under certain circumstances. After a momentary exposure (too short for eye movement) that is followed by a blank field the viewer preserves an iconic image of the input pattern for some fraction of a second. George Sperling of the Bell Telephone Laboratories has shown that a signal given during this postexposure period can serve to direct a viewer's attention to any arbitrary part of the field, just as if it were still present.

The displays used in Sperling's experiments consisted of several rows of letters—too many to be reported from a single glance. Nevertheless, subjects were able to report any *single row*, indicated by the postexposure signal, rather well. Such a signal must come quickly; letters to which the observer does not attend before the brief iconic memory has faded are lost. That is why the observer cannot report the entire display: the icon disappears before he can read it all.

Even under these unusual conditions, then, people display selectivity in their use of the information that reaches the eye. The selection is made from material presented in a single brief exposure, but only because the experimental arrangements precluded a second glance. Normally selection and construction take place over a series of glances; no iconic memory for individual "snapshots" can survive. Indeed, the presentation of a

second stimulus figure shortly after the first in a brief-exposure experiment tends to destroy the iconic replica. The viewer may see a fusion of the two figures, only the second, or an apparent motion of the figures, depending on their temporal and spatial relations. He does not see them separately.

So far we have considered two kinds of short-term memory for visual information: the iconic replica of a brief and isolated stimulus, and the cumulative schema of the visible world that is constructed in the course of ordinary perception. Both of these processes (which may well be different manifestations of a single underlying mechanism) involve the storage of information over a period of time. Neither of them, however, is what the average man has in mind when he speaks of memory. Everyday experience testifies that visual information can be stored over long periods. Things seen yesterday can be recalled today; for that matter they may conceivably be recalled 20 years from now. Such recall may take many forms, but perhaps the most interesting is the phenomenon called visual imagery. In a certain sense one can see again what one has seen before. Are these mental images like optical ones? Are they revived copies of earlier stimulation? Indeed, does it make any sense at all to speak of "seeing" things that are not present? Can there be visual experience when there is no stimulation by light?

To deal with these problems effectively we must distinguish two issues: first, the degree to which the mechanisms involved in visual memory are like those involved in visual perception and, second, the degree to which the perceiver

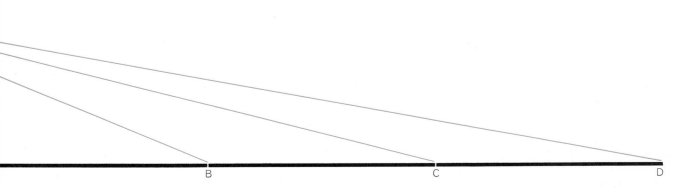

B   C   D

object in view increases. The texture elements of a distant surface are also projected closer together than similar elements nearby.

Thus a textured surface slanting away from the viewer is represented optically as a density gradient (*see illustration on next page*).

is willing to say his images look real, that is, like external things seen. Although the first issue is perhaps the more fundamental—and the most relevant here —the second has always attracted the most attention.

One reason for the perennial interest in the "realness" of images is the wide range of differences in imaging capacity from person to person and from time to time. When Francis Galton conducted the first empirical study of mental im-

agery (published in 1883), he found some of his associates skeptical of the very existence of imagery. They assumed that only poetic fancy allowed one to speak of "seeing" in connection with what one remembered; remembering consisted simply in a knowledge of facts. Other people, however, were quite ready to describe their mental imagery in terms normally applied to perception. Asked in the afternoon about their breakfast table, they said they could see it clearly, with

colors bright (although perhaps a little dimmer than in the original experience) and objects suitably arranged.

These differences seem to matter less when one is asleep; many people who report little or no lifelike imagery while awake may have visual dreams and believe in the reality of what they see. On the other hand, some psychopathological states can endow images with such a compelling quality that they dominate the patient's experience. Students of per-

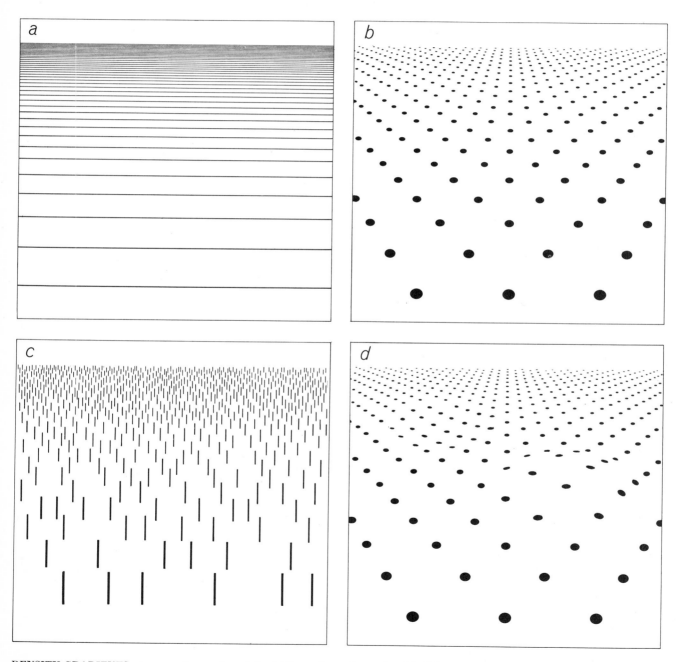

DENSITY GRADIENTS convey an impression of depth. Depending on the size, shape and spacing of its textural elements, the gradient may create the impression of a smooth flat surface (a, b), a rough flat surface (c) or a surface broken by an elevation and a depression (d). Like the gradients depicted, the textured surfaces of the visual world (by structuring the light that falls on the retina) convey information concerning the orientation of the surface. Textured surfaces also provide a scale for gauging the size of objects.

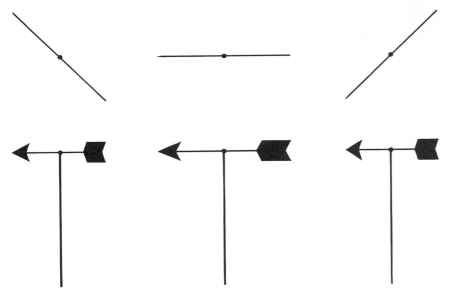

AMBIGUOUS VISUAL INPUT can arise from a stationary weather vane. The weather vane in three different orientations is shown as it would be seen from above (*top*) and in side view (*bottom*). If the vane begins to rotate, its real length will become apparent.

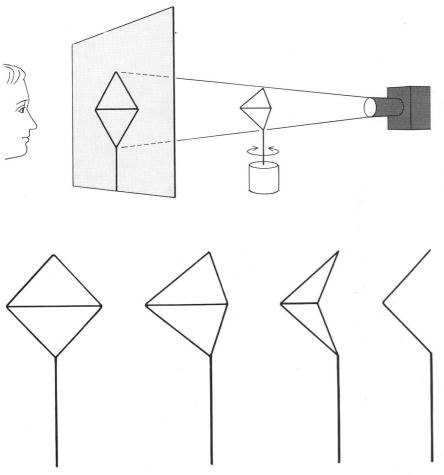

KINETIC DEPTH EFFECT shows how movement can endow perceived objects with three-dimensional shape. The shadow of a bent wire form (*shown at bottom in four different orientations*) looks as flat as the screen on which it is cast so long as the form remains stationary. When it is swiveled back and forth, the changing shadow is seen as a rigid rotating object with the appropriate three-dimensionality. The direction of rotation remains ambiguous, as in the case of the weather vane in the illustration at top of the page.

ception have often disregarded dreams and phantasms, considering them "hallucinatory" and thus irrelevant to normal seeing. However, this is a difficult position to defend either logically or empirically. Logically a sharp distinction between perception and hallucination would be easy enough if perceptions were copies of the retinal image; hallucinations would then be experiences that do *not* copy that image. But since perception does more than mirror the stimulus (and since hallucinations often incorporate stimulus information), this distinction is not clear-cut. Moreover, a number of recent findings seem to point up very specific relations between the processes of seeing and of imagining.

Perhaps the most unexpected of these findings has emerged from studies of sleep and dreams. The dreaming phase of sleep, which occurs several times each night, is regularly accompanied by bursts of rapid eye movements. In several studies William C. Dement and his collaborators have awakened experimental subjects immediately after a period of eye motion and asked them to report their just-preceding dream. Later the eye-movement records were compared with a transcript of the dream report to see if any relation between the two could be detected. Of course this was not possible in every case. (Indeed, we can be fairly sure that many of the eye movements of sleep have no visual significance; similar motions occur in the sleep of newborn babies, decorticated cats and congenitally blind adults.) Nevertheless, there was appreciably more correspondence between the two kinds of record than could be attributed to chance. The parallel between the eye movements of the dreamer and the content of the dream was sometimes striking. In one case five distinct upward deflections of the eyes were recorded just before the subject awoke and reported a dream of climbing five steps!

Another recent line of research has also implicated eye movements in the processes of visual memory. Ralph Norman Haber and his co-workers at Yale University reopened the study of eidetic imagery, which for a generation had remained untouched by psychological research. An eidetic image is an imaginative production that seems to be external to the viewer and to have a location in perceived space; it has a clarity comparable to that of genuinely perceived objects; it can be examined by the "*Eidetiker,*" who may report details that he did not notice in the original presentation of the stimulus. Most *Eidetikers*

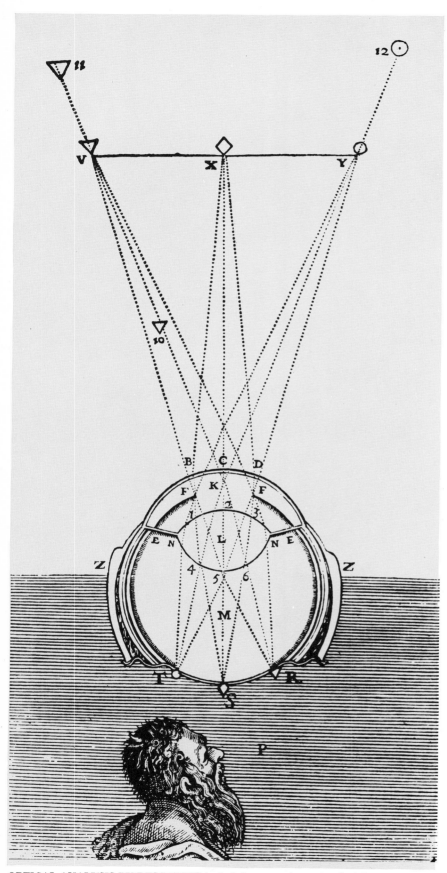

OPTICAL ANALYSIS BY DESCARTES included an experiment in which he removed the eye of an ox, scraped the back of the eye to make it transparent and observed on the retina the inverted image of a scene. The illustration is from Descartes's essay *La Dioptrique*.

are children, but the developmental course of this rather rare ability is not well understood. What is most interesting about these images for the present argument is that the *Eidetiker* scans them with his eyes. Asked about a detail in one or another corner of the image, he moves his eyes to look at the appropriate part of the blank wall on which he has "projected" it. That is, he does just what anyone would do who was really looking at something.

Are these esoteric phenomena really relevant to the study of vision? It might be argued that they do not provide a safe basis for inference; dreaming is a very special physiological state and eidetic imagery is restricted to very special types of people. It is not difficult, however, to show that similar processes occur in persons who do not have vivid visual imagery at all. A simple demonstration suggested by Julian Hochberg of New York University helps to make this point: Try to remember how many windows there are in your own house or apartment.

If you have never considered this question before, it will be hard to find the answer without actively looking and counting. However, you will probably not need to look at the windows themselves. Most people, even those who say they have no visual imagery, can easily form and scan an *internal representation* of the walls, counting off the windows as they appear in them. This process evidently uses stored visual information. It seems to involve mechanisms much like those used for seeing and counting real windows.

We can draw three conclusions from this demonstration. First, seeing and imagining employ similar—perhaps the same—mechanisms. Second, images can be useful, even when they are not vivid or lifelike, even for people who do not have "good imagery." Third, mental images are constructs and not copies. This last point may have been obvious in any case—you might just as well have been asked to imagine a gryphon and to count its claws—but it bears further emphasis. All the windows could not have been optically imaged on the retina simultaneously, and they may not even have appeared there in rapid succession. The image (or series of images) developed in solving this problem is new; it is not a replica of any previous stimulus.

The first two of these points have received additional confirmation in a recent experiment by Lee R. Brooks of McMaster University, whose method puts imagery and visual perception in direct competition. In one of his studies the subjects were shown a large block *F* and told to remember what it looked like. After the *F* was removed from view they were asked to describe the succession of corner points that would be encountered as one moved around it, responding "Yes" for each point that was either on the extreme top or the bottom of the *F*, and "No" for each point in between. This visual-memory task proved to be more difficult when the responses were made by *pointing* to a printed series of yeses and noes than when a spoken "Yes" or "No" was allowed. However, the difficulty was not intrinsic to the act of pointing; it resulted from the conflict between pointing and simultaneously visualizing the *F*. In another of Brooks's tasks the subjects had to respond "Yes" for each noun and "No" for each non-noun in a memorized sentence.

In this case they tended to rely on verbal-auditory memory rather than visual memory. As a result spoken response was the more difficult of the two.

We would not have been surprised to find a conflict between visually guided pointing and corner-counting on an *F* the viewer was *looking at*. After all, he could not be expected to look in two places at once. Even if the *F* had appeared on the same sheet of paper with the yeses and noes, interference would have been easy to understand: the succession of glances required to examine the corners of the *F* would have conflicted with the visual organization needed to point at the right succession of responses. What Brooks has shown, rather surprisingly, is that this conflict exists even when the *F* is merely imagined. Visual images are apparently produced by the same integrative processes that

make ordinary perception possible.

In short, the reaction of the nervous system to stimulation by light is far from passive. The eye and brain do not act as a camera or a recording instrument. Neither in perceiving nor in remembering is there any enduring copy of the optical input. In perceiving, complex patterns are extracted from that input and fed into the constructive processes of vision, so that the movements and the inner experience of the perceiver are usually in good correspondence with his environment. Visual memory differs from perception because it is based primarily on stored rather than on current information, but it involves the same kind of synthesis. Although the eyes have been called the windows of the soul, they are not so much peepholes as entry ports, supplying raw material for the constructive activity of the visual system.

14

Movements of the Eye

E. Llewellyn Thomas   *August 1968*

To look closely at something is to turn one's eyes so that the image falls on the fovea, a specialized area smaller than the head of a pin that lies near the center of the retina. Only in this tiny region are the receptor cells concentrated with sufficient density to provide detailed vision. As a result not more than a thousandth of the entire visual field can be seen in "hard focus" at a given moment. Yet the human eye is capable of discerning in considerable detail a scene as complex and swiftly changing as the one confronting a person driving an automobile in traffic. This formidable visual task can be accomplished only because the eyes are able to flick rapidly about the scene, with the two foveae receiving detailed images first from one part of the scene and then from another.

Therefore most of the time our eyes are jumping from point to point. These movements and fixations can be recorded in various ways. One method is to photograph the bright spot you can see when a light shines on the eye. This bright spot is the reflection from the convex surface of the cornea. Because the radius of curvature of the cornea is smaller than the radius of the spherical eyeball, the angle of reflection changes when the eyeball rotates and the bright spot appears to move. These movements can be correlated with the movements of the eye's line of sight.

When such a photographic record is combined with a motion picture of the scene ahead of the viewer, it reveals the features that attracted his notice, held it or were overlooked. Such records have useful applications, for example in the design of highway signs and radar displays. They can show how critical details in an X-ray plate or an aerial photograph are sometimes overlooked, even when the viewer thinks he has scanned

the picture carefully. In our laboratory at the University of Toronto we have been using developments of this method to study how the human eye attacks such visual problems. We have also been interested in how the patterns of eye movement are affected by psychological disturbances and drugs, and how a sequence of eye movements and fixations can be related to the processing of information in the brain.

The most common major eye movement is the saccade: the rapid jump the eye makes as it moves from fixating one part of a scene to fixating another. The fixations themselves usually last less than half a second, but their duration depends on the character of the scene and what the viewer is doing. The jump between fixations takes only a few milliseconds. Vision is greatly reduced not only while the eye is actually moving during the saccade but also for a short period before it starts to move. One can appreciate this reduced vision if one tries to observe one's own eye movements in a mirror.

The speed of the saccade depends on the saccade's length and direction, and the speed also differs from individual to individual. The flick may be so rapid that the eye's angular velocity may reach more than 500 degrees per second. This

velocity is not under conscious control; an effort to slow it will only break the saccade into a series of shorter movements. If at the end of the saccade the fovea is not "on target," the eye adjusts by making one or more small corrective jumps. The path the eyes follow between two fixation points may be straight, curved or even hooked, but once the eye is launched on a saccade it cannot change its target. It is as if the points in the visual field were recorded as a set of coordinates in the brain. The difference between the coordinates of a fixation point at one instant and the coordinates of the next fixation point constitutes an "error" signal to the eye-movement control centers, and the resulting movement of the eye is directed in a manner analogous to what an engineer would call a simple position servomechanism.

The eye moves so frequently and rapidly that the pattern it weaves can be recorded only by instruments. Methods of recording eye movements include contact lenses, suction cups and photoelectric devices. When the head must be left as unencumbered as possible (as in recording the eye movements of astronauts during flight or in recording eye movements under closed lids), the method of choice is the electro-oculograph. Early investigations of eye movements in reading (by Raymond Dodge) and in the ex-

VIEW THROUGH WINDSHIELD, shown in the sequence of photographs on the opposite page, indicates (*white spot*) where the viewer inside the automobile was looking as it moved along the street. The photographs were made with a device that records both the scene before a viewer's eyes and a spot of light reflected from one of his eyes. This device is worn on the viewer's head, as shown on page 151. A vertical line in the lens system of the device appears at the center of each photograph. It indicates, by its position with respect to the scene, when the observer's head has moved. Reading from left to right and top to bottom, the features of the scene that drew the eye were (*1*) the street pavement, (*2*) a pile of snow, (*3*) the broken line painted on the pavement, (*4*) a parked automobile, (*5*) the street pavement, (*6*) a moving automobile, (*7*) a patch of snow in the street, (*8*) a storefront, (*9 and 10*) an automobile as it is overtaken, (*11*) the base of a telephone pole, (*12, 13 and 14*) the shoulder and face of a pedestrian and (*15*) the side of the road ahead.

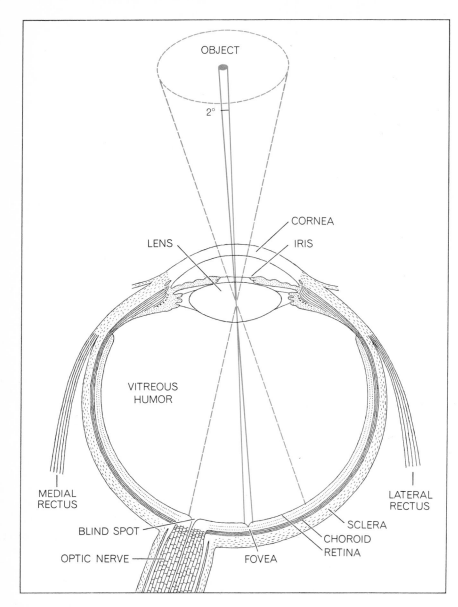

DISTINCT VISION is limited by the size of the fovea, a region of the retina where the receptor cells are tightly packed together. Whereas the retina as a whole covers a visual angle of approximately 240 degrees, the fovea subtends an angle of only about two degrees. Consequently, to perceive the details of a scene the two foveae of the eyes must be moved.

amination of pictorial material (by A. E. Brandt and Guy T. Buswell) were made by photographing with a stationary camera the moving corneal reflection of a viewer whose head was firmly fixed. Then the record had to be rather laboriously related to the scene being viewed.

The problem of continuously relating the eye to a changing scene was solved by Norman H. Mackworth and Jane F. Mackworth. The system they developed (at the Applied Psychology Research Unit in Cambridge, England) employed one television camera to record a magnified image of the corneal reflection and a second television camera to record the

scene in front of the viewer. On the television monitor the combined output of the two cameras showed the scene with the bright spot of the corneal reflection moving over it.

The next step was to allow the viewer to move his head and body so that it would be possible to study the many situations in which the scene is constantly changing and the viewer is moving his head and body as well as his eyes. To accomplish this Norman Mackworth and I, working at the Defence Research Medical Laboratories in Toronto, contrived an optical system mounted on a helmet; this system enabled us to record a com-

posite motion picture showing the changing scene in front of the wearer together with where he was fixating within the scene and his head and body movements. At various times we used fiber optics to transfer the combined image to a 16-millimeter motion-picture camera or mounted a small television camera on the helmet. The most convenient apparatus for studies outside the laboratory, however, was a "homemade" eight-millimeter camera weighing only a few ounces that we mounted on the helmet behind the optical system. The overall accuracy of this system is two degrees of solid angle, which is about the same as the area of acute vision subtended by the fovea (the size of a dime held at arm's length).

Such a system obviously has its limitations. The viewer has to wear equipment weighing several pounds on his head. His vision in one eye is reduced by the half-silvered mirror that picks up the corneal reflection. There is the possibility of the helmet's moving on the viewer's head during the experiment and upsetting the calibration. There is also the problem of the convergence of the eyes when one is viewing close objects, and of parallax errors. The useful field of the recording is limited to about 30 degrees in the horizontal. Nonetheless, for the study of real-life situations in which head and body movements usually play an important part, and in which the scene is continuously changing, some device such as the Mackworth camera is necessary.

Mervyn Thomas, Jane Mackworth and I used the camera to obtain some very interesting motion pictures of the eye movements of drivers in actual traffic. We saw how the driver's eyes dart about in their search for information. When an automobile is moving, the driver's eyes are constantly sampling the road ahead. At intervals he flicks quickly to the near curb, as if to monitor his position, but for such monitoring he seems to rely chiefly on the streaming effect—the flow of blurred images past the edges of his field of vision. The edges of other vehicles and sudden gaps between them attract visual attention, as do signs along the roadside and large words printed on trucks. If something difficult to identify is encountered, the fixations are longer and the eyes jump back to view it again.

The faster the automobile is moving or the heavier the traffic, the more frequent are the saccades. When the driver stops at a traffic signal, his eyes seem to move less often and rather aimlessly, but they jump toward anything novel that appears. On a main highway the cars passing in the opposite direction attract quick glances. A broken white line along the center of the road sometimes gives rise to vertical flicking movements. The eyes are also drawn to objects on the skyline such as tall buildings.

One of the strongest visual attractions seems to be flashing lights, such as those of a turn indicator on a vehicle ahead or of a neon sign at the side of the road. This demonstrates an important characteristic of human vision. When the image of an object strikes the periphery of the retina, the eyes swing involuntarily so that the object is focused on the two foveas and can be perceived in detail. Although the periphery of the retina is poorly equipped for resolving detail, it is very sensitive to movement seen in the "corner of the eye." A flashing light therefore serves as a powerful visual stimulus. On several occasions during our experiments a driver continued to glance in the direction of the flashing indicators of a car ahead, even after it had made its turn (a phenomenon Norman Mackworth had observed earlier in simulated driving studies with the television eye-marker).

I noticed another example of peripheral attraction when we recorded the eye movements of a pilot landing a small aircraft. At touchdown the pilot usually maintained his sense of direction by the streaming effect while looking rather aimlessly ahead up the runway. I believe this aimless looking reflects a readiness to react visually to the unexpected. On one occasion the pilot's eyes flicked away to fixate repeatedly on an object at the side of the runway in a flurry of rapid saccades. His eyes continued to be drawn over even after he must have identified the object as one of the spruce seedlings used on that airfield as snow markers, which our record showed he was fixating accurately.

This sensitivity to a moving or novel object at the edge of the scene demonstrates that the retina functions as an effective wide-angle early-warning system, and that a strong peripheral signal will continue to pull the eyes. This, I suppose, is the objective of the designer of flashing neon signs. If so, it would seem

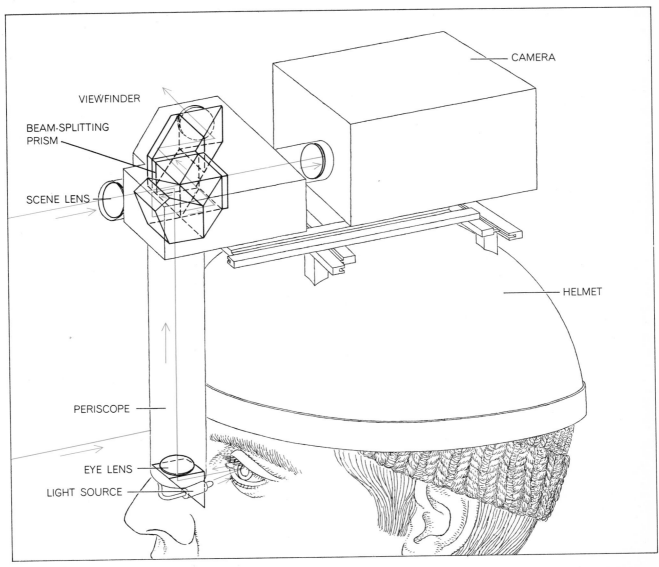

EYE-MARKER CAMERA tracks and records the eye's glance. The image of a spot of light, reflected from the cornea, is transmitted by an optical system in the periscope through a series of prisms. This serves to superpose the eye-marker image on the scene image. The combined image can be monitored through the viewfinder as it is photographed by the motion-picture camera.

better for him to exercise his skill elsewhere than along the sides of a highway.

Certain hazards in the operation of an airplane have been reduced by studying the visual behavior of the pilot. It is obviously desirable that the instruments in the cockpit be located so that the most important ones come most easily to the pilot's eyes, in the same way that the important controls come most readily to his hands. During the time it takes to make a single fixation an aircraft will have traveled several hundred yards. Nevertheless, in the past engineering considerations often took precedence over human ones. By making motion pictures of the pilot's eye and head movements during flight, Paul M. Fitts, J. L. Milton and R. E. Jones (in a study for the U.S. Air Force in 1951) identified the instruments that were used more often and the pattern in which they were viewed in various phases of flight. From this study and similar investigations in human-factors engineering, standardized layouts for instruments and controls were drawn up. Their wide adoption has helped to reduce what were two of the leading causes of aircraft accidents: misreading instruments and operating the wrong control.

In reading, as in driving an automobile, the predominant eye movement is the saccade, but the saccade of reading is initiated in a different way. When one gazes at a line on a printed page, only three or four words can be seen distinctly. If every word in the line is to be read, the eyes must jump two or three

times. How often they jump depends not only on the reader's ability to process the visual information but also on his interest in what he is reading. Thus the reading saccade is initiated not so much by the image on the periphery of the retina as by a decision made within the central nervous system. Fixation times lengthen as the material becomes harder to comprehend. The eyes may return at intervals to words scanned earlier; these regressions indicate the time it has taken the reader to recognize that his processing of the information was incomplete or faulty. Because we have long experience with the English language we anticipate common sequences of words and so may fixate only the first few words of a phrase.

When people of Occidental cultures read, they habitually move their eyes from left to right and top to bottom, and so they usually look first at the upper left-hand part of a page. This may not apply, however, if the format of the page is broken up, as it is in a newspaper. When someone is looking at pictures or groups of pictures, the scanning patterns seem to be individualistic. They are also consistent, but there is no preferred sequence in which areas are inspected. As Mackworth has remarked, the order of visual fixations seems to matter no more than the sequence in which a series of shots is taken for an amateur motion picture: "Shoot now and think later."

Harley Parker and I recorded and compared the visual behavior of an artist and a nonartist as they examined a series of paintings. The pitfalls in reporting such subjective studies are obvious, but

there seems no doubt that many painters are highly successful in directing the movements of our eyes. The artist viewer appeared more sensitive to this, particularly with respect to more abstract pictures. The eyes of both men, however, were drawn to discontinuities, including the edges of the picture itself.

This agrees with recent neurophysiological findings that contours and borders, such as those in a checkerboard, are strong stimuli of the evoked voltages that can be measured in the brain when such items are presented to the eye. This might also be expected from the fact that the border defines the shape and is a key information element in a scene. The visual pull of such borders may constitute an impediment if the viewer is searching for a low-contrast feature, such as an abnormality in an X-ray film of the chest. Edward L. Lansdown and I recorded the eye movements of a group of student radiologists as they inspected a selection of chest X rays. Our records showed that the students had carefully examined the edges of the heart and the margins of the lung fields, and indeed these are important regions for signs of disease. But large areas of the lung fields were never inspected by most of the students in the group, even though they thought they had scanned the films adequately.

To be sure, the students who had made the most complete visual examinations were the ones with the most experience in X-ray interpretation. Nevertheless, William J. Tuddenham of the University of Pennsylvania School of Medicine and L. Henry Garland of the

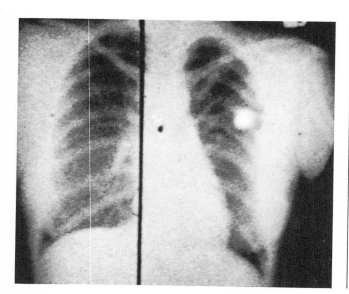
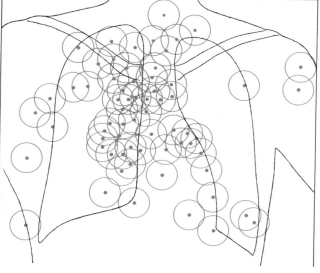

X-RAY SEARCH, made by student radiologists looking for signs of pathology, was studied by means of the eye-marker camera. Appearing on an X-ray plate of the chest (*left*) is the mark of a single eye fixation (*white spot*) made by one of the students. A drawing of the lung area (*right*) displays a summary of the eye fixations of a student who was engaged in the rapid examination of a single X ray. The area of sharp vision is indicated (*circle*) around each fixation point. Large areas of the lung fields were not explored.

Stanford University School of Medicine tested groups of trained radiologists and found that they missed 25 to 30 percent of "positive" chest X rays under conditions in which their errors must have been largely due to failures of perception. Joseph Zeidner and Robert Sadacca of the Human Factors Research Branch of the U.S. Army have reported similar failures in the interpretation of aerial photographs by a group of skilled military photointerpreters: the interpreters neglected to report 54 percent of the significant signs. It appears that the structure of the image under examination may obliterate the pattern of scanning an observer intends to follow; his gaze is drawn away, so that he literally overlooks areas he believes he has scanned. Moreover, low-resolution peripheral vision often determines where the viewer does not look. Here the potentiality for errors is obvious, particularly in a task performed under pressure.

In this connection there are some interesting differences between the way children and adults look at pictures. Norman Mackworth and Jerome S. Bruner, working at the Center for Cognitive Studies at Harvard University, have found that children show more short eye movements and concentrate on less informative details. They are less consistent in their viewing patterns, and sometimes they visually trace out simple contours that adults process by peripheral vision. All of this suggests that children concentrate visually on detail more than had previously been thought.

The link between the image and the mind is a difficult one to investigate because the brain does not receive information passively but partly controls what reaches it from the eyes. Our gaze is averted from something that is distasteful; alternatively, something that has been perceived only too well may be barred from fully conscious awareness. Studies undertaken at the University of Pennsylvania by Lester Luborsky, Barton J. Blinder and Norman Mackworth have shown that people tend to avoid accepting and remembering visual information that is associated with heightened emotion (as measured by an increase in the well-known galvanic skin response). They may deny that they ever looked at some emotionally charged feature, even when their eye-movement record shows that they had.

This rejection of visual information may reach pathological levels, the most extreme example being hysterical blindness. Eugene Stasiak and I explored the visual reactions of a group of patients at

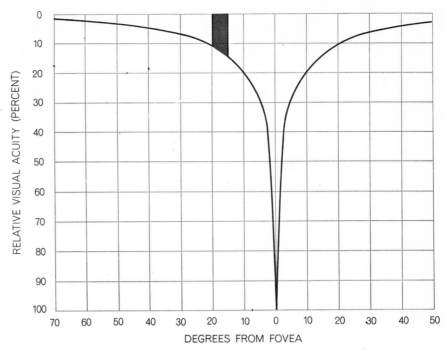

VISUAL ACUITY is greatest in the foveal region of the retina. At the point where the optic nerve passes through the inner coat of the eyeball (*gray area*) there is no vision.

the Lakeshore Psychiatric Hospital in Toronto. We recorded the patients' eye movements while they were looking at life-size photographs of themselves and other people. We found that the scanning patterns of the patients differed significantly from those of people in a nonpatient control group. Whereas the people in the control group (whether they were looking at pictures of themselves or at pictures of others) paid most attention to the face, the psychiatric patients avoided looking at the face. The duration of the patients' fixations on the photographs also differed, at times being markedly shorter than the average time of the control group and on occasion distinctly longer. We believe both the different fixation times and the avoidance of the face reflect a tendency on the patients' part to reduce their intake of information. This tendency may arise from distortions of perception or from differences in interpretation. With several patients there appeared to be a relation between psychiatric history and viewing pattern; for example, the patient's eyes might return again and again to a part of the body significant in his own psychiatric history.

In other experiments Hyam Day and I investigated the intake of visual information by subjects who were not suffering from a psychological disturbance but

FIXATIONS ON INKBLOT were shown by eye-marker camera to fall chiefly on the blot's margin. The border of a form presents a high contrast and a strong visual stimulus to certain of the retinal cells. This may serve to draw the eye from other areas in the scene.

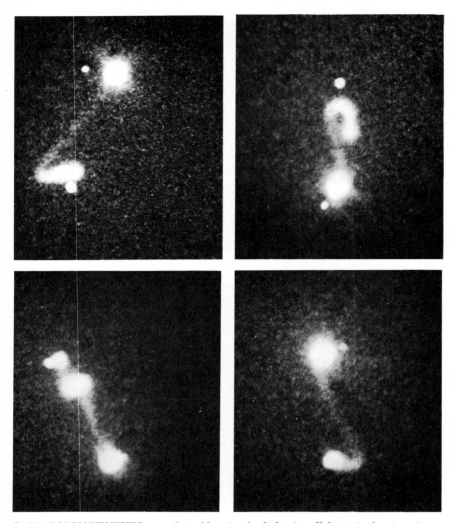

SACCADIC MOVEMENTS were elicited by stimulus lights (*small dots*). As the viewer's eye moved from a fixation on one stimulus light to a fixation on another, the path of the saccade, or eye flick, was photographed. The hook that appears in three of the paths suggests that one of the muscles that moves the eyeball operates later than the others. The experiment was arranged so that the path image would be displaced from the image of the stimulus lights.

attention shifts to the mouth; apparently everyone reads lips to some extent.

On a motion-picture screen the center of visual interest is also the face. To study the effects of observing violence, Richard H. Walters of the University of Waterloo and I showed a group of subjects a knife-fight scene from a motion picture. This appeared to increase the subjects' aggressive behavior (as measured by a test given the viewers immediately after the film was shown). To gain some idea of which elements in the film were most active in this regard, we recorded the eye movements of several subjects while they were watching it. The subjects spent the greatest part of the time following the faces of the two central characters; the knives themselves and the other actors received only an occasional glance.

Such movements of the eyes as they explore the environment are largely outside conscious control. Records of the movements can therefore provide insights into the processing of visual information by the brain. For example, Norman Mackworth has observed a phenomenon that he calls "looking without seeing." His subjects had been given the task of finding one number among a matrix of numbers. Mackworth noted that at times a subject's eyes would fixate on the number he was seeking, but even so he would continue the search. His eyes might make several fixations around the number, thereby breaking the scanning pattern, and then resume their searching movements. That there was recognition of the number at some level in the nervous system was indicated by the variation in scanning pattern. The subject was not consciously aware, however, that he had found what he was seeking.

In a later study Norman Mackworth, Ira T. Kaplan and William Metlay asked a group of people to watch two dials and report each time the reading on either dial had changed. The visual records of the group indicated that about a third of the dial changes that had not been actually reported had been fixated. In our studies of automobile drivers there was an instance that appeared to be similar: a driver looked straight at a red light and then started to drive right through it.

A great deal of the information that arrives at the brain from the retina fails to obtrude on the consciousness. In this connection it is startling to watch a film of one's own eye movements. The record shows hundreds of fixations in which items were observed of which one has not the slightest recollection. Yet the

who had been given the stimulant dextroamphetamine. Two abstract pictures, one more complex than the other, were simultaneously presented to the subject, once after he had been given a capsule of dextroamphetamine and on another occasion after he had been given an inert capsule. The film of the subjects' visual reactions showed that they spent more time examining the complex picture after they had been given the drug. This result suggests that the drug increases willingness to seek and accept visual information. Whether it also affects the ability to process the information is another question.

It is evident from other studies that when an observer's interest is aroused by what he sees, his eyes move more often. The eyes of a group of healthy young men moved nearly twice as frequently in examining photographs of attractive young women as they did during the inspection of inkblots. Incidentally, the curved edge of the female form attracts the male eye—a logical assumption for which it is pleasant to have experimental verification. Not only do the eyes move more often when the viewer is more interested; there are also more corrective jumps serving to bring the image of the object of interest toward the center of the fovea. There are, moreover, fewer eye blinks, the eyes are opened wider and the pupils are dilated [see "Attitude and Pupil Size," by Eckhard H. Hess; SCIENTIFIC AMERICAN Offprint 493].

In this way the eyes demonstrably reveal emotion. The direction of a glance may also reveal intention. It is not surprising, then, that when a person looks at the face of another person, he tends to look most at the eyes. When the other person starts to speak, however, visual

signals must have reached the brain because one took motor action and even made rather complex decisions based on the information that was received during the forgotten fixation. Parts of the brain appear to function rather like a secretary who handles routine matters without consulting her employer and apprises him of important points in incoming letters—but who at times makes mistakes.

Some insight into the brain's processing of information can be gained by examining the eye movements of a person who is engaged in solving a problem. For example, I have recorded the eye movements of two mediocre chess players who were studying an end-game problem. The visual patterns of the two players differed greatly; still, it was clear that both were in effect shifting the pieces to various positions on the board as they tried out a series of possible moves.

A more sophisticated approach to problem-solving was displayed by another subject, an engineer whose eye movements were recorded as he analyzed an electronic circuit. After he had studied the circuit, which I had drawn on a blackboard, I changed some of the components and asked him to decide how the alterations would affect the circuit's operation. In looking at the circuit before it was changed the eyes of the engineer had traced the essential pathway. In viewing the altered circuit he did not again explore the pathway but went directly to the parts that would be the most affected. At another time the same subject examined a series of differential equations in which I had made planned (and unplanned) errors. His eyes rapidly singled out the mistakes, making a series of short jumps that effectively narrowed down the area of his attention until they had centered on the critical terms.

The length of time that is spent in looking at a scene must obviously be related in some way to the amount of information about the scene that the viewer receives. Certain of our studies suggest that a lengthening fixation time may be associated with a diminishing intake of information. The subjects were shown Rorschach inkblots and were asked to write down what the blots reminded them of. At first their eyes darted over the entire area of the blot, making numerous fixations. As time went on the fixations became decidedly longer. Perhaps these fixation times reflect a process in which the viewer, having realized that the blot offers little or no genuine information, is adding or generating meaning rather than merely accepting it.

V

Beyond the Visible: X-ray to Radio Waves

Beyond
the Visible:
X-ray to
Radio Waves

Electromagnetic waves come in all sizes: the long radio waves used for radio broadcasting, the short waves used for long-distance communications, the very-high-frequency and ultra-high-frequency waves used for television broadcasting, as well as microwaves, infrared rays, visible rays, ultraviolet rays, X-rays, and gamma rays. The many different names suggest that the properties of the various waves differ greatly, and they do. The most basic reason for the differences is that the amount of energy in one quantum increases as the frequency of the radiation increases. In a gamma ray, each individual quantum is so large that it is usual to count them one by one, like particles. At the other extreme, in the radio-frequency waves, quanta are so small and numerous that we seldom notice their discreteness. Because of such differences, the study of different wave regions has naturally emphasized and revealed very different aspects of the nature of electromagnetic radiation.

Sir Lawrence Bragg's article is not concerned with the quantal nature of X-rays, but rather with the wave aspects. As Bragg was one of the first to show, the wavelengths of X-rays approximate the spacing between atoms in a crystal. Thus X-ray waves scattered from such atoms interfere with each other, like light waves, to produce a regular pattern of beams. From these diffraction patterns, it is possible to infer the arrangement of atoms within the crystal. But any such crystallographic analysis is difficult, and requires both skill and ingenuity. It is an amazing story that Bragg recounts. In the course of his scientific career, X-ray crystallography was originated and has evolved from the study of simple crystals like rocksalt to the analysis of the molecular structures of enormously complex biological molecules.

X-rays can penetrate some materials that are opaque to ordinary light, but there is no material as transparent to X-rays as air is to visible light. Thus most of what we know about the astronomical universe comes from the visible and near-visible wavelength regions. To observe X-rays from beyond the atmosphere, we must use sounding rockets or satellites. The atmosphere is also opaque to most infrared wavelengths, which are longer than visible waves. However, there are a few infrared wavelengths that can penetrate the atmosphere, but these our eyes cannot see, although we may feel them as heat if they are strong enough. Some photographic materials can record near infrared wavelengths just beyond the visible. Most of the detectors that have been developed for scientific and technological use in the infrared wavelength region are small units that must be scanned across an image to record the details. With them, it is now possible to survey the sky from the ground at selected infrared wavelengths, and at other wavelengths from high-altitude balloons.

Bruce C. Murray and James A. Westphal, in their article, review the history of infrared detection and some of the beginnings of infrared astronomy. By the methods that have been developed, we can now measure the surface temperatures of the moon and planets, and can study the changes in those temperatures.

A massive object must be quite hot if it is to emit visible light, but can emit infrared radiation at comparatively low temperatures. Do such infrared emitters exist in space? If they do, how strong and how numerous are they? These are the questions investigated by G. Neugebauer and Robert B. Leighton, who made a systematic survey of the sky in the wavelength region between 2 and 2.4 micrometers, the infrared region to which the atmosphere is transparent. In their survey Neugebauer and Leighton observed thousands of infrared-emitting stars, many of which had never been seen before. Some of these are genuinely cool objects; others appear red because their light has ben dimmed and reddened as a result of passing through interstellar dust. It seems likely that these studies will give us new insights into the problem of the creation and aging of stars.

Men have always been able to look up at the sky, but only in recent years, with the development of aircraft and satellites, have they been able to look down at the earth. In their aerial observations of the earth's surface they have made good use of the wavelengths beyond the visible; the shorter ultraviolet waves, the longer infrared, and even the radio waves. Whether the information is collected point by point, or whether an entire area is photographed directly, the data are usually assembled to form a picture or a collection of pictures in different wavelengths of light. In a single picture, several visible wavelengths can be represented by their colors, and several infrared or ultraviolet wavelengths can be represented by arbitrarily chosen false colors. With the appropriate combination, certain features of the landscape under observation—such as particular crops or rock formations—can be made to appear more prominently than in an ordinary photograph. Robert N. Colwell shows how these new techniques can help us to assess the nature and possibilities of regions of the earth.

Radio waves are of particular value for communication, broadcasting, and radar, but they can also be used for spectroscopy. Since tunable electronic oscillators for these wavelengths are available, it is common to use them as sources of radiation and to measure the relative power absorbed at various wavelengths by the material being investigated. However, tuning the oscillator, that is, the source rather than the spectrometer, creates a less essential difference than that produced by the smallness of the quanta at these low frequencies. Since the quanta are so small, an ordinary oscillator provides many of them, and it can easily supply enough to excite all the available absorbing atoms, so that at radio frequencies, saturation, occurs easily. Thus attention was drawn to the fact that radiation can change the relative population of energy levels. Under some circumstances, it was found to be possible to put more atoms in a high energy level than in a lower level. This is known as "population inversion" or "a negative temperature" since it is just the reverse of the situation in equilibrium at any positive temperature. When there are more atoms in the higher energy state, radiation is amplified rather than absorbed; this, too, is exactly the opposite of what ordinarily occurs.

Great advances in radio-frequency spectroscopy were made in the years following 1945. Most of the pioneers in this field were men experienced in electronics. Several of them, including Willis Lamb, Jr. and Joseph Weber, recognized that population inversion in atomic or molecular systems might be utilized to provide an alternative to conventional electronic amplifiers. But the amplification obtainable from any such device seemed slight. However, in 1951, Charles H. Townes found a new way to induce stimulated emission in ammonia molecules and to enhance the effects by putting the molecules in a metal resonator tuned to the frequency that the atoms could amplify. Townes and his associates, James P. Gordon and Herbert J. Zeiger, used these findings to construct the first molecular oscillator, which produced a very steady, pure, single frequency in the microwave region. This device they called a MASER (an acronym for Microwave Amplification by Stimulated Emission of Radiation). At about the same time, Nikaloi G. Basov and Aleksandr M. Prokhorov independently proposed a similar device. Townes, Basov, and Prokhorov shared the Nobel prize in 1964 for this discovery. Gordon, in his article, tells of the discovery and describes the uses of masers.

15

X-ray Crystallography

Sir Lawrence Bragg   July 1968

Fifty-six years ago a new branch of science was born with the discovery by Max von Laue of Germany that a beam of X rays could be diffracted, or scattered, in an orderly way by the orderly array of atoms in a crystal. At first the main interest in von Laue's discovery was focused on its bearing on the controversy about the nature of X rays; it proved that they were waves and not particles. It soon became clear to some of us, however, that this effect opened up a new way of studying matter, that in fact man had been presented with a new form of microscope, several thousand times more powerful than any light microscope, that could in principle resolve the structure of matter right down to the atomic scale. The development of X-ray crystallography since 1912 has more than fulfilled our early expectations. It not only has revealed the way atoms are arranged in many diverse forms of matter but also has cast a flood of light on the nature of the forces between the atoms and on the large-scale properties of matter. In many cases this new knowledge has led to a fundamental revision of ideas in other branches of science. A culmination of sorts has been reached in the past few years with the successful structural analysis of several of the basic molecules of living matter—the proteins—each of which consists of thousands of atoms held together by an incredibly intricate network of chemical bonds.

The purpose of this article is to go back to the beginning and broadly summarize the course of X-ray crystallography over the past half-century or so. In so doing I shall try to answer two key questions: Why X rays? Why crystals?

X-ray crystallography is a strange branch of science. The result of an investigation lasting many years can be summed up in a "model." I have often been asked: "Why are you always showing and talking about models? Other kinds of scientists do not do this." The answer is that what the investigator has been seeking all along is simply a structural plan, a map if you will, that shows all the atoms in their relative positions in space. No other branch of science is so completely geographical; a list of spatial coordinates is all that is needed to tell the world what has been discovered.

The atomic structure of a crystal is deduced from the way it diffracts a beam of X rays in different directions. A crystal is built of countless small structural units, each consisting of the same arrangement of atoms; the units are repeated regularly like the pattern of a wallpaper, except that in a crystal the pattern extends in three dimensions in space. The directions of the diffracted beams depend on the repeat distances of the pattern. The strengths of the diffracted beams, on the other hand, depend on the arrangement of atoms in each unit. The wavelets scattered by the atoms interfere to give a strong resultant in some directions and a weak resultant in others. The goal of X-ray analysis is to find the atomic arrangement that accounts for the observed strengths of the many diffracted beams.

This brings us to the question of why X rays, of all the available forms of electromagnetic radiation, are indispensable for this method of investigation In order for the interference of the diffracted beams to produce marked changes in the amount of scattering in different directions, the differences in the paths taken by reflected beams must be on the order of a wavelength. Only X rays have wavelengths short enough to satisfy this condition. For example, the distance between neighboring sodium and chlorine atoms in a crystal of sodium chloride (ordinary table salt) is 2.81 angstrom units (an angstrom is 10^{-10} meter), whereas the most commonly used wavelength in X-ray analysis is 1.54 angstroms.

Actually crystals came into the picture only because they are a convenient means to an end. The resultant scattering of X rays would be hopelessly confused and impossible to interpret if the scattering units were randomly distributed in all orientations. In a crystal the units are all similarly oriented and hence scatter the X rays in the same way; as a result a total scattering measurement made with a whole crystal leads directly to a determination of the amount scattered by an individual unit.

The Condition for Diffraction

The easiest way to approach the optical problem of X-ray diffraction is to consider the X-ray waves as being reflected by sheets of atoms in the crystal. When a beam of monochromatic (uniform wavelength) X rays strikes a crystal, the wavelets scattered by the atoms in each sheet combine to form a reflected wave. If the path difference for waves reflected by successive sheets is a whole number of wavelengths, the wave trains will combine to produce a strong reflected beam. In more formal geometric terms, if the spacing between the reflecting planes is d and the glancing angle of the incident X-ray beam is θ, the path difference for waves reflected by successive planes is $2d \sin \theta$ [*see upper illustration on page 163*]. Hence the condition for diffraction is $n\lambda = 2d \sin \theta$, where n is an integer and λ is the wavelength.

I first stated the diffraction condition in this form in my initial adventure into research in a paper presented to the Cambridge Philosophical Society in

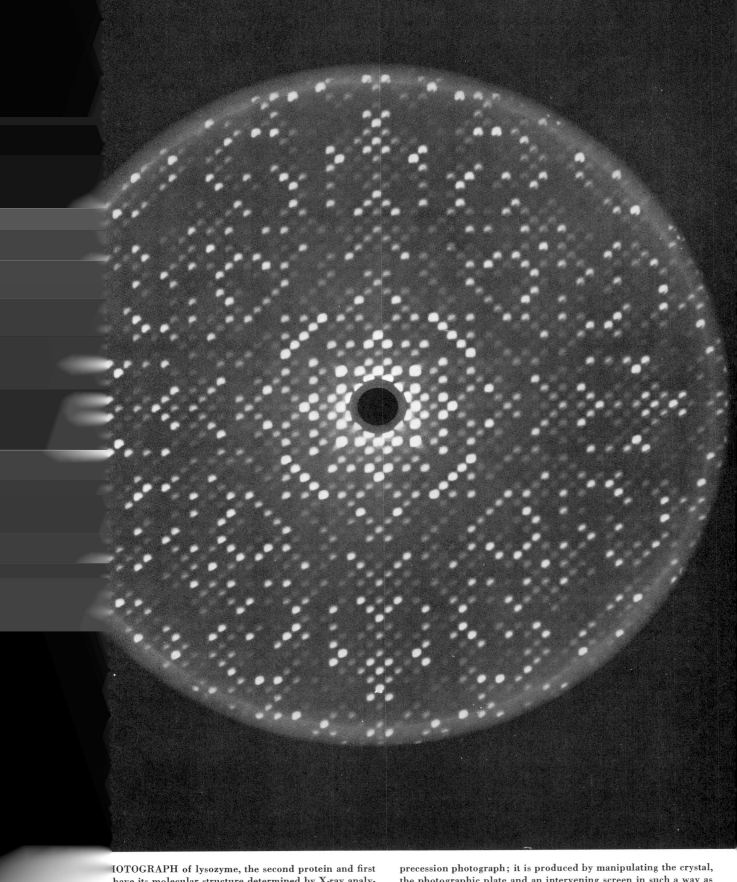

IOTOGRAPH of lysozyme, the second protein and first have its molecular structure determined by X-ray analyzes the recent achievements of the X-ray technique. The ts correspond to various orders of diffracted waves pro-radiating the lysozyme crystal with a beam of monochro-ys. This particular type of X-ray photograph is called a precession photograph; it is produced by manipulating the crystal, the photographic plate and an intervening screen in such a way as to hold one of the three indices of the diffracted beams constant while recording the values of the other two indices in the form of a rectilinear pattern. The lysozyme molecule contains 1,950 atoms and measures approximately 40 angstrom units in its largest dimension.

1912, and it has come to be known as Bragg's law. It is, I have always felt, a cheaply earned honor, because the principle had been well known for some time in the optics of visible light.

The atoms of a given crystal can be arranged in sheets in a number of differ-

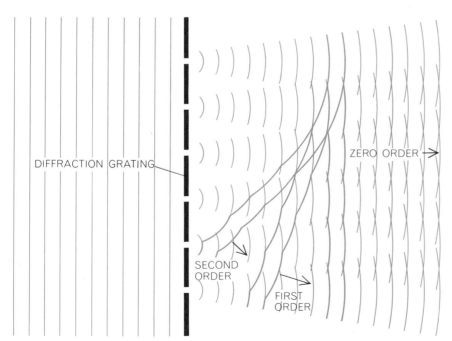

BRAGG'S LAW, first formulated by the author in 1912, states the condition for diffraction of an incident beam of monochromatic X rays by the successive sheets of atoms in a crystal. In general terms the law states that if the path difference for waves reflected by successive sheets of atoms is a whole number of wavelengths, the wave trains will combine to produce a strong reflected beam. In more formal geometric terms, if the spacing between the reflecting planes of atoms is d and the glancing angle of the incident X-ray beam is θ, the path difference for waves reflected by successive planes is $2d \sin \theta$. In this diagram the extra path followed by the lower ray (heavy colored line at bottom) is four wavelengths long, which is exactly equal to the path difference of $2d \sin \theta$ between the two diffracted rays (upper right).

ent ways; three possible arrangements of the sheets in a crystal of sodium chloride are indicated in the illustration on the opposite page. The equation for reflection can be satisfied for any set of planes whose spacing is greater than half the wavelength of the X rays used; this

DIFFRACTION ORDERS are illustrated here for the comparatively simple case of a ruled optical diffraction grating. In this case the diffracted waves are defined by a single integer n in the equation $n\lambda = a \sin \theta$, where λ is the wavelength of the incident radiation and a is the spacing between the lines of the grating. In the case of a crystal, on the other hand, the pattern repeats in three dimensions, and so the order of the diffracted X-ray waves must be defined by three integers, which are represented generally by the letters h, k and l.

condition sets a limit on how many orders of diffracted waves can be obtained from a given crystal using an X-ray beam of a given wavelength.

In the case of an optical diffraction grating with an interlinear spacing a, the orders of the diffracted waves are defined by a single integer n in the equation $n\lambda = a \sin \theta$; the diffracted waves are referred to as first-order waves, second-order waves and so forth [see lower illustration at left]. In the case of a crystal, on the other hand, the pattern repeats in three dimensions, and so the order of the diffracted waves must be defined by three integers, which are represented generally by the letters h, k and l.

In the structural diagrams of sodium chloride on the opposite page the axes of the structure are denoted by the letters OA, OB and OC, these being the intervals at which the pattern repeats. In the diagram at the left the first reflection to appear from the planes perpendicular to OA will be one for which there is a path difference of the two wavelengths between O and A, since there are two sheets of atoms in this distance. With respect to the spacing OA, then, this initial reflection is a second-order reflection; with respect to the spacings OB and OC, however, the same reflection is a zero-order reflection, since the reflecting planes are parallel to both OB and OC. Therefore this type of reflection, or diffraction, is assigned the order (200), indicating $h = 2$, $k = 0$ and $l = 0$. Similarly, the initial reflection to appear from the planes in the diagram at the center is (220), whereas for the diagram at the right it is (111). Higher orders of reflection would of course have higher integer values of h, k and l.

An Example of X-Ray Analysis

The structure of sodium chloride is a simple arrangement of cubic symmetry in which sodium and chlorine atoms occur alternately in three directions at right angles, like a chessboard in three dimensions. How was this structure derived?

The analysis will be gone into in some detail here, because it is generally representative, even though this particular case is so very simple. A glance at the structural diagrams of sodium chloride shows that the planes represented there are of two kinds. The reflections, or orders, designated (200), (400), (600) and so on, and those designated (220), (440), (660) and so on, arise from sheets of atoms that are identical, each containing equal numbers of sodium and chlorine

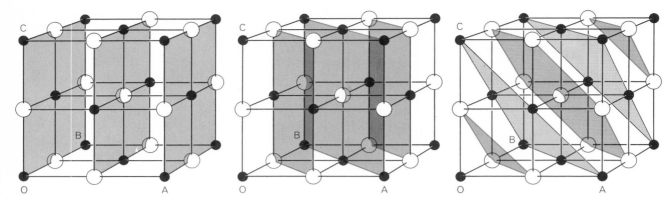

THREE POSSIBLE ARRANGEMENTS of the reflecting sheets of atoms in a sodium chloride crystal are indicated by the colored planes. The axes of this simple cubic crystal are denoted by the letters OA, OB and OC. In the diagram at left the first reflection to appear from the planes perpendicular to OA is assigned the order (200), since there is a path difference of two wavelengths between O and A while the reflecting planes are parallel to OB and OC. (In this case $h = 2$, $k = 0$ and $l = 0$.) Similarly, the initial reflection to appear from the planes in the diagram at center is designated (220), whereas for the diagram at right it is (111) with respect to chlorine planes. In general, orders with even indices arise from sheets that are identical and hence result in strong, in-phase reflections, whereas orders with odd indices arise from alternately occupied sheets and hence result in weak, out-of-phase reflections.

atoms. One would expect the sequence of successive orders to fall off regularly in intensity. As the diagram at the right on this page shows, however, the reflection (111) comes from a more complex set of planes, in that the sheets are alternately occupied by sodium and chlorine atoms. Since for (111) there is a path difference of one wavelength for the strongly reflecting chlorine planes, the waves reflected from the weaker sodium planes halfway between them will be opposite in phase. The order (111) will be weak, since the sodium contribution partially offsets the chlorine contribution. On the other hand, for (222) the contributions will be in phase and the order will be strong.

In this type of space lattice, as it is called, there are identical points at the face centers as well as at the corners of the cube; this implies that the indices must be either all odd or all even. These observations can be generalized by stating that orders with even indices, such as (200), (220) and (222), should form a strong sequence, whereas those with odd indices, such as (111), (113) and (333), should be comparatively weak.

This is the effect that is actually observed. The illustration on page 7 shows a very early set of measurements of sodium chloride and potassium chloride made with the ionization spectrometer, a device invented by my father, W. H. Bragg, in 1913. The abscissas measure the glancing angle, the ordinates the strength of the reflection. The two peaks seen on each order are the $K\alpha$ and $K\beta$ "lines" in the spectrum of the palladium anticathode, the $K\alpha$ line being the stronger of the two. The orders are re-

flected from crystal faces with crystallographic indices (100), (110) and (111). As the curves show, the order (111) for sodium chloride is anomalously small, whereas (222) fits into the same sequence with (200) and (220). For potassium chloride, on the other hand, the scattering powers of the potassium atoms and the chlorine atoms are so nearly the same that the order (111) is too weak to be observed. It was on the basis of such evidence that the structural arrangement of both of these alkaline halides was confirmed.

Although the preceding analysis is somewhat simplified, it is a typical example of the method used in the early determinations of crystal structure. A number of orders of diffracted waves were measured, either with the ionization spectrometer or on a photographic plate, and an attempt was then made to find an atomic arrangement that accounted for the relative intensities of the various orders.

The Significance of $F(hkl)$

The quantity $F(hkl)$ is the cornerstone of X-ray analysis, and its determination is the final aim of all experimental methods. This quantity is a measure, for each order (hkl), of the intensity of the beam scattered by the whole unit of a pattern expressed in terms of the amount scattered by a single electron as a unit. For instance, the quantity $F(000)$ is scattered in the forward direction through zero angle, so that there are no path differences to cause interference; $F(000)$ is therefore the total number of electrons in the unit of pattern. For higher orders

there is a reduction in intensity owing to interference.

It is important to note that $F(hkl)$ is a dimensionless ratio, characteristic only of the crystal structure. It is independent of the wavelength of the X rays. If a smaller wavelength is used, the orders appear at lower angles and path differences are reduced, but phase differences remain the same. Thus $F(hkl)$ depends only on the distribution of scattering matter in the unit cell, which it is the object of X-ray analysis to determine.

The theoretical basis for measuring values of $F(hkl)$ was laid down by C. G. Darwin in two brilliant papers soon after the discovery of X-ray diffraction. In those early days the experimental observations were too approximate for a test of his theory, and a number of years elapsed before it could be applied.

Darwin's first calculation assumed the crystal to be "ideally perfect." Rough tests showed, however, that the efficiency of reflection was many times stronger than his theory indicated. Darwin correctly reasoned that the cause of the discrepancy was the departure of the crystal from perfection. It is a curious paradox that imperfect crystals reflect more efficiently than perfect crystals. In the latter case the reflection, which is almost complete over a few seconds of arc, comes from a thin superficial layer only; planes at greater depths cannot contribute because the uppermost layers have robbed the radiation, so to speak, of the component the lower layers would otherwise have reflected. Actual crystals, however, are in general far from perfect. They are like a three-dimensional crazy quilt of small blocks that differ slightly in orientation; as a result the crystal reflects over an appreciable angular range. Within this range rays penetrate into the crystal until they encounter a block at the correct angle for reflection, and the contributions from all such blocks add to the total reflection.

Darwin's second formula, therefore, applies to what is called an "ideally imperfect" crystal, and it is the formula always used. The intensity of the incident beam, or the amount of radiation per unit of time, is compared with the total amount of radiation received by the recorder as the crystal is swept through the reflecting range at a constant angular rate; this enables all elements of the mosaic to make their contribution to the reflection.

When calculating a value of $F(hkl)$ for a postulated atomic arrangement, it is necessary to know the contributions from individual atoms, which depend on the characteristic distribution of electrons in each atom. These distributions were calculated by Douglas R. Hartree in 1925 and are expressed as "F curves" typical of each atom. Intensity measurements were the subject of an extensive study by the University of Manchester

school, culminating in the paper by Reginald James, Ivar Waller and Hartree on the zero-point energy of the rock-salt lattice. Amplitudes of thermal vibration can be measured by their effects in reducing F values; by extrapolating to absolute zero it was found that the atoms still had a vibration corresponding to a half-quantum, as theoretical studies had indicated.

Experimental Measurements

When a diffracted X-ray beam is recorded by an ionization chamber, a Geiger counter or a proportional counter, the orders are recorded one by one, by setting the crystal and the chamber at suitable angles. Alternatively the beams can be recorded as spots on a photographic plate or film by turning the crystal during the exposure so that a number of planes can reflect. In the early crystal determinations the ionization spectrometer measured orders individually. As more complex crystals were attempted and more orders had to be measured, the photographic method was favored because a single exposure registered a large number of orders. Recently auto-

mation has obviated the tedium of making numerous individual measurements, and the most advanced analyses are now performed with counters as recorders.

The original X-ray spectrometer designed by W. H. Bragg is a typical example of the first method [*see illustration below*]. A collimated beam from the X-ray tube fell on the face of the crystal and was reflected through slits into the recording ionization chamber, which was filled with a heavy gas (methyl bromide) to increase ionization. The outer case was at a potential of several hundred volts, and the ionization was measured by driving the charge onto a coaxial wire connected to a tilted gold-leaf electroscope. It was with this instrument that my father made his pioneer investigations on the X-ray spectra from anticathodes of a number of different metals, a project that formed the basis for H. G. J. Moseley's subsequent work on atomic number; the early determinations of crystal structure, for which I was mainly responsible, were also made with this instrument.

Considering the crudeness of the apparatus by modern standards, it gave surprisingly accurate results. A main trouble arose from the vagaries of the X-ray

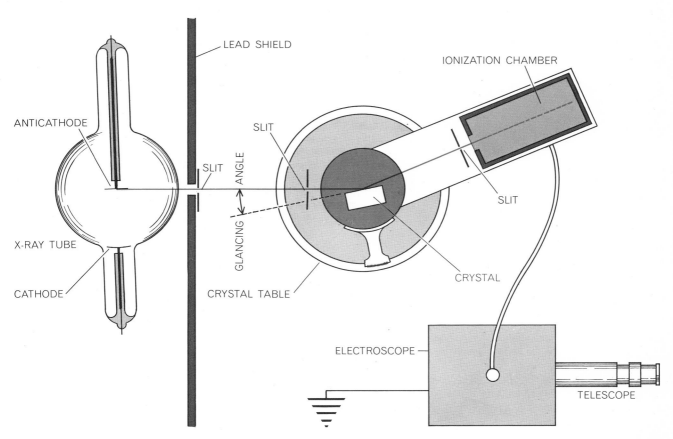

IONIZATION SPECTROMETER was the instrument used by the author's father, W. H. Bragg, to conduct the first investigations of the X-ray spectra from various metallic anticathodes and later by the author to make the early determinations of crystal structure.

tubes in those days. The tube was energized by a Rumkorff coil, first with a hammer switch and later with a mercury switch, which gave a steadier discharge. If the X rays from the tube got too hard, one held a match under a fine palladium tube attached to the main tube, which allowed some gas to diffuse in; if they got too soft, one sparked to a bunch of mica sheets inside, which absorbed some gas. The gold-leaf electroscope was also a tricky instrument for accurate work. I think that one of the main reasons why X-ray analysis developed in my father's laboratory at the University of Leeds, even though the fundamental discovery had been made in Germany, was that my father had so much experience in making accurate ionization measurements with the primitive apparatus then available.

When the diffracted beams are measured one by one, the indexing presents no difficulty because the crystal orientation that produces each beam is known. When many beams are recorded at the same time on a photographic plate, however, each of them must be identified. A number of ingenious methods have been devised for this purpose.

In general two types of X-ray photograph have been widely used. One type is called a "rotation" photograph [*see top illustration on next page*]. In this method the X rays fall on a small crystal, which is rotated around an axis that coincides with one of its principal crystal axes, and the diffracted beams are recorded on a cylindrical film. The images of the diffracted beams all lie on "layer lines"; for instance, if the crystal axis is along *OC*, the layer lines correspond to $l = 0$, $l = 1$, $l = 2$, and the spots have all values of h and k. If the spots are very numerous, it may be too difficult to sort them out and a Weissenberg camera is used. In this technique one layer line is singled out by a slit, and the film is translated as the crystal turns. If the film has been translated horizontally, the displacement of a spot along the horizontal axis tells the angle of setting of the crystal when it was recorded and so defines the other indices [*see illustration on page 169*].

Another elegant device in this category is the precession camera. Crystal, photographic plate and screen perform a sinuous dance in such a way that those spots, for instance, with a definite value of l and all values of h and k are recorded as a rectilinear net [*see illustration on page 162*]. This method is particularly suitable for crystals with large unit cells and consequently numerous values of the indices.

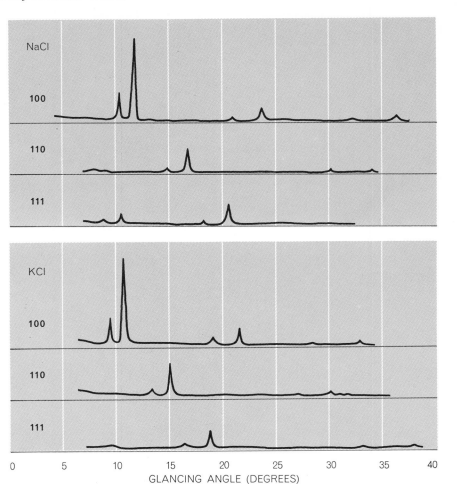

EARLY MEASUREMENTS of the intensity of the reflected X rays from sodium chloride (*top*) and potassium chloride (*bottom*) were made with the ionization spectrometer. The orders were reflected from crystal faces with crystallographic indices (100), (110) and (111). The two peaks seen on each order are the $K\alpha$ and $K\beta$ "lines" in the spectrum of the palladium anticathode, the $K\alpha$ line being the stronger of the two. For sodium chloride the order (111) is anomalously small, because the weak sodium contribution partially offsets the strong chlorine contribution, whereas for potassium chloride the order (111) is too weak to be observed, because the scattering powers of the potassium atoms and the chlorine atoms are so nearly similar. This comparison confirmed the structures assigned to the crystals.

The second general method of X-ray photography is the powder method, developed independently in 1916 by Peter J. W. Debye and Paul Scherrer in Switzerland and by Albert W. Hull in the U.S. [*see bottom illustration on next page*]. The powder method is used when the material is available only in microcrystalline form. The X rays fall on a mass of tiny crystals in all orientations, and the beams of each order (*hkl*) form a cone. Arcs of the cones are intercepted by a film surrounding the specimen. In the powder photographs of sodium chloride and potassium chloride on page 168 one can see that in sodium chloride there is a weak series for odd (*hkl*) values, whereas in potassium chloride these disappear because the scattering powers of the potassium atoms and the chlorine

atoms are so similar. In addition potassium chloride has a larger spacing than sodium chloride, hence the displacement of the arcs to smaller angles. The powder method has found its main use in the study of alloys.

Symmetry

The pattern of every crystal has certain symmetry elements that form a three-dimensional scaffolding on which the atoms are arranged, and these elements can be uniquely determined by the X-ray-diffraction method. In the early days of X-ray analysis, when the ionic compounds that were being studied often had a high symmetry, this fact was of great assistance in arriving at a solution. The possible schemes of symmetry

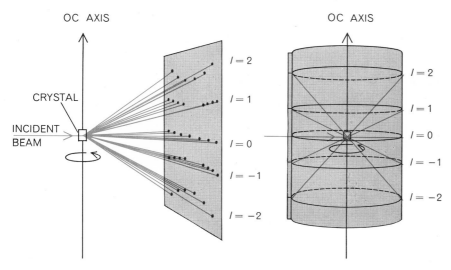

ROTATION PHOTOGRAPHS ARE MADE by aiming the X rays at a small crystal, which is rotated around an axis that coincides with one of its principal symmetry axes; the diffracted beams are recorded on either a flat plate (*left*) or a cylindrical film (*right*). The images of the diffracted beams all lie on "layer lines"; in this case the crystal axis is along OC, the layer lines correspond to $l = 0$, $l = 1$, $l = 2$ and the spots have all values of h and k.

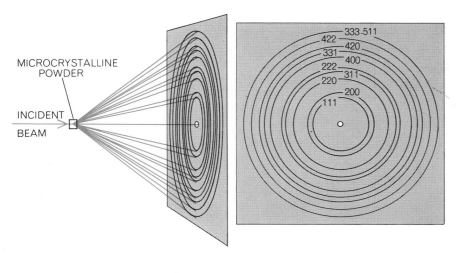

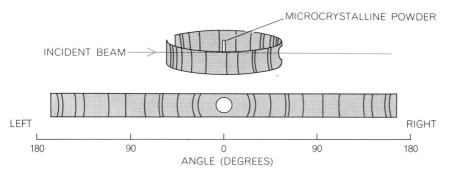

POWDER PHOTOGRAPHS ARE MADE by aiming the X rays at a mass of tiny crystals in all orientations. The diffracted beams of each order (hkl) will then form a cone. If recorded on a plate perpendicular to the incident beam, each diffraction order will appear as a ring surrounding the central spot (*top*); the positions of the rings shown are typical of a face-centered-cubic crystal lattice. It is usually more convenient to employ a cylindrical photographic film whose axis is perpendicular to the incident radiation (*bottom*). Arcs of the cones are intercepted at all angles up to nearly 180 degrees; the film is then unrolled.

are limited by geometry, just as the possible number of regular solid figures are limited, although in the case of crystal symmetries the number, 230, is quite large. Symmetry axes and symmetry planes can be identified by noting regular absences of diffracted-wave orders; the presence or absence of symmetry centers can be determined by a statistical survey of intensities, as was first shown by A. J. Wilson; crystals with symmetry centers characteristically have many more weak reflections than crystals with no symmetry centers.

Finally, X rays can tell "which way around" a structure is. Optically active molecules can have two forms, one of which is the reflection of the other (the dextro and levo forms of the chemist). In general when the waves scattered by the atoms have phases as if coming from atomic centers, these two forms give identical X-ray diffraction, that is, the reflection from the right-hand side has the same amplitude as that from the left, although the phase is reversed. When the wavelength of the X rays is close to an absorption edge of an atom, however, there is an appreciable phase change. The atom scatters as if at one location for the one side and at another location for the other side, so that the resultant amplitudes are different. This enables dextro and levo to be distinguished; for instance, in the classic case of a tetrahedron with four different corners one could tell for each orientation whether one was looking at an apex or a base. J. M. Biyvoet was the first to distinguish between dextro and levo forms of the tartrate ion. There was a 50 : 50 chance that the traditional chemical convention for representing dextro and levo was correct; luckily it turned out to be right!

Inorganic Compounds

The first crystals to be analyzed by means of X rays were simple types. An approximate measure of the complexity of a crystal is the number of parameters that must be determined in order to define the positions of the atoms. In the case of an atom at a symmetry center, for instance, no parameters are needed; it must be exactly at the center. If the atom lies on an axis, its position along the axis is fixed by one parameter; if on a reflection plane, by two; if in a position of no symmetry, by three.

The early determinations were limited to one or two parameters; in fact, it was doubted whether more complicated crystals would ever be analyzed. The break-

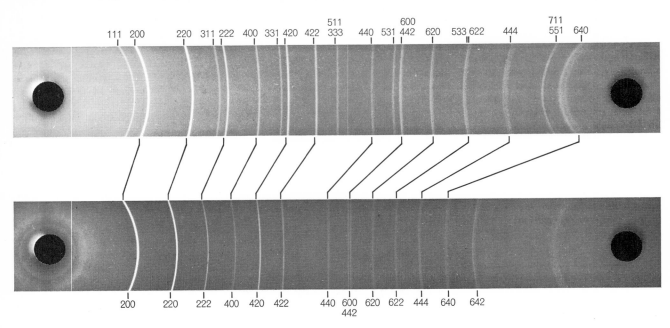

POWDER PHOTOGRAPHS of the diffracted X rays from sodium chloride (*top*) and potassium chloride (*bottom*) confirm the earlier findings made with the ionization spectrometer: In sodium chloride there is a weak series for odd (*hkl*) values, whereas in potassium chloride these orders disappear. Potassium chloride has a larger spacing; hence the arcs are displaced to smaller angles.

through into much more complex structures was made in the early 1920's by the Manchester school, where analysis was extended to cases of 10 or 20 parameters, a great advance at that time. It was made possible by quantitative measurements and increasing experience in the nature of inorganic compounds.

One of the first successes of X-ray analysis was to show that these compounds are not built of molecules. They are ionic in character, with a regular alternation of positive and negative ions held together by electrical attraction. For instance, in the sodium chloride structure there are no sodium chloride groups but rather a chessboard pattern of positive sodium ions and negative chlorine ions. It was difficult in the early days to reconcile the new view of ionic compounds with classical chemical ideas, but once accepted the ionic view afforded a much fuller understanding of the construction of such compounds.

In an ionic compound the ions pack together as if they had characteristic sizes. Their dimensions are not completely fixed, but they vary only over a small range. On the whole the negative ions are by far the largest, because their electrons are more loosely held.

The packing of ions of characteristic size is a very useful concept when postulating various atomic arrangements, particularly when combined with a knowledge of the symmetry elements. The hexagonal symmetry of the crystal beryl

($Be_3Al_2Si_6O_{18}$), for instance, is of a high order, with sixfold, threefold and twofold axes, symmetry planes and symmetry centers. An atom cannot overlap itself, so that it must either lie exactly on one of these symmetry elements or be just off it. This restriction is so demanding that the structure of beryl could be immediately deduced once the symmetry was determined. The top illustration on page 170 shows the only possible way of packing the atoms of the beryl formula into the network of symmetry elements.

The laws governing the structure of inorganic compounds, established by Linus Pauling in 1929, afford another guide in seeking a solution. They also explain why some compounds are stable, whereas others that seem equally plausible from a chemical point of view do not actually exist. Pauling's rule is based on the requirement that for stability the energy of the compound must be as low as possible. Each small positive ion lies inside a cluster of larger negative ions; for instance, very small positive ions such as beryllium or boron are each surrounded by three oxygen atoms; silicon is surrounded by four oxygens, magnesium and iron by six oxygens and still larger ions by eight or more oxygens. If we picture electric fields in terms of lines of force, suppose the number of lines representing the charge on the positive ion is divided equally between the negative ions coordinated around it. Pauling's rule states that the total number of lines com-

ing to the negative ion from all its positive neighbors just balances its charge. This might seem at first sight a simple rule, but it is powerful in excluding improbable structures. Its significance is that when Pauling's rule is obeyed, the lines of force between positive and negative ions stretch only over the very short distances between nearest neighbors, so that the energy of the electric field is at a minimum and the structure is stable.

The study of inorganic compounds culminated in the determination of all the common mineral forms, in particular the silicates. These compounds obey Pauling's rule rigorously, because they must be very stable in order to exist as minerals. The explanation of their composition proved to be very interesting. Their nature is determined by the silicon-to-oxygen ratio, ranging from SiO_4 in the basic rocks to SiO_2 in quartz. Although the ratio varies widely, the silicon ion is always surrounded by four oxygen atoms; the silicon-oxygen tetrahedrons may, however, share no corners, one corner, two corners, three corners or four corners by having an oxygen atom in common. In the SiO_3 silicates, for example, there are long strings of SiO_4 groups that run endlessly through the structure, representing infinite linear negative ions bound laterally by the positive ions. The silicate groups occur as sheet ions in the micas and clays, and as three-dimensional-network ions with metals in their interstices in the feldspars. This unexpected feature of minerals explains their composition in a simple and elegant way; it is one of the important new conceptions introduced by X-ray analysis.

Alloys

After the nature of inorganic compounds had been clarified, the next achievement of X-ray analysis was to explain the nature of metallic alloys, which had hitherto been so mysterious. The pioneer investigations into alloy structure were made by Arne F. Westgren in Sweden. They were developed by Albert J. Bradley and his pupils at Manchester, for the most part between 1925 and 1935. The powder method was used perforce, because the material was in microcrystalline form, and in Bradley's hands it reached a peak of perfection that has hardly been equaled since. The ground covered was so extensive that it is only possible to give the briefest summary.

In the first place, the determination of

alloy structure provided the foundation on which a theory of alloy chemistry could be developed. When two metals unite in varying composition, they form a series of phases. These compounds are non-Daltonian, that is, they are not composed of some simple ratio of elements; on the contrary, each exists over a range of composition. William Hume-Rothery first pointed out that in different binary systems phases with very similar physical properties tend to have the same ratio of free electrons to atoms in their composition. Structure determinations showed that such phases have a closely similar atomic arrangement but with curious characteristics. The essential similarity lies in the positions occupied by atoms, not in the way the kinds of atoms are distributed among the places. Apparently the relation of atom to atom is relatively immaterial; it is the position of the atoms that is all-important. This in turn was explained by theoretical physicists in terms of Brillouin zones. Treating the free elec-

trons as standing waves, the system has a low energy if the electrons of shortest wavelength are just too long to be reflected by the most marked reflecting planes in the phase structure. In the stable phase the atoms take up arrangements that create the strongly reflecting planes required for low energy. To put it broadly, an alloy is not a compound between one metal and another but rather a compound between all the metal atoms on the one hand and all the free electrons on the other. It is perhaps not too much to say that the X-ray determination of alloy structures led for the first time to a rational theory of metal chemistry.

Equilibrium systems, or the phases produced by variations of composition, had previously been deduced from studies of polished and etched specimens, but they can be mapped out far more directly by X-ray analysis. Phases can be recognized by their powder photographs and the composition of the phase in any given case can, after some preliminary trials, be fixed by noting which spacings of the unit cell vary over the range. Ternary and even quaternary systems, which would hardly be amenable to metallographic methods, can be tackled by X-ray methods.

An interesting application in this area was found in the "order-disorder" systems. An example of such a system is the copper-gold alloy Cu_3Au, first studied by Gudmund Borelius of Sweden. At high temperatures all the points of the face-centered-cubic lattice of this alloy are occupied at random by gold or copper atoms; at low temperatures after slow annealing the gold atoms segregate into the cube corners, leaving the face centers to the copper atoms. The progress of the segregation can be followed by the appearance of new lines, corresponding to greater spacings, in the powder photographs. The variation of segregation with temperature presents interesting thermodynamic problems of second-order phase change, and the X-ray work did much to stimulate the study of corresponding changes in other systems.

Another phenomenon studied intensively by Bradley was the splitting of a phase into regions with slightly different composition, which were nonetheless united in having a continuous crystal lattice. Such segregation sets up intense internal strains. It is characteristic of alloys used as strong permanent magnets, because the strains give the material a high magnetic retentivity.

In general, X-ray analysis has provided a powerful new tool for examining the properties of alloy systems, an achieve-

WEISSENBERG PHOTOGRAPH is a type of rotation photograph that is used when the spots are too numerous to sort out by the conventional method. In this technique one layer line is singled out by a slit, and the film is translated as the crystal turns. The displacement of a spot along the translation axis (in this case the horizontal axis) tells the angle of setting of the crystal when it was recorded and so defines the other reflection indices of the crystal.

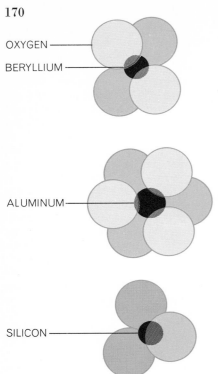

OXYGEN

BERYLLIUM

ALUMINUM

SILICON

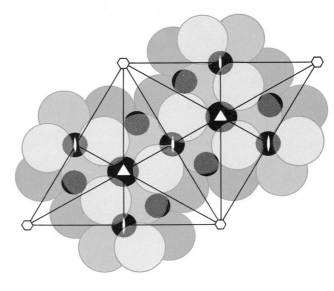

VERTICAL-ROTATION AXES

◊ TWO-FOLD AXIS

△ THREE-FOLD AXIS

⬡ SIX-FOLD AXIS

STRUCTURE OF BERYL (*right*), a complex inorganic compound with the formula $Be_3Al_2Si_6O_{18}$, was deduced from a knowledge of the packing of the constituent ions (*left*) as soon as the basic hexagonal symmetry of the crystal was determined by X-ray diffraction. Since an atom must lie exactly on one of the symmetry elements or be just off it, there could be only one way of packing the atoms of the beryl formula into the network of symmetry elements. A key to the symmetry axes of the crystal is given at bottom.

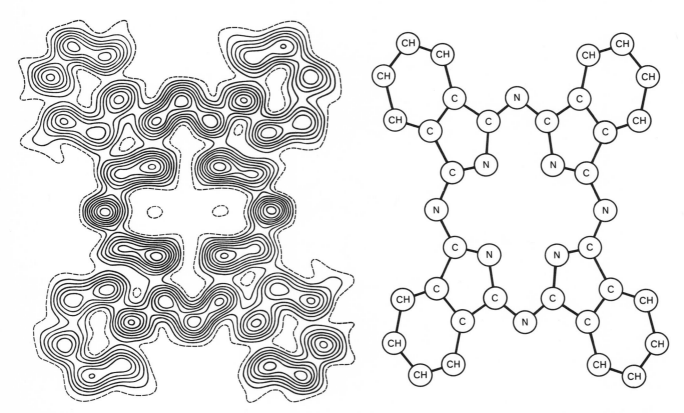

FOURIER REPRESENTATION of the electron-density distribution in a molecule of phthalocyanine (*left*) was used to construct the atomic model of the molecule (*right*). The Fourier "density map" is arrived at by treating a molecular structure not as a cluster of individual atoms but as a continuous electron distribution capable of scattering X rays. The density distribution of the molecule as a whole is obtained by adding together the terms of a Fourier series, a mathematical expression that can be used to represent the periodic variation of sets of electron-density sheets in all directions. The Fourier method is ideal for analyzing organic molecules.

ment that has great technical importance as well as scientific interest.

The Fourier Method

Another method of X-ray analysis attacks the solution of the crystal structure from a quite different angle. So far the crystal has been regarded as a pattern of atoms, each of which scatters X rays as if from its center with an efficiency determined by Hartree's *F* curves. The resultant of the waves scattered by these atoms is then compared with the observed amplitude of reflection, the position of the atoms being adjusted to give the best fit.

This method was successful as long as the number of atoms in the unit cell was small. As increasingly complex crystals were studied, however, it became more and more difficult to try adjustments of so many parameters simultaneously,

even when the structure was approximately known. The refining of the structure to get the best fit became extremely laborious.

The Fourier method is in a sense a complete reversal of this process. A structure is treated not as a cluster of atoms but as a continuous electron distribution capable of scattering X rays. The investigator seeks to map this continuous distribution, and, if he is successful, he can then recognize the positions of the atoms by noting where the electron density rises to peak values. There is no juggling with the positions of atoms one by one; the density map shows the best position for all of them, however large their number.

The density distributions are mapped by adding together the terms of a "Fourier series," a mathematical expression that can be used to represent any quan-

tity that varies periodically. Since a crystal is a periodic pattern in three dimensions, the electron density can be represented by a three-dimensional Fourier series. Each element of the series is a set of electron sheets, or strata, that vary periodically in density, and if the amplitudes and phases of these sheets (which crisscross in all directions) are known, they can be added and the result is a plot of the density distribution.

My father first pointed out, in his Bakerian Lecture to the Royal Society of London in 1915, that each of these periodic components reflects one corresponding order and only that order; moreover, the amplitude of the reflected waves is proportional to the amplitude of the Fourier component. Since changes in the phase of the reflected waves can still give the same X-ray effects, however, the only way of choosing the right phase

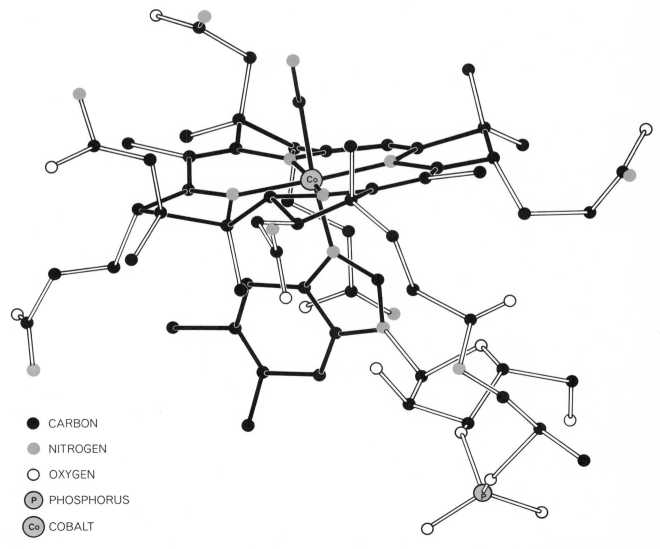

● CARBON

● NITROGEN

○ OXYGEN

(P) PHOSPHORUS

(Co) COBALT

STRUCTURE OF VITAMIN B-12, solved by Dorothy Crowfoot Hodgkin in 1955, represented one of the outstanding achieve- ments of what might be called the classical methods of X-ray analysis. The formula of vitamin B-12 molecule is $C_{63}H_{84}N_{14}O_{14}PCo$.

is to introduce some criterion of reality leading to a picture with the right number of atoms of the right kind in the unit cell. The Fourier method therefore centers around a "phase hunt." Once the phases are known the structure is "in the bag."

Organic Molecules

From 1930 onward the Fourier method was recognized as being ideal for analyzing organic molecules, and many were determined in this way. The first organic structures, naphthalene and anthracene, had been outlined by W. H. Bragg in 1922 at the same time that the study of inorganic structures was pursued at Manchester, and his laboratory at the Royal Institution concentrated on the organic field.

Initially most of the studies dealt with crystals that had symmetry centers. This is a great simplification of the problem, because the phases of the Fourier components with respect to such a center must by symmetry be either 0 or π; in other words, $F(hkl)$ must be either plus or minus. The advantage here is that calculations on the basis of a quite rough approximation of the structure generally make it clear which is the right sign, particularly in the case of the strong and therefore important orders. A Fourier series can then be calculated, the position of the atoms can be improved, further signs that were formerly doubtful can be fixed and a new Fourier can be summed. This process of refinement is rapidly convergent, and after a few stages the structure is accurately determined.

A three-dimensional Fourier series is a formidable affair, and in these attacks on organic structures the less ambitious task of using two-dimensional series and getting a projection of the structure on a plane was more usually undertaken. Projections on the three principal planes define the positions of the atoms in space. A pretty example of this was the analysis of phthalocyanine with 60 parameters, where the signs of the F's were found without any guesswork as to the nature of the structure [*see bottom illustration on page 170*].

It is possible to substitute a heavy atom at the center of the phthalocyanine molecule without any alteration in the crystal lattice. If a spot becomes stronger when the heavy atom is introduced, its original F value with respect to the center of the molecule must have been positive; if the spot becomes weaker, the F value must have been negative. All the signs were determined in this way and

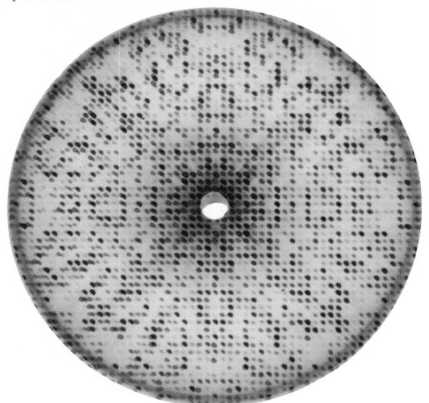

ADDITION OF A HEAVY ATOM at a specific place among the molecules in a protein crystal provided the key that has led to the recent solution of several protein structures. In this illustration of the method two precession photographs of the same crystal of lysozyme are superposed with a slight relative displacement. The set of spots due to the native protein is printed in black. The set of spots due to the protein with the heavy atom is printed in color. Numerous changes in the intensities of corresponding spots can be detected.

used in a two-dimensional Fourier series. The result is shown as a contour plot of the electron densities.

In most cases the results of X-ray analysis confirmed the topography assigned to the molecules by organic chemistry, but the X-ray findings determined the bond distances and bond angles with great accuracy and so cast much light on the nature of the bonds.

The next stage in the study of organic molecules was to tackle far more complex structures, some of which had defeated the efforts of organic chemists to elucidate their stereochemistry. A forerunner of this stage was the solution of strychnine by Biyvoet in 1948, published independently at almost the same time that Sir Robert Robinson's researchers at the University of Oxford arrived at an identical structure by purely chemical reasoning. The outstanding examples are the solution of penicillin and vitamin B-12; in each case Dorothy Crowfoot Hodgkin of Oxford was the leader of the research. The latter investigation was a saga of X-ray analysis that took eight years. Not only was much chemical information about the molecule lacking

but also conclusions arrived at on chemical grounds were actually misleading. The molecule, of formula $C_{63}H_{84}N_{14}O_{14}PCo$, is shown in the illustration on the preceding page.

The solution illustrates the curious and unique character of X-ray analysis, which is reminiscent of the solution of a code, or of an ancient form of writing such as Egyptian hieroglyphics or Minoan Linear B. It was first assumed that the phases of the F's were those of the cobalt atom (Co) at the center of the molecule and a Fourier series was formed on this hypothesis. Although it turned out that this is far from true, the phases are, as it were, weighted in this direction because the cobalt atom is so heavy compared with the other atoms. Fourier series have a surprisingly obliging way of trying to tell the investigator something with the most sketchy basis of information, and in this case the series outlined in a shadowy way the molecular structure immediately surrounding the cobalt atom. The information was used to adjust the phases, and a further series was formed and so the structure gradually began to emerge from the cobalt atom outward. The calculations would have been impossibly onerous had it not been for the availability of electronic computing of structure factors and three-dimensional Fourier series. The solution of vitamin B-12 represented the highest flight of what might be called the classical methods of X-ray analysis, and the Nobel prize awarded to Mrs. Hodgkin in 1964 was a well-deserved acknowledgment of her achievement.

Biochemical Molecules

We now come to a most dramatic turning point in the history of X-ray analysis. When vitamin B-12 was analyzed, with 181 atoms in the molecule, it seemed hard to imagine that much more complex structures could ever be tackled; it had taken eight years to complete and the difficulties increase as a high power of the number of atoms. And then, as the result of an investigation that had lasted for some 20 years, a way was finally found to solve the structure of the immensely more complicated molecules of living matter, the proteins. The first of these to be analyzed, by John C. Kendrew in 1955, was myoglobin, which has 2,500 atoms in its molecule.

By a curious paradox, the very size of such a molecule has opened up a new line of attack that is not possible in the case of simpler types, leading to a direct determination of phases without any element of guesswork or trial and error. The principle is the same as in the case of phthalocyanine described above, where the substitution of a heavy atom in the molecule enabled the signs of the F values to be found. A discovery made by M. F. Perutz in 1953 made it possible to generalize this method for the proteins.

He found that heavy atoms such as mercury and gold, or complexes containing such atoms, can be incorporated at specific places in the framework of the protein crystal without affecting the arrangement of the molecules, which are so large and loosely packed that the added groups find places in the interstices. Further, Perutz showed that the added heavy atom produces changes in the F values large enough to be accurately measurable. It might at first sight appear strange that the addition of one heavy atom of mercury to a protein molecule with 2,500 atoms of carbon, oxygen and hydrogen should make an appreciable difference; it does so because the scattering comes from one center, whereas the random contribution from n atoms ranging over all phases is proportional to $\sqrt{n}$, not to n. The changes in intensity caused by the addition of a heavy atom can be seen when two precession photographs made with the same crystal are superposed with a slight relative displacement [*see illustration on preceding page*]. The black set of spots is due to the native protein, the colored set to the protein with a heavy atom, and a close examination will show numerous changes in the intensities of corresponding spots.

It is necessary to find some three or four heavy atoms that can be attached to definite sites on the molecule. Although the structure is initially unknown, direct methods are available for finding the relative positions of these "staining" atoms. The phase difference between the F value H due to the heavy atom and the F value P due to the protein can be found by comparing $F(P)$ with $F(P + H)$, because $F(P + H)$ must be the vectorial resultant of $F(P)$ and $F(H)$; the knowl-

edge of the phase difference for several heavy atoms pins down the position of the Fourier component.

Because the solution is direct it can be found by giving instructions to a computer. The computer is essential because the complexity is so great. Some 100,000 or 200,000 intensities must be measured accurately by means of an automatic machine that sets the crystal and the recorder at the right positions for one order after another and lists the results. A corresponding number of equations must be solved to find the phases, and the Fourier series of many thousands of terms must be formed. This long series must be summed at perhaps a quarter of a million places in the unit cell to give the density at each point. The information is then automatically turned into contours, which are plotted on stacked transparent sheets, and the investigator has then to translate the density distribution into atomic arrangement.

The final result is impressive. Some half-dozen protein structures have so far been analyzed and they are already beginning to yield valuable information on such vital biochemical processes as the operation of enzymes. The second protein molecule to be analyzed successfully (after myoglobin) was the enzyme lysozyme (by David C. Phillips). The most recent success has been hemoglobin (by Perutz); the model of this protein contains 10,000 atoms. I confess that when I contemplate one of these models, I can still hardly believe that it has been possible to work out all its details by the optical principles of X-ray analysis, which half a century ago claimed sodium chloride as its first success.

16

Infrared Astronomy

Bruce C. Murray and James A. Westphal   *August 1965*

The basic task of the astronomer is to record samples of the radiation emitted and reflected by celestial objects. The obstacles to the fulfillment of this task are numerous. Historically they have included ignorance of the kind of radiation to look for, ignorance of the filtering action of the earth's atmosphere, and lack of instruments to detect radiation of certain wavelengths.

In this article we shall describe briefly how the obstacles have largely been surmounted in the infrared region of the spectrum. The radiation in this region, which lies between the visible spectrum and the microwave region of the radio spectrum, carries information needed to determine the surface temperature of the moon and some of the planets and the nature of planetary atmospheres; it also bears unique clues to the nature of luminous objects throughout the universe—from very cool stars to the extraordinarily brilliant quasi-stellar sources.

Until World War II advances in infrared astronomy were few and far between. Since then there has been rapid progress in infrared techniques and in the volume of new findings. Up to now the most important work has been done with earth-based instruments. The next stage, which is just beginning, is the use of balloons to carry instruments above most of the earth's atmosphere. Eventually, when satellite laboratories are large enough and reliable enough, they may make a valuable contribution. There is no danger, however, that ground-based observers will soon be unemployed: their infrared techniques are still being developed much faster, and yielding richer dividends, than those associated with balloons and space vehicles.

Infrared astronomy had its origin in observations made by Sir William Herschel in 1800, long before there were photographic plates or other means for recording radiation. Using his eye as a detector, he observed the sun through "differently coloured darkening glasses" (that is, filters). "What appeared remarkable," he wrote, "was that when I used some of them, I felt a sensation of heat, though I had but little light; while others gave me much light, with scarce any sensation of heat."

This prompted Herschel to conduct a famous experiment in which he used a prism to separate sunlight into its various colors and compared the temperature at different points in the spectrum by means of a glass thermometer whose mercury bulb had been blackened with ink. Two other thermometers located out of the path of the sun's rays served as controls. Herschel was surprised to find that the sunlit thermometer showed a steady increase in temperature as he moved it from the violet end of the spectrum to the red end—and that the temperature remained high for some distance beyond the visible red. Herschel subsequently demonstrated that this "infra-red" radiation was produced not only by the sun but also by other sources, and that it obeyed the same laws of reflection and refraction that apply to visible light.

Today the term "infrared radiation" is commonly used to describe electromagnetic radiation whose wavelength lies between .75 micron (750 millimicrons), which is just beyond the red end of the visible spectrum, and roughly 3,000 microns (three millimeters), the beginning of the region that can be detected by microwave radio techniques. The distinction between infrared astronomy and radio astronomy is therefore an arbitrary one, based entirely on differences in detection techniques. In radio astronomy celestial radiation that has been collected by an antenna system is fed into a device that operates as a wave detector. Although strenuous efforts have been made to reduce the wavelengths at which such detectors operate, progress has been slow. World War II radar technology pushed the detectable wavelength down to 1.2 centimeters, or 12 millimeters. After 20 years of effort the shortest operating wavelength for a wave detector has been lowered to about three millimeters. Between .75 micron and three millimeters the only practical detectors are those the infrared astronomer can use in conjunction with optical telescopes, so this piece of the electromagnetic spectrum remains his by right of occupancy. The region between 22 microns and 1,000 microns is still almost entirely unexplored, however, largely because little radiation in this region can penetrate the earth's atmosphere. The transparency of the earth's atmosphere to infrared radiation of various wavelengths is plotted at the top of the illustration on page 176.

For convenience infrared astronomers have labeled portions of the infrared region according to the mode of detection or to the bandwidth of particular "windows" in the atmosphere. Thus the region from .75 micron to 1.2 microns is called the photographic infrared, because photographic emulsions still respond to radiation of such wavelengths. In fact, the first photograph in the infrared was made by Sir John Herschel (Sir William's son) in 1840, before suitable silver-salt emulsions were available. He recorded a portion of the infrared spectrum of the sun by exposing paper that had been soaked with alcohol containing particles of carbon black; the heat of the infrared radiation evaporated the alcohol in such a way as to leave a detectable image. Some 100 years later the photographic infrared provided the first evidence of carbon dioxide on Venus, water vapor and carbon dioxide on Mars and hydrogen on Jupiter. These and other landmarks in the history of infrared astronomy are listed in the illustration on the next page.

All astronomical observations beyond 1.2 microns are currently made with one-dimensional detectors, that is, detectors that respond only to the radiant energy collected at a single point in the image. The region from 1.2 to 5.2 microns is usually called the near infrared. In the region from 5.2 to 8 microns the earth's atmosphere is completely opaque. There is then a window between 8 and 14 microns, loosely described as the long-wavelength infrared; the term can be stretched to include radiation that enters through still another window from about 17 to 22 microns. No important astronomical measurements have yet been made in the region between 22 and 1,000 microns, but it is suspected that somewhere in this large expanse of the spectrum there are a few windows of potential significance for ground-based astronomy.

The first of the one-dimensional infrared detectors was the thermocouple, which consists of a junction of two dis-

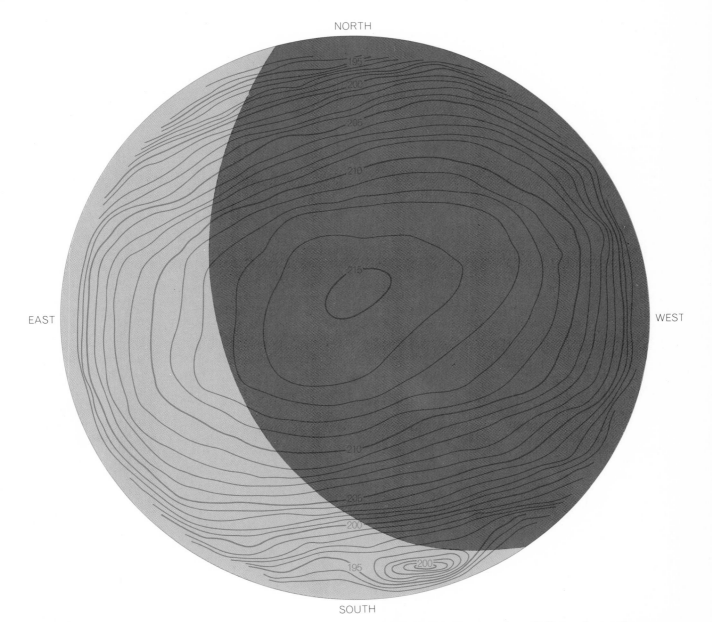

INFRARED MAP OF VENUS was made by the authors and Robert L. Wildey of the California Institute of Technology, using an 8-to-14-micron infrared detector in conjunction with the 200-inch Hale telescope on Palomar Mountain. The infrared radiation that can be observed by scanning the disk of Venus at 8 to 14 microns is thermal radiation emitted by the sun-heated atmosphere. The figures in the diagram represent in degrees Kelvin (degrees centigrade above absolute zero) the "brightness temperature" of Venus. The brightness temperature is equivalent to the actual temperature if an object emits at all wavelengths as though it were a black body. On the Kelvin scale the range from 195 to 220 degrees represents a range from —78 to —53 degrees C. These are temperatures in the upper atmosphere of Venus; the surface temperature is believed to be above the boiling point of water. Note that the temperature across the disk does not change at the terminator: the dividing line between the sunlit hemisphere (left) and the dark hemisphere.

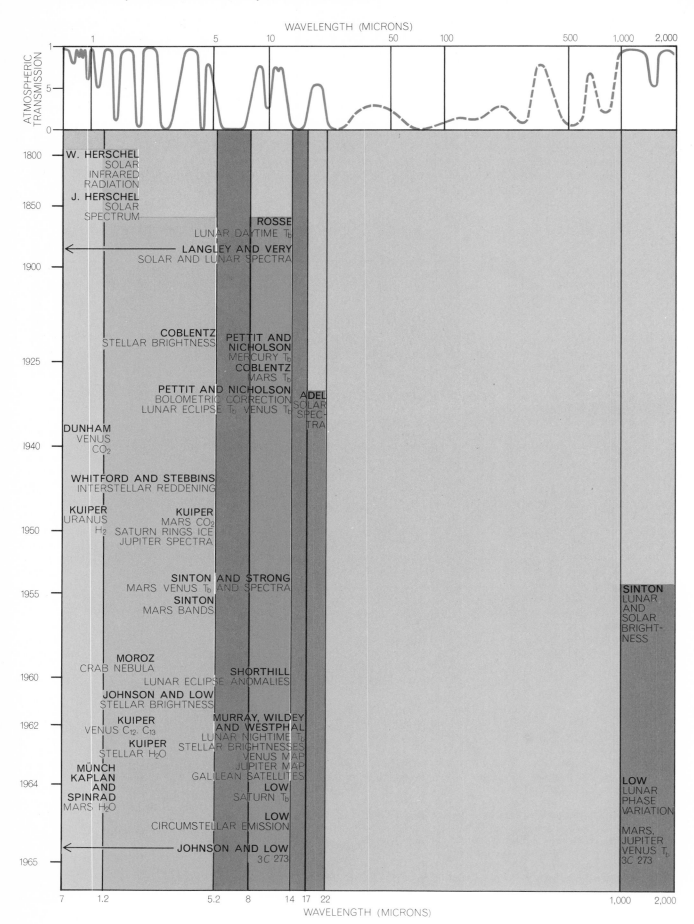

WAVELENGTH (MICRONS)

ATMOSPHERIC TRANSMISSION

1800 W. HERSCHEL
SOLAR
INFRARED
RADIATION
1850 J. HERSCHEL
SOLAR
SPECTRUM
ROSSE
LUNAR DAYTIME T_b

← LANGLEY AND VERY
SOLAR AND LUNAR SPECTRA

1900

COBLENTZ
STELLAR BRIGHTNESS
PETTIT AND
NICHOLSON
MERCURY T_b
1925 COBLENTZ
MARS T_b
PETTIT AND NICHOLSON
BOLOMETRIC CORRECTION
LUNAR ECLIPSE T_b, VENUS T_b
ADEL
SOLAR
SPEC-
TRA
DUNHAM
VENUS
CO_2
1940

WHITFORD AND STEBBINS
INTERSTELLAR REDDENING

KUIPER
URANUS
H_2
KUIPER
MARS CO_2
SATURN RINGS ICE
1950 JUPITER SPECTRA

SINTON AND STRONG
MARS VENUS T_b AND SPECTRA
SINTON
1955 MARS BANDS
SINTON
LUNAR
AND
SOLAR
BRIGHT-
NESS

MOROZ
CRAB NEBULA
SHORTHILL
LUNAR ECLIPSE ANOMALIES
1960 JOHNSON AND LOW
STELLAR BRIGHTNESS

KUIPER
VENUS C_{12}, C_{13}
1962 KUIPER
STELLAR H_2O
MURRAY, WILDEY
AND WESTPHAL
LUNAR NIGHTIME T_b
STELLAR BRIGHTNESSES
VENUS MAP
JUPITER MAP
GALILEAN SATELLITES
LOW
SATURN T_b
MÜNCH
KAPLAN
AND
SPINRAD
MARS H_2O
1964 LOW
LUNAR
PHASE
VARIATION
LOW
CIRCUMSTELLAR EMISSION
MARS,
JUPITER
VENUS T_b
3C 273
← JOHNSON AND LOW
3C 273
1965

WAVELENGTH (MICRONS)

similar metals; heating of the junction generates a small flow of electric current. A parallel array of thermocouples is known as a thermopile; it was first used in astronomy almost 100 years ago by William Parsons (Lord Rosse) to measure the 8-to-14-micron radiation emitted by the full moon and collected by a reflecting telescope. (The glass lenses in a refracting telescope will not transmit radiation much beyond 1.5 microns.) In 1880 Samuel Pierpont Langley invented another one-dimensional detector: the bolometer, a device that measures the increase in electrical resistance that results when a blackened metal foil is heated by absorbing radiation. With the bolometer Langley and Frank Washington Very made crude measurements of the infrared spectra of the sun and moon out to about 14 microns.

Early in this century the sensitivity of the thermocouple was increased by placing it in a vacuum. This improvement enabled W. W. Coblentz to measure the near-infrared emission of stars for the first time. In the late 1920's Edison Pettit and Seth B. Nicholson introduced the concept of the stellar bolometric correction, a correction applied to estimates of the energy output of stars that is based on infrared measurements out to 14 microns. They also took the first infrared readings of the moon during an eclipse. Soon thereafter Arthur Adel pushed infrared measurements of the solar spectrum out to about 22 microns.

The next big advance in infrared detectors was the Golay cell, invented by Marcel J. E. Golay in 1942. In this device the heating of a confined gas creates a pressure that slightly distorts a mirror against which a beam of light is directed; thus any change in temperature within the cell results in a displacement of the beam of reflected

LANDMARKS in the history of infrared astronomy are listed in this chart, which is vertically logarithmic in time backward from the present. The surnames of the major investigators are given, together with short identifications of their achievements. The transparency of the earth's atmosphere to infrared radiation of various wavelengths is plotted at top. The symbol "T_b" signifies brightness temperature. The label "3C 273" (bottom) denotes a quasi-stellar radio source, or quasar. Light gray region is unexplored; very little radiation in this region can penetrate the earth's atmosphere.

INFRARED RADIATION WAS DISCOVERED by Sir William Herschel in 1800 with the experimental apparatus depicted in this contemporary engraving. Herschel used a prism (D) to separate sunlight into its various wavelengths and compared the temperature at different points in the spectrum by means of a glass thermometer whose mercury bulb had been blackened with ink (1). Two other thermometers (2 and 3) located out of the path of the sun's rays served as controls. He was surprised to find that the sunlit thermometer showed a steady increase in temperature as he moved it from the violet end of the spectrum to the red end and, moreover, that the temperature remained high beyond the visible red.

light. With the Golay cell, shortly after World War II, William M. Sinton and John Strong made new measurements of the 8-to-14-micron radiation from Venus and Mars and brought up to date the values Coblentz had obtained some 30 years earlier for the "brightness temperature" of these planets. The brightness temperature of an object is equivalent to its kinetic (that is, actual) temperature only if the object emits at all wavelengths as if it were a black body. The emissivity of a planet is influenced, however, by such things as the roughness of its surface. If the planet has an atmosphere, the transparency and the temperature of the atmosphere also contribute to the planet's overall brightness temperature. For Venus, Sinton and Strong obtained a brightness temperature near the center of the planet's disk of 235 degrees Kelvin (38 degrees below zero centigrade, the freezing point of water). For Mars they confirmed Coblentz' estimate that the surface temperature is only a few degrees above the freezing point of water (273 degrees Kelvin).

The Golay cell in its present form

approaches the limit of sensitivity attainable by any detector operated in thermal equilibrium with a room-temperature environment. An uncooled and unshielded detector responds to all the infrared radiation that impinges on it. When the background brightness of the sky is also taken into account, the infrared astronomer's situation can be compared to the one in which a visible-light astronomer would find himself if he tried to observe the stars by day with a luminous telescope.

The infrared emission of the earth's atmosphere is particularly strong in the 8-to-14-micron region of the spectrum [see bottom illustration on next page]. In a typical case photons of these wavelengths will strike an uncooled detector at a rate of 10^{15} per second. The statistical fluctuation under such circumstances will be about 3×10^7 photons per second; therefore any signal of this strength or less cannot be distinguished from "noise" in one second of observing time. By lengthening the observing time and integrating the detector output the effect of noise can be reduced, but to obtain an improvement

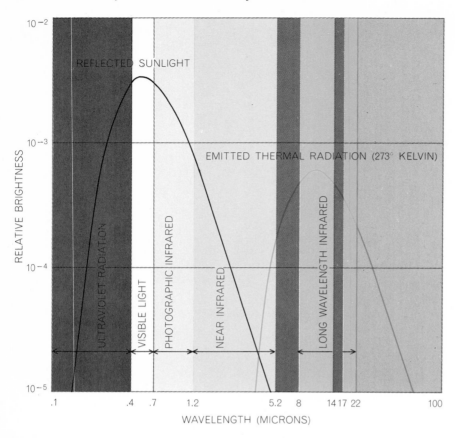

RADIATION FROM MARS falls into two main categories, reflected solar radiation (*left*) and emitted thermal radiation (*right*), which overlap in the near-infrared region of the spectrum. "Windows" in the earth's atmosphere that admit infrared radiation are in color. The peak of the emitted radiation happens to be centered in the 8-to-14-micron window.

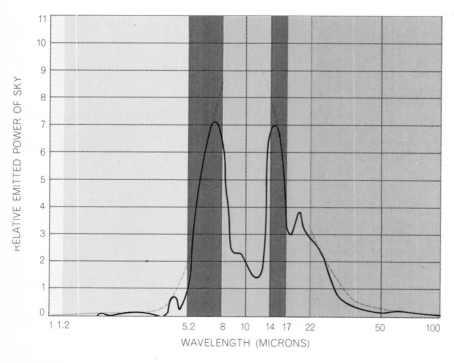

RADIATION EMITTED BY EARTH'S ATMOSPHERE (*black curve*) is substantial at 8 to 14 microns. If, however, the atmosphere emitted as much radiation as a black body does at 300 degrees K. (*colored curve*), the 8-to-14-micron window would be all but useless.

by a factor of 10 the observing time must be increased by a factor of 100.

The long-sought goal of producing a cooled and shielded thermal detector was attained in 1960 by Frank J. Low at the firm of Texas Instruments, Incorporated. Low, who is now associated with the National Radio Astronomy Observatory in Greenbank, W.Va., developed a bolometer that operates at a few degrees K., the temperature at which liquid helium evaporates. The bolometer is at the bottom of a cylindrical metal shield that is refrigerated by liquid nitrogen. Thus few infrared photons can reach the detector except those defined by the cylinder's field of view. (An arrangement similar to the one used by Low is illustrated at the bottom of the opposite page.) With his cooled detector Low was successful in observing the 8-to-14-micron radiation from Saturn for the first time; he has also measured the one-millimeter emission from Jupiter and other objects.

E fforts since World War II to exploit the infrared region of the spectrum for military purposes have led to the development of an entirely new class of detector that uses semiconducting crystals. These devices, known as quantum infrared detectors or photoconductive detectors, have the ability to absorb individual infrared photons and to release a unit of electric charge for each photon absorbed. The conductivity of the crystal depends on the number of charge carriers released; thus conductivity can be used as a measure of infrared flux. Although the new detectors are noisier than Low's bolometer, they have been steadily improved, are easy to obtain and have given a great impetus to infrared astronomy. For the first time detector sensitivity is no longer the most serious limitation in carrying out infrared observations with earth-based telescopes.

A standard arrangement for using sensitive detectors in infrared astronomy is illustrated at the top of the opposite page. The detector is exposed alternately to two beams; one beam consists of radiation from the celestial object and the surrounding sky, the other of radiation from the sky alone. A rotating chopper blade determines which beam reaches the detector. If the infrared flux of the two beams is different, the detector will produce a fluctuating signal proportional to differences in radiation energy in the two beams; in this way a steady sky background is eliminated. The signal is rectified to yield a direct-current voltage, which is then recorded. Finally, after suitable calibration of the instrument, the observed voltage is used to compute the infrared flux intercepted by the aperture of the telescope. The major remaining source of error in such measurements is a persistent uncertainty involving the irregular transparency of the atmosphere to radiation of various wavelengths. To reduce this uncertainty to a negligible level will require an intensive study of the absorption and emission properties of the atmosphere at various times of the day and in various seasons.

Let us now turn to some of the things that have been accomplished in infrared astronomy with the new detectors. Among the topics that have received much attention is the composition of the atmospheres of the nearby planets. Because Mars has long seemed to be the planet most hospitable to life it has been intensively studied. One discovery, which caused a considerable stir at the time of its announcement in 1956, has since been shown to have an explanation other than the one first proposed, but it provides a good example of the pitfalls that abound in this new and difficult field.

In 1956 Sinton, then at the Smithsonian Astrophysical Observatory, conceived of a way to test the hypothesis that the dark regions of Mars, which change in appearance with the Martian seasons, may consist of vegetation. If the vegetation contains complex compounds of carbon and hydrogen, they should absorb infrared radiation at characteristic wavelengths. Such absorption is a general property of organic compounds, whether they are produced by living organisms or not.

Sinton therefore examined the sunlight reflected from Mars to see if any of the incident radiation in the region between 3 and 4 microns might be missing. If it were, one could assume that it had been absorbed by vegetation, particularly if the absorption changed with the seasons. When Sinton compared the sunlight reflected from a typical bright region on Mars with that from a dark region, he found that the latter had seemingly absorbed a small amount of infrared radiation at 3.43, 3.56 and 3.67 microns, which suggested the presence of complex organic compounds [*see top illustration on page 181*]. Sinton repeated his observations again in 1958 with more sensitive equipment and found he had to make a slight upward revision of .02 micron in

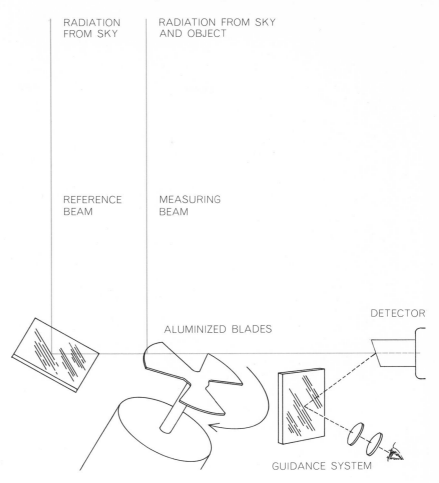

OPTICAL SYSTEM used in infrared astronomy exposes a sensitive detector (*right*) alternately to two beams; one beam consists of radiation from the celestial object and the surrounding sky, the other of radiation from the sky alone. A chopper blade determines which beam reaches the detector. If the infrared flux of the two beams is different, the detector yields a fluctuating signal, which is then rectified to produce a direct-current reading.

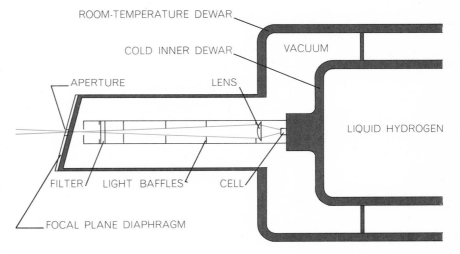

COOLED AND SHIELDED DETECTOR provides a very sensitive means for measuring infrared radiation. The diagram at the top of the page shows how the whole device is located in an optical system. The detector is placed at the bottom of a cylindrical metal shield that is refrigerated by liquid hydrogen, which boils at about 20 degrees K. So shielded, few infrared photons can reach the detector except those defined by the cylinder's field of view.

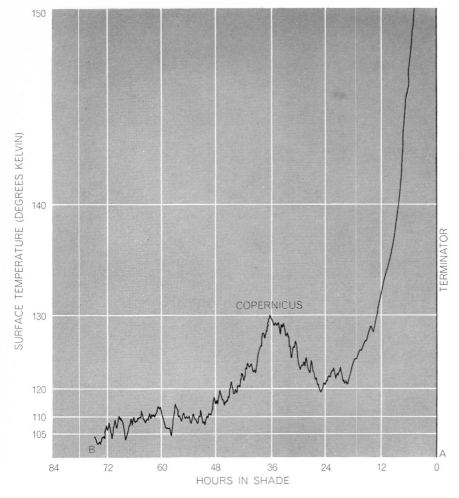

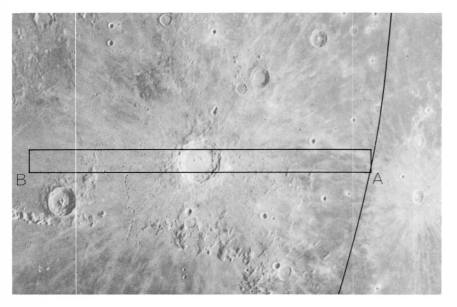

LUNAR NIGHTTIME COOLING CURVE (*top*) shows that the surface of the moon normally cools rapidly after the sun has gone down. This smooth decline is interrupted in this case by an anomaly in the region of the crater Copernicus (*see photograph at bottom*), which cools more slowly. Presumably such regions consist of bare rock, or of rock that is at most only thinly covered by the otherwise ubiquitous lunar dust. When this observation was made, nighttime was to the left, daytime to the right of the terminator line, which was itself moving to the right. Infrared radiation in the 8-to-14-micron range was recorded.

the wavelength of each of the three absorption bands. For several years these "Sinton bands" lent considerable support to the hypothesis that there was vegetation on Mars.

Early this year James S. Shirk, William A. Haseltine and George C. Pimentel of the University of California at Berkeley pointed out that deuterium oxide (heavy water) could account for the two most prominent bands (at 3.58 and 3.69 microns) if it were present in large amounts in the Martian atmosphere. This explanation, however, seemed unsatisfactory. Finally, in March, D. G. Rea and B. T. O'Leary of the University of California at Berkeley, together with Sinton himself, reported their conclusion that deuterium oxide present in the earth's own atmosphere had not been adequately taken into account in the Mars observations. The presence of the third band at 3.45 microns remains to be explained.

Another kind of investigation of Martian atmospheric absorption bands seems well substantiated and has led to a sharp revision in estimates of the density of the Martian atmosphere. In 1963 Lewis D. Kaplan, Guido Münch and Hyron Spinrad of the California Institute of Technology used the 100-inch reflecting telescope on Mount Wilson to make new measurements of the carbon dioxide absorption bands in the photographic infrared radiation reflected from Mars; they concluded that carbon dioxide is less plentiful than had been indicated by earlier and less accurate measurements. This implied that the pressure of the atmosphere at the surface of Mars is only about .37 pound per square inch, or 2.5 percent of the earth's atmospheric pressure of 14.7 pounds per square inch at sea level. The Martian atmosphere therefore may be too rarefied to support either a winged vehicle or a parachute, both of which had been considered for landing instrument capsules from spacecraft. Now it appears that a large fraction of the payload available for landing a first probe on Mars may have to be taken up by a structure for absorbing impact or by braking rockets. Thus the whole approach to the problem of exploring the Martian surface in the near future has been influenced by the results of ground-based infrared astronomy.

Perhaps the most fascinating—and certainly the most perplexing—results in infrared astronomy have to do with the surface temperatures of the moon and planets as indicated by their infrared thermal emission. As long ago as 1926 Pettit and Nicholson had shown that the moon cools with unexpected rapidity during a lunar eclipse. The surface temperature falls from about 390 degrees K. (117 degrees C.) to about 150 degrees K. in a few hours. Evidently the heat stored immediately below the surface is prevented from moving upward to replace the heat radiated into space. It appears, therefore, that the moon is covered by a millimeter or so of material 100 times more insulating than any substance that occurs naturally on earth. This observation provided the original basis for the belief that there is at least a thin layer of dust on the moon.

In 1960 Richard W. Shorthill, Howard C. Borough and Joseph M. Conley of the Boeing Aircraft Company made the additional discovery, with the aid of the 60-inch reflecting telescope on Mount Wilson, that the lunar crater Tycho cools more slowly than the surrounding areas during a lunar eclipse. This was the first detection of a geographical variation in the thermal properties of the lunar surface.

In the summer of 1962 we and Robert L. Wildey, one of our colleagues at the California Institute of Technology, extended the search for such thermal variations to the cooling that occurs during the normal lunar night. Ours was the first study of the moon to be made with a quantum infrared detector in the 8-to-14-micron region. Using the detector in conjunction with a special 20-inch telescope, we found that the kind of anomalous cooling discovered by Shorthill and his associates persisted more than 60 hours after the sun had set on an anomalous area [see illustration on opposite page].

Our observations strongly suggest that the slow-cooling areas, in particular the large rayed craters, consist partly of bare rock, or of rock that is at most only thinly covered; this would allow heat from below to reach the surface readily. Moreover, our nighttime cooling curves supply clues to the nature of the lunar surface at a depth measured in centimeters rather than in millimeters—the depth to which cooling is limited during the brief period of a lunar eclipse. We and others have been surprised to find that the physical model that best satisfies the eclipse observations does not fit the nighttime cooling observations. In fact, it does not appear that any simple homogeneous model for the lunar sur-

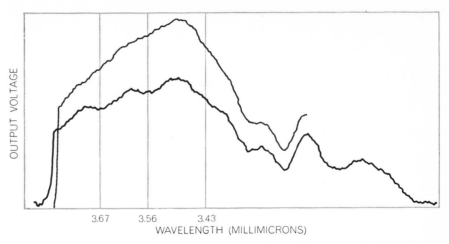

ERRONEOUS EVIDENCE for the presence of vegetation on Mars was obtained by William A. Sinton in 1956. When he compared the sunlight reflected from a typical bright region on Mars (curve at top) with that from a typical dark region (curve at bottom), he found that the latter had seemingly absorbed a slight amount of infrared radiation at 3.43, 3.56 and 3.67 microns, suggesting the presence of complex organic compounds. It now seems that the last two bands represent deuterium oxide (heavy water) in the earth's atmosphere.

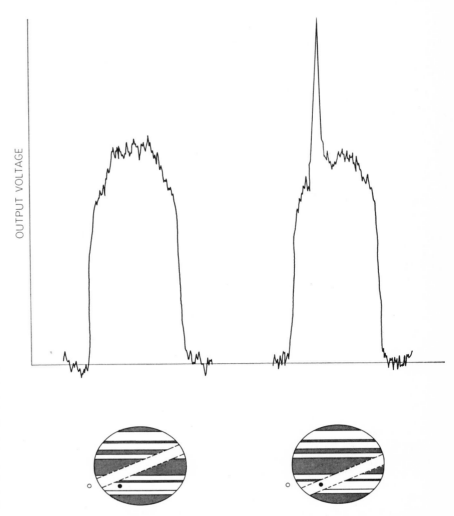

BAFFLING PHENOMENON was first observed by Wildey in 1962 while he was mapping the 8-to-14-micron radiation from Jupiter with the 200-inch telescope. When the scanning field included the shadow of one of the four largest moons of Jupiter (right), the infrared flux was enhanced by as much as thirtyfold directly under the moon's shadow. A normal scan is at left. The strange phenomenon was observed twice and has not been seen since.

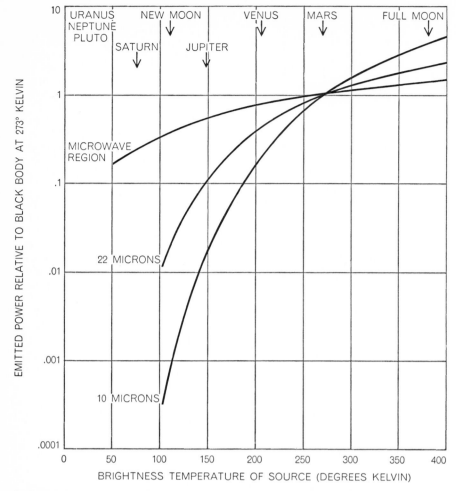

RELATIVE POWER EMITTED at three wavelengths is plotted against the brightness temperature of the source. The response at each wavelength is taken to be unity when the recording system is aimed at a black body of large angular size whose temperature is 273 degrees K. The brightness temperatures of the moon and planets are indicated at top. The graph shows that longer wavelengths are desirable for observing the colder planets.

series of observations, that *more* 8-to-14-micron radiation is emitted from the totally dark side of Venus than from the sunlit side. Once again observations have outstripped theory.

An interesting feature of the 8-to-14-micron map of Venus shown on page 175 is the small hot spot near the south pole. This was one of several that came and went within a period of about 24 hours. It seems reasonable to describe them as storms in the upper reaches of Venus' atmosphere.

We have also carried out infrared surveys of Jupiter with the 200-inch telescope. Photographs of Jupiter made with visible light show that the atmosphere of the giant planet is divided into a number of distinct horizontal bands, the pattern of which shifts with the passage of time. One might therefore expect to find some evidence of these bands in infrared maps of the planet. Instead maps of Jupiter's emission at 8 to 14 microns contain few distinctive features of any kind.

In our 1962 observations of Jupiter we twice detected phenomena that were completely baffling and that to our further surprise have not recurred since. As we were scanning the image of the planet to map its 8-to-14-micron emission, our detector happened to pass across a region darkened by the shadow of one of Jupiter's four largest moons. We were astonished to find that the infrared flux was enhanced by as much as thirtyfold at a point directly *under* the moon's shadow [*see bottom illustration on preceding page*]. Since the last observation of this curious phenomenon was made in 1962, it has not been detected again.

In the compass of this article we have had to make a somewhat arbitrary selection of the work that has been done at infrared wavelengths. For example, we have barely mentioned infrared studies of stars and other objects beyond the solar system. This omission can perhaps be justified on the basis that some of the most interesting work is so recent that it is only now reaching the technical journals. Infrared observations of stars and of objects that are of interest to radio astronomers—such as radio galaxies and the remnants of supernovae—are of considerable importance for the development of astrophysical theory.

One supernova remnant, the Crab nebula, has already been extensively studied in the infrared region by the Soviet astronomer V. I. Moroz [*see illus-*

face will be able to explain our observations. Evidently the lunar surface is more heterogeneous under its thin veneer of dust than anyone had thought. This is one of several instances in which the observations of infrared astronomers have outrun the ability of theorists to provide explanations.

Later in 1962 we trained our 8-to-14-micron detector on the surface of Venus, this time using radiation collected by the 200-inch reflector on Palomar Mountain. The surface of Venus, of course, is obscured by a dense atmosphere that reflects and absorbs most of the sun's incident radiation. The infrared radiation that can be detected by scanning the disk of Venus at 8 to 14 microns is thermal radiation emitted by the sun-heated atmosphere. It had been discovered as early as 1927 by Coblentz that the infrared brightness temperature across the disk does not

change at the terminator: the dividing line between the sunlit and the dark hemisphere. This was confirmed in our more detailed survey [*see illustration on page 175*].

Our 1962 observations also showed clearly that the temperature is highest at the equator of Venus and falls considerably (about 20 degrees C.) toward the poles. The temperature also decreases generally toward the edge of the disk. Known as limb-darkening, this phenomenon is characteristic of emission from planetary atmospheres. (The atmosphereless moon, for example, does not show limb-darkening.)

It was originally surprising to discover that the distribution of heat within the atmosphere of Venus—and possibly at the surface of the planet—is practically independent of the location of the sun. It was even more surprising to discover last year, in our most recent

tration below]. At the University of Arizona, Harold Johnson and Low have made the first recording of the infrared emission of the brightest quasi-stellar radio source—3C 273. Low has also recorded the source's emission at one millimeter. These objects, now commonly called quasars, are among the brightest and most distant objects in the universe. The incentive to study their infrared emission is great, and they will doubtless receive increasing attention in the years ahead.

The future should also see major efforts to explore the infrared region between 22 and 1,000 microns, in which no important astronomical observations have yet been made. In this region the only major source of opacity in the earth's atmosphere arises from water vapor, the absorption bands of which are broadened by atmospheric pressure. The magnitude of this pressure-broadening at very high, dry sites has still not been investigated with care. It may well be that there are adequate win-

dows at various places in the long-wavelength infrared region all the way to the radio-astronomy portion of the millimeter region. If such windows can be found, it should be possible for ground-based instruments to close the present gap between the domains of infrared astronomy and short-wavelength radio astronomy.

Perhaps the principal problem that each infrared astronomer must solve for himself is where to place his detectors in order to get the greatest return on his investment of time and energy. Should he operate with ground-based telescopes or should he send his instruments aloft in balloons and perhaps into space with rockets? Each platform has its advantages and disadvantages. Our own feeling is that balloons have many advantages over space vehicles for making a spectral reconnaissance of the infrared regions that cannot be explored from the ground. At an altitude of from 80,000 to 100,000 feet a bal-

loon is above virtually all the components of the atmosphere that absorb infrared radiation. The fact remains that if a detailed inspection of a planet's thermal emission is desired, there is no substitute for a suitably instrumented space vehicle, preferably one placed in orbit around that planet.

The advantages offered by ground-based telescopes, however, are hard to duplicate on small, remote moving platforms. These advantages include the ability to make long exposures and the ability to use complicated instrument systems, such as those that must be cooled by liquid nitrogen and liquid helium. The greatest advantage of all is the ability to repeat one's observations and to pursue a program until a satisfactory level of reproducibility has been obtained. Thus we feel reasonably sure that ground-based instruments will provide the major volume of infrared observations, and perhaps the observations of greatest significance, for decades to come.

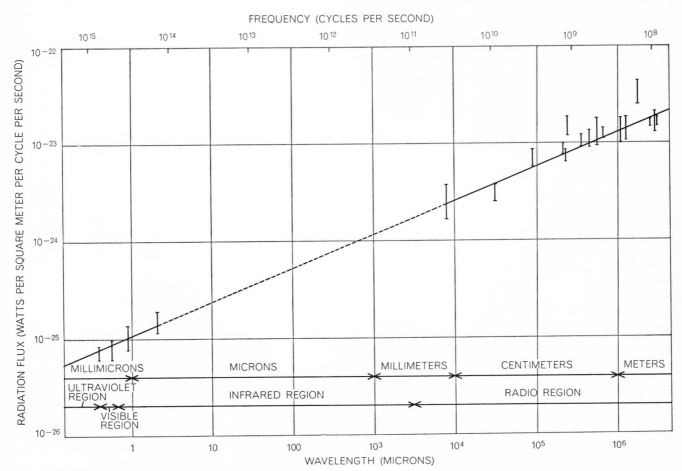

SYNCHROTRON EMISSION SPECTRUM of the Crab nebula includes the observed intensities (*solid black line*) and the interpolated intensities (*broken black line*) for the entire range of the electromagnetic spectrum from the visible to the radio wavelengths. The longest wavelength infrared observation, at 2.2 microns, was made by the Soviet astronomer V. I. Moroz, from whose paper this illustration has been adapted. Synchrotron radiation is caused by the rapid gyration of charged particles in a strong magnetic field.

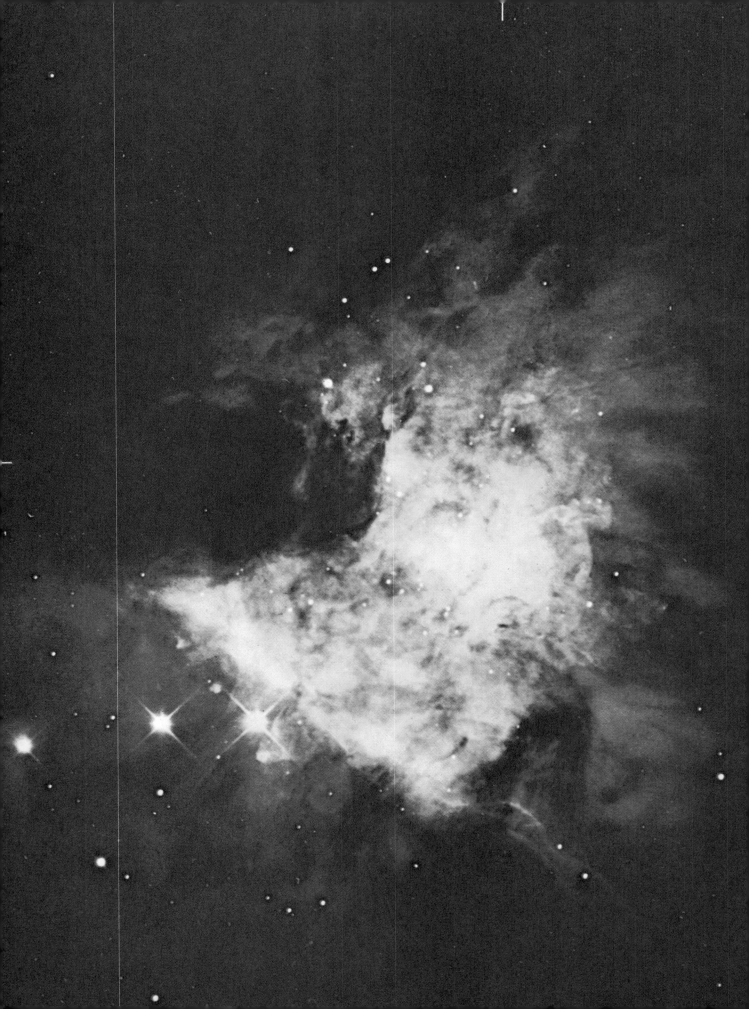

17

The Infrared Sky

G. Neugebauer and Robert B. Leighton   *August 1968*

Astronomers have long been aware that if we could see the night sky with eyes sensitive to infrared radiation, it would probably look much different from the sky dominated by the Big Dipper, Orion, Pegasus, Cygnus and other familiar constellations. Until two years ago, however, no one really knew how the night sky would look to an "infrared eye" or what kinds of objects besides stars might appear in it. Although one could be reasonably sure that the few thousand stars visible to the unaided eye would probably not dominate the infrared sky, no one could say how drastically different the infrared sky might look.

To find out we and our associates at the California Institute of Technology have used a specially built 62-inch reflecting telescope on Mount Wilson to conduct a comprehensive survey of infrared sources embracing approximately 75 percent of the celestial sphere. The principal wavelength we used was centered on 2.2 microns, about four times the wavelength of yellow light. The survey disclosed about 20,000 infrared sources in all. As we expected, the great majority are stars. If, in order to proceed with

maximum confidence, we count only sources that have 2.5 times the minimum detectable brightness, we are still left with 5,500 sources. For purposes of comparison, a total of about 6,000 stars could be counted in a visual survey made with the unaided eye at the same latitude. In short, our survey has employed an infrared "eye" that detects about as many stars as one can see in the night sky with the unaided eye.

Are they mostly the same stars or mostly different ones? The answer is mostly different. The number of stars visible to both kinds of detector, visual and infrared, is less than 2,000. Thus about 70 percent of the 6,000 stars visible to the unaided eye cannot be detected by our 62-inch infrared eye; similarly, about 70 percent of the 5,500 brightest sources in our survey are not visible to the unaided eye. If man had viewed the night sky with infrared-sensitive eyes, he would have constructed an entirely different assortment of constellations.

Early Infrared Surveys

It is largely an accident of uneven technological development that the sky was extensively surveyed at radio wavelengths more than 20 years before this could be done at two-micron wavelengths in the infrared. Prior to our work infrared studies at two-micron wavelengths were carried out mainly on individual objects such as the sun, the planets and a selection of bright stars [see "Infrared Astronomy," by Bruce C. Murray and James A. Westphal, which begins on page 174 in this book].

As long ago as 1840 Sir William Herschel demonstrated that the sun emits invisible radiation beyond the red end of the visible spectrum. The visible spectrum of course covers only a tiny fraction

of the total range of possible wavelengths, which is theoretically infinite. The wavelengths of visible light lie between .4 micron (violet) and .7 micron (red). The peak of the sun's energy falls near the middle of this region, at about .5 micron. Stars cooler than the sun, which has a surface temperature of 5,700 degrees Kelvin, would emit most of their energy in the infrared region beyond .7 micron. Stars as cool as 3,000 degrees K. are well known and a few stars cooler than 2,000 degrees had been found before our survey.

Estimates of the relative numbers of stars of various kinds per unit volume of space have consistently shown that the coolest stars—red dwarfs and the dark companions of hotter stars—account for most of the stellar matter in space. This suggested the possibility that even more matter might be in the form of "dark stars": stars too cool to emit visible light. Astronomers have also believed that protostars (stars in the process of formation) should exist and might be detectable with the appropriate equipment. The temperature of protostars might be as low as a few hundred degrees K. It has been to search for such objects and to extend knowledge of infrared sources in general that astronomers have long sought to push their observations as far into the infrared part of the spectrum as possible.

In the late 1930's Charles W. Hetzler of the Yerkes Observatory searched for cool stars using photographic plates sensitive to the near infrared in conjunction with the 40-inch Yerkes refractor. Perhaps because he never completed the survey, his work did not make much of an impact. He did, however, find a number of stars whose temperatures were between 1,000 and 2,000 degrees K.

Our interest in making an infrared sky survey was more directly stimulated by

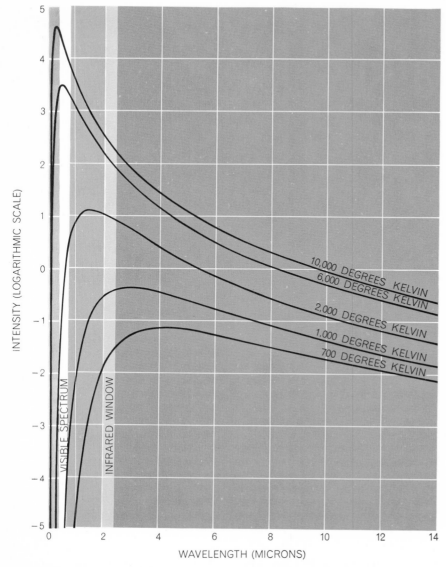

WAVELENGTH OF RADIATION emitted by heated bodies varies with the absolute temperature and follows Planck's law of black-body radiation. Ordinary stars range in temperature from about 2,500 degrees to 25,000 degrees Kelvin. Only about 1 percent of the radiation emitted by a 2,500-degree star is in the visible region, whereas about 10 percent lies in the band between two and 2.4 microns, chosen by the authors for their infrared survey.

the work of Freeman F. Hall, Jr., of the International Telephone and Telegraph Corporation, who mounted an array of infrared detectors cooled by dry ice on a 24-inch reflecting telescope. Using this instrument in the San Fernando Valley, Hall scanned some 20 percent of the Northern Hemisphere sky looking for cool objects. He seemed to find a number of sources not shown on star maps, but he also failed to detect some stars that were expected to be very bright in the infrared.

Building an Infrared Telescope

About five years ago we decided it would be worthwhile to make a comprehensive, and thus unbiased, search of the sky for infrared emission using sensitive detectors coupled to the largest possible telescope. It was evident that the existing large astronomical telescopes were unsuited for such a survey, both because of the large amounts of time that would be needed and because of the telescopes' relatively narrow field of view. We therefore decided to build a telescope specially suited to the problem.

It is well known that the free surface of a liquid, rotating uniformly around a vertical axis, assumes the shape of a paraboloid, which is precisely the surface needed to bring parallel rays to a focus by reflection. Exploiting this fact, we poured a slow-setting epoxy resin

on a rotating aluminum "dish" that had first been shaped on a lathe to approximately the right configuration. A constant rate of rotation was maintained for three days while the epoxy hardened. After considerable effort and several attempts the technique provided us with a usable 62-inch mirror having a 64-inch focal length. Although the mirror is somewhat lacking in perfection, its aluminized epoxy surface is satisfactory for the long wavelengths and coarse detectors used in infrared astronomy. With the help of students we built a telescope mounting and a small building to house it on Mount Wilson [*see bottom illustration on opposite page*].

Of equal importance to the design of an efficient telescope is the choice of the spectral region to be studied and the design of the detector system to be used. Astronomers who want to observe the infrared emission from celestial objects face several handicaps. One is the lack of sensitive infrared-detection systems. This limitation has been alleviated in the past 10 years, but infrared detectors are still less sensitive than good visible-light detectors by a factor of at least 1,000. If infrared detectors were as sensitive as visible-light ones, we could have made our survey with a two-inch mirror.

A more fundamental limitation is that gases in the earth's atmosphere, chiefly water vapor, absorb most of the incoming infrared radiation. Beyond the .7-micron limit of the visible spectrum the atmosphere remains fairly transparent out to about 1.3 microns, beyond which it is opaque except for a few transmission "windows." The first few of these are centered at the following wavelengths in microns: 1.65, 2.2, 3.6 and 4.8. There is a relatively broad window between eight and 14 microns and another between 17 and 22 microns. From 22 microns to 1,000 microns (one millimeter) the atmosphere is largely opaque. The last good window available to the infrared astronomer, the region from one millimeter to three millimeters, carries him into the domain of the radio astronomer, who employs antennas and wave detectors rather than the photodetectors that are normally used in conjunction with optical reflecting telescopes.

A final problem confronting the infrared astronomer is that the entire world radiates. Opaque nonmetallic bodies radiate energy whose wavelength is distributed according to Planck's law of black-body radiation [*see illustration on this page*]. The spectral distribution of black-body radiation depends on the absolute temperature (T) of the body in such a way that the maximum energy (per unit wavelength interval) is radiated at a wavelength (λ_{max}) given by Wien's displacement law ($\lambda_{max}T \cong 3,000$, where λ_{max} is in microns and T is in degrees Kelvin). Thus the peak of the sun's energy, corresponding to its temperature of 5,700 degrees K., is at about .5 micron, whereas objects at room temperature (300 degrees) radiate with a maximum intensity near 10 microns and emit negligible radiation at visible wavelengths. Therefore the infrared astronomer faces a problem comparable to that of an optical astronomer working in a lighted dome with a luminescent telescope.

We selected the window between two and 2.4 microns for our sky survey. Factors that influenced this choice were the favorable response characteristics of lead-sulfide photoconductive detectors, the good transparency of the atmospheric window at this wavelength and the fact that it provides a significant step beyond the visible. Stars with temperatures around 1,000 to 1,500 degrees K. would emit the peak of their energy in this wavelength region. In order to cover a suitably wide swath in the sky, a linear array of lead-sulfide detectors was used. In addition a silicon photodetector was employed to measure the incoming radiation between .7 and .9 micron, providing a basis for defining a "color" of the detected objects. All the detection is done electronically; no visual observations are made with the telescope.

To eliminate sky emission and the background radiation of objects at room temperature the mirror is rocked gently at 20 cycles per second while the telescope and detectors remain fixed. The background radiation, being constant over a large part of the focal plane, gives rise to a steady, or direct, current in the detector. On the other hand, a small focused source, being shifted alternately on and off the detector by the vibration of the mirror, gives rise to an alternating current. The subsequent amplification of the signal current is arranged to ignore the direct-current component and to enhance the alternating one. This scheme works so well that at two microns it is possible to detect stars almost as effectively during the day as at night. (The Rayleigh scattering of sunlight, which is responsible for the blue color of the sky, is almost 100 times weaker at two microns than at .5 micron.) At .7 to .9 micron, however, there is too much background radiation during the day to allow daytime operation.

The entire telescope is automatically

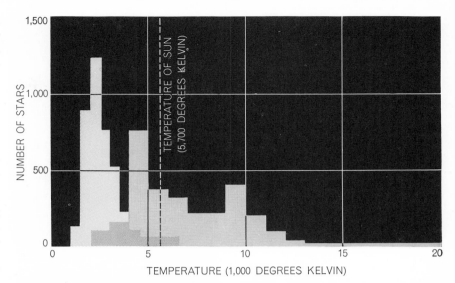

APPARENT TEMPERATURE RANGE of the 5,500 brightest stars in the authors' infrared survey is represented in color. Judged solely by their redness, most fall between 1,500 degrees and 3,500 degrees K. The temperature range of some 6,000 stars visible to the unaided eye is shown by the gray area. The areas overlap slightly between 2,000 and 6,500 degrees K.

INFRARED SURVEY TELESCOPE on Mount Wilson has a 62-inch plastic-on-aluminum mirror with a 64-inch focal length. The mirror's parabolic surface was formed by pouring liquid epoxy resin on an approximately contoured aluminum disk and rotating the disk at constant speed for three days while the epoxy hardened. The epoxy surface was then aluminized. The infrared sensors, chilled by liquid nitrogen, are supported on four legs at the focus of the mirror. When the telescope is not in use, the eight petal-shaped flaps are lowered to protect the mirror. The corrugated roof can be slid forward to provide a weatherproof housing for the instrument. The telescope and the housing were designed and built by the authors with the help of students at the California Institute of Technology.

programmed to scan the sky in a raster pattern. The telescope sweeps east to west through 15 degrees of arc at about 20 times the rotation rate of the sky and then steps north by 15 minutes of arc; it sweeps 15 degrees in the opposite direction, again steps 15 minutes north, and so on. In this way, during each hour of observing, a strip of sky measuring three degrees from north to south and 15 degrees from east to west is covered. During the course of a year the instrument can survey essentially all but the 25 percent of the sky that is too close to, or below, the southern horizon. It has now been used to scan the entire northern sky twice.

Analysis of the Infrared Survey

As we have noted, some 20,000 infrared sources have been detected with our 62-inch infrared telescope. Only the 5,500 brightest sources will be compiled into a catalogue of infrared stars. Those that are less than 2.5 times the minimum detectable brightness will be omitted, because it is important, particularly for statistical work, to have confidence in the completeness of such a survey. Relatively few of the 5,500 (fewer than 30 percent) emit enough visible light to be seen with the unaided eye on a clear night. And approximately a third have visual magnitudes fainter than 10.5, which means they are about 100 times too faint to be seen with the unaided eye.

Whether or not a given star detected in our survey is among the 6,000 that can be perceived visually depends on its temperature—at least its apparent temperature. Typical stars range in temperature from about 2,500 to 25,000 degrees K. For a star with a temperature of 25,000 degrees roughly 2 percent of the total energy output is in the visible region, and less than .05 percent is in the infrared band observed in our survey. In contrast, only 1 percent of the radiation emitted by a 2,500-degree star is in the visible region, whereas 10 percent is in the two-micron infrared band. As a result a star that is on the threshold of detection in our survey would be easily visible as a second- or third-magnitude star if its temperature were about that of the sun, but if its temperature were 1,000 degrees, it would be invisible to a visual observer even with the 200-inch telescope!

These ideas become more concrete if we plot the apparent temperatures of the stars in our infrared survey and the apparent temperatures of the unaided-eye stars [see top illustration on preceding page]. It then becomes clear that

1. SIRIUS
2. CANOPUS*
3. ALPHA CENTAURI*
4. VEGA
5. CAPELLA
6. ARCTURUS
7. RIGEL
8. PROCYON
9. ACHERNAR*
10. BETA CENTAURI*
11. ALTAIR
12. BETELGEUSE
13. ALPHA CRUCIS*
14. ALDEBARAN
15. POLLUX
16. SPICA
17. ANTARES
18. FOMALHAUT
19. DENEB
20. REGULUS

stars that are bright in the infrared are cooler than stars that are bright visually. These temperatures cannot always be interpreted, however, as kinetic, or actual, temperatures.

A very red and apparently cool star need not be cool. It is well known that interstellar dust will scatter blue light and make a star appear redder, and thus cooler, than it actually is. This effect, however, provided another reason why a search of the sky in the infrared might turn out to be extremely revealing: the extinction of starlight in the infrared is much less than in the visible. In fact, in the direction of the center of our galaxy radiation of two-micron wavelength is attenuated by a factor of only 10, whereas we estimate that visible radiation is attenuated by a factor as large as 10 billion. Not only can stars be reddened by interstellar dust but also their spectral distribution may depart from Planck's law of black-body radiation. The general trends of temperature are nonetheless correct.

The illustrations on these two pages show the distribution in the sky of the brightest stars observed visually and the brightest stars observed at a wavelength of 2.2 microns; about 300 stars in each category are represented. Although the familiar constellations are no longer evident in the infrared, both distributions look more or less random and qualitatively the same. A few of the well-known bright reddish stars, such as Betelgeuse, are present on both charts, but as one would expect the hotter white stars do not stand out conspicuously in the infrared.

The distribution of the 300 faintest stars seen with the unaided eye and of the 300 faintest stars observed in the infrared survey are plotted together in the top illustration, pages 190 and 191.

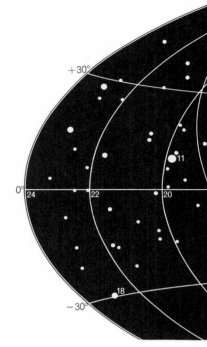

BRIGHTEST VISIBLE STARS, meaning stars visible to the unaided eye, are distributed more or less at random. The numbers

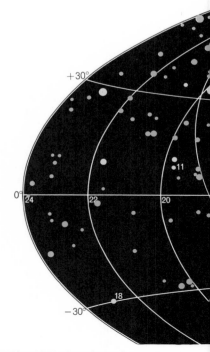

BRIGHTEST INFRARED STARS, meaning stars that are brightest at the survey wavelength of two to 2.4 microns, are also dis-

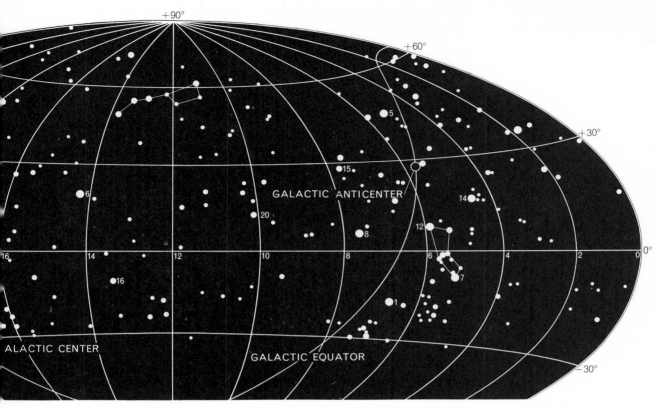

identify 15 of the 20 brightest stars of all; their names are given at the top of the adjacent column. Five, marked by asterisks, are not shown in the sky chart because they are permanently below the southern horizon at the latitude of Mount Wilson. In this and subsequent sky charts the number of stars plotted is about 300. Numerals on the horizontal axis represent right ascension in hours.

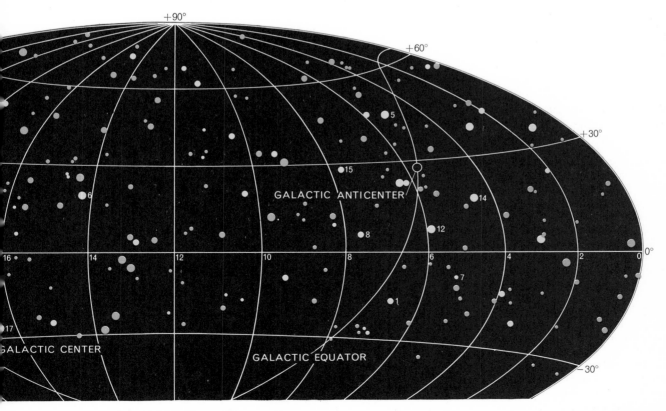

tributed more or less randomly, but only about 20 percent of them (*pale color*) are among the 300 brightest visible stars. Some of the others, however, would be visible as faint stars to the unaided eye. A star may appear red because it is genuinely cool or because its light has passed through interstellar dust, which preferentially scatters and reduces the blue component of the original light.

Only three stars are common to the two categories. Although the distributions are again roughly similar, the randomness is gone and the Milky Way—the central plane of our galaxy—begins to stand out. Perhaps it is even a little more pronounced in the infrared than it is in the visual. The Milky Way becomes very conspicuous if we plot the distribution of stars selected on the basis of redness, as is done in the bottom illustration on these two pages. In this illustration it is apparent that the survey can be used as a powerful tool for probing the structure of the galaxy.

The increasing importance of the Milky Way in the plots of the fainter stars can be explained on a simple basis. On the average the bright stars are relatively close to us and we see roughly the same number in any direction, since within this range of observation the galaxy is nearly uniform. The fainter stars, however, are generally so far away that we can see them well beyond the confines of the galactic disk when we look at right angles to its central plane. In this direction we run out of stars to be seen. On the other hand, when we look along the galactic plane, the density of stars remains high as far as the telescope can see; in fact, the gradual increase in the density of stars in the direction of the galactic center, and the decrease in the direction of the anticenter, stand out clearly.

By means of indirect arguments the facts given above can be used to delineate certain features of the galaxy as it is viewed in the infrared. For example, the cool stars observed in the survey enable us to estimate that the thickness of the galactic disk is approximately 400 parsecs (one parsec is 3.26 light-years), which is about the same as has been estimated on the basis of hotter stars. Another finding is that in the plane of the galaxy our telescope can detect very red giant stars out to an unexpectedly great distance: some 2,000 parsecs. Over the range observed we find that the galaxy thins out with distance from the galactic center: near the sun, which is about 10,000 parsecs from the center, the star density decreases by a factor of 2.5 with each 1,000 parsecs. To be sure, these simple concepts are confused by interstellar reddening, and we have had to make some guess as to how this reddening affects the data. Whereas the effects of the reddening and the question of the intrinsic redness of objects cannot be separated out uniquely, the infrared data should be much less confused by reddening than similar visual data are.

Infrared star counts may also have a bearing on the structure of the galaxy. It is known that at our distance from the galactic center the galaxy makes a complete turn in about 200 million years. On this basis, and from the size and shape of the galaxy, one can compute how much mass the galaxy must have. It turns out that less than half of the mass required by this analysis can be accounted for by detectable stars, gas and dust. One suggestion that has been made is that invisible stars—perhaps infrared stars—may be quite numerous and might account for a significant part of the total mass. The absence of large numbers of faint but randomly distributed stars in our survey indicates that such objects are either absent or lie below the detection threshold of our equipment. The faintest infrared stars we do see, being intrinsically bright stars but at a great distance, account for a very small part of the total mass. Thus the missing mass remains unaccounted for.

The Coolest Objects Observed

Although the statistical results that have come from the survey have been valuable, we have been most interested in the individual very red objects detected. At first we expected that most of these objects would belong to the family of cool variable stars with periods ranging from a few months to several years. (One reason the sky was surveyed in two different years was to estimate how many stars might have been missed on a single survey because they were at a low point of their light curve; another was to obtain a statistical measure of the fraction of survey stars that are variable.) We thought if we were lucky we might also be able to detect protostars. These objects might be in the form of extended blobs of dust and gas at a temperature of only a few hundred degrees K., and might represent a turbulent mass of matter assembled by its own gravitational attraction just before the formation of one or more stars. The survey was designed to detect concentrated objects as cool as 400 degrees K., which meant that we could hope to detect stellar objects that were only a little above the boiling point of water (373 degrees), if any such objects existed in the sky and were near enough to us.

Of the 5,500 stars observed, 450 are so red that at least 97 percent of their total energy output is in the infrared beyond one micron, which corresponds to black-body temperatures below about 1,700 degrees. Almost all these stars are, as we had expected, long-period vari-

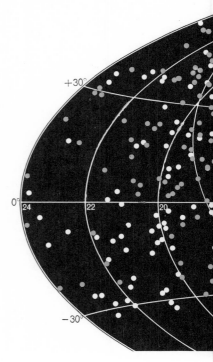

FAINTEST STARS, both visible (*white*) and infrared (*color*), tend to be more numerous near the galactic equator for the

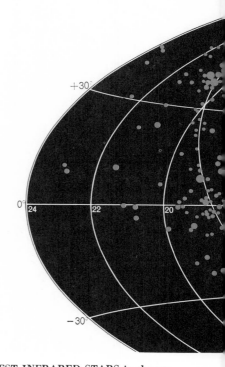

REDDEST INFRARED STARS in the survey show an unmistakable concentration along the galactic equator and particularly

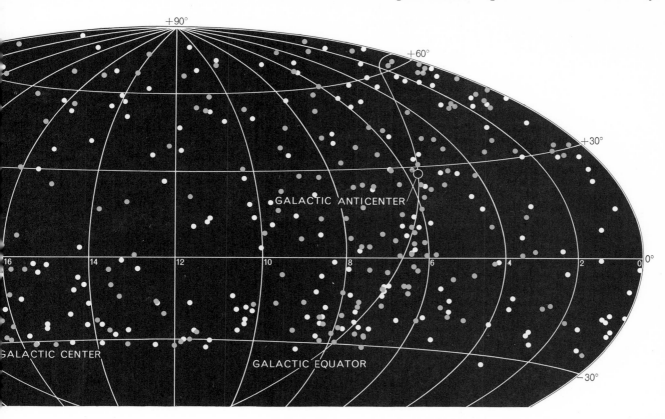

simple reason that there are more stars to be seen when looking into the galactic plane than when looking at right angles to it. Only three of the 300 faintest infrared stars in the survey are in-cluded among the 300 faintest visible stars. Among the 5,500 bright-est infrared stars in the survey, about 30 percent are among the 6,000-odd stars visible to the unaided eye from the same latitude.

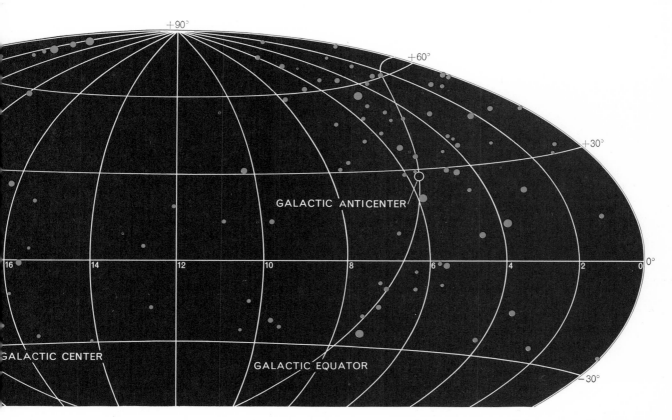

in the general direction of the galactic center. It is estimated that interstellar dust dims visible starlight originating near the center of the galaxy by a factor as large as 10 billion. Infrared radiation of two-micron wavelength, however, is attenuated by a factor of only about 10. The apparent temperature of all the stars plotted here is below 1,700 degrees K. Many are found to be long-period variables.

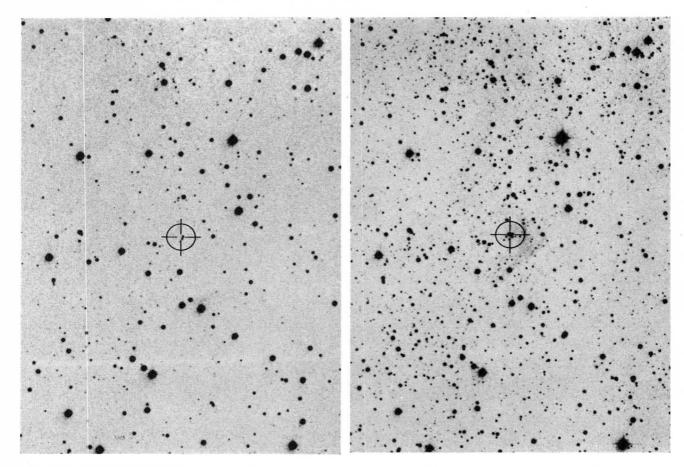

INFRARED SOURCE IN CYGNUS emits as much radiation at two microns as does Vega, the fourth-brightest star. The object is invisible on blue-sensitive plates (*left*) taken with the 48-inch Schmidt telescope on Palomar Mountain. It stands out clearly, however, on red-sensitive plates (*right*). At a wavelength of 20 microns the Cygnus source outshines every known stellar object except the sun.

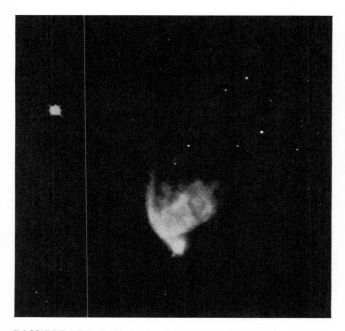

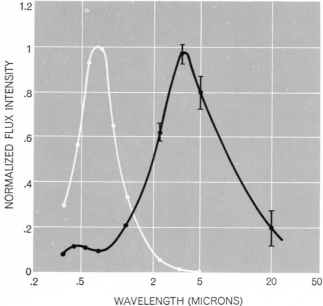

POSSIBLE PREPLANETARY SYSTEM coincides with an object at the head of Hubble's variable nebula (*left*). In this photograph from the Lick Observatory, the infrared object, known as R Monocerotis, looks like the head of a diving bird. The object had been classified as a T Tauri star until Eugenio E. Mendoza of the Tonanzintla y Tacubaya Observatory in Mexico found that the spectrum of R Monocerotis (*black curve at right*) has a large maximum near four microns. White curve shows the spectrum of the sun.

ables. Over three years of observation the brightness of some stars at 2.2 microns has been observed to change by a factor of nearly 10. This in itself is a significant finding because the coolest variable stars previously measured (the Mira variables) change brightness very little in the infrared.

Some of the very red stars are not long-period variables, however. In fact, one of the reddest (and coolest) stars so far detected does not vary. This star, located in the vicinity of Cygnus [*see top illustration on opposite page*], is as bright at two microns in the infrared as Vega, the fourth-brightest star in the sky. Frank J. Low of the University of Arizona has found that at 20 microns the Cygnus source is brighter than any other known stellar object except the sun. Its energy distribution seems to be similar to the one expected from a star whose temperature is about 1,000 degrees. Fred F. Forbes of the University of Arizona has found that its radiation in the near infrared is about 5 percent polarized.

What is this cool object? We do not yet know, except that it seems to be unique in the combination of its great brightness, extreme redness and lack of variability. Harold L. Johnson and V. C. Reddish of the University of Arizona have argued that it may be an extremely bright supergiant star that has been reddened by either interstellar dust or a circumstellar envelope of some kind. If this

is the case, the supergiant would be of a kind never before observed. Other workers, notably M. V. Penston of the Royal Greenwich Observatory, have suggested that stars in the process of formation should be surrounded by a shell of cool dust. Hence the Cygnus source may be an example of a protostar, although it is not accompanied by other young stars as one would expect.

Almost all the other bright, very red objects that have been studied more closely after their detection in the survey have been shown either to vary in brightness or to be stars highly reddened by interstellar dust. Thus one important but essentially negative result of the survey has been to establish that extremely red objects that might be associated with star formation, and that are also very bright at two microns, are not common.

A Preplanetary System?

It was our desire to avoid the bias involved in preselecting certain areas of the sky or categories of objects judged to be "interesting" that led us to survey the entire sky. Our goal was to find out what was there. More conventional telescopes equipped with infrared detectors can be much more sensitive than our simple survey telescope. With such instruments several exciting new discoveries have been made on close examination of particular objects.

One of these objects is R Monocerotis, which lies at the head of the comet-shaped nebula called Hubble's variable nebula [*see bottom illustration on opposite page*]. For many years R Monocerotis had been classified as a T Tauri star on the basis of its optical spectrum [see "The Youngest Stars," by George H. Herbig; SCIENTIFIC AMERICAN, August, 1967]. In 1966 Eugenio E. Mendoza of the Tonanzintla y Tacubaya Observatory in Mexico found that the spectrum of R Monocerotis has a second maximum in the infrared that actually accounts for most of the total energy radiated by the object. The peak of this infrared component is around four microns; the entire energy distribution corresponds roughly to that of a black-body source at 750 degrees K. except for a curious excess at 22 microns. Low, who has made most of the astronomical observations at 10 microns and beyond, and Bruce J. Smith have suggested that this energy distribution may be produced by a dust cloud surrounding the star that absorbs the short-wavelength radiation and reemits the energy at the longer infrared wavelengths. Low and Smith further suggest that this object may be an example of a preplanetary system. It may be significant that T Tauri stars are known to be among the very youngest stars in the galaxy.

A quite similar object has been found in the Great Nebula in Orion, which has

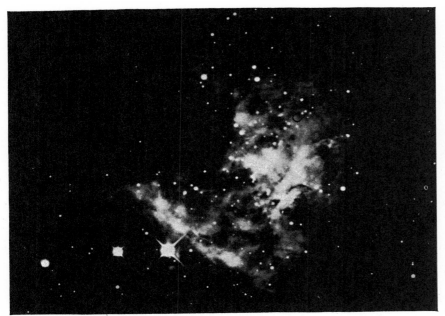
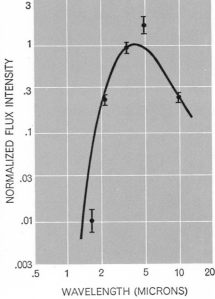

INFRARED STAR IN ORION was discovered by Eric E. Becklin of the California Institute of Technology, using the standard 60-inch telescope on Mount Wilson. The location of the object is shown by the small colored circle in the Lick photograph at the left. Within it no star can be seen even with the 200-inch telescope. The infrared source seems to be a point embedded in a larger region that also emits in the infrared. The radiation curve of the point source (*right*) conforms to that of a black body at 650 degrees K.

been suspected as being a breeding ground for new stars [*see illustrations on preceding page and page 184*]. The object was found by our colleague, Eric E. Becklin, using the Mount Wilson 60-inch telescope. At photographic wavelengths this object is quite invisible even with the 200-inch telescope, but in the infrared it is almost bright enough to appear on our sky survey. Although the source seems to be a point, it is surrounded by an extended distribution of infrared radiation that is centered on it.

The emission of the point source has been measured at various infrared wavelengths out to 13.5 microns. These measurements yield a radiation curve that conforms closely to that of a black-body whose surface temperature is around 650 degrees K. Again we must consider whether the object really has this temperature or whether it is a normal star whose visible component of radiation has been absorbed and scattered by dust. One can calculate that if it were a red supergiant it would have to be hidden behind enough dust to dim it by a factor of 100 trillion to create the observed appearance. This explanation seems to us most unlikely. We believe the object is a star with an extremely cool surface—quite possibly a protostar. If reasonable guesses are made as to its size and mass, one finds that observable changes should occur in much less than 1,000 years, a short time by astronomical standards.

Last year Low and Douglas E. Kleinmann attempted to study the Orion infrared star at 20 microns. They were unable to detect a measurable signal from the point source but found, adjoining the point source but apparently distinct from it, an extremely bright extended source. Indeed, at 22 microns this infrared "nebula" turns out to be the brightest known object in the sky with the exception of the sun and the moon. We can only guess at its temperature, but from the relative absence of energy at other wavelengths one can estimate that it is less than 150 degrees K., or about 120 degrees below zero Celsius. Again the current belief is that the nebula is an example of a dense cloud in which stars are forming.

A further exciting fact was added recently when Ernst Raimond and Baldur Eliasson of Cal Tech, working with the radio telescope at Owens Valley, Calif., discovered that the Orion infrared point source is also emitting line radiation characteristic of the hydroxyl radical (OH). With this clue, known OH-emission sources are now being examined in the infrared to see if other such instances can be found.

The Galactic Center in Infrared

Many other galaxies exhibit a definite nucleus when they are observed at visible wavelengths. In the case of our own galaxy the interstellar extinction is so great that one cannot see into the galactic center, although several studies have shown the presence of a central "bulge." Several years ago, however, radio astronomers found a radio source, Sagittarius A, whose location coincides quite closely with the point identified as the galactic center on the basis of stellar-mo-

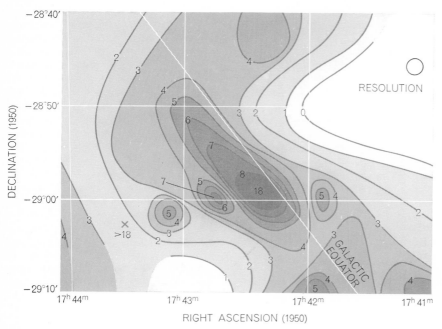

INFRARED MAP OF GALACTIC CENTER shows intense emission at 2.2 microns slightly to the left of the galactic equator. Slightly farther to the left is an intense point source, marked by a colored cross. The zero line represents the sky background radiation. The other lines are labeled in units of 5.2×10^{-10} watt per square centimeter per micron per steradian.

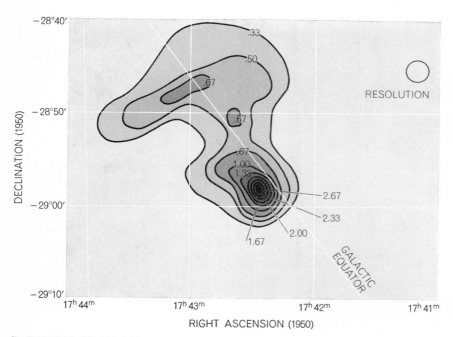

RADIO MAP OF GALACTIC CENTER is plotted to the same scale as the infrared map at the top of the page. Both survey methods locate the galactic center in very nearly the same place. The numbers on the contour lines represent the antenna temperature in degrees Kelvin. A slight correction was made for extinction by dust. The survey was made at a wavelength of 1.9 centimeters by D. Downes, A. Maxwell and M. L. Meeks, using the 120-foot antenna at the Lincoln Laboratory, operated by the Massachusetts Institute of Technology.

tion studies. When we started our survey, we hoped to detect the center of the galaxy by its infrared radiation.

An infrared source we now believe to be the center of our galaxy did in fact show up on the survey. It was so inconspicuous, however, that we recognized it only after it had been found by Becklin with a 2.2-micron photometer on a 24-inch telescope on Mount Wilson. After this initial success further measurements were made at .9, 1.65, 2.2 and 3.4 microns using the 60-inch Mount Wilson telescope and the 200-inch telescope on Palomar Mountain. These observations reveal an extended source of infrared radiation centered on the dynamical center of the galaxy or very near it. On a larger scale a weak background is also seen, the pattern of which is quite complex [*see upper illustration on page 194*]. We currently believe most of the secondary features arise from localized changes in interstellar absorption rather than from multiple strong emitters at the galactic center. The gross appearance in the infrared agrees with radio maps of the region [*see illustration on page 194*].

The radiation from the galactic center can be interpreted by comparing it with radiation from the nucleus of the Great Nebula in Andromeda, which is believed to closely resemble our own galaxy. In fact, if infrared observations of our galaxy's nucleus are plotted to the same scale as infrared observations of the Andromeda galaxy's nucleus, the similarity between the two intensity profiles is striking [*see illustration at right*]. If this comparison is valid, and we believe it is, then in all likelihood the infrared radiation recorded from the center of our galaxy is produced by millions of ordinary stars densely packed into a region whose dimensions are only a few parsecs across. Inside the central core, about one parsec in diameter, the number of stars per unit volume may be about 10 million times what it is in the neighborhood of the sun. This means that the stars in the core are 200 times closer together than the stars familiar to us, so that if we lived there the stars in the sky would appear some 40,000 times (more than 11 magnitudes) brighter than those we normally see. Even so, the nearest stars would be, on the average, several thousand times more distant than Pluto, the solar system's outermost planet. As we have mentioned, the galactic center cannot be seen visually because the visible radiation from it is cut down by a factor of 10^{10}.

Close to the center of the main body of radiation there is a particularly strong infrared object that appears to be a point source. If, as seems likely, this source is located at the galactic center 10,000 parsecs away, it must be less than .1 parsec in diameter. Yet it has a total radiative output estimated to equal that of 300,000 suns. The true nature of this source is still open to debate, and no explanation put forward so far is satisfactory. Here we cannot draw an analogy between our galaxy and others because none of them is close enough for us to distinguish such a small point within the nuclear region surrounding it. If the source were a single bright star, it would be among the two or three intrinsically brightest stars ever measured. Alternatively, if it were a cluster of stars rather like the sun, the stars would have to be so close together that two of them would collide every 1,000 years or so, and the cluster would have an expected lifetime of only 1,000 million years—a span much shorter than the age of the galaxy.

The results we have described have come from observations made primarily at the near-infrared wavelengths. What would the sky look like if we used a much longer wavelength such as 20 microns? We cannot tell without an un-biased search, but perhaps a hint is given by observations of unusual objects such as quasars.

Much too faint to be detected by our survey telescope, quasars have been recently examined in the infrared both at the University of Arizona by Low and Johnson and at Cal Tech. Although measurements beyond two microns have been published for only the brightest quasar, 3C 273, it is clear that in this object and quite a few other quasars the bulk of the energy is radiated in the infrared wavelengths. Furthermore, Low and others at the University of Arizona have studied Seyfert galaxies, galaxies that have a starlike nucleus, and have found that here also the bulk of the energy is emitted in the infrared. In fact, Low finds that at least one Seyfert galaxy has its maximum emission intensity at 20 microns. How this radiation is produced is still unknown. Quite possibly it is nonthermal, meaning that the energy originates in a process entirely different from the one that produces the radiation in ordinary stars. Such results make us confident that infrared astronomy holds important clues to understanding the universe.

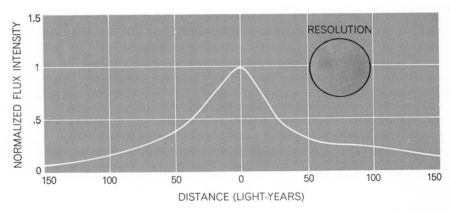

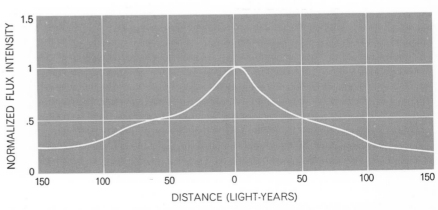

GALACTIC NUCLEI, the Andromeda galaxy at the top and our own galaxy at the bottom, exhibit similar profiles when scanned by infrared detectors at a wavelength of 2.2 microns. The resolution of the lower scan was degraded to match that for the Andromeda galaxy.

18

Remote Sensing of Natural Resources

Robert N. Colwell   January 1968

As pressures on natural resources increase, because of growing populations and rising standards of living, it becomes steadily more important to manage the available resources effectively. The task requires that accurate inventories of resources be periodically taken. Until as recently as a generation ago such inventories were made almost entirely on the ground. Geologists traveled widely in exploring for minerals; foresters and agronomists examined trees and crops at close hand in order to assess their condition; surveyors walked the countryside in the course of preparing the necessary maps. The advent of aerial photography represented a big step forward. Within the past few years the making of aerial photographs has been augmented by a new technique, in which sensing is done simultaneously in several bands of the electromagnetic spectrum. The name often given the technique is remote sensing. In its fullest form the technique ranges through the spectrum from the very short wavelengths at which gamma rays are emitted to the comparatively long wavelengths at which radar operates. In this way one can secure far more information about an area than can be obtained with conventional photography, which is limited to the visible-light portion of the spectrum.

Remote sensing can be done from aircraft or spacecraft, including unmanned satellites. It employs cameras and a number of other sensing devices. To some extent the data obtained by the sensing devices can be processed and interpreted automatically, so that a large volume of information can be dealt with rapidly.

The information thus obtained is useful to investigators in many disciplines. Geologists use remote sensing to find deposits of minerals and petroleum, to improve their understanding of the distribution and origin of major geological features and to study the exchanges of energy associated with such crustal disturbances as earthquakes and volcanic eruptions. Soil scientists can take inventory of the important physical and chemical characteristics of soils by relating these characteristics to the geological features and the types of vegetation found on images obtained by remote sensing. Foresters and agriculturists can determine what kinds of trees and plants are growing in an area, can assess the health of the forest or crop and can estimate harvests. Similar information can be obtained by workers interested in populations of livestock, wildlife and fish.

By means of remote sensing hydrologists can locate useful aquifers and can estimate the volume of surface and subsurface flow in watersheds. Oceanographers can map the movements of ocean currents, marine organisms and water pollutants. They can study in detail the daily and seasonal changes in tides, shorelines and the state of the sea. Geographers can analyze land-use patterns over broad areas and can study the interplay of climate, topography, plant life, animal life and human activity in a particular area. Engineers planning large construction projects such as highways, airports and dams can obtain data on landforms, rock materials, soils, types of vegetation and conditions of drainage. It goes almost without saying that remote sensing in various parts of the spectrum is invaluable to map makers in their efforts to identify ground features and to position them accurately.

The earliest aerial photographs, made somewhat more than a century ago, suffered from the deficiencies of the cameras and emulsions and from the necessity of using such unsteady vehicles as balloons and kites for platforms. Today the array of equipment available for remote sensing can be matched to almost any requirement. Whatever the platform—helicopter, airplane or satellite—the camera can be mounted so that it is stabilized against roll, pitch and yaw and insulated against vibration. The aberrations of the lenses in cameras have been greatly reduced so that sharp images can usually be obtained. Roll film of high dimensional stability has almost entirely replaced emulsion-coated glass plates. Several kinds of color film are available to augment or replace black-and-white film in both the visible and the infrared portion of the spectrum.

Remote-sensing Equipment

Among the many types of equipment developed for remote sensing, six show the most value or promise for the inventory of natural resources. They are the conventional aerial camera, the panoramic camera, the multiband camera, the optical-mechanical scanner, sidelooking airborne radar and the gamma ray spectrometer.

A conventional aerial camera has four basic components: a magazine, a drive mechanism, a cone and a lens [*see top illustration, page 200*]. The magazine

CENTRAL AUSTRALIA'S characteristic topography appears in the photograph on the opposite page, made from the *Gemini V* spacecraft on August 27, 1965. The spacecraft was at an altitude of 165 miles; the area shown is west of Alice Springs. An experienced interpreter can use such a photograph to obtain information about a variety of natural resources and land uses. Some ways the photograph can be interpreted are illustrated on pages 56 and 57.

MAIN FEATURES of the *Gemini* photograph (*see key on opposite page*) include two geological formations indicative of sedimentary rocks. *A*, at left, shows steeply dipping beds in the MacDonnell Range; *B*, at right, shows eroded rocks in the Waterhouse Range.

FURTHER INTERPRETATION of the *Gemini* photograph led to the conclusion that *C*, known as Gosse's Bluff, is a meteorite crater (*left*). The region marked *D* on the spacecraft photograph and shown at right above has several features that indicate alluvial soil.

SOIL RESOURCES ascertained from study of the *Gemini* photograph include *E*, shown in a low-angle view at left; dunelike patterns suggest a sandy soil. *F*, at right, is a dry lake bed; there the interpreter would predict the existence of heavy clay soils.

VEGETATION BOUNDARIES appear more distinctly in the *Gemini* photograph than in low-angle views. *G*, at left, is a boundary between mulga, a type of acacia tree, and spinifex, a grass. *H*, at right, is a boundary between Mitchell grass (*yellow*) and spinifex.

is the light-tight box that holds the film. Usually it can be detached from the rest of the camera. The film is ordinarily in the form of a continuous roll 9½ inches wide and 200 feet long. Such a roll will accommodate about 250 exposures, each nine inches square.

The drive mechanism is a series of cams gears and shafts designed to move the film from the supply spool to the take-up spool. As the film moves, rollers guide it over the front surface of a locating plate. One of the rollers is designed to meter the amount of film passing from the supply spool to the take-up spool between exposures, thereby providing a correct and uniform spacing of exposures on the roll of film.

During an exposure, suction is created behind the locating plate by means of a venturi tube or a special vacuum-cylinder-and-piston apparatus built into the magazine. The suction, transmitted to the film through small perforations and grooves in the locating plate, holds the film in a flat plane against the locating plate at the instant of exposure. In this way distortions that would be caused by wrinkles in the film at the moment of exposure are minimized.

The cone is a light-tight unit that holds the lens in the correct relation to the film. The length of the cone is governed by the focal length of the lens, which is essentially the distance from the center of the lens to the film. It is not unusual for a magazine to have interchangeable cones to accommodate lenses of differing focal lengths. Most of the aerial photography done for the inventory of natural resources uses focal lengths of six, 8¼ or 12 inches.

The lens is a compound one that is carefully designed to cast an undistorted image on the large area of the film. Aerial cameras usually have fixed-focus lenses with the focus at infinity; the camera is used so far above the ground that such a focus will provide a sharp image of all objects on the ground. In most aerial cameras the shutter is between the front and the rear elements of the lens. The drive mechanism of the camera recocks the shutter automatically after an exposure.

The panoramic camera [*see bottom illustration on next page*] makes it possible to photograph a large area in a single exposure at very high resolution, meaning with a high degree of sharpness of image in every part of the photograph. The camera meets a need but creates some special problems. In order to get a sharp image when photographing large areas, one paradoxically needs a narrow angular field so as to minimize

aberrations of the lens. Such a field is provided in the panoramic camera by a narrow slit in an opaque partition near the focal plane of the camera. The slit is parallel to the camera platform's line of flight. With such a slit, however, one will be able to photograph only a narrow swath of terrain unless the optical train of the camera is equipped to pan, or move from side to side, as the aircraft advances. The optical train of the panoramic camera is designed to make such movements.

On the other hand, for the panoramic camera to maintain a uniformly clear focus as the optical train moves, the frame of film being exposed must be held in the form of an arc instead of being kept flat as in a conventional camera. With the film in an arc the pho-

tographic scale becomes progressively smaller as the distance of objects on the ground increases to the left and right of the flight path. In some applications the scale problems outweigh the advantage of a panoramic field of view, so that it is preferable to use a conventional camera.

Related Devices

The multiband camera makes photographs simultaneously in several bands of the spectrum. In essence it provides a variety of lens, filter and film combinations, each designed to obtain maximum information from a particular band. A typical camera might have nine such combinations [*see illustrations on page 201*]. Together the lenses give the camera a capacity to sense in the range of

PRINCIPAL FEATURES of the *Gemini* photograph on page 55 are identified. The arrows show direction in which the low-angle aerial photographs on the opposite page were made.

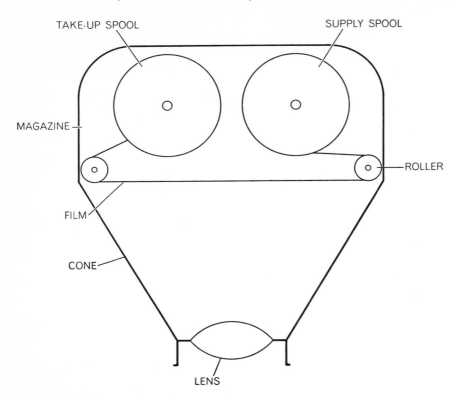

CONVENTIONAL AERIAL CAMERA uses film in roll form and can make about 250 exposures, each nine inches square. Magazine holds the film. Cone positions lens with respect to the film, at a distance governed by the focal length of the lens. Film being exposed is held flat against a locating plate to minimize distortions and provide uniformly sharp images.

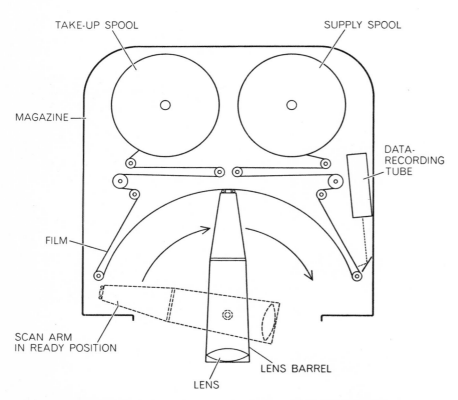

PANORAMIC CAMERA was developed to provide sharp aerial photographs of large scale. Since the camera must have a long focal length it must also have a narrow angular field. As a result it requires a scanning mechanism that moves the lens barrel to left and right. At any instant during the course of a scan only light passing through a narrow slit falls on the film.

wavelengths from .4 to .9 micron, which is to say throughout the visible spectrum and into the very near infrared. All nine shutters click simultaneously, thus yielding nine photographs, each with tonal values that are distinctive for its portion of the spectrum. Study of distinctive tonal values in nine photographs of an area enables the interpreter to determine a "tone signature" for each type of object. As a result he obtains much more information about the area's natural resources than he could obtain from any one of the photographs.

The optical-mechanical scanner meets the need for a device that will sense farther in the infrared—in what is commonly called the thermal infrared region. Ordinary photographic film is not sensitive to wavelengths in the thermal infrared region. It would be possible to coat a film with a material sensitive to such wavelengths, but then the problem would arise of protecting the film from the thermal energy being emitted by the camera. Just as the conventional camera must be a light-tight box to keep light-sensitive film from fogging, so a thermal infrared camera would have to have a heat-tight box to keep heat-sensitive film from fogging. In fact, the box would have to be continuously cooled almost to absolute zero, which is a practical impossibility for a large airborne sensing device.

Thus a "camera" that translates thermal energy directly onto film is out of the question. It is possible, however, to obtain photographic images of thermal energy indirectly, and that is what the optical-mechanical scanner does. The device uses a detector that consists of a coating of some infrared-sensitive material such as copper-doped or gold-doped germanium on the end of an electrical conductor. The material occupies an area no bigger than a pinhead. It is entirely feasible, even in an airborne system, to cool this small detector with liquid nitrogen for sensing at wavelengths of from three to six microns and with liquid helium for longer wavelengths.

A rotating mirror directs to the detector energy emanating from the terrain. At any instant the mirror views only a small segment of terrain. Infrared photons striking the detector generate an electrical signal that varies in intensity according to the amount of thermal energy coming from the part of the terrain then being viewed by the mirror. The signal, by being converted to a beam of electrons, can generate visible light, such as the moving luminous spot on the face of a cathode-ray tube. The spot grows brighter or dimmer in direct

MULTIBAND CAMERA has nine lenses and nine film-filter combinations, each designed to function best in one part of the spectrum. Camera permits more positive identifications to be made of certain natural resources from their multiband "tone signatures."

MULTIBAND EXPOSURE was made with a multiband camera. The wavelengths of energy represented range from .38 micron (*top left*) to .9 micron (*bottom right*), which covers not only the visible spectrum but also parts of the ultraviolet and near-infrared regions.

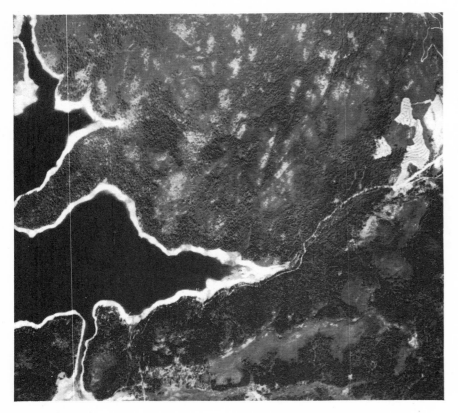

PANCHROMATIC VIEW of the Bucks Lake area of the Sierra Nevada was obtained with panchromatic film, meaning film that is sensitive to the entire visible spectrum. Such a photograph is particularly useful for estimating the density of vegetation and for identifying certain species of vegetation. The area is part of the one shown in color on page 205.

RADAR VIEW of the same area is especially useful for discerning types of vegetation that appear less clearly in panchromatic view. Radar also shows drainage networks more clearly.

proportion to the strength of the electron beam. An image of the light is recorded on photographic film, and the analyst obtains what is in effect a thermal map of the ground.

The scanner is not limited to sensing in the thermal infrared region of the spectrum. It can provide multiband imagery in any band from the near ultraviolet through the visible and photographic infrared regions and into the thermal infrared. Moreover, in "photographs" made by the instrument the general shape of ground features is essentially the same in every band, so that the images can be superposed or otherwise compared readily.

Side-looking airborne radar, commonly called SLAR, brings to remote sensing such valuable attributes as all-weather and around-the-clock usefulness and the ability to penetrate a cover of vegetation. Because radar operates at much longer wavelengths than the other equipment I have described, however, it does present difficulties in obtaining high resolution. Recent developments such as SLAR equipped with a synthetic aperture system have brought about large improvements in the quality of radar imagery.

In the SLAR system a transmitting antenna in the airplane sends a short pulse of microwave energy out one side of the plane. The energy strikes a roughly circular area on the ground, and a receiving antenna collects the energy reflected back to the plane. The greater the distance from the aircraft to any portion of the target, the greater the time delay in the return of the reflected signal. By accurately measuring the time delay, SLAR differentiates the echoes that return to it from various small concentric rings. Each ring represents the locus of all points within the large circle that are roughly equidistant from the plane.

Within any ring there is a spot just opposite the aircraft that moves along at the same speed as the aircraft. At any given time the distance from the aircraft to all other points on the ring is either increasing or decreasing. Here the Doppler effect comes into play: the frequency of the reflected signal changes according to whether the plane is approaching a given point or receding from it. As a result the microwave energy reflected back to the aircraft from such points differs in frequency from the energy transmitted to them. The radar receiver is designed to accept energy of approximately the same frequency as the initial pulse and to reject significantly different frequencies.

Because of the two discriminating effects—one depending on time delay and the other on the Doppler effect—the radar receiver accepts at any given instant only the energy that meets two conditions: that it be from the narrow ring within which the time delay is such that the energy is at that instant striking the receiving antenna, and that it be in the particular part of the ring that is directly opposite the aircraft—the part having almost no relative velocity with respect to the aircraft and thus exhibiting no Doppler effect. Together the two discriminating features provide the synthetic aperture. The technique greatly improves the spatial resolution of the system.

Radar images are transformed into photographic images in the same way that photographic images are produced by the optical-mechanical scanner. The microwave energy is converted to an electron beam that operates a cathode-ray tube, and the light is recorded on film. The density on each portion of exposed film is in proportion to the brightness of the radar signal coming from the corresponding spot on the terrain.

The gamma ray spectrometer functions at very short wavelengths—a millionth of a micron or less, compared with the billion microns or more at which radar and other microwave sensors operate. The spectrometer is excellent for locating radioactive substances, even when it is operated at altitudes of several thousand feet above the ground. It is therefore useful in prospecting for minerals. Moreover, a gamma ray spectrometer can be designed to operate in as many as 400 different channels, or wavelength bands, so that the instrument has considerable ability to differentiate each of several radioactive minerals.

Analysis of Data

Remote sensing of natural resources rests on the fact that every feature of the terrain emits or reflects electromagnetic energy at specific and distinctive wavelengths. The analyst cannot hope to accomplish much in the way of interpreting the data, however, until he takes the time to determine what spectral response pattern—what multiband tone signature—to expect from a given feature. The best means of accomplishing this is to set up a test site in which each type of feature that is to be identified by remote sensing is exhibited. By studying multiband images obtained from the test site the analyst will equip himself to recognize, by their unique spectral response patterns, the features that are of interest to him in a sensing mission. Ideally at least one such test site should be includ-

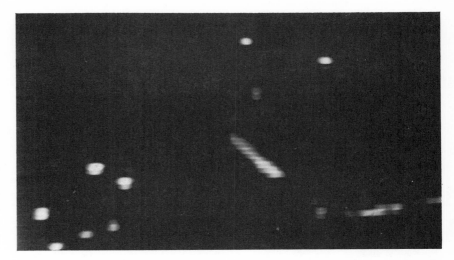

THERMAL INFRARED image of a site in Yosemite Valley shows several campfires better than sensing in other bands would. Thermograph, which senses infrared wavelengths and uses them to govern a source of visible light that is recorded on film, was about a mile above the valley. Smallest fire detected was one charcoal briquette less than a cubic inch in size.

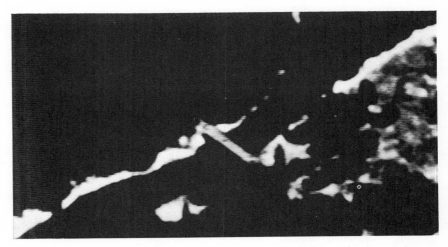

ADDITIONAL VIEW of the Yosemite Valley site from the same station was made with the thermograph set to function at wavelengths of eight to 14 microns and so brought out vegetation in meadows (right). The fire-sensing thermograph functioned at three to five microns.

TIMBER RESOURCES stand out in this thermal infrared view of same site. Thermograph was set for eight to 14 microns but the image was obtained by day rather than by night.

MANGROVE TREES in a swamp near Brisbane, Australia, appear normal in this panchromatic aerial photograph. Sensing in another part of the spectrum told a different story.

INFRARED VIEW of the same mangroves shows that the trees at upper left have been damaged. Mud had been pumped into the basin. Unhealthy trees and crops have a dark tone in infrared because of a previsual loss in reflectance at infrared wavelengths of .7 to .9 micron.

ed in each sensing flight for calibration purposes.

Eventually it may become possible to identify every feature in a given area. The technique of sensing in a variety of wavelengths promises to speed progress toward that objective. As the number of spectral bands used in remote sensing is increased, the identifying response pattern for each natural resource becomes more complete and more reliable.

At the same time the increase in spectral bands sensed means that the task of analyzing data grows larger. It can become unmanageable unless the analyst has equipment that helps him to correlate the multiband images. The problem is that he confronts several black-and-white images, each with distinctive tone values for particular features. He can find himself in confusion if he interprets one image, goes on to another, refers back to the first and so on for a number of images.

One way to deal with the problem is to reconstitute the various multispectral black-and-white images into a single, composite color image. The usual technique is to project each black-and-white image through a colored filter. A battery of projectors is used so that all the images can be superposed simultaneously on the screen.

In such a composite image the tone or brightness of a ground feature as recorded in any given spectral band is used to govern the intensity of one of the colors used in the composite. By varying the selection of colored filters the analyst can change the color contrast of the composite. Often by this means he finds that one combination of filters provides the best interpretability of one kind of feature, whereas other filters provide better interpretability of other features. The bottom two illustrations on page 206 are composites made in this way.

A second way of correlating multiband images is to use a battery of photoelectric sensors to scan all the black-and-white images simultaneously. The sensors record degrees of brightness. For each spot scanned the sensors automatically determine a tone signature, which in theory will be identifiable with some signature established from the test site. By this means the analyst can identify what features the remote-sensing equipment detected on the ground.

In its ultimate form the technique will result in a tape printout indicating the objects and conditions encountered at every spot in the multiband imagery. The method has not been developed to that stage, but even at its present stage of development it is able to provide

WILD-LAND RESOURCES are studied in a test area in the Bucks Lake region of the Sierra Nevada. This photograph was made from a camera station on a rock 2,000 feet above the lake. The station is used to make simulated aerial photographs of a known area. Such terrestrial photographs can be used as guides in interpreting simi- lar photographs, obtained from aircraft or spacecraft, of regions where the wild-land resources need to be identified. A normal color photograph is only one of several types of photograph used for evaluating resources. Sensings can also be made in other wave- length bands of the spectrum to detect different physical features.

SAME AREA of the Sierra Nevada is photographed in infrared. The film used to make both this photograph and the one on the cover of this issue contains a red dye that is sensitive to near-infra- red wavelengths of .7 to .9 micron. The false colors often provide more scope for interpretation than is possible with other film. Largest amounts of infrared energy produce the reddest color.

ROCK TYPES are differentiated more clearly in an infrared photograph (*right*) than in a full-color photograph (*left*) of the same area. The technique may aid in identifying rocks on moon that contain hydrated salts and could be a source of water for astronauts.

LIVESTOCK can often be identified more precisely in an infrared photograph than in normal color. Here the same group of livestock is photographed in normal color (*left*) and in infrared (*right*). Test panels appear at the left and right sides of the photograph.

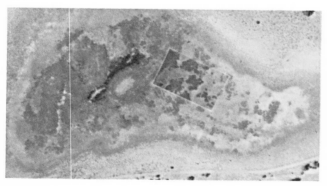

RANGELANDS merit study in both normal color and infrared photography. Two types of forage, bitterbrush and big sage, appear more clearly in infrared photograph at right than in the normal-color photograph at left. Bitterbrush is bright red; sage, dark.

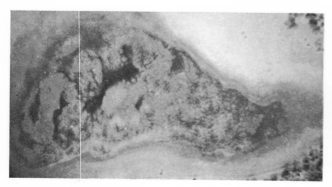

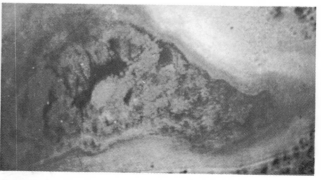

SAME AREA of rangeland is shown in a multiband technique. Black-and-white pictures, exposed at various wavelength bands, are projected separately with filters of different colors; the projections are combined in single images that bring out significant features.

enough automatic analysis of images to reduce considerably the amount of work done by the analyst. The illustrations at right show the results of photoelectric scanning of an aerial photograph.

In a third technique the multiband sensing system records on magnetic tape, rather than on photographic film, the signal strength from each object in each spectral band. Thereafter the procedure is essentially the same as it is in the photoelectric scanning technique. The third method provides a complete inventory only moments after the remote sensors have been flown over the areas of interest. It also makes possible an analysis of the signal strengths emanating directly from the sensed objects, whereas in the second method the analysis is of signals that may have been degraded in the process of forming multiband images of the objects.

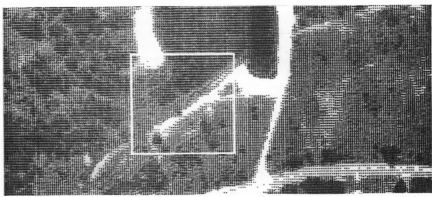

Some Applications

Against the background of sensing equipment and analytical techniques that I have described it is possible to consider in more detail some of the ways in which remote sensing can contribute to the management of natural resources. Several of the possibilities are illustrated in the photograph on page 197 which was made from the spacecraft *Gemini V* and shows a large area of central Australia. The principal features of the area are identified by letters in the black-and-white reproduction of the photograph on page 199.

The southern part of the MacDonnell Range [*A in the photograph on page 199*] has steeply dipping parallel beds that the geologist would recognize as indicating the presence of folded sedimentary rocks varying in hardness and in susceptibility to erosion. The characteristics of the northern part of the range would suggest to the geologist that the rocks there are igneous or metamorphic. Evidence of faulting appears in the linear ridge that runs through the northern part of the range. The characteristics of the Waterhouse Range [*B in the illustration*] suggest sedimentary rocks that long ago were folded into an anticline, or upfolded structure, and have since been eroded to varying degrees. Careful study of shadow detail in the vicinity of the circular structure known as Gosse's Bluff [*C*] reveals that it is a hollow outcropping of rocks that probably resulted from the impact of a large meteorite.

From even this crude interpretation of the photograph a mineralogical prospector would be able to deduce that some of the best prospects for metallic

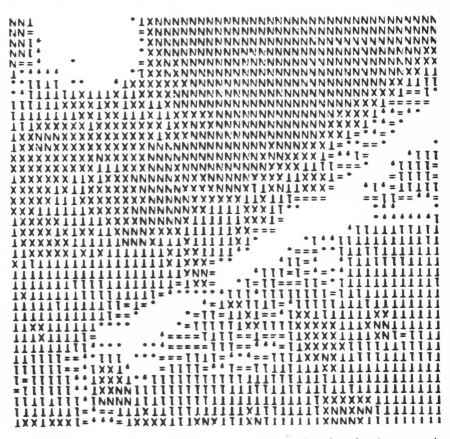

AUTOMATIC ANALYSIS of tonal qualities can be done with a photoelectric scanner. At top is a photograph made with a multiband camera. At center is a scanner's print in which "N" shows darkest tones and other symbols represent lighter tones. At bottom is an enlargement of the outlined area. Since each natural resource tends to have a unique multiband tone signature, automatic encoding of tones may lead to automatic resource inventories.

minerals are to be found along the discernible fault lines in the MacDonnell Range. The petroleum geologist would be interested in the folded anticline of the Waterhouse Range. It is equally significant that the searchers for both metals and petroleum often can eliminate nearly 90 percent of the vast area shown in a small-scale photograph as being unworthy of detailed mineralogical or petroleum surveys. Important deposits of either kind are rarely found in areas that photographically show little geologic evidence of their presence.

The *Gemini* photograph is also helpful in assessing the soil resources of the area. For example, it can be assumed that most of the central region [D] has deep alluvial soils because there are nearby mountain ranges from which alluvial deposits are likely to have come, because the pattern of streams indicates that a considerable amount of outwashing ac-

tivity has taken place even though the area now seems arid, and because in the outwash plains geologic features have become so deeply buried, presumably by deposited soil, as to be indiscernible. In the top left portion of the photograph [E] the presence of sandy soil is suggested by the dunelike patterns, which continue appreciably beyond the edge of the photograph. A dry lake bed [F] is likely to contain heavy clay soils.

The photograph is of further usefulness in determining the vegetational resources of the area. Even though the photographic scale is small, several vegetational boundaries can be seen. One of considerable significance [H] shows two types of grass: Mitchell grass on the left and spinifex on the right. Areas of Mitchell grass are far better than other grassland for maintaining livestock. Moreover, they normally are indicative of the

most fertile soils in an area, a point of great importance if the objective is to find new land to put to the plow.

In mapping vegetational boundaries the lack of fine detail in a photograph such as the *Gemini* one may actually be helpful. The fact is evident if one looks at the area marked G in the *Gemini* photograph and at the corresponding oblique aerial photograph at the bottom left on page 198. The boundary is between mulga (a type of acacia tree) and spinifex. In the *Gemini* photograph the boundary is clear; in the oblique photograph it is difficult to follow even though more detail is discernible there.

Recently I accompanied Ray Perry of the Commonwealth Scientific and Industrial Research Organization in a check of the ground shown in the *Gemini* photograph. We made the oblique aerial photographs that appear on page 198. The check showed the interpretations

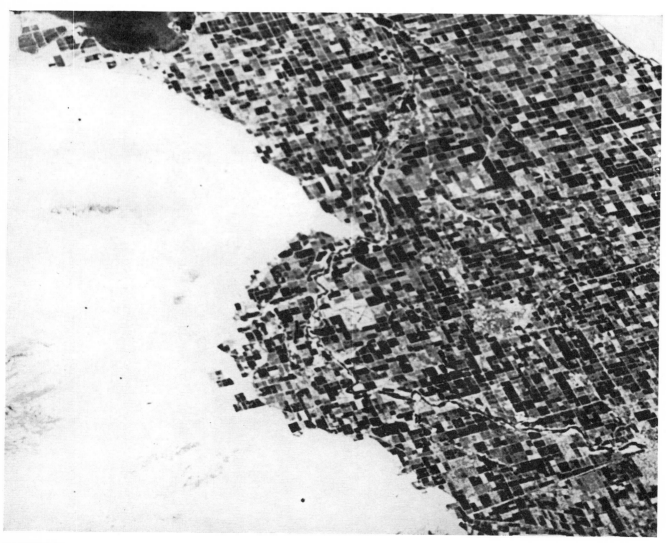

SALTON SEA AREA of southern California appears in a photograph made from a Gemini spacecraft. The pattern is made by farmland. Individual fields as small as 40 acres can be distinguished. Many kinds of farm crops can be identified in such a photograph.

previously made from the *Gemini* photograph were correct in all respects.

I have dwelt at length on this single *Gemini* photograph in order to suggest the capabilities of spacecraft photography in the remote sensing of natural resources. Since the whole of an area as big as Australia can be depicted in a short time with a few photographs from a spacecraft, the possibilities of the technique are enormous, particularly for the vast areas of the world that are yet to be developed. Australia is a case in point. According to Australian scientists, virtually all the significant geologic, soil and vegetational features found in approximately 70 percent of the continent's arid regions are represented in the *Gemini* photograph that I have described. It seems evident that one of the best ways to produce suitable reconnaissance maps for the remainder of underdeveloped Australia and for other underdeveloped

areas of the world would be through the use of space photography, supplemented as necessary with large-scale aerial photographs and with field checks.

Additional Applications

The catalogue of uses for remote sensing is extensive. In forestry, for example, it is possible in small-scale photographs, such as those from spacecraft, to delineate the timberland, brushland and grassland in a wild area. With proper film and filter it is possible to differentiate the three major types of timber—hardwood, softwood and mixed wood. In larger-scale photographs one can determine the size of trees, the density of growth and the volume of timber. Foresters also use aerial photographs to detect trees that are diseased or infested with insects. Aerial photographs can be used to help in the planning of forest

roads and of means for fighting forest fires.

The management of rangelands is assisted by remote sensing. From photographs one can learn the species of vegetation in an area, together with their volumes and their forage value. Photographs also reveal other data pertinent to range management, such as watering places, salt ground, plants that are poisonous to livestock, highly erodible sites and areas that need reseeding.

Wildlife managers can use aerial photographs for censuses of various kinds of animals and fish. The information is important in determining the impact of hunting, fishing and the works of man on fish and wildlife populations.

Administrators of agricultural programs need information on the type of crop growing in each field of a large area, the vigor of each crop and the probable yield. Where crops lack vigor, the agri-

RADAR IMAGE of farmland in Kansas shows certain types of crops more clearly than images from other bands of the spectrum could. Lightest fields, for example, contain sugar beets. Clear radar images can be obtained day and night and through clouds.

ADVANTAGE OF RADAR in penetrating a dense cover of vegetation to reveal the geologic structure of the terrain appears in a radar view of an area in the Sierra Nevada. The longer the wavelength at which radar operates, the better the radar penetrates vegetation.

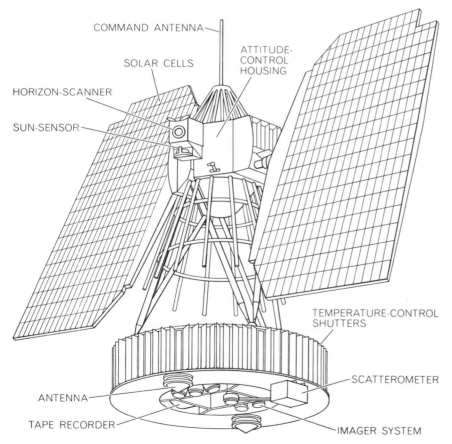

UNMANNED SATELLITE that will sense data in several wave bands and transmit the information to earth by television may be in operation by 1970. The U.S. Department of the Interior and the National Aeronautics and Space Administration have been working on plans for such a spacecraft, to be known as EROS for Earth Resources Observation Satellite.

culturist wants to know what is wrong. All such information can often be obtained through the interpretation of aerial photographs if the photographs have been made under appropriate conditions, including the scale, the type of filter and film and the seasonal state of development of the crops.

Work already done along these lines has indicated that the classification of crops and land use in six categories will suffice for the preliminary assessment of almost any agricultural area. The categories are orchard crops, vine and bush crops, row crops, continuous cover (such as alfalfa and cereal crops), irrigated pasture crops and fallow ground. Each of these categories can be recognized by an experienced interpreter of photographs; usually he can also make further identifications of specific crop types within each of the six categories.

Let us consider the matter of crop vigor a little further. The first photographic evidence of loss of vigor due to black stem rust in wheat and oats or to blight on potatoes is to be found in the near infrared part of the spectrum, where reflectance rather than emission phenomena are of primary importance. On positive prints made from infrared photography the unhealthy plants register in abnormally dark tones. The technique is successful even in photographs made from spacecraft. Moreover, haze does not interfere appreciably with the technique because haze is easily penetrated by the long wavelengths used in making infrared photographs.

Water resources are susceptible to a degree of management through remote sensing. Aerial photography can show the area and depth of snowpacks on important watersheds at various times of the year. By following seasonal changes in the snowpack hydrologists can more intelligently regulate the impounding and release of water in reservoirs. Watershed managers also need to keep track of vegetation in order to estimate the loss of water to plants.

Vast ocean areas, about which a great deal remains to be learned, can be surveyed by remote sensing, particularly from spacecraft. Typically a camera in a satellite orbiting the earth can photograph a strip 3,000 miles long in 10 minutes, so that it is easily possible to keep track of changes over huge reaches of ocean. Among the phenomena that can be followed are the flow of currents, the course of tidal waves and the movements of marine animals, kelp beds and icebergs.

Many other applications of remote

sensing come to mind; I can only touch on them. Numerous archaeological sites have been discovered through conventional aerial photographs; it is probable that spacecraft photographs will reveal still more sites. Tax authorities can use aerial photographs to update maps showing land use and to spot efforts to change a land use without detection, such as by turning timberland into farmland while leaving a strip of forest along the road that a ground-based tax assessor might be expected to travel. Violations of law often show up in photographs; examples are illegal mining or logging in remote areas, pollution of waters by illegal dumping of chemicals, release through industrial smokestacks of materials that contribute to smog, and fishing in waters where fishing is prohibited. The analysis of such disasters as floods, fires and hurricanes can be assisted by the study of remote-sensing data, and the information so obtained can be used in making emergency decisions and in combating future catastrophes of a similar nature.

Techniques of remote sensing are in a fairly early stage of development. Many of the applications I have suggested are therefore yet to be realized in practice. Their success, and the achievement of still other applications, will depend heavily on further research into the kinds of data that can be obtained from remote sensing—in learning, for example, where in the spectrum a certain plant disease will appear most distinctly. My colleagues and I have found it helpful to set up arrays of various natural resources and photograph them from high but stationary places, such as water towers and the tops of cliffs. The work helps to determine, economically and under controllable conditions, the bands of the spectrum that might best be used in remote sensing directed at finding the same resources.

A Prospect

I can foresee the possibility that the techniques for remote sensing will evolve into a highly automatic operation, in which an unmanned satellite orbiting the earth will carry multiband sensing equipment together with a computer. Thus equipped the satellite could, for any particular area, take inventory of the resources and produce a printout that would amount to a resource map of the area. The computer could then use the inventory data in conjunction with preprogrammed factors (such as what ratio of costs to benefits would be likely to result from various resource management practices) and could reach a decision for the optimum management of the resources in the area. The decision would be telemetered to the ground for whatever action seemed necessary.

As a simple example, the satellite's sensors might spot a fire in a large forest. Its computer might then derive information on the location and extent of the fire and could assess such factors as the type and value of the timber, the direction and speed of the wind and the means of access to the fire. On the basis of the assessment the computer would send to the ground a recommendation for combating the fire.

Capabilities of this kind need not be limited to emergencies. Many routine housekeeping chores now done manually by the resource manager could be made automatic by electronic command signals. Examples might include turning on an irrigation valve when remote sensing shows that a field is becoming too dry and turning off the valve when, a few orbits later, the satellite ascertains that the field has been sufficiently watered.

A satellite of such capabilities may seem now to be a rather distant prospect. After a few more years of developing the techniques for remote sensing the prospect may well have become a reality.

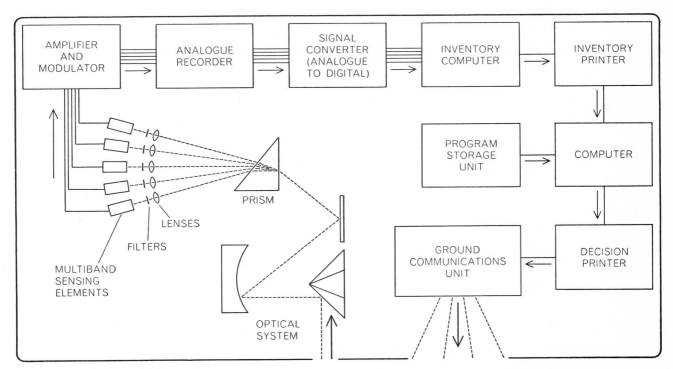

COMPUTERIZED SATELLITE is a prospect for the future. It would sense resources in several wave bands, automatically identify them, weigh them against previously programmed data on the cost effectiveness of various management possibilities and send to the ground a decision on what should be done. It also could be used to monitor developing situations, such as a forest fire, suggesting how ground crews might fight it, and to perform automatically such tasks as turning irrigation valves on and off as required.

19

The Maser

James P. Gordon   December 1958

The 50-foot radio telescope at the Naval Research Laboratory in Washington, D.C., recently acquired a strange accessory. Mounted just behind the antenna, at the center of the telescope's parabolic reflector, is an oblong box containing a synthetic ruby and some standard microwave equipment. A bath of liquid helium chills the ruby to the temperatures of the cold reaches of space which the telescope surveys. With the help of this refrigerated gem astronomers hope to extend their range of observation far beyond its present limits, perhaps far enough to clear up once and for all the mysteries of the size and geometry of the universe.

The ruby is part of a new microwave device called the "maser." The letters of this odd word stand for Microwave Amplification by Stimulated Emission of Radiation. The maser represents the ultimate in high-fidelity amplifiers. The best previous amplifiers, using vacuum tubes, put out a mixed signal which combined an amplified version of the input with a wide assortment of oscillations originating in the tubes themselves. If the input signal becomes weaker, the percentage of noise in the output increases, and the resemblance between input and output diminishes. Eventually a point is reached where the input, though still amplified, can no longer be recognized in the output. The great virtue of the maser is that it generates practically no noise. It can detect much weaker signals than other amplifiers can, and hence pick up radio waves from far more distant points in space. As we shall see, it is also finding a number of other important applications in science and technology.

What makes the maser so quiet? It is perhaps helpful to ask first: What makes vacuum tubes so noisy? Vacuum tubes utilize a stream of agitated electrons which are boiled out of a cathode and sent crashing into a collecting plate by an outside voltage. The signal to be amplified imposes its variations on the electron stream. But the particles have their own random variations, which are inevitably part of the output of the tube. It is a tribute to the ingenuity of electrical engineers that, in improvements such as the traveling-wave tube, they have been able to go so far toward muffling the effects of unruly electrons. The least noisy of these tubes, however, leaves a lot to be desired.

The maser dispenses with streams of electrons altogether. Instead it makes use of certain intrinsic oscillations in many types of material particles. These oscillations are basic phenomena of nature. The idea of harnessing them for useful work occurred independently a few years ago to several workers in the field of microwaves, including C. H. Townes of Columbia University, N. G. Basov and A. M. Prokhorov in the U.S.S.R. and J. Weber of the University of Maryland.

To appreciate what led to this notion we should briefly consider the interaction between high-frequency radiation and matter. Every student of elementary physics has witnessed the experiment in which light from a sodium lamp is shined into a container of cool sodium vapor and is completely absorbed. At the same time light of a different frequency—that is, color—from some other source passes through the container undimmed. The classical explanation is that every atom and molecule has certain natural vibrations which occur at sharply defined frequencies. When the oscillations of light or of other electromagnetic waves coincide with one of these frequencies, the radiation gives up energy to the atom or molecule, causing it to vibrate like a pendulum which has been set swinging by a series of properly timed pushes. Conversely, if atoms or molecules can be made to vibrate by some other means, say by thermal agitation, they will emit electromagnetic waves of the same characteristic frequency. In the experiment just mentioned, waves from hot, vibrating sodium molecules are absorbed by the cold molecules. Waves whose frequency does not correspond to the frequency of the sodium vibrations pass through unaffected.

If the reader is wondering how such a mechanism can be made to amplify the energy in a wave, he may as well stop. If the "classical"—that is, pre-quantum mechanical—explanation were completely correct, there would be no maser. (As a matter of fact, there would be no atoms. On the classical theory electrons revolving around atomic nuclei would continuously radiate away their energy and spiral into the nucleus. All of ordinary matter would thus collapse.)

To discover the secret of the maser we must turn to the quantum picture of matter and radiation. In this view atoms and molecules exist most of the time in one of a number of stable, nonradiating states. Each state corresponds to a fixed quantity of energy. Radiation, on the other hand, consists of the particles called photons, carried by a sort of guiding wave. The frequency of the wave is a measure of the energy of the photons, according to Max Planck's famous equation $E = hf$. A particle of radiation is produced when an atom falls from a higher to a lower energy state, and the energy of the photon is exactly equal to the difference in energy between the states. When an atom jumps the other way, from a lower to a higher energy state, it absorbs a photon of the same frequency. Thus

SOLID-STATE MASER is mounted at the focus of the 50-foot radio telescope of the Naval Research Laboratory in Washington, D.C. By largely eliminating the "noise" inherent in conventional amplifiers, the maser enables the telescope to detect very faint signals.

when radiation passes through an assembly of atoms, one of three things can happen. If the energy of the photons does not equal the difference between a pair of energy levels in the atoms, there is no interaction. If the energies match, and a photon collides with an atom in the lower of the two states, the radiation will be absorbed and the atom will be "excited" to the higher state. If the photon collides with an atom in the higher state, it will cause the opposite jump, down to the lower state, and a new photon will be emitted. Thus there will now be two photons where before the collision there was only one.

In any assemblage of atoms there is always some traffic between low- and high-energy states. The atoms keep hopping up and down in their energy states, boosted by energy received in chance collisions and falling because of their natural tendency to seek the lowest energy level. Under ordinary conditions the lower states are always more densely populated than the higher ones. Thus when radiation of the appropriate fre-

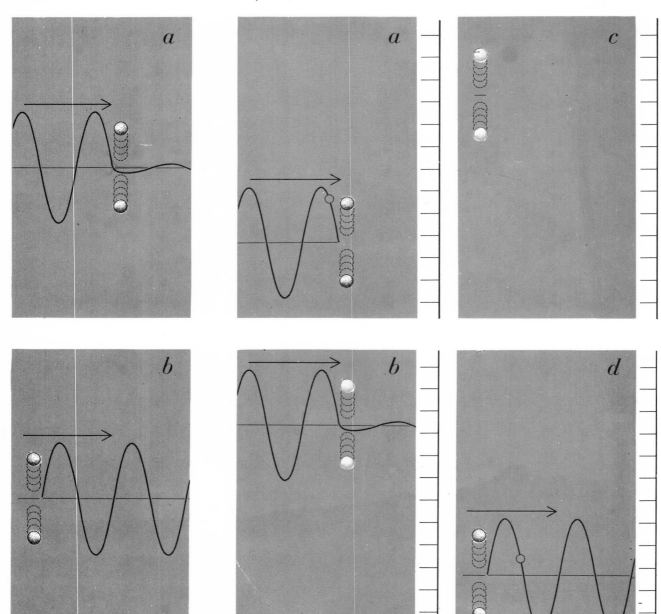

CLASSICAL VIEW of the interaction of electromagnetic radiation and matter is depicted. At top an electromagnetic wave (*wavy line*) of the appropriate frequency sets a two-atom molecule (*balls*) to vibrating. The process absorbs energy from the wave. At bottom a molecule spontaneously emits energy (*wavy line*) of characteristic frequency.

QUANTUM-MECHANICAL VIEW of the interaction is similarly depicted. Here the electromagnetic radiation is regarded not as a wave but as a photon (*white dot*) guided by a wave. The frequency of the guiding wave is related to the energy of the photon. The molecule does not vibrate; the broken circles merely indicate that the atoms are regarded as simultaneously occupying a number of positions. At top left the molecule is at a lower energy level. At bottom left the molecule has been "excited" by a photon of the appropriate energy, and raised to a higher energy level. At top right the molecule is at the higher energy level. At bottom right it has fallen to the lower energy level and emitted a photon of characteristic energy. Scale at right of these four illustrations suggests energy levels.

quency passes through the assemblage of atoms, more photons will be absorbed than new ones created, and the outgoing beam will be weaker than the incoming beam.

But suppose it were somehow possible to change the distribution of energy levels so that there were more atoms in the higher of two states than in the lower. Then a beam of photons of the appropriate frequency would produce more downward jumps than upward ones; the net effect would be that more photons would come out than went in. In other words, the output wave would have more energy than the input wave. This is the secret of how the maser amplifies.

The first of the masers to be developed is based on the molecule of ammonia. For reasons we shall mention in a moment, the ammonia maser is more useful as an oscillator and a timekeeper than as an amplifier. It is in any case a remarkable device: a simple metal chamber, into which only a little ammonia gas is admitted, which yields a weak microwave signal of almost unbelievable purity. Its output wave falls short of a mathematically perfect sine curve by less than one part in 100 billion!

The molecule which produces this perfect monotone has the shape of a pyramid. At the apex of the pyramid is a nitrogen atom; at the base, three hydrogen atoms [see illustrations at right]. The nitrogen atom is able to move through the plane of the hydrogen atoms. thus turning the pyramid inside out. On the classical theory we picture the nitrogen atom flipping back and forth at a characteristic frequency of about 24,000 million vibrations per second, or 24,000 megacycles per second. At any given instant the nitrogen atom is on one side of the hydrogens or on the other. From the quantum point of view the nitrogen has at a given time a certain probability of being on either side—in a sense it is partly on both sides. Moreover, the molecule as a whole has two distinct energy states. The difference in energy between the states equals the energy of a photon with a frequency of 24,000 megacycles per second.

Now it happens that ammonia molecules in the higher state are repelled by strong electrostatic fields, whereas those in the lower state are attracted. Thus we have a method for segregating the high-energy molecules and getting maser action. The separator is a cylinder of charged rods [see illustration at top of page 218]. Proximal to the rods the field is strong; along the axis of the cylinder the field is weak. When a beam of

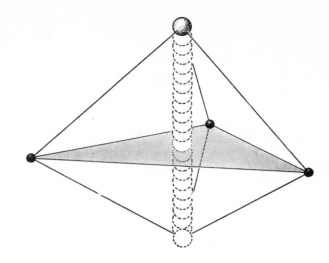

CLASSICAL VIEW OF THE AMMONIA MOLECULE is that its single nitrogen atom (*large ball*) vibrates back and forth across the plane of its three hydrogen atoms (*small balls*).

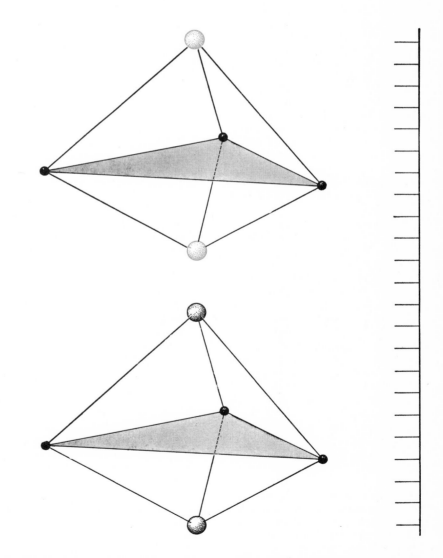

QUANTUM-MECHANICAL VIEW OF THE MOLECULE is that, in a sense, the nitrogen atom is simultaneously on both sides of the plane of the hydrogen atoms. The molecule may occupy either a higher energy level (*top illustration*) or a lower energy level (*bottom*).

ammonia molecules is sent through the separator, those in the upper state are attracted to the axis, while those in the lower state are pulled toward the electrodes and dispersed. Out of the far end comes a stream of molecules, virtually all of which are in the upper energy-state. If these molecules are irradiated with 24,000-megacycle microwaves, only downward transitions will be induced. Energy will be given up by the molecules to the microwave field, and the incoming wave will be amplified.

In the actual instrument ammonia gas at low pressure escapes from a nozzle into an evacuated chamber containing the separator and a resonant cavity. After passing through the separator, molecules in the upper state enter the cavity, into which the microwave signal is fed through a waveguide.

The resonant cavity is simply a metal box with highly reflecting walls. Each incoming photon can bounce back and forth across the chamber thousands of times before it escapes again, greatly increasing its chance of interacting with a molecule in the beam.

Whenever there is a collision, a new photon is born. It too is trapped in the chamber for a time and may collide with another molecule, producing a second new photon, and so on. If there are enough molecules in the cavity, this chain reaction becomes self-sustaining; the amplifier turns into an oscillator, generating its own wave without any input signal.

The ammonia maser is an extraordinarily stable oscillator. Its virtually unvarying sine waves can be used as a "pendulum" to regulate an almost perfect clock [see "Atomic Clocks," by Harold Lyons; SCIENTIFIC AMERICAN Offprint 225]. Although such timepieces have not yet been fully tested, it has been demonstrated that two ammonia masers will maintain their frequencies with respect to each other for at least a year with an accuracy of one part in 10 billion. A maser-regulated clock should gain or lose no more than one second in a few hundred years.

As an amplifier the ammonia maser has a remarkably narrow band-width: it will not amplify waves which depart from its central frequency by more than 3,000 to 5,000 cycles. The ammonia maser is not readily tunable; the central frequency cannot easily be changed. This means that it is not really a practical amplifier. If it were used in a communications channel, it could transmit only one voice at a time; it could not come close to receiving a television station. The ammonia maser was, however, the

instrument which first demonstrated the great potentialities of maser amplifiers. Moreover, studies of its resonance curve have contributed important information about the magnetic fields within the ammonia molecule.

It was not until the invention of masers that utilize solids rather than gases that practical low-noise microwave amplifiers became a reality. Solid-state masers have a noise level even lower than that of the ammonia maser. Furthermore they are tunable, they have much broader band-widths and they put out much more power. The fact that their frequencies can be varied makes them unsuitable as standards of frequency or of time, but it adds considerably to their general usefulness as amplifiers.

The action of the solid-state maser also depends on quantum jumps, but they are jumps of electrons within individual atoms rather than energy transitions of whole molecules. It is by now a familiar fact that every electron is in effect a small spinning magnet. In most atoms, which are nonmagnetic, the electrons are paired off with their poles opposed to each other so that their magnetism is canceled out. There are a few substances, however, in whose atoms the cancellation is incomplete; some electrons are unpaired and the material as a whole is magnetic, or, in technical terms, paramagnetic.

It is the behavior of unpaired electrons placed in an external magnetic field that makes the solid-state maser possible. As usual, there are two ways to describe this behavior: the classical way, which has the advantage of being easy to visualize but the drawback of being incomplete; and the quantum way, which is implausible but correct. Classically we imagine that the spin axis of the electron wobbles, or precesses like a top around the direction of the field [see diagram at left in illustration at top of opposite page]. In quantum terms we say that the spinning electron can have just two positions: one in which its axis points in the same direction as that of the field; the other in which it points in the opposite direction. The two positions constitute different quantum states, the higher of which is represented by the electron whose axis points in the direction of the field. As in the case of molecules, the difference between the levels corresponds to the energy of a photon whose frequency equals that of the classical vibration. Also as in the case of molecules, there are normally more electrons at lower levels than at higher.

To make a maser we simply need to

find a way of reversing the normal distribution and putting the majority of electrons in the upper state. Then if they are irradiated with photons of the correct frequency, they will jump down, amplifying the incoming beam.

The first type of solid-state maser that was developed is known as the two-level paramagnetic maser. In some versions the paramagnetic material is a silicon crystal containing some impurity atoms, such as those of phosphorus, which have one more electron than they need to satisfy their role in the crystal lattice. In other versions it is a quartz crystal which has been subjected to neutron bombardment to release unpaired electrons. The crystal is placed between the poles of a strong magnet and cooled to a temperature a few degrees above absolute zero in a bath of liquid helium, so that most of its unpaired electrons fall into the lower of their two possible energy states. Then it is subjected to a fairly high-powered microwave pulse, which briefly raises the majority of the electrons to the higher state. While this "inverted population" of electrons lasts, it can act as an amplifier for a weak microwave signal. In silicon the amplifying period lasts about a minute after each "pumping" pulse; in quartz, only a few thousandths of a second.

The difference between the energy of the upper and lower levels depends upon the strength of the magnetic field. Hence by adjusting the strength of the magnet, the maser can be tuned over a wide range of frequencies. With very strong fields it may be possible to reach the never-never land of waves a fraction of a millimeter long.

In a solid crystal the outside field is not the only one to act on unpaired electrons. The electrons are also influenced by the magnetism of neighboring atoms. The internal magnetic effect varies from point to point in the crystal, so that not all the electrons are subjected to exactly the same field. Thus they respond to slightly different frequencies, and this is the reason for the wider band-width of the solid-state devices.

The chief disadvantage of the two-level maser is that it can be operated only in bursts; its amplifying action stops each time its electrons drop down again to the lower level. This problem has been overcome with the development of the newest member of the maser family: the three-level paramagnetic maser.

Conceived by Nicolaas Bloembergen of Harvard University, the three-level paramagnetic maser has a basic element

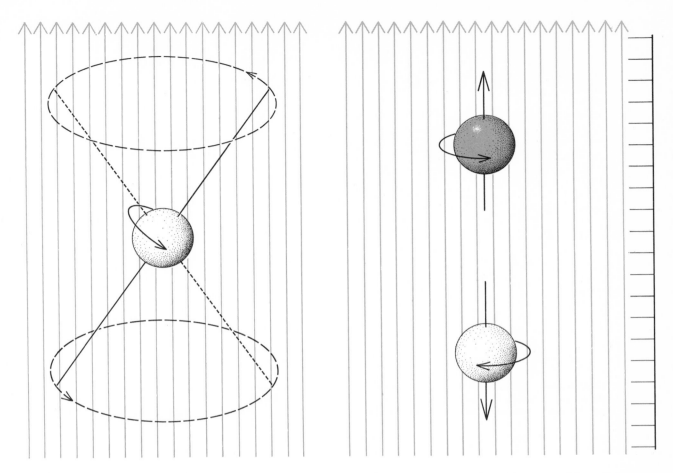

ELECTRON IN A MAGNETIC FIELD (*colored arrows*) is depicted from the classical standpoint (*left*) and from the quantum-mechanical (*right*). In the classical view the axis of the electron's spin precesses, or wobbles, around the direction of the magnetic field at a frequency related to the strength of the field. In the quantum-mechanical view the electron has a higher energy state (*top right*) in which its "south" magnetic pole is pointed in the direction of the field, and a lower energy state (*bottom right*) in which the pole is pointed in the opposite direction. The difference in the energy levels is related to the strength of the field.

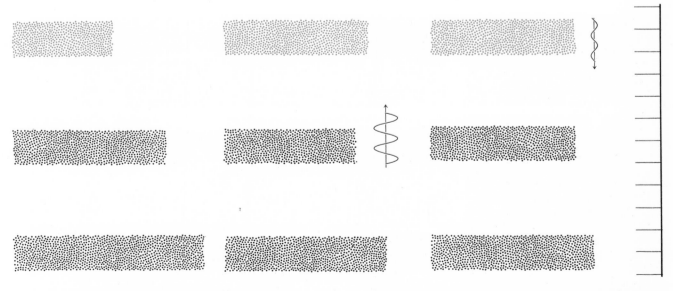

THREE-LEVEL SOLID-STATE MASER is considered. At left are electrons in three energy states; the largest number of electrons is in the lowest state, the smallest number is in the highest state. In the middle electrons are "pumped" from the lowest state to the highest by microwave energy of the appropriate frequency. At right electrons drop from the highest state to the middle state, emitting microwave energy of a lower frequency. Thus energy put into the maser at the latter frequency can be amplified.

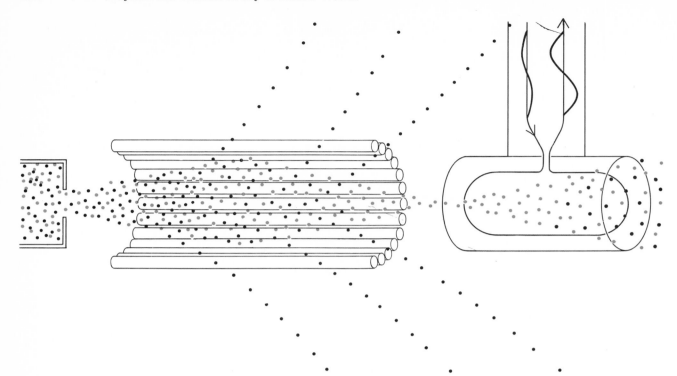

AMMONIA MASER sends ammonia molecules in two energy states through a cylinder of electrically charged rods. The molecules in the lower state (*black dots*) are pulled toward the rods; the mole-cules in the higher state (*colored*) are attracted to the axis of the cylinder. The molecules in the higher state then enter a resonant cavity (*right*), where they may be used to amplify a microwave signal.

consisting of atoms with more than one unpaired electron apiece. Atoms of this kind are found in the naturally paramagnetic elements such as iron and chromium, in which one of the interior shells of electrons is not filled. Quantum mechanics tells us that in many such atoms there is one more energy level than the number of unpaired electrons. For ex-ample, chromium atoms, which make up part of the ruby crystal, possess three unpaired electrons and thus have four energy levels.

Any three of the available levels can be used. When the crystal is cooled to very low temperatures, the atoms distribute themselves among the energy states in the usual way, each higher level containing fewer atoms than the one below it [*see illustration at bottom of preceding page*]. Now we irradiate the solid with microwaves of the proper frequency, causing a jump from the lowest of our three levels to the highest. By this pumping action the top level is kept fuller than the middle one. Therefore a weak signal whose frequency corre-

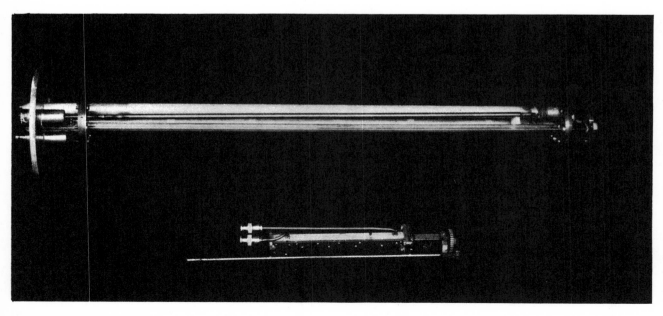

COMPONENTS OF A THREE-LEVEL MASER appear in the photographs on these two pages. The object at top in the photo-graph at left is essentially a waveguide through which microwaves are conducted to the maser cell. The object at bottom in the same

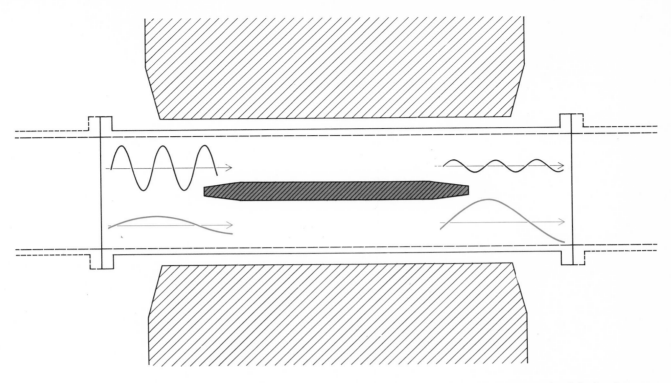

SOLID-STATE MASER consists essentially of a crystal (*center*) between the poles of a magnet (*top and bottom*). Microwave energy of an appropriate frequency (*black curve at left*) pumps electrons in the crystal to a higher state. An input signal (*colored curve at left*) of lower frequency is amplified (*colored curve at right*) at the expense of the pumping energy (*black curve at right*).

sponds to the energy gap between the top and middle levels will cause more downward than upward transitions, and the signal will be amplified. Pumping and amplification can go on at the same time, and so the maser operates continuously.

The first three-level maser was built at Bell Telephone Laboratories. Since then numerous masers of this kind, incorporating a variety of different crystals, have gone into operation at many other laboratories. One of them, as we have indicated, is already attached to a radio telescope. Soon they will be appearing in other applications.

There are jobs to be done by all the members of the maser family. In addition to simply telling time, ammonia and other gas-maser clocks will help explore some of the basic questions of physics. One plan is to recheck the celebrated Michelson-Morley experiment, which demonstrated that the speed of light is constant. Turning the maser's beam of molecules in two directions—along the path of the earth's travel and against it—

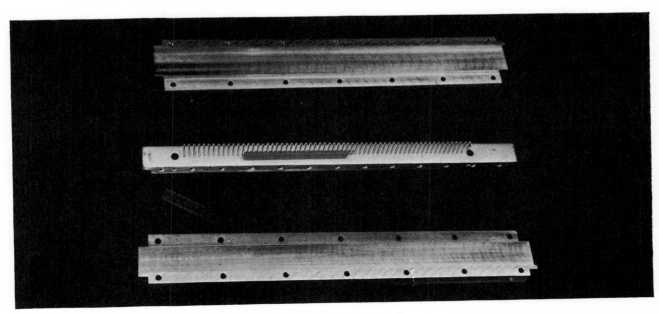

photograph is the maser cell, which is mounted at the right end of the waveguide. In the photograph at right the maser cell is dissected. One section of the large synthetic ruby of the maser stands against the row of pins in the middle; another one is to the left.

should result in no change of the output frequency, if light travels at a constant rate regardless of the motion of the observer. If there is a difference, it is too small to show up on Michelson's light interferometer. But the maser may be able to detect it. [At the time that this article first went to press, it was announced that the experiment had been performed by Townes, working with J. P. Cedarholm, G. F. Bland and B. L. Havens of the International Business Machines Watson Laboratory at Columbia University. No difference was detected.]

Another project is a check on the general theory of relativity, which predicts that clocks are slowed up by gravi-

tational fields. Artificial satellites will soon be circling the earth at distances where its gravity is noticeably weaker than at the surface. An atomic clock mounted in one of these vehicles could demonstrate the effect, if it exists.

Maser amplifiers may greatly simplify long-distance radio and television communication. As an example of what may be in the cards, suppose a ring of balloon satellites were made to circle endlessly around the earth. They would be permanent reflectors, from which signals could be bounced from any point on the earth's surface to any other. The received signals would be very weak. But the cold and lonely satellites would not

contaminate them with much noise. Thus the sensitive, almost noiseless maser amplifiers could pick them up and boost them to useful levels without degrading them beyond recognition.

French workers have applied the maser principle to build a super-sensitive magnetometer for measuring the earth's field. In other laboratories people are thinking of using masers to produce beams of infrared radiation with an extremely narrow band of frequencies. The list is not exhaustive, and there are probably important applications that no one has thought of as yet. Quantum mechanics is adding a new dimension to "classical" electronics.

COMPLETE THREE-LEVEL MASER is photographed at Bell Telephone Laboratories. In center, between the poles of a large electromagnet, is a silvered flask which is filled with liquid helium. The maser cell is inside the flask between the two magnet poles.

VI
Lasers

Lasers

At the time of the invention of the first maser, Townes was trying to discover a new way to produce electromagnetic oscillations at frequencies higher than the oscillations that could be produced by electron tubes. Many others were intrigued by this possibility, and they began to invent names for future stimulated-emission devices for producing oscillations in various frequency regions: RASER (radio-frequency), IRASER (infrared), LASER (light), UVASER (ultraviolet) and XRASER (X-ray). All of these would be variants of the maser, utilizing the same principle, and it seemed that their development would be possible if no unexpected obstacles were encountered.

At that time it was generally thought that the next step might be a maser that would operate in the far infrared region, at wavelengths a little shorter than the shortest radio waves. Yet when Townes and I studied the problems in detail it seemed easier to bypass most of the infrared and to construct instead a maser in the visible or near-visible region. We were able to show that it was possible to excite enough atoms for an optical maser, and also proposed a new kind of maser resonator that would cause the output to be a narrow beam.

As soon as these ideas were published, many attempted to build optical masers of various kinds. There seemed to be so many alternate possibilities that it was hard to know which was the easiest. The first successful operation of an optical maser was achieved by Theodore H. Maiman in 1960. Soon afterward, others were successful, and there were four additional kinds before the end of that year. Maiman called his device a LASER; others continued to use the term optical maser. The principles on which lasers operate undoubtedly place them in the family of masers, but in structure, properties, and applications they are quite different from their microwave predecessors. Thus, the more compact term, laser, has become the common usage.

In the first two articles in this section, I have described the structure, the properties, and some early scientific applications of lasers. Three years after the development of the first laser, short pulses with peak powers of a billion watts had been achieved. Many wavelengths had been generated, and many new research areas had been opened to exploration. The applications of the laser include hole drilling, eye surgery, spectrochemical analysis, and laser gyroscopes. Progress in the development and application of lasers continues to be rapid.

In addition, new methods of obtaining laser action have been devised. A new kind of laser can often make possible new experiments, some of which in turn point the way to other new lasers. For a number of these lasers, the medium consists of electrical discharges in gases—not unlike the kind used for neon signs—with the addition of a pair of mirrors to define the beam. Since such common gas discharges can be used as laser media, some workers have tried to use luminescent flames. This idea of a completely nonelectrical laser, consisting of some kind of flame whose light is directed by mirrors, is an attractive one, but so far the realization of it has eluded researchers, although several kinds of lasers have been powered by the light from a chemical flame or explosion. The lasers in which the use of pure flame is most closely approximated are those described in the article by George C. Pimentel. They derive their excitation from chemical combination during a fast gaseous reaction, and are not quite true chemical lasers only because they require ignition by an electrical impulse. It does seem that a purely chemical laser would indeed be both powerful and efficient. However, before we can successfully design such a device, we must learn much more about the processes that govern chemical reactions.

Since lasers have been made from solids and gases, why not from liquids? There are many transparent liquids that can be obtained in large quantities in which fluorescing substances can be dissolved. One drawback is that a molecule in a liquid is being constantly and severely buffeted by its neighbors, causing the optical spectra of most substances to be greatly broadened when they are dissolved in liquids. Also, in some solutions the interaction of the atoms or molecules with the liquid quenches the light emission. In spite of these difficulties a number of liquid laser systems that operate with good efficiency have been designed. Since they can be made as large as desired, liquid lasers may prove to be among the most powerful. Alexander Lempicki and Harold Samelson review the problems and progress in the construction and use of liquid lasers. Since their article was written, there has been much research, with some successful results, on a different class of liquid laser—one with a medium of organic dyes. The output wavelengths of these dye lasers can be adjusted by varying the composition of the dye.

Most high-power lasers are of the optically excited type, powered by some kind of a lamp. Whether the active medium is a solid or a liquid, the laser can use only a limited range of wavelengths, and this range seldom covers more than a few percent of the light from the lamp. For this reason, these optically excited lasers are generally inefficient, and the dissipation of excess heat severely limits their ability to produce sustained high power outputs. Most gas lasers that have thus far been developed are also quite inefficient, with the single remarkable exception of the carbon-dioxide gas lasers, which have produced much higher continuous power outputs than any other kind. The principles of operation and the properties of this infrared laser are described in the article by C. K. N. Patel.

20

Optical Masers

Arthur L. Schawlow   June 1961

For at least half a century communications engineers have dreamed of having a device that would generate light waves as efficiently and precisely as radio waves can be generated. The contrast in purity between the electromagnetic waves emitted by an ordinary incandescent lamp and those emitted by a radio-wave generator could scarcely be greater. Radio waves from an electromagnetic oscillator are confined to a fairly narrow region of the electromagnetic spectrum and are so free from "noise" that they can be used for carrying signals. In contrast, all conventional light sources are essentially noise generators that are unsuited for anything more than the crudest signaling purposes. It is only within the last year, with the advent of the optical maser, that it has been possible to attain precise control of the generation of light waves.

Although optical masers are still very new, they have already provided enormously intense and sharply directed beams of light. These beams are much more monochromatic than those from other light sources; at their best optical masers rival the very finest electronic oscillators as a source of a single frequency. The development of optical masers is moving so rapidly that they should soon be ready for a wide variety of applications. These may range from space communications and radar to accelerating specific reactions in chemical technology.

To appreciate the limitations of light waves as they are ordinarily found, let us consider how they are produced. All light sources—incandescent lamps, arcs and so on—are essentially hot matter. In the familiar neon tube, it is true, the glass walls remain cool, but the electrons and gas atoms within the tube are accelerated to the high speeds normally

associated with high temperatures. The atoms are continuously "pumped" to an excited state; then they fall back, losing energy and radiating visible light. They fall back, however, one atom at a time. The disorderly atomic motion we associate with a heated gas is paralleled by a disorderly outpouring of light quanta, or photons. Just which atoms radiate at any instant is purely a random affair. The excited electrons in the hot tungsten filament of an incandescent lamp also radiate randomly and independently.

Thus the light that comes from any conventional light source is called spatially incoherent. This means that the light emerges in a jumble of tiny, separate waves that reinforce or cancel each other in random fashion; the wave front so produced varies from point to point and changes from instant to instant. The wave front resembles one that would be produced by throwing a handful of pebbles into a pool. If, on the other hand, only a single pebble were dropped into the pool, a coherent circular wave front would be produced. By the same token one can imagine a point source of light that could generate coherent waves whose fronts would form spherical surfaces. Alternatively, a suitable source might generate coherent light waves whose fronts were plane surfaces; at every point on the plane the strength of the electric field would be the same. As the wave fronts traveled past a given point in space, the field strength would be seen to rise and fall smoothly and rhythmically in phase, swinging from positive to negative in value.

If a conventional electronic oscillator that produces radio waves is connected to a small radiator of suitable design, the radiator will send out spherical coherent waves. If one wishes, the oscillator can be connected to feed a number of radiat-

ing antennas that will send out a directional wave, much like a plane wave.

To obtain a directional wave from an incoherent light source one must start with a source of small dimensions. Then, by placing a screen with a hole in it some distance from the source, we can select the segment of the wave that happens to be going in the desired direction. Alternatively, the light emitted by a small source can be focused with a larger mirror or lens to yield a beam with sides that are roughly parallel. The sides of a beam produced by an arc lamp and a six-foot mirror diverge at an angle of about one degree. As we shall see, the output of an optical maser is both more directional and more coherent.

Perhaps the most important limitation of ordinary light sources is their inherent low brightness. No matter how high their temperature, they cannot emit more energy than a perfect radiator. The theoretical output of a perfect radiator, called a black body, is given by the famous black-body radiation curve first derived by Max Planck. The visible surface of the sun, for example, behaves much like a black body with a temperature of 6,000 degrees centigrade. The sun's total radiation, at all wavelengths, is seven kilowatts per square centimeter of its surface, and no matter how we collect and concentrate sunlight it is impossible to achieve any greater radiation density.

Although seven kilowatts may seem a substantial amount of energy, it is really not very much if one considers the tremendous width of the solar spectrum. To bring this point home let us compare the width of the visible portion of the electromagnetic spectrum with the width of a standard television channel, which is four megacycles. A little calculation

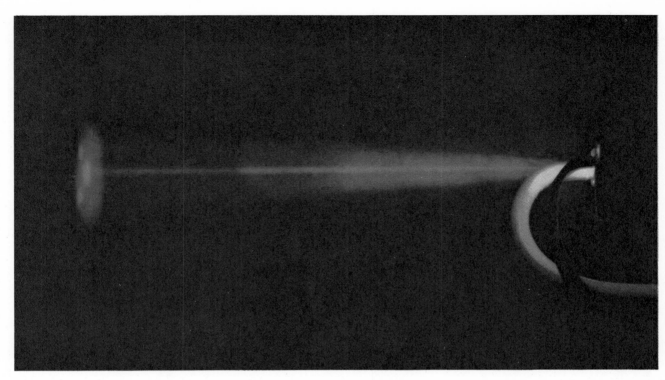

BEAM FROM RUBY OPTICAL MASER makes a thin streak of red light as it passes through smoke. Upper end of curved cooling tube at right is attached to front end of the maser housing, which here cannot be seen. The ruby crystal is mounted in the housing.

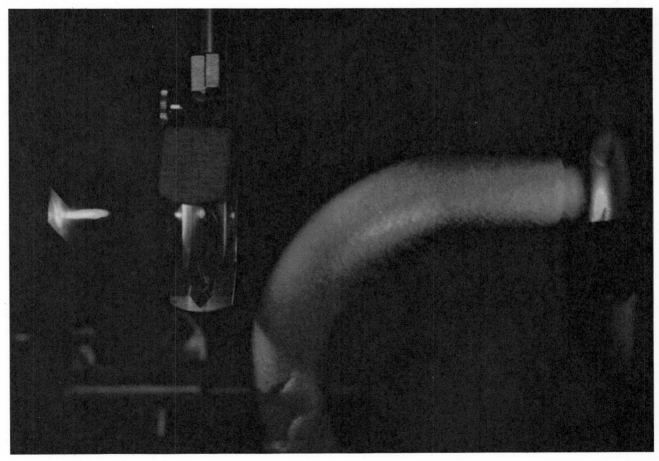

BRILLIANT BLUE-WHITE FLAME at left is incandescent carbon vapor produced by focusing a ruby-maser beam on a carbon target. The beam heated a spot on the target to about 8,000 degrees centigrade in .0005 second. The large curved object to the right is the same cooling tube seen in the photograph at top. The small lens used to focus the beam is mounted at the left of the tube.

GAS OPTICAL MASER employs a helium-neon mixture to produce an infrared beam. Reddish glow results from gas discharge of mixture. The gas maser, designed by Ali Javan, W. R. Bennett, Jr., and D. R. Herriott, was the first to operate continuously.

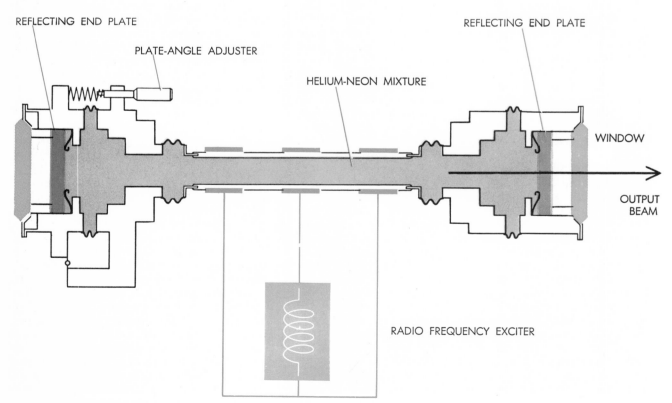

REFLECTING END PLATE

PLATE-ANGLE ADJUSTER

REFLECTING END PLATE

HELIUM-NEON MIXTURE

WINDOW

OUTPUT BEAM

RADIO FREQUENCY EXCITER

OPERATION OF GAS MASER depends on right mixture of helium and neon gases to provide an active medium. Radio frequency exciter puts energy into the medium. The output beam is built up by repeated passes back and forth between reflecting end plates.

shows that the visible region between the wavelengths of 4,000 and 7,000 angstrom units could contain 80 million television channels. In other words, each angstrom unit is about 100,000 megacycles wide. If one were able to filter out a narrow band of green light one megacycle wide from the region where the sun has its peak energy output (4,800 angstrom units), one would find that each square centimeter of solar surface produces only .00001 watt. To obtain as much as a single watt of green light one megacycle wide one would have to collect and filter the output from 10 square yards of solar surface. In contrast, man-made transmitters operating in the television region of the radio spectrum can easily generate 10,000 watts in a band much less than one megacycle wide.

Ordinary light sources are like the sun: they are broad-band noise generators that spread their output over a wide range of frequencies without supplying much power at any particular frequency. Even gas-discharge lamps, which emit light at a restricted number of narrow lines in the spectrum, do not approach the best electronic oscillators as sources of power at a single frequency.

There has been, of course, a great effort to extend electronic oscillators to shorter wavelengths. The length of the shortest waves that can be generated by electronic means is about one millimeter, or 10 million angstrom units. Any attempt to reach shorter wavelengths with conventional electronic designs meets with formidable difficulties. Foremost among these is the difficulty of fabricating the resonant structures that tune the oscillator. These structures can seldom be much larger than a wavelength in size. At millimeter wavelengths they are already so small that they are hard to make with uniform accuracy. To produce optical wavelengths, which are three orders of magnitude shorter, a radically different approach is needed.

An attractive solution to the problem would be to stop trying to build these tiny resonators and to replace them by atomic or molecular resonators. Nature has provided us with a wide variety of such resonators through the entire infrared, visible and ultraviolet spectrum. Indeed, engineers are accustomed to using atomic oscillators in gas-discharge lamps. A single atom, however, radiates very little power, and that only intermittently. What is needed is some way to synchronize a large number of atoms so that they can work together to produce a powerful, coherent wave.

Such an approach has been made pos-sible by the maser principle, discovered by Charles H. Townes at Columbia University [see "The Maser," by James P. Gordon, which begins on page 212 in this book]. Maser stands for "microwave amplification by stimulated emission of radiation." The original maser, completed in 1954 by James P. Gordon, H. J. Zeiger and Townes, used the vibrations of ammonia molecules to provide microwave oscillations of precisely determined frequency. Subsequently Nicolaas Bloembergen of Harvard University indicated a practical way to build the so-called three-level solid-state maser for use as a low-noise microwave amplifier. The first maser of this type was built at the Bell Telephone Laboratories by George Feher, H. E. D. Scovil and H. Seidel, and since then many others have been constructed. Radio astronomers have found them extremely valuable for amplifying very faint radio signals from space. Last year masers were also used to amplify the weak signals received on the bounce from the *Echo* satellite.

Stimulated emission, which is the basis of maser operation, is the reverse of the process in which electromagnetic waves, or photons, are absorbed by atomic systems. When a photon is absorbed by an atom, the energy of the photon is converted to internal energy of the atom. The atom is then raised to an "excited" quantum state. Later it may radiate this energy spontaneously, emitting a photon and reverting to the "ground" state or to some state in between. During the period in which the atom is still excited it can be stimulated to emit a photon if it is struck by an outside photon having precisely the energy of the one that would otherwise be emitted spontaneously. As a result the incoming photon, or wave, is augmented by the one given up by the excited atom. More important and more remarkable, the wave, upon release, falls precisely in phase with the wave that triggered its release. This phenomenon lies at the heart of the maser principle [*see illustration on following page*].

The problem in designing a maser is to prepare an "active medium" in which most of the atoms can be placed in an excited state, so that an electromagnetic wave of the right frequency passing through them will stimulate a cascade of photons. There must be an excess of excited atoms to enable stimulated emission to predominate over absorption. Atoms are raised to an excited state by injecting into the system electromagnetic energy at a wavelength different from the stimulating wavelength; the activating process is called "pumping."

Once an active medium has been prepared it can be enclosed in a reflecting box, or cavity resonator. Then a wave that starts out at one wall of the box will grow in amplitude until it reaches another wall, where it will be reflected back into the mass of excited atoms. Inevitably there are losses at the walls due to imperfect reflection. If the amplification by stimulated emission is great enough to make up for these reflection losses, a steady wave will build up in the box. At centimeter wavelengths it is not difficult to build a box having the dimensions of a wavelength and so designed that the wave will build up with only one mode of oscillation. A single mode of oscillation corresponds to a single frequency of output; extraneous modes create extra frequencies, or noise, and compete with the desired mode in extracting energy from the supply of excited atoms.

At optical wavelengths a single-wavelength resonator would have dimensions inconveniently small. To surmount this problem, Townes and the author proposed in 1958 that a maser for optical wavelengths could be built by making a special kind of resonator with dimensions thousands of times greater than the emission wavelength but which nevertheless would favor a particular mode of oscillation. In the optical maser the reflecting box is replaced by a device or structure with two small mirrors facing each other. A wave that starts out near one mirror and travels along the axis of the system will grow by stimulated emission until it reaches the other mirror. There it will be reflected back into the active medium so that growth can continue. If the gain on repeated passages is enough to make up for the losses at the mirrors, a steady wave will be built up. If one of the mirrors is semitransparent, a portion of the wave can escape through it, constituting the output of the maser.

It is perhaps evident that a wave inclined at an angle to the axis will leave the system after only a few reflections, or perhaps without ever striking one of the mirrors. Such a wave will not have the same opportunity to build up as does a wave that travels straight along the axis of the system. Like other maser oscillators, the optical maser Townes and I described would be triggered off by the first photons to be emitted spontaneously after the system had been "pumped up" to the active state. (A maser designed to operate as an amplifier, on the other hand, uses an input signal as a stimulating wave.)

We had every reason to expect that the output of an ideal optical maser constructed in this manner would be extremely directional, very powerful, essentially monochromatic and, above all, coherent. The output would be directional because the only waves emitted would have had to make repeated passages—perhaps thousands—without deviating very far from the axis of the maser. It would be very powerful because stimulated emission forces excited atoms to radiate much earlier than they would spontaneously. It would be very monochromatic because stimulated emission is a resonant process and takes place most strongly at the center of the band of frequencies that can be emitted in spontaneous radiation. These favored frequencies will in turn cause emission at the same frequency, so that the wave built up in the maser will contain only an extremely narrow range of frequencies or wavelengths.

Finally, the output of the optical maser, if it is a good approximation of a plane wave traveling in a single direction, will be spatially coherent because all the wave fronts are planes perpendicular to the direction of propagation. Since the maser output is nearly monochromatic, it also has time coherence. This means that there is a fixed phase relation between the portion of the wave emitted at one instant and the wave emitted after a fixed time interval. For a wave whose period is one second, crests follow each other at one-second intervals. On the other hand, if the frequency varies, the interval between crests is irregular. The more nearly the wave holds to a single, fixed frequency, the more nearly it exhibits time coherence.

Testing these predictions required preparation of an active medium that would actually display maser action in the optical region of the spectrum. The first announcement of success was made last July by T. H. Maiman of the Hughes Aircraft Company, whose device used a ruby crystal. Between July and the end of 1960 four other substances were tested successfully by various investiga-tors. These devices all embodied the concept of reflecting end walls, described above. At last count optical maser oscillations had been obtained at 11 different wavelengths. It seems likely that these wavelengths will soon be joined by many others.

Maiman's ruby maser is typical of those using crystals. Ruby is aluminum oxide in which a few of the aluminum atoms have been replaced by chromium atoms; the more chromium, the deeper the color. Maiman used a pale pink ruby containing about .05 per cent chromium. The color results from the fact that the chromium atoms in the crystal absorb a broad band of green and yellow light, along with ultraviolet light, and let only the red and blue pass through. Moreover, the light that is absorbed raises the chromium atoms to an excited state from which two steps are required to carry them back to the ground state. In the first step they give up some of their energy to the crystal lattice and land temporarily in what is called a metastable state. If they are not subjected to stimulation, their stay at this level lasts a few milliseconds while they drop at random to the ground state. Photons emitted during this final drop have a wavelength (at room temperature) of 6,943 angstrom units, which accounts for the characteristic red fluorescence of ruby crystals. In an optical maser, however, the first few photons released at this wavelength stimulate the still excited chromium atoms to give up photons and tumble to the ground state much sooner than they would normally; the result is a cascade of photons all at the 6,943-angstrom wavelength.

For use in an optical maser the pink ruby is machined into a rod about four centimeters long and half a centimeter across. Its ends are polished optically flat and parallel and are partially silvered. The rod is placed near an electronic flash tube that provides broadband pumping light. What Maiman discovered before anyone else is that the most powerful of these lamps, when connected to a large power supply, is capable of raising most of the chromium atoms to the excited state. Up to a certain critical flash intensity, all that happens is that the ruby emits a burst of its typical red fluorescence spread over the usual decay period for the excited atoms. But above a critical level maser action takes over, and an intense red beam, lasting for about half a thousandth of a second, flashes out from the partially silvered ends of the rod. This shows that a

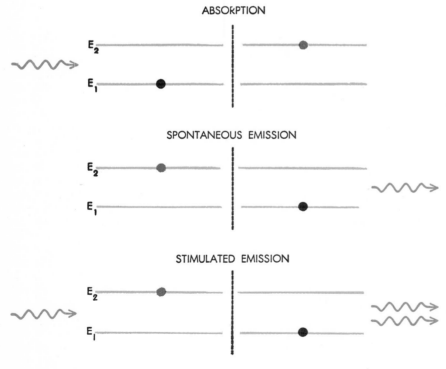

ABSORPTION

SPONTANEOUS EMISSION

STIMULATED EMISSION

STIMULATED EMISSION of photons (*bottom*), the basis of maser operation, is contrasted with absorption (*top*) and spontaneous emission (*middle*). When an atom in the "ground" state (*black dot at top left*) absorbs a photon (*wavy colored arrow*), it is excited, or raised to a higher energy state (*gray dot at top right*). The excited atom (*middle left*) may then radiate energy spontaneously, emitting a photon and reverting to the ground state (*middle right*). An excited atom (*bottom left*) can also be stimulated to emit a photon when it is struck by an outside photon. Thus in addition to the stimulating photon there is now a second photon of the same wavelength (*bottom right*) and the atom reverts to the ground state.

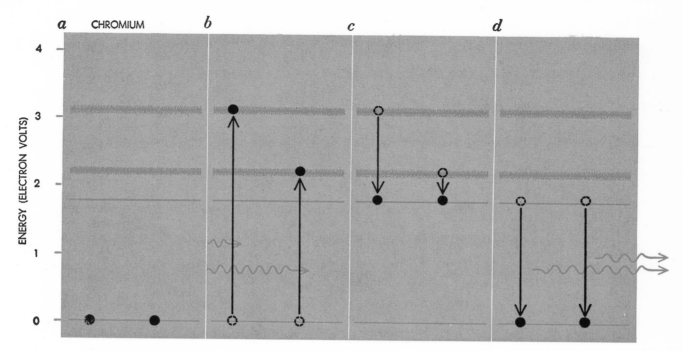

CHROMIUM ATOMS (*black dots*) in a ruby maser crystal are "pumped" to higher energy levels and then stimulated to emit photons, producing a maser beam. Atoms in the ground state (*a*) absorb photons (*wavy colored arrows*), which pump them to one of two energy "bands" (*b*). The atoms give up some of their energy to the crystal lattice and fall to a metastable energy level (*c*). When stimulated by photons from other chromium atoms, they emit photons of a characteristic wavelength and fall to ground state (*d*).

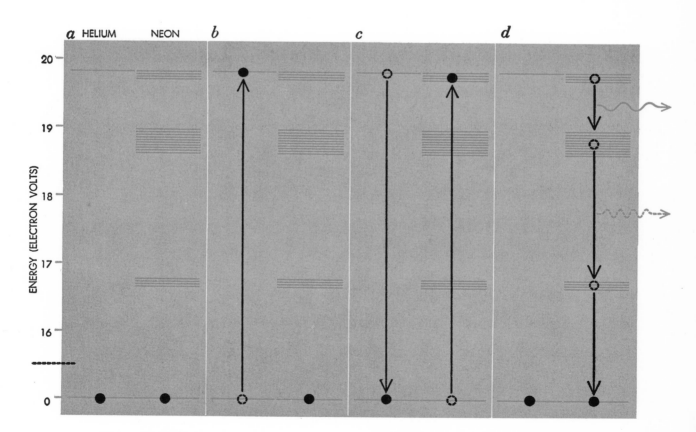

HELIUM AND NEON ATOMS (*black dots*) constitute the active medium of the gas maser. At the start both are in the ground state (*a*). Electron bombardment pumps helium to a higher energy level (*b*). When helium and neon atoms collide, the helium loses its energy to the neon, which is raised to one of four distinct energy levels (*c*). When stimulated by an outside photon, the neon contributes a photon (*wavy colored arrow at top in "d"*) to the maser beam and falls to one of 10 energy levels. The neon then reverts to the ground state in steps; the photon emitted in the first step (*wavy broken arrow*) does not contribute to the maser beam.

sufficient excess of atoms has been pumped up to the excited state to make up for the losses at the ends.

In 1959 the author had predicted that it should be possible to build an optical maser using a dark red ruby that contains about 10 times as much chromium as the pink ruby. It was predicted that at this higher concentration maser action would take place simultaneously at two different wavelengths—7,009 and 7,041 angstroms [*see illustration on opposite page*]. This mode of operation was recently·demonstrated in a maser built by G. E. Devlin and the author, and in another built by I. Wieder and L. R. Sarles of Varian Associates. Still other solid optical masers, using samarium or uranium ions in a calcium fluoride crystal, have been constructed by P. P. Sorokin and M. J. Stevenson of the International Business Machines Research Laboratory. These masers oscillate at wavelengths of 7,080 and 25,000 angstroms respectively.

All these masers were first operated in short bursts, but they seem potentially capable of continuous operation. The active medium used by Maiman, however, is less well suited than the others in which the stimulated emission comes in a transition to an intermediate energy level that is some distance above the ground state. It is not necessary, there-

fore, to expend a lot of energy pumping half the atoms out of the ground state so that emission can predominate over absorption. In the newer materials the intermediate state—where the atoms land after emitting photons of the desired frequency—can be emptied simply by cooling. Hence the active medium contains very few atoms "tuned" to absorb the photons produced by maser action. Only enough pumping is needed for this action to begin.

A totally different way to obtain excited atoms for an optical maser employs gas atoms in an electric glow-discharge under very special conditions. In a mixture of helium and neon gas it is possible to secure maser oscillation at several wavelengths in the infrared region around 10,000 angstroms. This system was proposed in 1959 by Ali Javan of the Bell Telephone Laboratories. A successful prototype, constructed by him in collaboration with W. R. Bennett, Jr., and D. R. Herriott, was demonstrated early this year. The principal feature of this maser is its ability to operate continuously and with a very low energy input—about 50 watts in the first model.

In Javan's maser the stimulated emission occurs when a neon atom falls between two intermediate levels, the lower of which is well above the ground state.

Only a modest input of energy is required to produce a gas discharge—essentially like that in an ordinary neon sign—and this in turn provides a continuous supply of neon atoms at the proper level of excitation needed to produce a continuous maser beam [*see illustrations on page 226*]. As in the ruby masers, the beam is built up and made coherent by bouncing back and forth between reflecting end plates.

The helium-neon maser exemplifies the increasing subtlety of maser designs. The energy needed to raise the neon atom to an excited state is not supplied directly by an incoming photon; it is supplied by collision with an excited helium atom. Many other possibilities remain to be explored. Energy levels suitable for masers may be found in many different kinds of system. For example, in the infrared region spectral lines are produced by vibrations of gas molecules, by vibrations of crystals and by electronic excitations of certain atoms in crystals. Which of these may be usable in a maser can be discovered only by a detailed study of a system's spectrum.

Now that optical masers have been built, how closely do they match expectations in power, directionality, coherence and the narrowness of the band of wavelengths produced? We know

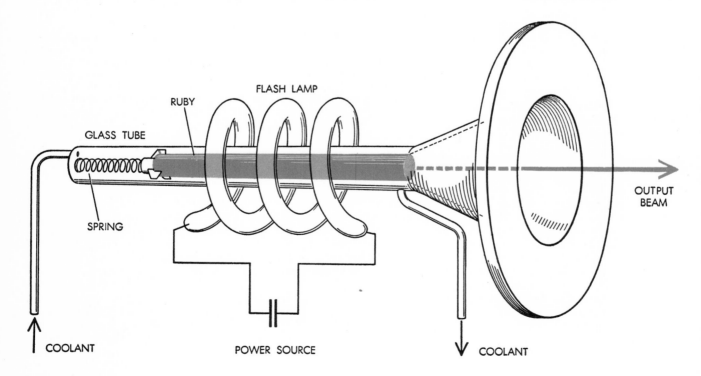

RUBY MASER is powered by a flash lamp, which provides pumping energy. Output beam is emitted through partially silvered end of ruby crystal; other end is completely silvered. Beam builds up by repeated reflection between the ends. Liquid nitrogen is used to cool the ruby, though it can also be operated at·room temperature. Only the front end of the maser housing (*right*) is shown.

most about the pink ruby. In short bursts its power output reaches 10,000 watts for a beam measuring less than a square centimeter in cross section. The sides of the beam are parallel to within less than half a degree; at lower power the divergence drops to about a twentieth of a degree. The latter divergence corresponds to a spread of only five feet per mile, and it could be reduced by running the beam through a telescope backward. With telescopic demagnification it should not be difficult to project on the moon a spot of light only two miles in diameter.

If desired, the maser's power can be focused to produce intense heating. For instance, a lens with a focal length of one centimeter will focus the beam to a spot only a hundredth of a centimeter in diameter, corresponding to an area of one ten-thousandth of a square centimeter. In this spot the maser beam will deliver power at a density of 100 million watts per square centimeter. Brief though the flash is, its power is thousands of times greater than could be obtained by focusing sunlight and is enough to melt or vaporize a spot on the surface of even the most refractory material. This was first demonstrated by my colleague W. S. Boyle [see bottom illustration on page 225].

It is not surprising that the ruby maser falls short of ideal performance in some respects, particularly in the narrowness of the band of wavelengths it produces. Because it is violently pulsed, the ruby rod heats appreciably. Nevertheless, when the maser threshold level is reached, the band of wavelengths narrows to about .02 angstrom, or about 1,000 megacycles. This is as narrow as the sharpest spectral line from any nonmaser light source.

The ruby is far surpassed in the narrowness of its output of wavelengths by the gas maser of Javan, Bennett and Herriott. This maser produces spectral lines less than one kilocycle wide at a carrier frequency of 100,000 megacycles. The gas maser's power output per kilocycle of band-width is about 100 million times that of a square centimeter of the sun's surface. It is possible that the frequency of a maser's output will drift slightly over a period of time, but over a short period it is remarkably stable; in the radio range this stability is equaled only by the finest frequency standards and by atomic clocks.

Of all the properties of the optical maser, none is more striking than the spatial coherence of its light. This is readily demonstrated by using the maser

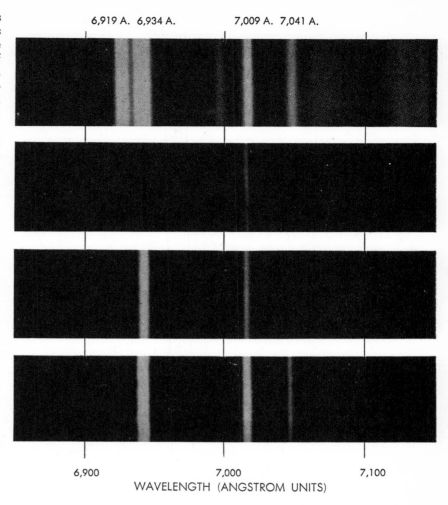

RUBY-MASER SPECTRA in three lower photographs are compared with spectrum of spontaneous (unstimulated) ruby fluorescence at top. As pumping power reaches first threshold for maser action (*second from top*), the ruby "mases" at 7,009 angstrom units (A.), at two wavelengths as power increases (*third from top*), then at three (*bottom*). Maser oscillation never occurs at 6,919 A. Sequence in which spectral lines appear varies with the maser crystal used and operating conditions. A 30-second exposure was required to photograph the fluorescent spectrum. Three lower photographs show single flashes of .0005 second.

to repeat the classic two-slit interference experiment first performed in 1806 by Thomas Young to show that light consists of waves. In Young's experiment light passes through two parallel slits and then falls on a distant screen. If light waves from one slit reach a point on the screen in phase with light waves from the other slit, the two sets of waves reinforce, producing a bright spot. At a nearby point on the screen, where the light from one slit has traveled half a wavelength farther than the light from the other slit, the waves cancel out, producing a dark spot. Thus a pattern of alternating light and dark spots appears on the screen.

As the experiment is usually performed, a small light source is placed some distance from the slits, so that the wave fronts reaching them travel nearly perpendicularly to their plane. If the source is too large or too close to the slits, the pattern fails to appear. Young's experiment is therefore a good test for the perpendicularity of wave fronts and for wave coherence.

When the experiment is performed with an optical maser, the slits can be placed directly against the surface from which the beam emerges and a clear interference pattern will result [see illustration, page 233]. The pattern agrees well with one calculated on the assumption of perfect coherence across the distance between the slits. Actually, in a ruby rod the region of coherence is usually limited by crystalline imperfections

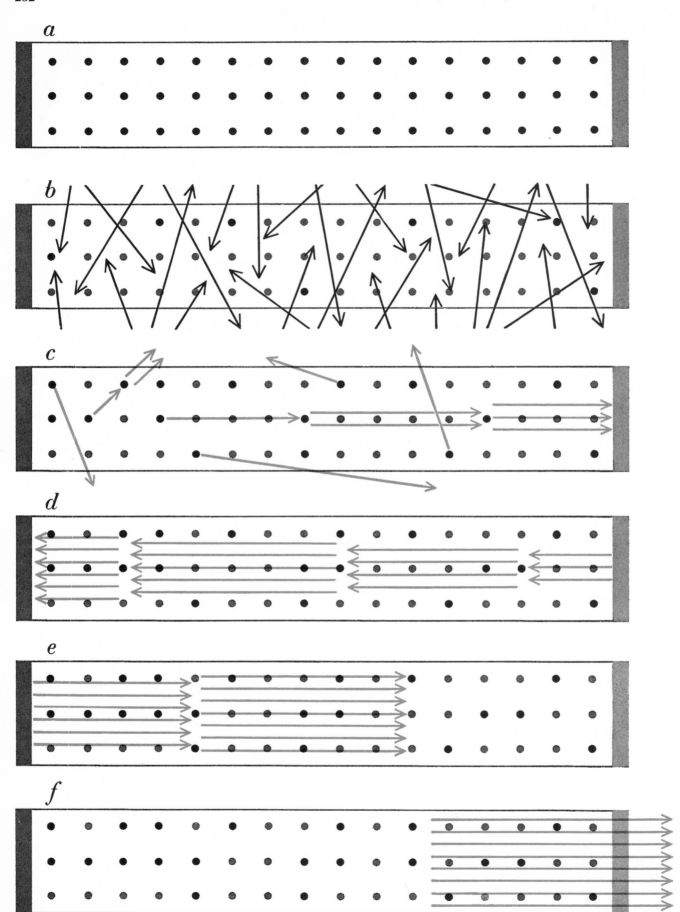

to about a tenth of the rod's diameter. In the gas maser, however, coherence extends across the whole width of the end plates.

The optical maser is such a radically new kind of light source that it taxes the imagination to canvass its possible applications. Message-carrying, of course, is the most obvious use and the one that is receiving the most technological attention. Signaling with light, although it has been used by men since ancient times, has been limited by the weakness and noisiness of available light sources. The amount of information light signals can carry is thereby quite limited. An ordinary light beam can be compared to a pure, smooth carrier wave that has already been modulated with noise by short bursts of light randomly emitted by the individual atoms in the light source. The maser, on the other hand, can provide an almost ideally smooth wave, carrying nothing but what one puts on it.

If suitable methods of modulation can be found, coherent light waves should be able to carry an enormous volume of information. This is so because the frequency of light is so high that even a very narrow band of the visible spectrum includes an enormous number of cycles per second; the amount of information that can be transmitted is directly proportional to the number of cycles per second and therefore to the width of the band. One must distinguish here between the spectral band-width of the unmodulated maser beam, or carrier wave (which, as we have seen, is extremely narrow), and the band-width after a signal has been impressed upon it.

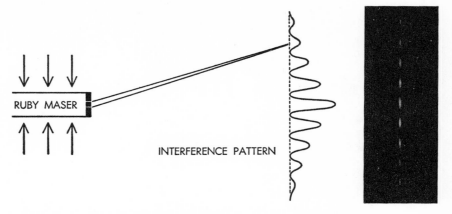

TWO-SLIT INTERFERENCE EXPERIMENT demonstrates that the light waves leaving a ruby maser are spatially coherent, or in step. When two coherent waves strike a screen, after traveling paths of slightly different length, they reinforce and cancel each other in symmetrical fashion to produce an interference pattern. The photograph of the interference pattern at right was made by D. F. Nelson and R. J. Collins of Bell Telephone Laboratories.

PHOTON CASCADE in a solid optical maser amplifies a light wave by stimulated emission. Before the cascade begins (a), the atoms in the maser crystal are in the ground state (*black dots*). Pumping light (*black arrows in "b"*) raises most of the atoms to the excited state (*gray dots*). The cascade begins (c) when an excited atom spontaneously emits a photon (*colored arrow*) parallel to the axis of the crystal. (Photons emitted in other directions pass out of the crystal.) The photon stimulates another atom to contribute a second photon. This process continues ("d" and "e") as the photons are reflected back and forth between the ends of the crystal. When the amplification is great enough, some of the beam passes out through partially silvered end of crystal (f).

In television transmission the carrier wave (which is also narrow) carries a signal that produces an effective band-width of four megacycles. A single maser beam might reasonably carry a signal with a frequency, or band-width, of 100,000 megacycles, assuming a way could be found to generate such a signal. A signal of this frequency could carry as much information as all the radio-communication channels now in existence. It must be admitted that no light beam will penetrate fog, rain or snow very well. Therefore to be useful in earthbound communication systems light beams will have to be enclosed in pipes.

There will certainly be other uses for optical masers. The very intense heat spot produced by focusing an optical maser might be used for fabricating all sorts of electronic devices. For instance, it would be possible to weld a small joint after the joint had been sealed inside a glass envelope. But, in addition to sheer power, the maser provides an intense source of coherent radiation with very high electric-field strength. In such strong fields atoms or molecules may react in strange and unpredictable ways. The beams should therefore be useful in many areas of research. One can also conceive of using maser beams in harmonic generators or mixers. With a suitable mixer one could put in two light waves of different frequency and take out a third wave whose frequency would be the difference of the two original frequencies. In this way it should be possible to synthesize wavelengths that cannot be produced directly. This should

lead eventually to superheterodyne receivers capable of translating optical wavelengths into any desired longer wavelength.

It has been known for some years that if one had a strong enough source of infrared radiation of the right frequency, it would be possible to excite vibrations in a particular species of molecule. Any other molecules that might be present would not be affected. Because the excited molecules would react more vigorously than the others, it should be possible to exert a highly selective control over some chemical reactions. Up to now all available light sources have been far too weak for such possibilities to be taken seriously, but optical masers may eventually make such control a reality.

It should be realized that we are talking about a whole family of devices embracing a wide range of frequencies, power ratings and band-widths. The family will include not only oscillators but also amplifiers. One type will be useful for amplifying a light signal that has been weakened by traveling a long distance, perhaps through pipes or through interplanetary space. Another type of amplifier will be able to intensify an entire image—for example, the faint image of a star—that is fed into it.

The list of potential applications of the optical maser could be extended almost indefinitely. With the advent of the optical maser, man's control of light has reached an entirely new level. Indeed, one of the most exciting prospects for workers in the field is that this new order of control will open up uses for light that are as yet undreamed of.

21

Advances in Optical Masers

Arthur L. Schawlow   July 1963

It is never possible to predict when a development in technology will fire the imagination of the scientific and engineering community. Fifteen years ago it was the transistor, which stimulated a worldwide flowering of solid-state physics. The latest device to fascinate the technical community is the optical maser, or, as it is now often called, the laser. The term is an acronym for "light amplification by stimulated emission of radiation." (In "maser" the "m" stands for "microwave.") The laser is a device for producing a powerful monochromatic beam of light in which the waves are coherent, or in step. The waves emitted by ordinary light sources, such as incandescent and fluorescent lamps, are incoherent and nonmonochromatic.

By conservative estimate about 500 research groups are engaged in laser development and exploitation in the U.S. alone. Much of this effort is directed toward the use of laser beams in communication systems. The amount of information that can be carried by a communication channel is proportional to its frequency, and in principle the visible region of the spectrum between the wavelengths of 4,000 and 7,000 angstrom units could accommodate 80 million television channels. The realization of this potential is still far in the future. Outside the field of communications—in chemistry, medicine and several other disciplines—many possible uses of a strong beam of monochromatic laser

light are being intensively explored.

The first theoretical analysis showing that it should be possible to build an optical maser was published in 1958 by C. H. Townes, then at Columbia University, and the author. Several years earlier Townes had worked out the principle of microwave amplification by stimulated emission of radiation. Our analysis showed that a device working in the optical region could be made using the same principles. Its structure, however, would be different, and many of its properties and uses would be quite different from those of its microwave ancestor. The first announcement of a working model of an optical maser was made just three years ago this month by T. H. Maiman, then at the Hughes Aircraft Company [see "Optical Masers," by Arthur L. Schawlow, which begins on page 224 in this book].

Maiman found that a suitable active component for a laser could be made from a single crystal of pink ruby: aluminum oxide colored pink by the addition of about .05 per cent chromium. A description of a typical early ruby laser will illustrate the atomic basis of laser action. For this purpose I will describe lasers built by Robert J. Collins, Donald F. Nelson, Walter L. Bond, C. G. B. Garrett and the author at the Bell Telephone Laboratories in the summer of 1960. The ruby was machined into a rod about four centimeters long and half a centimeter across. Its ends were polished optically flat and parallel and were

partially silvered. A powerful electronic flash tube was coiled around the ruby to provide an intense source of "pumping" light. Normally the chromium atoms in the ruby absorb ultraviolet radiation and a broad band of green and yellow light. The light raises the atoms to an "excited" state, from which they drop back to the "ground" state in two steps. In the first drop, to a metastable state, the atoms give up some of their energy to the crystal lattice and no light is emitted. The second drop, however, is accompanied by emission of energy in the form of photons, or quanta of light, with a wavelength (at room temperature) of 6,943 angstroms, which is a deep red. The drop to the metastable state is almost instantaneous, but the drop from there to the ground state occurs at random over a period of a few thousandths of a second. This delay is helpful in achieving maser action. An atom in the metastable state can be stimulated to emit a photon and fall to the ground state instantaneously if it absorbs a photon carrying the same energy it would normally release in its fall. Conversely, an atom in the ground state can be raised to the metastable state by the same sort of photon. To obtain laser action, then, there must be more atoms in the upper state than in the lower, otherwise absorption will predominate over emission. If the required population inversion can be attained, the first few photons released (at random) by atoms dropping to the ground

JUNCTION-DIODE LASER built by Nick Holonyak, Jr., and S. F. Bevacqua of the General Electric Company is the first such device to operate in the visible region of the spectrum; this makes it possible to photograph its beam in color. The wavelength of the red light, aimed at the camera, is about 7,000 angstrom units. The center of the beam looks yellow owing to its intensity, which has overexposed the film. The laser and its supporting structure appear blue because blue light was used for general illumination.

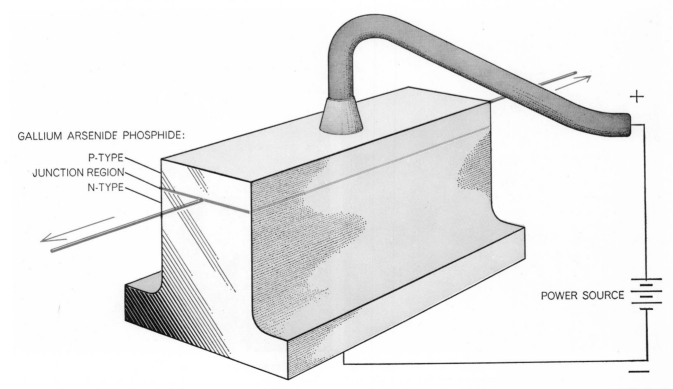

STRUCTURE OF DIODE LASER resembles that of ordinary junction diodes. The active material is a crystal of gallium arsenide phosphide. Small amounts of impurities create p (positive) and n (negative) regions. At the junction electrons drop into "holes," emitting photons in the process. Front and rear faces of the diode are polished to favor build-up of light emission along one axis.

ELECTRICAL BREAKDOWN OF AIR is produced by the focused beam of a giant-pulse ruby laser. Such lasers incorporate a shutter to postpone stimulated emission, thereby raising beam intensity. When the shutter is opened, a giant pulse of millions of watts is delivered for 10 to 25 billionths of a second. The photograph was made at the Scientific Laboratory of the Ford Motor Company.

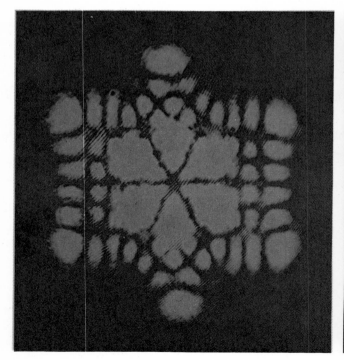

OSCILLATION MODES of a gas-discharge laser yield vivid symmetrical patterns. The emerging beam is about half a centimeter in diameter. Patterns show where light waves reinforce or cancel. The photograph was made by Bell Telephone Laboratories.

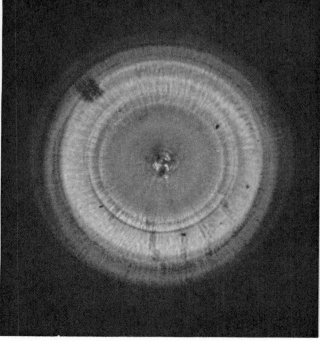

STIMULATED RAMAN EFFECT is seen when the output of a giant-pulse laser is focused in benzene. The vibration frequency of the benzene molecule adds to the laser frequency, yielding the colored rings. The photograph is by R. W. Terhune of Ford.

state will trigger off a cascade of photons all the same wavelength and all in step. This inversion is achieved by making the pumping light suitably intense. Because the ends of the ruby rod are partially silvered, photons are reflected back and forth parallel to the long axis of the laser, forcing the cascade to develop in a single direction. At the peak of the cascade an intense beam of red light flashes out from the ends of the rod.

Since Maiman's first announcement in July, 1960, many new laser materials have been discovered. They include crystals other than ruby, glasses, plastics, liquids, gases and even plasmas (the state of matter in which some of the atomic electrons are dissociated from the atoms). New materials are being discovered almost weekly. The only general requirement for a laser system is that it provide an upper energy state into which atoms can be pumped and a lower state to which they will return with the spontaneous emission of photons. The system must also allow a population inversion between the two states. Since the emission wavelength is controlled by the characteristic resonances of the particular material used in the laser, only a limited number of wavelengths can be generated by a given material. Consequently in order to cover the full spectrum of optical frequencies new materials will be needed unless some radically different approach can provide a device that is tunable over a wide range.

At present optical masers exist with output wavelengths from about 5,900 angstroms (.59 micron) in the yellow-orange portion of the spectrum out to 35 microns in the middle of the infrared. There have been observations of stimulated emission at wavelengths as short as 3,100 angstroms (.31 micron) in the ultraviolet, but no one has yet reported true maser action as indicated by the production of a well-defined beam. The ratio between the longest optical-maser wavelength (35 microns) and the shortest (.59 micron) is almost 60 to 1. Between 35 microns and the beginning of the microwave region at about one millimeter, where conventional electronic oscillators can take over again, there is a gap in which there is as yet no means for producing coherent radiation. Since this gap represents a wavelength ratio of only about 30 to 1, it is smaller than the region now covered by optical masers.

The search for new laser materials is essentially a search for elements that possess an atomic state with a suitable range of energy levels. As we have seen,

the active ion in the first optical maser was chromium. Its chief drawback is that its terminal level for laser action is identical with the ground state. Because the ground state is normally fully populated, its depopulation requires a great expenditure of energy. This means that it is very difficult to operate a ruby laser except in pulses. Continuous operation, however, has been achieved at Bell Laboratories by Willard S. Boyle and Nelson.

Several recent masers, operating in the 6,100-angstrom region, use trivalent (triply charged) ions of the rare-earth element europium, whose suitability was recognized in the original 1958 paper by Townes and the author. Europium ions fluoresce in sharp, strong spectral lines, and some of the strongest lines end on a terminal level well above the ground level. This terminal level is almost empty at moderate temperatures; any atoms put into it fall quickly to the ground state. Thus if relatively few atoms can be raised to the upper state, emission can be stimulated without competitive absorption by atoms already in the terminal state. Unfortunately it is hard to excite even a few atoms to the upper state because in most crystals the europium ion has no broad absorption bands to intercept the pumping radiation. Most of the light from the pumping lamp passes uselessly through the material.

One way around this difficulty is to put the europium ion into an organic compound known as a chelate, which acts as a kind of molecular cage. The chelate has strong, broad absorption bands in the near ultraviolet, and much of the energy that is absorbed is quickly transferred to the trapped europium ion, exciting it to the state required for maser action.

The possibility of combining europium with a chelate to produce a laser has been recognized for at least three years. The first success was reported only this February by Alexander Lempicki and H. Samelson of the General Telephone and Electronics Research Laboratories. The successful material was europium benzoylacetonate and it was used not as a crystal, or even a glass, but as a liquid solution in alcohol. The achievement was particularly surprising because one would expect the molecules in a liquid to be so buffeted by thermal agitation that the spectral emission lines would be broadened too much to sustain laser action. The europium ion, however, is not very sensitive to such buffeting, and it is somewhat shielded by the outer portions of the chelate molecule.

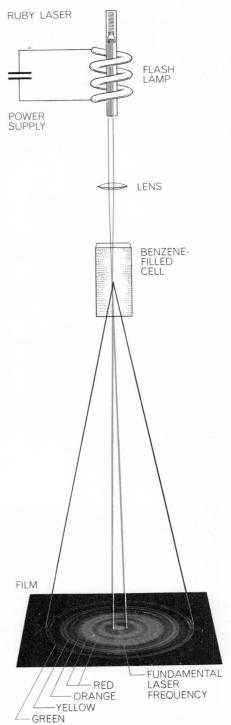

RUBY LASER

FLASH LAMP

POWER SUPPLY

LENS

BENZENE-FILLED CELL

FILM

FUNDAMENTAL LASER FREQUENCY

RED
ORANGE
YELLOW
GREEN

RAMAN LASER EFFECT is created by focusing an intense laser beam in benzene and recording the result directly on film (*see picture at bottom right on opposite page*). The frequency of the laser beam is both downshifted and upshifted by multiples of the vibration frequency of the benzene molecule. The downshifting yields infrared frequencies, which do not show on color film. The upshifting by one, two, three and four multiples of the benzene molecular vibration frequency produces respectively the red, orange, yellow and green rings.

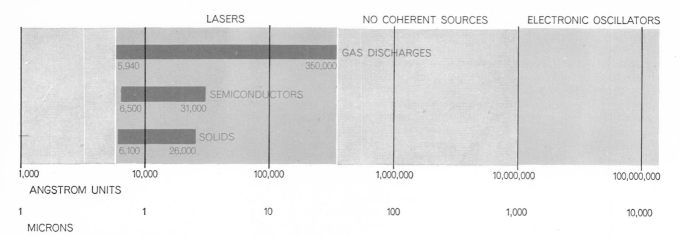

LASERS   NO COHERENT SOURCES   ELECTRONIC OSCILLATORS

GAS DISCHARGES
5,940   350,000

SEMICONDUCTORS
6,500   31,000

SOLIDS
6,100   26,000

1,000   10,000   100,000   1,000,000   10,000,000   100,000,000

ANGSTROM UNITS

1   1   10   100   1,000   10,000

MICRONS

LASER FREQUENCIES now extend from 5,940 angstrom units, in the yellow-orange part of the visible spectrum, to 350,000 angstroms (35 microns) in the far infrared. The colored bars indicate the minimum and maximum frequencies for different types of lasers. To date, gas-discharge lasers have produced the greatest number of different wavelengths: over 160. Although it is believed that semiconductor lasers can generate the whole range of frequencies from 6,500 to 31,000 angstroms, this is still to be demonstrated.

Almost simultaneously N. E. Wolff and R. J. Pressley at the RCA Laboratories announced operation of another europium chelate laser in which the chelate was suspended in an acrylic plastic. The plastic laser can be made to operate either in the usual rod configuration or in the form of long fibers. Both the liquid and the plastic are pumped optically with a strong lamp and produce coherent laser light at the characteristic europium-ion wavelength near 6,100 angstroms.

Other materials that respond with optical-maser action when optically pumped include many crystals and glasses and at least one gas: cesium vapor. The cesium has two output wavelengths, one near three microns and the other near seven microns. Because of their high density of active ions, the solids usually produce more intense beams than gases do.

The attractive feature of gas lasers is that they can be designed to produce output beams over a wide range of wavelengths. Except for the cesium-vapor laser, gas lasers are pumped electrically rather than optically. It turns out that the conditions for amplification by stimulated emission, at some wavelength or other, are satisfied in an electric discharge through almost any gas. Moreover, such masers operate continuously rather than intermittently. The noble gases—helium, neon, argon, krypton and xenon—have been the most thoroughly investigated, and each has provided maser action at more than one wavelength. The longest optical-maser wavelength generated so far—35 microns —was produced by xenon; this result was obtained in a series of studies conducted

at Bell Laboratories by W. R. Bennett, Jr., W. L. Faust, R. A. McFarlane and C. K. N. Patel.

These studies reveal that, in the process of collision with fast electrons in the discharge, atoms are likely to be excited to some atomic states more than to others. These favored states can then serve as upper levels for maser transitions to lower terminal states. If the atoms are allowed to linger in the terminal states, however, they can absorb radiation of the same frequency and return to the upper state. Therefore they must be forced to lose energy so that they will fall from the terminal state to a still lower ground state. Since this transition is promoted if the atoms collide frequently with the walls of the discharge tube, it generally helps to use tubes with rather small diameters. By reducing the diameter to about six millimeters and using mirrors with high reflectivity in the visible, but not in the infrared, J. D. Rigden and A. D. White of Bell Laboratories have designed a gas laser with an output of 6,328 angstroms. This particular laser should provide a simple and convenient source of continuous monochromatic light, with a sharply defined beam, for many laboratory applications.

Neither the gas-discharge masers nor the optically pumped solid-state masers are very efficient. Their output energy is usually less than 1 per cent of the input. Last fall, however, this limitation was unexpectedly lifted by the discovery of a class of semiconductor junction lasers. They promise conversion efficiencies well above 10 per cent and possibly even approaching 100 per cent.

The new class of laser was reported almost simultaneously by three groups of workers: Robert N. Hall, G. E. Fenner, J. D. Kingsley, T. J. Soltys and R. O. Carlson of the General Electric Company; T. M. Quist, R. H. Rediker, Robert J. Keyes, William E. Krag, Benjamin Lax, Alan L. McWhorter and Herbert J. Zeiger of the Lincoln Laboratory of the Massachusetts Institute of Technology; and M. Nathan, W. P. Dumke, Gerald Burns, F. H. Dill and Gordon Lasher of the International Business Machines Corporation.

For some years there had been discussion and speculation about the possibility of obtaining maser action from a semiconductor. According to quantum theory the electrons in a solid can occupy two broad energy levels: a lower level called the valence band and an upper level called the conduction band. To carry an electric current a solid must be well supplied with electrons in the conduction band; a semiconductor is less well supplied. Any electron in the conduction band possesses an excitation energy at least equal to the energy gap between the two bands. In principle the electron could be stimulated to radiate this energy in the form of a photon. In the commonly used semiconductors such as germanium and silicon, however, the electrons in the conduction band have crystal momentum, which must also be given up in the transition. Since this requires the co-operation of lattice vibrations, it is a relatively unlikely process. For this reason such semiconductors— known as indirect-gap semiconductors —emit light feebly and so far have not produced maser action.

There is another class of direct-gap

semiconductors, typified by gallium arsenide, in which the transition can take place without help from lattice vibrations. In these an electron can drop from the conduction band and occupy, or recombine with, a "hole" in the valence band. This recombination can take place spontaneously with the emission of a photon. When there is sufficient density of excited, or conduction-band, electrons, the spontaneous emission gives way to stimulated emission and maser action can result. The required electron densities can be achieved in the junction region of a "p-n" junction diode [*see illustration "c" at right*]. In the *p* (positive) region there is an excess of electrons in the valence band. In the *n* (negative) region there is an excess of electrons in the conduction band. If free electrons are fed into the *n* region, they travel to the junction region; there they drop into the holes of the *p* region, emitting photons. Since most of the free electrons lie near the plane of the junction, recombination radiation grows if it propagates along this plane, and the light emerges strongly where the junction meets the side walls of the crystal [*see illustrations on page 235*].

To impart directionality to the emitted light it is necessary only to provide parallel reflecting mirrors on two opposite sides of the crystal. This can be done by polishing two faces of the crystal: the crystal-air boundary provides a natural reflecting surface. The natural cleavage faces of the crystal also make excellent mirrors. Only two opposite faces need be mirror-like; the other faces are left roughly ground or are deliberately etched.

Because large numbers of excited electrons are produced in a junction diode when a current flows, only a small diode is needed to produce laser action. Typically the area of the junction is about one square millimeter. Junction-diode lasers are very efficient because nearly every electron injected across the junction contributes a useful photon, and the losses are mainly the electrical-resistance losses in the rest of the diode. The devices built to date have been small and output has been limited to less than one watt, but there seems nothing to prevent the building of much larger units.

In pure gallium arsenide at room temperature the laser light has a wavelength around 9,000 angstroms, in the near infrared. At lower temperatures the output wavelength decreases to around 8,400 angstroms. The output can therefore be tuned over a considerable range

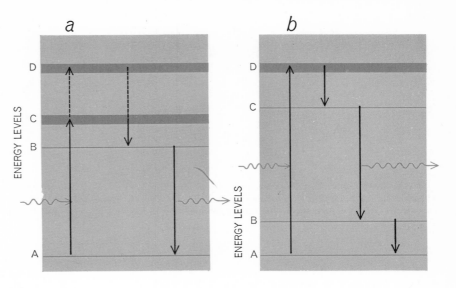

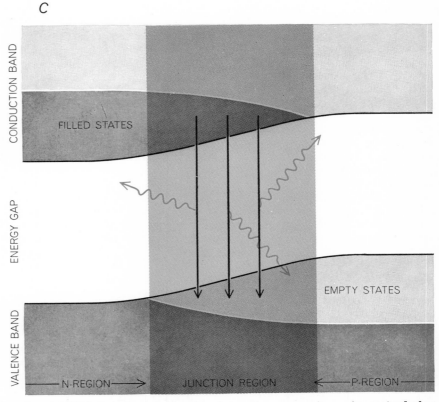

LASER ACTION depends on the fact that photons (*wavy arrows*) are often emitted when electrons drop from higher to lower energy states. In solid and gas-discharge lasers the electrons are bound to "excitable" atoms. In semiconductor lasers the electrons are unbound. In the original ruby laser (*a*) "pumping" light raises an atom from "ground" state *A* to *C* or *D*. The atom falls promptly to metastable state *B*. The final fall to *A*, which is normally a random process, can be stimulated if the atom is struck by a photon like the one it would emit. When *B* contains more atoms than *A*, stimulated emission predominates over absorption. In other solid lasers and in gas-discharge lasers (*b*) the terminal state *B* is slightly above the ground state, hence is normally lightly populated. Thus an excess of atoms in *C* is readily attained. In the semiconductor, or junction-diode, laser (*c*), electrons are injected at a higher level and fall to a lower level in a crystal "sandwich" containing *p* and *n* regions. The pumping energy is supplied by electricity. At the junction, electrons drop into holes, empty states at edge of the *p* region. This recombination of electron and hole, which leads to the emission of a photon, can be stimulated by another photon of the same energy. Spontaneous photons travel in all directions. But those traveling in the plane of the junction are most likely to stimulate recombination and produce laser action.

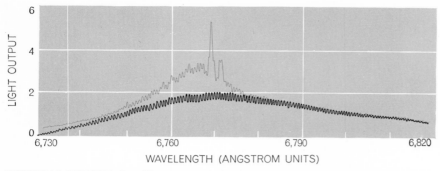

SPECTRAL OUTPUT of a gallium arsenide phosphide diode laser is shown near threshold (*black curve*) and just after a single mode of oscillation has begun to predominate (*colored curve*). The curves are for one of the lasers constructed by Holonyak and Bevacqua of G.E.

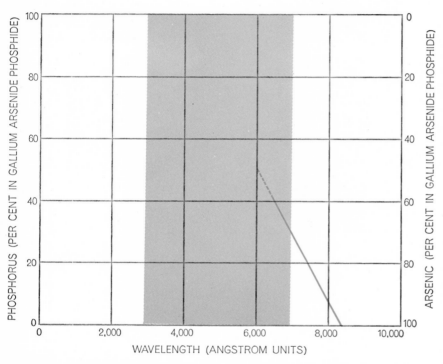

OUTPUT *V*. COMPOSITION is shown for the ternary mixture of gallium arsenide phosphide. Percentages refer just to the arsenide-phosphide fraction of the mixture; gallium is always present. When phosphorus exceeds arsenic in the mixture, laser action begins to fail.

by varying the temperature. Nick Holonyak, Jr., and S. F. Bevacqua of General Electric have shown that still further change in wavelength can be achieved by using three-element alloy mixtures such as gallium arsenide phosphide. Depending on the ratio of arsenic to phosphorus, such a diode will operate between 6,100 and 8,400 angstroms. A three-element mixture of gallium indium arsenide shows promise of operating from 8,400 out to 31,000 angstroms, in the infrared. By adjusting the temperature of operation the output can be brought close to any wavelength desired. This easy tunability makes diode lasers less suitable than others for the generation of an accurately reproducible wavelength. They do, however, have the ad-

vantages of compactness, simplicity and efficiency. Also, their output power can be easily and quickly controlled by changing the supply voltage, so that a signal can be impressed on the light beam.

For high output power ruby and certain glasses containing neodymium ions seem to be best. Here the excited ions are provided by a brilliant flash of light, usually from a xenon discharge lamp. As larger rods have become available, larger output energies have been obtained. Total flash energies as high as several hundred joules are delivered in one or two milliseconds. (A joule is one watt for one second.) For this brief period the energy released is equivalent

to the output of several thousand 100-watt lamps. Such a flash can be focused to penetrate a steel plate an eighth of an inch thick. This is a considerable advance over the early lasers, which could penetrate one or two razor blades; their output was rated in "gillettes." There is nonetheless a great gulf between existing laser beams and the sort of heat ray, envisioned by some people, that would be able to destroy a ballistic missile. Even a thousand joules will not boil a single gram of water. But when the laser beam is properly focused it can weld, melt or vaporize a small amount of any substance.

Enormously high peak powers and very short pulses have been made possible by the giant-pulse technique first proposed by R. W. Hellwarth of the Hughes Aircraft Corporation. In this method, sometimes known as "Q-spoiling," a fast-acting shutter is interposed between one end of a laser rod and the mirror normally found there. The shutter is closed during most of the pumping-light flash so that light from the end of the rod cannot reach the mirror and be returned to the rod. Since the light path is blocked, laser oscillations cannot start even though a large number of atoms are put into the upper state of the laser transition. Once the rod has been excited into this highly amplifying state, the shutter is quickly opened. As soon as the shutter is open and light can reach the mirror, laser oscillation builds up almost instantly. Under these conditions most of the excitation energy stored in the rod is delivered in one huge burst of light. This giant pulse can deliver up to 50 megawatts lasting for about 10 nanoseconds (billionths of a second). Moreover, the beam from a giant-pulse laser is highly directional. The divergence of the beam can be less than three minutes of arc.

Laser beams of still higher intensity can be obtained by amplifying the output of the giant-pulse laser. The amplifier consists of another rod without mirrors; in fact, to keep the amplifier from oscillating spontaneously the ends of the amplifying rod must be treated to prevent reflection. The amplifier is pumped by its own flash lamp, therefore it is ready to amplify by stimulated emission the instant the giant pulse is delivered.

The intense wave of the giant pulse stimulates all available atoms in the amplifying rod to emit almost as soon as the light pulse begins to pass through them; that is, the leading edge of the pulse is amplified and uses up all the excited atoms. There are then no excited atoms left to reinforce the remainder of the

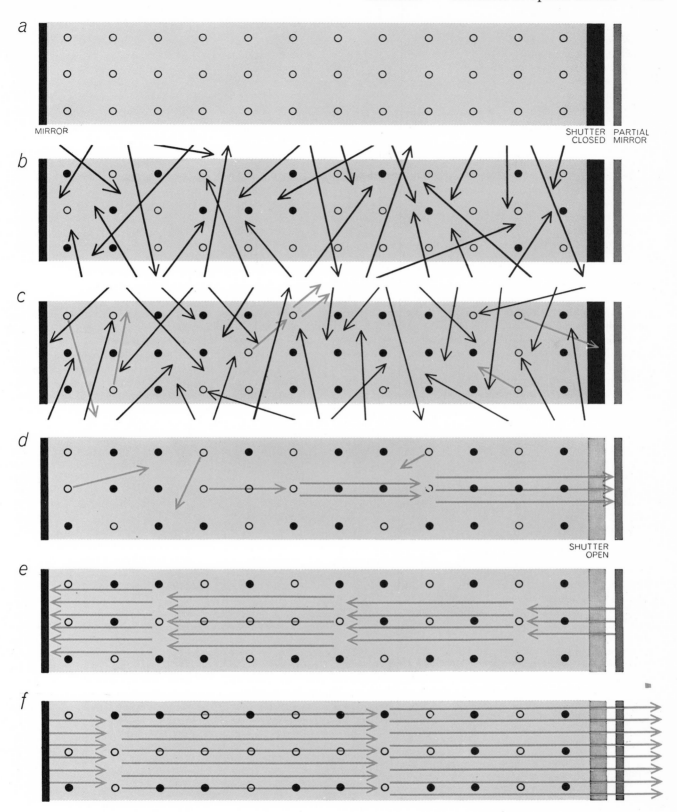

a

MIRROR

SHUTTER CLOSED PARTIAL MIRROR

b

c

d

SHUTTER OPEN

e

f

GIANT-PULSED RUBY LASER employs a shutter to delay laser action until a large population of atoms has been raised to an excited state. Before the pumping light is turned on (*a*), the atoms are in the ground state (*open circles*). The light (*black arrows in "b," "c"*) raises atoms to the excited state (*black dots*). If an emitted photon (*colored arrow*) strikes another excited atom, it stimulates further emission. This stimulation is limited until the shutter is opened (*d*). Then photons traveling precisely parallel to the long axis of the laser are reflected back and forth between the two mirrored surfaces, stimulating a cascade of photons. The cascade culminates in a coherent beam of light, which flashes through the partially silvered mirror with an intensity of millions of watts.

light pulse. As a result amplification makes the giant pulse not only more intense but also briefer.

So far the peak power reported is approximately 500 million watts in a beam whose cross section is less than one square centimeter. Assuming that the beam intensity is about a billion watts per square centimeter, the intensity of the corresponding electric field is nearly a million volts per centimeter in the unfocused beam. A good lens with a focal length of one centimeter could focus the beam to a spot a thousandth of a centimeter in diameter. The beam intensity in this focal spot would be a million billion (10^{15}) watts per square centimeter, and the optical-frequency electric field would be about a billion volts per centimeter. This is more than the electric fields binding the outer electrons in most atoms and would cause severe disruption even in transparent substances. Usually one thinks of the radiation pressure of light as being negligibly small, but in such a focused beam it would be over 15 million pounds per square inch.

Even at ordinary laser intensities transparent materials, which are usually nonconductors, react in an unusual manner. By means of laser experiments it has been shown that the dielectric constant (a measure of insulating ability) depends not only on the material and the light frequency but also on the instantaneous magnitude of the electric field. In other words, the response to high electric fields is nonlinear. When a wave of any pure single frequency passes through such a nonlinear medium, the wave shape is distorted. It can be shown by Fourier analysis that such a distorted wave is equivalent to the original wave with the addition of one or more harmonic waves. These harmonics have two, three or more times the frequency of the original.

The generation of laser harmonics was first observed by Peter A. Franken, A. E. Hill, C. W. Peters and G. Weinreich of the University of Michigan. They focused the 6,943-angstrom light from a ruby maser onto a block of quartz and observed harmonic radiation at twice the frequency, that is, at a wavelength of 3,472 angstroms. In these early experiments the intensity of the harmonic was very low—less than one part per million of the fundamental. Subsequent improvements, principally by J. A. Giordmaine of Bell Laboratories and by P. D. Maker, R. W. Terhune, M. Nisenoff and C. M. Savage of the Scientific Laboratory of the Ford Motor Company, have led to harmonic-generation efficiencies as high as 20 per cent.

Other nonlinear phenomena have been produced by the high intensity of laser beams. These include mixing of light waves to obtain "sum" and "difference" frequencies. It is thereby possible to get intense coherent light at many new wavelengths by combining the outputs of individual lasers. This sort of mixing has long been familiar in the radio-frequency region, but it is new in optics. N. Bloembergen, Peter S. Pershan and their associates at Harvard University have recast a large part of the theory of optical wave propagation to take into account these nonlinearities. All the laws of optics are modified to some extent at the high intensities produced by pulsed lasers.

A different sort of nonlinear effect was observed almost accidentally by E. J. Woodbury of Hughes Aircraft. He was working with a giant-pulse laser in which the shutter was a Kerr cell containing nitrobenzene. (Such a shutter either passes or blocks light in response to an electric field.) Woodbury found that the output beam contained, in addition to the ruby wavelength of 6,943 angstroms, additional wavelengths a few hundred angstroms to the red side of the ruby wavelength. These additional wavelengths were as coherent and as well collimated as the main beam. Careful investigation showed that the new wavelengths were shifted in frequency from the ruby light by amounts equal to the various vibrational frequencies of the nitrobenzene molecule. Such a shift in light frequency is known as the Raman effect. In this case it resulted when the ruby light frequency mixed with the molecular vibrations. The ordinary Raman effect yields incoherent light of low intensity. The Raman laser lines are coherent and intensities up to half that of the original beam have been observed [see illustration at bottom right on page 236]. The discovery of Raman laser action makes available new wavelengths of high-intensity coherent light. It also provides a new way of quickly getting information about the frequencies at which molecules vibrate and perhaps about the frequencies at which they rotate.

With these and other radical advances appearing literally every few days, there has been little chance to do the careful, detailed development work needed to realize practical applications. Some of the proposed applications, particularly military ones, require much higher output energies than those now available. Until the efficiency and the average output power (in contrast to the peak power) are increased, it will not be practical to use lasers for large-scale cutting and welding. There is no apparent reason in principle why this cannot be done. High-efficiency lasers do exist, and they run continuously, but they do not yet deliver high power.

This being so, the first applications will be those in which one of the other properties of lasers, such as high peak power or very monochromatic spectral output, is important. For at least one application a beam of light lasting less than one millisecond and delivering a fraction of a joule is ideal. The application is in medicine: when the retina of the eye is torn or injured, it is possible to "weld" the retina to its support by coagulation with an intense spot of light and thus prevent it from becoming detached. Indeed, following the work of D. G. Meyer-Schwickerath of the University of Bonn, ophthalmologists have used intense light beams from conventional lamps during the past few years for retinal coagulation.

One advantage of the laser for coagulation is that its flash takes less than a thousandth of a second, compared with about half a second for coagulation by ordinary light. In the shorter period there is no opportunity for the eye to move and it does not have to be immobilized, as it does at present. N. S. Kapany and N. A. Peppers of Optics Technology, Inc., and the Palo Alto Medical Research Foundation have designed a compact laser for this purpose that fits into the handle of an ophthalmoscope. Preliminary tests on animals by Harold C. Zweng and Milton Flocks of the Palo Alto Foundation and the Stanford University School of Medicine have shown how to regulate the output of the laser for various eyes. The device is found to be easy to use. If it proves equally successful with human patients, it could encourage ophthalmologists to seek out and repair retinal lesions at an early stage.

Some other potential applications exploit the extraordinary monochromaticity of the laser beam. For example, at the Massachusetts Institute of Technology, Ali Javan, T. S. Jaseja and C. H. Townes have recently used helium-neon gas-discharge lasers to repeat the classic Michelson-Morley experiment with a new order of accuracy. This experiment, first performed in 1881 by A. A. Michelson and E. W. Morley, showed that the velocity of light is unaffected by the motion of the earth through space. The

ACTIVE MATERIAL (AND VALENCY STATE)	OUTPUT WAVELENGTHS (MICRONS)	HOST MATERIAL	OPERATING MODE	OPERATING TEMPERATURE (DEGREES CENTIGRADE)
EUROPIUM (3+)	.61	YTTRIUM OXIDE PLASTIC CHELATE IN ALCOHOL	PULSED	20
CHROMIUM (3+)	.70	ALUMINUM OXIDE	CONTINUOUS	20
SAMARIUM (2+)	.71	FLUORIDES OF CALCIUM STRONTIUM	PULSED	—196
YTTERBIUM (3+)	1.02	GLASS	PULSED	—196
PRASEODYMIUM (3+)	1.05	CALCIUM TUNGSTATE	PULSED	—196
NEODYMIUM (3+)	1.06	VARIOUS FLUORIDES MOLYBDATES GLASS	CONTINUOUS	20
THULIUM (2+)	1.12	CALCIUM FLUORIDE	PULSED	—253
ERBIUM (3+)	1.61	CALCIUM TUNGSTATE	PULSED	—196
THULIUM (3+)	1.91	CALCIUM TUNGSTATE STRONTIUM FLUORIDE	PULSED	—196
HOLMIUM (3+)	2.05	CALCIUM FLUORIDE CALCIUM TUNGSTATE GLASS	PULSED	—196
DYSPROSIUM (2+)	2.36	CALCIUM FLUORIDE	CONTINUOUS	—196
URANIUM (3+)	2.4–2.6	VARIOUS FLUORIDES	CONTINUOUS	20
HELIUM			CONTINUOUS	
NEON			CONTINUOUS	
KRYPTON			CONTINUOUS	
XENON	160 WAVELENGTHS BETWEEN 5,940 ANGSTROM UNITS (.594 MICRON) AND 35 MICRONS		CONTINUOUS	
CARBON MONOXIDE			CONTINUOUS	
OXYGEN			CONTINUOUS	
OTHER GASES			CONTINUOUS	
GALLIUM ARSENIDE PHOSPHIDE	.65–.84		PULSED	—175
GALLIUM ARSENIDE	.84		PULSED CONTINUOUS	20 —196
INDIUM PHOSPHIDE	.91		PULSED CONTINUOUS	—153 —253
INDIUM ARSENIDE	3.1		PULSED CONTINUOUS	—196 —269

Row labels (vertical): SOLID OR IONIC LASERS · GAS-DISCHARGE LASERS · SEMICONDUCTOR INJECTION LASERS

TABLE OF LASER TYPES shows the output frequency associated with various active materials, mode of operation and maximum operating temperatures. Included among the solid lasers is one liquid laser, an alcohol solution of trivalent europium held in a cagelike compound called a chelate. Not listed is one gas laser, using cesium vapor, that is optically pumped and operates at two wavelengths: 3.2 and 7.2 microns. With this one exception gas lasers are all activated by an electric discharge through the gas.

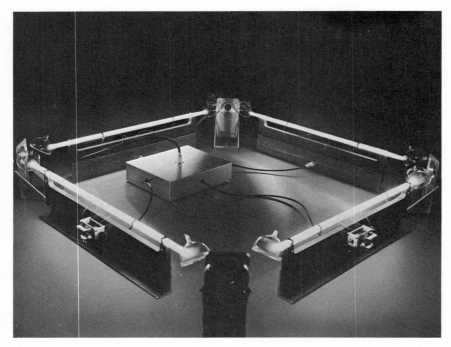

RING LASER has been built by Warren M. Macek and his associates at Sperry Gyroscope Company. Two laser beams circulate around the apparatus in opposite directions (*see diagram below*). If the apparatus is rotated, one beam rises in frequency, the other falls.

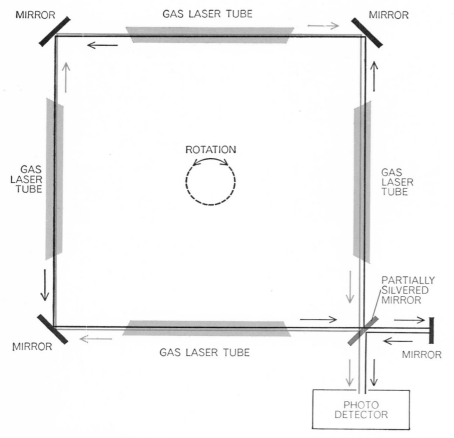

OPERATION OF RING LASER exploits the stable frequency produced by four gas-discharge tubes linked to act as a single laser. The frequency of the two circulating beams is compared by the photodetector at lower right in the diagram. If the ring laser is rotating to the right, for example, the clockwise beam must travel farther to make a complete circuit and its frequency falls. The counterclockwise beam correspondingly rises in frequency.

experiment laid to rest the idea that light waves are propagated through an all-pervading "ether" (in which case the velocity would not have been constant) and set the stage for Einstein's theory of relativity.

To repeat the experiment the M.I.T. group has installed its lasers in a wine cellar on Cape Cod, far removed from automobile traffic. On a day when the weather is calm and the earth is quiet, the frequency of the laser beam will remain constant within a few thousand cycles out of 10^{14} cycles. The relative drift between two lasers is sometimes as small as one part in 10^{13} per second. To achieve such stability the laser structure must be extremely rigid. A change in frequency of one part in 10^{13} would be produced by a change in length of one part in 10^{13}. Since the mirrors at the ends of the laser are separated by about one meter, this means a change in length of 10^{-13} meters, or a thousandth the diameter of an atom.

Javan and his colleagues have repeated the Michelson-Morley experiment by turning their lasers in different directions with respect to the earth's motion. Any change in the velocity of light would change the time required for the laser beam to travel between the two end mirrors and would show up as a change in frequency of the output beam. The apparatus is sensitive enough to detect a change in the velocity of light as small as three millimeters per second. Preliminary results show that the change, if any, is less than this value. Ultimately the apparatus may be sensitive enough to detect a change as small as .03 millimeter per second. The limit of accuracy attained by Michelson was about 150 millimeters per second and, using his methods, his successors were able to improve the accuracy by a factor of about 10.

Another classic experiment of Michelson's has also been repeated in a new way with the aid of optical masers. This is an experiment, first proposed by Michelson in 1904, to detect the absolute rotation of the earth. By means of mirrors light is made to circulate in both directions around the four sides of a square. The time taken for a complete circuit is the same in either direction as long as the square is at rest. But if the square is rotated about an axis perpendicular to its plane, a ray traveling in the direction of rotation will take longer to complete the trip than one traveling against the rotation. The reason is that the mirrors are retreating from the first ray and approaching the second.

The effect produced by the earth's rotation is, of course, tiny because light travels so much faster than the mirrors move. At a latitude of 40 degrees the rotation of the earth produces a shift of a hundred-thousandth of a wavelength in a horizontal square three meters on each side. Michelson felt that the effect would be too small to be measured. In 1914, however, G. Sagnac of France was able to detect the effect with the four mirrors mounted on a rotating platform. Then in 1925 Michelson and H. G. Gale did the experiment on a heroic scale with evacuated pipes forming a square 450 meters on a side and showed that the earth's rotation caused a shift of a quarter of a wavelength.

With the advent of optical masers it was realized by the late Adolph H. Rosenthal of the Kollsman Instrument Corporation and Warren M. Macek of the Sperry Gyroscope Company that the experiment could be done in a new and more sensitive way. The method uses four helium-neon gas-discharge laser tubes, one mounted on each side of a square [*see illustrations on opposite page*]. Mirrors are placed at the four corners of the square so that light leaving one end of a gas-discharge tube goes around the circuit and returns to its starting point. The entire perimeter of the square in effect constitutes a single laser, which means that light travels around the square in both directions. The time taken for one circuit controls the laser oscillation frequency. When the square is rotated about its axis, the laser produces two slightly different light frequencies corresponding to the two directions in which light travels around the square.

These two oscillations can be combined on a photodetector and the difference between their frequencies measured. For example, a square one meter on a side, operating at a wavelength of 1.1 microns, was shown recently by Macek and Daniel T. M. Davis, Jr., of Sperry to give a beat frequency of 500 cycles per second when the square was rotated at a rate of two degrees per minute. At the latitude of New York the earth's rotation produces a laser rotation rate of about a sixth of a degree per minute, which should show up as a beat frequency of 40 cycles per second. This should be readily detectable. Since this "ring laser" can perform the same function as a gyroscope, it may eventually be useful for navigational purposes.

It will be noted that the few scientific and technical applications I have mentioned are as yet only in the stage

of being probable. Most other proposed applications are not even that far advanced. Embarrassed by riches, scientists and engineers have had trouble deciding the laser applications on which to concentrate.

In the end, radically new sources of electromagnetic radiation will have many uses. It has by now been shown that lasers can produce beams of visible or infrared light of almost any wave-

length, that they can produce enormous peak powers, that they can be stable and monochromatic and that they can be quite efficient. But no single device combines all these attributes. The engineering task is to select the proper combination of properties for any proposed application and to design the particular optical maser to fit it. One can also be sure that there will continue to be surprising innovations and advances.

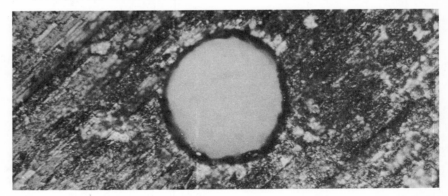

NOVEL SPECTROSCOPE employs a pulsed ruby laser to vaporize a microscopic amount of any material for spectrographic analysis. The photograph at top shows a specimen being vaporized by the laser beam. For successful analysis the vaporized material must be superheated. This is achieved by allowing the vapor to produce a short circuit between two electrodes (*middle photograph*). The micrograph shows the 50-micron crater produced by the laser. The instrument was developed by Jarrell-Ash Company, Newtonville, Mass.

22

Chemical Lasers

George C. Pimentel   April 1966

The current scientific literature reflects a virtual population explosion among the wavelengths at which laser action has been observed. A recent summary lists some 330 such wavelengths; they span the spectrum from the near-ultraviolet region to the far infrared. The rapid growth of the roster of lasers is paralleled by a rising number of applications of these remarkable light sources.

The laser exploits the fact that an atom or a molecule that has been excited by a source of energy can be stimulated to emit some or all of its extra energy in the form of a photon, or quantum of light. The stimulation can be provided by an incoming photon that has precisely the energy of the photon the excited atom or molecule is ready to emit. As a result of the stimulated emission the incoming photon is augmented by the emitted photon. The process is described by the words that give rise to the acronym "laser": light amplification by stimulated emission of radiation.

To be of significant magnitude the process requires a large population of molecules in an excited state. This situation is achieved by injecting energy into the system, a procedure known as "pumping." In most of the lasers designed so far the pumping energy has been supplied by an intense source of light or by electron bombardment. Such lasers obviously require an outside "feed" in the form of electric power. Moreover, the efficiency of these systems is rather poor; the output of energy achieved by the laser effect is much less than the input of energy required for pumping.

An idea that has intrigued a number of investigators for some years is the possibility that the energy released in chemical reactions could be used for pumping. This release of energy is associated with the making and breaking of chemical bonds. In principle the chemical reactions, once initiated, could proceed without an outside source of power. In other words, a chemical laser could be self-pumping. It could also be highly efficient and hence would act as an extremely intense laser: a concentrated source of light at a single wavelength.

By the fall of 1964 interest in this possibility had increased to such an extent that a symposium was organized in California solely for the discussion of chemical lasers. The proceedings of the symposium have been published as a supplement to the journal *Applied Optics;* this valuable document contains 21 articles and is 215 pages long. The authors of these articles represent four countries, seven universities, one government laboratory and 10 industrial laboratories. The articles clearly indicate the important principles—yet the publication is remarkable for the fact that none of the articles describes the successful operation of a chemical laser.

Nonetheless, one editor of the supplement, Kurt E. Shuler of the National Bureau of Standards, felt optimistic enough to express the belief that "the chemical laser has something in common with the four-minute mile: once the barrier is broken, successful operation of chemical lasers will be announced regularly." Only a week before the symposium Jerome V. V. Kasper of our laboratory first operated a chemical laser successfully. We call it a "photodissociation laser"; it is based on the breakdown of organic compounds containing iodine. Shortly thereafter we discovered the second chemical laser. It could be called an "explosion laser," because it involves the violent reaction between hydrogen and chlorine. Now that the

chemical laser has achieved its four-minute mile, we are optimistic about the fulfillment of Shuler's prediction. We are also confident that the chemical laser will prove to be an extremely valuable instrument for assessing some aspects of chemical reactions that hitherto have eluded analysis.

The significant feature of a laser is the enormous difference between the character of its light and the light from an ordinary light source such as the sun, a flame or an incandescent lamp. In these thermal light sources atoms and molecules are continuously being excited by collisions, and many of them release their energy by emitting light. When one molecule thus spontaneously emits light, it does so without influence from light emitted by other molecules. Hence this kind of independent and spontaneous emission in a population of molecules consists of photons that encompass a wide range of frequencies. Moreover, the photons possess no wave coherence: the constructive superposition of waves, crest on crest. Wave coherence is a property uniquely associated with lasers.

The high degree of coherence of laser light is obtained because stimulated emission synchronizes the radiation of individual molecules. A photon from an excited molecule stimulates another molecule to contribute a second photon with the same wavelength as the first and precisely in phase, or in step, with it. In a large population of excited molecules the process occurs repeatedly and produces a cascade of emissions, which take the form of an increasingly intense light wave.

This cascade process can be augmented still further if the coherent light is reflected back and forth through the excited molecular population by a pair of mutually aligned mirrors. Such an arrangement of mirrors is called an optical cavity. For a gas laser the cavity could be merely a slender tube with mirrors at each end. A light wave traveling along the axis of the tube will be enhanced by stimulated emission; when it reaches either of the mirrors, it will be reflected back and so will give rise to further stimulated emissions. In a properly designed reflecting system the gain on repeated passages will be greater than the losses. Such losses occur, for example, because mirrors are not perfect reflectors and because some of the light travels at an angle to the axis of the tube and so escapes from the system.

If one of the mirrors is semitransparent, a portion of the wave can escape through it. This is the output of the laser: a beam of light that is markedly directional, powerful, monochromatic and coherent. Light with these characteristics opens up possibilities that do not exist with ordinary light—both in research on the properties and effects

of light and in practical applications such as the transmission of signals.

Essentially the laser has three components: a suitable set of energy levels, a pumping system and an optical cavity. The set of energy levels is supplied by an atomic or a molecular system, and it provides a means of storing energy for concerted release in the form of monochromatic light. I have already touched on pumping, but the topic merits closer attention.

In most materials under most conditions nearly all the molecules are in a low energy state, usually called the "ground" state. Such molecules will absorb energy rather than emit it; therefore under ordinary conditions—that is, whenever molecules in the ground state outnumber molecules in excited states—absorption predominates. One of the central problems in designing a laser is to achieve an inversion of the normal situation, so that a preponderance of the molecules are in an excited state. There

must be an excess of excited molecules to enable stimulated emission to predominate. It is this excess that must be achieved by pumping.

Much of the current research on lasers is directed toward the first component: the energy-level system. This research seeks to discover new energy systems to fill gaps among the wavelengths now generated by lasers and to extend these wavelengths farther into the ultraviolet and infrared regions of the spectrum [see illustration on page 253]. For this purpose, and for their own fundamental interest, new pumping methods are also being sought. The discovery of more effective means of inverting an energy-level population results in lasers with more intense emission of light.

The search for new methods of pumping leads to the chemical laser. Chemical pumping is unique in that the first component of a laser (the energy-level system) intrinsically supplies the second (the pumping). Other tech-

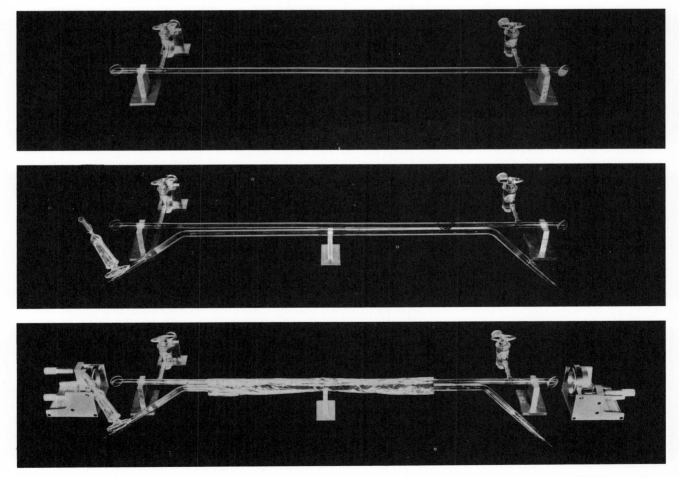

LASER APPARATUS used for investigating chemical-laser effects has as its basic part a quartz tube (top). The stopcocks near the tube ends are used to fill it with gas. In investigations of a laser based on the breaking of an iodine bond a flash tube is needed (middle) to give a pulse of light that initiates the reaction. The bottom photograph shows the apparatus with the laser mirrors in place opposite the ends of the tube and aluminum foil wrapped around the two tubes. The foil serves as a reflector to concentrate the light flash.

niques start with an energy-level system and pump it with an outside source of energy; in a chemical system the pumping is achieved with energy generated by the reactions that produce the energy-level system.

The chemical reactions that are most promising for laser action are those known as exothermic, meaning that they produce heat. As a general statement the desired kind of reaction can be written $A + BC$ yields $AB + C$ + heat. The letters stand for atoms or molecular fragments. The statement describes a reaction in which the molecular bond between atoms B and C is broken, a new bond is formed between A and B and heat is evolved because the net effect of the breaking and making of these chemical bonds releases energy.

Chemists would like to observe such a reaction in slow motion to see just how this energy is released. Initially all the energy is contained in the product fragments AB and C and is distributed in varying degrees among four forms of excitation: electronic, vibrational, rotational and translational [see top illustration on opposite page]. Electronic excitation involves changes in the spatial distribution of the electrons that bind the atoms of a molecule together; achieving it calls for high energy at the frequencies of ultraviolet radiation or visible light and results in emissions at those frequencies. In vibrational excitation the atoms of the molecule vibrate in relation to each other. This kind of excitation requires less energy than electronic excitation; it can be accomplished by energy at the frequencies of infrared radiation and results in emissions at those frequencies. Rotational excitation involves rotation of the entire molecule. The input and output energies of this

excitation are still lower, occurring at microwave frequencies. There is always a subcomponent of rotational energy in vibrational excitation. Translational excitation, in which the whole molecule moves from one place to another, is the kind commonly associated with heat.

As the reaction proceeds, collisional processes—the banging of atoms into one another—inevitably redistribute the energy among the four forms of excitation, the system approaches equilibrium and the temperature rises. In the case of electronic and vibrational energy, however, these collisional processes of de-excitation can be rather slow. This is why the energy produced in the reaction is not instantly evolved as heat. The fact that some of the reaction energy remains in the form of electronic and vibrational excitation lies at the heart of chemical-laser systems. It is

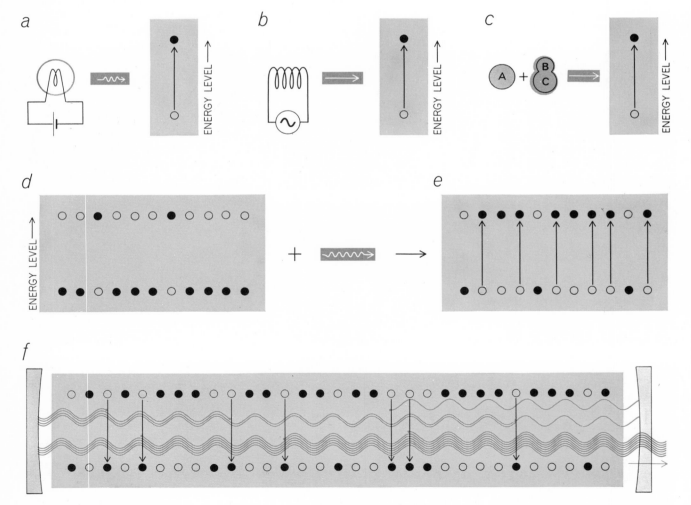

ESSENTIAL COMPONENTS of a laser are a pumping system, an energy-level system and an optical cavity. Pumping injects energy into a population of atoms or molecules; it can be done by light (a), electron bombardment (b) or the energy released in a chemical reaction (c). Pumping raises molecules from a state of low energy (d) to higher levels (e) where each molecule can be stimulated by a photon, or quantum of light, to release part of its energy as another photon of the same wavelength. In the optical cavity (f) photons are reflected back and forth many times, stimulating more emissions and producing a growing wave of highly intense light.

this excitation, this brief storage of energy, that makes the atoms and molecules ripe for stimulated emission.

It is now appropriate to recast slightly the general statement about the chemical reactions of interest for lasers so that it reads $A + BC$ yields $AB^* + C^*$. The asterisks represent products in a state of excitation. The statement says that a chemical reaction can yield products that are born excited in an energy-level system suitable for laser action. Here in a shorthand form is the unique aspect of chemical pumping: the energy-level system intrinsically supplies its own pumping.

Two other advantages of the chemical laser can be cited. One is that in principle the excitation of AB or C is obtained on the initiation of the chemical reaction and without any external power supply. The reaction can be started by the mere mixing of reactants. Alternatively, one can begin with a premixed sample and start the reaction explosively by some means such as a spark or a flash of light.

A much more important advantage, however, is the potential population inversion that chemical pumping can achieve in an energy-level system. It is conceivable—indeed, it may be happening in some of our experiments—that the distribution of energy in an energy-level system following a chemical reaction might result exclusively in excited states, either electronic or vibrational. Until the slow de-excitation process occurred there would be no lower-state population at all! The implication is that chemical lasers could be extremely efficient.

The reader may have detected a somewhat tentative quality in these statements. He must remember that the chemical laser is in a very early stage of development, and that its advantages must be stated more as potentialities than as facts. Moreover, it must be recorded that there are some inherent limitations in chemical lasers. If the reaction is set off explosively, the light source is inherently pulsed, or momentary. A second pulse can be obtained only after the vessel in which the reaction occurs has been flushed out and recharged. On the other hand, if the reactants are continuously mixed, the mixing rate and the rate of reaction might be limiting factors.

Lasers based on vibrational excitation suffer an additional disadvantage because of the fact that each excited vibrational state has a variety of rotationally excited sublevels. These sublevels are generally occupied in accordance

TYPE	ENERGY LEVEL	EXCITATION	MECHANISM
ELECTRONIC	100,000 TO 200,000 CALORIES PER MOLE	VISIBLE OR ULTRAVIOLET LIGHT	
VIBRATIONAL	500 TO 10,000 CALORIES PER MOLE	INFRARED LIGHT	
ROTATIONAL	.1 TO 100 CALORIES PER MOLE	MICROWAVE LIGHT	
TRANSLATIONAL	ANYTHING ABOVE 0	HEAT	

EXCITATION OF MOLECULES as a result of pumping takes four forms, each of which is related to the amount of energy required to achieve the excitation. The energy is expressed here in terms of calories per mole; a mole represents a standard number of molecules. Electronic excitation requires the highest input of energy, equivalent to that in ultraviolet or visible light. The other forms of molecular excitation require less energy.

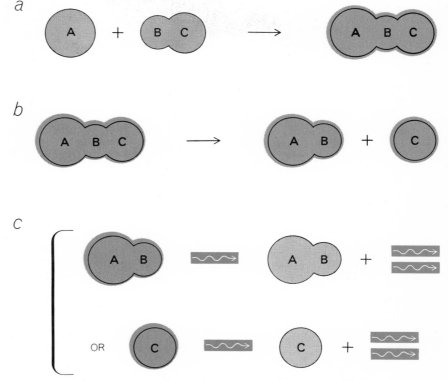

CHEMICAL PUMPING is based on the energy released in the making and breaking of chemical bonds. For example (a), atom A might combine with a molecule consisting of atoms B and C to produce an intermediate and transient molecule (color) possessing extra energy. This molecule could separate into two molecular fragments (b); either might be excited and could be stimulated to drop to a lower energy level (c), emitting a photon.

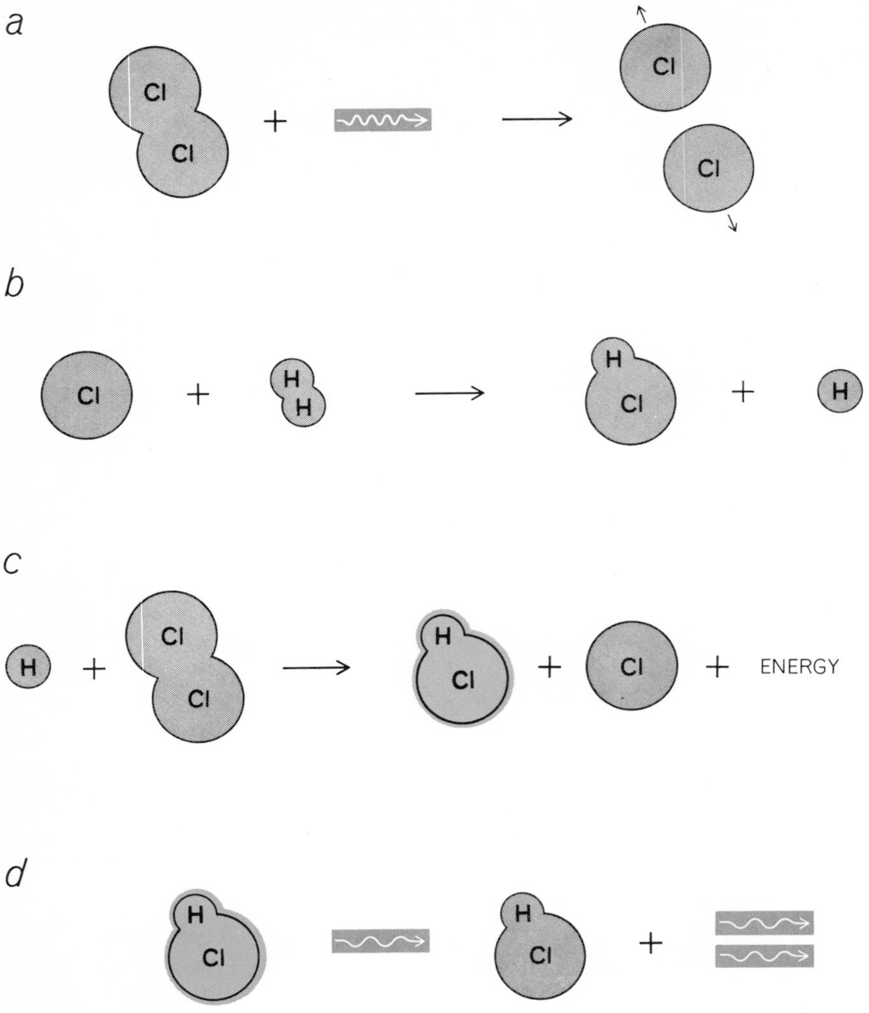

a

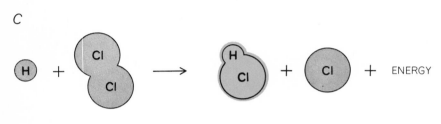

b

c

d

REACTIONS between hydrogen and chlorine in an explosion provide pumping for a chemical laser. A trigger of light (*a*) separates a chlorine molecule into two chlorine atoms; one of them (*b*) combines with a hydrogen molecule to yield a hydrogen chloride molecule and a free hydrogen atom, which reacts as shown at *c* to produce an excited hydrogen chloride molecule (*color*) that thereupon (*d*) emits a photon of infrared radiation.

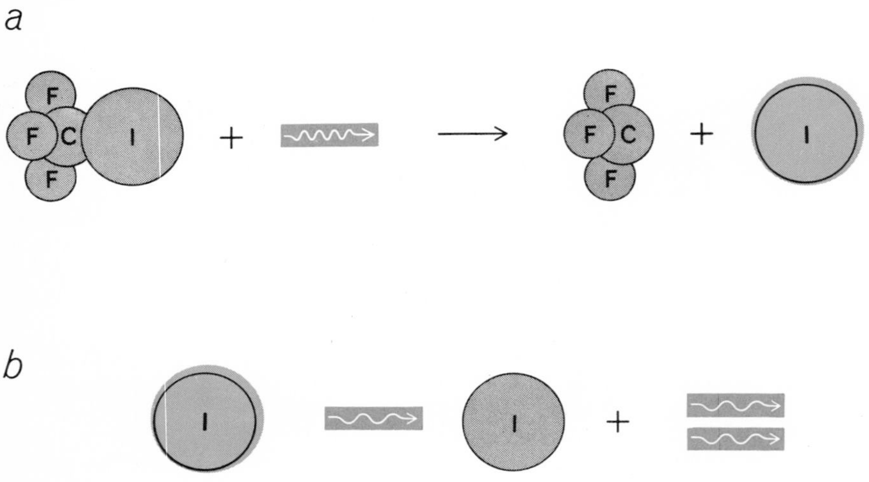

a

b

IODINE LASER derives its pumping from the dissociation by light of a molecule consisting of a carbon atom, three fluorine atoms and an iodine atom (CF_3I). In rupture of the carbon-iodine bond an excited iodine atom (*color*) is born and can release a photon (*b*).

with the surrounding temperature, and they tend to dilute the possible occupancy of any particular level from which laser action is sought. Such dilution reduces the potential gain of the laser action.

A final limitation of chemical lasers is not intrinsic but has to do with the state of knowledge. There are very few chemical reactions for which the distribution of energy is known in sufficient detail to allow a prediction of whether or not laser action will occur. This limitation, however, is precisely the reason chemical lasers are of such great interest to a chemist. When laser action is achieved in a chemical reaction, the chemist gains new information about the distribution of energy at the time of reaction—about what is usually called the microscopic distribution of energy. Chemical lasers contribute a new weapon to a sparsely equipped arsenal for learning this crucial information. Chemists need to know the microscopic distribution of energy at the time of reaction in order to understand fully the dynamics of chemical reactions.

Considerations of this nature brought about the widespread interest in chemical lasers and led to our own experiments. As is so often the case, our success in these experiments grew out of some special conditions. As is also often the case, these special conditions involved a portion of particular capability, a portion of persistence, a portion of creativity and a portion of luck.

The portion of particular capability was furnished by a rapid-scan infrared spectrometer constructed by Kenneth C. Herr, then a graduate student in our laboratory. This instrument was designed for studies of the chemical species produced transiently by flash photolysis: chemical decomposition caused by an intense burst of light. Herr's spectrometer scans in approximately 200 microseconds the portion of the infrared region of the spectrum that is characterized by wavelengths of from one to 15 microns. On its first successful operation it was faster by two orders of magnitude than any earlier instrument capable of scanning this region.

As the potentiality of this instrument became apparent, Kasper, who was also a graduate student at the time, began investigating infrared fluorescence that occurred shortly after flash-initiated decompositions. Our intention was to examine the distribution of energy among chemical-reaction products at their birth and to follow the subsequent equilibration of energy. Kasper designed a

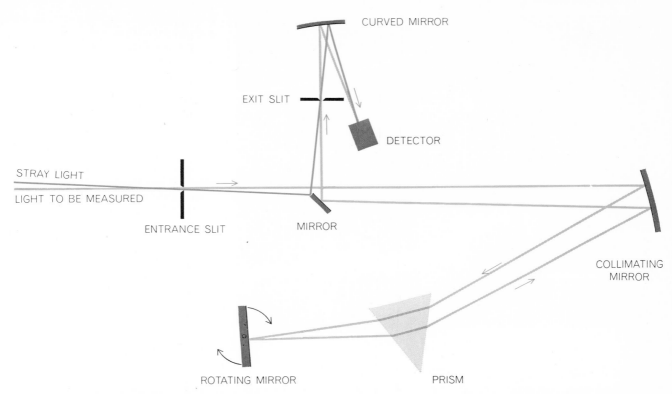

RAPID-SCAN SPECTROMETER provided the first indication that stimulated emission was occurring in molecules excited by chemical reactions. It was designed to scan infrared radiations produced by flash photolysis: chemical decompositions resulting from an in-tense burst of light. Stray emissions (*dark color*) appearing among the expected emissions (*light color*) proved to be highly intense near-infrared radiation deflected from the edges of a mirror and caused by stimulated emissions among excited molecular fragments.

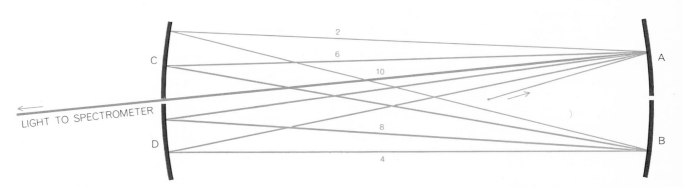

MULTIPLE-REFLECTION CELL acted as an optical cavity. Four mirrors (*A, B, C* and *D*) that could be focused independently reflected light back and forth; some of the traversals are numbered. With this arrangement there would be an increasing gain in intensity per traversal if stimulated emission were occurring and a decreasing gain if it were not. Stimulated emission was observed.

multiple-reflection Raman cell—a stainless steel cylinder about a foot in diameter and a meter long with two independently focusable halves of spherical mirrors at each end [*see lower illustration above*]. This arrangement provided an effective path length exceeding 40 meters for the travel of light (or other radiation) and made possible the efficient collection of light from a diffuse emitting gas.

Kasper began his studies by initiating explosions in hydrogen-chlorine (HCl) mixtures with flashes. This energy-level system was selected in direct response

to promising work at the University of Toronto by J. C. Polanyi and his co-workers, who had observed and systematically elucidated infrared fluorescence in reactions between hydrogen and chlorine and had thought the HCl system might provide a basis for a chemical laser. Kasper observed emissions of infrared radiation, but it was confusing because it occurred at unpredictable frequencies and times, which should not have been the case with the stimulated emissions expected from the HCl system. For a time we thought that stimulated emissions might be occurring in

carbon dioxide impurities in the system. The system was finally shelved, after many experiments, when it was found that periodic shock waves in the multiple-reflection experimental cell were causing some of the fluctuations in intensity.

We then turned to the idea of substituting such halogens as fluorine and iodine for the hydrogen atoms in organic compounds in the expectation that the halogen-substituted compounds would provide likely energy-level systems for infrared fluorescence. One of the first molecules we selected was trifluoro-

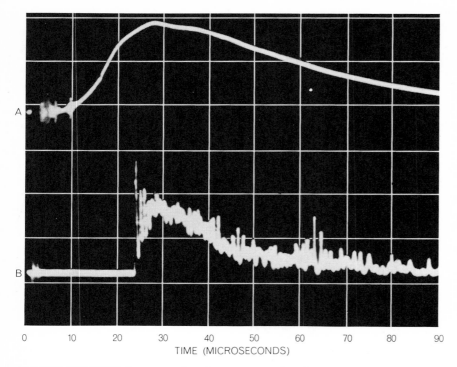

0   10   20   30   40   50   60   70   80   90

TIME (MICROSECONDS)

INTENSE EMISSION from excited iodine atoms produced these traces on an oscilloscope. Line *A* records the flash that set off the photodissociation reaction in which iodine atoms were separated from molecules; line *B* shows the stimulated emission that resulted.

methiodide (CF_3I). The intent was to search for vibrational excitation in the CF_3 fragment produced by photolysis. We expected this excitation to be left as the electronically excited CF_3I molecule underwent rupture of the carbon-iodine bond.

In this system, as in the HCl system, emission was observed after flash photolysis, but once again it was not reproducible in terms of frequency or time. The only certain thing at this point was that Kasper's work was in a frustrating phase. The time for persistence, creativity and luck (if we were to have any) had arrived.

Kasper provided the persistence and creativity by continuing his attack on the CF_3I problem. During a crucial week he recognized that his spurious and nonreproducible signals were not in the infrared region that he was scanning. He found that instead they originated with intense bursts of near-infrared radiation. The pulses of radiation were so intense that energy scattered from the edges of the spectrometer's mirrors would reach the detector no matter what the position of the spectrometer's rotating mirror. (This mirror was designed to restrict the light reaching the detector to a narrow frequency range.) Hence the pulses were observed at various locations in the

spectrum [*see upper illustration on preceding page*]. Kasper measured the frequency of the intense bursts and found that the emitter was not CF_3, as we had sought and expected, but the iodine atom! The reaction was producing this atom preferentially in a state of electronic excitation. This intense excitation of an atom that we had not expected to be excited was our portion of luck.

By increasing the length of the light path in the multiple-reflection cell we ascertained that the emission was amplified in a way that identified it as stimulated emission. This emission displayed laser threshold behavior in spite of the unconventional geometry of the optical cavity, which was the multiple-reflection cell. The energy levels were provided by iodine atoms; the pumping, by the dynamics of bond rupture in the electronically excited CF_3I.

Here, then, was the discovery of the first photodissociation laser: laser action achieved by the breaking of a molecular bond following the absorption of light by the system. It can be argued that this is a somewhat loose definition of a chemical laser because the reaction has to be initiated by absorption of light and is not self-sustaining. In spite of this legitimate semantic distinction there is strong chemical interest in the photodissociation laser because the population inversion is brought about by the

distribution of energy that accompanies the rupture of chemical bonds.

The clarification of the confusing behavior of the CF_3I system gave meaning to all the similar spurious signals that had been recorded in the studies of HCl explosions. Kasper returned to the HCl system and was able to establish quickly that here again the emission was stimulated emission. In this case the photolysis acts only as a trigger. The pumping occurs during the chemical reactions of the ensuing explosion. Accordingly the HCl laser satisfies a more rigorous definition of a chemical laser.

The first part of the cycle begins when a chlorine atom reacts with a hydrogen molecule to produce a hydrogen chloride molecule (HCl) and a free hydrogen atom. The free hydrogen atom is available to engage in the reaction that constitutes the second part of the cycle: the hydrogen atom and a chlorine molecule (Cl_2) react to produce an excited hydrogen chloride molecule and a free chlorine atom, which is thus available to allow a repetition of the first part of the cycle [*see top illustration on page 250*]. This reaction releases a large amount of energy, a portion of which is left in vibrational excitation of the HCl product. Another portion is in the form of rotational motions; the remainder goes directly into translational motion. (There is not enough energy to produce electronic excitation.) We estimate that about 15 percent of the energy goes into the vibrational excitation that is so crucial for laser action.

After establishing that these two forms of emission were stimulated emissions, we investigated them in an optical cavity of more conventional geometry [*see illustration on page 247*]. This cavity consisted of a quartz tube fitted with quartz end windows tilted at a carefully calculated angle that minimizes reflection losses in the cavity. Reflection is provided by two spherical mirrors 86.5 centimeters apart. Front-surfaced gold mirrors are used to provide high reflectivity in the infrared. About 6 percent of the radiation in the cavity is deflected to the outside by a flat piece of quartz and focused on a fast-response detector. For photodissociation experiments we place a flash tube alongside the laser tube and, to concentrate the flash further, wrap an aluminum reflector around the two tubes.

One of the interesting discoveries made with this apparatus is that the intensity of the iodine laser emission can be very high. Under certain circumstances one can obtain power at the kilowatt level. This level of power implies that there is a high gain of energy in the system. We were able to demonstrate such a gain experimentally: the laser emission could still be obtained with only five centimeters of the length of the tube exposed to the flash and with a filter inside the optical cavity that absorbed 71 percent of the energy! These findings indicate that in a single trip down the tube one photon entering the tube at one end can give rise to 10 billion photons at the other end. This is one of the highest gains ever reported for any gas laser.

With our chemical lasers we have been able to investigate a number of intriguing questions in chemistry. I have already mentioned the value of the laser in yielding data about the microscopic distribution of energy in chemical reactions. Another investigation has provided information about why the laser emission of iodine terminates so suddenly. It turns out that the temperature rises so rapidly that new chemical reactions become important. We have also been interested to find that a number of organic iodides besides CF_3I produce laser emission and even more interested to find that some do not. These exceptions present particularly challenging problems to the chemist.

What of the future? I think it reasonable to expect that chemically activated vibration-rotation lasers will someday be numerous. Many chemical reactions occur with changes of bond lengths, and such reactions will almost surely leave the products in vibrationally excited states. On the other side of the ledger, it must be noted that the conversion of vibrational energy into rotation and translation occurs more rapidly as the size of the molecules involved increases. Therefore most vibration-rotation lasers will have to be based on gaseous molecules with only two to five atoms. We can also expect that such lasers will be difficult to operate in the far infrared, using rotational excitation. The very rapid change of rotational energy into translational energy will be quite an obstacle. Electronic excitation of reaction fragments resulting in laser emission seems more likely to be fruitful, even in the far infrared, than pure rotation lasers.

The search for a chemical laser that will operate continuously remains a challenge. One would think that flames, in which excited molecules are known to exist, could provide a basis for such a laser. Yet careful studies of this question, such as those conducted by R. Bleekrode and W. C. Nieuwpoort at the Philips Research Laboratories in the Netherlands, have so far been unsuccessful. Here too my colleagues and I lean toward the expectation that, as more chemists enter this interesting area, the problems will become clearer

and success will eventually be attained.

The extremely large gain achieved by the iodine-atom laser gives promise that high power levels may be one of the special virtues of chemical lasers. It should be noted, however, that the gain and power of the HCl laser are relatively low. This laser does not even approach the limiting power once calculated by Polanyi, who showed that a vibration laser with chemical pumping could in principle achieve an output as high as 100 billion watts. Polanyi foresaw, however, that dilution of occupancy by the many rotational states would prevent achievement of such astronomical power levels, and this problem has proved to be significant. As investigators of chemical lasers proceed to heavier molecules, where the rotational levels are closer together, the dilution will be even greater.

For these reasons I cannot hold out such prospects as an astronaut mixing two liquids to turn on the laser headlights of his spacecraft. A more realistic prospect for the chemical laser is that it will furnish a tool, equivalent to a new chemical microscope, that will focus on the distribution of energy in elementary reactions, revealing the exact energetic state of the product species as they are born during a reaction. In this role the laser will somewhat relieve, although only momentarily, the chemist's insatiable desire to know more about how chemical reactions occur.

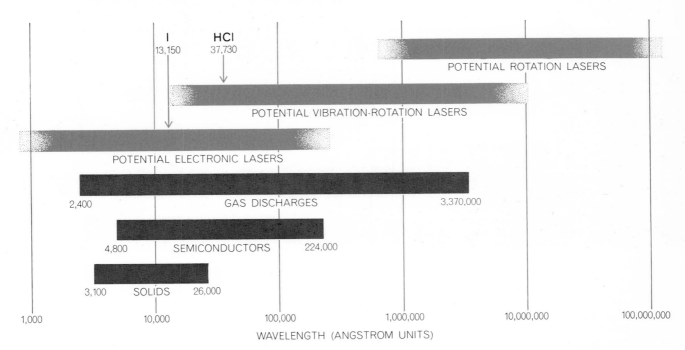

AREA OF SPECTRUM spanned by existing lasers (gray) ranges from 2,400 angstrom units in the ultraviolet region to 3,370,000 angstroms in the far infrared. Two chemical lasers (colored arrows) have been operated; other chemical lasers might extend into the microwave region (right). Frequencies range from 100,000 waves per centimeter at far left to one wave per centimeter at far right.

INVISIBLE BEAM of infrared radiation from a pulsed liquid laser (*inside box at left*) was made visible for this photograph by first passing it through a crystal of potassium dihydrogen phosphate (*inside mounting at center*), which halved the wavelength of the beam from 10,550 angstrom units (infrared) to 5,275 angstroms (green). Since the green beam was still highly collimated and directed only to the right, it could not be recorded directly by the camera. A shallow trough containing water and a few drops of milk was therefore placed in the path of the beam; light scattered from the particles of milk in suspension was then visible to the camera. The green color in the trough represents the accumulated effect of 15 separate bursts of light, spaced about two minutes apart. A burst consists of several pulses, each lasting between 20 and 50 nanoseconds (billionths of a second). The photograph was made at the General Telephone & Electronics Laboratories. A photograph of the entire optical bench is shown at the top of pages 256 and 257.

23

Liquid Lasers

Alexander Lempicki and Harold Samelson   June 1967

A few years ago the laser could be aptly characterized as a solution in search of a problem. This situation is in the process of changing rapidly as new applications of lasers are announced almost daily in various areas of science, technology and medicine. All this activity has generated a growing demand for lasers with greater power, efficiency and stability. The lasers currently in use have as their active mediums either gases or solids, and a major part of the effort to overcome the deficiencies of existing laser systems has been devoted to the search for new gases and solids to serve as laser materials. This article concerns another approach altogether: the use of a liquid as the active medium in a laser.

One of the most important characteristics of a laser medium, and one that strictly limits its performance, is its degree of optical perfection, or freedom from local irregularities. Most gas systems have a high degree of optical perfection, simply because the density of the gas is uniform and at low pressures the refractive index (the tendency to bend a light beam) of the gas is not sensitive to changes in temperature. In condensed systems—solids and liquids—a high degree of optical perfection is more difficult to attain. Crystals and glasses are usually formed at high temperatures and require considerable effort and expense to be freed of the many "frozen in" imperfections that can lower their optical performance.

Liquids, of course, are not subject to such defects. On the other hand, liquids are particularly prone to large changes in refractive index brought about by changes in temperature. By circulating a liquid, however, one can effectively eliminate such temperature gradients and hence any associated variations in refractive index. Circulation entails no loss of optical quality due to variations in density, since liquids are incompressible. Furthermore, in very-high-power lasers, solids tend to crack or shatter, whereas liquids naturally do not. Finally, the cost of a solid-state laser rises rapidly with its size, which is limited in any case by the method of fabrication. No such inherent limitation exists for liquid lasers.

All these advantages of the liquid medium are somewhat offset by the fact that liquids generally have a much larger coefficient of expansion than solids do. Although this property can cause problems, they are not insurmountable. From these preliminary considerations alone liquid lasers would appear to be worthy of serious consideration. Recent findings have brightened this promising picture, suggesting that liquid lasers may soon become competitive in many areas with solid-state lasers.

The theoretical foundation for the laser was laid by Albert Einstein, who perceived in 1917 that an excited atom or molecule can emit a photon, or quantum of light, by either of two mechanisms. In the first process photons are emitted in the absence of any external perturbation. This process, called spontaneous emission, has a probability of occurrence that is characterized by a definite lifetime. In the second process a photon emitted spontaneously from an atom or a molecule can trigger another excited atom or molecule to emit its photon prematurely. This process, called stimulated emission, has a probability that is dependent on the density of the photons. If the density of the excited atoms and photons is high enough, the stimulated-emission process will predominate, and laser action will result.

(The word "laser" is an acronym for "light amplification by stimulated emission of radiation.")

For laser action to occur one must first achieve a "population inversion," that is, the higher, or excited, states of the atoms or molecules must be more densely populated by electrons than the lower, or terminal, states are; otherwise the absorption of photons by unexcited atoms will prevent the dominance of the stimulated-emission process. In addition it is always helpful and usually necessary to enclose the laser medium in a structure that prevents the photons from leaving the scene of the action too soon. This can be accomplished by a pair of mirrors, one of which is slightly transmissive to allow the extraction of the stimulated emission to the outside world, where it can be studied or put to use.

Laser radiation is characterized by three main properties: the waves are coherent (all in step), highly monochromatic (all with the same wavelength) and capable of being propagated over long distances in the form of well-collimated beams. Since laser action is initiated by a spontaneous process, the spontaneous lifetime cannot be too long lest the reaction "breed" too slowly. Furthermore, the conversion of absorbed excitation energy to emitted light energy must be reasonably high. Because the "avalanche" of electrons from excited states to terminal states will start only when enough photons are available, it is important that photons not be absorbed by impurities or scattered by optical imperfections in the medium. In other words, the optical losses of the material must be small.

These general requirements for the onset of laser action were first formulated and expressed in a compact mathe-

LIQUID LASER AND ASSOCIATED COMPONENTS rest on an optical bench consisting of a slab of granite four feet long. The wide glass tube containing the active liquid (a solution of neodymium ions in selenium oxychloride) can be seen through the open door of the box. The tube is surrounded by three narrower tubes containing xenon, which are used to excite the ions in the liquid. When the laser is in operation, the door is closed in order to shield the experimenters from the intense white light produced by the xenon flash tubes. The small fan at the back of the box helps to cool the laser. Just to the left of the box is a mirror that reflects

matical equation in 1958 by Arthur L. Schawlow and Charles H. Townes, then respectively at the Bell Telephone Laboratories and Columbia University [see "Optical Masers," by Arthur L. Schawlow, which begins on page 224 in this book]. Given the characteristics of the laser system (the width of its band of wavelengths and the lifetime of the emission, as well as the optical losses), the Schawlow-Townes equation predicts what minimum population inversion must be reached before anything spectacular is likely to happen. The knowledge of this minimum-inversion threshold is extremely important, because it is this factor that determines the minimum number of active atoms or molecules per unit volume needed for laser action; if the concentration of active particles is less than the minimum inversion threshold, nothing will happen, regardless of the other factors. The minimum-inversion factor is also used to determine how much one has to excite a laser medium in order to bring it to the point where the avalanche of electrons can start feeding on itself. Beyond this threshold stimulated emission takes over, and all the emitting atoms respond together to the electromagnetic field bouncing between the mirrors.

Schawlow and Townes thus established the criteria a luminescent system must satisfy to be considered a potential laser material. First, the emitted light should be confined to a few bands of the spectrum, the ideal case being a single narrow band, or line, of high intensity. If the band is too broad, the photons within the laser cavity would be spread over a wide range of energies and would therefore be less effective in stimulating emission. Second, the conversion efficiency of the material must be high. For example, if the excited atoms do not generate enough photons and instead dissipate their energy in the form of heat, the avalanche process will never start. Finally, the necessity of keeping the loss of photons to a minimum requires both a high degree of optical perfection in the laser material and a good alignment of the reflecting mirrors.

How does one excite a laser medium? There are several possible ways, depending on the structure of the laser and the properties of the active medium. A gas laser or a solid-state laser can be excited by passing an electric current through it, by bombarding it with electrons or by illuminating it. Although there is no fundamental reason why any of these methods could not be used with a suitable liquid, only the last method, called optical pumping, has been employed so far. In this method the active particles are pumped from their "ground" state to an excited state by the absorption of light. The most suitable pumping light may differ from material to material, but xenon flash lamps, which emit white radiation, have been widely employed for optically pumped

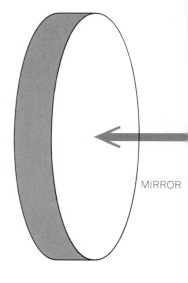

MIRROR

XENON FLASH TUBES (*white*) are used to "pump" electrons in the active liquid (*color*) from lower to higher energy states.

the escaping laser beam back into the active medium. Just to the right of the box is the apparatus that was used to make the photograph on page 254. At far right is a photodetector for studying the laser radiation.

pulsed lasers. Continuously emitting lasers, on the other hand, have utilized a variety of pumping sources, including incandescent tungsten filament lamps and mercury or xenon arc lamps. The liquids studied by our group at the General Telephone & Electronics Laboratories have

all been optically pumped by a conventional xenon flash source.

In trying to devise a liquid laser medium one must first survey materials that show luminescence in the liquid form. In the early days of lasers organic materials were preferred, largely because luminescence is a rather common phenomenon in the organic domain. Some early reports of success were later shown to be premature, and the achievement of stimulated emission from organic systems proved to be far more difficult than had been anticipated. In fact, operation of a purely organic laser was first reported only last year by Peter Sorokin and John Lankard of the International Business Machines Corporation. Their laser has a number of novel properties and will be subject to much further research. In its present form it requires the use of extremely intense, short pulses of exciting radiation, which can be obtained only from "giant pulse" ruby lasers or from flash tubes used in conjunction with specialized circuitry. These organic lasers operate in a pulsed mode and have a potentially high repetition rate. The output consists of a short burst of radiation with a high peak power. Although this class of liquid lasers is very interesting, there are special problems and properties that set it apart from other kinds of lasers. In this article we are concerned primarily with liquid lasers whose characteristics more closely parallel those of solid-state devices.

Outside the organic domain liquid

luminescence is not a particularly common phenomenon. In the search for a liquid laser it was therefore natural to take a cue from the materials used in the solid state. In most of these lasers the active atoms (those that participate in the emission process) are dispersed in a host substance, which is either a crystal lattice or a glassy framework. In liquids the counterparts would be the active solute and the host solvent. In solid systems the active components have most commonly been the lanthanide, or rare-earth, ions and certain metal ions. The electrons responsible for the optical properties of the rare-earth ions are situated deep within the ion's electron cloud and are usually well shielded from external perturbing influences.

It is just this property that gives rise to the characteristically sharp line emission of such ions and accounts for their success in laser applications. It is quite natural, therefore, to consider their use in liquids. When introduced into solution as "free" ions (in the form, say, of a rare-earth halide dissolved in water), however, their fluorescence efficiency is very low. The agitation of the solvent molecules is too much even for the shielded electrons, and the absorbed energy is dissipated as heat rather than emitted as photons. In order to use these materials it is necessary to find some way to make this nonradiative dissipation of energy noncompetitive with the radiative path. For the rare-earth ions this

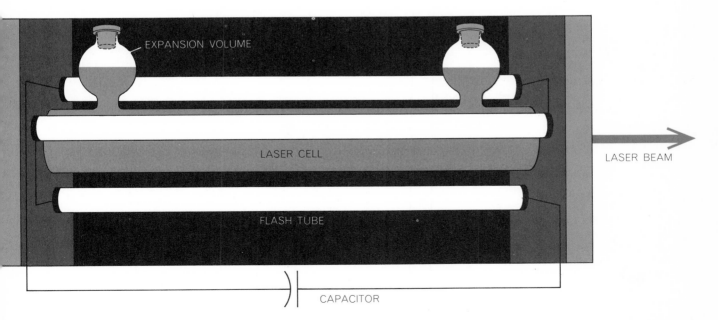

When an electron returns spontaneously to the lower state, the photon of light it emits can trigger another electron to emit its photon prematurely, setting off the "avalanche" process that characterizes laser action. Expansion volumes protect the laser against damage caused by the thermal shock wave generated in the liquid by the flash. Flash tubes are connected in series to a capacitor (bottom).

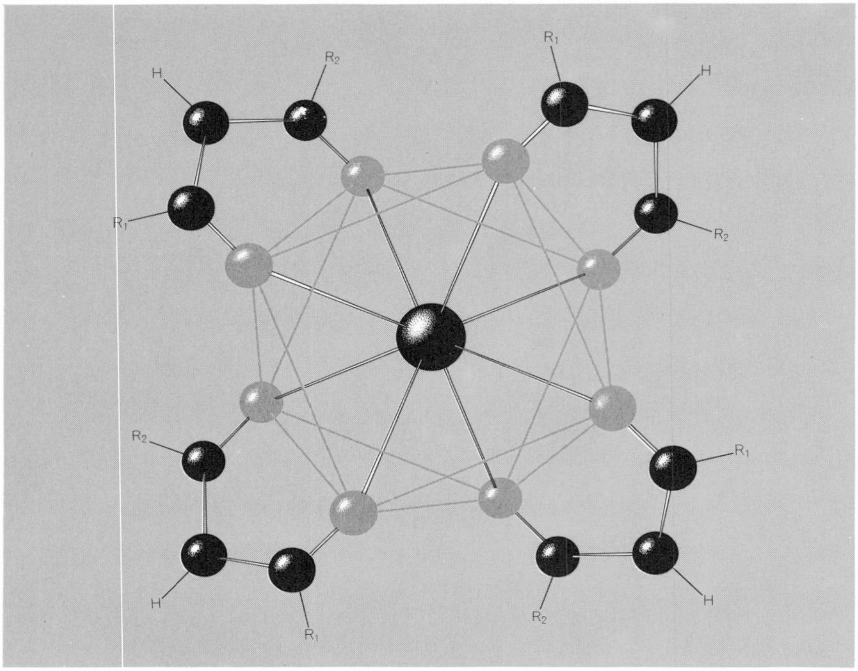

CHELATE CAGE consisting of eight oxygen atoms (*colored balls*) shields the active rare-earth ion (*black ball at center*) from the agitation of the solvent molecules (*not shown*) in one class of liquid-laser materials. In this particular organic molecule the oxygens are arranged in the form of an antiprism (*colored lines*). Each of the organic groups, called ligands, is bonded to the central rare-earth ion by two oxygen atoms, which together with three carbon atoms (*gray balls*) constitute the basic ligand chain. The groups designated R_1 and R_2 are further organic components of the ligands; in the benzoylacetonate molecule R_1 is a benzene ring (C_6H_5) and R_2 is a methyl group (CH_3), whereas in the benzoyltrifluoroacetonate molecule R_1 is a benzene ring and R_2 is a trifluoromethyl group (CF_3).

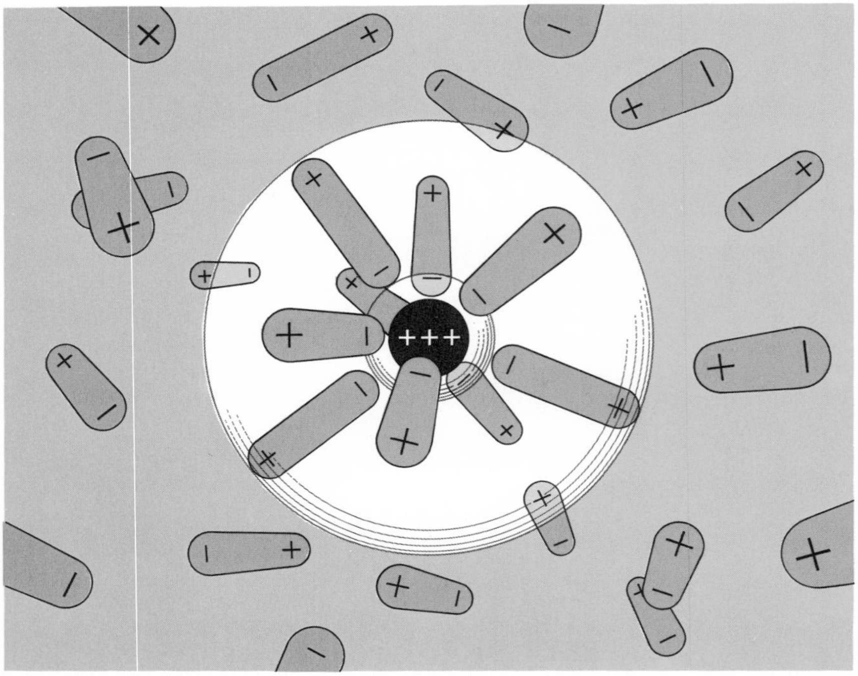

"SOLVATION SHELL," consisting of an array of inorganic solvent molecules (*color*), forms around a "free" rare-earth ion (*black*) in solution, effectively isolating it from interactions with the solvent. The solvent molecules are represented schematically here as simple elongated electric dipoles. The best liquid-laser material of this general type discovered to date is a solution of trivalent neodymium ions (Nd^{+3}) in selenium oxychloride ($SeOCl_2$).

can be accomplished by incorporating the ion into a cagelike molecule that provides additional shielding, or by giving the solvent a special structure. These two approaches to the problem of energy dissipation have led to two different classes of liquid lasers.

A number of cagelike structures are known to chemists; in one type, called a chelate, the rare-earth ion exhibits intense fluorescence with a comparatively sharp line spectrum. In a chelate molecule (the name is derived from the Greek word meaning claw) the rare-earth ion is bonded to a number of organic groups called ligands. The particular ligands that are effective with rare-earth ions have two points of bonding and are called bidentate. Typical among such ligands are the benzoylacetonate group (CH_3–CO–CH–CO–C_6H_5)$^-$ and the benzoyltrifluoroacetonate group (CF_3–CO–CH–CO–C_6H_5)$^-$. Each of these ligands is bonded to the rare-earth ion by two carbonyl (CO) groups. In the completed structure the ion is surrounded by the ligand oxygens, with the remainder of the organic structure providing further isolation from the solvent.

The most effective of these compounds contain four bidentate ligands, making a cage of eight oxygens in the immediate vicinity of the rare-earth ion. The total number of atoms in such a complex can easily exceed 100. An important feature of the structure is that the oxygens are placed in well-defined positions forming a polyhedron around the central ion. Several such structures are possible and have been identified; a typical one is shown in the top illustration at the left. The significant point here is the similarity between the immediate surroundings of the rare-earth ion in a chelate molecule and the situation in some crystal lattices. Although the bulky molecule interacts with the solvent, the central ion is principally "aware" of the oxygen cage and in some ways behaves as if it were in a crystal lattice.

It would be misleading, however, to disregard the organic structure beyond the oxygens. In fact, it can and frequently does play a major role in promoting laser action. Each ligand can be regarded as an organic molecule with its own electronic structure and energy levels. Although organic molecules have vastly different geometries, sizes and structures, their energy-level structure is generally similar. A common characteristic is that these molecules readily absorb radiation, usually in the blue or ultraviolet region of the spectrum. Electrons raised to an excited "singlet" state by this absorption can return to the ground state directly; this gives rise to a short-lived organic fluorescence [*see illustration below*]. On the other hand, the electron may make an internal transition to a long-lived metastable state, called the "triplet" state, and then return to the ground state. This emission is called phosphorescence. Which path is ultimately dominant depends on the structure of the molecule, its surroundings and the temperature.

In particular, when the molecule happens to form a ligand to a rare-earth ion, the path involving the metastable triplet is strongly favored. Furthermore, in such a chelate structure the electron in the triplet state, instead of returning to the ground state radiatively, may transfer its energy to the rare-earth ion. For this to occur there must

be a close match in energy between the ligand triplet state and the excited ion state, with the former being somewhat higher. Such an energy transfer can be extremely efficient and result in a greatly improved chance of exciting the rare-earth ion. Photons in the pumping source that would not be absorbed by the rare-earth ion itself can now be usefully employed. The pumping bands of a chelate complex are very much wider than those for the free rare-earth ion. Thus the decrease in nonradiative loss, achieved by the shielding effect of the ligand, and the improved pumping resulting from the energy transfer from the ligand greatly facilitate the attainment of population inversion.

The first liquid laser, based on a chelate structure, was successfully operated by our group at General Telephone & Electronics in January, 1963. The active component was a europium

ion at the center of a cage consisting of four benzoylacetonate ligands. The solvent was a mixture of ethyl and methyl alcohols. These solutions have the property of becoming more viscous as the temperature is lowered. At −160 degrees centigrade, a convenient operating temperature for the laser, the solution is quite viscous, somewhat like thick honey, and the optical quality is excellent. Although laser action can be achieved only at low temperatures with this particular chelate, the results demonstrated that laser action can take place in a liquid and that the speculations involved in evaluating the merits of the chelates were correct. With a sufficiently intense pulse of excitation from the flash tube, the beam of red light emitted at a wavelength of 6,131 angstrom units indeed had all the properties attributable to solid-state lasers. These properties include high spectral purity, beam collimation and the characteristic "spik-

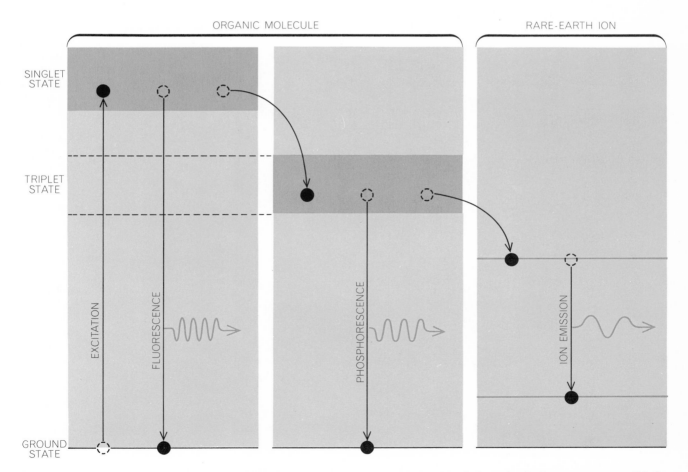

ORGANIC MOLECULE

RARE-EARTH ION

SINGLET STATE

TRIPLET STATE

EXCITATION

FLUORESCENCE

PHOSPHORESCENCE

ION EMISSION

GROUND STATE

ENERGY LEVELS of the electrons in a rare-earth chelate molecule are arranged in such a way as to favor the internal transition of electrons from the first excited "singlet" state of the ligands (*left*) to a long-lived metastable "triplet" state (*center*), from which they can be transferred to a closely matched excited state of the rare-earth ion (*right*). Electrons that return to the "ground" state of the

organic molecule directly from the singlet state are responsible for organic fluorescence; those that return to the ground state directly from the triplet state account for the characteristic emission called phosphorescence. The energy transfer from the organic molecule to the active rare-earth ion greatly facilitates the attainment of the "population inversion" required for the onset of laser action.

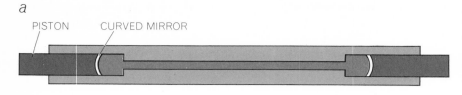

a

PISTON   CURVED MIRROR

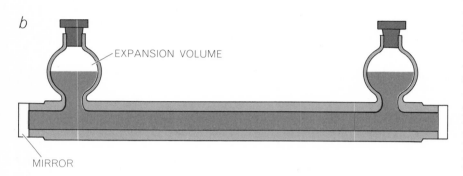

b

EXPANSION VOLUME

MIRROR

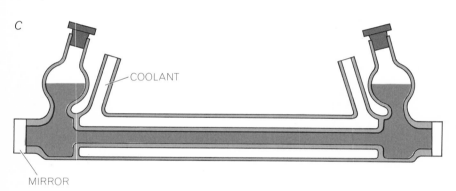

c

COOLANT

MIRROR

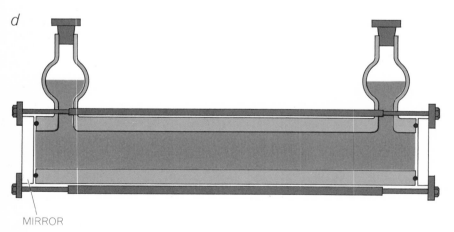

d

MIRROR

TYPICAL LIQUID-LASER CELLS have undergone several modifications in design. Cell *a* was used in early chelate lasers, which operated only at very low temperatures. Since the chelate liquid contracts considerably when it is cooled, it was necessary to devise some structure that would keep the mirrors in alignment during the contraction. This was accomplished by outfitting the cell with two close-fitting quartz pistons whose opposed interior faces were optically ground and polished. Drawn inward by surface tension, the pistons followed the contracting liquid, maintaining their alignment. Cell *b* is similar to the one installed in the inorganic liquid laser shown on pages 82 and 83. The bulbs serve as expansion volumes and are also used for filling the cell. Cell *c* is surrounded by a glass jacket through which a cooling liquid is circulated. Cell *d* is a recent demountable version of *b*. In *b*, *c* and *d* the mirrors can be either evaporated on the end windows of the cell or placed outside.

ing," or pulsation, of the output as a function of time [*see illustration on opposite page*].

There are many possibilities for constructing such chelate complexes and many different solvent combinations that can be used. Indeed, after the first demonstration of a successful chelate laser a number of other systems were introduced. A major problem was to find a chelate that retained its fluorescent intensity and structural integrity at higher temperatures, ideally at room temperature. Such a chelate, it was discovered, is formed by the ligand benzoyltrifluoroacetonate and the solvent acetonitrile. Trivalent (triply ionized) europium formed a complex with this ligand, and when it was dissolved in this solvent, it constituted a chelate laser capable of operating at room temperature.

All the chelate lasers discussed so far use ligands that belong to the general class designated as beta-diketone, in which the carbonyl group is principally responsible for the interesting spectroscopic and energy-transfer properties of the ligands. The singlet absorption of this group is so intense, however, that the exciting radiation is absorbed within a few tenths of a millimeter after entering the solution. This places a very serious limitation on the performance of a chelate laser; only a small amount of the material is involved in the laser action, and the energy and power outputs are much smaller than those of the more conventional solid-state lasers. Thus the use of beta-diketone chelate cages, although it is effective in achieving the first liquid laser, ultimately limits this device as a practical system.

To find a way out of the dilemma we were obliged to go back and seek another way to isolate the ion and prevent the nonradiative losses. This involved giving up the energy-transfer property of the beta-diketone ligands. This sacrifice would be fatal for a rare-earth ion with weak pumping bands of its own, such as europium, but it is of small consequence to other rare-earth ions, such as neodymium, which is known to "lase" in many solid materials without assistance from energy transfer.

Following this line of reasoning, Adam Heller of our group succeeded in constructing neodymium chelate complexes free of the absorption limitation and giving rise to laser action. In these chelates, however, the nonradiative losses are still large enough to limit the

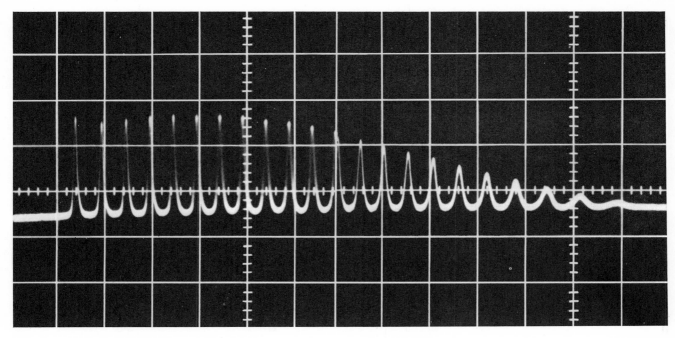

CHARACTERISTIC "SPIKING," or pulsation, of the output of a pulsed laser as a function of time can be observed in this oscillo- scope trace produced by a chelate liquid laser. The active medium was a europium-benzoylacetonate chelate in an alcohol solution.

performance of the resulting laser. Major advances therefore depended on a still greater reduction of these losses. To show how this was achieved we return to the more fundamental problem of the luminescence of the "free" ion in solution.

We have mentioned briefly that essentially "free" ions display rather weak luminescence, if it is detectable at all. The key word in this context is "free," and one must understand the sense in which we use the word. In chelates the ions are definitely bonded to the ligands. In solvents such as water the "free" ion is surrounded by solvent molecules that form a "solvation shell" [see bottom illustration on page 258]. The resulting complex is not essentially different from a chelate, inasmuch as it can have considerable stability and a well-defined geometry. The low efficiency of luminescence in such systems (for instance neodymium ions solvated by water) must therefore be attributed to a deactivation of the ion by the solvation shell. Instead of radiating as photons the excitation energy of the ion is somehow dissipated into heat, or— what is synonymous—into vibrational motions of the shell and outlying solvent molecules.

A detailed study of this process led Heller to understand how the nonradiative loss could be controlled and minimized. The interchange of energy be- tween the ion and the solvent can be pictured as a disappearance of a single large quantum of electronic energy localized on the ion and a simultaneous appearance of a number of smaller vibrational quanta localized somewhere in the solvation shell or beyond. The probability of such nonradiative losses depends on the number of the vibrational quanta that must be created and decreases rapidly as this number increases. This effect can be demonstrated by substituting deuterium oxide, or heavy water, for ordinary water. Because of the increase of mass the vibrational quantum of energy associated with the deuterium-oxygen bonds is lowered and more quanta must be excited to deactivate the ion. The result is a definite increase in luminescent yield.

The energy of the vibration is primarily determined by the lightest atom in the bonding group. It occurred to Heller that nonradiative losses could be prevented by the use of solvents having no hydrogen or deuterium atoms at all. This requirement alone seriously limits the number of choices; it eliminates virtually all organic solvents. Further requirements are even more restrictive: the solvent must be transparent to the emission wavelength and should be transparent to most of the pumping radiation. In addition the solvent must have a high dielectric constant in order to dissolve sufficient amounts of the active ionic compounds.

The liquid selenium oxychloride ($SeOCl_2$) has met all these requirements. In its pure form it is a nearly colorless, highly toxic liquid with a density comparable to that of glass, a low refractive index and a high dielectric constant. By itself it is capable of dissolving only limited amounts of substances such as neodymium oxide and neodymium chloride. The solubility of these substances can, however, be greatly increased by adding such compounds as tin tetrachloride ($SnCl_4$) or antimony pentachloride ($SbCl_5$). Mixtures of these compounds with selenium oxychloride form very strong aprotic acids (acids that do not contain protons, or hydrogen ions); these acids can then chemically react with the neodymium compound. In the dissolution of neodymium oxide the highly polar selenium oxychloride molecules presumably form a solvation shell around the trivalent neodymium ion. Since the vibrational energy is inversely proportional to the square root of the mass, and since the lightest atom in the system is oxygen (16 times heavier than hydrogen), the vibrational energies are likely to be about four times lower than in hydrogen-containing solvents.

In this system the ion is effectively isolated from interactions with the solvent, and the nonradiative dissipation of its electronic excitation energy is greatly reduced. Early observations indeed showed that trivalent neodymium

INTENSITY →

6.160   6.150   6.140   6.130   6.120

WAVELENGTH (ANGSTROM UNITS)

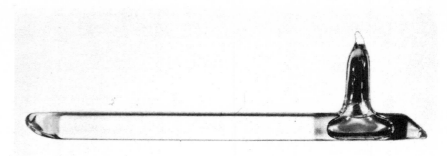

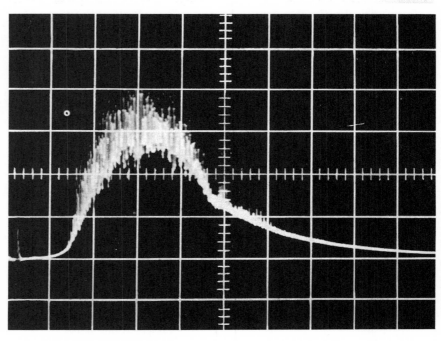

SIMPLEST TYPE of liquid-laser cell consists of a Pyrex tube with its ends flame-sealed to minimize reflection (*top*). Laser action takes place in the absence of the usual end mirrors, as shown by the characteristic spiking on the oscilloscope trace of the laser's output (*bottom*). The laser cell is filled with a solution of neodymium ions in selenium oxychloride.

in selenium oxychloride exhibits an extremely intense fluorescence. The principal line emission of this ion, which occurs at 10,550 angstroms in the infrared region of the spectrum, was shown at room temperature to exceed in intensity even the line emissions found in high-quality laser crystals and glasses. The width of the spectral line

SPECTRAL OUTPUT characteristic of laser action is graphically illustrated by these two curves, one of which shows the fluorescence spectrum of a chelate laser just below the threshold for laser action (*black*), whereas the other shows the spectrum just above the threshold (*color*). The spectral output of the laser suddenly shrinks to a narrow, intense line at 6,131 angstroms.

in this fluorescence is significantly broader than the lines observed in crystals but narrower than those in glasses. Perhaps even more important, the absorption bands used for optical pumping are broader than the absorption bands of crystals and comparable to the bands of glasses.

The remarkable spectroscopic properties of the material indicated that it could be incorporated into a comparatively simple laser cell. This proved to be the case: the solution contained in a simple Pyrex glass tube crudely sealed at both ends showed the characteristic laser spiking [*see the illustration above*]. Input energy of only 30 joules to the flash tube was required to attain the threshold of laser action. No mirrors were necessary because total internal reflection (due to the fact that the solution has a higher index of refraction than glass) trapped enough radiation for laser action to result.

A laser cell with no mirrors has a limited usefulness because the stimulated radiation leaks out of the cell in all directions and does not form a collimated beam. To achieve such a beam one must use precision-made cells with properly aligned mirrors. The performance of a number of six-inch cells with a quarter-inch inside diameter was evaluated and found to be quite comparable to the performance of commercial glass laser rods of similar dimensions. Output energies of several joules per pulse are readily obtainable; the peak power of individual spikes reaches 10 to 20 megawatts. Furthermore, the spectral output is far purer than those character-

istic of glass lasers. This performance is particularly impressive if one compares it with that of the chelate laser, whose output and efficiency are respectively at least 1,000 and 10,000 times lower.

From this result it appears that a liquid medium with nearly ideal fluorescence properties has finally been found. This, however, completes only the first part of the task. Among the many problems that remain the foremost is the problem of the thermal expansion coefficient of liquids, which is about 1,000 times larger than it is in solids. A thermal shock wave generated in the medium by the flash can lead to disastrous consequences for the cell. The simple expedient of providing volumes for expansion at both ends is effective, but better designs are being developed. Heating of the liquid caused by the exciting flash is also accompanied by a

change of refractive index, which distorts the path of the rays and thereby leads to losses in the cavity. Here circulation of the liquid may prove to be of great importance, particularly for lasers that are operated continuously or at high pulse rates.

It is in the class of "free" ion liquid lasers that the advantages and disadvantages of the liquid state in laser technology are most likely to receive a critical test. The achievement of continuous operation and high-energy, high-power pulsed operation appears to be only a matter of time. Liquid lasers have thus reached a stage of development at which they promise to be competitive with the more conventional lasers. In short, a new way has been found; now the whole technology of using the liquid medium and exploiting its advantages must be developed.

CARBON DIOXIDE LASER 178 FEET LONG, shown in operation at the U.S. Army's Redstone Arsenal in Huntsville, Ala., is capable of producing a continuous beam of coherent light with an output power as high as 2.5 kilowatts. The glow inside the laser tube is caused by the electric discharge used to excite the carbon dioxide gas. The laser beam itself is infrared and hence invisible.

24

High-Power Carbon Dioxide Lasers

C. K. N. Patel   August 1968

Until quite recently it was generally assumed that the most powerful lasers that would ever be built would be solid-state lasers, for the simple reason that in a solid the "lasing" particles are much more concentrated than they are in a gas. Nevertheless, it was recognized almost from the beginning that solid-state lasers have their drawbacks. With respect to two important criteria of laser performance—the spectral purity and the spatial coherence of the output light beam—solid-state lasers rate rather poorly. Moreover, most high-power solid-state lasers operate only in the pulsed mode; in other words, their power output consists of short, intense bursts of light rather than a continuous beam. In contrast the original atomic-gas lasers produced continuous beams with excellent spectral purity and spatial coherence, but their power output was very low compared with the power output from the solid-state lasers.

This situation has changed entirely with the advent of the molecular-gas lasers. The outstanding example of this new class of lasers is the carbon dioxide laser, which can produce a continuous laser beam with a power output of several kilowatts while at the same time maintaining the high degree of spectral purity and spatial coherence characteristic of the lower-power atomic-gas lasers. A carbon dioxide laser was recently used to produce an infrared beam with an output power of 8.8 kilowatts—the most powerful continuous laser beam achieved to date. The significance of such a power output is vividly demonstrated by the fact that a focused infrared beam of a few kilowatts is capable of cutting through a quarter-inch steel plate in a matter of seconds [see illustration at right].

Because of their high power output in the infrared region of the electromagnetic spectrum, the carbon dioxide gas lasers have opened up a whole new range of wavelengths for the study of nondestructive optical interactions with gases, liquids and solids. Such optical interactions include nonlinear processes whereby one can generate a coherent source of infrared radiation that is continuously tunable over a range of frequencies. There are in addition a variety of other applications for which high-power carbon dioxide lasers promise to be useful. Perhaps the most important potential application is in the area of optical communications and optical radar. The carbon dioxide laser is particularly suited for use in both terrestrial and extraterrestrial communication systems because the infrared beam it produces is only slightly absorbed by the atmosphere. In this article I shall attempt to explain the physics underlying the operation of this new type of high-power gas lasers.

In general a gas laser consists of a low-pressure gas-filled vessel (called the laser tube) located between two mirrors that form an "optical cavity." The gas in

HIGH-POWER INFRARED BEAM from the Redstone Arsenal carbon dioxide laser is shown burning a hole through a quarter-inch-thick stainless-steel plate—a job that takes about 10 seconds. The infrared beam emerges through the slanted Brewster window at the end of the laser tube (left) and passes through a partially reflecting end mirror before striking a concave mirror (right), which focuses it on the steel plate (center). The thermal applications of the high-power carbon dioxide lasers hold considerable promise for industry but are regarded as secondary to the potential use of such lasers in optical communication systems.

the tube (called the laser medium) can consist of atoms, metallic vapor or molecules. Laser action is usually obtained in the gas by subjecting it to an electric discharge; the energetic electrons provided by the discharge collide with the active gas particles, exciting them to higher energy levels from which they spontaneously descend to lower energy levels, emitting their excess energy in the form of photons, or light quanta. In order to achieve the optical "gain" that characterizes laser action it is necessary that the "population density" of particles in the upper energy level exceed that in the lower energy level. This condition is known as population inversion, since it is the inverse of the normal, or nonexcited, state of affairs. In order to achieve a high output power on a given transition between a pair of energy levels, it is also necessary that the absolute number of atoms excited to the upper laser level be large and that the gas particles leave

the lower laser level just as fast as they arrive from the upper level. In other words, the "depopulation," or de-excitation, of the particles in the lower laser level is just as important as the excitation of particles from the ground state to the upper laser level, since a particle that has already contributed to the laser output must return to the ground state before it is available again for excitation to the upper level in order to produce additional laser power.

The energy expended by particles in dropping from the lower laser level back to the ground state contributes nothing to the power output of the laser. Hence a certain amount of energy is wasted for every particle that makes the laser transition. This fact suggests an obvious yardstick for judging the efficiency of a particular laser system. The amount of energy wasted by a particle in returning from the lower laser level to the ground state is equal to the difference between

the energy needed to excite the particle to the upper laser level and the energy of the photon of light that is emitted when the particle makes the transition from the upper laser level to the lower laser level. It follows that the ratio of these two quantities—the emitted energy divided by the excitation energy—is a measure of the efficiency with which a given laser system can operate. The situation in which every particle that is excited to the upper laser level contributes one photon of laser radiation is of course ideal; it assumes that other mechanisms, such as transitions to other lower energy levels, are negligible for de-exciting a particle in the upper laser level. Thus the ratio of the energy of the emitted photon to the energy of excitation is actually the absolute maximum efficiency (or, as it is sometimes called, the quantum efficiency) of the laser system.

In practice the efficiency of an operating gas laser is considerably lower than its quantum efficiency, since no perfect means exist for selectively exciting the gas particles from the ground state to the upper laser level. Take the case of excitation by means of a collision between an atom and an energetic electron in a gas discharge. The electron must have a certain energy to excite the atom to the upper laser level. Unfortunately in a gas discharge the electrons do not all have the same kinetic energy; instead they are distributed continuously over a wide range of kinetic energies. Hence one cannot help but excite atoms not only to the upper laser level but also to other levels (either higher or lower than the upper laser level), from which they would not contribute to the laser output. The result is that only a fraction of the input electric power needed to produce the discharge is effective in exciting the atoms to the upper laser level. If we define the working efficiency of a laser as the ratio of the output power of the laser beam to the input power of the electric discharge, then the working efficiency will always be much lower than the quantum efficiency. The closer a laser approaches the ideal system in terms of the selectivity of the excitation mechanism, the closer the working efficiency will approach the quantum efficiency. Or, in a somewhat different perspective, a high quantum efficiency, combined with a selective excitation mechanism, is the prescription for obtaining a high working efficiency in a practical laser.

The first gas laser was operated at the Bell Telephone Laboratories in 1961. It operated on a transition between two

CARBON DIOXIDE MOLECULE (a) is linear and symmetric in configuration and has three degrees of vibrational freedom. In the symmetric stretch mode (b) the atoms of the molecule vibrate along the internuclear axis in a symmetric manner. In the bending mode (c) the oscillation of the atoms is perpendicular to the internuclear axis. In the asymmetric stretch mode (d) the atoms vibrate along the internuclear axis in an asymmetric manner. The vibrational state of the molecule is accordingly described by three quantum numbers, v_1, v_2 and v_3, and is usually written in the form $(v_1v_2v_3)$, where v_1 describes the number of vibrational quanta in the symmetric stretch mode, v_2 the number of vibrational quanta in the bending mode and v_3 the number of vibrational quanta in the asymmetric stretch mode.

excited states of atomic neon and produced a strong laser oscillation at a wavelength of 1.15 microns. Laser action has since been obtained using almost all the elements and covering the wavelength range from 2,000 angstrom units (.2 micron) in the ultraviolet region of the spectrum to 133 microns in the infrared region.

The energy-level spectra of molecular gases are considerably more complicated than those of atomic gases. In addition to the familiar electronic energy levels, a molecule can also have energy levels arising from the vibrational motion and the rotational motion of the molecule [see illustration at right]. Thus for a given electronic configuration of a diatomic (two-atom) molecule, say, there are several almost equally spaced vibrational energy levels, and for each of the vibrational levels there are a number of rotational levels. The spacings of the electronic energy levels for molecules are comparable to those for atoms, but the vibrational and rotational spacings are typically smaller by factors of 20 and 500. As a result the energy-level scheme of a molecular gas is extremely complicated.

The first molecular-gas laser oscillation was obtained from electronic transitions of a number of diatomic gases. Obviously, however, one can also have transitions between two different vibrational levels of the same electronic level of the molecule. Such transitions in turn actually occur between two rotational levels belonging to the two different vibrational levels. Moreover, because of the increasing spacing of the rotational levels in a vibrational level and because of a quantum-mechanical selection rule that in the simplest case allows only those transitions involving a change in the rotational angular momentum equal to $\pm h/2\pi$ (h is Planck's constant), such transitions between two vibrational levels result in a vibrational-rotational band [see illustration on next page]. The center of the band corresponds to the spacing between the vibrational levels in the absence of any rotational energy; the transitions on the long-wavelength side correspond to a change of $+h/2\pi$ in angular momentum and are called the P-branch transitions, whereas those on the short-wavelength side involve a change of $-h/2\pi$ in angular momentum and are called the R-branch transitions. As the illustration shows, the P-branch and R-branch transitions are almost equally spaced. These vibrational-rotational transitions, which usually result in infrared emission, are the basis of all the current breed of high-power molecular-gas lasers.

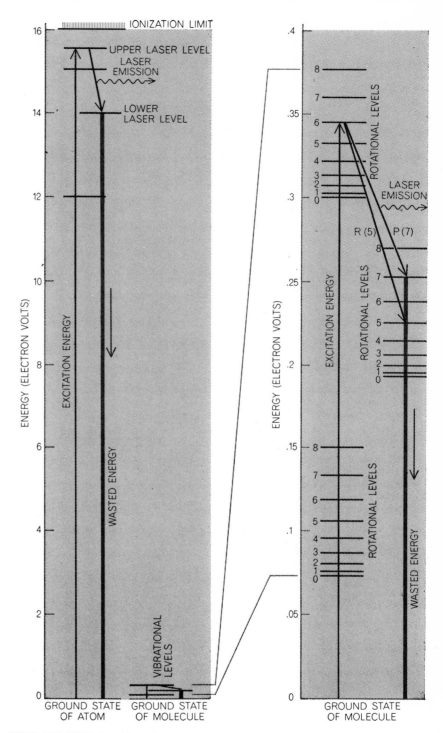

ENERGY-LEVEL DIAGRAMS of an atom and a molecule are compared. In an atom the electronic energy levels between which infrared transitions can occur are situated near the atomic ionization limit—far above the ground state of the atom. As a result the atom has to be excited to a very high energy in order to produce laser action, which in turn results in the emission of a photon with a comparatively small amount of energy. Thus the use of atomic gases wastes a great deal of energy and results in a low quantum efficiency. In a molecule, on the other hand, the vibrational levels of the electronic ground state are very close to the ground level of the molecule; hence the photon energy is a sizable fraction of the total energy needed to excite the molecule from the ground state to the upper laser level. This results in a much higher quantum efficiency. The enlargement at right shows that the vibrational levels of the molecule's electronic ground state are in turn composed of a number of rotational energy levels due to the rotation of the molecule. The number with each level indicates that level's rotational angular momentum in units of $h/2\pi$. Two of the allowed infrared transitions between the rotational levels belonging to two different vibrational levels are indicated.

I should like to explain now how it was that I came to build and operate the first continuous-wave molecular-gas vibrational-rotational laser at Bell Laboratories a few years ago. In the course of our investigation of laser action in atomic gases it became clear that if the aim was to obtain large power output in the infrared region (that is, at wavelengths longer than a few microns), the atomic gases were far from the ideal system. This is primarily so because for most atomic gases the electronic energy levels between which infrared transitions can occur are situated close to the atomic ionization limit—far above the ground state of the atom. As a result the atom has to be excited to a very high energy level in order to produce laser action, which in turn results in the emission of a photon with a comparatively small amount of energy. Thus the use of atomic gases results in a low quantum efficiency and consequently a low working efficiency.

Such a system has another very serious drawback. Close to the ionization limit of an element the energy levels corresponding to different electronic configurations are situated in a very small energy range; as a result electron-impact excitation, which is the mechanism for producing laser action in gas discharges, would be highly nonselective and the population density of atoms in the upper laser level would be very small. This will further limit the power output and result in an even lower working efficiency, since a significant fraction of the energetic electrons capable of exciting atoms to the upper laser level are lost in exciting atoms to other levels nearby. Typically an atomic-gas laser operating at a wavelength of about 10 microns produces only a few milliwatts of power and

has a working efficiency of about .001 percent.

The situation is entirely different when one is dealing with molecules; the vibrational-rotational levels belonging to the electronic ground state of a molecule are ideal for efficient and powerful laser systems in the infrared region. The vibrational levels of the electronic ground state are very close to the ground level of the molecule and thus the laser photon energy is a sizable fraction of the total energy needed to excite the molecule from the ground state to the upper laser level. The result is a very high quantum efficiency compared with that of an atomic-gas infrared laser. In addition, since the vibrational levels are close to the ground state of the molecule, almost all the electrons present in a discharge will be effective in the required excitation process. This fact ensures a high working efficiency as well as a high power output, because now one can obtain a large population density of molecules in the upper level.

It was on this basis that I originally decided to investigate the possibility of laser action using the vibrational-rotational transitions of the electronic ground state of carbon dioxide. Diatomic molecules appeared to be less suitable for continuous-wave laser oscillation because of the unfavorable lifetime of diatomic molecules excited to the various vibrational levels of the electronic ground state. Carbon dioxide was chosen for two reasons: it is one of the simplest of the triatomic molecules, and a large amount of spectroscopic information already existed about its vibrational-rotational transitions. The carbon dioxide molecule is linear and symmetric in con-

figuration and has three degrees of vibrational freedom [see illustration on page 266]. In one degree, atoms of the molecule vibrate along the internuclear axis in a symmetric manner. This mode of vibration is called the symmetric stretch mode and is denoted v_1. In another symmetric mode of vibration the oscillation of the atoms is perpendicular to the internuclear axis. This mode is called the bending mode and is denoted v_2. Finally, there is an asymmetric stretch mode of vibration along the internuclear axis; this mode is denoted v_3. By the rules of quantum mechanics the energies of the vibrations are quantized and are all different.

In the first approximation these three modes of vibration are independent of one another. As a consequence the carbon dioxide molecule can be excited to have any linear combination of the three individual modes of vibration. Therefore the vibrational state of the molecule must be described by three quantum numbers, v_1, v_2 and v_3, which represent the quanta of the v_1, v_2 and v_3 modes of vibration to which the molecule is excited. The description of a given vibrational level would accordingly take the form $(v_1 v_2 v_3)$, where v_1 describes the number of vibrational quanta in the symmetric stretch mode, v_2 the number of vibrational quanta in the symmetric bending mode and v_3 the number of vibrational quanta in the asymmetric stretch mode.

In the energy-level diagram of some of the low-lying vibrational states of carbon dioxide [see illustration on opposite page] the rotational substructure of each of the vibrational levels has been excluded in order to keep the diagram relatively uncluttered. The rotational levels are spaced much closer than the vibrational

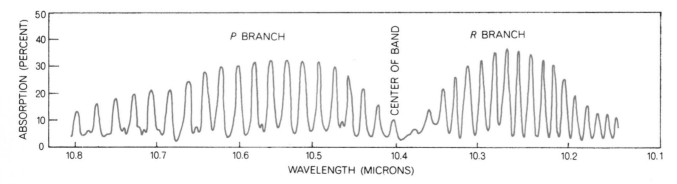

LASER OSCILLATION arising from transitions between two rotational energy levels belonging to two different vibrational levels of the same electronic level of carbon dioxide leads to the emission of infrared light at a number of different wavelengths, which form what is called a vibrational-rotational band. The curve shows the positions of the transitions as observed in the absorption spectroscopy of unexcited carbon dioxide gas. The center of the band corresponds to the spacing between the vibrational levels in the absence of any rotational energy; the transitions on the long-wavelength side correspond to a change of $+h/2\pi$ in rotational angular momentum and are called the P-branch transitions, whereas those on the short-wavelength side involve a change of $-h/2\pi$ in rotational angular momentum and are called the R-branch transitions (h is Planck's constant). The band shown here produces 10.6-micron radiation.

states. The various vibrational levels with different quanta in modes v_1, v_2 and v_3 form almost equally spaced ladders, although only the lowest states (those with only one or two quanta of vibrational energy) are shown. For a number of reasons, such as the lifetime of carbon dioxide molecules in various states and the probability of excitation by electron impact from the ground state, the level designated 001 is suitable for the upper laser level, and the 100 and 020 levels form the lower laser levels. The molecules that arrive at the lower levels decay to the ground state through radiative and collision-induced transitions to the lower 010 level, which in turn decays to the ground state. The $001 \rightarrow 100$ vibrational-rotational transitions produce infrared radiation near 10.6 microns, and the $001 \rightarrow 020$ transitions produce infrared radiation near 9.6 microns. Accordingly the quantum efficiency of a $001 \rightarrow 100$ laser would be nearly 40 percent, whereas that of a $001 \rightarrow 020$ laser would be about 45 percent. It is this high quantum efficiency and the possibility of selective excitation to levels that are close to the ground level that originally made the system attractive to investigate and that has made it possible for us to reach practical efficiencies on the order of 20 to 30 percent.

In our earliest experiments the laser tube was filled with pure carbon dioxide at a pressure of about one torr (one millimeter of mercury). The electric discharge was produced by applying a high-voltage direct current across a section of the tube. In such a discharge a large number of collisions occur between energetic electrons and the carbon dioxide molecules. A few of the most energetic electrons cause the carbon dioxide molecules to dissociate, that is, to break up into carbon and oxygen atoms. The threshold for this process, however, is quite high, and the number of electrons possessing this large amount of kinetic energy is very small. The lower-energy electrons, which far outnumber the high-energy electrons, cause the carbon dioxide molecules to be excited to various vibrational levels. As it happens, the electrons preferentially excite the carbon dioxide molecules to the $00v_3$ levels, that is, to the almost equally spaced levels of the v_3 ladder.

It should be remembered that the upper level for the laser oscillation at 10.6 microns is the one with v_3 equal to 1. Does this mean that the carbon dioxide molecules that are excited to the higher states of $00v_3$ (those with v_3

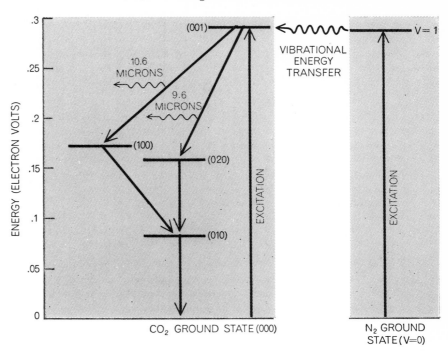

ADDITION OF NITROGEN GAS to a carbon dioxide laser results in the selective excitation of the carbon dioxide molecules to the upper laser level. Since nitrogen is a diatomic molecule it has only one degree of vibrational freedom; hence one vibrational quantum number (v) completely describes its vibrational energy levels. Nitrogen molecules can be efficiently excited from the $v=0$ level to the $v=1$ level by electron impact in a low-pressure nitrogen discharge. Since the energy of excitation of the $N_2(v=1)$ molecule nearly equals the energy of excitation of the $CO_2(001)$ molecule, an efficient transfer of vibrational energy takes place from the nitrogen to the carbon dioxide in collisions between $N_2(v=1)$ molecules and $CO_2(000)$ molecules. In such a collision the nitrogen molecule returns from the $v=1$ level to its ground state by losing one quantum of its vibrational energy, thereby exciting the carbon dioxide molecule from its ground state to the 001 level. The carbon dioxide molecule can then radiatively decay to either the 100 level or the 020 level, in the process emitting infrared light at 10.6 or 9.6 microns respectively.

greater than 1) will not contribute to laser action, thereby reducing the efficiency and power output of the system? In reality this does not happen because the $00v_3$ levels are almost equally spaced, and as a consequence a collision between a $CO_2(00v_3)$ molecule and a $CO_2(000)$ molecule results in an efficient transfer of vibrational energy from the excited molecule to the unexcited molecule. The $CO_2(00v_3)$ molecule loses one quantum of v_3 vibrational energy and becomes a $CO_2(00v_3 - 1)$ molecule, while the $CO_2(000)$ molecule gains that quantum of energy and becomes a $CO_2(001)$ molecule, or in other words a molecule in the upper laser level [see upper illustration on next two pages].

This process is resonant in the sense that there is a redistribution of the energy of the excited molecule without any loss of the total internal energy by its conversion into kinetic, or thermal, energy. This means that the efficiency of converting the $CO_2(00v_3)$ molecules into $CO_2(001)$ molecules with no loss of energy is very high. Therefore in practice

one should be able to excite carbon dioxide molecules to the required upper laser level quite efficiently by electron impact in a gas discharge.

The $CO_2(001)$ molecules can now, for example, emit a laser photon at 10.6 microns and go to the 100 level, from which they have to be returned to ground state before the molecule can be utilized again for producing a laser photon. The molecules at the lower laser level are de-excited essentially through collisions with other molecules. Again the possibility of resonant vibrational energy transfer plays an important role. The lower laser level has nearly twice the energy required to excite the carbon dioxide molecule to the 010 vibrational level. As a result a collision that involves a $CO_2(100)$ or $CO_2(020)$ molecule with a $CO_2(000)$ molecule will efficiently redistribute the vibrational energy between the two molecules by exciting both of them to the $CO_2(010)$ level [see lower illustration on next two pages].

Because of the resonant nature of this collision the vibrational de-excitation of the lower laser level is quite efficient. The de-excitation process is not yet complete, however. The $CO_2(010)$ molecules still must be de-excited to the ground state before they can again take part in the laser emission. The de-excitation of $CO_2(010)$ is also governed by collisions, but this time the collisions are nonresonant ones in which the energy of the $CO_2(010)$ molecules has to be converted into kinetic energy. Such collisions can involve other CO_2 molecules, foreign gas particles or the walls of the laser tube.

Because of the nonresonant nature of this vibrational energy conversion into kinetic energy the de-excitation of the $CO_2(010)$ molecules can be slow and cause a "bottleneck" in the overall cycle

of excitation and de-excitation, thereby reducing the efficiency and the power output. Even for the pure carbon dioxide laser I originally tested, the de-excitation mechanism was sufficiently fast to allow strong laser oscillation on the $001 \rightarrow 100$ and the $001 \rightarrow 020$ vibrational-rotational transitions respectively at 10.6 and 9.6 microns. It was found that because of their larger emission probability the 10.6-micron transitions are stronger than the 9.6-micron transitions by about a factor of 10. For the rest of the article we shall be concerned only with these 10.6-micron transitions.

It is quite clear that electron-impact excitation that occurs in a pure carbon dioxide discharge cannot produce

the highly selective excitation of the molecules to the upper laser level that is required for obtaining a practical efficiency approaching the quantum efficiency of the system. The reason is that the electrons can also excite the carbon dioxide molecules to levels other than the $00v_3$ level, causing a reduction in efficiency as well as power output. For high efficiency what is needed is some form of selective excitation of the carbon dioxide molecules to the upper laser level. Such a selective excitation occurs when nitrogen gas is added to the carbon dioxide laser.

The usefulness of nitrogen can be explained by referring to the energy-level diagram of the low-lying vibrational

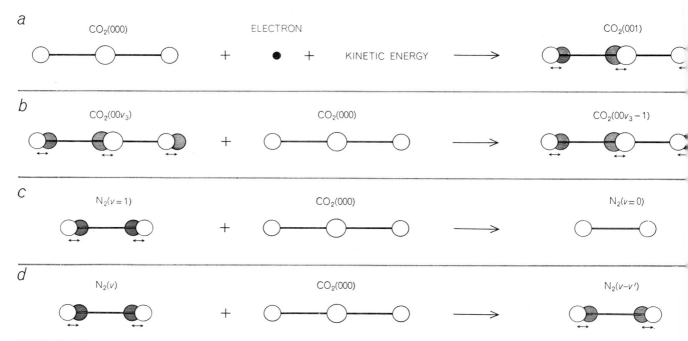

EXCITATION MECHANISMS capable of raising carbon dioxide molecules to the upper laser level (in this case the 001 level) are shown. In an electric discharge the collision of an unexcited, or 000, molecule with an energetic electron can raise the carbon dioxide molecule to the 001 level directly (a). Alternatively such a collision can excite the 000 molecule to a $00v_3$ level, where the v_3,

or asymmetric stretch, mode has more than one quantum of vibrational energy; in this case subsequent collisions with unexcited molecules result in the transfer of single quanta of vibrational energy to the unexcited molecules, raising them to the 001 level (b). In a carbon dioxide–nitrogen laser collisions between vibrationally excited nitrogen molecules and unexcited carbon dioxide molecules

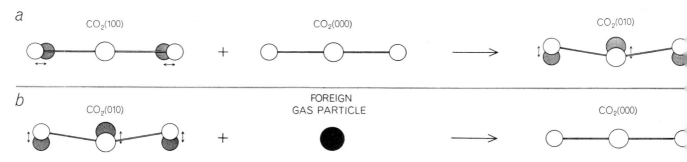

DE-EXCITATION MECHANISMS capable of "depopulating" the lower vibrational levels of carbon dioxide can result in an increased laser power. Two such de-exciting collisions are shown

here. In a the collision of an excited 100 molecule with an unexcited 000 molecule leaves both molecules at the 010 level. In b a molecule at the 010 level can in turn collide with foreign gas particles

levels of the electronic ground state of molecular nitrogen [see *illustration on page 269*]. Since nitrogen is a diatomic molecule, it has only one degree of vibrational freedom; its vibrational energy levels are described by quanta of energy arising from vibrations along the internuclear axis alone. Accordingly one vibrational quantum number completely describes the vibrational levels of the nitrogen molecule. Because nitrogen is a homonuclear, diatomic molecule, molecular nitrogen excited to various vibrational levels of the electronic ground state cannot decay radiatively or through collisions, and it is therefore extremely long-lived.

Nitrogen molecules are efficiently ex-

ELECTRON

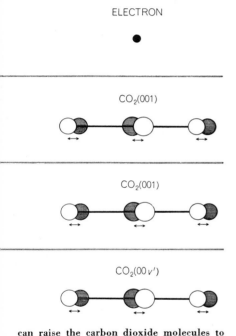

ELECTRON

$CO_2(001)$

$CO_2(001)$

$CO_2(00v')$

can raise the carbon dioxide molecules to the 001 level by transferring one quantum of vibrational energy from the nitrogen molecule, which can have initially either one (c) or more than one (d) quanta of vibrational energy going into the collision.

$CO_2(010)$

FOREIGN
GAS PARTICLE

● + KINETIC ENERGY

(or with the walls of the laser tube) and thereby return to the ground state, where it is available to be excited once again.

cited from the $v = 0$ level to various higher vibrational levels primarily by electron impact; they can also be excited by cascading from higher electronic states and by the recombination of dissociated nitrogen atoms. In a low-pressure nitrogen discharge one can excite approximately 30 percent of the nitrogen molecules to the $v = 1$ level. Since the energy of excitation of the $N_2(v = 1)$ molecule nearly equals the energy of excitation of the $CO_2(001)$ molecule, one would expect an efficient transfer of vibrational energy from the nitrogen to the carbon dioxide in collisions between the $N_2(v = 1)$ molecule and the $CO_2(000)$ molecule. In such a collision the nitrogen molecule returns from the $v = 1$ level to its ground state by losing one quantum of its vibrational energy and the carbon dioxide molecule is excited from its ground state to the 001 level. Because of the resonant nature of this collision process, the selective excitation of carbon dioxide molecules to the upper laser level should be very efficient.

Furthermore, the higher vibrational levels of the nitrogen molecule are nearly equally spaced, as are the $CO_2(00v_3)$ levels. Hence, in collisions involving $N_2(v)$ and $CO_2(000)$ molecules efficient vibrational energy transfer can take place in which the excited $N_2(v)$ molecule loses v' quanta of vibrational energy and is deexcited to the $N_2(v - v')$ level while the $CO_2(000)$ molecule gains the v' quanta of vibrational energy and is selectively excited to the $CO_2(00v_3 = v')$ level. Since the spacing between the energy levels of the $N_2(v)$ ladder and the $CO_2(00v_3)$ ladder is nearly equal, these collisions involve resonant vibrational energy transfer and the process is very efficient. The $CO_2(00v_3 = v')$ molecules are then converted into $CO_2(001)$ molecules (that is, into the upper-laser-level molecules) through the resonant collisions discussed earlier. In the end one has efficient selective excitation of carbon dioxide molecules to the upper laser level, and one should expect a significant increase in efficiency and power output from a carbon dioxide–nitrogen laser as compared with a pure carbon dioxide laser.

The first experiments to verify this hypothesis were carried out in the system shown on page 274. The gases in the system are continuously flowing. There is no electric discharge in the interaction region, where the laser action is expected to take place. Nitrogen enters through one port and passes through the excitation region, where an electric dis-

charge is produced by means of an oscillating electric field or a high-voltage direct current. The nitrogen molecules are excited to various vibrational levels of the electronic ground state as the nitrogen passes through the discharge region.

Since this is a continuous-flow system, the nitrogen molecules that have been subjected to the discharge are pumped into the interaction region in times that are short compared with the average lifetime of a vibrationally excited nitrogen molecule. Hence the nitrogen gas entering the interaction region will contain a significant fraction of nitrogen molecules that are still excited and that remain in the vibrationally excited levels of the electronic ground state. Carbon dioxide entering through another port mixes with the nitrogen coming through its port. As described above, vibrational energy transfer from nitrogen to carbon dioxide results because of the collisions involving the vibrationally excited nitrogen molecules and the ground-state carbon dioxide molecules. Carbon dioxide molecules are thus selectively excited to the upper laser level. Notice that there is no other form of excitation in the interaction region for exciting the carbon dioxide.

Strong laser oscillation can be obtained in this system on the vibrational-rotational transitions of carbon dioxide even though no discharge is present in the interaction region. After the carbon dioxide molecules have contributed to laser oscillation the continuous-flow system pumps out all the de-excited molecules, and fresh nitrogen discharge products and carbon dioxide enter to continue the laser oscillation. The strength of the laser oscillation proved the effectiveness of using vibrationally excited nitrogen molecules for selective excitation of carbon dioxide molecules to the upper laser level. By mixing nitrogen and carbon dioxide together in a laser tube, with the discharge in the laser region, conversion efficiencies as high as 5 percent have been demonstrated.

Increasing de-excitation of the lower laser levels by removing the "bottleneck" at the 010 level of carbon dioxide can also result in increased power output as well as higher efficiency from the carbon dioxide laser. Earlier I mentioned that de-excitation of the $CO_2(010)$ molecules takes place by conversion of the energy of the $CO_2(010)$ molecule into kinetic energy during a collision with another particle. The rate at which this de-excitation process proceeds depends on the nature of the other particle. For example, carbon dioxide itself has about 100 de-exciting collisions per second at a pressure of one torr, whereas helium atoms have some 4,000 (and water molecules some 100,000) de-exciting transitions per second at the same pressure. Thus we have another method for increasing the power output and efficiency of the nitrogen–carbon dioxide laser system.

It was found that in order to obtain an extremely high continuous power output at a high efficiency it is necessary to use additional gases in the discharge tube. Gases such as oxygen, water vapor, hydrogen and helium give rise to increased power output. The increase is understood in terms of two effects: (1) the increased rate of de-excitation of the lower vibrational levels of the carbon

dioxide molecules and (2) the increase in the rate at which carbon dioxide molecules are excited to the 001 level, either directly by electron-impact processes or indirectly by increasing the excitation rate of the vibrationally excited nitrogen molecules. Both processes for increasing the excitation of the carbon dioxide molecules to the upper laser level are likely if the density of electrons in the discharge is increased and also if the energy distribution of the electrons changes to make it more favorable for exciting the carbon dioxide molecules to the 001 level directly and for faster production of $N_2(v)$ molecules.

Helium seems to be important on both counts and is the most widely used third gas. Water vapor and hydrogen are useful only in terms of the first effect. Car-

bon monoxide seems to be important from both the excitation and the de-excitation points of view. Using a carbon dioxide pressure of three torr, a nitrogen pressure of three torr and a helium pressure of about 20 torr, a continuous-wave power of some 80 watts per meter of discharge length has been obtained at a wavelength of 10.6 microns. The working efficiency in this case is in excess of 20 percent.

At present most of the high-power carbon dioxide lasers have the gases flowing at a slow rate through the laser tube. Some of our early experiments at the Bell Laboratories and more recent experiments at the Philips Research Laboratory in the Netherlands have shown, however, that it is possible to make sealed-off carbon dioxide lasers if sufficient care is taken in preparing the tube and if the proper gas mixtures are used. These lasers are capable of producing just as much power output as the flowing-gas systems, and the efficiency is quite comparable.

Typical carbon dioxide lasers are about two meters long and can produce continuous-wave laser power of about 150 watts. There is nothing to prevent one from making a very long laser in order to obtain much higher power outputs, since the power output increases linearly with length. In fact, workers at the Raytheon Company have constructed a "folded" carbon dioxide laser that is 600 feet long. This laser has produced continuous-wave power as high as 8.8 kilowatts. The power output of the laser has thus finally caught up with the fantasies of science fiction, and the thermal effects of such output are certainly awesome.

The experimental setup illustrated at the top of page 274 is useful in studying laser action in molecular gases that are unstable, that is, gases that dissociate easily under direct-discharge excitation and/or require an extremely selective excitation for continuous laser operation (for example the diatomic gases). The advantage here is that there is no discharge in the laser region and thus the only levels of the active gas that can be excited are those whose energy coincides with the vibrationally excited nitrogen molecules. In this way continuous laser oscillation was achieved on vibrational-rotational transitions of carbon monoxide (CO) at five to six microns, in nitrous oxide (N_2O) on the 001 → 100 transitions near 10.8 microns and in carbon disulfide (CS_2) on the 021 → 120 transitions near 11 microns.

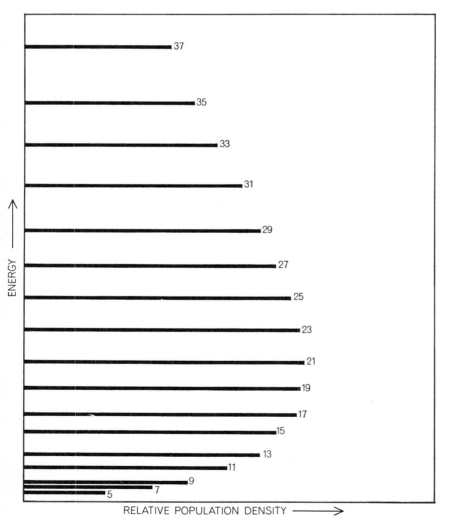

ENERGY →

RELATIVE POPULATION DENSITY ⟶

BOLTZMANN DISTRIBUTION of the population densities of the rotational energy levels of the 001 vibrational level of carbon dioxide results from the fact that during its lifetime in a given vibrational level a molecule undergoes a large number of rotational thermalizing collisions, hopping around from one rotational level to another about 10 million times per second. The horizontal scale shows the population densities of the rotational levels at about 400 degrees Kelvin. Vertical energy scale shows the position of each rotational level.

The carbon monoxide laser is particularly interesting from the spectroscopic point of view. We are now able to observe transitions among vibrational levels as high as $v = 25$ in the electronic ground state—transitions that have never been observed before. Nitrous oxide, which is similar in its vibrational modes to carbon dioxide, has the capability of generating high continuous-wave power at an efficiency comparable to that of the carbon dioxide system; it has not, however, been investigated in detail as yet. In any case, the technique of selective excitation for obtaining high power output and high efficiency appears to be generally applicable.

Other techniques for obtaining vibrational excitations in molecules include chemical reactions, heating of gases by flames or burners and optical excitation by matching optical radiation obtained from discharge or flames. These other means have not yet been exploited to any great extent but they do hold promise. The fact that the discharge excitation of the carbon dioxide laser is capable of a conversion efficiency of more than 20 percent, however, poses a formidable challenge to new techniques in terms of practical applications.

So far I have described the mechanisms of excitation and de-excitation that result in the extremely high power output of carbon dioxide lasers, but I have said nothing about the spectrum of the power output. As I have mentioned, the transitions between two vibrational levels occur in the form of a band consisting of P and R branches, because of the closely spaced rotational levels of both the upper and the lower laser vibrational levels. Does this imply that the power output from the carbon dioxide laser occurs at a number of frequencies corresponding to the discrete P-branch and R-branch transitions simultaneously? If the power output were to occur at a number of frequencies, the laser beam would not be truly monochromatic and its usefulness in areas such as communications would be limited. In reality the power output from a high-power carbon dioxide laser can usually be made to occur on a single P-branch transition, usually $P(20)$ at 10.5915 microns, without any trouble, in spite of the fact that the $001 \rightarrow 100$ vibrational band contains a number of possible P-branch and R-branch transitions. This is accomplished by exploiting some rather subtle "competition effects" that take place between the P-branch and the R-branch transitions—a stratagem that in-

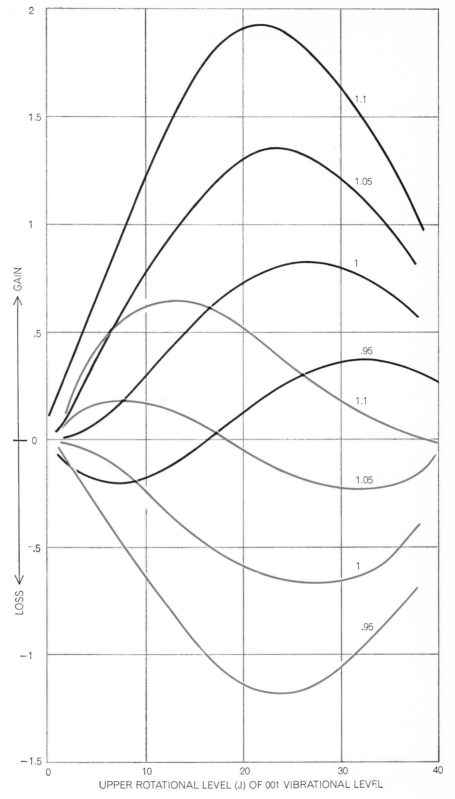

COMPETITION EFFECTS among the various possible vibrational-rotational laser transitions of carbon dioxide usually result in one P-branch transition dominating. This set of curves shows the amount of gain (or loss) on a number of P-branch transitions (*color*) and R-branch transitions (*black*) of a given vibrational band. The number associated with each curve gives the ratio of the total population density in the upper, or 001, vibrational laser level to the total population density in the lower, or 100, vibrational laser level.

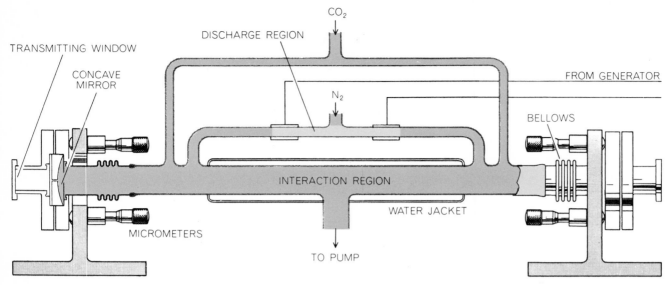

CO₂

DISCHARGE REGION

FROM GENERATOR

TRANSMITTING WINDOW

N₂

CONCAVE
MIRROR

BELLOWS

INTERACTION REGION

WATER JACKET

MICROMETERS

TO PUMP

CONTINUOUS-FLOW SYSTEM was used by the author to verify the hypothesis that a carbon dioxide–nitrogen laser would be more efficient than a pure carbon dioxide laser. Strong laser oscillation was obtained in this system on the vibrational-rotational transitions of carbon dioxide even though no electric discharge was present in the interaction region, thereby proving the effectiveness of using vibrationally excited nitrogen molecules for selective excitation of carbon dioxide molecules to the upper laser level.

creases the usefulness of the carbon dioxide laser tremendously.

It is important to observe that the energy spacings between the various vibrational levels are usually much greater than the kinetic energy of the molecules (which is on the order of .025 electron volt at room temperature). The spacing of the rotational energy levels, on the other hand, is smaller than the kinetic energy. Thus the population density of a particular rotational level in a given vibrational level is not independent of the population density of other rotational levels, since every single collision can result in an exchange of energy equal to the rotational-level spacings. As a result the molecule can jump around from one rotational level to another very frequently. The frequency of this hopping around (also known as the rotational thermalization rate) is in excess of 10 million hops per second for the gas pressures at which the lasers operate. Since the spacing of the vibrational energy levels is much larger than the kinetic energy of the molecules, however, the vibrational thermalization rate is very small: about 1,000 per second. The vibrational-level lifetime, including radiative and collisional relaxation, is about a millisecond whereas the rotational thermalization time is considerably shorter: about 10^{-7} second. This implies that during its lifetime in a vibrational level a molecule undergoes a very large number of rotational thermalizing collisions. This gives rise to a Boltzmann distribution of the molecules among the

various rotational levels of a vibrational level [*see illustration on page 272*].

Under the above conditions governing the population densities of the rotational levels one can calculate the amount of gain (or loss) on the various P-branch and R-branch transitions of a given vibrational band [*see illustration on preceding page*]. From such a calculated set of curves the following useful conclusions can be easily reached: (1) Some P-branch transitions show gain even when the total vibrational population density in the lower laser level exceeds that in the upper level. This situation is called "partial inversion," since the R-branch transitions do not show gain. (2) When the total vibrational population density in the upper laser level exceeds that in the lower laser level, both P-branch and R-branch transitions show gain. This is called "complete inversion." (3) Even for the case of complete inversion, an R-branch transition always has less gain than a P-branch transition starting from the same upper rotational level.

Let us now see what practical effects one can observe from the above conclusions. While it is true that gain occurs on a large number of transitions simultaneously, the existence of a Boltzmann distribution requires that the change of population density of one rotational level affect the population density of all rotational levels in order to maintain the Boltzmann distribution. The rotational transition with the highest gain—in this case transition $P(22)$—will start oscillating first. This will be the strongest P-

branch transition, since the R-branch transitions have lower gain. When this occurs, the rate at which molecules are removed from the $J = 21$ rotational level increases because of the stimulated emission on the $P(22)$ transition. But the requirement of the Boltzmann distribution will result in a transfer of molecules from other rotational levels to the $J = 21$ level and the population density of all the rotational levels decreases even though the laser oscillation on $P(22)$ drains the molecules from the $J = 21$ level. This results in a very strong competition among the possible laser transitions and usually one P-branch transition dominates.

As a result of our newfound mastery of these competition effects, the power output from a high-power continuous-wave carbon dioxide laser can be made to occur on a single rotational transition of the $001 \rightarrow 100$ band, thereby ensuring that the high-power output is both extremely coherent and extremely monochromatic.

Oscillation is possible on the weaker P-branch or R-branch transitions provided there is sufficient gain and a wavelength-selecting element such as a grating or a prism is introduced in the laser cavity to prevent the stronger transition from oscillating. Because of the strong competition, one obtains nearly the same amount of power output on any transition that one selects for oscillation, using the wavelength-selecting device.

In addition, because of the long lifetime of the vibrational levels responsible for laser oscillation in carbon dioxide, we can store energy in the discharge medium for about a millisecond by blocking the path of the laser beam within the resonator and thereby preventing the laser oscillation. If the block is suddenly removed, then the output from the laser occurs in the form of a sharp pulse whose peak power is usually 1,000 times larger than the average continuous-wave power obtainable from this laser. This mode of operation is called Q-switching. The Q-switching is most easily accomplished by replacing one of the laser-cavity mirrors with a rotating mirror [*see illustration below*]. The laser operates every time the rotating mirror lines up with the opposite stationary mirror, putting out an infrared pulse at 10.6 microns. With such a Q-switching scheme a carbon dioxide laser capable of producing approximately 50 watts of continuous-wave power will produce nearly 50 kilowatts of pulsed power in bursts approximately 150 nanoseconds long and at a rate of about 400 bursts per second. Such high pulsed-power output with the coherency afforded by gas lasers is particularly useful in nondestructive physical investigations.

An ideal source of coherent radiation is one that can be continuously "tuned," that is, one whose frequency can be changed and controlled continuously. Tuning a high-power molecular laser is not strictly possible, but the number of discrete vibrational-rotational transitions that can be made to oscillate is extremely large. For example, in carbon monoxide alone there are about 200 transitions that oscillate between five and six microns; in carbon dioxide about 100 transitions with high-power output

can be made to oscillate between nine and 11 microns. In short, the high-power molecular lasers, although not continuously tunable, offer a wide range of discrete wavelengths at which one can work.

The high continuous-wave and Q-switched power made available by the carbon dioxide lasers has many applications. Focusing the coherent infrared output into an area of approximately a thousandth of a square centimeter can give an intensity of a million watts per square centimeter for a continuous-wave laser and an intensity of a billion watts per square centimeter for a Q-switched laser. Continuous-wave powers in excess of one kilowatt have obvious thermal applications such as metal cutting and welding. A strange "softening" of granite rock is also reported when the rock is irradiated with a kilowatt of power from a carbon dioxide laser. The output from the carbon dioxide laser at 10.6 microns, although invisible to the eye, is just as devastating as that from any other powerful laser. The thermal applications of the carbon dioxide lasers command considerable industrial interest.

More important, however, are the nonthermal applications of the carbon dioxide laser. These potential applications include optical communications both on the earth and in space. The main attraction here is the low-loss optical "window" that exists between eight and 14 microns for transmission through the earth's atmosphere. The high efficiency and high power of the carbon dioxide lasers at 10.6 microns make them ideal candidates for such applications. The

carbon dioxide laser is also ideal for use in optical radar systems, again because of low-loss transmission through the atmosphere. Another possibility is the use of a carbon dioxide laser to investigate optical interactions with matter at a wavelength of 10.6 microns, since many semiconductors that are opaque in the visible portion of the spectrum are transparent at this wavelength. Still another application of the high-power carbon dioxide laser is the use of the 10.6-micron radiation as a "pump" for studying nonlinear properties of new materials with the aim of making a really tunable source of infrared radiation. In this connection my colleagues and I have performed a number of interesting experiments, which include second-harmonic generation, parametric amplification of far-infrared radiation, two-photon electron-hole pair production in semiconductors, nonlinearities arising from conduction electrons in semiconductors and Raman scattering from Landau-level electrons in semiconductors. Some of these mechanisms are strong enough to enable us to make a tunable laser oscillator in the infrared portion of the spectrum. Such a tunable laser, pumped with the fixed-frequency carbon dioxide laser, can be used as a local oscillator in an optical communication or radar system. Moreover, such a tunable infrared source would completely revolutionize infrared spectroscopy. The description of these experiments will perhaps be the subject of a future article. In conclusion, it suffices to say that the carbon dioxide lasers have already opened up avenues of physical investigation undreamed of before, and they promise many more fruitful experiments in the future.

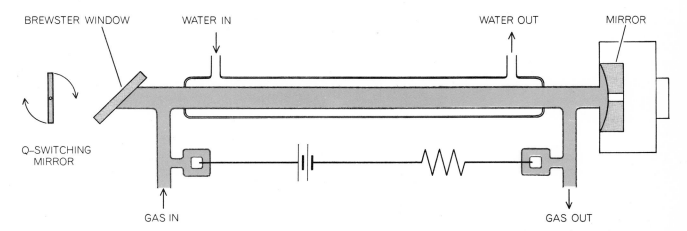

Q-SWITCHING, a technique for operating a normally continuous-wave laser in a pulsed mode, is accomplished by replacing one of the laser-cavity mirrors with a rotating mirror. The laser operates every time the rotating mirror (*left*) lines up with the opposite stationary mirror (*right*). A carbon dioxide laser capable of producing approximately 50 watts of continuous-wave power will produce nearly 50 kilowatts of Q-switched power in bursts approximately 150 nanoseconds long and at a rate of about 400 bursts per second.

VII

Properties and Applications of Laser Light

The applications of the light from a laser depend on the properties of that light, which in turn depend on the type and construction of the laser. The properties of the light generated by the various lasers and some of the applications that they make possible were discussed in several of the articles in the preceding section.

In the first article in this section, I have reviewed the basic ways in which laser light differs from ordinary light: laser light is more monochromatic, powerful, directional, and coherent. These properties are defined, and the extent to which each can be achieved in particular kinds of lasers is discussed. The importance of each is best illustrated by descriptions of some of the kinds of scientific experiments they make possible: coherence, for example, is important if the phase of waves is to be compared, as in interference experiments. In addition, some further advances in laser techniques are reported, such as the generation of intense light pulses so short that their duration is measured in picoseconds (10^{-12} seconds).

One large and important area of physics, nonlinear optics, would not exist if it were not for the development of intense laser light. The term "nonlinear" refers to the relation between the response of a transparent material and the electromagnetic field of the light. If the light is of ordinary intensity nearly all of it that emerges from a transparent medium has the same wavelength as it did before it entered the medium. But the high-intensity laser light can rapidly alter the optical properties of the medium, causing intense beams of new wavelengths to be generated.

At the time that the 1961 article "Optical Masers" (Section VI) was published, it could be said only that "one can also conceive of using maser beams in harmonic generators or mixers." Just as those words were being printed, the first report of successful generation of an optical harmonic appeared—red light had been converted into ultraviolet. By 1963, as much as 20 percent of the red light could be converted into the second harmonic, and it was discovered that the Raman effect could be stimulated by laser light. A thorough review of nonlinear optics is given in J. A. Giordmaine's article. As a beam of intense light traverses a medium, it alters the refractive index of the medium and so affects the propagation of another beam. Giordmaine discusses a number of the forms that this interaction can take, and points out other possibilities. Since publication of his article in 1964, some of these possibilities, such as stimulated Brillouin scattering, have indeed been observed; they are discussed briefly in the first article of the section, "Laser Light."

Some of the similarities between light waves and radio waves are enhanced by lasers. Thus, it is now possible to have so many quanta in a light wave that we can ignore the discreteness of the energy in it. We can also apply short, intense pulses, like those achieved at radio frequencies, to atomic or molecular systems, and thus observe transient effects of short duration. Some of these effects were first studied in nuclear resonance at radio frequencies. When a suitable radio-frequency pulse was applied at the nuclear-resonance frequency, it was found that the nuclei could be made to precess vigorously and to emit an after-signal. After several pulses had been applied echo pulses were observed. To generate an echo pulse, the pulses must deliver enough radio-frequency

Properties and Applications of Laser Light

279

energy to cause a transition between energy states, but they must do so in a period of time shorter than that required by the nuclei to settle into the final state.

Similar phenomena have now been observed at optical frequencies, even though relaxation is usually so rapid that extremely short pulses are needed. In the optical region, where the test samples are much larger than a wavelength, new three-dimensional effects have been found in the echo process. This new field, which is described in Sven R. Hartmann's article, can be expected to expand as a result of the recent availability of picosecond light pulses.

In addition to their scientific application, lasers have been found to have considerable practical value, and they have facilitated a number of operations that, previously, were extremely difficult, or even impossible. For some of these, such as drilling holes through hard objects like diamonds and ceramics, the laser is used as a source of intense heat. For others, such as measurement applications and holography, laser light's coherence is the decisive factor. In still other applications the directionality or monochromaticity of the light is needed. The steadily lengthening list of these applications is discussed in the article by Donald R. Herriott.

Light has been used for signaling for many centuries. But engineers who work with radio waves have learned much more effective ways to use electromagnetic waves for communication. Signals are impressed on a steady pure wave train of a single frequency, by altering either the amplitude or the frequency of each successive wave. The higher the wave frequency, the more rapidly the waves succeed each other, and the more rapidly successive bits of information can follow each other. Thus, ordinary broadcast frequencies of, say, a million cycles per second, can transmit only voice and music, but frequencies of about 50 million cycles per second can transmit enough details for television pictures. The extremely high carrier frequencies of visible light make it theoretically possible to transmit enormous amounts of information in one optical channel —as much information as all the radio channels now existing can handle. But there are problems: since light does not penetrate rain, snow, or fog very well, methods must be developed for protecting light beams from the weather, as well as for channeling them around bends. Some of the promise of lasers for communication, the problems, and the solutions are discussed in the article by Stewart E. Miller.

If we are ever to take full advantage of the laser beams' potentially enormous capacity, we must devise ways to impress information on the light. That is, develop efficient methods for broad-band modulation of light. Most of the basic ways of controlling light by the application of electric or magnetic fields to certain materials have been known for some time, but new configurations and new materials can increase the speed of operation and decrease the amount of signal power required, and new methods of light modulation, like injection of charges into semiconductors, are now being studied. Donald F. Nelson reviews these methods in his article.

280

One of the most visually spectacular applications of lasers is that of making and viewing holograms. A typical hologram is a piece of photographic film or glass plate on which the naked eye can discern only a gray blur and occasional irregular blotches. But when laser light shines on the hologram, one can look through it, as through a magic window, and see a fully three-dimensional reconstruction of the scene encoded on the film. Holography was conceived and demonstrated before lasers, but because it requires light sources with considerable coherence lasers have stimulated great advances in holography, and have made it much easier and more practical. New methods, such as the use of an off-axis reference beam to avoid confusing secondary images, have been developed. In their article, Emmett N. Leith and Juris Upatnieks describes the theory and the method of holography, illustrating the excellent reconstructions that can be obtained by it.

Holography, like nonlinear optics, is an exciting and active field, in which continual progress is being made: some of this progress is described in Keith S. Pennington's article. With pulsed laser sources, instant holograms have been made of three-dimensional volumes that contain, for example, a fog-like suspension of small particles. Once the image has been reconstructed, a microscope can be focused on an individual particle, and particles can be studied and counted. Double-exposed holograms display interference fringes, which show whether an object has moved as little as a fraction of a wavelength of light between the exposures. Multicolor holograms, which utilize the fact that the photographic emulsion has thickness, have also been made. Just as the reflection of X-rays in a crystal can reveal the atomic spacing within that crystal (see the article by Bragg in Section V), successive layers in the emulsion can reflect a particular color strongly if their spacing is right for that color and angle of illumination. The holographic process is arranged to record the necessary layers in the emulsion. As a result of the advances in understanding that have come from holographic research with lasers, it is possible to make these color holograms viewable in a beam of ordinary, nonlaser light.

As the articles of this section illustrate, lasers are making possible many new ways of probing the properties of matter. Their scientific applications have been greater than anyone could have imagined. Many practical applications, some of them surprising, have been demonstrated as well, but laser technology has not yet caught up with the imagination of the comic-strip artist. Until a laser that is not only powerful, but also efficient, compact, and inexpensive is invented, many possible applications will remain impractical. But there is every reason to believe that the development of such a laser is just a matter of time: no fundamental obstacles are evident, and each of the necessary qualities has been attained in at least one separate type of laser. We can, therefore, look forward confidently to major advances in laser technology—advances based on principles already established—that will lead to new and important applications of what has already proved to be a basic tool of science.

281

25

Laser Light

Arthur L. Schawlow   *September 1968*

How does laser light differ from ordinary light? In brief, it is much more intense, directional, monochromatic and coherent. The light emitted by an ordinary source such as a candle or an incandescent lamp consists of uncoordinated waves of many different lengths, that is, it is incoherent and more or less white. The waves of laser light are coordinated in space and time and have nearly the same length. This coherence and chromatic purity, and also the intensity of laser light, results from the fact that in a laser excited atoms are stimulated to radiate light cooperatively before they have had time to do so spontaneously and independently. The directionality of laser light arises from the geometry of the laser. These properties of laser light suggest many uses for it not only in technology [see "Applications of Laser Light," by Donald R. Herriott, page 313] but also in physics.

Most lasers consist of a column of active material that has a partly reflecting mirror at one end and a fully reflecting mirror at the other. In a typical solid laser material, a ruby crystal, the active ingredients are chromium atoms interspersed in the crystal lattice of aluminum oxide. The laser is primed by pumping these atoms, by means of a flash of intense light, to an excited state. With a preponderance of atoms in that state the system can be stimulated to produce a cascade of photons, all the same wavelength and all in step, by triggering the emission of energy that drops the atoms from the excited state to a lower energy state. A photon carrying this quantum of energy, on striking an excited atom, causes it to emit a photon at the same frequency, and the light wave thus released falls in step with the triggering one. Waves that travel to the sides of the column leave the system, but

those that go to the ends of the column along its axis are reflected back and forth by the mirrors. The column, whose length is a whole number of wavelengths at the selected frequency, acts as a cavity resonator, and a beam of monochromatic, coherent light rapidly builds in intensity as one atom after another is stimulated to emit photons with the same energy and direction [*see illustration on page 288*]. It is as if tiny mechanical men, all wound up to a certain energy

and facing along the axis of the laser enclosure, were successively set in motion by other marchers and fell into step until they became an immense army marching in unison row on row (the plane wave fronts) back and forth in the enclosure. After the laser light has built up in this way it emerges through the partly reflecting mirror at one end as an intense, highly directional beam. Light intensities as high as a billion watts per square centimeter have been produced.

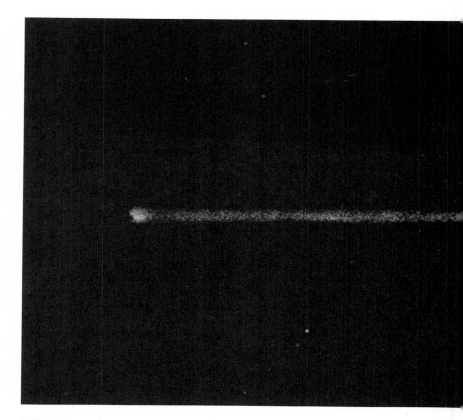

SHORTEST LASER PULSES EVER PHOTOGRAPHED were discovered by workers at the Bell Telephone Laboratories to be components of what was previously believed to be one long pulse from a high-power neodymium-glass laser. The pulses appear as a series of bright

The output from the first solid laser was in the form of brief pulses. A continuous beam can now be produced by several kinds of solid laser, but such a beam is more easily generated by a gas laser. A common laser of this type contains helium and neon, with neon as the active material. A continuous glow discharge is used to pump the neon atoms to a certain energy level, and they are stimulated to emit photons that drop them to the next lower level (not the ground state, or lowest level). As in a solid laser, the beam builds up and is made coherent by being bounced back and forth between end mirrors. Among the many other kinds of laser system are those based on laser action in semiconductors, liquids and molecular gases such as carbon dioxide.

Laser light shows itself to be different from ordinary light even when it merely illuminates a surface. The surface looks grainy and seems to sparkle. The graininess is so distracting that when a printed page is illuminated by laser light, it is hard for the eye to focus on the writing. The reason lies in the coherence of the laser light waves. As the waves are scattered from neighboring points on the paper they interfere with one another everywhere, producing bright spots where the waves overlap and reinforce one another in phase, and leaving dark spots where they cancel one another out of phase. The interference pattern depends on the angle at which the paper is viewed; the pattern changes with a slight movement of the eyes or head and the shifting bright spots seem to sparkle. Ordinary light does not produce such interference because the light waves are unrelated to one another in phase. The waves' mutual interference is chaotic and consequently produces no diffraction pattern.

Interference is of course one of the most basic properties of waves. When two waves arrive in the same phase, they will add to a higher intensity than either wave alone can. If, on the other hand, the waves arrive in opposite phase, the resulting intensity is less and can even be zero. Yet it is contrary to all ordinary experience to shine two beams of light on a surface and find darkness where they overlap. This does not happen because the phases of the light waves in the two beams are not fixed but fluctuate randomly. The reason is that in ordinary light sources the waves come in short bursts emitted independently by enormous numbers of individual atoms. Even if the beams come from nearby places in the same source, there is little or no phase correlation between them.

It is nonetheless possible to demonstrate interference with ordinary light, if we filter out those waves that happen to have related phases. If we have a wave that travels in a definite direction, the wave fronts form planes at right angles to the rays. At any two points on such a wave front the phase of the wave is the same. If we now take waves from two parts of the front and direct them so that they overlap, they will interfere. This is the way Thomas Young first did the celebrated experiment in which he demonstrated the wave aspect of light [see "Light," by Gerald Feinberg, page 4]. In that experiment a plane wave falls on two narrow slits, side by side and fairly close together. Part of the wave passes through each slit, and since the slits are narrow the beams spread out and overlap on a distant screen. On the screen a pattern of light and dark bands can be seen, corresponding to the places where the waves from the two slits arrive in phase or out of phase.

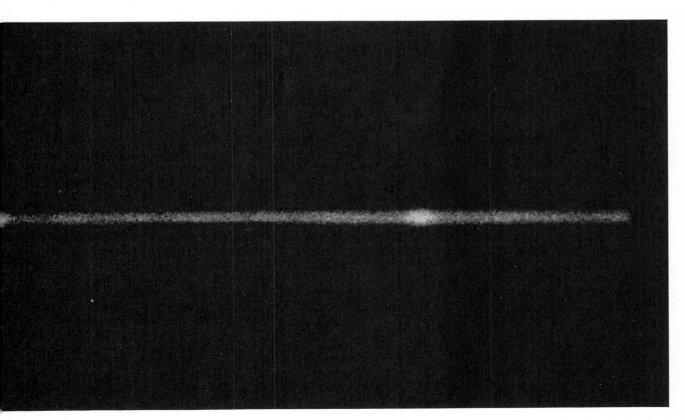

spots on a background track. Each pulse is about three-tenths of a millimeter in length and less than a picosecond, or trillionth of a second, in duration. The technique used to photograph the pulses is illustrated on the next page. The extremely high peak powers that can be got in picosecond pulses from such "mode-locked" lasers promise fresh insights into interactions of light and matter.

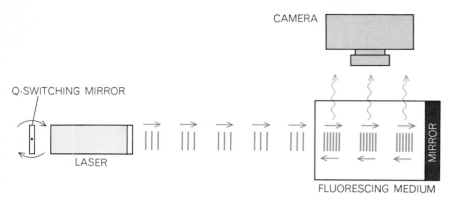

CAMERA

Q-SWITCHING MIRROR

LASER

MIRROR

FLUORESCING MEDIUM

TECHNIQUE used to record the picosecond laser pulses shown in the photograph on the preceding two pages is illustrated in this schematic drawing. The neodymium-glass laser is mode-locked by a rotating mirror (*left*), producing intense bursts of light, each of which in fact consists of a train of closely spaced picosecond pulses. The pulses enter a glass cell containing a highly transparent fluorescent liquid solution and are reflected back on themselves by a mirror at one end (*right*). The molecules in the solution are such that they emit a photon of light only after absorbing two photons from the laser. As a result intense fluorescence from the release of a large number of photons occurs only in the regions where a pulse traveling toward the mirror overlaps a pulse reflected from the mirror. Fluorescent spots are photographed and their length is measured in order to determine their duration.

If Young's experiment is tried by placing an ordinary light source near the pair of slits, it will not work. The screen will be uniformly illuminated because the phases of the light waves coming through the slits fluctuate randomly. If a laser is placed near the slits, however, it will produce an interference pattern because its light is coherent. To perform Young's experiment we can produce nearly coherent light from ordinary sources, but only by discarding most of the light and selecting a small portion of it. Thus there was coherent light before lasers. Even the sparkling appearance of a surface under coherent illumination was observed and explained before lasers.

Ordinary lamps cannot produce light that approaches true monochromaticity. The light from even a single spectral line of the best low-pressure gas lamp is spread over a band of frequencies that typically is at least 1,000 megacycles wide. Light from a gas laser, on the other hand, can be confined within a single megacycle in breadth, which amounts to a frequency spread of considerably less than one part in a million. In a gas laser with a mirror spacing of 30 centimeters a round trip between the mirrors covers about a million wavelengths. Accordingly a shift in frequency of only one part per million will convert the laser from one mode of resonance to another. Typically there are a dozen or more such modes within the frequency range of the laser medium. If certain precautions are not taken, the laser may oscillate on many or all of these frequencies simul-

taneously. For most applications this is undesirable; for example, a frequency spread of less than one part in two million is essential if two beams of light are to interfere sharply after traveling paths that differ in length by one meter (two million wavelengths).

There are several ways to refine the output of a gas laser to the desired purity. One is to use an etalon as an end mirror in the laser. The etalon is a piece of glass, quartz or sapphire with parallel surfaces that form a resonant cavity much shorter than the laser as a whole. The resonant frequencies of this short cavity are much more widely spaced than the frequencies of a long cavity, and the cavity can be designed so that it will allow only one mode of oscillation in the band of possible laser frequencies. The best gas lasers now generate light that is restricted almost entirely to a single wavelength.

With this exquisitely refined instrument it has become possible to examine materials and physical phenomena in new ways. Among the interesting applications of the laser is the probing

of materials by the study of their Brillouin scattering of light.

In 1915 the French physicist Louis Brillouin suggested that light traveling through a material must undergo slight changes in wavelength as the result of encounters with the high-frequency sound waves that arise from the ordinary thermal vibrations of atoms in the material. He published a brief account of his calculations leading to this conclusion and then entered the French army. After the war he decided to publish a more complete report on this work but found himself unable to understand his old notes. He then found a pictorial way to describe the phenomenon he had originally deduced by mathematical means, and this led to an illuminating view of the subject.

The sound waves from the vibrating atoms fan out in all directions, and since the vibrations may vary considerably in frequency the waves have a wide range of frequencies up into the infrared. Like other sound waves, they consist of alternate compressions and expansions in the direction of the wave propagation. Since the velocity of such a wave is much slower than that of a light wave, it follows that the sound wave is much shorter than an electromagnetic wave of the same frequency. Hence a wave of visible light passing through a liquid in the same direction as a sound wave of the same frequency will encounter regularly spaced maximal compressions and expansions of the sound wave. A small part of the light will be reflected from each sound-wave crest, and if the spacing between the crests is just half the wavelength of the light, the reflections will add in phase to produce an appreciable amount of light. Because of the Doppler effect the reflected light will be shifted to a slightly lower frequency, since it is reflected from a moving "mirror" traveling in the same direction as the incident light beam. Conversely, light reflected from sound waves moving in the opposite direction will be shifted to a higher frequency. The magnitude in each case is readily calculable: it is twice the velocity of sound divided by

ORDINARY LIGHT AND LASER LIGHT are compared in the illustration on the opposite page. In an ordinary thermal light source, such as an incandescent lamp (*a*), the atoms radiate independently, producing light waves that are both spatially incoherent (out of step) and temporally incoherent (with various wavelengths). A pinhole can be used to obtain spatially coherent light from the ordinary light, but only by sacrificing most of the power output of the lamp (*b*). Similarly, a color filter can be used to obtain temporally coherent light from the ordinary light, but again a large part of the lamp's power is lost (*c*). By combining a pinhole and a filter one can obtain a light beam that is both spatially and temporally coherent, but its power output will be a tiny percentage of the total output of the lamp (*d*). In contrast, all the light produced by a laser is both spatially and temporally coherent (*e*).

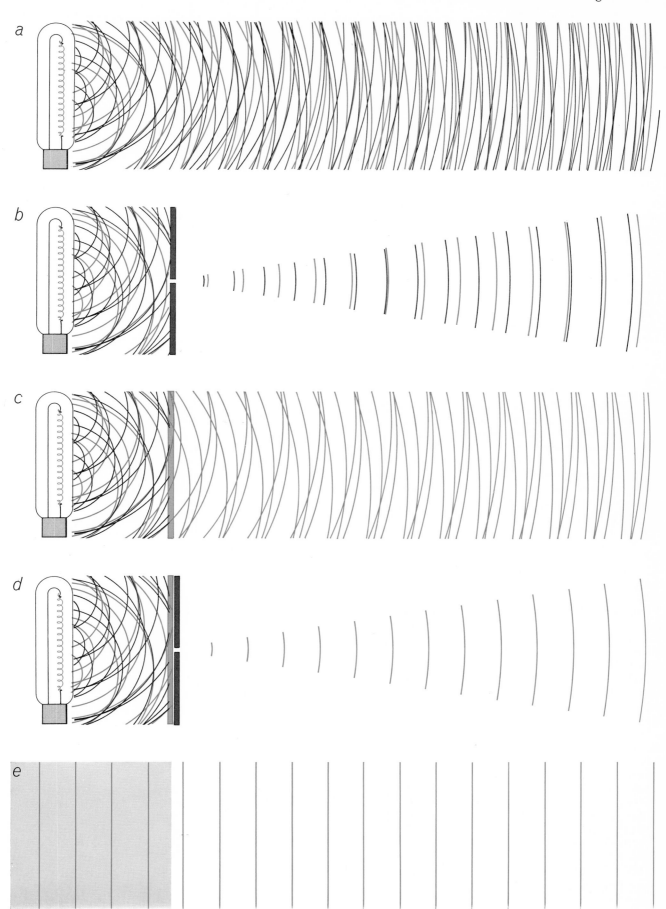

---

the velocity of light, and it amounts to a frequency shift of about 10 parts in a million.

The formula for Brillouin scattering makes it possible to measure the velocity of sound at various wavelengths in any liquid and thus to study important properties of materials. Observation of the scattering is so difficult with ordinary light sources, however, that little work was done along this line before the laser became available. With a laser beam, thanks to its monochromaticity and directionality, it is now relatively easy to observe Brillouin scattering. In 1964 George B. Benedek, Joseph B. Lastovka, Klaus Fritsch and Thomas Greytak of the Massachusetts Institute of Technology and Raymond Y. Chiao and Boris P. Stoicheff of the University of Toronto used gas lasers to study Brillouin scattering in a number of liquids and solids. They found that in some substances the velocity of sound depends on the sound-wave frequency. For example, in liquid benzene high-frequency compression waves, at five billion cycles per second, travel 15 percent faster than those at low frequencies.

By bringing together the incident laser beam and the scattered light on the cathode of a phototube, extremely small shifts in the frequency of the scattered light can be measured. The phototube current shows a beat signal at the dif-

ference frequency, even when the shift amounts to only a few cycles per second. Benedek and N. C. Ford of M.I.T. and S. S. Alpert, David Balzarini, Robert Novick, Lester Siegel and Yen Yeh of Columbia University have measured shifts of a few hundred cycles per second in light of 10^{14}-cycles-per-second frequency; these shifts arise from thermal fluctuations in a liquid near its boiling point. Herman Z. Cummins, Norman Knable and Yeh at Columbia have observed similarly small shifts in a dilute solution of polystyrene.

The laser is being applied to probe the internal structure and behavior of molecules, by examining the light-scattering phenomenon known as the Raman effect. In this effect, discovered by C. V. Raman of India in 1928, the light frequency shifts as photons take up or give energy to molecular vibrations, rotations and other motions. It is evidenced in frequency shifts that are much larger than those from Brillouin scattering, but the shifted light is much weaker, so that the intense, monochromatic light of the laser is of great value in studying it. Gas lasers employing neon, argon or krypton as the active material, which can provide continuous beams at powers up to several watts, are used in these studies.

Before the advent of the laser the Raman effect could be seen only in liquids, a few solids and (with difficulty)

in large volumes of certain gases. With a laser Sergio P. S. Porto (then at the Bell Telephone Laboratories) and Alfons Weber, Leonard E. Cheesman and Joseph J. Barrett of Fordham University have been able to observe Raman scattering even in small samples of gas at ordinary pressure—one atmosphere or less. The spectra they have obtained clearly resolve the fine structure of light-scattering produced by the rotation of molecules. The sensitivity made possible by the laser has also disclosed motions at a finer level than the rotation or vibration of the molecule itself. For example, in crystals of manganese fluoride at cryogenic temperatures Porto, P. A. Fleury and Rodney Loudon at Bell Laboratories have detected Raman scattering produced by waves from the spin of atoms. In praseodymium chloride J. T. Hougen and S. Singh at the National Research Council of Canada have even observed a Raman effect arising from the motions of electrons.

When one thinks of lasers, one usually thinks of a very bright light source. Actually all but the most powerful continuous-beam lasers put out scarcely more total visible light than a flashlight. The laser, however, puts all its output into light with one narrowly defined wavelength. Thus its power per interval of wavelength is much greater

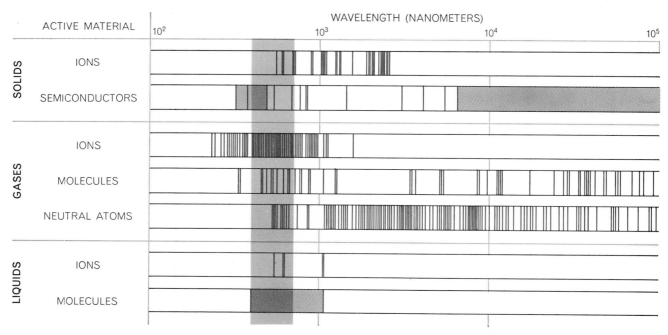

LASER LIGHT IS NOW AVAILABLE at a large number of wavelengths, ranging from the ultraviolet region (*left*) to the far-infrared region (*right*) of the electromagnetic spectrum. (The visible region is indicated by the vertical band in color.) Most of the wavelengths obtained to date from a variety of solid, gaseous and liquid materials are represented in the chart. The chart does not include those additional wavelengths that can be obtained from nonlinear optical processes by passing a laser beam through certain substances. Solid-state lasers of the semiconductor type and liquid lasers that use organic dye molecules as the active medium can be "tuned" over a range of wavelengths (*gray bands*) by changing the proportions of the active materials in the host material.

than the power available from other sources simply because of its greater monochromaticity.

An additional advantage of the laser in this regard arises somewhat independently from its high coherence. All the light from the entire diameter of the end of the laser is in phase. It can therefore be focused to a single point with a startling increase over any other optical source in power per square meter within the focused spot.

To date the only continuous laser that is capable of a large power output is the carbon dioxide type, whose "light" is in the infrared [see "High-Power Carbon Dioxide Lasers," by C. K. N. Patel; page 265 in this book]. Carbon dioxide lasers can generate up to 8,800 watts of continuous power. The unfocused beam from a carbon dioxide laser at a few hundred watts of power will cause a wooden board to emit a flaming jet almost instantly. It will cut through a hacksaw blade within seconds. (Incidentally, at the time the motion picture *Goldfinger* was produced its demonstration of a laser's power was ludicrous in terms of existing lasers; the performance it showed did not become possible until several months after the

motion picture's release, when Patel invented the carbon dioxide laser.)

Even the early lasers could, to be sure, produce a great deal of power in a short pulse. The very first operating laser, the ruby laser constructed by Theodore H. Maiman of the Hughes Aircraft Company, had a power output of several thousand watts for about half a millisecond. The beam from such a laser can vaporize a speck of substance within microseconds. The heating is so rapid, however, that it is only superficial; vaporization carries away the heat before it has had time to penetrate below the surface by conduction. With a laser pulse it is possible to vaporize ink from paper or even from an inflated rubber balloon without appreciably heating the underlying material.

The power of the pulse from some solid lasers (including ruby) can be built up to several hundred million watts by using a kind of shutter that delays the release of the energy stored in the active pulse until it has reached its peak power. Then, when the shutter is opened, the laser emission can proceed. In one version of this method (known as the *Q*-switching technique) a light-absorbing but bleachable dye is interposed before

the end mirror where the laser beam is to emerge. Blocked by the shutter, the optical energy emitted spontaneously and incoherently by the excited atoms grows until the shutter is bleached; then all the stored energy is released from the laser in a giant coherent pulse, lasting about 10 billionths of a second.

At power levels in the millions of watts per square centimeter the electromagnetic wave's electrical effects on a material become important. A visible laser beam with 100 million watts of power per square centimeter, for example, produces an electric field amounting to 100,000 volts per centimeter. Such a field modifies the properties of any material through which the beam passes. As a result the monochromatic wave may become distorted so that harmonic waves are generated at two or more times its frequency. Infrared wavelengths may be converted in this way into visible light, and visible light into ultraviolet rays. Moreover, intense laser light can increase the refractive index of material through which it passes, by compressing the material, by aligning its molecules or by other mechanisms. The changes in refractive index have important consequences, some of which can be put to good use.

By producing changes in the refractive index within the laser medium, very intense laser light can greatly magnify the effects of Brillouin or Raman scattering. For example, when thermal fluctuations cause Brillouin reflection, the reflected beam adds to the laser light at some places and partly cancels it at others. At those places where the intensity is highest, the refractive index is increased most, and these are just the places where the index was already high. Thus above a threshold intensity very strong light reflection occurs, at the downward-shifted Brillouin frequency. Indeed, most of the laser light can be reflected in this stimulated Brillouin scattering, as was first demonstrated for solids by Elsa Garmire and Charles H. Townes at M.I.T., and for liquids by Richard G. Brewer and Klaus E. Rieckhoff of the International Business Machines Corporation. Stimulated Raman scattering can also occur and had been observed earlier by Eric J. Woodbury and N. W. Ng of the Hughes Aircraft Company. In both cases the light drives strong vibrations in the material and the stimulated light beam has a wavelength different from that of the laser. In a solid the vibrations induced by laser light can be strong enough to cause fracturing. John L. Emmett of Stanford University

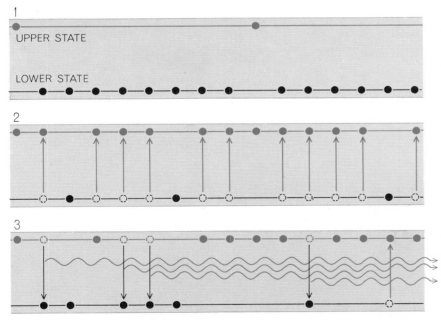

ENERGY-LEVEL PICTURE of laser action begins with the normal, or unexcited, state of affairs in the laser medium (1), in which the vast majority of atoms are in a lower energy state. The medium is then subjected to some external excitation (2), which "pumps" a sizable percentage of atoms into an upper energy state. This situation is known as population inversion. An atom falling spontaneously from the upper level to the lower level can then emit a photon of light that is capable of stimulating other atoms to emit photons with the same frequency and phase (3). Since a stimulating photon can just as easily be absorbed by an atom in going from the lower level to the upper level (*at right in 3*), it is important that population inversion be maintained, so as to make absorption less likely to occur than stimulation. As long as this condition is satisfied, the output will continue to be amplified.

1

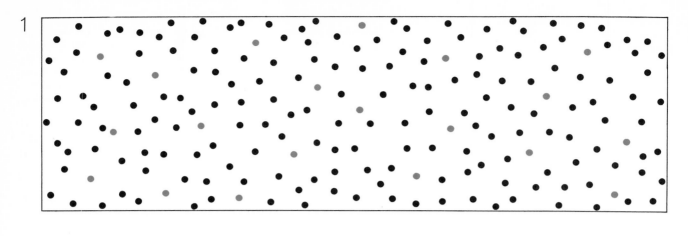

2

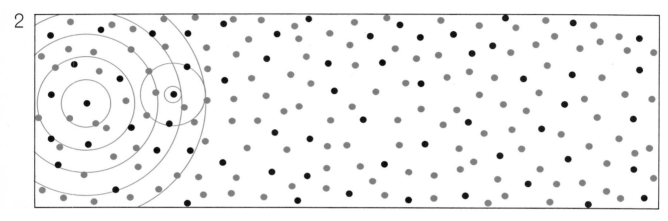

3

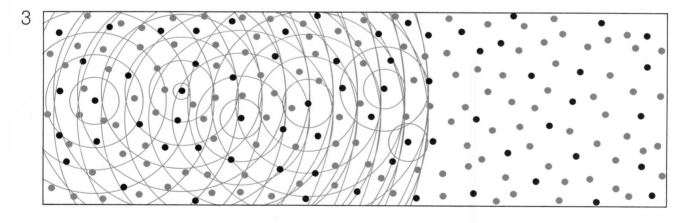

4

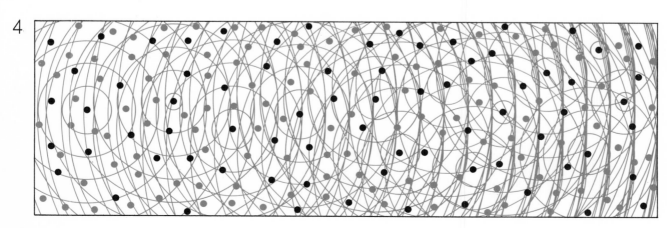

WAVE PICTURE of laser action also begins with most atoms in the laser medium in the unexcited state (1). Unexcited atoms are in black, excited atoms in color. After an external excitation has created a condition of population inversion (2) the spontaneous emission of a photon by a single atom can again begin the process of light amplification by stimulating coherent emission from other excited atoms (3, 4). Usually the energy of the laser beam is built up further by reflecting it between two end mirrors.

found that by using a cylindrical lens to focus the laser light along a line transverse to the direction of the laser beam, the stimulated reflected beam could be made to emerge transversely along the line of the focus. The stimulated beam could then be studied without being obscured by the intense laser light.

Curiously, in the investigation of the nonlinear effects produced by high laser

intensity—the generation of harmonic frequencies and the stimulation of Brillouin and Raman scattering—it was found that these effects generally occurred at laser intensities considerably lower than one should have expected them to be on the basis of the known physical processes at work. Chiao, Mrs. Garmire and Townes discovered a phenomenon that accounts for this apparent anomaly. In a powerful laser beam the refractive index of the medium is increased most at the center of the beam. Consequently the medium acts as a converging lens, focusing the beam to narrower dimensions and thereby increasing its intensity. This self-focusing process quickly gives the beam the intensity required for the nonlinear effects. Actually the light breaks up into a large number of small filaments, and within a filament it is bright enough to cause all the nonlinear scattering processes. Thus

nearly as soon as the light is strong enough for self-focusing the stimulated Brillouin or Raman scattering begins.

Several groups of investigators are now working on the development of coherent light sources that are tunable, that is, sources whose wavelength can be changed. The main approach is being made through the construction of optical-frequency parametric amplifiers and oscillators. Such devices allow the amplification of a variable low frequency at the expense of power put in at a fixed higher frequency. Their operation calls for a medium with an unusually large nonlinear response and at the same time high optical and mechanical quality. A tunable parametric oscillator that operates in the near infrared has been built at Bell Laboratories by R. G. Smith, J. E. Geusic, H. J. Levinstein, Singh and L. G. van Uitert. A parametric oscillator in

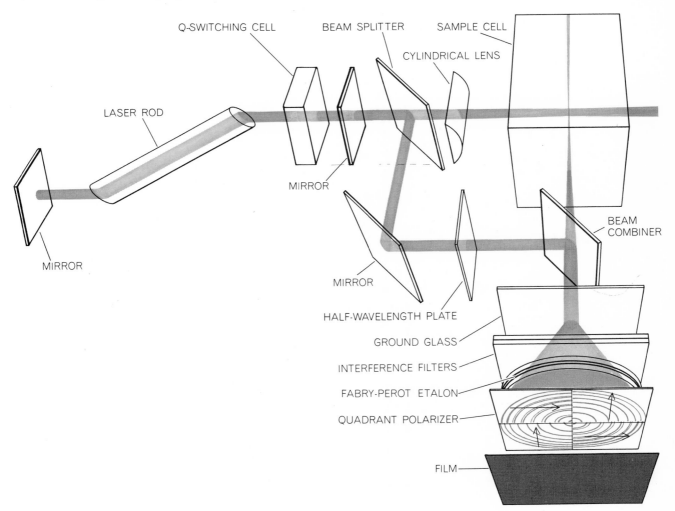

EXPERIMENTAL ARRANGEMENT used to study stimulated Brillouin scattering of laser light by sound vibrations in various materials was devised by John L. Emmett and the author at Stanford University. The distinguishing feature of their arrangement is the use of a cylindrical lens to converge the laser beam to a line focus, so that the scattered light is stimulated to emerge transverse to the beam; thus the scattered beam can be studied without being obscured by the intense laser light. The interferometric system and quadrant polarizer shown in the illustration are used to produce a photographic image in which the interference fringes that are due to the scattered light can be compared directly with the interference fringes due to the laser light (*see illustration on page 290*).

the visible range that produces tunable beams at a power of half a milliwatt has been constructed at Stanford by R. L. Byer, M. K. Oshman, J. Young and S. E. Harris.

Another current development in the refinement of lasers is the production of extremely short pulses. The pulses from most solid lasers range in duration from thousandths to millionths of a second. It has now been found possible to generate pulses whose length is measured in picoseconds (10^{-12} second). The technique employed is known as mode-locking. A laser beam can comprise waves of several slightly different wavelengths, such that one wave undergoes precisely one more cycle than another in the round trip between the mirrors. These components are called the modes of the beam. The trick in generating very short pulses is to bring all the modes into synchronization at some point in the laser column so that they produce a single, sharp maximum of intensity at that point. They can be "locked" in this cyclic pattern by placing a bleachable dye at the synchronizing point; the dye is bleached sufficiently for the waves to pass through most easily only when they all arrive simultaneously, and the laser therefore generates a brief pulse just at that moment at the end of each round trip of the waves.

In a picosecond light travels three-tenths of a millimeter. Hence the train of light waves in a picosecond pulse is only three-tenths of a millimeter long and contains only a few hundred cycles of the wave. Since pulses of such extreme brevity place relatively little strain on the laser material, the laser can be raised to high peak powers. Nikolai G. Basov and his associates in the U.S.S.R., using a mode-locked laser of neodymium glass and three subsequent stages of amplification, have produced laser pulses of more than a trillion watts. The pulses were so powerful that they attacked the nuclei of atoms; focused on a target of lithium deuteride in a vacuum, the pulse somehow caused neutrons to be released from the nuclei.

It seems likely that picosecond laser pulses will be highly useful in exploring the interior of atoms. When such a short light pulse is absorbed, the entire encounter is usually over before there is time for the absorbing atoms to be perturbed by the surroundings. Many kinds of transient effect showing the inertia of the absorber should therefore be observable. Most atoms in solids "relax" in less than a nanosecond, so that the transient effects are observable only with shorter pulses. Thus the interaction of many media may be quite different for picosecond pulses from what it is for longer wave trains.

There are now hundreds of masers and lasers, generating frequencies over most of the electromagnetic spectrum, from the radio region far into the ultraviolet. Indeed, it seems that before long the art of stimulating emission will be extended into the X-ray region. Most likely the visible-frequency laser will be employed to pump atoms to the energy levels necessary for X-ray emission, as radio generators are used to pump the gas laser. Very intense excitation will be needed to raise atoms to the X-ray emission level, because excited atoms spontaneously shed their energy more and more promptly as they go up the quantum ladder of energies. It can be shown that the power required to simultaneously boost enough atoms for stimulated X-ray emission may be as high as a million billion watts per cubic centimeter. That is well within the range, however, of what can be attained by focusing a pulsed laser. An X-ray laser might consist of a column of active material only a millimeter long and about a micron in diameter. Even without mirrors such a column should produce a fairly directional X-ray beam. Presumably the wavelengths of the output would be in the range of just a few angstroms, but precisely what emissions would come out of such a system is not easy to predict; it is a matter of record that most gas lasers were discovered experimentally.

Meanwhile the development of visible-light lasers is providing excitement enough. As we go to higher and higher powers, laser light is demonstrating extraordinary nonlinear phenomena in its interactions with matter. Some of the lasers now under development in the laboratory, such as the tunable and picosecond versions, are showing us that lasers so far have been rather simple devices only because we are just entering the stage of learning why and how to make complicated ones.

BRILLOUIN-SCATTERING PHOTOGRAPH obtained using the experimental arrangement shown on page 289 is essentially a Fabry–Perot interferogram with the interference fringes due to the scattered light occupying the quadrants at upper right and lower left and the interference fringes due to the laser light occupying the quadrants at upper left and lower right. The two sets of fringes can be measured directly to determine the amount of Brillouin scattering associated with a given liquid or solid material. This knowledge in turn can be analyzed to yield information about the structure and properties of the material.

26

The Interaction
of Light with Light

J. A. Giordmaine *April 1964*

One of the best-known characteristics of light is that the transmission, refraction and reflection of a beam of light in a transparent material are not affected by the intensity of the light or the presence of a second beam. According to James Clerk Maxwell's theory of electromagnetism the behavior of a light beam can be predicted solely from the wavelength of the light and its velocity in the material. Now, however, that we have lasers to generate intense beams of coherent light—light whose waves are all in step —many new and striking properties of light can be demonstrated.

It has recently been shown, for example, that in transparent materials an intense beam of light can generate harmonics, or overtones, of the original light frequency. It has also been shown that in the presence of matter two light beams can interact with each other. There is good reason to expect small but observable interactions of intense light beams even in a vacuum. These, however, have not yet been demonstrated, and it is not likely that they are within reach of existing lasers.

One type of interaction of light with matter has been known since 1927, when it was discovered by the Indian physicist C. V. Raman. In the Raman effect a quantum of light gives up some of its energy to a molecule and reappears as a scattered quantum with a lower frequency. It has now been discovered that the ordinarily weak Raman-scattered light is strongly enhanced if it is coupled to an intense beam of laser light.

The electromagnetic wave that constitutes light is made up of an electric component and a magnetic component; these components are locked in

step at right angles to each other and oscillate together. It is possible to alter the velocity of light in a transparent material by applying an additional electric or magnetic field to the material. As early as 1845 Michael Faraday, whose experiments touched almost every aspect of electricity and magnetism, discovered that a static magnetic field affects the way light travels through glass. He showed that the plane of polarization of a beam of light is rotated as the light travels along the lines of force in a magnetic field. Thirty years later the Scottish physicist John Kerr produced double refraction of light in glass by applying a strong electric field. In these two experiments the application of either an intense magnetic field or an intense electric field slightly changes the refractive index of the material, that is, the ratio of the velocity of light in a vacuum to the velocity of light in the material. In the Faraday experiment a beam of plane-polarized light acts as if it were composed of two circularly polarized beams rotating in opposite directions. The application of the magnetic field makes the index of refraction of the glass for one of the beams different from that for the other.

The Faraday and Kerr effects, as well as later experiments, suggest that by virtue of its own electric and magnetic field, light of sufficient intensity can change the refractive index of the medium supporting it, affecting its own propagation and that of other light beams present. It is evident that alterations in the refractive index, if produced, will have a periodicity, or frequency, equal to the optical frequency of the light beam that has created them. This implies that if a second beam of light of a different frequency is simultaneously present, its

velocity will be altered periodically by the high-frequency changes in refractive index produced by the first beam. As a result of this interaction one light beam should be able to modulate another, producing sum and difference frequencies.

In the language of the quantum theory of radiation, according to which light propagates in discrete bundles called photons, these processes represent interactions of photons. For example, two photons can be annihilated to produce a new photon embodying the energy of the two that disappeared. Since the frequency of a photon is proportional to its energy, the new photon will exhibit the sum frequency of the two annihilated photons. Other interactions of light beams can be regarded as the collision and scattering of pairs of photons.

Such "nonlinear" interactions have not been observed in experiments with ordinary light sources because the electric and magnetic fields associated with these sources are too small. The electric field of sunlight at the surface of the earth has an amplitude of about 10 volts per centimeter, enough to change the refractive index of glass in the Kerr effect by only about one part in 10^{15}. The magnetic field of sunlight is about a thirtieth of a gauss, less than a tenth of the strength of the earth's magnetic field and enough to change the refractive index of glass in the Faraday effect by only one part in 10^{12}. Although brighter sources such as the carbon-arc lamp and high-pressure discharge lamps have been available, their broad emission spectra, like that of the sun, make the search for nonlinear effects difficult. For the effects to be readily observable a great deal of energy must be concentrated in a narrow band of wavelengths, the narrower the better. Without such mon-

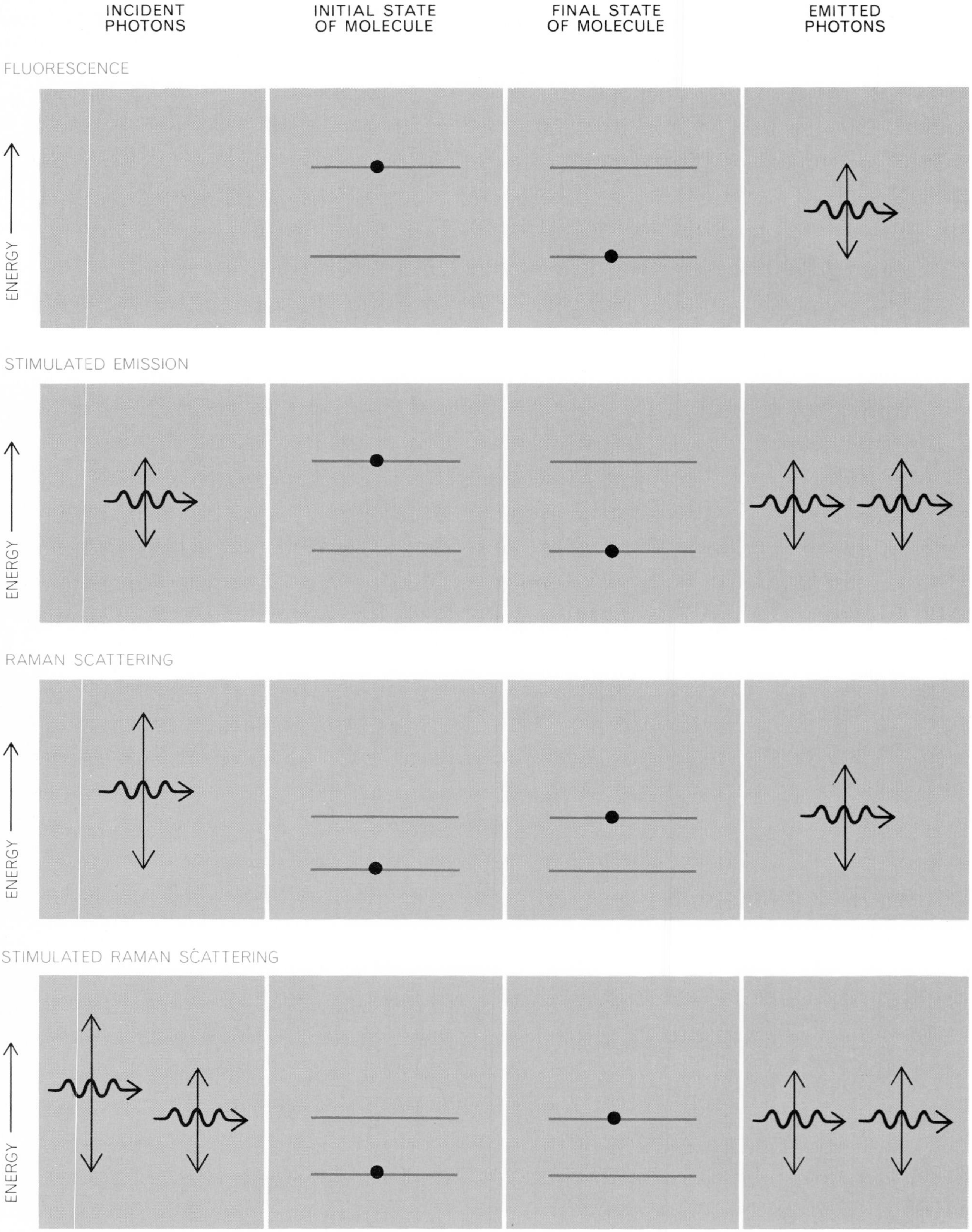

| | INCIDENT PHOTONS | INITIAL STATE OF MOLECULE | FINAL STATE OF MOLECULE | EMITTED PHOTONS |

FLUORESCENCE

STIMULATED EMISSION

RAMAN SCATTERING

STIMULATED RAMAN SCATTERING

ENERGY

RADIATION PROCESSES involve transitions between two excited states of a molecule or atom. In fluorescence a photon is spontaneously emitted with energy equivalent to that lost by the molecule. In stimulated emission a photon with exactly the excitation energy of the molecule stimulates it to emit another photon of like energy. In the presence of many excited molecules a chain reaction, or laser action, can occur. In Raman scattering a molecule that is in a de-excited state absorbs a photon of arbitrary energy and re-emits it after subtracting the energy needed for excitation. In stimulated Raman scattering the production of a scattered photon is stimulated by the presence of a photon of exactly the same energy. Consequently a chain reaction can occur.

ochromatic and coherent radiation there is no opportunity for the waves to interact with matter or with each other in an orderly way.

With the development of the laser in 1960, physicists finally obtained a light source that seemed capable of producing nonlinear optical effects. Its output was concentrated in a narrow band of frequencies and its waves were highly coherent [see "Optical Masers," by Arthur L. Schawlow, beginning on page 224 in this book]. In the summer of 1961 a search for nonlinear effects was undertaken by Peter A. Franken, Allen E. Hill, C. W. Peters and Gabriel Weinreich of the University of Michigan. They focused onto a quartz crystal the beam of a ruby laser that emitted a three-kilowatt pulse of red light at a wavelength of 6,943 angstrom units. Of the light striking the crystal one part in 10^8 was converted to second-harmonic light with a wavelength of 3,471.5 angstroms; this wavelength, which lies in the ultraviolet region of the spectrum, is exactly half the wavelength and therefore twice the frequency of the laser light [see illustrations on next page]. The possibility that the emitted light might be some kind of ultraviolet fluorescence induced by the laser beam could be ruled out because its wavelength was precisely half the laser wavelength and because it was emitted in as highly directional a beam as the incident laser beam.

Many related experiments and some

"SECOND HARMONIC" ULTRAVIOLET LIGHT is generated when red light from a ruby laser passes through a crystal of potassium dihydrogen phosphate (KDP). The laser beam, which has a wavelength of 6,943 angstrom units, originates at the right off the edge of the photograph. The blocklike assembly at the right houses a rotating partially reflecting mirror that is part of the laser mechanism. A fully reflecting mirror at the other end of the laser's optical path is fixed. Laser action does not occur until the rotating mirror and the fixed mirror are parallel. If this alignment is postponed until the population of excited atoms in the ruby laser rod has reached a peak, laser action is intensified. Between the rotating mirror and the triangular crystal of KDP there is a diaphragm and red filter to exclude stray light. Inside the crystal about .1 per cent of the laser beam is converted to ultraviolet light of 3,471.5 angstroms, which is exactly half the wavelength of the incident light. The unconverted red light is removed by a deep blue filter mounted to the left of the crystal. The second-harmonic ultraviolet light, here barely visible, creates a bright flash when it strikes the fluorescent screen at far left. The experiment was photographed in the author's laboratory.

FIRST DEMONSTRATION that ultraviolet light could be generated by the intense flash of a ruby laser was made with this experimental arrangement in 1961 at the University of Michigan. The investigators were Peter A. Franken, Allen E. Hill, C. W. Peters and Gabriel Weinreich. The quartz crystal converted only a hundred-millionth of the incident light to ultraviolet light. On being passed through a prism the ultraviolet is bent more than the red laser light and the two can be photographed separately (*see below*).

3,471.5   6,943

FIRST PHOTOGRAPHS of second-harmonic ultraviolet light were made by Franken and his associates. In each case the amount of ultraviolet (*small spots at 3,471.5 angstroms*) is roughly proportional to the square of the amount of red light at 6,943 angstroms.

unexpected developments quickly followed. Up to 20 per cent efficiency has been obtained in converting laser light to harmonic frequencies. By means of nonlinear processes coherent light has been made available at hundreds of new wavelengths in the ultraviolet, visible and infrared regions of the spectrum. The nonlinear optical effects show themselves in a variety of striking ways and represent a new branch of optics of considerable technological promise.

To understand how harmonic light was generated in the experiment of the Franken group it is necessary to understand how the electric field of the laser light wave acted on electrons in the crystal of quartz. A free atom consists of a positively charged nucleus surrounded by a cloud of one or more electrons; when there are several electrons, they form a series of discrete shells. The electrons in the outermost shell are loosely bound and are called valence electrons. When one atom is close to another, as it is in a crystal, the valence electrons are available to be shared by, or transferred to, other atoms. The result of this process is to fill completely the outer shells of adjacent atoms, which are thereby bound together. Some crystals, such as sodium chloride, are termed ionic because electrons are transferred from atoms that have one or a few electrons in excess of a complete shell to atoms whose outer shells lack electrons. Both the lenders and the borrowers of electrons are left with a net electric charge, either positive or negative. These ions arrange themselves regularly in a lattice in such a way that oppositely charged ions are as close together as possible. Other kinds of crystals, such as diamond, are called covalent because the outermost electrons are shared among atoms to provide each with a filled outer shell. In both ionic and covalent crystals the over-all crystal is electrically neutral.

Let us see what happens when visible light waves pass through a transparent crystal. One component of the light wave is an alternating electric field. The nuclei of atoms are too heavy to respond to this rapidly alternating field, and the inner electrons are too tightly bound to the nuclei to respond significantly. The weakly bound valence electrons, however, redistribute themselves in step with the field [see upper illustration on this page]. Their redistribution involves a polarization, or a displacement of negative charge, inside the crystal. This polarization induced by light is not to be confused with the polarization that can be induced in a light beam by the use of a polarizing filter. The periodically changing polarization inside the crystal corresponds to an oscillating motion of the negative charge density and therefore to a weak alternating current at the light frequency.

As long as the optical electric field is small compared with the cohesive electric fields within the crystal, the polarization current faithfully follows the electric field of the light wave [see upper illustration on next page]. The crystal now behaves like a highly directional antenna, supporting a wave of current that travels through the crystal precisely in step with its parent light wave and radiating primarily in the same direction. The energy in the light wave is not significantly changed; the only effect of the polarization and subsequent reradiation is to slow down the velocity of light in the medium.

The situation is quite different for intense light. The focused light from certain lasers has an electric field as strong as 10 million (10^7) volts per centimeter. Such strong fields are comparable to the cohesive local electric fields in the crystal, which are of the order of 10^8 to 10^{10} volts per centimeter. Consequently when intense laser beams enter a transparent crystal, they cause a massive redistribution of the electrons and the resulting polarization is no longer proportional to the optical electric field. In fact, at optical fields of 10^7 volts per centimeter and higher many materials break down completely.

The simplified diagram at the bottom of this page illustrates the characteristic response when an intense optical electric field travels through a nonlinear, or ionic, material. It shows that an intense field in the "right" direction is more effective in polarizing the material than a field in the "left" direction. Such a situation can occur only in a crystal that has a "one-wayness" in its structure, or, to be more precise, one that has no center of symmetry. Of the crystals found in nature only about 10 per cent fall in this class, and they usually exhibit the phenomenon called piezoelectricity. When a piezoelectric crystal is subjected to mechanical pressure, its asymmetry leads to unequal distortions in the distribution of positive and negative charge and a voltage appears across the faces of the crystal.

The distorted polarization wave produced by an intense laser beam travels at the same velocity as the light wave. It can be shown, moreover, that the dis-

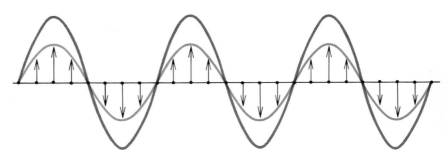

LINEAR POLARIZATION WAVE (color) is created when a light wave of moderate intensity passes through a transparent medium. The light wave carries an optical electric field (black curve), which causes a symmetrical displacement of loosely bound electrons (black arrows). The displacement takes place in step with the optical electric field and forms an optical polarization wave. The wave radiates a light wave of its own frequency.

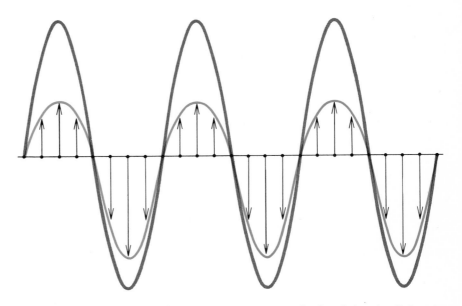

NONLINEAR POLARIZATION WAVE (color) is created when light of sufficient intensity passes through certain crystals with a "one-wayness" in their structure. Loosely bound electrons are moved more easily to one side than to the other by the light's optical electric field (black curve). The result is a distorted polarization wave that gives rise to light containing a second harmonic, or overtone, of the fundamental wave frequency.

torted wave is the sum of three components: a wave at the fundamental frequency (*f*) of the light wave, a wave at the second-harmonic frequency (2*f*) and a third component that corresponds to a "direct current," or steady, polarization [*see illustration on the next page*].

The second-harmonic polarization wave travels in step with the fundamental, or *f*, light wave and radiates light at frequency 2*f* in the same direction. In almost all materials, however, the velocity of 2*f* light is slower by a few per cent than the velocity of *f* light. This is another way of saying that a material's refractive index for high-frequency light is usually greater than it is for light of lower frequency. It is this variation in refractive index that creates a spectrum when white light is passed through a prism. The variation in refractive index with wavelength is called normal dispersion.

The difference in velocity between fundamental (*f*) light and harmonic (2*f*) light means that the harmonic light radiated from the 2*f* polarization wave will travel at a velocity a few per cent slower than the 2*f* polarization wave itself. It is evident that the light radiated by the 2*f* polarization wave at any instant will be slightly out of step with the light it radiated a fraction of a second earlier; the two radiated waves will begin to interfere destructively [*see top illustration on page 298*]. The distance required for the 2*f* polarization wave and its radiated light to get completely out of phase is called the coherence length; it is only about a thousandth of a centimeter. If the crystal thickness is made equal to the coherence length, or any even multiple of it, the harmonic radiation disappears completely. As a result of the interference it is usually impossible to make use of crystals longer than about a thousandth of a centimeter in generating harmonics.

A number of techniques have been proposed to overcome this difficulty in practical experiments. The one most commonly used exploits the double refraction exhibited by certain crystals. The technique was developed independently by Paul D. Maker, Robert W. Terhune, Martin Nisenoff and Carleton

M. Savage of the Scientific Laboratory of the Ford Motor Company and by the author at the Bell Telephone Laboratories.

Certain asymmetric crystals such as calcite are doubly refracting because in them light can travel at two different velocities, described as ordinary and extraordinary. These velocities actually vary with propagation direction and polarization as well as with wavelength. Ordinary and extraordinary velocities in potassium dihydrogen phosphate (KDP), a piezoelectric crystal commonly used for harmonic generation, are illustrated in the middle diagram on page 298. The diagram shows that at an angle of 50 degrees to the optic axis of the crystal, ordinary fundamental light at 6,943 angstroms travels at exactly the same velocity as extraordinary harmonic light at 3,471.5 angstroms. When this direction is used for harmonic generation, the retardation of the ultraviolet harmonic light due to dispersion is precisely compensated by the higher velocity of extraordinary light at the harmonic wavelength.

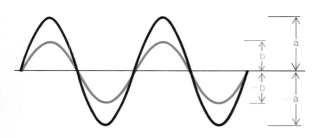

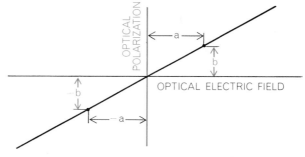

WHEN CRYSTAL RESPONSE IS LINEAR, the optical polarization wave (*color*) is directly proportional to the optical electric field (*black*). When values of the wave and field are plotted against each other, as shown at right, the result is a straight line.

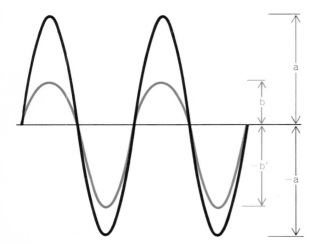

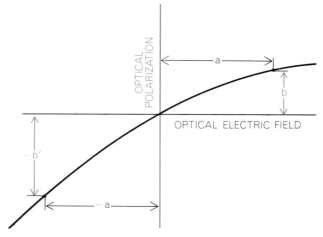

WHEN CRYSTAL RESPONSE IS NONLINEAR, the optical polarization wave (*color*) is no longer proportional to the optical electric field (*black*). When values of the wave and field are plotted against each other (*right*), the resulting curve is nonlinear.

This technique has made possible an increase in coherence length from a thousandth of a centimeter to more than a centimeter and has led to a million-fold increase in conversion efficiency. In KDP a 20 per cent conversion efficiency from red to ultraviolet has been observed by Maker, Terhune and Savage with a million-watt pulsed laser. Arthur Ashkin, Gary D. Boyd and Joseph M. Dziedzic of the Bell Laboratories, also using KDP, have observed harmonics from a continuously operating gas laser at power levels as low as 50 millionths of a watt.

A second method of avoiding the interference problem has been developed by Robert C. Miller of the Bell Laboratories and is applicable in ferroelectric crystals such as barium titanate. Ferroelectric crystals can be obtained in the form of a multilayered sandwich in which the layers are regions, called domains, that have different properties. In barium titanate adjoining domains are completely equivalent except that one is inverted with respect to the other. The phase of the harmonics generated in successive domains is reversed, with the result that the interference effect is partially offset and harmonic generation greatly enhanced. Franken, Hill and Peters have observed similar enhancement with stacked quartz plates that have axes pointing in alternate directions.

Franken and his associates have also detected the "direct current" polarization mentioned earlier as the third component of the distorted polarization wave that can be produced by intense laser beams. The direct-current signal can be detected simply by connecting plates to opposite surfaces of a piezoelectric crystal that is transmitting the light output from a laser. The direct-current signal appears as a voltage pulse proportional to the laser intensity. The crystal action in this experiment is analogous to that of a vacuum-tube (or crystal) diode in rectifying, or "detecting," a radio signal. Detailed theories of all the above processes, as well as others, have been presented by Nicolaas Bloembergen, Peter S. Pershan, John A. Armstrong and J. Ducuing of Harvard University and also by David A. Kleinman of the Bell Laboratories.

Included in these new theories is an analysis of the interaction that takes place when two light beams of different frequencies are sent through a transparent medium in different directions. When intense monochromatic beams are used, they "beat" together to produce new frequencies that correspond to the

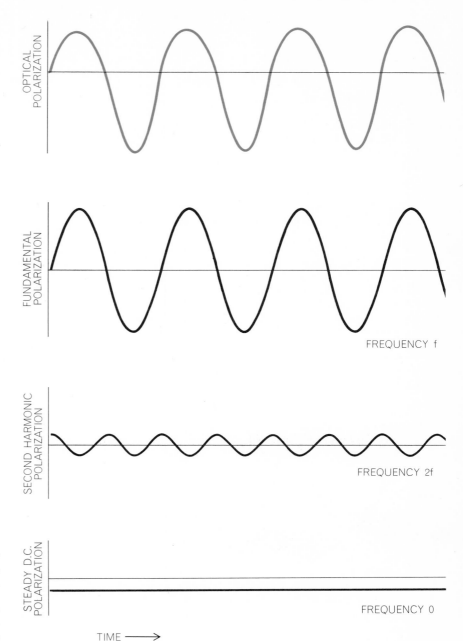

ANALYSIS OF NONLINEAR POLARIZATION WAVE (top) shows it to be the sum of three components: a wave at the fundamental frequency (f) of the light wave that created it, a wave at the second-harmonic frequency (2f) and a component that corresponds to a steady polarization (bottom). The first and second of these components radiate their own light waves at frequencies of f and 2f respectively. In almost all materials the velocity of 2f light is a little slower than that of f light, with result shown at top of page 298.

sum and difference frequencies of the primary beams. This phenomenon has been observed in independent experiments by Franken and his colleagues, by A. W. Smith and Norman Braslau of the International Business Machines Research Center, by Miller and Albert Savage, as well as by the author. A novel feature of the Smith-Braslau experiment is that one light source was the 5,461-angstrom green line of a standard

mercury-arc lamp. Its beats with the red ruby laser (6,943 angstroms) occur in the ultraviolet at 3,056 angstroms. If these wavelengths are expressed as frequencies, it is apparent that the first two add to produce the third.

How this addition of frequencies comes about is illustrated at the top of page 299. The diagram shows the superposition of two light waves of different frequencies and wavelengths. The super-

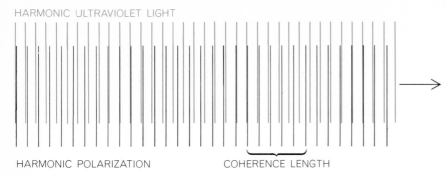

HARMONIC ULTRAVIOLET LIGHT

HARMONIC POLARIZATION   COHERENCE LENGTH

DESTRUCTIVE WAVE INTERFERENCE occurs in a crystal because the polarization wave (*black*) normally travels a little faster than its harmonic radiation (*color*). The polarization and its radiation get completely out of step in a distance called the coherence length.

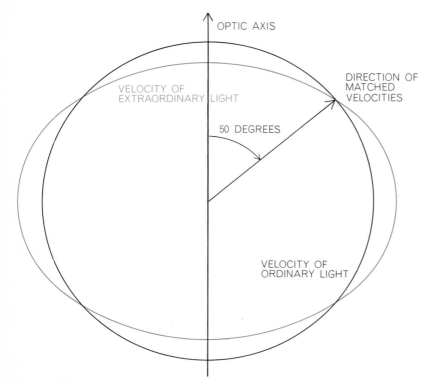

OPTIC AXIS

VELOCITY OF
EXTRAORDINARY LIGHT

DIRECTION OF
MATCHED
VELOCITIES

50 DEGREES

VELOCITY OF
ORDINARY LIGHT

INTERFERENCE CAN BE OVERCOME by generating harmonic light in a crystal that exhibits double refraction such as KDP. The black circle represents the velocity of ruby laser light of 6,943 angstroms polarized perpendicularly to the page. The colored oval represents the velocity of second-harmonic light of 3,471.5 angstroms polarized in the plane of the page. At 50 degrees to the optic axis both waves travel at the same velocity.

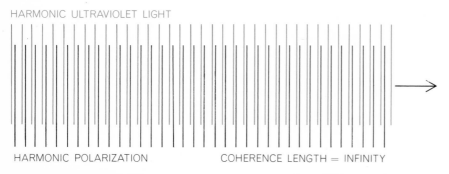

HARMONIC ULTRAVIOLET LIGHT

HARMONIC POLARIZATION   COHERENCE LENGTH = INFINITY

ELIMINATION OF WAVE INTERFERENCE is achieved by sending a ruby laser beam into a crystal of KDP at 50 degrees to the optic axis. Now the harmonic polarization wave (*black*) and the harmonic ultraviolet light it radiates (*color*) stay in step indefinitely.

position produces a moiré pattern in which the crossover points identify regions of maximum electric field strength. The two sets of moiré lines drawn through these regions of maximum electric field identify the crests of two new nonlinear polarization waves that propagate through the medium. It can be seen in the geometry of the moiré pattern that one of the new waves has a frequency equal to the sum of the frequencies of the two primary waves. The other new wave has a frequency equal to the difference in frequency between the primary waves.

The illustration also identifies a quantity called the propagation vector and designated K. The K vector of any wave points in the direction of the wave motion and has a length proportional to the reciprocal of the wavelength (that is, 1 divided by the wavelength). Just as one of the new polarization waves has a frequency equal to the sum of component frequencies, so too it has a K vector equal to the sum of component K vectors. The other polarization wave has a K vector equal to the difference between component K vectors.

In the quantum theory of radiation the frequency of a light wave is proportional to the energy of a photon and the propagation vector K is proportional to its momentum. When two photons interact, both energy and momentum must be conserved. In the case where two beating waves interact to produce a wave whose frequency is the sum of the frequencies of the primary waves, the conservation is straightforward: the sum-frequency photon appears with the combined energy and momentum of the two primary photons that have been annihilated.

In the case where two beating waves interact to produce a wave whose frequency is the difference between the frequencies of the primary waves, energy and momentum have to be conserved in a rather curious way. Let us say that the two primary photons have frequencies of f_1 and f_2 and that the difference photon has a frequency f_3 equal to f_1 minus f_2. In the interaction of f_1 and f_2 only the f_1 photon is annihilated. In its place appear another f_2 and an f_3 photon. In being transformed into an f_2 photon the f_1 photon gives up enough energy to create an f_3 photon. In other words, it can be predicted that such an interaction will yield as many new photons of f_2 light as of f_3 light. Because a great deal of primary f_2 light is needed to make the interaction take place, it will be quite difficult to observe the small amount of additional f_2 light produced.

All the experiments described so far make use of the asymmetric properties of piezoelectric crystals to produce nonlinear optical effects. It is appropriate to ask if such effects can also be obtained with ordinary symmetrical crystals and isotropic materials such as glass and liquids. The answer is yes. As one might expect, all materials become nonlinear in the presence of sufficiently intense fields, but the effects are much weaker than those found in asymmetric materials.

Because symmetrical materials lack an intrinsic one-wayness, the polarization wave produced by an intense light beam is not skewed left or right as it is in asymmetric materials. Instead the electronic charges in the material are displaced equally to the left and to the right. The nonlinearity arises from the fact that the displacement can no longer follow in exact proportion as the electric field rises to peak intensity. When this sort of distorted polarization wave is analyzed into its components, it is found to consist mainly of a pure wave of the fundamental frequency and a weak third-harmonic wave. The third harmonic of ruby laser light (6,943 angstroms) occurs in the far ultraviolet at 2,314 angstroms. It has been produced in calcite by Terhune of the Ford Laboratory; the conversion efficiency was three parts per million.

In the intense electric fields of laser light not only the transmission of light but also its reflection and refraction begin to depart from the classical rules of optics. Bloembergen and Pershan have shown that the laws of reflection and refraction must be generalized to include harmonic generation at surfaces. Ducuing and Bloembergen have observed harmonic generation of light on reflection from piezoelectric crystals such as tellurium that are opaque at both the fundamental and second-harmonic frequencies.

At high intensities the absorption of light also exhibits new features. In 1961 W. Kaiser and C. G. B. Garrett of the Bell Telephone Laboratories showed that intense laser light is absorbed in transparent materials that normally absorb light only at twice the laser frequency. In this process two photons are absorbed simultaneously, leaving an atom in the excited state that would be produced by absorption of a single photon of twice the frequency. (The process

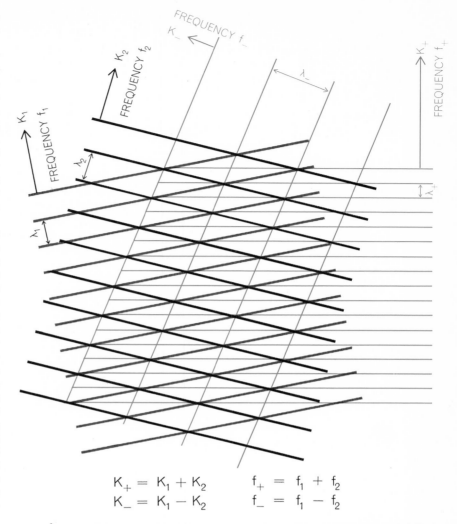

$$K_+ = K_1 + K_2 \qquad f_+ = f_1 + f_2$$
$$K_- = K_1 - K_2 \qquad f_- = f_1 - f_2$$

MOIRÉ PATTERNS are produced by the interaction of two light waves of different frequencies. Their frequencies and wavelengths are labeled f_1 and f_2 and λ_1 and λ_2 respectively. Their propagation vectors designated K_1 and K_2 point in the direction of the wave motion and have a length proportional to the reciprocal of the wavelength. The points where the wave fronts intersect identify regions of maximum electric field strength. Moiré lines drawn through these maxima identify the crests of two new nonlinear polarization waves that radiate light. One wave radiates light of frequency f_+, which is the sum of f_1 and f_2. The other wave radiates light of frequency f_-, which is the difference between f_1 and f_2. New K vectors, K_+ and K_-, are likewise produced by sum and difference.

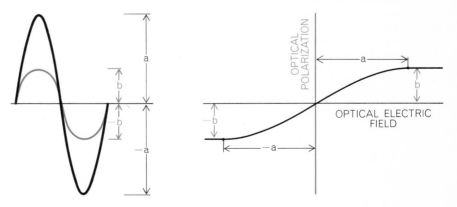

NONLINEAR POLARIZATION WAVE (*color*) can be created in liquids and symmetrical solids as well as in asymmetric crystals. Polarization wave is plotted against optical electric field (*black*) at right. Components of polarization wave appear at top of next page.

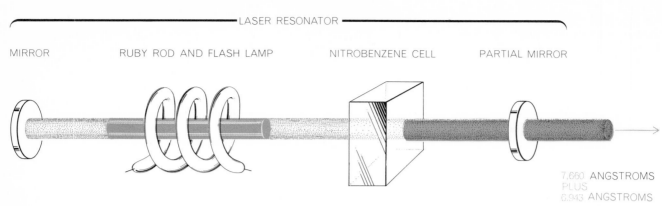

RAMAN LASER ACTION is an enhanced form of the effect first observed in 1927 by the Indian physicist C. V. Raman. In this effect a photon of light is absorbed by a molecule and re-emitted at a lower frequency. In the diagram laser photons of 6,943 angstroms are reflected back and forth through nitrobenzene. After losing energy to nitrobenzene a portion of the beam emerges at 7,660 angstroms. Raman laser action was discovered in 1962 by Eric J. Woodbury and Won K. Ng of the Hughes Aircraft Company.

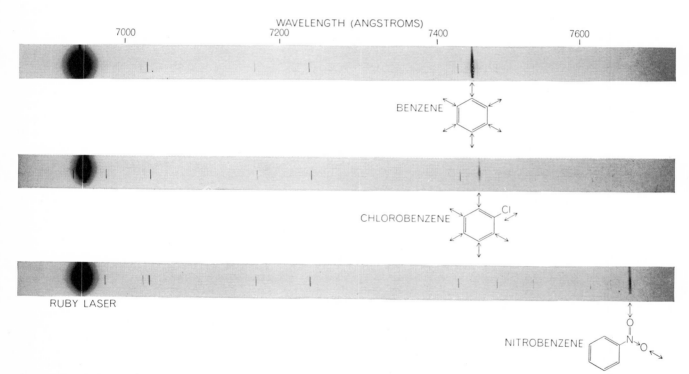

STIMULATED RAMAN SPECTRA are shown for three similar molecules. Each molecule tends to vibrate in only one or two of its strongest modes. The many narrow, short lines are produced by materials used for calibration. The Raman emission of the upper two molecules represents the synchronous vibration of the entire benzene ring. The vibration in the bottom spectrum is characteristic of the nitro (NO_2) group attached to the benzene ring. The spectra were photographed by John A. Howe and the author.

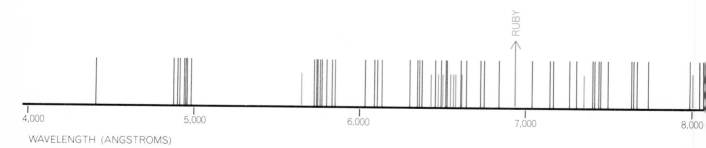

OVER 100 COHERENT LIGHT SOURCES have now been produced by Raman laser action in various materials. The black lines identify wavelengths created by using pulses from ruby lasers; the colored lines are wavelengths available from neodym-

was predicted theoretically in 1931 by Maria Goeppert Mayer, who last year won a Nobel prize for her work on the structure of the atomic nucleus.) John A. Howe and the author have found that many normally transparent materials become opaque to intense laser light as a result of nonlinear processes. Recent work by John J. Hopfield, John M. Worlock and Kwangjai Park of the University of California at Berkeley has shown that the two-photon absorption process can provide information about excited states in solids not obtainable from ordinary spectroscopy.

One of the more interesting potential applications of the laser is its use as a source of "pump" light to generate far-infrared radiation. The far-infrared region, which holds great interest for spectroscopists, has been largely inaccessible for lack of tunable strong infrared sources. Proposals for using lasers together with nonlinear processes to remedy this shortcoming have been outlined by Robert H. Kingston of the Lincoln Laboratory of the Massachusetts Institute of Technology, Norman M. Kroll of the University of California at San Diego and Bloembergen.

The principle they propose involves the "parametric" process diagrammed at bottom left, which shows how a voltage wave can be amplified in an apparatus that contains condenser plates. If the plates are pulled apart slightly at each voltage peak against the electric forces tending to pull them together and are returned to their original position at the times of zero voltage when the electric forces are absent, the mechanical work done goes into amplifying the voltage wave. In a device that uses laser light for pumping, some dielectric material would be substituted for the condenser plates. A periodic change in the dielectric constant would serve the same function as moving the plates.

Notice that if the plates are pulled apart at frequency f, the voltage wave being amplified has the subharmonic frequency $f/2$. More significantly, it is possible to pump at frequency f and amplify any two lower frequencies f_1 and f_2 whose sum is equal to f. Several laboratories are now trying to develop a pumping device that will produce useful quantities of coherent infrared light at suitable pairs of infrared frequencies using a laser as a pump.

A laser-driven process that is already being put to practical use in spectroscopy is stimulated Raman emission, which was discovered two years ago by Eric J. Woodbury and Won K. Ng of the Hughes Aircraft Company. In the course of precise measurements of the light emitted from a million-watt pulsed ruby laser it was observed that about 10 per cent of the expected light at 6,943 angstroms seemed to be missing. The missing light was soon found to be emerging as a coherent beam at a new wavelength: 7,660 angstroms in the infrared region [see top illustration on opposite page].

The new emission occurs at a frequency differing from the laser frequency by 4×10^{13} cycles per second. This difference was subsequently identified as the frequency of a characteristic vibration of the nitrobenzene molecule by Woodbury in collaboration with another group at Hughes Aircraft (Gisela M. Eckhardt, Robert W. Hellwarth, Frederick J. McClung, Jr., Steven E. Schwarz and Daniel Weiner). Woodbury had just happened to use a laser arrangement that included a cell of nitrobenzene as an optical component. Although Raman laser emission had been predicted a few years earlier by Ali Javan, now at the Massachusetts Institute of Technology, its discovery was a happy accident.

In the Raman effect a photon of incident light is absorbed by a molecule and re-emitted at a lower frequency. The energy removed from the light beam appears as mechanical energy of vibration or rotation of the molecule. The striking new feature of the Woodbury-Raman effect is that if enough photons are emitted in the ordinary Raman effect and if they are prevented from escaping too quickly (by being reflected back and forth inside a resonator), they begin to stimulate further Raman emission [see bottom diagram, page 292]. This stimulation is similar to the process by which light is amplified in a laser, except that prior excitation of the molecules is unnecessary. In the chain reaction that follows, a large fraction of the incident laser light is converted into Raman light of lower frequency. With the Woodbury-Raman effect it is possible to photograph a Raman spectrum in a single burst of laser light lasting a ten-millionth of a second; by conventional techniques the exposure would require from a minute to an hour.

It has recently been discovered that when intense laser pulses are focused in solids, liquids and high-pressure gases, the stimulated Raman process can occur even without a resonator cavity. These advances have been made by Terhune, Robert W. Minck and William G. Rado of the Ford Laboratory and by Gisela Eckhardt, David P. Bortfeld and Myer Geller of Hughes Aircraft. Near the focus, where the light intensity can exceed one billion watts per square centimeter, the amplification of Raman light is as high as 10^{50} per centimeter, enough to amplify stray background light up to the 100,000-watt level in one pass through the focus.

A new feature of the focused-light experiments is that the molecular vibrations stimulated by the Raman effect become so violent that the refractive index of the material oscillates strongly at the molecular-vibration frequency. Light passing through the focus acquires a modulation at this frequency. As a result the characteristic vibration frequency of the molecule is not simply

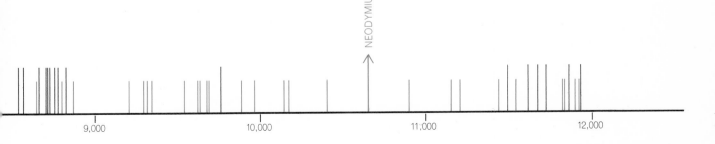

ium lasers. By interacting these sources in nonlinear crystals of the KDP type one can obtain, by sum and difference combinations, more than 5,000 light sources of distinctively different wavelengths. Ultimately they should be useful in spectroscopic investigations.

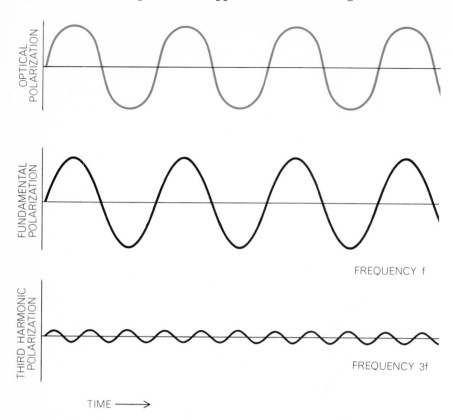

OPTICAL POLARIZATION

FUNDAMENTAL POLARIZATION

FREQUENCY f

THIRD HARMONIC POLARIZATION

FREQUENCY 3f

TIME ⟶

ANALYSIS OF DISTORTED WAVE (*top*) **created by intense light in a symmetrical medium shows that it can be broken down into two components: a pure wave at the fundamental frequency** (*f*) **and a low-amplitude wave at the third-harmonic frequency** (*3f*).

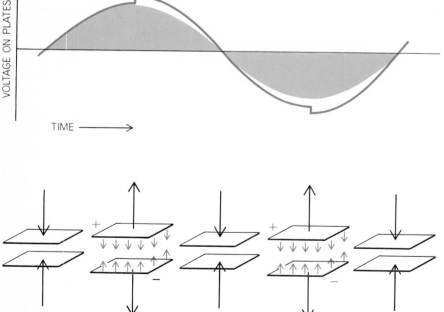

VOLTAGE ON PLATES

TIME ⟶

"PARAMETRIC" AMPLIFIER PRINCIPLE suggests a way in which visible laser light could be used to produce coherent infrared radiation. The diagram demonstrates the principle with capacitor plates, which are mechanically pushed apart (*black arrows*) **when an alternating voltage applied to the plates is at a peak. Such peaks coincide with the maximum electric force** (*colored arrows*) **acting to pull the plates together. The plates are moved together when the voltage and electric force are zero. The motion of the capacitor plates at frequency *f* amplifies the electric signal at a frequency of half *f*.**

subtracted from the laser frequency but is added to it as well. These shifted frequencies, called upper and lower side bands, are emitted in sharply defined directions determined by the conservation of momentum condition described earlier. The large variety of substances showing the Raman effect provide hundreds of new coherent sources of light from the ultraviolet through the infrared [*see bottom illustration on these two pages*].

Charles H. Townes and his associates at the Massachusetts Institute of Technology have predicted further that in an intense light beam a Raman-like process should also lead to the generation of intense waves of high-frequency sound. In this process the energy lost by a photon of light should reappear as a quantum of sound.

All the effects described so far involve the interaction of light with light in a material medium. It has been recognized for some time, however, that interactions of intense light beams should occur even in a vacuum. From the viewpoint of quantum electrodynamics a vacuum is a polarizable medium with a refractive index slightly different from 1. Gamma ray photons can interact in a vacuum to create electron-positron pairs, if the photons have sufficient energy to make up the rest mass of the created particles (about a million electron volts). Although optical photons, which have energies of only one to three electron volts, lack the energy to produce electron-positron pairs, two optical photons can interact to form what is called a virtual pair. Such a pair can be observed only indirectly when they annihilate to yield two new photons with the same total energy as the original photons, which can go off in directions different from either of the colliding photons. This rather unlikely type of scattering occurs as if the refractive index of the vacuum underwent small changes in response to the presence of intense electric and magnetic fields carried by light. Estimates show, however, that this scattering would be impossibly difficult to observe with existing lasers.

The nonlinear optical experiments that have been performed to date have suggested a variety of new optical techniques that would be of use in spectroscopy. Beyond that, together with the laser they bring closer the time when the entire electromagnetic spectrum will be manipulated with the precision and usefulness of modern electronic and radio techniques.

27

Photon Echoes

Sven R. Hartmann   April 1968

For the past few years my colleagues and I at Columbia University have been investigating a curious optical phenomenon called the photon echo. Our basic experimental technique is quite simple. When we illuminate a ruby crystal with two short bursts of coherent light from a ruby laser, we sometimes observe not two but three equally spaced light pulses emerging from the other end of the crystal! The first two output pulses are simply the original laser pulses transmitted through the crystal. The third pulse, on the other hand, is spontaneously emitted by the crystal as a delayed by-product of the passage of the first two pulses. It is this third light pulse that we refer to as the photon echo. (In quantum theory the photon is the quantum, or energy unit, of light.)

The photon-echo experiment is one of a large class of echo experiments in which the excitation of a system by two energy pulses separated by a certain time interval (*t*) leads to the spontaneous emission of a third energy pulse *t* seconds after the second excitation pulse. The effect of the first pulse is to induce a macroscopic excitation in the irradiated system that is quickly (but only apparently) dissipated. The second pulse, *t* seconds later, modifies the state of the excited system in such a way that its previous excitation experience is in effect "recalled." When the time elapsed after the transmission of the second excitation pulse is equal to the time separation of the two excitation pulses, the macroscopic excitation induced by the first pulse is re-formed by the irradiated system and a signal is thereby radiated to the outside world. As a general rule the amplitude, or intensity, of the echo signal decreases as the time interval between the first two pulses is increased.

The detailed behavior of such echo signals yields important information about the relaxation characteristics of a system (that is, the ways in which a system returns to normal after being subjected to a shock). Moreover, the inherent memory represented by the echo has been recognized for some time as being potentially useful as a storage system for a computer.

Although the photon-echo experiment is easy to describe, its explanation is rather subtle and should best follow a short discussion of some of the earlier echo experiments.

The earliest-known echo effect—called the nuclear-spin echo—was discovered in 1950 by E. L. Hahn at the University of Illinois in the course of some nuclear-magnetic-resonance experiments. Hahn found that when he applied two resonant bursts of an oscillating magnetic field to a sample containing a large number of paramagnetic atomic nuclei placed in a large constant magnetic field, the paramagnetic nuclei generated an echo signal. The echo-generating mechanism in this case is comparatively easy to visualize. A paramagnetic nucleus is one that has a magnetic moment parallel to its axis of spin. Such a nucleus behaves rather like a tiny spinning dipole magnet. When a paramagnetic nucleus is placed in a magnetic field, its magnetic moment precesses around the direction of the magnetic field in much the same way that the axis of a spinning top precesses around the direction of the earth's gravitational field. In a crystal lattice, however, the spins of many nuclei interact with one another and with the lattice so that they eventually become polarized with their magnetic moments effectively lined up along the magnetic field. If one now applies a small circularly polarized mag-

netic field that is rotating at the frequency of the precessing nuclei in a plane perpendicular to the constant magnetic field, the nuclei will undergo a complicated motion as they precess around the resultant of the rotating field and the constant field [*see illustration on pages 304 and 305*]. An important characteristic of this motion is that at any instant the angle between the direction of the magnetic moments and the direction of the transverse rotating magnetic field remains the same.

The downward spiral motion executed by each nuclear magnetic moment eventually brings it into the transverse plane, whereupon the rotating magnetic field is turned off. The magnetic-field pulse in this case is called a 90-degree pulse, since the magnetic moment precesses through an angle of 90 degrees around the direction of the transverse rotating field. The magnetic moments of all the nuclei in the sample are now oriented at right angles to the constant magnetic field and are rotating together in the transverse plane at the resonance frequency. As a result the coil that houses the sample will have induced in it an electrical signal, just as a motor generator induces an electric current in its coil.

The induced signal is quickly reduced to zero, however, since there is a spread in the resonance frequencies of the nuclear spins owing to spin-spin interactions and inhomogeneities in the applied magnetic field. As time progresses the individual magnetic moments will precess at different rates and hence fan out in the transverse plane. Since the magnetization of the sample is the vector sum of all the nuclear magnets, it is clear that the net magnetization will soon disappear.

If a second resonant magnetic-field

pulse is now applied with twice the intensity of the first (or with the same intensity but for twice as long as the first), then each magnetic dipole will again precess in a spiral motion around the resultant of the rotating field and the constant field. In this case, however, the pulse is called a 180-degree pulse, since each magnetic moment precesses 180 degrees around the direction of the transverse rotating field. The important feature of the new dipole configuration is that the relative phase angle of any two dipoles is exactly the negative of what it was before the second pulse. Accordingly the dipoles that precess fastest are now last, whereas the ones that precess slowest are now first. It is clear that after a time interval equal to the time it took for the dipole moments to fan out in the first place they will all be precessing together again in the transverse plane. As soon as this macroscopic oscillating dipole moment is reformed, the coil housing the sample will again detect a temporary electrical signal. This signal is the nuclear-spin echo.

The occurrence of a spin echo usually requires that the local magnetic fields at the various lattice sites remain more or less constant during the time the echo is formed, so that the phase "memory" is easily restored. Nuclear-spin echoes have been detected in many solids, liquids and gases, and they are usually characterized by a simple dependence of echo amplitude on pulse-separation time. The decay of the echo yields information regarding spin-spin interactions, which are very difficult to study in any other way.

The preceding analysis for a nuclear-

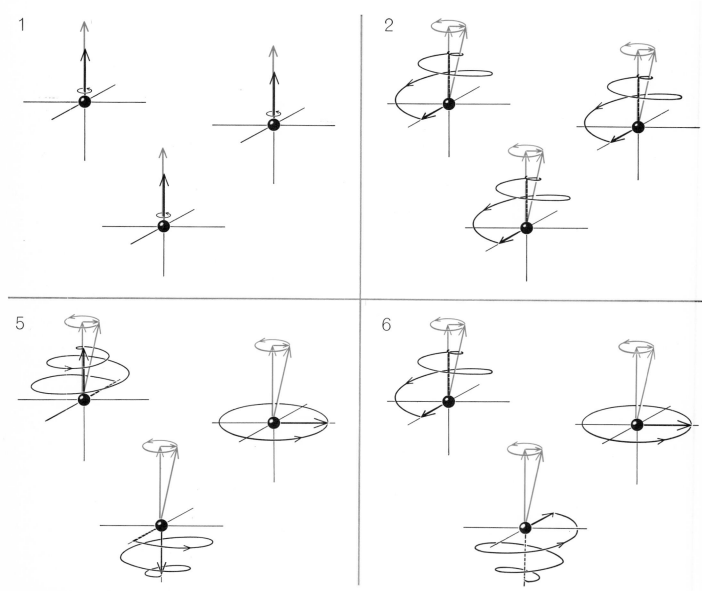

ECHO-GENERATING MECHANISM is demonstrated for the comparatively simple case of the nuclear-spin echo, a phenomenon that is similar in many respects to the photon echo. When a crystal containing a large number of paramagnetic atomic nuclei is placed in a large constant magnetic field (vertical colored arrows), the nuclei ultimately become polarized so that their magnetic moments (heavy black arrows) are all effectively lined up along the magnetic field (1). If one now applies a small circularly polarized magnetic field (horizontal colored arrows) that is rotating at the precession frequency of the nuclei in a plane perpendicular to the constant magnetic field, the nuclei will precess around the resultant of the two magnetic fields (2). The downward spiral motion executed by each nuclear dipole moment eventually (after several hundred turns) brings it into the transverse plane, whereupon the rotating magnetic field is turned off (3). The magnetic moments of all the nuclei in the sample are now oriented at right angles to the constant magnetic field and are rotating together in the transverse plane at the resonant frequency. As a result the coil that houses the

spin echo was made for a particular pulse sequence that had the effect of rotating the magnetic moments through angles of 90 degrees and 180 degrees successively. Almost any other pulse sequence will lead to an echo; the other echoes are weaker, however, and not as easy to explain. Although we have considered only the interaction of the nuclear magnetic moment with an applied magnetic field, the same analysis holds for other nuclear interactions as well.

Electrons also spin and have a magnetic moment; accordingly one can observe electron-spin echoes. The behavior of these echoes is quite striking in that one usually observes large fluctuations in the intensity of the echo as the separation between the excitation pulses is increased. These fluctuations in intensity are caused by the fact that the local magnetic field at each electron site is disturbed by the precessing nuclear magnetic moment of the neighboring atoms. Nonetheless, it is possible to obtain strong electron-spin echoes, since the time variation of the local fields has some regularity to it; by spacing the excitation pulses carefully with respect to the precession period of the neighboring nuclei one can enable the electron spins to recover their "lost" phase.

So far we have considered only echoes produced by easily visualized precessing magnets. If we generalize our results, however, we find that we are dealing with systems that contain a finite number of energy levels capable of being excited by a direct resonant interaction. For example, the simple case of echoes produced by protons in water

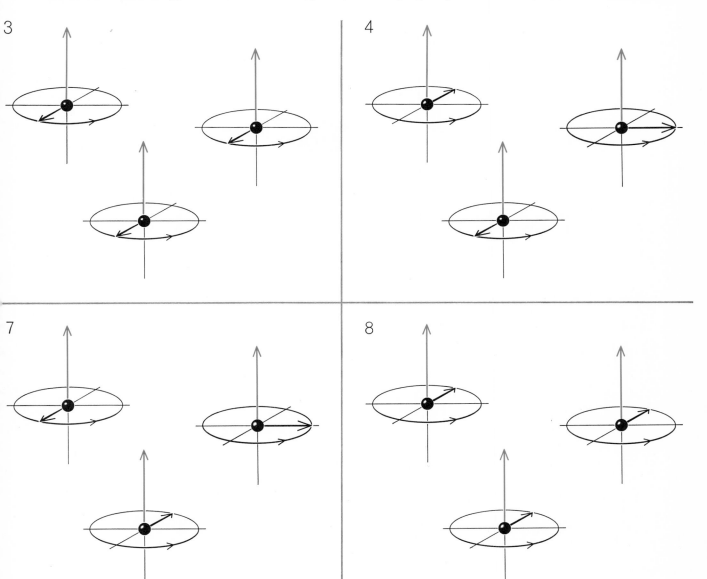

sample will have induced in it an electrical signal. The induced signal is quickly reduced to zero, however, since spin-spin interactions and inhomogeneities in the applied magnetic field will cause the individual magnetic moments to precess at different rates and hence fan out in the transverse plane (4). If a second resonant magnetic-field pulse is now applied for twice as long as the first, then each magnetic moment will precess around the initial direction of the resonant field by an angle of 180 degrees and end up once again in the transverse plane (5, 6). (If a magnetic moment happens to be coincident with the initial direction of the resonant field, it simply continues to rotate in the transverse plane at the resonant frequency.) The important feature of the new dipole configuration is that the relative phase angle of any two dipole moments is exactly the negative of what it was before the second pulse (7). After a time interval equal to the time it took for the dipole moments to fan out in the first place, they will all be precessing together again in the transverse plane (8). The coil housing the sample will again detect a temporary electrical signal representing the nuclear-spin echo.

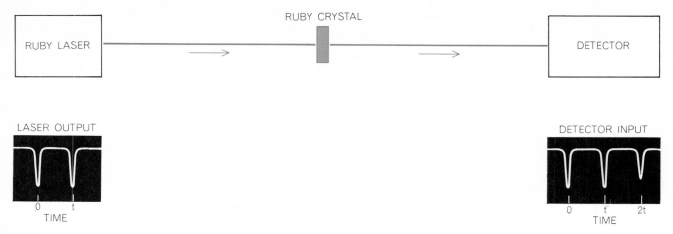

LASER OUTPUT

0   t
TIME

DETECTOR INPUT

0   t   2t
TIME

PRINCIPLE OF PHOTON-ECHO EXPERIMENT is illustrated by this schematic diagram. Two short bursts of coherent light from a ruby laser (*left*) are directed at a ruby crystal (*center*); under the right conditions three light pulses are detected emerging from the other end of the crystal (*right*). The third pulse is the spontaneously emitted photon echo. The stylized oscilloscope traces at bottom show that the time interval between the second excitation pulse and the echo is equal to the interval between the two excitation pulses.

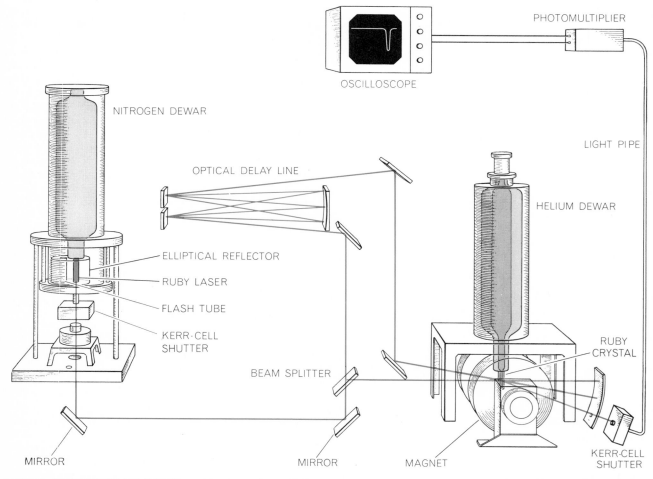

ACTUAL EXPERIMENTAL SETUP used by the author and his colleagues at Columbia University to study the photon echo is depicted here. To ensure against thermal excitations the ruby crystal is cooled to 4.2 degrees Kelvin (degrees centigrade above absolute zero) by suspending it from the base of a Dewar vessel containing liquid helium; the ruby laser is cooled to 77 degrees K. by means of another Dewar vessel containing liquid nitrogen. The ruby laser rod is mounted in an evacuated elliptical cavity at one of the foci; a flash tube at the other focus is used to optically "pump" the ruby rod. A Kerr-cell shutter serves to provide short, intense pulses. Two pulses are obtained by passing the light through a beam splitter, allowing the reflected light to impinge directly on the ruby crystal while diverting the transmitted light into an optical delay line. When the second pulse emerges from the delay line (between 30 and 400 billionths of a second later), it too is directed at the ruby crystal. Because the output pulses are not parallel, the two excitation pulses can be blocked by a screen in order to prevent them from desensitizing the photomultiplier used to detect the echo. The echo pulse passes through a hole in the screen and along a flexible "light pipe"; the detected signal is displayed on an oscilloscope.

can be analyzed in terms of an ensemble of two-level systems, since protons have only two energy states (corresponding to "spin up" and "spin down") that can be coupled by an interaction of the proton's magnetic dipole moment and an external magnetic field. Using the methods of quantum mechanics, one can readily show that in such a situation one should expect to obtain a spin echo.

Another situation that is formally similar to that of a proton in a magnetic field is that of an isolated atom, either in a gas or as an impurity in a crystal lattice. Such atoms are characterized by certain well-defined energy states, and these states can always be coupled by some interaction. An example of such a system is the chromium impurity that makes an aluminum oxide crystal a ruby. When the chromium impurity ions in ruby are excited by circularly polarized light, it is possible to consider the chromium system as an ensemble of two-level systems coupled by an interaction of the electric dipole moments of the ions with the rotating electric-field vector of the circularly polarized light. The transition between the two levels is accomplished by irradiating the chromium ions with resonant light pulses that are capable of exciting only two of the ions' many energy levels, making it possible to neglect the rest. This formal connection between the chromium-atom systems and the nuclear systems leads to the prediction of an echo phenomenon similar to the nuclear-spin echo. The echoes produced by the chromium ions will be light pulses formed by a macroscopic oscillating electric dipole moment without the need for any applied constant field to provide an axis for the dipoles to precess around. The small wavelength of the expected radiation with respect to the size of the sample also suggests a new kind of echo phenomenon.

Our group at Columbia, consisting of Isaac D. Abella, Norman A. Kurnit and myself, began our search for this new echo in 1964. We quickly decided that the experiment should be performed using a ruby laser as a light source and a ruby crystal as the medium in which to form the echo. To ensure against thermal excitations that would relax the echo and prevent us from observing it, we cooled the ruby crystal to 4.2 degrees Kelvin (degrees centigrade above absolute zero) in a bath of liquid helium. The cooling of the ruby crystal to such low temperatures caused us some inconvenience: we then had to cool the laser crystal, since the frequency of the excitation pulse from the ruby laser is temperature-dependent. This dependence arises from the fact that as the temperature increases, thermal excitations shake the chromium atoms in their environment and modify their effective interactions with the neighboring atoms. Fortunately we had to cool the laser crystal only to 77 degrees K., the temperature of liquid nitrogen.

The ruby laser rod was supported from the base of a nitrogen-filled Dewar vessel and was contained in an evacuated elliptical cavity at one of the foci [see bottom illustration on page 306]. At the other focus of the cavity a flash lamp was placed to optically "pump" the ruby rod. In order to obtain short, intense pulses a Kerr-cell shutter was employed to "Q-switch" the ruby; this enabled us to obtain high-energy pulses with a small cross section and a duration of about 15 billionths of a second. Two pulses were obtained by passing the light through a beam splitter, which is nothing more than a thin flat plate that partially reflects and partially transmits light that impinges on it. The reflected light is aimed directly at the ruby crystal, and the transmitted light is diverted into an optical delay line. The optical delay line consists of an arrangement of spherical mirrors that provides a long optical path for the second light pulse so that it emerges delayed by a time equal to the distance traveled divided by the velocity of light. Typical delay times were between 30 and 400 billionths of a second. When the second pulse emerges from the delay line, it is aimed at the same point on the ruby crystal where the first pulse struck.

We wanted the light pulses to be as closely spaced in time as possible to avoid relaxation effects. This caused a problem, because the initial pulses can desensitize the photomultiplier used to detect the echo. That is what happened even when we put a Kerr-cell shutter in front of the photomultiplier to try to block the excitation pulses and allow only the echo through. Here we were fortunate because a calculation showed that, when the light pulses are not parallel, the echo is radiated in a direction different from that of either of the excitation pulses. This effect enables us to use nonparallel light pulses and to block the path of the excitation pulses by placing a screen in front of the photomultiplier, allowing only an opening for the echo to get through.

The calculation that led to this conclusion is quite straightforward, and its essence can be explained simply. The first pulse, whose lines of constant phase lie in parallel planes, stimulates a spatial excitation with a similar plane-wave character. The second pulse, which strikes the crystal from a slightly different angle, superposes its corresponding planes of constant phase on those of the first pulse. The echo will then be propagated in a direction that is perpendicular to the planes in which the rephased dipole moments are in phase. These planes are obtained by requiring that the phase angle of the first excitation pulse vary twice as fast spatially as the phase angle of the second excitation pulse [see illustration on next page].

The experiment described above was performed repeatedly without success until we decided to apply a large magnetic field. All studies of electron-spin relaxation in the "ground" state and the excited states of ruby had been conducted with high magnetic fields, and although extrapolation of these results indicated that for our experiment a magnetic field was not necessary, we decided to play it safe and apply a magnetic field anyway. Because of the crystal structure of ruby there is a direction called the optic axis in which the index of refraction is independent of polarization. It seemed that if we did apply a magnetic field, then for reasons of "symmetry" we should apply it along the optic axis. We did so and we immediately detected the photon echo. We found that as the spacing between the excitation pulses was increased, so was the spacing between the excitation pulse and the echo [see illustration on page 311]. When we turned off the magnetic field, the echo disappeared. We also found to our surprise that when the applied magnetic field was rotated a few degrees away from the optic axis, the echo disappeared.

After we had convinced ourselves that we had detected an actual photon echo and not some spurious reflection, we submitted a paper to Physical Review Letters for publication. I mention this because shortly after it was submitted we found that we were unable to obtain any more photon echoes! A week passed with no success until we found that the trouble was caused by the extreme sensitivity of the orientation of the magnetic field with respect to the optic axis. We had again doubled the time between the excitation pulses and the importance of the field orientation had drastically increased. The crystal and the magnetic field had to be aligned to within a degree, which was difficult to do with our experimental configuration.

In subsequent experiments we have shown that one can obtain photon ech-

308

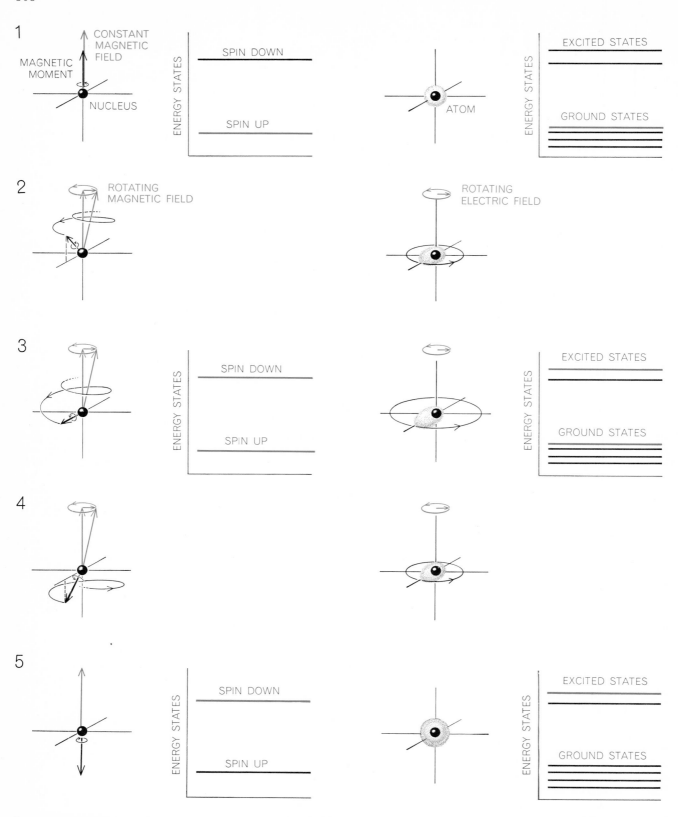

SIMILARITY between the permitted energy states of a nucleus spinning in a magnetic field (*left*) and of an isolated impurity atom in a crystal lattice (*right*) led to the prediction of the photon echo. As the energy-level diagrams accompanying the drawings show, both systems can be regarded as two-level systems capable of being excited by a direct resonant interaction. (Occupied states are indicated by colored lines, unoccupied states by black lines.) In the case of a proton excited by a rotating magnetic field the "spin up" and "spin down" energy states are coupled by an interaction of the proton's magnetic dipole moment with the applied magnetic fields. In the case of a chromium impurity ion in a ruby crystal excited by circularly polarized light, two of the ion's many energy levels are coupled by an interaction of the ion's electric dipole moment with the rotating electric-field vector of the light. The electric dipole moment of the atom arises from the induced polarization of its electric-charge distribution represented by the positive nucleus and the negative electron cloud. The nuclear-spin echo is detected as an electrical signal; the photon echo, as a light pulse.

oes in the absence of a magnetic field. The magnetic field inhibits the neighboring aluminum nuclei from "flipping" the electron spin of the chromium ion or modulating the energy separation of the atomic states that are responsible for the echo. By making the time separation between the excitation pulses small enough, however, it is possible to observe an echo signal before it has time to relax completely. A sharp rise in echo amplitude takes place at an applied magnetic field of about 10 gauss, which is approximately the magnetic field at the chromium lattice sites attributable to the aluminum neighbors [*see top illustration at right*]. The dips at higher fields are due to "level crossings" in the ground state and arise because the ruby system is not an ideal two-level system but rather a more complicated system with four levels in the ground state alone.

The critical dependence of the orientation of the magnetic field with respect to the optic axis is now being studied in our laboratory with the help of electron-spin echoes. In an experiment with Daniel Grischkowsky we found that the ordinary electron-spin echoes of chromium ions in ruby are also strongly dependent on the orientation of the magnetic field. A detailed analysis of this simpler problem has shown that the critical dependence on orientation is due to an enhanced quantum-mechanical interaction that arises when the component of the precessing nuclear moments of the aluminum atoms that lies in the average direction of the spin of the chromium electron fluctuates in time. Accordingly the echoes last longest when the aluminum nuclei precess around an axis that is parallel to the average spin direction of the chromium ions, a condition that is not met when the applied magnetic field is either too weak or tilted away from the optic axis. Although the aluminum nuclei are effectively free, the chromium ion is strongly perturbed by the crystalline fields, with the result that its magnetic moment only points along the magnetic-field direction when it is parallel to the optic axis, whereas at lower applied magnetic fields the nonuniform dipolar field of the chromium ion makes a sizable contribution to the magnetic field at the aluminum sites, with the result that the aluminum nuclei then precess about nonparallel axes. The occurrence of the echo dips at higher fields is thus caused in part by the extreme sensitivity of the spin orientation of the chromium ion with respect to the magnetic-field direction in the

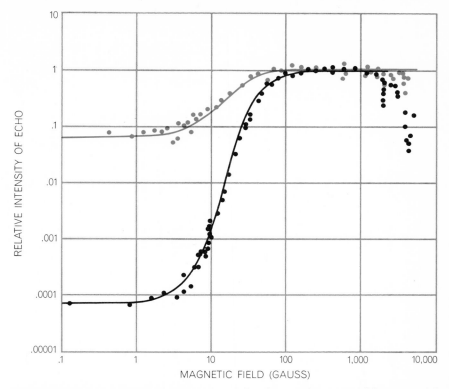

SHARP RISE in the amplitude, or intensity, of the photon echoes emitted by an excited ruby takes place at an applied magnetic field of about 10 gauss, which is approximately the magnetic field at the chromium lattice sites that can be attributed to the neighboring aluminum atoms. The dips at higher fields are due to "level crossings" in the four-level ground state of the ruby. The two sets of points were obtained for experiments in which the pulse separations were 34 billionths of a second (*color*) and 75 billionths of a second (*black*).

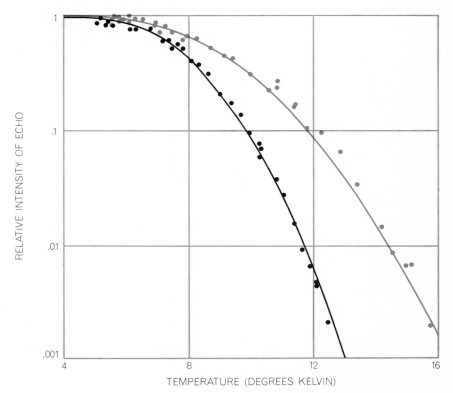

RELAXATION EFFECTS can be studied by means of photon echoes. In this example the intensity of the two sets of echoes decreases as the temperature of the ruby is raised. The pulse separations for the two sets were 50 billionths of a second (*black*) and 103 billionths of a second (*color*). Quantized lattice vibrations called phonons cause the echo to decay.

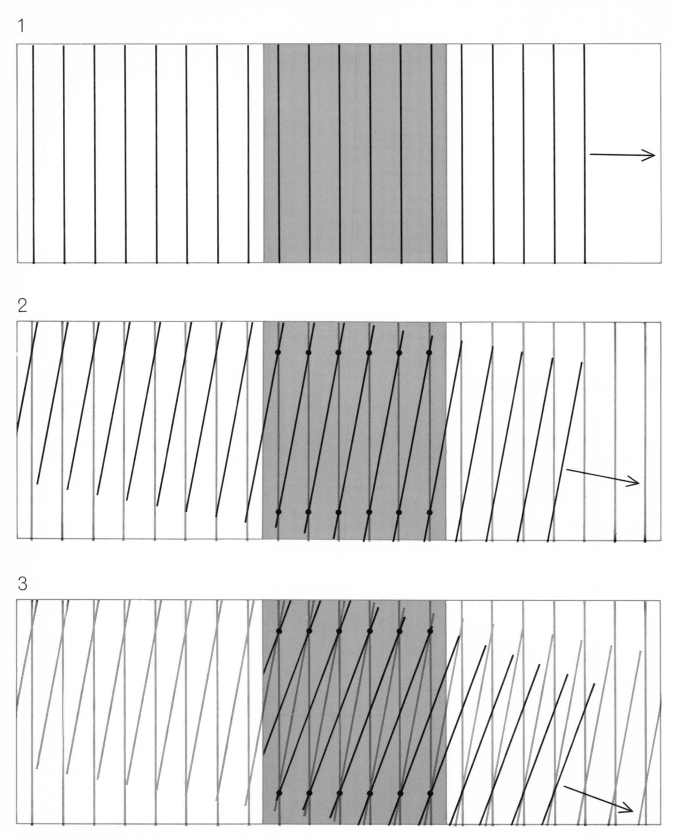

PHOTON ECHO IS PROPAGATED in a direction different from either of the two excitation pulses when the excitation pulses are not parallel. The first light pulse, whose lines of constant phase lie in parallel planes, stimulates a macroscopic excitation in the ruby crystal with a similar plane-wave character (1). The second pulse, which strikes the crystal from a slightly different angle, superposes its corresponding planes of constant phase on those of the first pulse (2). The echo will then be propagated in a direction perpendicular to the planes in which the rephased dipole moments are in phase (3). These planes are obtained by requiring that the phase angle of the first excitation pulse vary twice as fast spatially as the phase angle of the second excitation pulse. The black dots in 2 and 3 indicate one family of points for which the rephased dipole moments of the macroscopic excitation will have the same phase.

energy region of the level crossings in the ground state.

The main use of the photon echo, like all other echo phenomena, is in the study of relaxation effects. As the temperature of the ruby sample is raised, for example, the amplitude of the echo decreases [*see bottom illustration on page 309*]. The quantized lattice vibrations called phonons interact with the excited chromium atoms and cause energy-level transitions that make the echo decay. A detailed study of this process enables one to understand the nature of the interaction of the chromium atoms and phonons.

It is not just the relative directions of the excitation pulses that are important; their relative polarizations are important also. If the two excitation pulses are plane-polarized at a certain angle with respect to each other, then it can be shown that the echo is plane-polarized with respect to the first pulse at an angle

that is twice as large as the angle between the excitation pulses. This circumstance enables one to select the echo in another way: by polarizing the excitation pulses at 90 degrees with respect to each other and then using a polarizer in front of the detector to eliminate the light from the second pulse. By doing this and letting the excitation pulses propagate in parallel directions, we obtained multiple echoes. In this case the echoes were so strong that they themselves acted as excitation pulses and produced further echoes. Up to three echoes were observed in this way. These echoes had not been seen previously since the directions in which they were propagating were not the same and only the first echo was reaching the detector.

It is now tempting to excite any system with two resonant shocks in the hope of seeing an echo, even when one may not be certain beforehand that an echo is theoretically possible. For ex-

ample, if one generates a plasma, or ionized gas, in a large magnetic field, the free electrons in the plasma will travel in helical paths whose axes are along the direction of the magnetic field. The frequency of the circulating electrons, called the cyclotron frequency, depends only on the value of the magnetic field and not on the velocity of the electrons. Now we again have a resonant magnetic system as we had with the nuclear spins, and one may wonder whether we can obtain echoes.

The answer is that we can, as was shown by Daniel E. Kaplan and Robert M. Hill of the Lockheed Research Laboratories, who employed a pulsed microwave generator to excite the cyclotron resonance. Their result was quite mystifying, however; a quick calculation shows that no echo should really be expected in this situation. The process by which cyclotron echoes are formed turns out to be different from the process associated with the spin or photon echoes. When nuclear magnets are excited by a resonant pulse of energy, one can at most invert the nuclear spins—any further increase in the energy of the excitation serves to bring them back to their initial state, and this in fact plays a central role in the formation of ordinary nuclear-spin echoes.

On the other hand, the resonant excitation of an electron in its cyclotron orbit can result in a continual increase in the electron's energy (or the radius of its cyclotron orbit). In contrast to the photon echo the cyclotron echo is explained in terms of a "bunching" of electrons in momentum space that is unbalanced by a velocity-dependent relaxation mechanism. This echo phenomenon offers a convenient way to study relaxation processes due to collision processes in a plasma.

Two-pulse echoes are not the only possible type. By exciting a system with three or more pulses one can obtain a whole series of additional echoes. Some of these echoes are produced by the mechanism described in this article; others are produced by different mechanisms and therefore decay with a different characteristic relaxation time.

With the advent of "mode-locked" lasers that can produce light pulses of extremely short duration (on the order of a ten-trillionth of a second), one can now visualize the possibility of using the photon-echo technique to make measurements of very short relaxation phenomena under almost ideal conditions or alternatively of using photon echoes for computational operations or for information storage in an extremely fast computer.

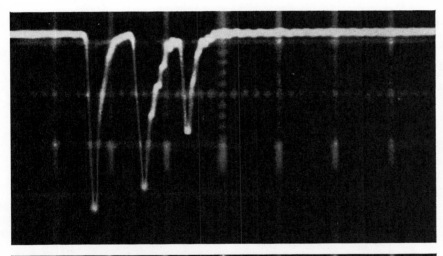
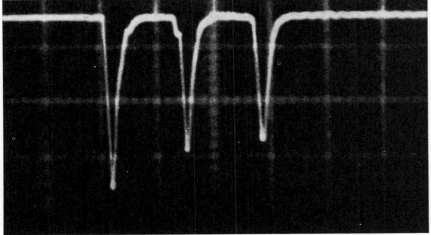

OSCILLOSCOPE TRACES of the photomultiplier response to two series of light pulses, each consisting of two excitation pulses and an echo, show that as the spacing between the excitation pulses was increased (*top to bottom*), so was the spacing between the second excitation pulse and the echo. Time increases to right at 100 billionths of a second per division.

PORT OF

28

Applications
of Laser Light

Donald R. Herriott   *September 1968*

Predicting what will eventually be done with lasers is risky. The prospects of the laser are qualitatively different, for example, from those of the transistor at the time of its invention 20 years ago. The transistor was, after all, essentially an improved device for performing existing functions, and its evolution was comparatively straightforward. The laser, on the other hand, produces light that is different in both quality and intensity from the light generated by any other source. As a result some of the more obvious uses of lasers in existing systems, such as convention-

al interferometers, may turn out to be less important than the development of new systems that take advantage of the unique characteristics of laser light to perform tasks either thought to be impossible or not even imagined.

The prime example of such an unpredictable development has been the recent burst of activity in the branch of interferometry known as holography, or photography by wave-front reconstruction. Here the advent of the laser, combined with a few critical refinements of an existing idea, has provided a completely new and unexpected capability.

Another aspect of this unpredictability is manifested by the fact that the use of laser light as the carrier wave for a long-distance communication system—a concept recognized quite early as one of the most important of the potential applications of the laser—is still a long way from being commercially implemented on a large scale. This is not for lack of a sound basis for this application but rather because of the broad range of auxiliary techniques required, and because of the existing high level of development in the competing technology.

In the meantime, as more and more people have become aware of this extraordinary new light source, a host of suggestions have been made for more prosaic applications of laser light, in fields as diverse as welding and surveying. A surprising number of these applications appear to be immediately feasible. Indeed, it is quite possible that some of the less sophisticated uses of the laser will in the long run prove to be among the most important, at least from an economic point of view. Here I shall outline the major areas in which applications of laser light can be grouped and describe some typical examples in each area.

There is a large class of laser applications that depend not so much on coherence or monochromaticity per se but rather on the unprecedented brightness, or energy per unit area, that can be obtained by focusing a laser beam with a lens. This brightness, which is a byproduct of the beam's coherence, is a unique feature of laser light and can be many orders of magnitude greater than the brightest light produced by conventional sources. To understand why this is so it is necessary to review briefly a few of the basic differences between the incoherent light produced by an ordinary

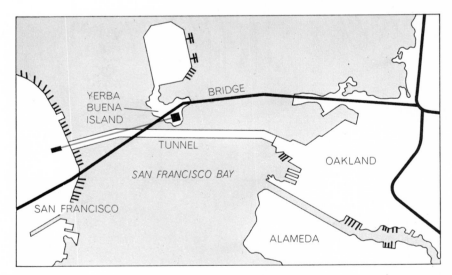

USE OF THE LASER in technology is symbolized by the photograph on the opposite page. The bright red spot near the center of the photograph was made by a helium-neon gas laser mounted on a surveyor's transit on the roof of the Ferry Building in downtown San Francisco. The laser is one of about a dozen used to align a fleet of dredging barges and other floating equipment being employed in the construction of the subway tube between San Francisco and Oakland, a major link in the projected Bay Area Rapid Transit system (BART). The photograph was made from Yerba Buena Island along one of the straight stretches of underwater trench being prepared for the tube (*see map above*). The laser beam is visible only to an observer standing directly in the path of the beam. The beam was about two inches wide at the laser and spread to a width of about nine inches by the time it reached the camera, approximately a mile and a half away. The square object with alternating red and white quadrants next to the laser on the roof is a target for another laser.

bright source and the coherent light produced by a laser.

In a conventional light source the atoms of a solid or a gas are agitated either thermally or electrically to higher energy states. When these atoms return spontaneously to their lower energy levels, they radiate some of their excess energy as light. Since each atom behaves independently at this stage, its emission is at a random time and in a random direction with a random polarization.

It follows that the light radiated in a single direction is the complex sum of all the light from the individual atoms. The phases of any two atoms will tend to cancel their radiation in some directions and enhance it in others. The total energy of the source will on the average be radiated uniformly in all accessible directions, and the amount of energy observed in a given direction will be proportional to the solid angle subtended by the observing device. The maximum total energy that can be radiated by a given source depends on two factors: the surface area of the source and the max-

imum temperature to which the source can be heated without melting (in the case of a solid) or the maximum pressure and temperature that can be sustained in a discharge lamp (in the case of a gas). Thus in practice the only way to increase the power output from an ordinary source beyond the limitations imposed by the source material is to increase the area of the source.

Power output, however, is only half the story. For many applications brightness, or concentrated power, is much more important than power itself. A 40-watt fluorescent lamp, for example, produces more light than a 40-watt incandescent lamp, but it would not make nearly as good a light source for a spotlight. It is therefore not surprising that students of optics have tried for centuries to get a brighter light source by reducing the size of a large source with a lens. They have discovered that the brightness of the source cannot be increased in this way, because even under ideal conditions the reduced area of the image just makes up for the reduced col-

lection angle that the lens intercepts from the source [see *illustration below*]. In other words, with a conventional source one cannot produce an image that is brighter than the source. The brightness can at best match that of the source, neglecting losses due to surface reflection, scattering and absorption by the lens elements.

In the case of a source that is smaller than the resolution limit of the lens, the size of the image is determined by the aperture and aberrations of the lens. For example, when a star is photographed through a telescope, the size of the image does not depend on the size of the object. Since the star is actually smaller than the size indicated by the image, the brightness of the image must always be less than the surface brightness of the star.

Now, in a laser light is also emitted when atoms drop from a higher energy level to a lower one, but in this case the atoms are triggered to emit in unison by the standing wave in the laser cavity. Enough of the light previously generat-

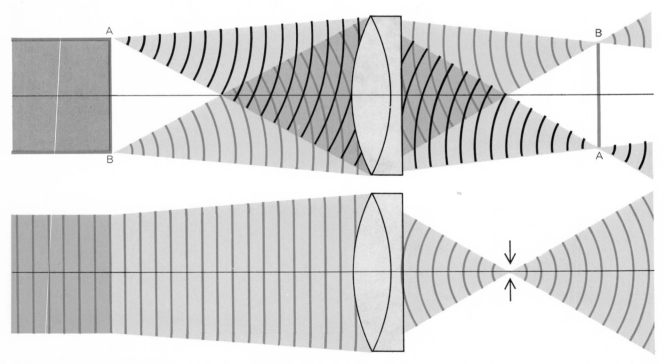

ADVANTAGE OF LASER LIGHT over ordinary light in forming an image with a high brightness, or energy per unit area, arises from the basic differences between the coherent light produced by the laser and the incoherent light produced by an ordinary source. In an ordinary source (*top*) light is emitted independently by each atom, so that the emissions from all the atoms of the source will be at random times and in random directions with random polarizations. As a result the total energy of the source will on the average be radiated uniformly in all accessible directions, and the amount of energy in any given direction will be proportional to the solid angle subtended by the observing device. Any attempt to increase the brightness of an image over the brightness of the source by re-

ducing the size of the source with a lens cannot succeed, because even under ideal conditions the reduced area of the image just makes up for the reduced collection angle that the lens intercepts from the source. In contrast, the coherent light produced by a laser (*bottom*) is generated over a sizable volume with the proper phase, so that when it is focused by a lens, all the individual contributions by the atoms in the laser medium are in the correct phase to add up. In a typical laser the directionality of the beam is limited only by diffraction by the laser aperture. Accordingly with a suitable lens all the energy of the laser can be concentrated into a diffraction-limited image that is only one micron in diameter, resulting in much greater energy density than the density of the source.

ed is retained in the reflective cavity to keep the new emission in the proper phase, polarization and direction. This standing wave interacts with the excited atoms and causes most of them to emit their excess energy in phase with the stimulating wave before they have a chance to emit it randomly. As a result the laser generates only light that travels in the direction of the standing wave. In a typical laser this directionality is limited only by the diffraction of the emerging beam by the laser aperture. It is important to realize that the laser does not violate the materials limitations of ordinary light sources; it simply concentrates all its energy into a single, diffraction-limited beam.

In effect the beam from a laser is the same as one from a distant small source, such as a star. When the beam is focused by a lens, its diameter at the point of sharpest focus depends only on the resolution limit of the lens. With a suitable lens all the energy from a typical laser can be concentrated into a diffraction-limited image that is only one micron in diameter, regardless of the size of the laser! This results in a tremendous energy density, one that is far greater than the energy density of the source. The key point is that inside the laser the radiation is generated over a sizable volume with the proper phase, so that when the radiation is focused by the lens, all the individual contributions are in the correct phase to add up.

The energy density of the image formed by a lens in a laser beam can be used to heat, melt or even vaporize small areas of any material. This capability promises to find wide use in the field of microelectronics. The main advantages here are the very small size of the focused image, the absence of contamination of the very pure materials required in such circuits and the precise control of the amount of energy used. For example, the image of the laser can be used to cut a narrow gap through a vapor-deposited film; by cutting such a gap along a meander path through a conducting film one can easily form a capacitor [see top illustration at right]. In the fabrication of integrated circuits the laser beam can also be used to weld connections between parts of the circuit, or to cut through connections and thereby tailor a general circuit to perform one of a variety of functions. This discretionary wiring can also be used to compensate for a small percentage of defective components and thus increase reliability. Discrete components such as a precision resistor can be adjusted in a

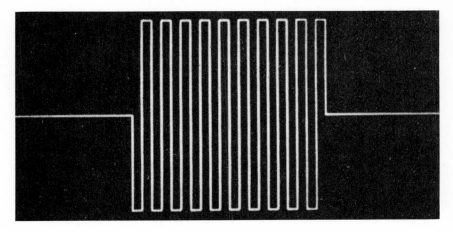

MICROCAPACITOR was made by using a beam from a solid-state laser to cut a meander path through a .3-micron-thick gold conducting film vapor-deposited on a sapphire substrate. The cut is six microns wide. The main advantages of laser light in the field of microelectronics are the very small size of the focused image, the absence of contamination of the very pure materials required in such circuits and the precise control of the energy used.

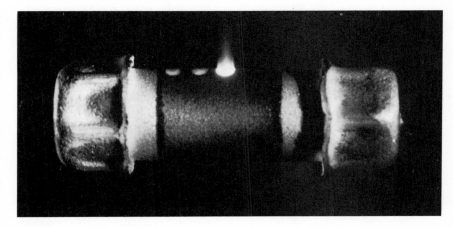

PRECISION RESISTOR is adjusted in value by means of a completely automatic machine that measures the resistance and pulses a laser to vaporize conductive material until the desired resistance is obtained. This photograph was made at the Western Electric Company.

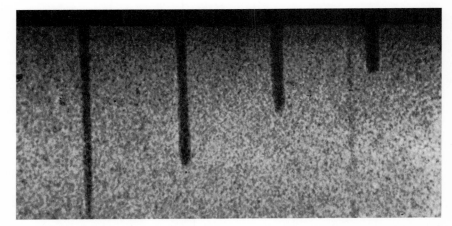

PENETRATING POWER of the focused light beam from a pulsed ruby laser is demonstrated by this X-ray photograph, which shows a number of holes drilled by such a laser in an alumina ceramic .062 inch thick. The diameter of the holes varies between .0015 inch and .003 inch. Twenty-four pulses each with an energy of a tenth of a joule were required to pierce a hole all the way through the ceramic. The reason narrow holes can be drilled to a depth greater than the depth of focus of the laser has not been adequately explained. This photograph and the one at top of the page were made at the Bell Telephone Laboratories.

completely automatic machine that measures the resistance and pulses the laser to vaporize conductive material until the desired resistance is obtained [*see middle illustration on preceding page*].

In a related application a pulsed laser has been used to pierce holes in diamond chips used in dies for drawing wire. A number of laser pulses are used to make the hole and to rough it into shape. The hole is then polished with olive oil and diamond dust to its final shape and finish.

Another interesting application that has already been demonstrated is the use of a pulsed laser to balance high-speed gyroscope motors as they run. Vibration sensors determine the amount and the exact orientation of the errors in balance, and the laser source is automatically pulsed to remove material at the proper places until balance is achieved. In fact, it is conceivable that high-power lasers will someday be used routinely to cut a wide range of materials, including wood, cloth and paper. The combustion of the adjacent material is usually not a problem because the heated material vaporizes almost instantaneously and hence dissipates heat rapidly.

The high intensity and directionality of a laser beam has made surveying one of the most direct and practical applications of the laser. The laser beam can be focused through a telescope to have the same width at any distance as the resolution of the telescope. Thus when the light beam formed in the telescope is measured at the target, the accuracy is the same as when, in conventional surveying, the image of the target is observed in the telescope. The principal advantage of the laser system is in saving labor and communications. In a typical surveying application a laser beam is positioned along the intended route for a pipeline. It is important in laying pipeline that the trench be dug to just the bottom of the pipe, since soil disturbed below this level will later settle and may rupture the line. As the shovel digs, its depth can be regularly measured with a stick. The stick is simply placed at the bottom of the cut and the height of the laser beam falling on the stick is read directly. The same technique can be used by the men cleaning up the trench to fit the actual shape of the pipe. Accuracies of a fraction of an inch are easy to maintain in this way. In the present procedure a telescope is set up in a similar manner, but then a man must stay at the telescope, take all the measurements and communicate them to the group doing the digging. This requires both an additional man at the telescope and communication of the results to the digging crew.

When property lines or power lines are being laid out through wooded land, it is common to clear broad rights-of-way along the entire path. With a laser surveying instrument the laser beam can be set up on the proper line and the beam can be observed as it falls on each obstruction. A man can then walk from the laser to the target, see immediately each branch or tree that the beam hits and remove only actual obstructions.

The high intensity and directionality of a laser beam can also be used to align jigs for mechanical tooling by photoelectric centering of a target. The person viewing a target through a telescope can resolve or distinguish two objects separated by the diffraction limit of the telescope (approximately one second of arc per inch of diameter). He can center a dark cross hair in the telescope on a white line on a suitable target pattern to three or five times that accuracy. A laser beam can be projected through the same telescope with a half-power width that is also about the same as the diffraction limit. By balancing the light in the two sides of the beam, the center of the beam can be found to better than a tenth of the half-power width. Under the best conditions a hundredth of this width would be possible.

Laser alignment systems are now be-

LASER "KNIFE" developed at Bell Laboratories has an articulated arm that allows the beam from a stationary laser to be moved freely for use in surgery, microcircuit fabrication or many other applications. The "elbows" of the hollow arm contain prisms that reflect the beam down the center of each section in spite of the free rotation of each joint.

ing used, and indeed are needed, for the alignment of jigs in the new large second-generation jet aircraft, where tolerances of a hundredth of an inch over distances in excess of 200 feet are involved. One or more laser sources can be set up in alignment along the length of the jig and each critical point can be measured with respect to the laser beams. This can be done over short distances without people at the laser sources. Detectors of the quadrant type, with servo drives that automatically center the detector on the beam both horizontally and vertically, are frequently employed.

If a laser beam is directed to scan an object, and a viewing telescope is made to track the intersection of the laser beam and the object from a different direction, the combination can survey the object in three dimensions. Angular readings can be taken from such an instrument to convey to a computer the form of an object such as an automobile model so that the computer can define the shape of the dies necessary to make the automobile body parts. It could also scan an aircraft to determine if its form properly agrees with the plans.

In the area of remote sampling it has been suggested that laser beams could be used to map the distribution and motion of pollutants. The idea here is to pulse a short burst of light from a laser through the atmosphere and observe the light scattered back to a receiving telescope, much as radar is used to observe clouds and rain. It will take a predictable amount of time for the light to travel to a particular sampled region and return. The signal observed at a given time after the laser pulse is dispatched will be a measure of the transmittance of the air along the path and the backscatter of the pollutant at the specific distance along the beam. It should be possible to analyze the returned beam to determine the concentration of a variety of pollutants at each point along the path of the beam. Thus one observing point in a large area could monitor pollution levels and identify the specific sources of pollutants.

So far we have considered the group of applications that are principally based on the high brightness of the laser source, which is an indirect result of the coherence of the light from the source. We shall now consider applications that directly exploit the spatial and temporal coherence of a laser source to extend the capability of a system beyond what can be done with coherent light from conventional sources.

The principal application of coherent light before the advent of the laser was in interferometry. Here two or more light beams are made to follow different paths through an optical system. The light is then combined so that interference can be observed. If the two beams are in phase when they recombine, the square of the sum of their amplitudes will be the observed intensity; if the beams are out of phase, the square of the difference of their amplitudes will be observed. In some interferometers these intensities will be observed as alternate light and dark fringes across a field of view, each indicating a half-wavelength shift in path length between the two paths through the interferometer. In other interferometers fringes caused by light traveling at various angles through the instrument are observed in angular space. In still others a single fringe covers the entire field, and changes in intensity of the field are caused by variation of phase between the beams with time. This last type of interferometer is commonly used with photoelectric detectors and records phase shift as a function of time.

In none of these conventional methods of interferometry is it mandatory that the two light beams come from a single source. The trouble is that if they do not come from a single source, their frequencies will vary with time, causing the fringes to shift so rapidly that they cannot be observed. Lasers have now provided sources whose frequency can be controlled so that interference between light from different sources is practical.

With two beams from a conventional source the light following the different paths must meet so that light from the same point on the source is superposed, and so that light emitted at the same time is recombined. Both the position and the time must be close enough so that the phases of the two effective sources are coherent. The distance along the beam between two points that have correlation adequate to give useful contrast will depend on the width of the spectral lines of the source. High-pressure mercury lamps require that the two paths be matched to within a fraction of a millimeter. Low-pressure isotope lamps can be used at a path difference of a good part of a meter. Laser sources, in contrast, are narrow enough in line width to be used over hundreds of miles. The importance of this lies in the fact that it frees one from the need to worry about the matching of path lengths. In making measurements on a 200-inch telescope with an interferometer one path of which is 50 feet long, for example, it is now possible to use a reference path of a few inches instead of having to build a reference path of the same 50-foot length as the path to the mirror.

The long coherence length afforded

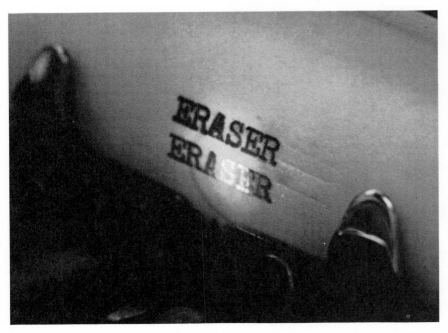

LASER ERASER invented by Arthur L. Schawlow of Stanford University is capable of vaporizing ink from paper without appreciably heating the paper. The heating of the black ink, which absorbs the laser pulse and becomes incandescent, is so rapid that the ink vapor carries away the heat before it can penetrate below the surface by conduction. The dark ring is a shadow of the end of the laser, produced by stray light from the laser flash lamp.

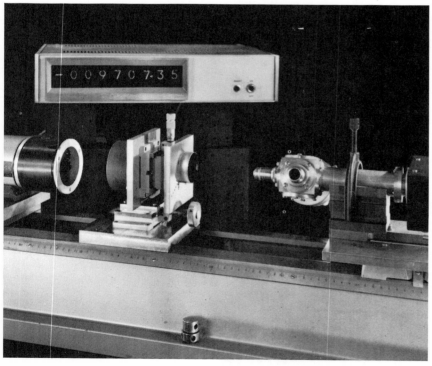

TWO LASER INTERFEROMETERS in the author's laboratory at Bell Laboratories are used to test polished lens surfaces for sphericity and to measure their radius of curvature. In this demonstration of the system's extreme sensitivity the laser interferometer at right is being used to position the slide carrying the lens, so that the focal point of the microscope objective at the end of the interferometer coincides first with the surface of the lens (*top*) and then with the center of curvature of the lens (*bottom*). In both of these situations one observes through the viewer attached to this interferometer a straight-line pattern of interference fringes rather than the usual curved pattern of such fringes. The laser interferometer at left is used independently to measure the displacement of the slide along the optical bench by counting automatically the number of interference fringes shifted in going from the position at top to the position at bottom. This fringe shift is in turn translated into a measurement of the lens's radius of curvature in units of eighths of a wavelength; the results are displayed on the face of the electronic counter above the optical bench.

by the laser has eliminated one of the routine requirements that have generally limited the practical applications of interferometry. For instance, a spherical test interferometer has been constructed in which a polished lens surface can be tested for sphericity without making a test glass of identical radius, a costly and time-consuming job [*see illustration at left*]. In a similar instrument constructed prior to the introduction of the laser, light from a low-pressure mercury-isotope lamp was converged at right angles to the surface of a reference glass and then to the surface being tested. The light reflected from the two surfaces was combined to give interference fringes that showed the regularity of the sample. The spacing between the reference glass and the surface of the lens was limited to two inches in order for adequate contrast to be observed. This required a separate interchangeable reference surface for every two inches of range of the instrument. The faint light from the low-pressure lamp required that the observer adapt his eyes to the dark for several minutes for adequate visibility. A laser source in the same instrument would provide all the light needed and allow a single reference surface to be used with the full range of lens radii. This would change an instrument used under only the most favorable conditions in the laboratory into one with everyday application in the optical shop.

The freedom from the need for path compensation in interferometers with laser sources has made many long-path interferometric measurements practical. Flexure in dams, drift along geologic faults and long-wave, low-frequency oscillations in the earth's crust can now be studied by this method.

To expand on just one of these examples, a dam should be an elastic structure; in other words, it should deflect in proportion to the water level behind it. If a dam shows hysteresis in its deflections (that is, if it remains partly deflected), or if it is slowly shifting, this is an indication that it will ultimately fail. A laser interferometer can be used to measure and record motions of points on a dam to fractions of a wavelength of light. This kind of information should help civil engineers to study such structures and determine their safety.

In one of the earliest determinations of a standard of length by means of interferometry A. A. Michelson manually counted the fringes in an "etalon" a tenth of a meter long and stepped this unit along repeatedly to cover a meter;

in this way he succeeded in determining the length of the meter in wavelengths of the red line of a cadmium discharge lamp. Automatic fringe-counting techniques have since eliminated the counting chore, but the low intensity of conventional light sources limits the counting rate, and the breadth of their spectral lines limits the range of measurement to inches. The laser removes both limitations. A fringe-counting interferometer can now count the fringes directly as a mirror is moved over distances of 20 meters or more at a velocity of many inches per second. This measurement is made in terms of the wavelength of the laser source and is therefore limited only by the stability of the laser.

It is well known that fringe-counting can be used to measure the velocity of one of the interferometer mirrors by means of the Doppler effect. With a laser as a light source, however, light scattered from a moving sheet of paper, a moving liquid or even a gas moving in a pipe or in the open atmosphere can be made to interfere with the original light to obtain beat frequencies that are an accurate measure of the velocity of the scattering target. The application of this new capability to the control of industrial processes will almost certainly be significant.

Let us turn now to the two principal applications of laser light that could not have been achieved without the brightness and the coherence of laser sources: optical communications and holography.

Communication with laser light is based both on the high brightness of the source and on the narrowness of its spectral lines. A suitable antenna system for optical communications consists of two identical large-aperture telescopes facing each other. The receiving telescope sees, from each part of its aperture, the aperture of the transmitting telescope with a uniform brightness equal to that of the source. Thus it is the high source brightness of the laser that is necessary to transmit enough energy to define broad-band information. This type of antenna system may be quite useful for communication in space, but on the earth atmospheric turbulence, smog, snow, airplanes, birds and so on jeopardize reliability. As a result major efforts are being made to devise a light conductor that can be installed (with a reasonable number of bends) for communication purposes. Lenses spaced periodically along a pipe would correct for some degree of misalignment. Gas lenses

promise similar guidance without the loss due to reflectance.

The monochromaticity of the laser beam is chiefly important in assembling and recovering the messages from the laser beam. Information modulated on a light beam should be at a frequency higher than the range of frequencies over which the carrier wave may wander, so that after mixing with a local source at the receiving end to retrieve the original signal the carrier-wave noise can be filtered from the signal. Laser beams have frequencies that are high enough and stable enough for this purpose.

Although at first laser communications will be confined to outer space or other special instances, lasers will prob-

ably fill a real need when the growing demand for communication facilities cannot be easily satisfied with lower-frequency systems and when better modulators, detectors and enclosed light guides are developed [see "Communication by Laser," by Stewart E. Miller, beginning on page 323].

The basic concept of holography, which is more than 20 years old, is simply that the diffraction pattern of light from an object is a transform, or coded record, of the object. If such a diffraction pattern could be stored, one should be able to reconstruct an image of the object.

The original problem with holography

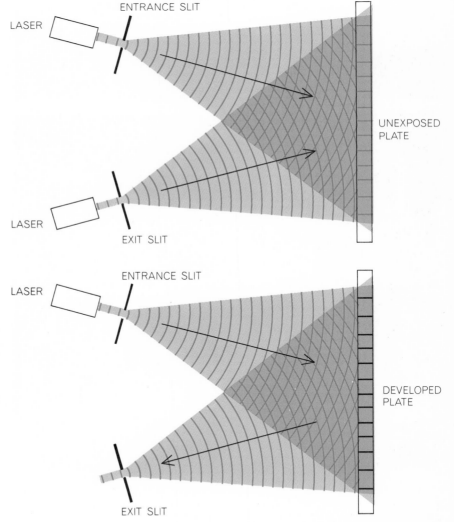

PRINCIPLE OF HOLOGRAPHY is elucidated by referring to this simplified diagram of an ordinary diffraction-grating spectroscope in which the grating has been replaced by a photographic plate. When a pair of laser beams are used to illuminate both the entrance and the exit slit of the spectroscope, characteristic double-slit fringes will be formed on the plate (*top*). When the plate is developed, it will then act as an inefficient grating (*bottom*). Using light of the same wavelength, the spacing of the fringes will be just right to diffract out the exit slit light entering the entrance slit, or to diffract out the entrance slit light entering the exit slit. In holography a more complex subject is substituted for one of the original laser beams and a correspondingly more complex fringe pattern results.

was that whereas it is easy to record the square of the amplitude of the diffraction pattern, the phase is usually lost, and without a record of the phase the holographic reconstruction is poor except for very special objects. The critical innovation, which came in 1963, was to have the diffraction pattern interfere with a reference beam of monochromatic laser light at a certain angle. The interference of the reference beam and the "subject" beam now results in a series of interference fringes whose contrast is a measure of the amplitude of the subject beam and whose position is a measure of the phase of the subject beam. When the developed photographic plate that has recorded the interference pattern is later illuminated with a laser beam identical with the reference beam, the diffracted light will have the same amplitude and phase characteristics as the original beam from the subject.

How a hologram works can be clarified by considering an experiment performed with an ordinary diffraction-grating spectroscope [*see illustration on preceding page*]. When a laser is used to illuminate both the entrance slit and the exit slit of the spectroscope, double-slit fringes will be formed on the grating. If the grating is replaced by a photographic plate, the plate can record the fringes, and when the plate is developed, it will act as an inefficient grating. Now it can be shown that if the same laser wavelength falls on the developed plate, the spacing of the fringes will be just right to diffract out the exit slit light entering the entrance slit, or to diffract out the entrance slit light entering the

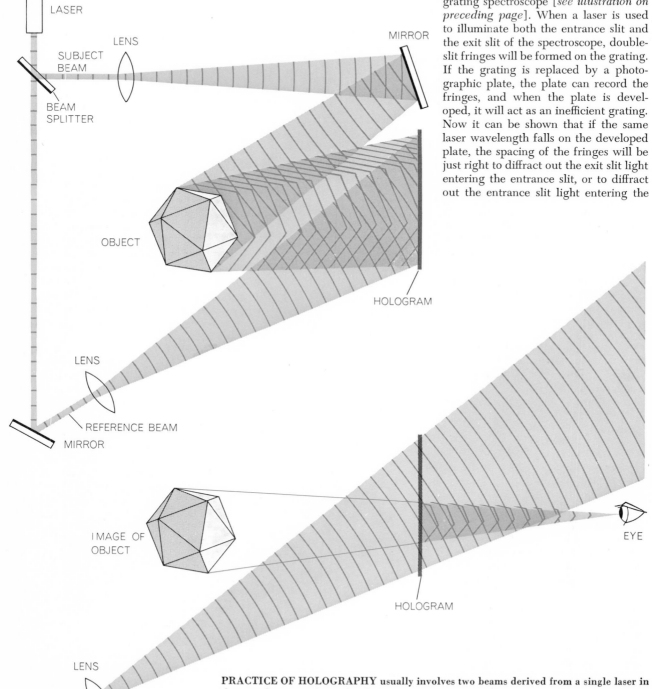

PRACTICE OF HOLOGRAPHY usually involves two beams derived from a single laser in the recording stage (*top*). One beam is used to illuminate the object, while the other is used as a reference beam. The reference beam and the light reflected from the object are then allowed to interfere, and the resulting interference pattern is recorded on a photographic plate, forming the hologram. In the reconstruction stage (*bottom*) the hologram is illuminated by the reference beam alone, producing replicas of the wave fronts reflected from the original object. The reconstructed wave fronts can be observed visually or with a camera.

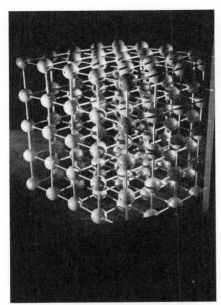

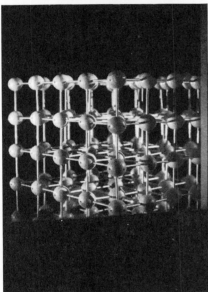

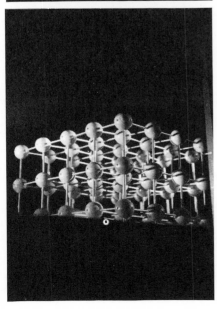

exit slit. If more than one slit were involved, a series of fringes would be superposed, with each fringe pattern having a contrast corresponding to the intensity of light from one point and a spacing to diffract the light to the correct position. If a more complex subject were used, a correspondingly more complex fringe pattern would result and the photographic plate would be called a hologram.

This storage of the phase and amplitude of light has led to a number of new applications. For example, the information stored in a hologram can be reconstructed at a later time to interfere with the object, now distorted or slightly moved, in the interferometer. Thus accurate interferometric measurements can be made of a casting as it ages or as its temperature changes.

Holograms can also be made between two complex wave forms. Here the reference beam does not have to be a plane wave; the beam from a second object can be used as the reference. When the resulting hologram is illuminated with light from either of the objects, the other object will be seen. More than one such hologram can be superposed in this way on one piece of photographic material. For instance, an *A* can be recorded with a spot of light in one position of the field for one exposure, and a *B* can be stored with the reference-beam spot at another point. Other letters can each be superposed with the reference source in a different position. If one now illuminates the developed hologram with light from one of the letters, only the spot that was used as the reference beam for that letter will appear bright. This can be used to associate the position of a spot of light in a field of view with the shape of a character and promises to be very useful as an "associated memory". system. Unfortunately some letters, such as *E* and *F* or *O* and *Q*, are so similar that both reference beams appear bright at the same time.

Other applications of holography take advantage of the extreme fidelity of the reconstructed holographic image of a scene. This fidelity makes it possible to "see around" objects in the image and to focus at various depths in the image. In fact, the broad range of possible developments in the field of holographic applications recalls the situation in the parent field of laser applications, and is a fascinating subject in its own right [see "Advances in Holography," by Keith S. Pennington, beginning on page 351 in this book].

The uses of laser light in spectroscopy straddle the borderline between the scientific and the technological applications of the laser. For instance, extremely small bits of a substance can be vaporized and excited in a laser beam to emit the wavelengths characteristic of the substance's energy levels for spectroscopic analysis. This makes it possible to study smaller samples than one could before, and it eliminates contamination of the substance by the electrodes needed in conventional spectroscopy.

The enormous power that can be generated with laser beams makes it possible to conveniently produce and examine the higher energy states of substances in the laboratory. Such states exist in the sun and the stars, but their effects are obscured over much of the visible spectrum by the earth's atmosphere. Excitation with conventional arcs and plasmas is more cumbersome and is limited in available energy.

Raman spectroscopy in which an intense monochromatic source is used to irradiate a sample has been greatly improved with the polarized, collimated beam from laser sources. The light is scattered so that new spectral lines characteristic of the substance are observed. The substance to be examined can be placed within the laser cavity or in other multiple-reflection arrangements to increase the excitation by 10 to 100 times.

Raman scattering has thus become a more useful tool with laser excitation and continuous recording than would have been possible even with very large conventional light sources or day-long exposures on photographic plates. Raman measurements that are now only scientific studies can be expected to become a standard control procedure in many chemical operations.

It is impossible to predict which of these various applications of laser light will be most important in the long run. Moreover, as I have indicated, the developments in this area so far suggest that what is most predictable about it is its unpredictability.

HOLOGRAM of a ball-and-stick model of the atomic structure of a simple cubic crystal was photographed from three different vertical directions to obtain the three different perspectives shown. Part of the hologram frame is visible in each photograph. The reconstructed three-dimensional holographic image has all the visual properties of the original atomic model, and in fact no known visual test can distinguish the two.

29

Communication by Laser

Stewart E. Miller   January 1966

The announcement in 1960 that a working model of a laser had been achieved was greeted with enthusiasm by workers in many fields, but none were more sanguine about the prospects of the new device than investigators interested in the problem of long-distance communication. The basis for their enthusiasm was the simple fact that the capacity of a communication channel is proportional to the width of its band of frequencies; thus a communication system utilizing electromagnetic waves in the visible region of the spectrum, where enormously wide bands of frequencies are available, should in principle be capable of carrying many times the amount of information carried by lower-frequency radio-wave systems.

The chief obstacle to the exploitation of light for communication before 1960 was the lack of a source that could produce light waves that were both coherent (in step) and monochromatic (with a single frequency). Since the light produced by a laser is both coherent and monochromatic, it was felt at the time that the laser was the answer to a communication engineer's prayer. Although a practical, working system of long-distance communication by laser has yet to be built, the initial enthusiasm has not waned. Today there are probably more physicists and engineers working on the problem of adapting the laser for use in communication than on any other single project

in the field of laser applications. At the Bell Telephone Laboratories many workers, including the author, are engaged in exploring the potential of the laser for communication. In this article I shall attempt to explain some of the advantages of a laser communication system and also some of the problems that remain to be solved before such a system can become an actuality.

There are available at present four proved electrical techniques for transmitting a large volume of messages over a long distance. The oldest of these is the coaxial-cable system, which still carries a large proportion of the communication traffic between cities in the U.S. The standard coaxial cable consists of a copper tube three-eighths of an inch in diameter with a single copper-wire conductor in the center; the cables are generally gathered in bundles of eight to 20. Depending on the amount of communication traffic to be carried, amplifying equipment must be located every two to four miles along the cable. Coaxial cables normally carry radio waves with wavelengths of from 600 to 15 meters and with frequencies of from 500,000 to 20 million cycles per second.

The largest share of the intercity communication traffic in the U.S. today is transmitted through the air by means of microwave-radio relay towers, spaced some 20 to 30 miles apart. This system employs beams of microwave

radiation, mainly in the frequency band between one billion and 10 billion cycles per second.

A third long-distance transmission technique, called wave guide, has been perfected in recent years but is not yet in widespread use. In wave guide a single hollow tube about two inches in diameter is used to transmit millimeter waves with frequencies of from 30 billion to 90 billion cycles per second. Eventually—if and when the need arises —a wave guide system would be able to handle appreciably more communication traffic than any other system currently available.

The fourth and newest long-distance electrical communication technique involves the use of artificial earth satellites. Broad-band communication by satellite—operating within the microwave-radio band—was first achieved experimentally between the U.S. and Europe with the Bell System's *Telstar* satellite and has now been introduced commercially by the Communication Satellite Corporation's *Early Bird*.

At the heart of every one of these long-distance communication systems is the principle called multiplexing —the simultaneous transmission of many different messages over the same pathway. A channel for transmitting an individual human voice, for example, requires a frequency band extending from 200 to 4,000 cycles per second. The information contained in this frequency

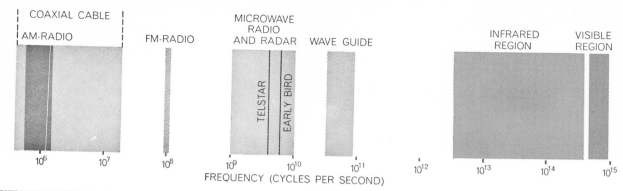

FREQUENCY BANDS in which several of the major electrical communication systems operate are shown in gray in this drawing of a section of the electromagnetic spectrum. Since the capacity of a communication channel is proportional to the width of its band of frequencies, an intercity communication system utilizing electromagnetic waves in the visible region of the spectrum (*extreme right*) should in principle be capable of carrying many times the amount of information carried by the lower-frequency radio-wave systems.

band, however, can be transmitted just as well in the band from 100,200 to 104,000 cycles per second—or for that matter in any other band that is 3,800 cycles per second wide. The act of transferring a signal from one frequency band to another is called modulation. In order to perform the function of modulation without adding noise, or interference, to the signal, an intercity communication system requires an oscillator capable of producing a carrier wave with a very narrow spectral width. This single-frequency carrier wave is then successively modulated by a large number of voice channels to create a new, composite signal wave [*see illustration on page 328*]. For example, 1,000 telephone channels, each with a nominal bandwidth of 3,800 cycles per second, can be transferred to a single signal wave that contains the band of frequencies extending from the frequency of the original carrier wave to that of the carrier wave plus 3.8 million cycles per second (1,000 times 3,800). Similarly, a second set of 1,000 telephone channels can be transferred to a second carrier wave to form another broad signal wave, and so on. Special electrical networks then combine several of these broad energy bands for simultaneous transmission over a single intercity pathway. At the other end of the line a similar network separates the single signal into its component broad bands, and these in turn are subdivided by means of a demodulation process into individual telephone signals.

The aim of the whole multiplexing process is economy; it is cheaper to transmit a single broad-band signal wave on a single coaxial cable, say, than it is to transmit many narrow-band signal waves on many coaxial cables. For this reason all the currently available

intercity transmission techniques employ some variation of the multiplexing process.

It should not be difficult at this point to see what is attractive to communication engineers about the visible portion of the electromagnetic spectrum. Since an individual communication channel requires the same bandwidth regardless of the region of the spectrum in which it is located, the higher-frequency regions, which have far more room for communication channels, have a much greater potential capacity than the lower frequencies. The frequency in the center of the visible region of the spectrum is about 100,000 times greater than the frequency of the six-centimeter waves used in the microwave-radio relay system; thus the theoretical com-

munication capacity of a typical light wave is about 100,000 times greater than that of a typical microwave. This fact has long been recognized by communication engineers, and attempts to exploit the vast potential of light for communication were made at the Bell Laboratories before 1950. After a brief period of exploration this work was deferred; to understand why, it is necessary to review briefly how carrier waves are produced by a conventional radio communication system and by light sources other than lasers.

Power for radio communication is produced by electrical circuits, each of which is made up of a number of passive tuning elements (coils and parallel-plate capacitors) in combination with an

LASER BEAM produced by a helium-neon gas laser (*left*) is focused by means of a "gas lens" (*center*) in this photograph made in the author's laboratory at the Bell Telephone Laboratories in Holmdel, N.J. As the beam emerges from the lens it decreases to minimum before expanding. The photograph was made in three stages. First the optical bench on which the various components are mounted was fully illuminated and exposed. Then the

active element (either a vacuum tube or a transistor) and a source of current. The active element serves as a kind of valve for transforming the current into one that pulsates at a frequency determined by the number of turns in the coils or the number of plates in the capacitors. A circuit of this type is called an oscillator.

Almost all of a radio oscillator's power is concentrated at a single frequency, which can be adjusted at will by changing the arrangement of the coils or the capacitors. When the output current from such an oscillator is fed into a suitably designed horn, the energy is radiated in the form of a beam that spreads at an angle roughly equal to the wavelength of the radiation divided by the diameter of the horn's aperture [see illustration on next page]. Because all the energy originates in circuits that are small compared with the length of the typical radio wave and because the energy is usually radiated from a horn with a wide aperture, the wave fronts of the beam are essentially plane, or flat, at the mouth of the horn and gradually assume a spherical shape as the beam progresses away from the horn.

Now consider how light is produced by an ordinary incandescent, or hot-wire, electric lamp [see illustration at top of page 327]. A current passing through the fine wire heats it to a high temperature, whereupon it emits electromagnetic energy in the form of visible light. The light from the hot wire ra-

diates in all directions; more precisely, each point on the wire radiates in all directions. This is an important difference between a radio oscillator and a hot-wire light source, and before the advent of the laser it was one of the main drawbacks to the use of light waves for communication. When one attempts to focus the light output from a hot-wire lamp into a beam, several undesirable effects ensue. First, only part of the radiation from the wire falls on the focusing lens; second, and more important, each radiating point produces a beam whose angle with respect to the axis of the main beam is proportional to the distance of that particular radiating point from the center of the wire. In order to make this angle as small as possible, "point sources"—for example carbon arcs—are used in searchlights and other lamps in which a narrow beam is essential. Even with a point source, however, the resulting beam spreads at an angle equal to the wavelength of the light divided by the diameter of the source. Obviously a point light source can supply only a small amount of power compared with a source that is not so restricted in size.

Another important difference between a hot-wire light source and a radio-wave source is the range of frequencies at which a given source radiates. The emission frequency of a hot-wire source varies with temperature; moreover, a hot-wire radiator spreads its power over a very broad spectral band—in sharp contrast to a radio oscil-

lator, which radiates steadily at a single frequency.

The inadequacy of a hot-wire light source as an oscillator for producing single-frequency carrier waves ultimately led to the deferral of early research on the exploitation of light for communication. Invariably the wide-band emissions from a series of hot-wire oscillators would overlap and cause mutual interference. In addition, within any given channel interference would occur among various individual voice signals. An attempt to avoid these problems could be made by selecting with a filter only the energy within a narrow band; although this would produce a more nearly monochromatic source, it would utilize only a tiny fraction of the original power of the lamp. The loss of efficiency involved in this step would make the whole procedure impractical.

The invention of the laser in the late 1950's by Arthur L. Schawlow and Charles H. Townes provided a way out of this dilemma. The principle on which the laser—as well as its parent, the maser—is based can be traced back as far as 1917, when Albert Einstein showed that "stimulated," or controlled, radiation could be obtained from an atom under certain conditions. (The term "laser" is an acronym for "light amplification by stimulated emission of radiation"; "maser" is an acronym for "microwave amplification by stimulated emission of radiation.")

In order to grasp the novelty of the

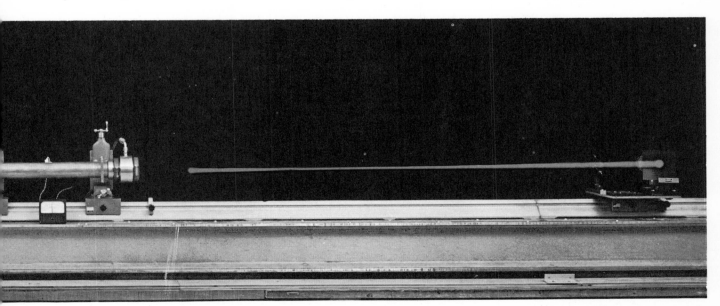

room lights were turned out and the laser itself was activated and exposed. Finally the laser was masked and a portion of the laser beam was photographed in color with the aid of a special device mounted on a sled on the optical bench (right). The device contains an ordinary glass lens for focusing the beam on a circular mirror, which in turn rotates the beam through an angle of 90 degrees toward the camera; the beam then strikes a translucent surface, where it is recorded as a circular image on the photographic film. When the sled is pushed along the optical bench, these successive circular images form a continuous image of the beam on the film.

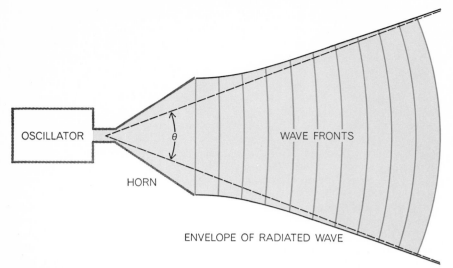

RADIO WAVES obtained from a radio oscillator (*left*) in the form of a pulsating current can be fed into a suitably designed horn (*center*), from which they are radiated into space in the form of a beam that spreads at an angle (θ) roughly equal to the wavelength of the radiation divided by the diameter of the horn's aperture. The wave fronts of the beam are essentially plane at the mouth of the horn and assume a spherical shape as the beam progresses away from the horn. The angle θ has been exaggerated here; normally it is less than 10 degrees.

concept of stimulated emission, let us first examine a little more closely how light is produced by an ordinary incandescent lamp and by a fluorescent lamp. In both cases radiation is the result of a change in the orbital arrangement of electrons in a molecule or around an atomic nucleus. According to the rules of quantum mechanics there are discrete orbital arrangements that a given set of electrons can assume; certain of these arrangements have more energy than others. When an electron drops from a configuration of higher energy to one of lower energy, the surplus energy appears as radiation, partly electromagnetic and partly acoustic, or vibrational. Since the possible energy levels are discrete, the electromagnetic radiation from any one type of change in electronic configuration always has the same frequency. In a hot solid, however, many different electronic configurations are possible, and the differences in energy among the permitted states are slightly different from one another. As a consequence light is emitted at many different frequencies. Further complications in the electromagnetic spectrum of an emitting hot wire are introduced by acoustic interactions, which will not be discussed here.

In a fluorescent lamp an electric current is passed through a gas rather than through a solid, but the radiative mechanism is essentially the same as in a hot-wire lamp. Electrons are raised from a lower energy state to a higher one, and when they fall back to the lower state, their surplus energy is emitted as light.

The situation is somewhat simplified in the case of a fluorescent lamp by the fact that acoustic interactions are negligible, and the frequency of the emitted light is related directly to the changes in the electronic energy levels. Moreover, a few types of energy change may tend to predominate, giving fluorescent tubes used in advertising signs their characteristic colors: yellow for sodium vapor, violet for mercury vapor and so on. Although the bandwidth is narrow enough to appear as a definite color, it is still very broad—on the order of 500 billion cycles per second for a sodium-vapor lamp.

The crucial difference between these conventional light sources and a laser lies in the extent to which the emission of surplus energy can be controlled. Einstein showed that when an atom or a molecule has somehow had its energy status raised, the release of this stored energy can be controlled by subjecting the atom or molecule to a small electromagnetic field of the proper frequency. (In contrast, the emissions of a hot-wire or fluorescent radiator occur spontaneously.) The controlled release of energy by the foregoing technique is called stimulated emission; the weak field doing the stimulating is enhanced by the energy of the stimulated radiation. In order to ensure that the stimulated emission is dominant, heat radiation must be kept to a minimum.

The number of possible frequencies emitted by a laser can also be restrict-

ed by selectively feeding power into a few specific changes in the electronic configuration of the emitting atoms. This situation is too complicated to explain in detail here, but in general it means that an emitting atom in a laser behaves ideally when it is suspended relatively far from its neighboring atoms. This isolation occurs naturally in a gas; it can also be achieved in a solid by mixing the emitting atoms or molecules very dilutely in a substance that is both transparent to the stimulated emission and passive in the frequency range of the emission, that is, in a solid in which no energy-level differences exist in the vicinity of the one responsible for the stimulated emission. By introducing energy that is specifically capable of raising the energy status of the isolated atoms only, the stimulated emission is kept to a narrow spectral band.

In a gas laser, such as the helium-neon laser shown in the top illustration on page 329, a steady electric discharge is maintained through the gas mixture. In the region of the discharge electrons associated with the neon atoms are raised to higher energy levels, from which they may drop spontaneously to lower energy levels with only a few discrete energy differences. One such energy difference accounts for the emission of red light with a wavelength of 6,328 angstrom units and a frequency of 473 trillion cycles per second. By sending a weak electromagnetic wave at exactly 473 trillion cycles per second through the laser tube one can stimulate emission from the excited neon atoms: the weak input wave will emerge as a more energetic output wave with the same frequency. Input energy at any other frequency will not stimulate this emission and will pass through the laser essentially unchanged. Moreover, if the input wave has plane wave fronts, so will the amplified output wave have them. The latter property, which is called spatial coherence, is in contrast to the series of broad, spherical wave fronts produced by the spontaneous, uncorrelated emissions of a hot-wire source.

A laser can be made to act as an electrical oscillator by adding two reflectors at the ends of the tube to form a resonant cavity [*see middle illustration on page 329*]. The light oscillating back and forth between the two mirrors at 473 trillion cycles per second is built up by additional stimulated emissions until it uses up all the excited electrons; some of the energy in the cavity is then re-

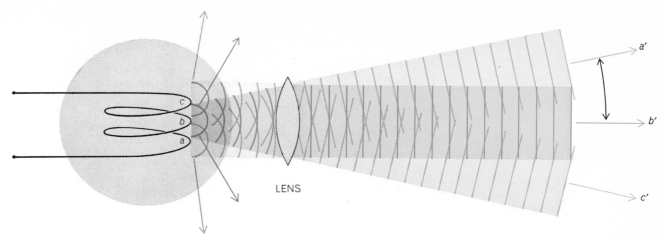

INCOHERENT LIGHT WAVES obtained from an ordinary incandescent, or hot-wire, electric lamp (*left*) radiate in all directions; stated more precisely, each point on the wire radiates in all directions. When one attempts to focus the light output from a hot-wire lamp into a beam, only part of the radiation from the wire falls on the focusing lens. Moreover, each radiating point produces a beam whose angle with respect to the axis of the main beam (*bb'*) is proportional to the distance of that particular radiating point from the center of the wire. These two drawbacks—and the fact that a hot-wire radiator spreads its power over a very broad spectral band—make the incandescent lamp unsuitable for use in a long-distance communication system based on light waves.

leased through one of the end mirrors, which is partially transparent. The output of such a laser is concentrated at a single frequency, with a maximum deviation from the fundamental frequency of only a few thousand cycles per second. As in the case of the laser amplifier, the output of this laser oscillator is spatially coherent.

The two properties of monochromat- icity and spatial coherence make the laser a potentially useful oscillator for intercity communication systems. What is more, the spatial coherence of a laser beam makes possible highly directional transmission unattainable by conventional radio techniques. A plane-wave laser source radiates a beam that is almost constant in width for a distance equal to the diameter of the source squared divided by four times the wavelength of the radiation [*see top illustration on page 330*]. Beyond this distance the beam gradually expands to form a cone, the angle of which is equal to the wavelength of the radiation divided by the diameter of the source. In other words, the spreading of a laser beam and a radio-wave beam is identical. Because of the vast differ-

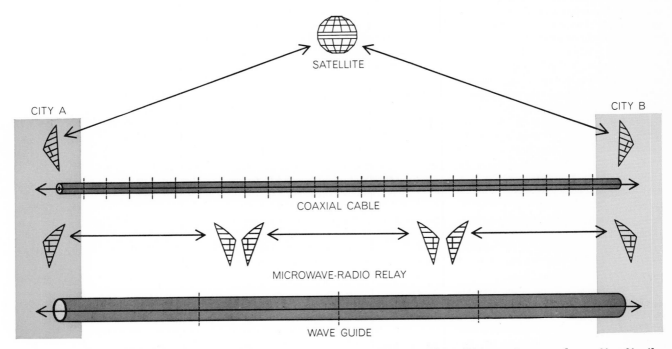

FOUR ELECTRICAL TECHNIQUES for transmitting a large volume of messages over a long distance are available at present. The newest technique involves the use of artificial earth satellites (*top*). The coaxial-cable system (*second from top*) still carries a large proportion of the communication traffic between cities in the U.S. The largest share of the intercity traffic in the U.S. is transmitted through the air by means of microwave-radio relay systems (*second from bottom*), with amplifying stations spaced some 20 to 30 miles apart. The wave guide technique (*bottom*), which has recently been perfected, will be able to carry more communication traffic than any other system currently available. Amplifiers (*short broken lines*) are spaced two to four miles apart in the coaxial-cable system and 10 to 15 miles apart in the wave guide system. Microwave-radio relay horns are actually 10 to 15 feet in diameter.

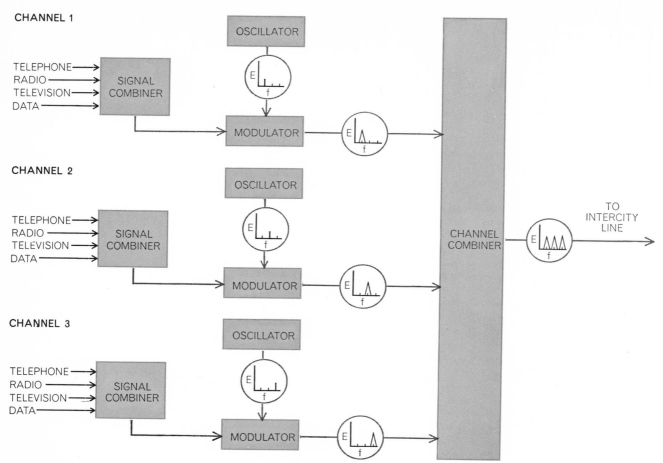

CHANNEL 1

TELEPHONE
RADIO
TELEVISION
DATA

SIGNAL COMBINER

OSCILLATOR

MODULATOR

CHANNEL 2

TELEPHONE
RADIO
TELEVISION
DATA

SIGNAL COMBINER

OSCILLATOR

MODULATOR

CHANNEL 3

TELEPHONE
RADIO
TELEVISION
DATA

SIGNAL COMBINER

OSCILLATOR

MODULATOR

CHANNEL COMBINER

TO INTERCITY LINE

MULTIPLEXING—a process for simultaneously transmitting many different messages over the same pathway—is employed in every long-distance electrical communication system. A single-frequency "carrier" wave produced by some kind of oscillator is successively modulated by a large number of individual signals to form a new, composite signal wave. This process is repeated for many different channels, using carrier waves of different frequencies. Special electrical networks then combine several of these broad energy bands for simultaneous transmission over a single intercity pathway. In each circled graph *E* stands for energy and *f* for frequency.

ence in wavelength, however, the practical implications of these formulas are quite different for the two radiations.

For example, in the case of a microwave-radio relay system the width of the antenna horn is typically 10 feet and the wavelength of the radiation is 7.5 centimeters. Applying the first formula yields 100 feet as the maximum distance over which the width of the beam remains constant. This means that a receiver with a 10-foot horn must be within 100 feet of the transmitter to receive most of the original beam. The normal practice in a microwave-radio relay system is to space the transmitter and the receiver 20 to 30 miles apart, with the result that the received power is about a hundred-thousandth of the transmitted power.

In the case of the laser, on the other hand, the beam width might be two inches and the wavelength of the beam on the order of 6,300 angstroms. This yields a maximum distance without beam expansion of about three-fifths

of a mile; thus a two-inch lens three-fifths of a mile from the laser would collect most of the transmitted power. For longer distances a series of two-inch lenses spaced three-fifths of a mile apart could be used to confine the beam and guide it to the receiver [*see second illustration at top of page 330*]. The power loss at each lens due to beam expansion could in principle be made as small as one part in 100,000, or even less by making the lens spacing 20 to 40 percent less than the maximum distance before beam expansion. Extremely long total distances would appear to be attainable before the net received power would drop to a hundred-thousandth of the transmitted power, as is the case in microwave-radio relay systems.

We have seen that the two basic properties of a laser beam—monochromaticity and spatial coherence—make it perfectly suited for use in a long-distance communication system. Nonetheless, many ticklish problems remain to be solved before this potential

can be effectively exploited. I shall now describe briefly the status of current research aimed toward solving these problems.

In order to build an efficient laser communication system, a large number of lasers are required to serve as oscillators. Their frequencies should be spaced far enough apart to avoid overlap when their modulated outputs are combined on an intercity line. On the other hand, too large a spacing between frequencies is undesirable, because this would waste valuable frequency space that could be used to carry communication traffic. Obtaining a properly spaced series of frequencies is by no means an easy task; laser frequencies are determined by discrete energy-level differences in the emitting atoms or molecules, and these are essentially fixed for a given material. A search is under way for an appropriate set of frequencies and for some rule by which such frequencies can be predicted. This research involves not only various gaseous mixtures but also solid laser materials, the emitting atoms of which are suspended as very dilute impurities in a transparent "host" solid.

Another problem arises from the fact that a given molecule may have more than one emission frequency. The helium-neon mixture mentioned earlier, for example, can emit at 261 trillion and 88.5 trillion cycles per second as well as at 473 trillion cycles per second. Since only one frequency is desired from each laser, techniques must be found for isolating a single emission frequency. Much remains to be done in this area, but so far laser outputs ranging from a few thousandths of a watt to millions of watts have been achieved, and hundreds of different laser frequencies have been observed. Recently at the Bell Laboratories a laser-like source with a continuously variable frequency was conceived and demonstrated; this device uses ambient-temperature control to vary the natural emission frequency through a 5 percent range in the vicinity of 300 trillion cycles per second.

The actual long-distance transmission of a laser beam is another challenge to which much current research is devoted. Although very low point-to-point transmission losses could be obtained in the near vacuum of outer space by using a highly directional beam, the earth's atmosphere is hostile to electromagnetic waves in the visible region. Rain, snow and fog can cause heavy power losses. When high reliability is a requirement of a particular transmission system, an unshielded atmospheric path does not seem feasible, but in special cases in which intermittent communication is acceptable unshielded pathways may suffice. Studies are under way to determine if an infrared laser would be more suitable for transmission through the atmosphere.

Guided laser transmission can be shielded from the atmosphere by putting the lenses in an airtight pipe, possibly underground. Here one has several options. The lenses can be spaced 300 feet or more apart and still contain the beam within a tube one inch in diameter. When this is done, high-quality optical lenses appear suitable for focusing, but some additional provision must be made to allow the beam to follow the curving path demanded by hills and horizontal turns. The laser beam will not follow a curved sequence of lenses for such large lens spacings. New techniques have been conceived for sensing the beam's position and, by means of a feedback mechanism, prop-

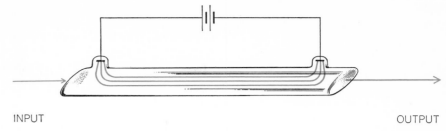

INPUT   OUTPUT

GAS LASER normally acts as an amplifier. A weak input wave stimulates emission from the excited gas atoms and emerges as a more energetic output wave with the same frequency.

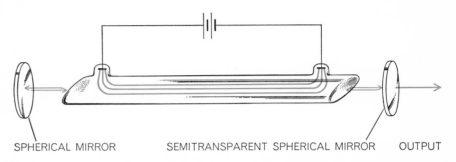

SPHERICAL MIRROR   SEMITRANSPARENT SPHERICAL MIRROR   OUTPUT

LASER ACTS AS OSCILLATOR when one adds two reflectors at the ends of the tube to form a resonant cavity. The light oscillating back and forth between the two mirrors is built up by stimulated emissions before it is released through one of the mirrors (*right*).

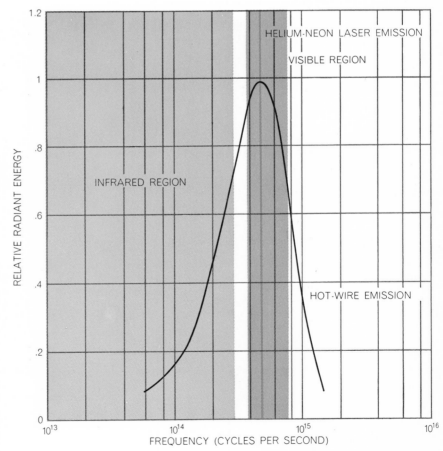

LASER EMISSION (*vertical colored line*) is concentrated at a single frequency, with a deviation from the fundamental frequency of only a few thousand cycles per second. In contrast, the emission from a hot-wire lamp (*black curve*) is spread over a broad spectral band.

erly directing the beam around the curve.

Alternatively, the lenses can be brought close together; quarter-inch lenses spaced a few feet apart will allow a beam to follow curves typical, say, of a modern superhighway. In this case the lenses must have a very low power loss, as there would be more than 1,000 lenses per mile. The best quartz optical lenses have far too much loss for this purpose, as a result of surface roughness and reflection from the interface between the quartz and the air.

In order to overcome these difficulties a new type of lens, called a gas lens, has been invented by Dwight W. Berreman of the Bell Laboratories and improved by some of his colleagues. In one model a gas—for example carbon dioxide—is passed through a heated

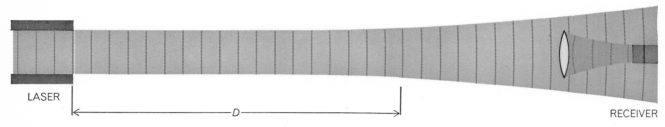

SPATIAL COHERENCE of a laser beam makes possible highly directional transmission. A plane-wave laser source radiates a beam that is almost constant in width for a distance (D) equal to the diameter of the source squared, divided by four times the wave-length of the radiation. Beyond this distance the beam gradually expands to form a cone. The expansion of the beam is greatly exaggerated here; in actuality D would be about three-fifths of a mile for a two-inch beam with a wavelength of some 6,300 angstrom units.

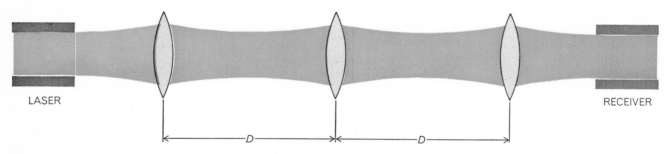

SERIES OF LENSES spaced at the distance D apart could be used to confine the laser beam and guide it to the receiver. The power loss at each lens due to beam expansion could in principle be made as small as one part in 100,000 or even less by making the lens spacing 20 to 40 percent less than D. Again the beam expansion has been greatly exaggerated and the horizontal scale compressed.

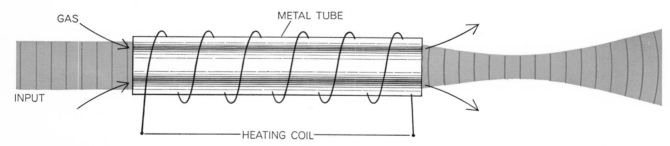

PRINCIPLE OF GAS LENS was invented by Dwight W. Berreman of the Bell Laboratories. A gas—for example carbon dioxide—is passed through a heated tube. Because the gas travels faster in the center of the tube, it is cooler there than near the wall. The cooler gas in the center is denser and hence a converging lens is formed. The great advantage of the gas lens is that there are no surfaces in the path of the laser beam, and the lens losses are limited to a very slight scattering of the light by the gas molecules. A gas lens is free from turbulence effects because the velocity of the gas is very low (about five miles per hour).

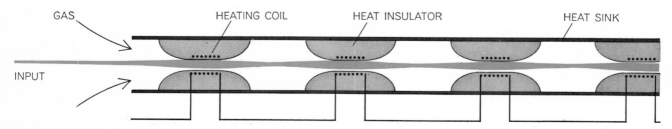

GAS-LENS WAVE GUIDE is one of several types already built by workers at the Bell Laboratories. Any lens wave guide must be built to meet extremely stringent tolerances, and further work will be needed to determine if the necessary accuracy can be achieved at a reasonable cost. The gas lens shown in the photograph on pages 324 and 325 uses air as the focusing medium.

tube. Because the gas travels faster in the center of the tube, it is cooler there than near the wall. The cooler gas in the center is denser and hence a converging lens is formed [*see third illustration from top on opposite page*]. Several different types of gas-lens wave guides have already been built. The great advantage of the gas lens is that there are no surfaces in the path of the light beam, and the lens losses are limited only to a very slight scattering of the light by the gas molecules. The light-guidance problem is much further from solution than this might suggest, however. A gas lens is free from turbulence effects because the velocity of the gas is low (about five miles per hour), but some aberrations appear nonetheless. Any lens wave guide must be built to meet extremely stringent tolerances, and further work will be needed to determine if the necessary accuracy can be achieved at a reasonable cost.

An essential component of any long-distance communication system is a modulator. In order to modulate the light output of a laser the light waves must be capable of being varied in synchronism with the broad-band radio wave produced by combining many individual telephone, television and radio signals. All the optical modulators devised so far have been based on variations in the refractive index of some substance in synchronism with the signal wave. In one of these devices [*see illustration on this page*] the laser output passes through a solid cylinder of potassium dihydrogen phosphate, which is placed in an electric field proportional to the signal wave. The index of refraction of the cylinder along the vertical axis differs from that along the horizontal axis by an amount proportional to this applied electric field. As a result the laser beam emerges from the far end of the modulator polarized at right angles with respect to the polarization of the input wave. In addition the amplitude of the modulator output wave varies according to the strength of the applied electric field.

Laser modulators of this type are operable but at present too inefficient to be entirely satisfactory. Similar devices based on modulation of the refractive index in semiconductor junctions are being examined.

Research is also being directed toward finding a suitable light detector for use at the receiving end of a laser-communication path. Vacuum tubes containing surfaces from which electrons are emitted in response to an impinging light beam—outgrowths of

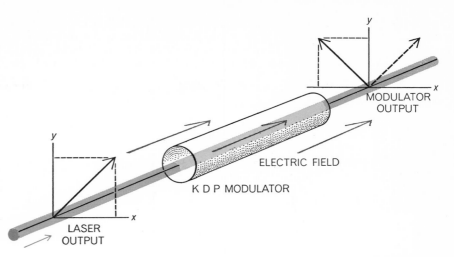

MODULATION OF LASER BEAM is based on variations in the refractive index of some substance in synchronism with the broad-band radio wave produced by combining many individual telephone, television and radio signals. In this particular modulator the laser output passes through a solid cylinder of potassium dihydrogen phosphate (KDP), which is placed in an electric field that is proportional to the signal wave. The index of refraction of the cylinder along the *x* axis differs from that along the *y* axis by an amount proportional to this applied electric field. As a result the laser beam emerges from the far end of the modulator polarized at right angles with respect to the polarization of the input wave.

the familiar photomultiplier tube—have been perfected and in the visible region of the spectrum are reasonably efficient. Their efficiency falls, however, at infrared frequencies. Another detector consists of a semiconductor junction that responds to light by releasing electrons into a low-frequency circuit in proportion to the energy of the impinging light wave.

A major part of the research effort devoted to finding better detectors, modulators and lasers involves new materials. Metallurgists, chemists and physicists are challenged to develop an understanding of the behavior of various materials and to devise techniques for deriving both purer materials and materials with carefully controlled traces of known "impurities" in otherwise pure and well-ordered crystals. Before the advent of the laser the need to study many of these properties of materials did not exist. Besides providing the need, the laser has provided a new capability for studying materials in ways not possible before. The essentially monochromatic nature of the laser output has made possible revealing spectroscopic studies of energy levels in a wide variety of substances.

In spite of the many advantages of the laser in long-distance communication, the economic competition from the present systems can be expected to be severe. The test of commercial success is not merely the feasibility of communicating in the visible region of the

spectrum. A combination of coaxial-cable, microwave-radio and wave guide systems can provide the equivalent of a single super-broad-band system. Such a composite system could provide the foreseeable communication needs of the world for many years to come and has the main advantage of diversification: less risk of losing the entire communication system as the result of an accident. In addition, any new system must not only do the job at a lower cost than existing systems but also anticipate various improvements in the existing systems. The transistor and other solid-state devices have revolutionized the existing communication systems in the past 10 years, and the laser must now compete in an era in which vacuum tubes with two-year life-spans have been replaced by solid-state devices with 20-year life-spans.

The laser, however, can also be expected to partake of the solid-state revolution. Solid-state lasers already exist, and although they have not had the spectral purity of gas lasers, this situation appears to be changing. The overriding trend in the history of electrical communication has been toward ever larger bandwidths and ever higher frequencies, because the use of wide-band systems has proved to be more economical than parallel narrow-band systems designed to achieve the same total communication capacity. Judging by this trend, we would expect the laser to play an important role in the communication systems of the future.

30

The Modulation of Laser Light

Donald F. Nelson   *June 1968*

Ever since the first laser was operated in 1960 the project that has attracted the most intense effort in the field of laser applications has been the attempt to exploit the potentially enormous information-carrying capacity of the laser beam for use in intercity communications [see "Communication by Laser," by Stewart E. Miller, which begins on page 323 in this book]. In general the problem can be broken down into five parts, corresponding to the five basic components essential to any long-distance electrical communication system. These components are: an oscillator to generate the carrier wave, a modulator to impress information on the wave, a transmission medium to convey the wave, a detector to receive the wave and a demodulator to extract the information from the wave.

In the past few years considerable progress has been made in the development of several of the components needed for laser communication. The most promising candidates for the oscillator now include such lasers as the helium-neon gas laser, the carbon dioxide gas laser and the neodymium-doped yttrium-aluminum-garnet crystal laser. The transmission medium may in some circumstances be simply the atmosphere, but the criterion of high reliability will probably require that the laser beam be transmitted through underground pipes containing numerous lenses to focus the beam periodically as well as mirrors to reflect the beam around corners. The

detector is likely to be a small semiconductor diode that generates an electric current when light strikes it.

Until recently the most serious obstacle to the construction of an optical communication system has been the lack of a suitable high-frequency modulator (and a compatible demodulator). Three new light modulators developed within the past year at the Bell Telephone Laboratories point the way to the eventual solution of this crucial aspect of the laser communication problem.

The modulation of a light wave means the controlled variation of some property of the wave such as its amplitude, frequency, phase, polarization or direction of propagation. Of these five possible approaches only modulation of the propagation direction is not currently envisioned for a laser communication system and so will not be discussed here. Polarization modulation has not been used by itself, but it does come into play as an intermediate step in two of the modulators that will be described later in this article.

We are left with the optical equivalents of the two best-known modulation methods of radio-wave and microwave communications, namely phase or frequency modulation (FM) and amplitude modulation (AM). As in the earlier technologies, amplitude modulation can be of two types. In one a small variation in the amplitude of the carrier wave is proportional to the electrical signal that is

supplied to the modulator. This type of modulation can be used to transmit an analogue signal, such as the signal provided by the human voice.

Another type of amplitude modulation, called pulse-code modulation (PCM), is currently finding increased use in communication technology; it is simply the abrupt turning on and off of the carrier wave [see "Pulse-Code Modulation," by J. S. Mayo; SCIENTIFIC AMERICAN, March, 1968]. This type of modulation is used to transmit digitized information that is manipulated by computer circuits. In PCM one "bit" of information is transmitted by the presence or absence of a pulse at a particular instant of time. In order to be carried by PCM the information must first be reduced to yes or no answers, that is, to a binary code.

The main attraction of an optical communication system is the large range of frequencies, or bandwidth, available for carrier waves. This means that far larger amounts of information can theoretically be transmitted by means of the visible portion of the electromagnetic spectrum than by all the radio-wave and microwave portions combined. Accordingly designers of optical communication systems are primarily concerned with systems that have a large bandwidth and hence a large capacity for information transmission.

Modulators for large-bandwidth systems must be capable of responding to electrical modulating signals with frequencies of hundreds or even thousands of megacycles per second. This would allow tens or even hundreds of television programs to be transmitted simultaneously. Thus the physical effect on which the modulator is based must be fast enough to respond to such frequencies. Electric and magnetic fields acting through the electro-optic and magneto-optic effects are sufficiently fast. Thermal methods and most mechanical methods of modulating light beams are too slow. Ultrasonic vibrations, which are mechanical in nature, may nonetheless be found useful in the future.

The physical effect that has received the most attention for laser-beam modulation is the electro-optic effect. In this effect the application of an electric field across a solid or liquid medium causes a small change in its refractive index. If the index is lowered, the light travels faster through the medium; if it is raised, the light travels slower. Furthermore, under the influence of an electric field the medium becomes birefringent, that is, light beams of two different linear polarizations travel through it at different velocities.

Since changing the light velocity affects the phase of the wave, an electro-optic modulator is basically a phase modulator. It can be converted to an amplitude modulator by a scheme that involves placing a light polarizer oriented at 45 degrees to the electric field in front of the electro-optic medium [see top illustration on page 336]. The orientation of the polarizer causes the resulting linearly polarized light to be equally divided between the two principal directions of the electro-optic medium. The electro-optic effect causes these two components to travel at different velocities and therefore to get out of phase with each other. After traversing the medium they no longer combine to give a linearly polarized light wave as they did on entering the medium. Instead their sum is an elliptically polarized light beam, that is, the tip of the optical electric-field vector traces out an ellipse in space once every cycle of the light wave. In this way two phase-modulated light components can be made to form a polarization-modulated light wave.

This wave can in turn be easily converted to an amplitude-modulated wave by passing it through another polarizer. The transmission axis of the second polarizer is placed at an angle of 90 degrees with respect to the axis of the first polarizer. Only the projection of the optical electric-field vector on the polarization axis is transmitted through the second

polarizer. If the proper amount of voltage is applied to the crystal, the output polarization can be made to be linear in a direction at 90 degrees to the input polarization. In this case complete transmission of the light through the output polarizer occurs. With no voltage applied, no light emerges. By alternating the voltage between these two values one can pulse-code-modulate the laser beam.

There are actually two types of electro-optic effect. For one type the change in the index of refraction is proportional to the square of the applied voltage. This is called the Kerr effect after John Kerr, a Scottish physicist who discovered it in liquids in 1875. The Kerr effect can also operate in any crystal. For the second type of electro-optic effect the change in refractive index is proportional to the first power of the applied voltage. It is called the Pockels effect after F. Pockels, a German physicist who made the first careful study of it in 1893. The Pockels effect can occur only in crystals that lack a center of symmetry, that is, lack a point through which every atom of the crystal can theoretically be reflected to obtain the identical crystal structure.

Kerr cells containing nitrobenzene have been used for years as light shutters in a variety of specialized applications. The first useful Pockels cell was made in 1949 from a crystal of potassium dihydrogen phosphate (KDP) by Bruce H. Billings, then at Baird Associates. None of these devices was capable of the extremely high-frequency operation needed for broad-band communications. In 1961 Ivan P. Kaminow of Bell Laboratories demonstrated a high-frequency modulator for lasers based on the Pockels effect in KDP. The Kaminow modulator required too much power for a practical communication system, but it served to stimulate a search for materials that would show a still larger effect. Many new crystals have been grown for this purpose since then. Lithium niobate, lithium tantalate, potassium tantalate-niobate (KTN) and potassium-lithium niobate are a few of the more promising materials. All of these exhibit a Pockels effect except KTN, which shows a Kerr effect. All are transparent to electromagnetic radiation in the visible portion of the spectrum and in a large portion of the infrared region and so can be used to modulate a great variety of lasers.

It is difficult to say which electro-optic material will ultimately be the best for a given laser wavelength, but already lithium tantalate has been in-

corporated into a very useful broadband modulator by Richard T. Denton, F. S. Chen and T. S. Kinsel at Bell Laboratories. This modulator is the most highly developed one at present. It differs in several important details from the generalized electro-optic modulator discussed above. First of all, by means of a reflector at one end of the crystal the light passes through the crystal twice [see bottom illustration on page 336]. This doubles the modulating effect for a given applied voltage. In addition, lithium tantalate is naturally birefringent. Even with no electric field present the two different linearly polarized light components travel at different velocities. They get out of phase during their passage through the crystal and emerge to produce a state of elliptic polarization. To prevent this another birefringent crystal in the form of a wedge is inserted in the path of the beam and adjusted so that in the absence of an electric field the beam is in the same state of linear polarization when it emerges as when it entered.

The birefringence of lithium tantalate creates another problem. When the temperature changes, the birefringence also changes and causes the output polarization to do so. This can be cured only by precise temperature control of the crystal. It has been found that the temperature must be held constant to within .04 degree centigrade. The metal blocks that apply the voltage to the crystal help to hold its temperature constant. They also perform a third function by reducing the amplitude of mechanical vibrations that the application of the voltage creates in the crystal by means of the piezoelectric effect.

The lithium tantalate crystal is long (one centimeter) and thin (quarter of a millimeter), since the change in phase brought about by the Pockels effect is proportional to the distance traversed by the light as well as to the electric field, the field being larger when the thickness over which the voltage is applied is reduced. Because of the small thickness of the crystal a lens is used to focus the parallel laser beam into the crystal and to re-form a parallel beam again after it emerges. The component of polarization at right angles to the input polarization is deflected by a birefringent element called a Rochon prism to form the output beam.

The lithium tantalate modulator has been used both in a conventional AM mode and in a PCM mode. In the AM mode it can produce 80 percent modulation of the intensity (the square of the amplitude of a wave) of a red helium-

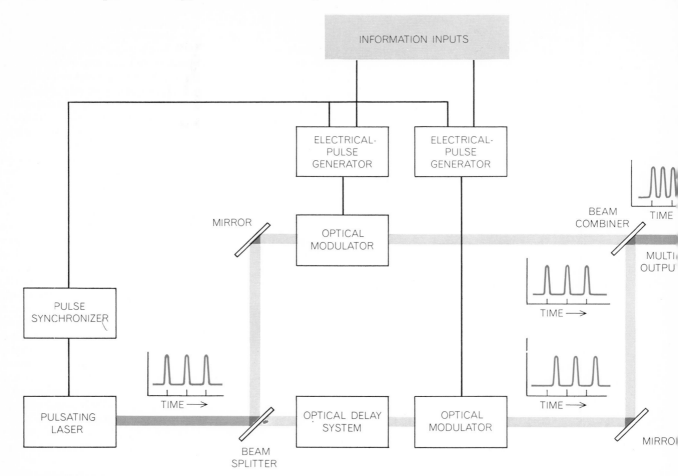

OPTICAL COMMUNICATION SYSTEM based on the pulse-code modulation of laser beams would make use of the principle of multiplexing: the simultaneous transmission of diverse information on the same beam. In the multiplexing operation (*left*) a beam of laser pulses is split and each part is modulated separately. One beam is delayed and then the two beams are recombined. The information-carrying capacity of the beam is thereby doubled. If the laser pulses are short compared with their spacing, this process can

neon laser beam over a bandwidth of 220 megacycles per second, using only 200 milliwatts of power from a transistorized amplifier. At present the effectiveness of the modulator is limited by the capabilities of this amplifier rather than by any characteristics of the modulator crystal. With an improved amplifier the bandwidth could be expanded to 1,000 megacycles per second.

The PCM mode of operation may prove to be the most practical for light modulators. It has the advantage that the amount of modulation need not be strictly proportional to the modulating electrical signal, as must be the case for conventional AM. Since information is conveyed in PCM by the presence or absence of a light pulse, such transmission is less affected by the presence of optical "noise" received with the signal. The third advantage is that PCM makes it easier to transmit simultaneously unrelated information, such as several television, telephone or data channels, over the same light beam. This mechanism of

simultaneous transmission of diverse information on the same beam is called multiplexing.

The lithium tantalate modulator has been used for PCM by applying to the crystal a train of voltage pulses, each of which is capable of producing an output polarization at 90 degrees to the input polarization. This polarization is deflected by a polarizing prism to form a train of output pulses. Thus the crystal acts as a gate with "on" and "off" positions. Although the device could modulate a continuous laser beam, it is more convenient for it to modulate a laser beam that consists of a regular train of pulses that are synchronized with the modulator and are narrow compared with their spacing in time. The modulator acts as a gate for these pulses by allowing some to pass and not others.

Additional information can be "time-multiplexed" into the pulse train by first splitting the laser beam into two pulse trains and then modulating each separately [*see illustration above*]. One of the beams is delayed with respect to the oth-

er and then the pulse trains are combined into one beam again. The narrower the pulses are compared with their original separation, the greater the number of separate beams that can be made, modulated, delayed and recombined, allowing greater information transmission. The demultiplexing process, illustrated on the opposite page, is essentially the reverse of this process.

The lithium tantalate modulator has already been operated at 224 million bits per second. With a pulsating helium-neon laser as a source fourfold multiplexing could be done to quadruple the rate of information transmission. Even higher rates are envisioned when pulsating lasers that have narrower pulses are used.

All the crystals that have been mentioned so far are dielectric crystals, that is, crystals that do not carry electric current. There are other crystals that have a sizable electro-optic effect but carry current when voltage is applied to them. This causes too much power

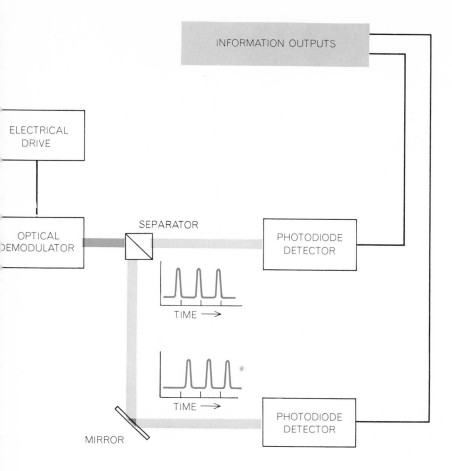

be repeated several times. In the demultiplexing operation (*right*) a demodulator changes the polarization of alternate light pulses, which are then separated from each other by the separator prism. Photodiodes then detect the two trains of pulses. Modulators consist of output polarizers plus electro-optic crystals; demodulators are just electro-optic crystals.

consumption for broad-band modulator use. One crystal of this type is the semi-conductor gallium phosphide, which exhibits a Pockels effect. F. K. Reinhart and I have found a way around this problem that involves the use of the electric field that exists within a *p-n* junction in gallium phosphide. A *p-n* junction is an electric potential barrier to the flow of current and is the heart of semiconductor diodes and transistors. This potential barrier must necessarily contain an electric field, even when no voltage is applied to the junction. If voltage is applied in what is called the reverse direction, no current flows but the electric field within the junction is increased. It can reach values close to a million volts per centimeter—a very strong field compared with what can be placed across large crystals. This strong electric field in turn leads to a large Pockels effect.

Along with this gain, however, comes a new problem. The *p-n*-junction region that possesses this huge field is less than a ten-thousandth of a centimeter wide.

This means that the laser beam that is to be modulated must be very carefully focused on the junction for it to pass along this thin, sheetlike region. Worse yet, because of the diffraction of light—the inherent tendency of light to spread out—one would expect it to be impossible to hold the light in the high-electric-field region where the Pockels effect occurs. Here, however, nature helps out and, for reasons that are not yet well understood, produces a "light pipe" effect that holds the light in the high-field region. A conventional light pipe, such as a plastic rod, prevents light within it from escaping through the sides by total internal reflection. In the *p-n* junction the "light pipe" has sides that are two parallel planes rather than the cylindrical surface of a rod. Such a structure is called a planar dielectric wave guide.

Apart from the narrowness of the electro-optic region and the necessity of lenses to direct the light into and out of this region, our arrangement is similar to other electro-optic modulators [*see top illustration on page 330*]. It should

be remembered that this modulator is on a much smaller scale, the *p-n* junction being only about a millimeter long. Another difference is that gallium phosphide is an orange crystal and will transmit only light of wavelengths spanning the green, yellow, orange, red and near-infrared spectral regions. This range does, however, include a number of prominent laser wavelengths.

Although the *p-n*-junction modulator has not yet been developed to the extent that the lithium tantalate modulator has, it has been studied enough for its capabilities and limitations to be known. The limitation on its modulation ability arises from the fact that power is dissipated within the diode crystal. This dissipation in turn arises from the charging and discharging of the junction's capacitance through the resistance of the bulk crystal. The power-dissipation limit places a limit on the product of the bandwidth of modulation times the voltage that is applied to the crystal, which determines the amount of the modulation. In addition, the junction's capacitance and the crystal's resistance also determine a practical upper limit to the modulation frequency, which is called the cutoff frequency.

Modulator diodes have been fabricated with cutoff frequencies as high as 7,000 megacycles per second. One 1.5-millimeter-long diode is capable of modulating the intensity of a red helium-neon laser beam as much as 80 percent with a power dissipation of only 1.5 milliwatts per megacycle per second of bandwidth. In the present mode of mounting about 150 milliwatts can be dissipated; this leads to a bandwidth of 100 megacycles per second. Improvements in the mounting to allow greater heat dissipation, and other improvements in the *p-n* junction itself, are expected to extend the bandwidth. If the light were passed through the junction twice as it is for the lithium tantalate modulator, the bandwidth could be extended by a factor of four for the same power dissipation. Further development work is needed to accomplish these improvements.

Although the gallium phosphide diode modulator can modulate light of wavelengths ranging from the green to the infrared, its efficiency for modulating the longer wavelengths is lower. It will modulate green laser light more effectively than the red laser light described above, and it will modulate infrared light more poorly. This points up the fact that eventually many light modulators will be needed; no one modulator can be optimal over the entire range of

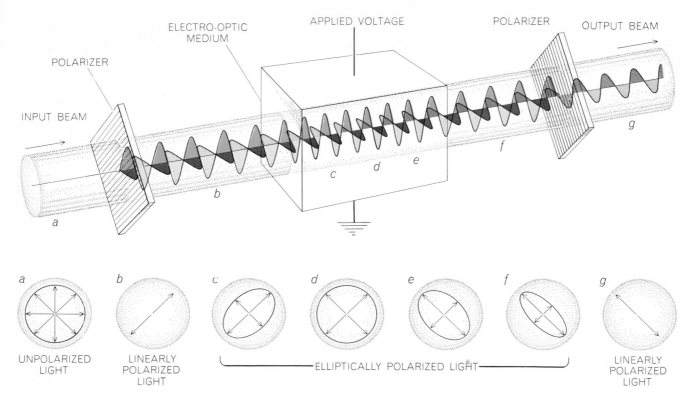

a UNPOLARIZED LIGHT

b LINEARLY POLARIZED LIGHT

c d e f — ELLIPTICALLY POLARIZED LIGHT —

g LINEARLY POLARIZED LIGHT

ELECTRO-OPTIC EFFECT is the basis for one class of laser-beam modulators. In general the electro-optic effect refers to the changes brought about in the light-refracting properties of a solid or liquid medium by the application of an electric field across the medium. In the demonstration at top a beam of unpolarized light from a laser is first sent through a polarizer. The linearly polarized light that emerges has its electric field oscillating in the plane defined by the axis of polarization of the polarizer. This linearly polarized beam can be represented by its vertical and horizontal components (*colored curves*), which are in phase. As the two components pass through the electro-optic medium they are slowed down at different rates and hence gradually become out of phase. They emerge from the medium to form an elliptically polarized light beam. Another polarizer placed in the path of this beam, with its polarization axis oriented at 90 degrees with respect to that of the first polarizer, allows only the component that is parallel to its transmission axis to be transmitted. By varying the applied voltage the polarization of the beam can be made more or less elliptic, and as a result the amplitude of the output beam can be changed accordingly. The cross sections of the beam at bottom show polarization at various stages.

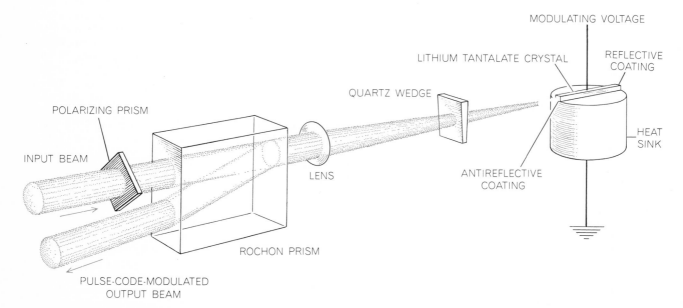

LITHIUM TANTALATE MODULATOR is the most highly developed electro-optic modulator. The laser beam passes through an input polarizer and is focused into the modulator crystal by a lens. It is reflected from the far end of the crystal and emerges in a state of elliptic polarization. After being re-formed as a parallel beam by the lens, the component of polarization perpendicular to the input component is deflected by a Rochon prism to form the output beam. When used for pulse-code modulation, the voltage on the modulator crystal is adjusted so that the light leaving the crystal is linearly polarized perpendicularly to the input polarization and so is entirely deflected by the Rochon prism. A wedge is inserted in the beam to offset the crystal's natural birefringence.

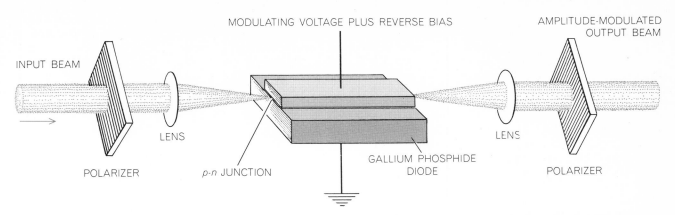

P-N-JUNCTION MODULATOR makes use of an electro-optic effect in a semiconductor crystal. Because the *p-n*-junction region is extremely narrow, careful focusing of the laser beam is required. A constant reverse bias is applied to augment the electric field across the junction and the modulating voltage is impressed on top of this constant field. The polarizers are at 90 degrees to each other.

wavelengths. For instance, the magneto-optic modulator described below is better in the near infrared than either the gallium phosphide diode or the lithium tantalate modulators.

I have mentioned that magneto-optic effects in crystals are fast enough to be used for large-bandwidth modulators of light. Recently such a modulator has been developed by R. C. LeCraw at Bell Laboratories using the Faraday effect. The Faraday effect is the rotation of the plane of polarization of a light wave as it travels through a substance in a direction parallel to an applied magnetic field. It can occur in a variety of gases, liquids and solids. It is named after Michael Faraday, who discovered the effect in glass in 1845.

The rotation of the plane of polarization of light is a phenomenon quite different from the conversion from linear to elliptical polarization described above. In a medium exhibiting Faraday rotation the states of polarization that are preserved on passage through the medium are the right-handed and left-handed components of circularly polarized light, not linearly polarized light as in the case of the birefringent medium discussed above. When a linearly polarized light wave is introduced into a medium exhibiting Faraday rotation, it divides into a combination of right and left circularly polarized waves of equal amplitude. These two states of circular polarization travel at different velocities in the magnetized medium. The resulting change of phase between them causes their sum to produce a state of linear polarization but with its plane of polarization rotated with respect to its initial orientation. The amount of rotation is proportional to the component of magnetization along the direction of propagation. This component can be varied by changing the applied magnetic field. The resulting variation of the plane of polarization can be converted to amplitude modulation by passing the beam through a polarizer.

An efficient magneto-optic modulator requires a material that gives the largest Faraday rotation per unit of optical loss from absorption. This ratio is large only for ferromagnetic materials. Until recently the best material on this basis was the crystal chromium tribromide, which has been studied by J. F. Dillon, Jr., at Bell Laboratories. From a practical viewpoint this crystal nonetheless had a crucial defect: it had to be cooled to within a few degrees of absolute zero in order to have the needed magnetic properties.

Recently a region of exceedingly high transparency in the near infrared has been found in the magnetic crystal yttrium-iron-garnet (YIG). Because of the low optical loss in this region, the ratio of Faraday rotation to optical loss is at least 30 times higher than it is for chromium tribromide. Furthermore, YIG can be used at room temperature. Its use in a high-frequency modulator is further aid-

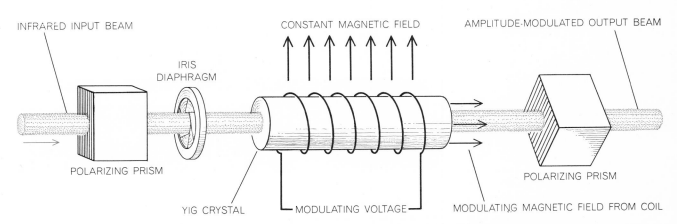

MAGNETO-OPTIC MODULATOR is based on the Faraday effect: the rotation of the plane of polarization of a light wave as it travels through a substance in a direction parallel to an applied magnetic field. In this particular modulator the plane of polarization of an infrared laser beam is rotated in a crystal of yttrium-iron-garnet (YIG). The amount of rotation is determined by the modulating magnetic field along the axis of the YIG rod. The second prism converts the polarization modulation to amplitude modulation.

ed by its having the lowest internal heating arising from rapidly varying magnetic fields of any known ferromagnetic material. The region of transparency of YIG lies between the wavelengths of 12,000 and 45,000 angstrom units in the near infrared. It is useful as a modulator throughout this region but will operate most efficiently at the short-wavelength end of the region. YIG is a synthetic insulating crystal that has ferromagnetic properties. It has the same crystal structure as the many types of gem-quality garnets found in nature. It was discovered in 1956 by two French workers, F. Bertaut and F. Forrat.

The magneto-optic modulator invented by LeCraw has been used to modulate a helium-neon gas laser whose output beam has a wavelength of 15,200 angstroms. This wavelength was chosen for study because it falls near the short-wavelength end of the high-transparency region and also because it is a wavelength to which high-speed germanium photodiode detectors are sensitive. After passing through a polarizer the beam encounters an iris diaphragm, which is used to define the beam diameter in its passage through the one-centimeter-long rod-shaped YIG crystal [*see bottom illustration on preceding page*]. In the final form of the device a lens would be used for this purpose to avoid any loss of light.

A constant magnetic field is applied across the axis of the rod. This field is sufficient to saturate the magnetization of the YIG crystal. This means that all the magnetization vectors of different "domains" in the crystal are forced to align themselves along the constant magnetic field. Current flowing through the coil that surrounds the YIG crystal creates an additional magnetic field parallel to the axis of the rod. This added magnetic field causes the magnetization vector to tilt toward the axis. The resultant component of the magnetization along the axis of the rod is responsible for the Faraday rotation. Hence varying the magnetic field produced by the coil around the YIG rod varies the magnetization direction and so varies the Faraday rotation. A second polarizer placed at the output end of the YIG rod converts the polarization modulation to amplitude modulation. Although this polarizer could be placed at many orientations, maximum linear modulation is obtained if it is at 45 degrees to the axis of the first polarizer.

The overall efficiency of the magneto-optic modulator is improved further by two alterations. First, the YIG rod is cut from a YIG crystal in a certain orientation with respect to the crystal axes. By so doing the magnetization vector finds it easiest to be tilted toward the rod axis, as is desired, and resists any tendency to be tilted in a plane perpendicular to the rod axis. Second, it has been found that incorporating a certain amount of gallium in the YIG crystal during growth greatly reduces the saturation magnetization, to which the power expended in the modulator is proportional, without significantly reducing the ability of the crystal to produce Faraday rotation.

With these two improvements the YIG modulator has been able to produce 20 percent amplitude modulation with a bandwidth of 200 megacycles per second at a power expenditure of less than .1 watt. Amplitude modulation of 40 percent has been obtained by passing the infrared light through the YIG crystal twice as was done in the lithium tantalate modulator. It is also worth pointing out that the YIG modulator can be used in a PCM mode of operation if desired.

Although the three modulators described above are the most promising ones now available, other approaches are being actively pursued in many laboratories. The use of ultrasonic vibrations in a crystal as a modulating mechanism was mentioned above. Still another approach is to perform the modulating function inside the laser itself rather than on the light beam after it has left the laser. K. Gürs and R. Müller at the Siemens and Halske research laboratory in Germany, for instance, have performed very interesting experiments on a modulator of this type. Only time will tell which modulators are finally used in optical communication systems, but enough is known now for one to predict confidently that the modulator problem will finally be solved.

MODULATED LIGHT BEAM is shown being transmitted in the shape of a thin sheet of light through the *p-n*-junction region of a gallium phosphide diode. The two micrographs represent the "on" and "off" modulation states of the *p-n* junction as seen through a polarizer on the output side of the diode. A light beam from a mercury-arc lamp is focused on the input side. In the "off" state (*top*) no bias voltage is applied to the diode through the contact wire at top and as a result very little light passes through the junction. In the "on" state (*bottom*) reverse bias is applied and more light emerges from the *p-n* junction.

31

Photography by Laser

Emmett N. Leith and Juris Upatnieks   June 1965

In spite of the steady refinement of photographic techniques and the invention of new photographic materials, the optical aspects of photography have changed little over the past 100 years. Reduced to its essential elements the photographic process consists of recording an illuminated three-dimensional scene as a two-dimensional image on a light-sensitive surface. The light reflected from the objects in the scene is focused on the sensitive surface by some kind of image-forming device, which can be a complex series of lenses or simply a pinhole in an opaque screen [*see upper illustration on page 342*].

This article deals with a radically different concept in photographic optics. Invented less than 20 years ago, this process, which can be called photography by wave-front reconstruction, does *not* record an image of the object being photographed but rather records the reflected light waves themselves. The photographic record, a hodgepodge of specks, blobs and whorls, is called a hologram; it bears no resemblance to the original object but nevertheless contains—in a kind of optical code—all the information about the object that would be contained in an ordinary photograph and much additional information that cannot be recorded by any other photographic process.

The creation of an intelligible image from the hologram is known as the reconstruction process. In this stage the captured waves are in effect released

from the hologram record, whereupon they proceed onward, oblivious to the time lapse in their history. The reconstructed waves are indistinguishable from the original waves and are capable of all the phenomena that characterize the original waves. For example, they can be passed through a lens and brought to a focus, thereby forming an image of the original object—even though the object has long since been removed! If the reconstructed waves are intercepted by the eye of an observer, the effect is exactly as if the original waves had been observed: the observer sees what to all appearances is the original object itself in full three-dimensional form, complete with parallax (the apparent displacement of an object when seen from different directions) and many other effects that occur in the normal "seeing" process.

The wave-front reconstruction process was discovered in 1947 by Dennis Gabor of the Imperial College of Science and Technology in London. During the next few years Gabor developed the method systematically, emphasizing particularly its applications to electron microscopy. Many other workers throughout the world have since made significant contributions—notably Hussein M. A. El-Sum and Paul Kirkpatrick of Stanford University—but their efforts were hampered by the lack of an adequate source of coherent light, that is, light whose waves are all in phase. The invention of the laser in 1960 opened the

way to new advances in wave-front reconstruction photography. Using a gas laser as a source of coherent light, as well as several other previously untried techniques, we have been able to obtain high-quality, three-dimensional hologram images in our laboratory at the University of Michigan. Partly as a result of our work and partly as a result of the largely unexplored potential of the laser as a source of coherent light, there has been a widespread resurgence of interest in the possible uses of this intriguing photographic process.

The basic optics of wave-front reconstruction photography differ from those of ordinary photography in three main respects. As in ordinary photography, the object is illuminated and a photographic plate is positioned so as to receive light reflected from the object. Unlike ordinary photography, however, no lens or other image-forming device is used and consequently no image is formed. Instead each point on the object reflects light to the entire photographic plate; conversely, each point on the plate receives light from the entire object [*see top illustration on page 343*]. The second departure from ordinary photography is the use of coherent light for illuminating the object, and the third is the use of a mirror to beam a portion of the coherent light directly to the plate, bypassing the object. This beam is called the reference beam, and it produces, by means of interference effects, a visible display of the wave pattern of the light impinging on the plate from the object; what is recorded on the plate is the resulting interference pattern.

Reflected light waves, like any other waves, are described by their amplitude (or intensity) and by their phase (or frequency). In the case of a point scatterer of light, the reflected waves travel outward from their origin in a series of ever expanding spherical shells, called wave fronts, that are concentric around the point of origin. These spherical waves are the three-dimensional analogue of the circular waves that appear on the surface of a still pond when a stone is dropped into the water. If the reflecting object is not a single point but a complex object, it can then be regarded as a collection of a large number of points, and the resulting wave pattern reflected from the surface of the object can be regarded as the sum of many such sets of spherical waves, each set concentric about its point of origin [see top illustration on page 345]. The exact form of the wave pattern reflected from an extended and irregular object is highly complex and cannot be described in detail here.

The central problem of wave-front reconstruction photography is to record this complex, signal-bearing pattern as it exists at a given plane at some instant of time. Such a record can be thought of as a "freezing" of the wave pattern; the pattern remains frozen until such time as one chooses to reactivate the process, whereupon the waves are "read out" of the recording medium. To capture the wave pattern completely both the amplitude and the phase of the waves must be recorded at each point on the recording surface. Recording the amplitude portion of the waves poses no serious problem: ordinary photographic film records amplitude by converting it to corresponding variations in the opacity of the photographic emulsion. The emulsion is entirely insensitive to phase relations, however, and one must assemble some appropriate apparatus that can convert these phase relations into a form in which they can be recorded photographically.

In wave-front reconstruction photography the phase relations are rendered visible to the photographic plate through the technique of interferometry, a standard and long-established way of converting phase relations into corresponding amplitude relations. We shall first consider how this is done in the comparatively simple case in which two

ORDINARY PHOTOGRAPH was made by illuminating a chessboard and a group of chessmen with normally incoherent light and recording a two-dimensional image of the scene on photographic film. Light reflected from chessmen is focused on film by camera lens.

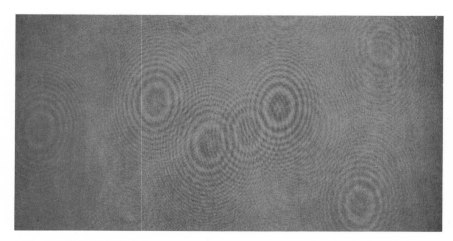

HOLOGRAM RECORDING of the scene shown in photograph at top of page was made in the first stage of the process of wave-front reconstruction photography. The visible structure of the hologram bears no resemblance to the original scene but nevertheless contains more information about the scene than would be contained in an ordinary photograph. The holograms used in this article were made by Albert Friesen of the University of Michigan.

RECONSTRUCTED IMAGE was made by directing a laser beam through the hologram. The reconstructed waves were then passed through a lens and brought to a focus, thereby forming an image of original scene, even though chessmen had long since been removed.

collimated light beams, whose wave fronts are successive planes perpendicular to the direction of the beams, interact to form a characteristic interference pattern; in terms of the shape of their wave fronts such waves are referred to as plane waves.

If two plane waves derived from a common source impinge at different angles of obliquity on an opaque surface, they will produce a set of uniform, parallel interference fringes on the surface. The spacing of the fringes will depend solely on the angle between the waves. At some places on the surface the waves will arrive in phase and their amplitudes will add to produce a resultant light intensity greater than would be produced by either wave acting alone. This process is called constructive interference and is responsible for the light fringes in the interference pattern. At other places the waves will arrive out of phase and will tend to cancel each other, the cancellation being complete if the two waves are of equal amplitude. This process is called destructive interference and is responsible for the dark fringes in the interference pattern. Where the waves are neither in nor out of phase, the resultant light intensity and corresponding fringe tone are intermediate between these two extremes.

A photographic recording of such a fringe pattern will yield a grating-like structure that can be regarded as a two-dimensional analogue of the sinusoidal wave produced by an electric oscillator. The important point of this analogy is that just as an electric wave can be modulated to serve as a carrier of information (about sound, say), so can the interferometrically produced wave pattern be modulated to serve as a carrier of information about the light waves that produced it.

Modulation of any kind of carrier wave can be accomplished in various ways, but the best-known and most commonly used methods are amplitude modulation (AM) and frequency modulation (FM). In amplitude modulation information is imposed on the carrier wave by causing the wave's amplitude to vary in accordance with some lower-frequency wave [see illustration on page 346]. In frequency modulation the amplitude of the carrier wave remains constant but spacing between the various cycles is altered. The effect can be described as a change in frequency: at some positions the cycles are compressed and the frequency is correspondingly increased, whereas at other positions the cycles are expanded and the

frequency is decreased. This kind of modulation can alternatively be described as phase modulation, since at any given time the phase, or the relative positions of the wave crests and troughs with respect to some stationary point, is different from what it would be in the absence of the modulation. (Although frequency modulation and phase modulation are not quite identical, the technical distinctions are not important here and will be disregarded.)

When the irregular wave pattern reflected from a complex object is made to interfere with a plane wave, the resulting interference pattern, instead of being uniform, has an irregularity that is related to the irregularity of the impinging wave fronts. At places where the signal-bearing waves have their greatest amplitude the interference fringes have the greatest contrast, whereas at places of low signal-wave amplitude the fringe contrast is low. Thus variations in the amplitude of the waves reflected from the object produce corresponding variations in the contrast of the recorded fringe pattern.

As we have noted, the spacing of the fringes is related to the angle between the signal-bearing waves and the reference waves. At places where the signal-bearing waves make a large angle with the reference waves the resulting fringe pattern is comparatively fine; at places where the waves meet at lesser angles the fringe pattern is coarser. Therefore the variations in the phase of the signal-bearing waves produce corresponding variations in the spacing of the fringes on the photographic record.

In brief, we have made two significant observations: both the amplitude and the phase of the signal-bearing waves can be preserved respectively as modulations in the contrast and spacing of the recorded interference fringes. All the information that can be carried by the light waves reflected from the object can be recorded on the interference grating produced by making these waves interfere with an obliquely impinging plane wave.

A hologram made in the manner just described has many of the properties of a grating produced on a ruling engine, but there are several important differences, the most important of which is the nonuniformity of the hologram grating slits as opposed to the precise uniformity attained in high-quality ruled gratings. Whereas the inadvertently produced irregularities in an imperfectly ruled grating give rise to false spectral lines, called "ghosts," the

deliberately induced irregularities in a hologram give rise, in the reconstruction process, to a complete, well-defined image.

When a grating consisting of uniformly spaced opaque and transparent slits is illuminated with a collimated beam of monochromatic light, a number of plane waves are generated by the interaction of the light with the grating structure. [see right side of top illustration on page 347]. These plane waves are radiated at various angles, which are determined by spacing of the slits in the grating. The "zero order" wave propagates in the same direction as the incident wave and can be regarded as an attenuated version of the incident wave. In addition, there are the two "first order" diffracted waves, one on each side of the zero-order wave. Beyond these occur the second-, third- and higher-order diffracted waves.

The generation of these diffracted waves can readily be explained by regarding the transparent slits as original sources, each radiating cylindrical waves. These elemental waves reinforce each other in certain directions, thereby giving rise to the various diffracted orders. The directions of reinforcement are obtained by drawing tangent lines to the various elemental wave fronts. The zero-order wave is formed by combining all the wave fronts that originated from the slits at the same time and are therefore all equidistant from the surface of the grating. By drawing a line tangent to all these corresponding cylindrical wave fronts the zero-order wave is obtained. This wave is parallel to the grating surface. One of the first-order diffracted waves is constructed by combining an elemental wave front from one slit with the previous wave front from the adjacent slit, then combining that with a still more previous wave front from the next adjacent slit, and so on. The other first-order diffracted wave is constructed in a similar way but in the opposite direction. The second-order diffracted waves are constructed by combining, from adjacent slits, wave fronts that are two wavelengths apart, and so on. From this construction method it is apparent that the closer the spacing of the grating lines, the greater the angle of diffraction.

When the spacing, or phase, of the grating slits is irregular, with some regions having closer line spacings than other regions, the localized variations in spacing give rise to corresponding local variations in the direction of the diffracted waves. Similarly, local variations in the contrast, or amplitude, of the fringes produce local variations in the amplitude, or intensity, of the diffracted wave. Thus the diffracted wave front is perturbed in a way that is related in a simple and predictable manner to the irregularities, both in spacing and contrast, of the hologram fringe pattern.

The reader will recall, however, that these fringe irregularities were produced by local variations in the amplitude and direction of the signal-bearing wave fronts that impinged on the hologram plate when the hologram was recorded. There is a kind of reversibility here: the distortions of the diffracted wave fronts by the fringe irregularities are precisely those distortions on the original wave front that gave rise to the fringe irregularities. For example, it was pointed out in the discussion of holo-

gram construction that places where the signal-bearing wave fronts made the greatest angle with the reference wave front corresponded to the most closely spaced fringes. These areas of the hologram grating in turn diffract light at greater angles.

Indeed, the manner of constructing the diffracted orders from the hologram diffraction grating is essentially the inverse of the process of constructing the interference pattern that is recorded on the hologram. The similarity of the two processes is true on a much more rigorous basis than we have described here and is the key concept underlying the wave-front reconstruction process. The two sets of first-order diffracted waves produced by the hologram are each an exact replica of the waves that issued from the original object. These waves

propagate outward from the hologram, behaving in all respects as the original waves would have done had they not been interrupted by the photographic plate placed in their path. A lens placed in the path of the diffracted waves can bring them to a focus, thereby forming an image of the original object, even though the original object is no longer present.

The two first-order waves differ from each other in one important respect. One diffracted order consists of waves that, when projected back toward the illuminating source, seem to emanate from an apparent object located where the original object was located. We say that these waves produce a virtual image, similar to the virtual images seen in a mirror. The other first-order diffracted waves are also accurate replicas

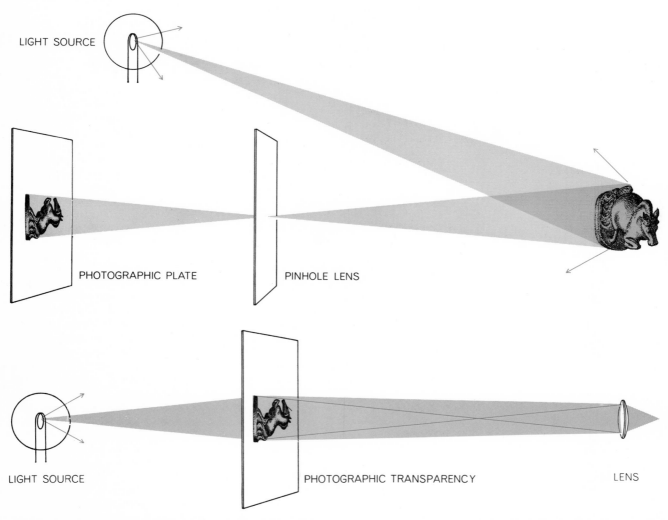

LIGHT SOURCE

PHOTOGRAPHIC PLATE

PINHOLE LENS

LIGHT SOURCE

PHOTOGRAPHIC TRANSPARENCY

LENS

DIFFERENCES between ordinary photography and photography by wave-front reconstruction are illustrated schematically on these two pages. Ordinary photography consists of recording an illuminated three-dimensional object as a two-dimensional image on a light-sensitive surface (*top left*). The light reflected from the object is focused on the surface by some kind of image-forming device, which may be simply a pinhole in an opaque screen. When ordinary incoherent light is shone through the photographic transparency (*bottom left*), the eye sees only a static, two-dimensional image of the original object. In the recording stage of wave-front reconstruction photography (*top right*) no lens or other image-forming device is used and consequently no image is formed. Instead each point on the object reflects light to the entire hologram; conversely, each point of the hologram receives light from the en-

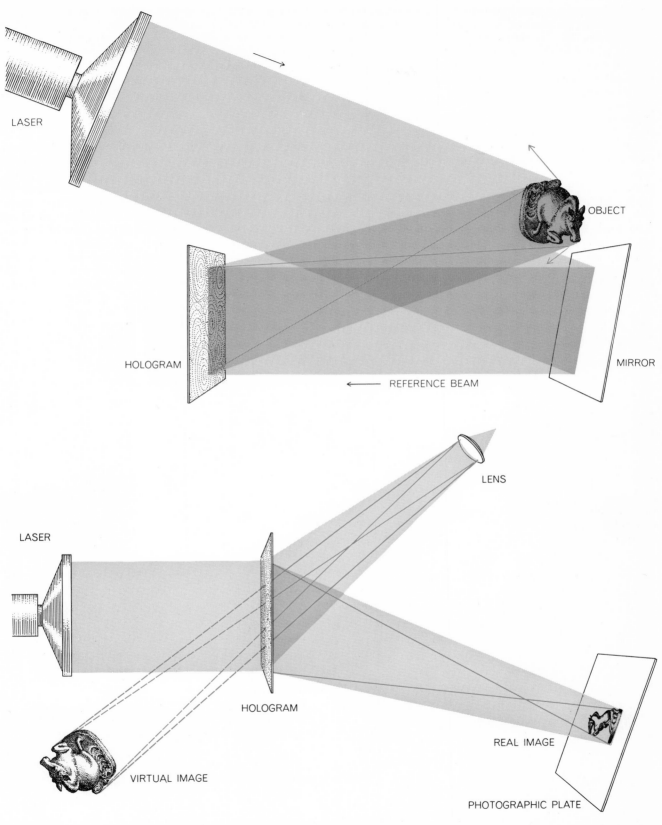

LASER

OBJECT

HOLOGRAM

MIRROR

REFERENCE BEAM

LENS

LASER

HOLOGRAM

VIRTUAL IMAGE

REAL IMAGE

PHOTOGRAPHIC PLATE

tire object. The reference beam produces, by means of interference effects, a visible display of the wave pattern of the light impinging on the hologram from the object. In the reproduction stage (*bottom right*) the hologram is illuminated with a collimated beam of monochromatic light and two images are produced by the "first order" diffracted waves emerging from the hologram interference grating. One diffracted order consists of waves that, when pro-

jected back toward the illuminating source, seem to emanate from an apparent object located at the position where the original object was located. These waves are said to produce a virtual image. The other first-order diffracted waves have conjugate, or reversed, curvature. These waves produce a real image, which can be photographed directly, without the need for a lens, by simply placing a photographic plate at the position of the image.

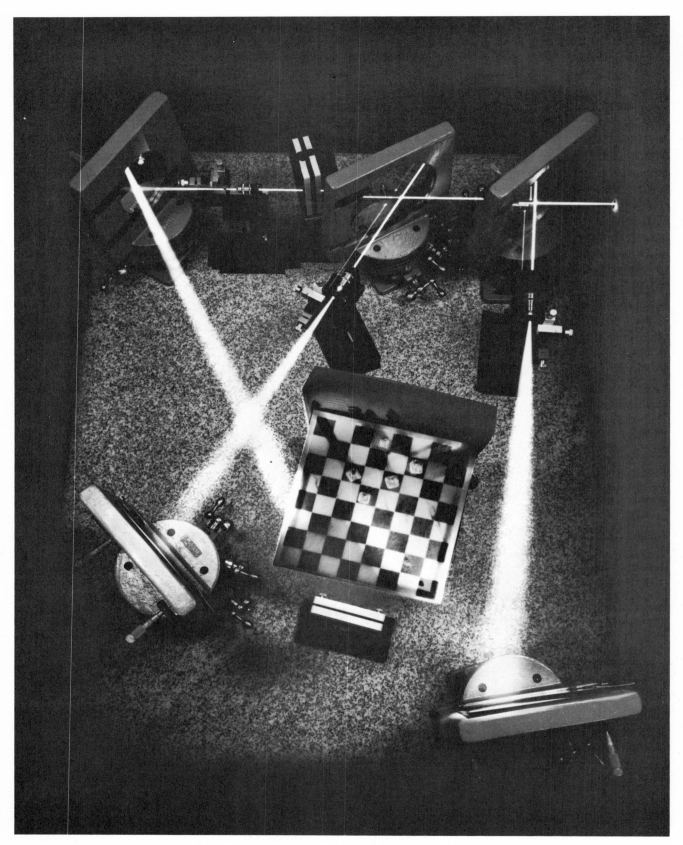

PHOTOGRAPHIC EQUIPMENT used in the first stage of the wave-front reconstruction process was photographed in the authors' laboratory at the University of Michigan. The laser beam enters from right at top and immediately passes through two partially reflecting and partially transmitting glass plates. The reflected parts of the beam are again reflected from two mirrors (*bottom left and right*) before being used to illuminate the chessboard (*center*). The transmitted part of the beam, called the reference beam, is reflected from another mirror (*top left*) and then impinges directly on the hologram plate (*sandwich-like object at bottom center*). Each beam passes through a microscope lens, which broadens the beam but has no effect on its valuable coherence properties.

LIGHT WAVES ARE REFLECTED from a point scatterer (*top*) in a series of ever expanding spherical shells, called wave fronts, that are concentric about the point of origin. If the reflecting object is complex (*bottom*), it can then be regarded as a collection of a large number of points, and the resulting wave pattern reflected from the surface of the object can be regarded as the sum of many such sets of spherical waves, each set concentric about its point of origin. The central problem of wave-front reconstruction photography is to record this pattern as it exists at a given plane at some instant of time.

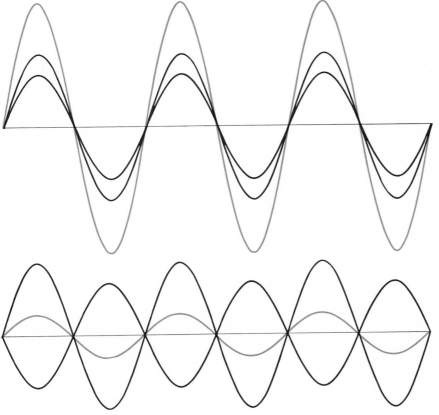

TWO KINDS OF INTERFERENCE of light waves are depicted. If two light waves of different amplitudes arrive at the recording surface in phase (*top*), their amplitudes will add to produce a resultant light intensity (*colored curve at top*) greater than would be produced by either wave acting alone. This process is called constructive interference and is responsible for the light fringes in the interference pattern. If the light waves arrive out of phase (*bottom*), their amplitudes will tend to cancel one another. This process is called destructive interference and is responsible for the dark fringes in the interference pattern.

of the original waves, except that they have conjugate, or reversed, curvature: originally diverging spherical waves from an object point are converted into converging spherical waves. These waves produce a real image, which can be photographed directly, without a lens, by placing a photographic plate at the image position.

Holograms and the images they produce have many curious and fascinating properties. The hologram on page 340, for example, is quite unintelligible and gives no hint of the image embodied within it. A cursory examination of it tempts one to identify the visible structures (concentric rings, specks and the like) with portions of the subject. Such an identification would be quite incorrect. The visible structure is purely extraneous and arises from dust particles and other scatterers on the mirror that supplies the reference beam. The pertinent information recorded on the hologram film can be seen only under magnification and consists of highly irregular fringes that bear no apparent relation to the subject. It is quite unlikely that one could learn to interpret a hologram visually without actually reconstructing the image.

When the hologram is placed in a beam of coherent light, however, the images embodied in it are suddenly revealed. The identity between the reconstructed waves and the original waves that impinged on the plate when the hologram was made implies that the image produced by the hologram should be indistinguishable in appearance from the original object. This identity is in fact realized. The virtual image, for instance, which is seen by looking through the hologram as if it were a window, appears in complete, three-dimensional form, and this three-dimensional effect is achieved entirely without the use of stereo pairs of photographs and without the need for such devices as stereo viewers.

The image has additional features of realism that do not even occur in conventional stereo-photographic imaging. For example, as the observer changes his viewing position the perspective of the picture changes, just as it would if the observer were viewing the original scene. Parallax effects are evident between near and far objects in the scene: if an object in the foreground lies in front of something else, the observer can move his head and look around the obstructing object, thereby seeing the previously hidden object. Moreover, one must refocus one's eyes when the observation is changed from a near to a more distant object in the scene. In short, the reconstruction has all the visual properties of the original scene, and we know of no visual test one can make to distinguish the two.

Similarly, the real image can be viewed by an observer, who will find it suspended in space between himself and the plate. This image has all the aforementioned properties, but it is somewhat more difficult to view, for reasons we shall not discuss here.

A hologram made in the manner just described has several interesting properties in addition to those having to do with the three-dimensional nature of its reconstruction. As an example, each part of the hologram, no matter how small, can reproduce the entire image; thus the hologram can be broken into small fragments, each of which can be used to construct a complete image. As the pieces become smaller, resolution is lost, since resolution is a function of the aperture of the imaging system. This curious property is explained on the basis of an observation made above: each point on the hologram receives light from all parts of the subject and therefore contains, in an encoded form, the entire image.

A second curious property of the wave-front reconstruction process is that it does not produce negatives. The hologram itself would normally be regarded as a negative, but the image it produces is a positive. If the hologram were copied by contact printing, the hologram would be reversed in the sense that opaque areas would now become transparent and vice versa. The image reconstructed from the copy, however, would remain a positive and would be indistinguishable from the image produced by the original except for the small degradation in quality that normally occurs in photographic copying. This curious property arises because the information is recorded on the film in the form of a modulated spatial carrier. Contact printing of the film results in only a reversal in the polarity of the carrier, and polarity reversals of a carrier do not affect the signal data contained on the carrier, a fact well known to electronic engineers. The reason for this insensitivity to polarity can be understood by recalling that the information on the grating carrier is embodied in the fringe contrast and in the fringe spacings; neither of these is altered by the reversal of polarity.

Another interesting property of wave-front reconstruction photography is that

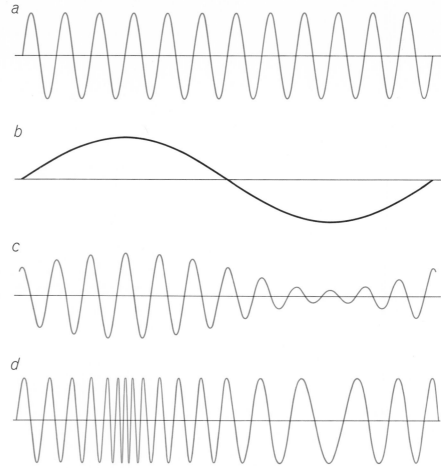

WAVES CARRY INFORMATION in various ways, but the best-known and most commonly used methods are amplitude modulation (AM) and frequency, or phase, modulation (FM). In amplitude modulation (c) information is modulated onto the carrier wave (a) by causing its amplitude to vary according to some lower-frequency wave (b). In frequency modulation (d) the amplitude of carrier wave remains constant but spacing between cycles is altered.

the reconstructed image has very nearly the same contrast rendition as the original object, regardless of the contrast properties of the photographic emulsion. Thus high-contrast plates, which in ordinary photography would be useful only for such objects as line drawings, can be used without losing any of the tonal properties of the object. The photographic plate containing the hologram may be capable of registering only two levels of density—transparent and opaque—but the tonal rendition of the reconstruction does not suffer. This mysterious property of wave-front reconstruction photography is not easily explained, but it is again related to the use of a carrier and also to the fact that each point on the object is recorded not on a single point of the hologram but on the entire hologram. Under these circumstances it can be shown that the failure to preserve a proper gray scale produces, as its main effect, higher-order diffracted waves. The first-order diffracted waves, which produce the reconstructed images, are to a first approximation unaffected by the distortion of the gray scale.

Still another interesting property of holograms is that several images can be superimposed on a single plate on successive exposures, and each image can be recovered without being affected by the other images. This is done by using a different spatial-frequency carrier for each picture, just as many radio messages can be transmitted between two sites simultaneously by the use of different carrier frequencies. The grating carriers can be of different frequencies, as in radio communication; moreover, since the film is two-dimensional there is still another degree of freedom, that of angle. Thus the grating carrier is specified both by the fringe spacing and by the fringe orientation. The fringe pattern can be vertical for one exposure, for example, and horizontal for another. In the reconstruction process the various

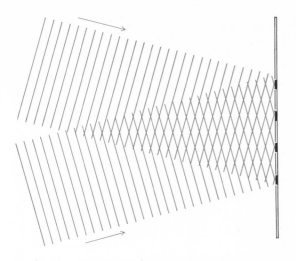
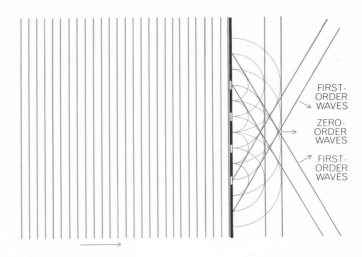

UNIFORM, PARALLEL FRINGES are produced by the interference of two plane waves derived from a common source and impinging at different angles of obliquity on an opaque surface (*left*). The spacing of the fringes depends solely on the angle between the waves. When the grating is illuminated with a beam of coherent light (*right*), a number of plane waves are generated by the interaction of the light with the grating. The "zero order" wave propagates in the same direction as the incident wave and can be regarded as an attenuated version of the incident wave. Beyond the two first-order waves occur second-, third- and higher-order waves.

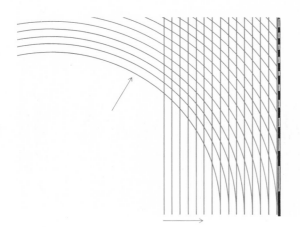
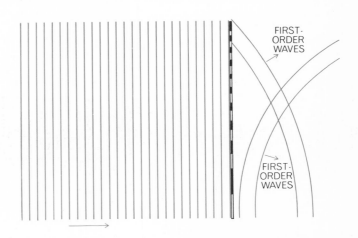

MODULATED FRINGES are produced by the interference of a plane wave and an irregular wave, in this case a cylindrical wave (*left*). Where the angle between the plane and the distorted wave fronts is large the fringe pattern is fine; where the angle is small the fringe pattern is coarse. When illuminated with a beam of coherent light, the modulated fringe pattern acts like an imperfect diffraction grating, producing diffracted waves that are distorted (*right*). The diverging first-order diffracted wave is responsible for the virtual image of the original object; the converging first-order diffracted wave is responsible for the real image of the object.

reconstructed waves will be diffracted in different directions and the reconstructed images will form in different locations.

Wave-front reconstruction photography, although appearing to offer exciting possibilities, has in the past been confined to the laboratory and for some time at least will remain so. The major reason for this is the strict coherence requirements for the light source used in the process. Ordinary light lacks this coherence property, and sources of coherent light are comparatively expensive and inconvenient to use.

There are two kinds of coherence—temporal and spatial—both of which are required for wave-front reconstruction photography. Temporal coherence, or monochromaticity, is required because the fringe pattern generated by the interference process is a function of the wavelength of the illumination. If the spectrum of the light is broad, each wavelength component produces its own separate pattern, and the resultant of all the wavelength components acting at once is to average out the fringes to a smooth distribution. A limited number of spectral components can be superimposed, however, as when three monochromatic waves, comprising the three primary colors, are used to achieve wave-front reconstruction imaging in color. The relaxation of the monochromaticity requirement cannot be carried very far, and each of the three color components must cover a quite narrow spectral band.

The other coherence requirement—spatial coherence—means that the light has been derived from a point source or that the light is capable of being imaged to a small spot or point. If the source lacks spatial coherence (that is, if it is broad), then each element of the source produces interference fringes that are displaced from those of other elements; the sum of many such sets of fringes averages to some very nearly uniform value, and the fringe pattern is absent.

It is possible to meet both coherence requirements using traditional sources, such as a mercury-arc lamp. Monochromaticity is obtained by passing the light through an optical device, such as a monochromator or a narrow-band color filter. This process discards all spectral components except those in a narrow band. Spatial coherence is obtained by focusing the light onto a pinhole. Since only a small fraction of the total light output of the lamp can be focused onto the pinhole, the traditional source is quite inefficient, and only an extremely small fraction of the total light emission is available for illumination of the object.

The light produced by a laser, on the other hand, is highly monochromatic and has extraordinary spatial coherence, thus making the wasteful processes described above unnecessary. The available light is several orders of magnitude greater than the monochromatic, spatially coherent light available from other sources. Hence the laser is greatly superior to all other known sources for wave-front reconstruction photography and is certainly in large part responsible for the interesting results that have already been achieved.

With a high-quality technique for producing fascinating and unusual images fully demonstrated, questions naturally arise as to what applications are to be found for it. Since its discovery by Gabor, many uses for the wave-front reconstruction process have been suggested, and more recently the number of proposed applications has grown rapidly.

Two applications that come to mind immediately are in television and motion pictures. It is possible in principle to produce a hologram television system, since a hologram can be recorded on the photosensitive surface of a television camera just as readily as on a photographic emulsion. Moreover, the hologram data can be transmitted and reconstructed in a receiver. Such a system would produce virtually the ultimate realism.

When the required system and component specifications are examined, however, it is found that they greatly exceed the present state of the art. Transmission bandwidths exceeding present television bandwidths by factors of several hundred are required, unless design compromises are made that result in a partial loss of the dramatic results attainable from holograms. Cam-

PARALLAX EFFECT is evident in these three virtual-image photographs, all made from the same hologram. The apparent displacement of the chessmen resulted from moving the hologram slightly. The same effect could have been obtained by keeping the hologram stationary and moving the camera or by keeping both stationary and moving the laser.

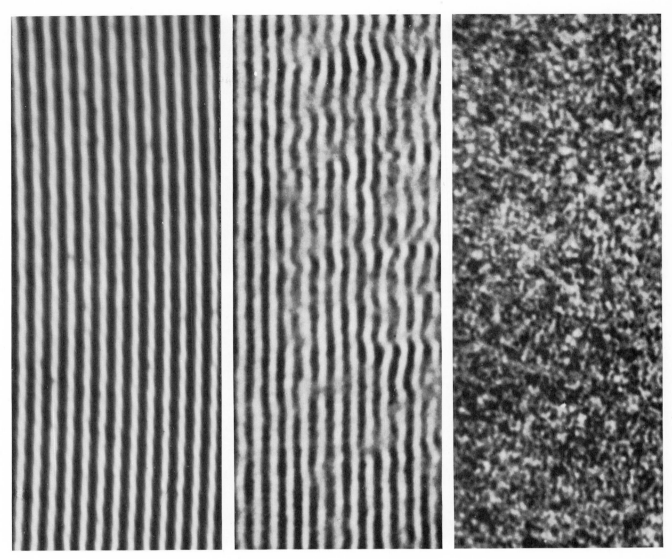

THREE INTERFERENCE PATTERNS show the effects of amplitude and phase modulation of a spatial carrier wave. The fringe pattern at left was formed by two plane waves impinging on a photographic plate at a slight angle to each other. One of the waves responsible for the pattern at center has been modulated to a small degree, producing slight variations in fringe contrast and irregularities in the shape of the fringe contours; the pattern is an enlarged section of a hologram of a comparatively simple photographic transparency. The interference pattern at right is an enlargement of section of a hologram of a diffusely reflecting, three-dimensional object. The degree of modulation is so great that the interference fringes have lost continuity and are no longer identifiable as fringes.

eras, picture tubes and associated components must also be much better than present-day equipment. In addition, the objects would have to be illuminated by laser light, and the receiver similarly would have to contain a laser; present lasers are inadequate for these tasks and would require improvement. The potential is great but the price is still quite high. Methods are being sought for reducing the stringent requirements on system bandwidths, with some initial success, but much remains to be done. For hologram motion pictures the problems are similar and even more severe.

As laser sources improve, wave-front reconstruction photography may emerge from the laboratory and become, through its remarkable three-dimensional imaging properties, an important photographic method for simulation and training devices and for applications in which a highly exact reproduction of the object is required.

Historically microscopy has been the primary area of application for the wave-front reconstruction method; Gabor's original applications were in this area. By the use of divergent beams of radiation Gabor, as well as El-Sum and Albert V. Baez at Stanford, have demonstrated that great magnification can be achieved with wave-front reconstruction, entirely without the use of lenses. Moreover, the hologram can be made with radiation of one wavelength and the reconstruction with another. Gabor proposed to produce a hologram with electron waves in an electron microscope and to make the reconstruction using visible light. By this means the highly developed methods of optical imagery can be applied to image formation in the domain of electron waves, where lens technique is less perfectly developed. Similarly, El-Sum and Baez have made holograms with an X-ray microscope and the reconstructions in visible light. This application holds much promise, because X rays can be focused only crudely and with extreme difficulty. The resolution achieved in X-ray microscopy falls several orders of magnitude short of what is theoretically possible, a condition that can be remedied by wave-front reconstruction methods. Technical difficulties have hampered progress in this area, but the difficulties—primarily the lack of X-ray sources of suitable intensity, monochromaticity and spatial coherence—do not appear insurmountable.

In an application developed by two of the authors' colleagues, Robert Powell and Karl Stetson, the vibratory motion of a complicated object can be measured with ease by the wave-front reconstruction method. The light reflected from such a vibrating object loses its coherence in a predictable manner. Consequently the image reconstructed from a hologram has superimposed on it a contour pattern of the vibrational amplitude; from this reconstruction the amplitude of vibration for each point on the object can be obtained at once by simple inspection of the hologram image.

Brian Thompson, George Parrent and their co-workers at Technical Operations, Inc., have developed an application that has a remarkable simplicity. They were faced with the problem of measuring the distribution by size and other properties of floating, foglike particles in a sample volume. Such particles generally do not remain stationary long enough for the observer to focus on them. In addition, it is often desirable to photograph all the particles in the volume at a given time. The wave-front reconstruction method offers an ideal solution to the problem. A hologram is made by illuminating the volume with a pulsed laser and photographically recording the transmitted light. A short-pulse laser is used to "freeze" the motion of the particles. In the reconstruction an image of the entire volume is produced, and the particle size, distribution and cross-sectional geometry can be measured by microscopic examination. (Although Thompson and Parrent have exploited both the three-dimensional imaging capabilities of the hologram process and the extraordinary coherence properties of the laser, their efforts are unrelated to ours and have developed the original ideas of Gabor along quite different lines.)

Additional applications should develop in time, particularly as advancing technology provides new devices that can facilitate the wave-front reconstruction method. In particular, high-power pulsed lasers with excellent coherence properties should bring about significant advances. It seems safe to predict that most future applications will center on the three-dimensional, highly realistic imagery that the method produces and that is unmatched in this respect by other photographic methods.

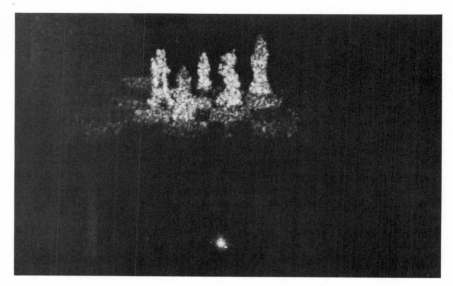

ENTIRE IMAGE of the original scene is reproduced by any part of the hologram, however small. At top the unbroadened laser beam, about a half-millimeter in diameter, is directed at the hologram (*faint rectangle in foreground of each photograph*). Since photographic resolution is a function of the aperture of the imaging system, the image appears blotchy and ill-defined at this aperture. As successively larger parts of the hologram are illuminated (*middle and bottom*) resolution is improved, but the depth of field of the image decreases.

32

Advances in Holography

Keith S. Pennington   *February 1968*

As is now widely known, the photographic technique called holography records a subject not by the direct process of ordinary photography, but by recording the pattern of wave fronts of light from the subject. This recorded information is then used to reconstruct an image of the subject.

Although these basic principles of holography were described as early as 1947 by Dennis Gabor, it was only after the introduction of the laser that this novel technique became truly practical. Indeed, the introduction of the laser, together with a modification of the original holographic technique, enabled Emmett N. Leith and Juris Upatnieks of the University of Michigan to record holograms that produced highly realistic images of three-dimensional objects [see "Photography by Laser," by Emmett N. Leith and Juris Upatnieks, beginning on page 339].

Since that time further exploration, actively undertaken in a number of research laboratories, is demonstrating that holography is even richer in possible applications than was at first supposed. In particular, techniques have been developed for making holograms that can be viewed with white light, and also holograms that reconstruct multicolored images. Holography has introduced additional flexibility into microscopic investigations and promises to be of particular importance in the study of biological subjects. Furthermore, holographic techniques have expanded the uses of interferometry into new areas and at the same time have introduced a new simplicity in some of the existing areas. At present a considerable amount of effort is being devoted to the possible use of holography in data-processing and the display of information.

In essence holography is not difficult to understand, and it is fairly easy to put into practice. Consider a beam of coherent laser light (in which all points on the wave fronts are related in phase) that is split in transit into two beams [see *upper illustration, page 353*]. One beam illuminates the subject to be recorded, and the light reflected from this subject falls on a photographic plate. The other beam, called the reference beam, is reflected from a mirror to the same photographic plate, where its wave fronts are superposed on those from the subject. This results in an interference pattern that, when the plate is developed, is recorded in the form of points of varying density—increased in density where the wave fronts arrived in phase and augmented each other, reduced in density where they were out of phase. The record on the photographic plate (the hologram) is simply a pattern of interfering wave fronts and shows no resemblance to the recorded subject. Nonetheless, the record contains "all the information" about the subject. When the record is "played back" by shining the reference beam alone through the hologram, the reconstructed wave fronts appear to diverge from an image of the subject. This image can then be viewed with the eye or other optical instruments or recorded with a camera [see *lower illustration on page 353*].

Since the hologram records all the information contained in a wave front, the images produced by means of holography are extremely realistic. With a single hologram one can examine a subject from different points of view and even focus at different depths throughout the image. Further, it is possible to observe the reconstructed images with such optical techniques as phase-contrast microscopy, schlieren techniques and interferometry. In fact, for optical purposes a hologram of a subject can often be as useful as the actual subject, and in many instances it can prove even more useful. In this article I shall review the areas in which holography has already been developed to working usefulness, namely microscopy, interferometry and multicolor holography (which is called "volume holography," referring to the technique employed).

In microscopy the holographic technique makes it possible to overcome a serious limitation. Subjects such as biological specimens suspended in a fluid must often be viewed under very high magnification. In studies of this type the microscope is restricted to an extremely small depth of field, which means that for any particular setting of the instrument only those parts of the subject in the immediate vicinity of a single plane will be in sharp focus. Consequently if the sample is to be viewed without drifting in and out of focus, it must be either thinned down to almost two dimensions or "frozen" into a solid. Often such sample preparations modify and distort the specimen.

Holographic techniques can remove these difficulties in a fairly straightforward manner. All that is necessary is to make a short-exposure hologram of the sample. This will freeze any motion and also ensure the formation of a hologram of good quality. Since the hologram records all the three-dimensional characteristics of the sample, it is not necessary to prepare samples artificially; thus the possibility of degrading the specimens contained in the sample is reduced. The resulting hologram image can then be examined at leisure with a microscope. The microscope can be focused at various planes throughout the depth of the hologram image; in this way the entire undistorted specimen can be studied. Moreover, in the reconstruction of the image from the hologram, it is still pos-

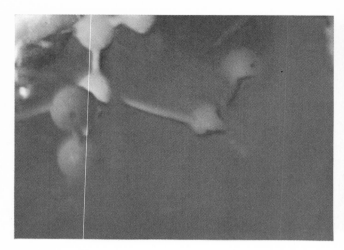

MONOCOLOR HOLOGRAM of a three-dimensional molecular model was illuminated with reflected white light from a zirconium-arc lamp and then photographed from two different angles to demonstrate the parallax effect, one of the distinguishing features of holography, or photography by wave-front reconstruction. In making the original hologram, the model was illuminated with a beam of coherent light from a helium-neon laser and the reflected inco-herent wave fronts were made to interact with a reference beam of coherent laser light to form an interference pattern, which was recorded throughout the depth of the photographic emulsion. The resulting "volume" hologram, in this case one that can be "read out" in white light, was made by G. W. Stroke and A. E. Labeyrie, then at the University of Michigan. The development of this technique has led to "white light" holograms that reconstruct in several colors.

MULTICOLOR HOLOGRAM of a small vase was illuminated with a pair of laser beams in order to make this photograph. The same wavelengths were used in recording and reconstructing the hologram: 6,328 angstrom units (red) from a helium-neon laser; 5,145 angstroms (green) and 4,880 angstroms (blue) from an argon-ion laser. The superposed volume holograms (one for each color) have color selectivity adequate to eliminate interaction between the red and the blue components and between the red and the green components. The faint "spurious" images displaced to the sides of the bright reconstruction at center, however, indicate a slight interaction between the blue and the green components. The hologram was made by A. A. Friesem and R. J. Fedorowicz, also at Michigan.

sible to use schlieren and phase-contrast techniques to bring out various details in the sample. Hence holography may provide an inexpensive and often preferable alternative to present techniques of sample preparation.

Holography promises to be an effective way to keep detailed records of biological and physical phenomena. It also gives one the opportunity to conduct many optical observations a second time on the "original" sample; similarly, it will allow one to make detailed comparisons of samples recorded at totally different times. The observation that one picture may be worth a thousand words can now be extended to say that one hologram may be worth a great many pictures.

Several investigators have applied holography to the study of biological specimens and have succeeded in producing highly magnified three-dimensional images of such subjects [*see top illustration on opposite page*]. Among those exploring this field of application are G. W. Stroke of the State University of New York at Stony Brook (formerly of the University of Michigan) and John F. Burke of the Harvard Medical School, who have used white-light-reconstructing holograms, and Raoul F. van Ligten of the American Optical Company, who has conducted some particularly interesting and varied work on biological samples.

In the area of microscopic examination of physical phenomena, Brian J. Thompson, George Parrent, Jr., and their co-workers at Technical Operations, Inc., have demonstrated that holography can be a powerful instrument for studying the properties of a gas containing a suspension of microscopic particles. By making high-speed holograms of particle suspensions with the light from a pulsed laser, and then examining the reconstructed image with a microscope, they were able to measure the distribution of the particles according to size and various other properties. Heretofore detailed information of this kind has not usually been available to direct observation; it could only be deduced in statistical terms. It appears that holography may now provide a means of checking theories concerning the scattering of light by suspensions of small particles.

Since holography consists of recording an interference pattern, it has probably occurred to the reader that it bears an uncommonly close resemblance to interferometry, that traditional field of physical optics. This resemblance, of course, is not a coincidence. The only basic difference between holography and conventional interferometry is that in holography one generally records extremely complex interference patterns. Perhaps even more important, holography at its conception was meant to be a technique for recording wave fronts, in contrast to the more common use of interferometers for analyzing wave fronts.

As is often the case, one of the first areas to benefit from the new technique was the area that gave rise to it. So it was that holography was responsible for introducing a new range of powerful methods to interferometry. Interferometry has commonly been used for the precise measurement and comparison of wavelengths, for measuring very small distances or thicknesses (of the order of wavelengths of light), for detecting disturbances or inhomogeneities in optical mediums, for determining the refractive indexes of materials, and so on. To these functions the technique of holographic interferometry adds capabilities for studying phenomena that were formerly considered virtually inaccessible. Furthermore, holography makes interferometry less complicated by relaxing some of the exacting requirements that have attended this technique. For example, holography eliminates the necessity of using optical components of extremely high quality. This advantage is particularly useful when the phenomena under study take place in a closed vessel and must be measured interferometrically through windows. Holography makes it possible to distinguish the relevant information from the spurious, and thus it permits accurate interferometric experiments on any material and in almost any environment.

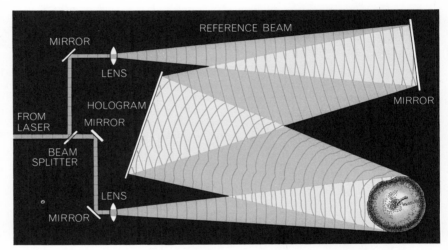

RECORDING STAGE of a simple holographic process is shown in this schematic drawing. Two beams are derived from a single laser by means of a beam splitter, such as a half-silvered mirror. One beam is used to illuminate the object, while the other is used as a reference beam. The reference beam and the light reflected from the object are then allowed to interfere, and the resulting interference pattern is recorded on a photographic plate, forming the hologram. Microscope lenses broaden both beams without affecting their coherence.

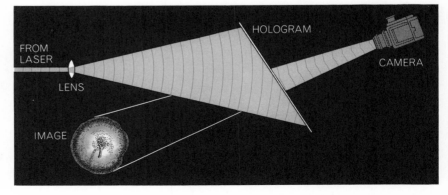

RECONSTRUCTION STAGE of the simple holographic process begun at top is shown here. The hologram is illuminated by the reference beam alone, producing replicas of the wave fronts reflected from the original object, even though the object may long since have been removed. The reconstructed wave fronts can be observed either visually or with a camera.

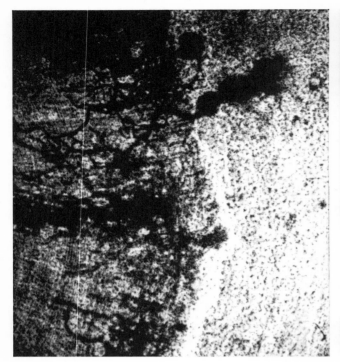

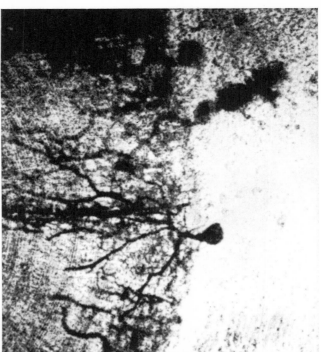

MICROSCOPIC HOLOGRAM of a stained biological specimen preserves the three-dimensional structure of the specimen, unlike an ordinary two-dimensional photomicrograph. The entire undistorted specimen can later be observed at leisure by selectively focusing the microscope at different depths in the holographic reconstruction of the specimen. In this case the reconstruction at left shows a network of nerves in which two "heads," or synaptic knobs, and some of the finer detail are in acceptable focus. The reconstruction at right, focused at a depth 40 microns away from that at left, shows a third "head" and its associated fibers more clearly. The smallest fibers visible are less than a micron in diameter. Hologram was made by Raoul F. van Ligten of the American Optical Company.

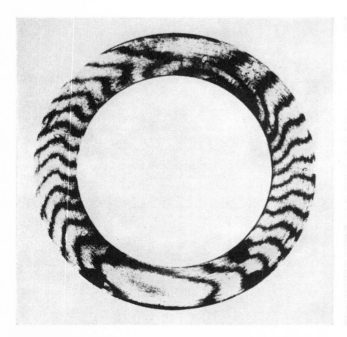

INTERFERENCE PATTERNS created by superposing the wave fronts from the holographic reconstruction of an object and the reilluminated object itself can reveal minute variations between the original dimensions of the object and its dimensions at some later time; the technique can also be used to distinguish between the original master of a machine tool and subsequent versions. In this case the object is an automobile cylinder viewed almost end on. The interference pattern observed on the inside surface of the cylinder wall at left is caused by interference between the reconstruction of the cylinder and the same cylinder viewed from the other end. The pattern at right is caused by interference between the reconstruction of one cylinder and an entirely different cylinder. Such interference patterns can be analyzed to detect slight differences in the radii of the two cylinders along their entire length. The tests were carried out by a group that included E. Archbold, J. M. Burch and A. E. Ennos of the National Physical Laboratory in England.

Let us consider, for example, a rerun on the reconstruction of a subject's image from a hologram. If the hologram and the subject are returned to precisely the same relative positions they had occupied during the original exposure, and both are again illuminated by the same direct and reference beams as before, we will observe the wave front from the subject superposed on the reconstructed wave front from the hologram. These two wave fronts are coherent and could interfere. If any change has taken place in the phase distribution of the light from the subject, there will be light and dark interference fringes that indicate the degree to which the phase of the light distribution has changed. This change will measure precisely any alteration that has taken place in the subject or in the density of the medium through which the beams have passed. Like other kinds of interferometry, the technique readily detects changes that produce optical-path differences of the order of a fraction of the wavelength of light. Unlike other kinds of interferometry, however, the technique makes it possible to perform experiments quite readily with almost any type of material.

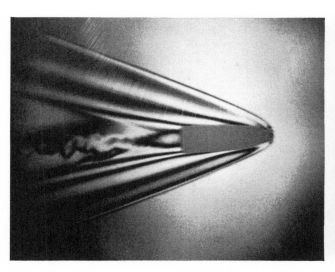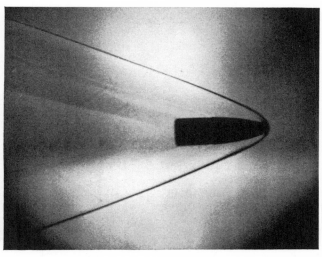

DOUBLE-EXPOSED HOLOGRAM of a bullet in flight (*left*) was made by a method called time-lapse interferometry. A pulsed ruby laser was used to record two high-speed exposures, the first with the bullet absent and the second with the bullet present. The resulting hologram (which actually consists of two superposed holograms) was then illuminated to reconstruct both the original and the changed wave fronts simultaneously. The interference of these respective wave fronts produced the image of the shock wave and the turbulence in the wake of the bullet. A singly exposed hologram of an identical bullet in flight is shown at right for contrast. Very little structure is visible in the shock wave and the wake is no longer discernible. Both bullets were traveling at a velocity of approximately 3,500 feet per second. The holograms were made by R. E. Brooks, L. O. Heflinger and R. F. Wuerker of TRW Inc.

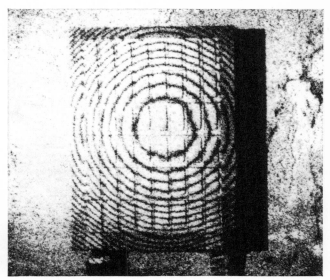

TWO OTHER EXAMPLES of double-exposed holograms made by the time-lapse interferometric technique are shown here. At left is a photograph of the reconstructed image of a fruit fly in flight, also made by the group at TRW Inc. A pulsed ruby laser was again used for the two exposures, the first with the fruit fly present and the second with it absent. The vertical streaks are part of the compressional wave produced by the beating of the fly's wings. At right is the reconstructed image of a bismuth-telluride thermoelectric device. The exposures were made with and without current passing through the device. The "bow type" distortion characterized by the circular interference fringes arises from the temperature gradient set up between the front and back surfaces when a current is applied. This work was performed by the author with R. A. Wolfe, R. J. Collier and E. T. Doherty of the Bell Telephone Laboratories.

The importance of this feature is more easily appreciated if one considers the degree of difficulty involved in studying any everyday object with the previously existing interferometric techniques. The surfaces of the subject are normally rough in terms of wavelengths of light, and there are often hundreds of such surface details per square millimeter of surface area. Consequently the interference between a wave front from such a subject and a simple plane wave would be extremely complex. We have all these interference fringes to observe even before we have deformed the object in some way. Deformation of the subject would likewise produce a highly complex interference pattern. The use of normal interferometric techniques has therefore left us with the difficult task of comparing and analyzing two extremely complex interference patterns.

The hologram, on the other hand, records all the information contained in the wave front of the subject even down to the smallest surface details. The interference between the reconstructed wave front from the hologram and the wave front from the deformed subject will show an overall interference pattern that reflects the manner in which the subject has changed as a whole. In short, the technique of holographic interferometry extracts the relevant information from a mass of spurious information and displays any changes in a readily observable way. By the same token, a holographic picture is not confused by minor flaws in the window or any other optical medium through which the subject is observed, as long as the flaws do not change.

This ability of holography to deal with complex subjects makes it feasible to conduct interferometric experiments on a great variety of materials and phenomena, such as concrete, rock specimens, metal objects, electronic components, flow lines and shock waves in wind tunnels, and so on. It should even be possible to follow the course of chemical reactions and diffusion.

Three techniques for employing holography in interferometric studies have been explored. They are called real-time interferometry, time-lapse interferometry and time-averaged interferometry. I have already described the method used for studies in real time; it allows us to observe changes in a subject as they occur.

The time-lapse technique records the situation before and after a change has taken place. Both views of the subject are recorded in the same hologram. The

hologram is a double exposure, with the second pattern of wave fronts superposed on the first; it reconstructs both wave fronts simultaneously. These wave fronts interfere and in doing so exhibit the changes that have occurred in the subject between the first and the second exposure.

Robert E. Brooks, Lee O. Heflinger and Ralph F. Wuerker of the TRW Systems Group have made several spectacular time-lapse holograms of subjects in very rapid motion. Using ruby lasers that emitted extremely brief pulses of light to freeze the motion, they obtained detailed pictures of the shock waves and

the wake from a bullet in flight [see upper illustration on page 355]; they also photographed the compressional wave produced by a fruit fly beating its wings [see illustration at lower left on page 355]. With time-lapse holography a group of us then working at the Bell Telephone Laboratories were able to picture the slight distortion that took place in a thermoelectric device as a result of temperature gradients that were set up when a current was applied [see illustration at lower right on page 355].

The third area, time-averaged interferometry, was actually the first of the

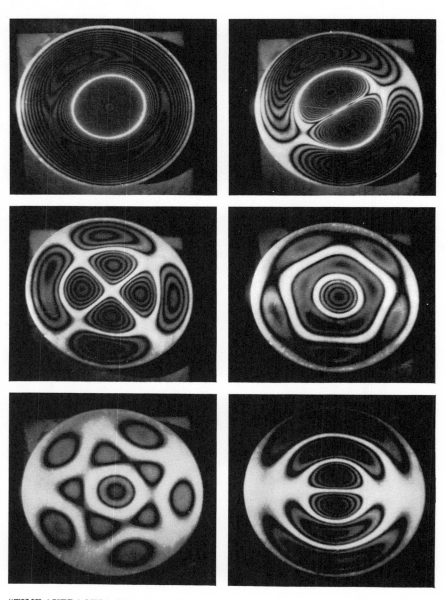

"TIME-AVERAGED" HOLOGRAMS of the vibrating bottom of a 35-millimeter film-can record the interference patterns associated with the modes of vibration of the can at six different resonant frequencies. The amplitude of each vibration can be measured by counting the number of fringes. The difference in amplitude in going from one bright fringe to the next bright fringe is approximately a half-wavelength of the light used to expose the hologram. The holograms were made by R. L. Powell and K. A. Stetson, then at Michigan.

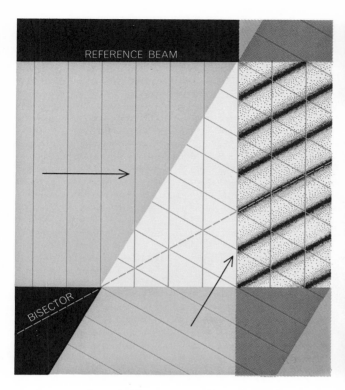

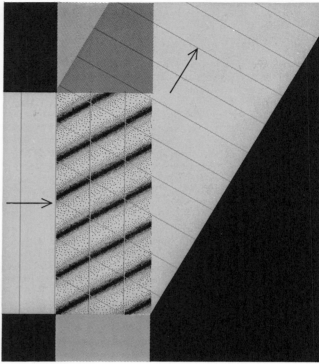

IN A VOLUME HOLOGRAM the fine details of the interference pattern are much smaller than the thickness of the photographic emulsion and hence are recorded throughout the depth of the emulsion. This makes it possible to record several colors as variations in the opacity of the emulsion throughout the depth. In the diagram at left two plane waves are shown interfering at a large angle in a silver-halide emulsion. The resulting hologram consists of a sinusoidal distribution of silver grains deposited in planes throughout the emulsion. The interference maxima lie along the bisector of the angle between the interfering beams. Reconstruction is accomplished by Bragg reflection from the interference planes (*right*). The volume hologram is illuminated with a plane wave that strikes the hologram at the same angle as the original reference beam did. At those wavelengths that satisfy the Bragg-reflection condition the waves reflected from successive planes are in phase and give rise to a replica of the other original plane wave.

three techniques to be demonstrated. This technique, which was reported by Robert L. Powell and Karl A. Stetson while they were at Michigan, is based on the use of long exposures to record an object's motion. It is used primarily to study a subject in rapid vibration. The technique is analogous to a time exposure of a swinging pendulum in ordinary photography. Whereas a long time exposure of a speeding car results in a photograph that is little more than a smear, a similar exposure of a pendulum produces recognizable images of the pendulum at the two ends of its swing. The reason, of course, is that the pendulum spends more time there than at any other point in the swing, so that the record in the photographic emulsion is densest at those two positions. Similarly, a hologram made with a long exposure (long in relation to the subject's oscillation period) will record wave fronts most densely at the two extreme positions of the subject's vibratory motion. It is natural to expect that the reconstructed wave front from a time-averaged hologram should approximate a double-exposed hologram in which the subject is record-

ed at the two extreme positions of its vibrating motion. The interference pattern would then provide a precise measure of the amplitude of vibration of the subject. It should be added that whereas the rigorous analysis of the subject is somewhat more complex, the general conclusions are similar. This technique, although not widely applicable, is highly useful for detecting and examining extremely rapid, short-amplitude vibrations [*see illustration on preceding page*].

In the applications I have discussed so far the hologram, or interference pattern, recorded in the photographic emulsion is essentially two-dimensional. Under certain conditions, however, the finest details of the interference pattern can be made so small that they have dimensions close to the wavelength of the light. In most cases this is far smaller than the thickness of the photographic recording medium. The recorded interference pattern must then be considered to possess depth, since the fringes are recorded throughout the thickness of the recording medium. We thus have a "volume hologram" that is in effect a three-

dimensional diffraction grating. Such a hologram will diffract light in much the same way that a crystal diffracts X rays. This property introduces new possibilities in the technique and applications of holography.

A volume hologram can be produced by directing the reference beam to the photographic plate from a direction such that the angle between the reference beam and the rays of light from the subject is fairly large [*see illustration above*]. The interference pattern will then have details smaller than the thickness of the photographic emulsion. As long as the emulsion has sufficient resolving capabilities, it will record these details throughout its entire thickness. As was indicated earlier, the resulting hologram diffracts light in the same way that a crystal diffracts X rays. As a result we can apply the classic Bragg reflection equations (derived from X-ray crystallography) to predict the nature of the wave front that will be reconstructed when we illuminate such a hologram.

The Bragg-reflection condition places restrictions on the reconstructed wave front. Unlike two-dimensional holograms, which will diffract all colors regardless of the angle of the incident illumination, volume holograms are both angle-selective and color-selective. When illuminated at a particular angle, volume holograms reconstruct in a particular color. By the same token, to reconstruct a volume hologram with a particular color beam it is necessary to illuminate the hologram at a particular angle. It is this relation between the angle of illumination and the wavelength of the illuminating source that is determined by the Bragg-reflection condition.

This can be illustrated by considering the simplest form of a volume hologram, which consists of a set of periodic planes of silver deposited in the photographic emulsion. Such a hologram could be formed by allowing two plane wave fronts to interfere at large angles in the photographic emulsion. If this volume hologram is illuminated by a beam containing a mixture of wave fronts (for example white light), a small fraction of the light will be "reflected" from each of the silver planes. At those wavelengths that satisfy the Bragg condition, however, the waves reflected from successive planes are in phase and give rise to a large diffracted amplitude. At other wavelengths the waves are not reflected in phase and therefore do not contribute appreciably to the total diffracted wave front.

The thicker the volume hologram, the narrower the spectral band of light that is diffracted at a given angle of illumination, that is, the more selective the hologram will be with respect to wavelength, or color. Hence a volume hologram of adequate thickness will select a narrow band of wavelengths from the beam of mixed light and yield a good reconstruction of the original recorded wave front. This situation differs considerably from the case of the two-dimensional hologram. As I have pointed out, such holograms will diffract all the wavelengths present in the illuminating source. The total diffracted wave front will give rise to a superposition of reconstructions at all wavelengths. Since the different wavelengths are diffracted at different angles, the resulting reconstruction will be an unrecognizable "rainbow" smear. This can be avoided and a good reconstruction obtained simply by passing the white light through a color filter. A volume hologram in effect performs this function of color-filtering internally.

L. H. Lin of Bell Laboratories and I were able to use these principles to form volume holograms in two colors that yielded a clear image of the subject. We used a beam containing blue light from an argon laser and red light from a heli-

um-neon laser. The light from the subject and the reference beam made an angle of approximately 90 degrees with each other at the photographic plate [*see upper illustration below*]. The emulsion in effect contained two holograms superposed on each other, one

made by interference in red, the other by interference in blue. If the hologram had been made in a single plane, the reconstructed picture would have contained three images: a correct image combining red and blue, a spurious image in red and a spurious image in blue [*see lower illus-*

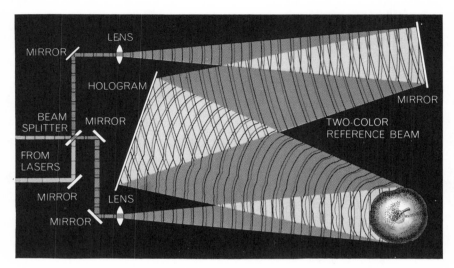

SIMPLE ARRANGEMENT for making multicolor volume holograms is represented in this schematic drawing. The subject is illuminated with a beam of light containing a blue component from an argon-ion laser and a red component from a helium-neon laser. The diffracted light from the subject is then allowed to interfere with a mixed reference beam derived from these two lasers. The large angle between the diffracted beam and the reference beam ensures that the smallest detail of the interference pattern is far smaller than the thickness of the photographic emulsion. The resulting hologram is actually a superposition of two holograms, one made by interference in red and the other by interference in blue.

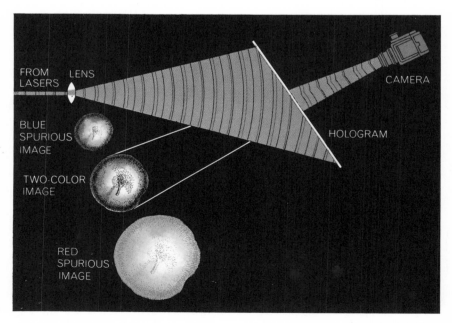

SPURIOUS IMAGES are generated in the reconstruction of a multicolor hologram when the photographic emulsion is insufficiently thick, as in the case of the so-called planar hologram shown here. The spurious blue image in this case is caused by the diffraction of blue light by the red part of the hologram, and the spurious red image is caused by the diffraction of red light by the blue part of the hologram. For an original n-color hologram the reconstruction would consist of one image with the correct color mix and $n(n-1)$ spurious images. The spurious images are eliminated by making the hologram sufficiently thick.

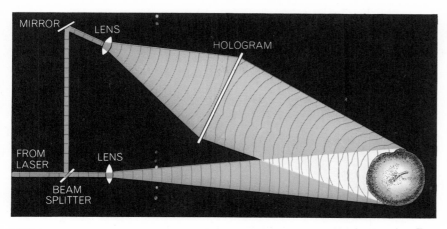

WHITE-LIGHT-RECONSTRUCTING HOLOGRAMS differ from other volume holograms in that the reference and subject beams are introduced from opposite sides of the photographic plate. The interference pattern recorded in the emulsion in this case will take the form of a series of planes almost parallel to the surface of the emulsion. Reconstruction of such holograms will again take place by Bragg reflection from the developed silver planes in the emulsion. However, because of the large angle at which the reconstructing beam will be reflected from the silver planes, interference will occur between waves that are backscattered by the planes. As a consequence the resulting hologram will diffract a fairly narrow band of wavelengths when illuminated by a small white-light source.

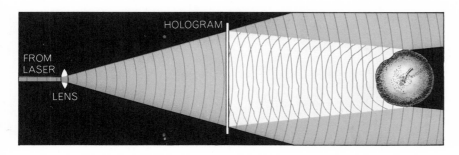

FIRST VOLUME HOLOGRAMS were made in 1962 by Yu. N. Denisyuk of the U.S.S.R., using an optical arrangement in which the light reflected from the subject interferes with the light traveling toward the subject. The resulting interference pattern is then recorded in the photographic emulsion. Although his technique was adequate to form volume holograms of simple subjects, the absence of a separate reference beam limited its applicability.

the photographic plate from opposite sides, forming an interference pattern whose planes were nearly parallel to the surface of the emulsion [*see upper illustration at left*]. Reconstruction of these holograms again takes place by Bragg reflection. Under these conditions, however, the holograms diffract a fairly narrow band of wavelengths when illuminated with a small white-light source. The subsequent development of this technique has led to formation of white-light volume holograms that reconstruct in several colors. Stroke and Burke have also used white-light holography to photograph specimens of biological tissue and have been able to produce high-resolution images over a wide field of view.

Historically the recording of interference patterns throughout the volume of a photosensitive material is a very old subject. As early as 1891 the eminent French physicist Gabriel Lippmann discovered a way to store information throughout the volume of a photographic emulsion. By recording standing waves in an emulsion (produced by a beam of light reflected back on itself), he was able to develop an early form of color photography. This technique, although interesting, proved to be impractical and for many years remained merely a scientific curiosity. In 1962 Yu. N. Denisyuk of the U.S.S.R. combined the Lippmann technique of recording standing waves with the original techniques of holography to make volume holograms [*see lower illustration at left*]. With this technique he was able to record holograms of fairly simple subjects. Denisyuk's technique, like the original holographic technique, had several disadvantages; it was the advent of the separate reference beam that indicated the way to a more general applicability of volume holograms.

Holography has been the scene of considerable activity in the past few years. It is perhaps needless to say that the activity has not been confined to the limited areas discussed in this article. Considerable effort has been expended in the area of data-processing and related subjects. These areas are exceedingly interesting in themselves and may yet prove to be the pot of gold at the end of the holography rainbow. Except for a few isolated cases, however, these areas of holography are also the ones that are presenting the most severe problems. In the meantime there are many areas in which holography could be exploited to great advantage by an investment in the necessary adaptation or further development of the techniques already available.

tration on preceding page]. This relation would hold for a two-dimensional hologram in any number of colors; such a hologram in n colors would yield $n(n-1)$ spurious images. Because of the Bragg-reflection condition our volume holograms eliminated spurious images. These early volume holograms could not reconstruct a clear image with white-light illumination. The emulsion we used was not thick enough to provide sufficient color selectivity at the angles of beam intersection we employed.

Experimenters at Michigan have also reported successful efforts in volume holography. A. A. Friesem extended the techniques of multicolor holography to compose a volume hologram in three colors: red, blue, and green [*see bottom illustration, page 352*]. He also successfully used volume holograms to suppress

the conjugate real image that appears in normal monocolor planar holograms. Leith and his co-workers have produced a sequence of volume holograms with the recording photographic plate set at different angles, so that when the plate was later rotated in the reference beam, the series of reconstructed pictures made an animated movie.

As work on volume holograms proceeded, Stroke and A. E. Labeyrie at Michigan, Charles M. Schwartz at the Battelle Memorial Institute and Leith and his colleagues at Michigan reported success in producing holograms from which good images could be reconstructed with white light. They achieved this not by increasing the thickness of the photographic emulsion but by enlarging the angle between the reference and subject beams. The beams were directed at

Biographical Notes and Bibliographies

I. LIGHT

1. Light

The Author

GERALD FEINBERG is professor of physics at Columbia University. He was graduated from Columbia College in 1953 and remained at the university from 1953 to 1956 as a National Science Foundation fellow. Obtaining his Ph.D. at Columbia in 1957, he spent a year as a member of the School of Mathematics of the Institute for Advanced Study in Princeton and two years as a research associate at the Brookhaven National Laboratory before returning to Columbia as a member of the faculty. During the academic year 1966–1967 Feinberg was at Rockefeller University. His major field of research is elementary particle physics. Another of his interests is treated in his forthcoming book, *The Prometheus Project*, which deals with ethical problems associated with technological advances.

Bibliography

A HISTORY OF THE THEORIES OF AETHER AND ELECTRICITY FROM THE AGE OF DESCARTES TO THE CLOSE OF THE NINETEENTH CENTURY. E. T. Whittaker. Longmans, Green and Co., 1910.

OPTICKS: OR A TREATISE OF THE REFLECTIONS, REFRACTIONS, INFLECTIONS & COLORS OF LIGHT. Sir Isaac Newton. G. Bell & Sons, Ltd., 1931.

THE PHYSICAL PRINCIPLES OF THE QUANTUM THEORY. Werner Heisenberg. Translated by Carl Eckart and Frank C. Hoyt. Dover Publications, Inc., 1949.

FUNDAMENTALS OF OPTICS. Francis A. Jenkins. McGraw-Hill Book Company, Inc., 1950.

2. How Light Interacts with Matter

The Author

VICTOR F. WEISSKOPF is professor of physics at the Massachusetts Institute of Technology. Born in Vienna, he received a Ph.D. in physics from the University of Göttingen in 1931. He worked in Europe until 1937, when he moved to the U.S. and joined the faculty of the University of Rochester. During World War II he was a group leader in the Manhattan project. He has been at M.I.T. since 1945, except for the period from 1961 to 1965, when he was director general of CERN, the European Organization for Nuclear Research. Weisskopf's research work deals with many aspects of theoretical physics, such as the quantum theory of interaction of light and atoms, the theory of the structure of the atomic nucleus and theoretical problems of elementary particles. With John M. Blatt he is the author of a textbook, *Theoretical Nuclear Physics*. He writes that his hobby is "finding clear and simple ways to explain modern physical theory."

Bibliography

ON THE TRANSMISSION OF LIGHT THROUGH AN ATMOSPHERE CONTAINING SMALL PARTICLES IN SUSPENSION, AND ON THE ORIGIN OF THE BLUE OF THE SKY. Lord Rayleigh in *The London, Edinburgh, and Dublin Philosophical Magazine and Journal of Science*, Vol. 47, No. 287, pages 375–384; April, 1899.

THE NATURE OF LIGHT AND COLOUR IN OPEN AIR. Marcellus Minnaert. Dover Publications, 1954.

OPTICS. Bruno B. Rossi. Addison-Wesley Publishing Company, 1957.

KNOWLEDGE AND WONDER: THE NATURAL WORLD AS MAN KNOWS IT. V. F. Weisskopf. Doubleday & Company, Inc., 1962.

OPTICAL PROPERTIES OF AG AND CU. H. Ehrenreich and H. R. Philipp in *Physical Review*, Vol. 128, No. 4, pages 1622–1629; November 15, 1962.

3. The Optical Properties of Materials

The Author

ALI JAVAN is professor of physics at the Massachusetts Institute of Technology. A native of Iran, now a U.S. citizen, he received a Ph.D. in physics from Columbia

University in 1954 and remained at Columbia for five years as a research associate. From 1958 to 1961, when he went to M.I.T., he was a member of the technical staff of the Bell Telephone Laboratories.

Bibliography

THE INTERACTION OF LIGHT WITH LIGHT. J. A. Giordmaine in *Scientific American,* Vol. 210, No. 4, pages 38–49; April, 1964.

THE MODERN THEORY OF SOLIDS. Frederick Seitz. McGraw-Hill Book Company, 1940.

OPTICAL MASER OSCILLATION IN A GASEOUS DISCHARGE. A. Javan in *Advances in Quantum Electronics,* edited by Jay R. Singer. Columbia University Press, 1961.

QUANTUM ELECTRONICS AND COHERENT LIGHT. Edited by P. A. Miles. Academic Press, 1964.

4. How Light is Analyzed

The Author

PIERRE CONNES is a spectroscopist at the Bellevue Laboratories of the French National Center for Scientific Research. After studying physics at the University of Dijon and teaching secondary school for two years he joined the Aimé Cotton Laboratory at the center. He designed and built several interferometric devices for high-resolution spectral analysis. His main field now is Fourier spectroscopy; his wife, Janine, specializes in the computation of the spectra. The Conneses first applied the Fourier technique to astronomy at the Mount Wilson and Kitt Peak observatories, while they were spending a year in the U.S. at the Jet Propulsion Laboratory of the California Institute of Technology. Connes writes that he is "currently engaged in the building of a large (but minimum-budget) infrared spectroscope for the Fourier spectroscopy of stars and planets."

Bibliography

NEW DEVELOPMENTS IN INTERFERENCE SPECTROSCOPY. P. Jacquinot in *Reports on Progress in Physics: Vol. XXIII.* The Physical Society, 1960.

TRANSFORMATIONS IN OPTICS. Lawrence Mertz. John Wiley & Sons, 1965.

COLLOQUE SUR LES MÉTHODES NOUVELLES DE SPECTROSCOPIE INSTRUMENTALE. Centre National de la Recherche Scientifique in *Journal de Physique,* Vol. 28, Conference C 2, supplement to No. 3–4; March–April, 1967.

5. Optical Pumping

The Author

ARNOLD L. BLOOM is director of theoretical research at Spectra-Physics, Inc., Mountain View, California. Previously he was a research physicist at the firm of Varian Associates in Palo Alto, Calif. He was born in Chicago, Ill., in 1923, and originally studied to become a concert pianist. Faced with the choice of several careers, he decided that his interest in physics would not allow him to pursue it "purely as a hobby." He took two degrees in physics at the University of California, receiving his Ph.D. in 1951. He has specialized in studies in nuclear and paramagnetic resonance. His interest in optical-pumping techniques dates from 1956.

Bibliography

MEASUREMENT OF THE EARTH'S MAGNETIC FIELD WITH A RUBIDIUM VAPOR MAGNETOMETER. T. L. Skillman and P. L. Bender in *Journal of Geophysical Research,* Vol. 63, No. 3, pages 513–515; September, 1958.

OPTICAL DETECTION OF MAGNETIC RESONANCE IN ALKALI METAL VAPOR. W. Bell and A. Bloom in *The Physical Review,* Vol. 107, No. 6, pages 1,559–1,565; September 15, 1957.

OPTICAL METHODS OF ATOMIC ORIENTATION AND OF MAGNETIC RESONANCE. Alfred Kastler in *Journal of the Optical Society of America,* Vol. 47, No. 6, pages 460–465; June, 1957.

SLOW SPIN RELAXATION OF OPTICALLY POLARIZED SODIUM ATOMS. H. G. Dehmelt in *The Physical Review,* Vol. 105, No. 5, pages 1,487–1,489; March 1, 1957.

Suggestions for Further Reading

THE SPEED OF LIGHT. J. H. Rush in *Scientific American,* August, 1955, p. 62.

LIGHT SCATTERED BY PARTICLES. Victor K. La Mer and Milton Kerker in *Scientific American,* February, 1953, p. 69.

LIQUID CRYSTALS. James L. Fergason in *Scientific American,* August, 1964, p. 76.

THE MICHELSON MORLEY EXPERIMENT. R. S. Shankland in *Scientific American,* November, 1964, p. 107.

THE THREE SPECTROSCOPIES. Victor F. Weisskopf in *Scientific American,* May, 1968.

STANDARDS OF MEASUREMENT. Allen V. Astin in *Scientific American,* June, 1961.

II. FORMING AND DETECTING IMAGES

6. How Images Are Formed

The Author

F. DOW SMITH is vice-president of the Itek Corporation, where he directs research programs and also does research in optics—particularly in interferometry, optical testing and the theory of image formation. Born in Canada, Smith took bachelor's and master's degrees at Queens University and a Ph.D. in optics at the University of Rochester in 1951. From 1951 until he joined Itek in 1958 he was at Boston University, beginning as instructor in physics and research assistant in the Physical Research Laboratories and ending as associate professor of physics, chairman of the department of physics and director of the Physical Research Laboratories.

Bibliography

OPTICAL IMAGE EVALUATION AND THE TRANSFER FUNCTION. F. Dow Smith in *Applied Optics*, Vol. 2, No. 4, pages 335–350; April, 1963.

APPLIED OPTICS AND OPTICAL ENGINEERING: COMPREHENSIVE TREATISE, VOLS. I–IV. Edited by Rudolf Kingslake. Academic Press, 1965–1967.

MODERN OPTICAL ENGINEERING: THE DESIGN OF OPTICAL SYSTEMS. Warren J. Smith. McGraw-Hill Book Company, 1966.

APPLICATION OF THE FAST FOURIER TRANSFORM TO THE CALCULATION OF THE OPTICAL TRANSFER FUNCTION. Steven H. Lerman in *Proceedings of the Society of Photo-Optical Instrumentation Engineers, Boston, March, 1968*, edited by Henry F. Sander (in press).

7. Fiber Optics

The Author

NARINDER S. KAPANY is president and director of research at Optics Technology, Inc. in Palo Alto, California. He graduated from Agra University in India in 1948, and for the next three years supervised the design, production and testing of optical instruments at the Ordnance Factory in Dehra Dun. He did graduate work in optics at Imperial College, London, and in 1952 joined the Barr and Stroud Optical Company in Glasgow as a lens designer. He was awarded a Royal Society scholarship to start research in fiber optics at Imperial College, and in 1954 received his Ph.D. from the University of London. Kapany was a member of the Institute of Optics at the University of Rochester from 1955 to 1957, and supervisor of optics research at the Armour Research Foundation of the Illinois Institute of Technology from 1957 to 1961. He has initiated considerable research in fiber optics, and has also worked in image evaluation, aspheric optics and interference microscopy.

Bibliography

FIBER OPTICS. PART I: OPTICAL PROPERTIES OF CERTAIN DIELECTRIC CYLINDERS. N. S. Kapany in *Journal of the Optical Society of America*, Vol. 47, No. 5, pages 413–422; May, 1957.

FIBER OPTICS. PART II: IMAGE TRANSFER ON STATIC AND DYNAMIC SCANNING WITH FIBER BUNDLES. N. S. Kapany, J. A. Eyer and R. E. Keim in *Journal of the Optical Society of America*, Vol. 47, No. 5, pages 423–427; May, 1957.

FIBER OPTICS. PART III: FIELD FLATTENERS. N. S. Kapany and R. E. Hopkins in *Journal of the Optical Society of America*, Vol. 47, No. 7, pages 594–598; July, 1957.

FIBER OPTICS. PART IV: A PHOTOREFRACTOMETER. N. S. Kapany and J. N. Pike in *Journal of the Optical Society of America*, Vol. 47, No. 12, pages 1109–1117; December, 1957.

8. How Images Are Detected

The Author

R. CLARK JONES is with the research laboratories of the Polaroid Corporation, which he joined in 1944 after three years at the Bell Telephone Laboratories. He writes: "Born 1916 in Ohio. Won a full-expense scholarship at Harvard. Covered all my expenses and I was not permitted to work. Held it seven years: A.B. in 1938, A.M. in 1939 and Ph.D. in 1941." Jones has a number of avocations, including riding in railroad locomotives ("I have traveled with the engineer on the locomotive a total of about 30,000 miles") and collecting cubic-inch samples of metals.

Bibliography

QUANTUM EFFICIENCY OF DETECTORS FOR VISIBLE AND INFRARED RADIATION. R. Clark Jones in *Advances in Electronics and Electron Physics: Vol. II*, edited by L. Marton. Academic Press, 1959.

PHOTO-ELECTRONIC IMAGE DEVICES: PROCEEDINGS OF THE THIRD SYMPOSIUM HELD AT IMPERIAL COLLEGE, LONDON, SEPTEMBER 20–24, 1965. Edited by J. D. McGee, D. McMullan and E. Kahan. *Advances in Electronics and Electron Physics: Vol. XXII*. Academic Press, 1966.

THE THEORY OF THE PHOTOGRAPHIC PROCESS. C. E. K. Mees. Third edition edited by T. H. James. The Macmillan Company, 1966.

ELECTRO-OPTICAL PHOTOGRAPHY AT LOW ILLUMINATION LEVELS. Harold V. Soule. John Wiley & Sons, 1968.

Suggestions for Further Reading

MAXWELL'S COLOR PHOTOGRAPH. Ralph M. Evans in *Scientific American*, November, 1961, p. 118.

PHOTOGRAPHIC DEVELOPMENT. T. H. James in *Scientific American*, November, 1952, p. 30.

ELECTRONIC PHOTOGRAPHY OF STARS. William A. Baum in *Scientific American*, March, 1956, p. 81.

MOIRÉ PATTERNS. Gerald Oster and Yasunori Nishijima in *Scientific American*, May, 1963, p. 54. Off print 299.

III. CHEMICAL AND BIOLOGICAL EFFECTS OF LIGHT

9. The Chemical Effects of Light

The Author

GERALD OSTER is professor of biophysics at the recently established Mount Sinai School of Medicine. Previously he spent 17 years at the Polytechnic Institute of Brooklyn, where he often collaborated with his wife, Gisela Oster, on work in photochemistry. He writes: "My current interests center around the application of physical chemistry to biology and medicine. In particular I am studying the role of trace metals in biological oxidation and the formation of free radicals. I am concerned with molecular changes in mucoid substances as they relate to disease and to sexual reproduction. I also toy with visual psychology and its related field, art. Exhibitions of my constructions were shown this summer in an art museum in Milwaukee and will be shown this fall in Chicago."

Bibliography

LIGHT-SENSITIVE SYSTEMS: CHEMISTRY AND APPLICATION OF NONSILVER HALIDE PHOTOGRAPHIC PROCESSES. Jaromir Kosar. John Wiley & Sons, 1965.

THE MIDDLE ULTRAVIOLET: ITS SCIENCE AND TECHNOLOGY. Edited by A. E. S. Green. John Wiley & Sons, 1966.

ENERGY TRANSFER FROM HIGH-LYING EXCITED STATES. Gisela K. Oster and H. Kallmann in *Journal de Chimie Physique et de Physico-Chimie Biologique*, Vol. 64, No. 1, pages 28–32; January, 1967.

PHOTOPOLYMERIZATION OF VINYL MONOMERS. Gerald Oster and Nan-Loh Yang in *Chemical Reviews*, Vol. 68, No. 2, pages 125–151; March 25, 1968.

FLASH PHOTOLYSIS AND SOME OF ITS APPLICATIONS. George Porter in *Science*, Vol. 160, No. 3834, pages 1299–1307; June 21, 1968.

10. Life and Light

The Author

GEORGE WALD is Harvard University's well-known authority on the chemistry of vision. Born in New York, he graduated from New York University in 1927, then did graduate work in zoology at Columbia University under Selig Hecht. After receiving his Ph.D. in 1932, he traveled to Germany on a National Research Council fellowship. While studying in Otto Warburg's laboratory at the Kaiser Wilhelm Institute in Berlin, Wald made his first notable contribution to knowledge of the eye—his discovery of vitamin A in the retina. After another year of postdoctoral study at the University of Chicago, he went to Harvard, where he is now professor of biology. He is a member of the National Academy of Sciences and was recently awarded the Nobel Prize for his work on the molecular basis of vision.

Bibliography

PHOTOSYNTHESIS AND RELATED PROCESSES. Eugene I. Rabinowitch. Interscience Publishers, Inc., 1945–1956.

RADIATION BIOLOGY. VOLUME III: VISIBLE AND NEAR-VISIBLE LIGHT. Edited by Alexander Hollaender. McGraw-Hill Book Company, Inc., 1956.

VISION AND THE EYE. M. H. Pirenne. The Pilot Press Ltd., 1948.

THE VISUAL PIGMENTS. H. J. A. Dartnall. Methuen & Co. Ltd., 1957.

11. How Light Interacts with Living Matter

The Author

STERLING B. HENDRICKS is chief scientist in the Mineral Nutrition Laboratory of the Agricultural Research Service of the U.S. Department of Agriculture. He obtained a Ph.D. in physical chemistry at the California Institute of Technology in 1926 and joined the Department of Agriculture in 1927 as a research scientist. In 1952 he was one of the discoverers of phytochrome, the pigment of photoperiodism that he describes in his article. He writes that he is "concerned with membrane function in all aspects of life but particularly with salt (nutrient) uptake by roots." Hendricks has been deeply involved in the development of knowledge about clays through his work on crystal structure with the techniques of X-ray and electron diffraction and about hydrogen bonding, which he has investigated through infrared spectroscopy. He has applied this knowledge to the properties of water in soils and to the isomerization of organic compounds.

Bibliography

CHEMISTRY AND BIOCHEMISTRY OF PLANT PIGMENTS. Edited by T. W. Goodwin. Academic Press, 1965.

PHOTORECEPTORS. *Cold Spring Harbor Symposia on Quantitative Biology: Vol. XXX.* Cold Spring Harbor Laboratory of Quantitative Biology, 1965.

PLANT BIOCHEMISTRY. Edited by James Bonner and J. E. Varner. Academic Press, 1966.

Suggestions for Further Reading

LIGHT AND PLANT DEVELOPMENT. W. L. Butler and Robert J. Downs in *Scientific American*, December, 1960, p. 56. Offprint 107.

THE ROLE OF LIGHT IN PHOTOSYNTHESIS. Daniel I. Arnon in *Scientific American*, November, 1960, p. 104. Offprint 75.

FLASH PHOTOLYSIS. Leonard I. Grossweiner in *Scientific American*, May, 1960, p. 134.

THE PATH OF CARBON IN PHOTOSYNTHESIS. J. A. Bassham in *Scientific American*, June, 1962, p. 88. Offprint 122.

ULTRAVIOLET RADIATION AND NUCLEIC ACID. R. A. Deering in *Scientific American*, December, 1962, p. 135. Offprint 143.

IV. LIGHT AND VISION

12. The Control of the Luminous Environment

The Author

JAMES MARSTON FITCH is professor of architecture at Columbia University. He studied architecture at Tulane University and at Columbia. For several years he worked as a designer and a housing analyst, and then he turned to architectural journalism. From 1936 to 1941 he was associate editor of *Architectural Record*. After a period of military service he became technical editor of *Architectural Forum*, where he worked from 1945 to 1949. He was architectural editor of *House Beautiful* from 1949 until he began teaching at Columbia in 1954. Fitch is the author of several books in his field, including a biography of Walter Gropius and a two-volume work entitled *American Building: The Forces That Shape It*. Another of his books is *Architecture and the Esthetics of Plenty*.

Bibliography

AMERICAN BUILDING: THE FORCES THAT SHAPE IT. James Martson Fitch. Houghton Mifflin Company, 1948.

PRIMER OF LAMPS AND LIGHTING. Willard Allphin. The Chilton Company, 1959.

ARCHITECTURAL LIGHTING GRAPHICS. J. E. Flynn and S. M. Mills. Reinhold Publishing Corp., 1962.

DESIGN WITH CLIMATE: BIOCLIMATIC APPROACH TO ARCHITECTURAL REGIONALISM, SOME CHAPTERS BASED ON COOPERATIVE RESEARCH WITH ALADAR OLGYAY. Victor G. Olgyay. Princeton University Press, 1963.

THE AESTHETICS OF FUNCTION. James Marston Fitch in *Annals of the New York Academy of Sciences*, Vol. 128, Part 2, pages 706–714; September 27, 1965.

13. The Processes of Vision

The Author

ULRIC NEISSER is professor of psychology at Cornell University. He received his bachelor's degree from Harvard College in 1950, his master's degree from Swarthmore College in 1952 and his Ph.D. from Harvard University in 1956. From 1957 to 1965 he taught psychology at Brandeis University; during much of that time he was also associated with the Lincoln Laboratory of the Massachusetts Institute of Technology as a summer staff member and as a consultant. From 1965 to 1967, when he went to Cornell, he was with the Unit for Experimental Psychiatry, which is affiliated with Pennsylvania Hospital and the University of Pennsylvania. He is the author of a book, *Cognitive Psychology*, which was published last year.

Bibliography

THE KINETIC DEPTH EFFECT. H. Wallach and D. N. O'Connell in *Journal of Experimental Psychology*, Vol. 45, No. 4, pages 205–218; April, 1953.

THE RELATION OF EYE MOVEMENTS, BODY MOTILITY AND EXTERNAL STIMULI TO DREAM CONTENT. William Dement and Edward A. Wolpert in *Journal of Experimental Psychology*, Vol. 55, No. 6, pages 543–553; June, 1958.

THE SENSES CONSIDERED AS PERCEPTUAL SYSTEMS. James J. Gibson. Houghton Mifflin Company, 1966.

COGNITIVE PSYCHOLOGY. Ulric Neisser. Appleton-Century-Crofts, 1967.

14. Movements of the Eye

The Author

E. LLEWELLYN THOMAS combines experience as a physician and an electrical engineer: he is professor of pharmacology in the faculty of medicine at the University of Toronto and associate professor of electrical engineering in the university's faculty of applied science and engineering. He is also associate director of the Institute of Bio-Medical Electronics, which the two faculties established in 1963 to investigate the application of engineering techniques and concepts to the biological sciences and vice versa. Born in England, Thomas received his engineering education at the University of London and his medical education at McGill University. He has worked as an engineer with the British army and the Montreal Neurological Institute and as a physician in Nova Scotia and also as an investigator of aerospace psychophysiology with the Defence Research Board of Canada.

Bibliography

EYE FIXATIONS RECORDED ON CHANGING VISUAL SCENES BY THE TELEVISION EYE-MARKER. J. F. Mackworth and N. H. Mackworth in *Journal of the Optical Society of America*, Vol. 48, No. 7, pages 439–445; July, 1958.

THE EVOLUTIONARY HISTORY OF EYE MOVEMENTS. G. L. Walls in *Vision Research: Vol. II*, edited by E. P. Horne and M. A. Whitcomb. National Research Council, 1962.

HEAD-MOUNTED EYE-MARKER CAMERA. Norman H. Mackworth and Edward Llewellyn Thomas in *Journal of the Optical Society of America*, Vol. 52, No. 6, pages 713–716; June, 1962.

EYE MOVEMENTS AND BODY IMAGES. E. Llewellyn Thomas and Eugene Stasiak in *Canadian Psychiatric Association Journal*, Vol. 9, No. 4, pages 336–344; August, 1964.

EYE MOVEMENTS AND VISION. Alfred L. Yarbus. Plenum Press, 1967.

Suggestions for Further Reading

THE EYE AND THE BRAIN. R. W. Sperry in *Scientific American*, May, 1956, p. 48.

EXPERIMENTS IN COLOR VISION. Edwin H. Land in *Scientific American*, May, 1959, p. 84. Offprint 223.

THE PERCEPTION OF NEUTRAL COLORS. Hans Wallach in *Scientific American*, January, 1963, p. 107. Offprint 474.

FLOATERS' IN THE EYE. Harvey E. White and Paul Levatin in *Scientific American*, June, 1962, p. 119.

EYE AND CAMERA. George Wald in *Scientific American*, August, 1950, p. 32. Offprint 46.

POLARIZED LIGHT AND ANIMAL NAVIGATION. Talbot H. Waterman in *Scientific American*, July, 1955, p. 88.

HOW WE SEE STRAIGHT LINES. John R. Platt in *Scientific American*, June, 1960, p. 121.

THE PERCEPTION OF MOTION. Hans Wallach in *Scientific American*, July, 1959, p. 56. Offprint 409.

THE PERCEPTION OF THE UPRIGHT. Herman A. Witkin in *Scientific American*, February, 1959, p. 50. Offprint 410.

SHADOWS AND DEPTH PERCEPTION. Eckhard H. Hess in *Scientific American*, March, 1961, p. 138.

THE ORIGIN OF FORM PERCEPTION. Robert L. Fantz in *Scientific American*, May, 1961, p. 66. Offprint 459.

STABILIZED IMAGES ON THE RETINA. Roy M. Pritchard in *Scientific American*, June, 1961, p. 72. Offprint 466.

ELECTRICAL EVENTS IN VISION. Louis J. and Margery J. Milne in *Scientific American*, December, 1956, p.113.

VISUAL PERCEPTION AND PERSONALITY. Warren J. Wittreich in *Scientific American*, April, 1959, p. 56. Offprint 438.

VISUAL PIGMENTS IN MAN. W. A. H. Rushton in *Scientific American*, November, 1962, p. 120. Offprint 139.

CONTROL MECHANISMS OF THE EYE. Derek H. Fender in *Scientific American*, July, 1964, p. 16. Offprint 187.

THE ILLUSION OF MOVEMENT. Paul A. Koers in *Scientific American*, October, 1964, p. 98.

VISION IN FROGS. W. R. A. Muntz in *Scientific American*, March, 1964, p. 110. Offprint 179.

VISUAL SEARCH. Ulric Neisser in *Scientific American*, June, 1964, p. 94. Offprint 486.

INHIBITION IN VISUAL SYSTEMS. Donald Kennedy in *Scientific American*, July, 1963, p.122. Offprint 162.

MOLECULAR ISOMERS IN VISION. Ruth Hubbard and Allen Kropf in *Scientific American*, June, 1967, p. 64. Offprint 1075.

V. BEYOND THE VISIBLE: X-RAY TO RADIO WAVES

15. X-ray Crystallography

The Author

SIR LAWRENCE BRAGG is retired director of the Royal Institution; he held the directorship from 1954 to 1966, and from 1953 until he retired he was also Fullerian Professor of Chemistry at the Royal Institution. Born in Australia, he took a degree in mathematics at the University of Adelaide in 1908 and a degree in physics at the University of Cambridge in 1911. In 1915, at the age of 25, he shared with his father, W. H. Bragg, a Nobel prize awarded for their work on the analysis of crystal structure by X rays. During World War I Sir Lawrence organized for the British Army the technique called sound ranging, which involved the detection of enemy guns by sound. In 1919 he succeeded Lord Rutherford as professor of physics at the University of Manchester. In 1938, after a year as director of the National Physical Laboratory, he succeeded Lord Rutherford as Cavendish Professor of Physics at the University of Cambridge. He has been a Fellow of the Royal Society since 1921.

Bibliography

THE ARCHITECTURE OF MOLECULES. Linus Pauling and Roger Hayward. W. H. Freeman and Company, 1964.

THE CRYSTALLINE STATE, A GENERAL SURVEY: VOL. I. Sir Lawrence Bragg. Cornell University Press, 1962.

CRYSTALS: THEIR ROLE IN NATURE AND IN SCIENCE. Charles Bunn. Academic Press, 1964.

ORIGINS OF THE SCIENCE OF CRYSTALS. John G. Burke. University of California Press, 1966.

16. Infrared Astronomy

The Authors

BRUCE C. MURRAY and JAMES A. WESTPHAL are respectively assistant professor of planetary science and senior research engineer at the California Institute of Technology. Murray received bachelor's, master's and doctor's degrees in geology from the Massachusetts Institute of Technology. He describes himself as "a geologist turned geophysicist turned planetary astronomer." His primary interest is "the use of ground-based telescopes to learn about the geology and geophysics—mostly the latter—of the moon, planets and larger satellites." His nonprofessional activities include lacrosse and local Democratic politics. Westphal is a graduate of the University of Tulsa. Before taking his present post in 1961 he did research for the Sinclair Oil Corporation.

Bibliography

COLLECTED SCIENTIFIC PAPERS OF SIR WILLIAM HERSCHEL: VOLUME II. Dulan and Co., Ltd., 1912.

THE DETECTION AND MEASUREMENT OF INFRA-RED RADIATION. R. A. Smith, F. E. Jones and R. P. Chasmar. Oxford University Press, 1957.

OBSERVATIONS OF JUPITER AND THE GALILEAN SATELLITES AT 10 MICRONS. Bruce C. Murray, Robert L. Wildey and James A. Westphal in *The Astrophysical Journal*, Vol. 139, No. 1, pages 986–993; April 1, 1964.

PLANETARY TEMPERATURE MEASUREMENTS. Edison Pettit in *Planets and Satellites*, edited by Gerald P. Kuiper and Barbara M. Middlehurst. The University of Chicago Press, 1961.

RECENT RADIOMETRIC STUDIES OF THE PLANETS AND MOON. W. M. Sinton in *Planets and Satellites*, edited by Gerald P. Kuiper and Barbara M. Middlehurst. The University of Chicago Press, 1961.

17. The Infrared Sky

The Authors

G. NEUGEBAUER and ROBERT B. LEIGHTON are respectively associate professor of physics and professor of physics at the California Institute of Technology. Neugebauer was graduated from Cornell University and obtained his Ph.D. from Cal Tech in 1960. After two years as an Army officer, during which time he served at the Jet Propulsion Laboratory, he returned to Cal Tech to pursue work in infrared astronomy. He participated in an infrared radiometric experiment flown past Venus on the spacecraft *Mariner II* and is preparing a similar experiment for the two Mariner spacecraft that will investigate Mars in 1969. Leighton was graduated from Cal Tech in 1941 and received his Ph.D. there in 1947. He worked on cosmic ray physics until about 1960, when his research interests turned toward solar physics and astrophysics. He participated in the television experiment carried out by *Mariner IV* and is working on a more comprehensive television experiment to be included in the Mars spacecraft next year. Neugebauer and Leighton cooperated in the construction and operation of an infrared telescope starting in 1963 and are now planning a larger instrument.

Bibliography

OBSERVATIONS OF EXTREMELY COOL STARS. G. Neugebauer, D. E. Martz and R. B. Leighton in *The Astrophysical Journal*, Vol. 142, No. 1, pages 399–401; July 1, 1965.

INFRARED PHOTOMETRY OF T TAURI STARS AND RELATED OBJECTS. Eugenio E. Mendoza V in *The Astrophysical Journal*, Vol. 143, No. 3, pages 1010–1014; March, 1966.

FURTHER OBSERVATIONS OF EXTREMELY COOL STARS. B. T. Ulrich, G. Neugebauer, D. McCammon, R. B. Leighton, E. E. Hughes and E. Becklin in *The Astrophysical Journal*, Vol. 146, No. 1, pages 288–290; October, 1966.

OBSERVATIONS OF AN INFRARED STAR IN THE ORION NEBULA. E. E. Becklin and G. Neugebauer in *The Astrophysical Journal*, Vol. 147, No. 2, pages 799–802; February, 1967.

DISCOVERY OF AN INFRARED NEBULA IN ORION. D. E. Kleinmann and F. J. Low in *The Astrophysical Journal*, Vol. 149, No. 1, Part 2, pages L1–L4; July, 1967.

INFRARED ASTRONOMY. A. G. W. Cameron and P. J. Brancazio. Gordon & Breach, Science Publishers, Inc. (in press).

18. Remote Sensing of Natural Resources

The Author

ROBERT N. COLWELL is professor of forestry at the University of California at Berkeley. A native of Idaho, he did his undergraduate work at Berkeley and acquired a Ph.D. in plant physiology there in 1942. During World War II and the Korean war he served as a photo-interpreter with various branches of the armed forces. He has also been active in the photo-interpretation aspects of the SAMOS and VELA UNIFORM military-satellite projects. Since joining the Berkeley faculty in 1947 Colwell has taught courses in photo-interpretation and photogrammetry and has conducted research on the civil uses of aerial photo-interpretation. He is currently chief of the Forestry Remote Sensing Laboratory (jointly supported by the National Aeronautics and Space Administration and the U.S. Department of Agriculture) and chairman of the National Research Council's Committee on Crop Geography and Vegetation Analysis.

Bibliography

BASIC MATTER AND ENERGY RELATIONSHIPS INVOLVED IN REMOTE RECONNAISSANCE. Robert N. Colwell, William Brewer, Glenn Landis, Philip Langley, Joseph Morgan, Jack Rinker, J. M. Robinson and A. L. Sorem in *Photogrammetric Engineering*, Vol. 19, No. 5, pages 761–799; September, 1963.

MANUAL OF PHOTOGRAPHIC INTERPRETATION. Edited by R. N. Colwell. American Society of Photogrammetry and George Banta Co., 1960.

RADAR REMOTE SENSING IN BIOLOGY. Richard K. Moore and David S. Simonett in *BioScience*, Vol. 17, No. 6, pages 384–390; June, 1967.

19. The Maser

The Author

JAMES P. GORDON was associated with C. H. Townes in the making of the first maser [see "Atomic Clocks," by Harold Lyons; SCIENTIFIC AMERICAN Offprint 225]. Gordon, then a graduate student under Townes at Columbia University, was especially concerned with investigating the properties of the ammonia molecule, which was the basic amplifying element of the early masers. Gordon comes from Scarsdale, N.Y., and is a graduate of the Massachusetts Institute of Technology. Upon receiving his Ph.D. from Columbia in 1955, he joined the staff of the Bell Telephone Laboratories, where he has worked on ammonia masers and on those questions of physics underlying the operation of solid-state masers.

Bibliography

ATOMIC CLOCKS. Harold Lyons in *Scientific American*, Vol. 196, No. 2, pages 71–85; February, 1957.

THE SOLID STATE MASER: A SUPER-COOLED AMPLIFIER. J. W. Meyer in *Electronics*, Vol. 31, No. 17, pages 66–71; April 25, 1958.

Suggestions for Further Reading

CHEMICAL ANALYSIS BY INFRARED. Bryce Crawford, Jr. in *Scientific American*, October, 1953, p. 42. Offprint 257.

GAMMA RAY ASTRONOMY. William L. Kraushaar and George W. Clark in *Scientific American*, May, 1962, p. 52.

RADAR ASTRONOMY. Von R. Eshelman and Allen M. Peterson in *Scientific American*, August, 1960, p. 50.

ROCKET ASTRONOMY. Herbert Friedman in *Scientific American*, June, 1959, p. 52.

ATOMIC CLOCKS. Harold Lyons in *Scientific American*, February, 1957, p. 71. Offprint 225.

THE X-RAY MICROSCOPE. Paul Kirkpatrick in *Scientific American*, March, 1949, p. 44.

MAGNETIC RESONANCE. George M. Pake in *Scientific American*, August, 1958, p. 58. Offprint 233.

RADIO STARS. A. C. B. Lovell in *Scientific American*, January, 1953, p. 17.

RADIO-EMITTING FLARE STARS. Sir Bernard Lovell in *Scientific American*, August, 1964, p. 13.

RADIO WAVES FROM JUPITER. K. L. Franklin in *Scientific American,* July, 1964, p. 34.

X-RAY ASTRONOMY. Herbert Friedman in *Scientific American,* June, 1964, p. 36.

INFRARED ASTRONOMY BY BALLOON. John Strong in *Scientific American,* January, 1964, p. 28.

X-RAY STARS. Riccardo Giacconi in *Scientific American,* December, 1967, p. 36.

VI. LASERS

20. Optical Masers

The Author

ARTHUR L. SCHAWLOW is professor of physics in the School of Humanities and Sciences at Stanford University and executive head of the physics department. He was graduated from the University of Toronto in 1941 and received his Ph.D. there in 1949. After two years as a postdoctoral fellow and research associate at Columbia University he became a research physicist at the Bell Telephone Laboratories. He went to Stanford in 1961. Schawlow's research has been in the fields of optical and microwave spectroscopy, nuclear quadrupole resonance, superconductivity and optical masers. He is coauthor with Charles H. Townes, now professor-at-large at the University of California, of the book *Microwave Spectroscopy* and of the first paper describing optical masers.

Bibliography

INFRARED AND OPTICAL MASERS. A. L. Schawlow and C. H. Townes in *The Physical Review,* Vol. 112, No. 6, pages 1940–1949; December 15, 1958.

THE MASER. James P. Gordon in *Scientific American,* Vol. 199, No. 6, pages 42–50; December, 1958.

POPULATION INVERSION AND CONTINUOUS OPTICAL MASER OSCILLATION IN A GAS DISCHARGE CONTAINING A HE-NE MIXTURE. A. Javan, W. R. Bennett, Jr., and D. R. Herriott in *Physical Review Letters,* Vol. 6, No. 3, pages 106–110; February 1, 1961.

POSSIBILITY OF OBTAINING NEGATIVE TEMPERATURE IN ATOMS BY ELECTRON IMPACT. A. Javan in *Quantum Electronics,* edited by Charles H. Townes, pages 564–571. Columbia University Press, 1960.

21. Advances in Optical Masers

The Author

For information on ARTHUR L. SCHAWLOW, see the preceding biographical note.

Bibliography

FREQUENCY STABILITY OF HE-NE MASERS AND MEASUREMENTS OF LENGTH. T. S. Jaseja, A. Javan and C. H. Townes in *Physical Review Letters,* Vol. 10, No. 57, pages 165–167; March, 1963.

LASERS. Bela A. Lengyel. John Wiley & Sons, Inc., 1962.

ROTATION RATE SENSING WITH TRAVELLING-WAVE RING LASERS. W. M. Macek and D. T. M. Davis, Jr., in *Applied Physics Letters,* Vol. 2, No. 3, pages 67–68; February, 1963.

SPECIAL ISSUE ON QUANTUM ELECTRONICS. *Proceedings of the Institute of Electrical and Electronic Engineers,* Vol. 51, No. 1, pages 1–294; January, 1963.

22. Chemical Lasers

The Author

GEORGE C. PIMENTEL is professor of chemistry at the University of California at Berkeley. He is a native Californian who did his undergraduate work at the University of California at Los Angeles and his graduate work at Berkeley, where he obtained a Ph.D. in 1949. He has been a member of the faculty at Berkeley since then, becoming professor in 1959. His particular interests are infrared spectroscopy, molecular structure, hydrogen bonding and the thermodynamic properties of hydrocarbons.

Bibliography

APPLIED OPTICS, SUPPLEMENT 2: CHEMICAL LASERS. Optical Society of America, 1965.

ATOMIC IODINE PHOTODISSOCIATION LASER. Jerome V. V. Kasper and George C. Pimentel in *Applied Physics Letters,* Vol. 5, No. 11, pages 231–233; December 1, 1964.

HCL CHEMICAL LASER. Jerome V. V. Kasper and George C. Pimentel in *Physical Review Letters,* Vol. 14, No. 10, pages 352–354; March 8, 1965.

IODINE-ATOM LASER EMISSION IN ALKYL IODINE PHOTOLYSIS. Jerome V. V. Kasper, John H. Parker and George C. Pimentel in *The Journal of Chemical Physics,* Vol. 43, No. 5, pages 1827–1828; September 1, 1965.

23. Liquid Lasers

The Authors

ALEXANDER LEMPICKI and HAROLD SAMELSON are with the General Telephone & Electronics Laboratories, Lempicki as manager of the quantum physics group and Samelson as senior scientist. Lempicki, a native of Poland, was active in the Polish underground movement during World War II. After the war he studied at the Jagiellonian University in Cracow, the University of Rome and the Imperial College of Science and Technology in London. He received a Ph.D. from the University of London in 1960, based on work he had done in his present laboratory since arriving in the U.S. in 1955. Samelson, who was graduated from Columbia College in 1947, went on to graduate school at Columbia and obtained a Ph.D. in 1952. He was at the Bell Telephone Laboratories for two years before joining General Telephone.

Bibliography

CHARACTERISTICS OF THE ND^{+3}: SEOCL$_2$ LIQUID LASER. Alexander Lempicki and Adam Heller in *Applied*

Physics Letters, Vol. 9, No. 3, pages 108–110; August 1, 1966.

A HIGH-GAIN ROOM-TEMPERATURE LIQUID LASER: TRIVALENT NEODYMIUM IN SELENIUM OXYCHLORIDE. Adam Heller in *Applied Physics Letters,* Vol. 9, No. 3, pages 106–108; August 1, 1966.

LASER ACTION IN RARE EARTH CHELATES. A. Lempicki, H. Samelson and C. Brecher in *Applied Optics, Supplement 2: Chemical Lasers,* pages 205–213; 1965.

ORGANIC LASER SYSTEMS. A. Lempicki and H. Samelson in *Lasers: Vol. I,* edited by Albert K. Levine. Marcel Dekker, Inc., 1966.

24. High-Power Carbon Dioxide Lasers

The Author

C. K. N. PATEL is a member of the staff of the Bell Telephone Laboratories. Born in India, he was graduated from the College of Engineering of the University of Poona in 1958. From 1958 to 1961 he did graduate work at Stanford University, receiving his master's and doctor's degrees in electrical engineering in 1959 and 1961 respectively. In 1961 he joined Bell Laboratories, where he has done extensive work on lasers. As a result of his work he received in 1966 the Adolph Lomb Medal of the Optical Society of America, which is awarded every two years to a person under 30 years old who has "made a noteworthy contribution to optics." At the time of the award his senior colleagues at Bell Laboratories were quoted as saying that "his theoretical and experimental contributions to gas lasers are equaled by very few scientists regardless of age."

Bibliography

ADVANCES IN OPTICAL MASERS. Arthur L. Schawlow in *Scientific American,* Vol. 209, No. 1, pages 34–45; July, 1963.

INTERPRETATION OF CO₂ OPTICAL MASER EXPERIMENTS. C. K. N. Patel in *Physical Review Letters,* Vol. 12, No. 21, pages 588–590; May 25, 1964.

RECENT DEVELOPMENTS IN CO₂ AND OTHER MOLECULAR LASERS. C. K. N. Patel in *Journal de Chimie Physique et de Physico-Chimie Biologique,* Vol. 64, No. 1, pages 82–92; January, 1967.

VII. PROPERTIES AND APPLICATIONS OF LASER LIGHT

25. Laser Light

The Author

For information on ARTHUR L. SCHAWLOW, see biographical note 20.

Bibliography

BRILLOUIN SCATTERING IN LIQUIDS. G. Benedek and T. Greytak in *Proceedings of the IEEE,* Vol. 53, No. 10, pages 1623–1629; October, 1965.

TWO-MAGNON LIGHT SCATTERING IN ANTIFERROMAGNETIC MNF₂. P. A. Fleury, S. P. S. Porto and R. Loudon in *Physical Review Letters,* Vol. 18, No. 16, pages 658–660; April 17, 1967.

ULTRASHORT LIGHT PULSES. A. J. De-Maria, D. A. Stetser and W. H. Glenn, Jr., in *Science,* Vol. 156, No. 3782, pages 1557–1568; June 23, 1967.

TRANSVERSE STIMULATED EMISSION IN LIQUIDS. J. L. Emmett and A. L. Schawlow in *The Physical Review,* Vol. 170, Second Series, No. 2, pages 358–362; June 10, 1968.

26. The Interaction of Light with Light

The Author

J. A. GIORDMAINE is a member of the staff of the Solid State Electronics Research Laboratory of the Bell Telephone Laboratories. He was born in Toronto in 1933 and received a B.A. in physics and chemistry from the University of Toronto in 1955. He did graduate work in physics at Columbia University under the direction of Charles H. Townes, obtaining a Ph.D. in 1960. He taught physics at Columbia from 1959 to 1961, when he took up his present post.

Bibliography

COHERENTLY DRIVEN MOLECULAR VIBRATIONS AND LIGHT MODULATION. E. Garmire, F. Pandarese and C. H. Townes in *Physical Review Letters,* Vol. 11, No. 4, pages 160–163; August, 1963.

INTERACTIONS BETWEEN LIGHT WAVES IN A NONLINEAR DIELECTRIC. J. A. Armstrong, N. Bloembergen, J. Ducuing and P. S. Pershan in *The Physical Review,* Vol. 127, No. 6, pages 1918–1939; September, 1962.

NONLINEAR INTERACTION OF LIGHT IN A VACUUM. J. McKenna and P. M. Platzman in *The Physical Review,* Vol. 129, No. 5, pages 2354–2360; March, 1963.

THEORY OF SECOND HARMONIC GENERATION OF LIGHT. D. A. Kleinman in *The Physical Review,* Vol. 128, No. 4, pages 1761–1775; November, 1962.

27. Photon Echoes

The Author

SVEN R. HARTMANN is associate professor of physics and an Alfred P. Sloan research fellow at Columbia University. He was graduated from Union College in 1954 and received a doctorate in physics from the University of California at Berkeley in 1961. After a year as a research physicist at Berkeley he joined the Columbia faculty. His special interests are magnetic-resonance effects, relaxation effects and echo effects.

Bibliography

ECHO BEHAVIOR IN RUBY. D. Grischkowsky and S. R. Hartmann in *Physical Review Letters,* Vol. 20, No. 2, pages 41–43; January 8, 1968.

EFFECTS OF DIFFUSION ON FREE PRECESSION IN NUCLEAR MAGNETIC RESONANCE EXPERIMENTS. H. Y. Carr and E. M. Purcell in *The Physical Review,* Vol. 94, Second Series, No. 3, pages 630–639; May 1, 1954.

PHOTON ECHOES. I. D. Abella, N. A. Kurnit and S. R. Hartmann in *The Physical Review,* Vol. 141, No. 1, pages 391–406; January, 1966.

SPIN ECHOES. E. L. Hahn in *The Physical Review,* Vol. 80, Second Series, No. 4, pages 580–594; November 15, 1950.

28. Applications of Laser Light

The Author

DONALD R. HERRIOTT is with the Bell Telephone Laboratories. Having studied physics at Duke University, optics at the University of Rochester and electrical engineering at the Polytechnic Institute of Brooklyn, he joined the Bausch & Lomb Optical Company in 1949 to work in research on thin films, interferometry and the measurement of the modulation transfer function of lenses. He continued this work after joining Bell Laboratories in 1956 and also participated in the development of optical systems for flying-spot storage of information and for picturephones. In 1960 he built the first gas laser in collaboration with Ali Javan and W. R. Bennett, Jr. He collaborated in the development of the spherical-mirror cavity, the folded optical delay line, the scanning spherical-mirror interferometer and a number of other interferometers using the laser source.

Bibliography

LASERS AND APPLICATIONS. The Antenna Laboratory of the Department of Electrical Engineering of the Ohio State University, edited by W. S. C. Chang. Ohio State University, 1963.

THE LASER. William V. Smith and P. P. Sorokin. McGraw-Hill Publishing Company, 1965.

LASERS AND THEIR APPLICATIONS. Kurt R. Stehling. World Publishing Company, 1966.

PROCEEDINGS OF THE SYMPOSIUM ON MODERN OPTICS. New York, N.Y., March 22, 23, 24, 1967. Edited by Jerome Fox. Polytechnic Press of the Polytechnic Institute of Brooklyn, 1967.

1967 CONFERENCE ON LASER ENGINEERING AND APPLICATIONS. *IEEE Journal of Quantum Electronics,* Vol. QE-3, No. 11; November, 1967.

29. Communication by Laser

The Author

STEWART E. MILLER is director of the Guided Wave Research Laboratory of the Bell Telephone Laboratories. He joined the Bell Laboratories in 1941 after receiving bachelor's and master's degrees in electrical engineering at the Massachusetts Institute of Technology. For eight years he did research on development of coaxial-cable carrier systems and on radar. Then he joined the radio research department, where he worked at first on components for microwave radio systems. In his present position he heads a group investigating communication techniques for wave regions ranging from the optical portion of the electromagnetic spectrum through waves of millimeter length.

Bibliography

ADVANCES IN OPTICAL MASERS. Arthur L. Schawlow in *Scientific American,* Vol. 209, No. 1, pages 34–45; July, 1963.

THE EVOLVING TECHNOLOGY OF COMMUNICATION. E. I. Green in *Electrical Engineering,* Vol. 78, No. 5, pages 470–480; May, 1959.

THE FUTURE OF MICROWAVE COMMUNICATIONS. S. E. Miller in *Proceedings of the IRE,* Vol. 50, No. 5, pages 1215–1219; May, 1962.

RESOURCE LETTER MOP-1 ON MASERS (MICROWAVE THROUGH OPTICAL) AND ON OPTICAL PUMPING. H. W. Moos in *American Journal of Physics,* Vol. 32, No. 8, pages 589–595; August, 1964.

30. The Modulation of Laser Light

The Author

DONALD F. NELSON is professor of physics at the University of Southern California. He did all his undergraduate and graduate work at the University of Michigan, where he received bachelor's and master's degrees in 1952 and 1953 respectively and a Ph.D. in 1959. From 1959 until he took his present position last year he was in the research division of the Bell Telephone Laboratories. Soon after joining Bell Laboratories he began experiments to explore laser action in solids. He collaborated in the first measurements of spatial coherence, relaxation oscillations, cavity loss and polarization of the pulsed ruby laser. Working with W. S. Boyle, he built the first continuously operating ruby laser. He has also been interested in a variety of optical properties of semiconductors.

Bibliography

ELECTROOPTIC LIGHT MODULATORS. I. P. Kaminow and E. H. Turner in *Applied Optics,* Vol. 5, No. 10, pages 1612–1628; October, 1966.

LIGHT MODULATION BY THE ELECTROOPTIC EFFECT IN REVERSE-BIASED GAP P-N JUNCTIONS. D. F. Nelson and F. K. Reinhart in *Applied Physics Letters,* Vol. 5, No. 7, pages 148–150; October 1, 1964.

ORIGIN AND USES OF THE FARADAY ROTATION IN MAGNETIC CRYSTALS. J. F. Dillon, Jr., in *Journal of Applied Physics,* Vol. 39, No. 2, Part II, pages 922–929; February 1, 1968.

A REVIEW OF ACOUSTOOPTICAL DEFLECTION AND MODULATION DEVICES. E. I. Gordon in *Applied Optics,* Vol. 5, No. 10, pages 1629–1639; October, 1966.

STABILIZATION AND MODULATION OF LASER OSCILLATORS BY INTERNAL TIME-VARYING PERTURBATION. S. E. Harris in *Applied Optics,* Vol. 5, No. 10, pages 1639–1651; October, 1966.

WIDE-BAND INFRARED MAGNETO-OPTIC MODULATION. R. C. LeCraw in *IEEE Transactions on Magnetics,* Vol. Mag-2, No. 3, page 304; September, 1966.

31. Photography by Laser

The Authors

EMMETT N. LEITH and JURIS UPATNIEKS are members of the staff of the Institute of Science and Technology at the University of Michigan. Leith is a research engineer and head of the optics group of the radar laboratory; Upatnieks is a graduate research assistant. Leith was born in Detroit; in 1950 he was graduated from Wayne State University, obtaining a master's degree in physics at the same institution two years later. Since then he has been at Michigan, working in radar, microwaves, communication theory, data processing and coherent optical systems. Upatnieks was graduated from the University of Akron in 1960 with a degree in electrical engineering. From 1957 to 1959 he was an engineer with the Goodyear Aircraft Corporation; he went to the University of Michigan in 1960.

Bibliography

ELIMINATION OF THE UNWANTED IMAGE IN DIFFRACTION MICROSCOPY. W. L. Bragg and G. L. Rogers in *Nature,* Vol. 167, No. 4240, pages 190–191; February 3, 1951.

A NEW MICROSCOPIC PRINCIPLE. D. Gabor in *Nature,* Vol. 161, No. 4098, pages 777–778; May 15, 1948.

RECONSTRUCTED WAVEFRONTS AND COMMUNICATION THEORY. Emmett N. Leith and Juris Upatnieks in *Journal of the Optical Society of America,* Vol. 52, No. 10, pages 1123–1130; October, 1962.

32. Advances in Holography

The Author

KEITH S. PENNINGTON is on the staff of the Thomas J. Watson Research Center of the International Business Machines Corporation. He was born in England and was graduated in 1957 from the University of Birmingham. In 1961 he obtained a Ph.D. in physics from McMaster University in Ontario. From 1961 to 1967 he was a member of the technical staff at the Bell Telephone Laboratories.

Bibliography

HOLOGRAPHY AND INTERFERENCE PROCESSING OF INFORMATION. L. M. Soroko in *Soviet Physics: USPEKHI,* Vol. 9, No. 5, pages 643–669; March–April, 1967.

AN INTRODUCTION TO COHERENT OPTICS AND HOLOGRAPHY. G. W. Stroke. Academic Press Inc., 1966.

PHOTOGRAPHY BY LASER. Emmett N. Leith and Juris Upatnieks in *Scientific American,* Vol. 212, No. 6, pages 24–35; June, 1965.

THEORY AND APPLICATIONS OF HOLOGRAPHY. John B. DeVelis and George O. Reynolds. Addison-Wesley Publishing Company, 1967.

Index